Selections from

The Arabian Nights

Sir Richard Burton's
famous translation of
THE THOUSAND NIGHTS AND A NIGHT
with modernized spelling and punctuation.

FIRST EDITION
of
The PROGRAMMED CLASSICS

Published by
Communication & Studies Inc.
Atlanta, Georgia

PRINTED IN THE UNITED STATES OF AMERICA

CONTENTS

STORY OF KING SHAHRYAR AND HIS BROTHER	1
The Tale of the Bull and the Ass	13

THE TALES OF SCHEHERAZADE

THE FISHERMAN AND THE JINNI	22
The Tale of the Ensorceled Prince	34
THE PORTER AND THE THREE LADIES OF BAGHDAD	44
The first Kalandar's tale	60
The second Kalandar's tale	67
The third Kalandar's tale	84
The eldest Lady's tale	102
THE TALE OF THE THREE APPLES	111
TALE OF NUR AL-DIN ALI AND HIS SON BADR AL-DIN HASAN	119
THE CITY OF MANY-COLUMNED IRAM	165
THE SWEEP AND THE NOBLE LADY	170
THE MAN WHO STOLE THE DISH OF GOLD WHEREIN THE DOG ATE	174
THE RUINED MAN WHO BECAME RICH AGAIN THROUGH A DREAM	177
THE EBONY HORSE	179

CONTENTS

THE ANGEL OF DEATH WITH THE PROUD KING AND THE DEVOUT MAN	205
SINDBAD THE SEAMAN AND SINDBAD THE LANDSMAN	207
First voyage of Sindbad Hight the Seaman	209
The second voyage of Sindbad the Seaman	216
The third voyage of Sindbad the Seaman	223
The fourth voyage of Sindbad the Seaman	232
The fifth voyage of Sindbad the Seaman	243
The sixth voyage of Sindbad the Seaman	250
The seventh voyage of Sindbad the Seaman	259
THE LADY AND HER FIVE SUITORS	268
KHALIFAH THE FISHERMAN OF BAGHDAD	275
ABU KIR THE DYER AND ABU SIR THE BARBER	305
THE SLEEPER AND THE WAKER	330
Story of the Larrikin and the Cook	332
ALADDIN; OR, THE WONDERFUL LAMP	355
ALI BABA AND THE FORTY THIEVES	439
CONCLUSION	464

Selections from
The Arabian Nights

THE ARABIAN NIGHTS' ENTERTAINMENTS
(*ALF LAYLAH WA LAYLAH*)
In the Name of Allah,
the Compassionating, the Compassionate!

PRAISE BE TO ALLAH • THE BENEFICENT KING • THE CREATOR OF THE UNIVERSE • LORD OF THE THREE WORLDS • WHO SET UP THE FIRMAMENT WITHOUT PILLARS IN ITS STEAD • AND WHO STRETCHED OUT THE EARTH EVEN AS A BED • AND GRACE, AND PRAYER—BLESSING BE UPON OUR LORD MOHAMMED • LORD OF APOSTOLIC MEN • AND UPON HIS FAMILY AND COMPANION TRAIN • PRAYER AND BLESSINGS ENDURING AND GRACE WHICH UNTO THE DAY OF DOOM SHALL REMAIN • AMEN! • O THOU OF THE THREE WORLDS SOVEREIGN!

AND AFTERWARD. Verily the works and words of those gone before us have become instances and examples to men of our modern day, that folk may view what admonishing chances befell other folk and may therefrom take warning; and that they may peruse the annals of antique peoples and all that hath betided them, and be thereby ruled and restrained. Praise, therefore, be to Him who hath made the histories of the past an admonition unto the present! Now of such instances are the tales called "A Thousand Nights and a Night," together with their far-famed legends and wonders.

Therein it is related (but Allah is All-knowing of His hidden things and All-ruling and All-honored and All-giving and All-gracious and All-merciful!) that in tide of yore and in time long gone before, there was a King of the Kings of the Banu Sasan in the islands of India and China, a Lord of armies and guards and servants and dependents. He left only two sons, one in the prime of manhood and the other yet a youth, while both were knights and braves, albeit the elder was a doughtier horseman than the younger. So he succeeded to the empire, when he ruled the land and lorded it over his lieges with justice so exemplary that he was beloved by all the peoples of his capital and of his kingdom. His name was King Shahryar, and he made his younger brother, Shah Zaman hight, King of Samarkand in Barbarian land. These two ceased not to abide in their several realms and the law was ever carried out in their dominions. And each ruled his own kingdom with equity and fair dealing to his subjects, in extreme solace and enjoyment, and this condition continually endured for a score of years.

But at the end of the twentieth twelvemonth the elder King yearned for a sight of his younger brother and felt that he must look upon him once more. So he took counsel with his Wazir about visiting him, but the Minister, finding the project unadvisable, recommended that a letter be written and a present be sent under his charge to the younger brother, with an invitation to visit the elder. Having accepted this advice, the King forthwith bade prepare handsome gifts, such as horses with saddles of gem-encrusted gold; Mamelukes, or white slaves; beautiful handmaids, high-breasted virgins, and splendid stuffs and costly. He then wrote a letter to Shah Zaman expressing his warm love and great wish to see him, ending with these words: "We therefore hope of the favor and affection of the beloved brother that he will condescend to bestir himself and turn his face usward. Furthermore, we have sent our Wazir to make all ordinance for the march, and our one and only desire is to see thee ere we die. But if thou delay or disappoint us, we shall not survive the blow. Wherewith peace be upon thee!"

Then King Shahryar, having sealed the missive and given it to the Wazir with the offerings aforementioned, commanded him to shorten his skirts and strain his strength and make all expedition in going and returning. "Harkening and obedience!" quoth the Minister, who fell to making ready without stay and packed up his loads and prepared all his requisites without delay. This occupied him three days, and on the dawn of the fourth he took leave of his King and marched right away, over desert and hillway, stony waste and pleasant lea, without halting by night or by day. But whenever he entered a realm whose ruler was subject to his suzerain, where he was greeted with magnificent gifts of gold and silver and all manner of presents fair and rare, he would tarry there three days, the term of the guest rite. And when he left on the fourth, he would be honorably escorted for a whole day's march.

As soon as the Wazir drew near Shah Zaman's court in Samarkand he dispatched to report his arrival one of his high officials, who presented himself before the King and, kissing ground between his hands, delivered his message. Hereupon the King commanded sundry of his grandees and lords of his realm to fare forth and meet his brother's Wazir at the distance of a full day's journey. Which they did, greeting him respectfully and wishing him all prosperity and forming an escort and a procession. When he entered the city, he proceeded straightway to the palace, where he presented himself in the royal presence; and after kissing ground and praying for the King's health and happiness and for victory over all his enemies, he informed him that his brother was yearning to see him, and prayed for the pleasure of a visit.

He then delivered the letter, which Shah Zaman took from his hand and read. It contained sundry hints and allusions which required thought, but when the King had fully comprehended its import, he said, "I hear and I obey the commands of the beloved brother!" adding to the Wazir, "But we will not march till after the third day's hospitality." He appointed for the Minister fitting quarters of the palace and pitching tents for the troops, rationed them with whatever they might require of meat and drink and other necessaries. On the fourth day he made ready for wayfare and got together sumptuous presents befitting his elder brother's majesty, and stablished his chief Wazir Viceroy of the land during his absence. Then he caused his tents and camels and mules to be brought forth and encamped, with their bales and loads, attendants and guards, within sight of the city, in readiness to set out next morning for his brother's capital.

But when the night was half-spent he bethought him that he had forgotten in his palace somewhat which he should have brought with him, so he returned privily and entered his apartments, where he found the Queen, his wife, asleep on his own carpet bed embracing with both arms a black cook of loathsome aspect and foul with kitchen grease and grime. When he saw this the world waxed black before his sight and he said: "If such case happen while I am yet within sight of the city, what will be the doings of this damned whore during my long absence at my brother's court?" So he drew his scimitar, and cutting the two in four pieces with a single blow, left them on the carpet and returned presently to his camp without letting anyone know of what had happened. Then he gave orders for immediate departure and set out at once and began his travel; but he could not help thinking over his wife's treason, and he kept ever saying to himself: "How could she do this deed by me? How could she work her own death?" till excessive grief seized him, his color changed to yellow, his body waxed weak, and he was threatened with a dangerous malady, such a one as bringeth men to die. So the Wazir shortened his stages and tarried long at the watering stations, and did his best to solace the King.

Now when Shah Zaman drew near the capital of his brother, he dispatched vaunt-couriers and messengers of glad tidings to announce his arrival, and Shahryar came forth to meet him with his wazirs and emirs and lords and grandees of his realm, and saluted him and joyed with exceeding joy and caused the city to be decorated in his honor. When, however, the brothers met, the elder could not but see the change of complexion in the younger and questioned him of his case, whereto he replied: " 'Tis caused by the travails of wayfare and my case needs care, for I have suffered from the change of water and air! But Allah be praised for reuniting me with a brother so dear and so rare!" On this wise he dissembled and kept his secret, adding: "O King of the Time and Caliph of the Tide, only toil and moil have tinged my face yellow with bile and hath made my eyes sink deep in my head."

Then the two entered the capital in all honor, and the elder brother lodged the younger in a palace overhanging the pleasure garden. And after a time, seeing his condition still unchanged, he attributed it to his separation from his country and kingdom. So he let him wend his own ways and asked no questions of him till one day when he again said, "O my brother, I see thou art grown weaker of body and yellower of color." "O my brother," replied Shah Zaman, "I have an internal wound." Still he would not tell him what he had witnessed in his wife. Thereupon Shahryar summoned doctors and surgeons and bade them treat his brother according to the rules of art, which they did for a whole month. But their sherbets and potions naught availed, for he would dwell upon the deed of his wife, and despondency, instead of diminishing, prevailed, and leechcraft treatment utterly failed.

One day his elder brother said to him: "I am going forth to hunt and course and to take my pleasure and pastime. Maybe this would lighten thy heart." Shah Zaman, however, refused, saying: "O my brother, my soul yearneth for naught of this sort, and I entreat thy favor to suffer me tarry quietly in this place, being wholly taken up with my malady." So King Shah Zaman passed his night in the palace, and next morning when his brother had fared forth, he removed from his room and sat him down at one of the lattice windows overlooking the pleasure grounds. And there he abode thinking with saddest thought over his wife's betrayal, and burning sighs issued from his tortured breast.

And as he continued in this case lo! a postern of the palace, which was carefully kept private, swung open, and out of it came twenty slave girls surrounding his brother's wife, who was wondrous fair, a model of beauty and comeliness and symmetry and perfect loveliness, and who paced with the grace of a gazelle which panteth for the cooling stream. Thereupon Shah Zaman drew back from the window, but he kept the bevy in sight, espying them from a place whence he could not be espied. They walked under the very lattice and advanced a little way into the garden till they came to a jetting fountain a-middlemost a great basin of water. Then they stripped off their clothes, and behold, ten of them were women, cuncubines of the King, and the other ten were white slaves. Then they all paired off, each with each. But the Queen, who was left alone, presently cried out in a loud voice, "Here to me, O my lord Saeed!"

And then sprang with a drop leap from one of the trees a big slobbering blackamoor with rolling eyes which showed the whites, a truly hideous sight. He walked boldly up to her and threw his arms round her neck while she embraced him as warmly. Then he bussed her and winding his legs round hers, as a button loop clasps a button, he threw her and enjoyed her. On like wise did the other slaves with the girls till all had satisfied their passions, and they ceased not from kissing and clipping, coupling and carousing, till day began to wane, when the Mamelukes rose from the damsels' bosoms and the blackamoor slave dismounted from the Queen's breast. The men resumed their disguises and all except the Negro, who swarmed up the tree, entered the palace and closed the postern door as before.

Now when Shah Zaman saw this conduct of his sister-in-law, he said to himself: "By Allah, my calamity is lighter than this! My brother is a greater King among the Kings than I am, yet this infamy goeth on in his very palace, and his wife is in love with that filthiest of filthy slaves. But this only showeth that they all do it and that there is no woman but who cuckoldeth her husband. Then the curse of Allah upon one and all, and upon the fools who lean against them for support or who place the reins of conduct in their hands!" So he put away his melancholy and despondency, regret and repine, and allayed his sorrow by constantly repeating those words, adding, "'Tis my conviction that no man in this world is safe from their malice!"

When suppertime came, they brought him the trays and he ate with voracious appetite, for he had long refrained from meat, feeling unable to touch any dish, however dainty. Then he returned grateful thanks to Almighty Allah, praising Him and blessing Him, and he spent a most restful night, it having been long since he had savored the sweet food of sleep. Next day he broke his fast heartily and began to recover health and strength, and presently regained excellent condition. His brother came back from the chase ten days after, when he rode out to meet him and they saluted each other. And when King Shahryar looked at King Shah Zaman, he saw how the hue of health had returned to him, how his face had waxed ruddy, and how he ate with an appetite after his late scanty diet. He wondered much and said: "O my brother, I was no anxious that thou wouldst join me in hunting and chasing, and wouldst take thy pleasure and pastime in my dominion!" He thanked him and excused himself.

Then the two took horse and rode into the city, and when they were seated at their ease in the palace, the food trays were set before them and they ate their sufficiency. After the meats were removed and they had washed their hands, King Shahryar turned to his brother and said: "My mind is overcome with wonderment at thy condition. I was desirous to carry thee with me to the chase, but I saw thee changed in hue, pale and wan to view, and in sore trouble of mind too. But now, Alhamdolillah—glory be to God!—I see thy natural color hath returned to thy face and that thou art again in the best of case. It was my belief that thy sickness came of severance from thy family and friends, and absence from capital and country, so I refrained from troubling thee with further questions. But now I beseech thee to expound to me the cause of thy complaint and thy change of color, and to explain the reason of thy recovery and the return to the ruddy hue of health which I am wont to view. So speak out and hide naught!"

When Shah Zaman heard this, he bowed groundward awhile his head, then raised it and said: "I will tell thee what caused my complaint and my loss of color. But excuse my acquainting thee with the cause of its return to me and the reason of my complete recovery. Indeed I pray thee not to press me for a reply." Said Shahryar, who was much surprised by these words, "Let me hear first what produced thy pallor and thy poor condition." "Know, then, O my brother," rejoined Shah Zaman, "that when thou sentest thy Wazir with the invitation to place myself between thy hands, I made ready and marched out of my city. But presently I minded me having left behind me in the palace a string of jewels intended as a gift to thee. I returned for it alone, and found my wife on my carpet bed and in the arms of a hideous black cook. So I slew the twain and came to thee, yet my thoughts brooded over this business and I lost my bloom and became weak. But excuse me if I still refuse to tell thee what was the reason of my complexion returning."

Shahryar shook his head, marveling with extreme marvel, and with the fire of wrath flaming up from his heart, he cried, "Indeed, the malice of woman is mighty!" Then he took refuge from them with Allah and said: "In very sooth, O my brother, thou hast escaped many an evil by putting thy wife to death, and right excusable were thy wrath and grief for such mishap, which never yet befell crowned king like thee. By Allah, had the case been mine, I would not have been satisfied without slaying a thousand women, and that way madness lies! But now praise be to Allah Who hath tempered to thee thy tribulation, and needs must thou acquaint me with that which so suddenly restored to thee complexion and health, and explain to me what causeth this concealment." "O King of the Age, again I pray thee excuse my so doing!" "Nay, but thou must." "I fear, O my brother, lest the recital cause thee more anger and sorrow than afflicted me." "That were but a better reason," quoth Shahryar, "for telling me the whole history, and I conjure thee by Allah not to keep back aught from me."

Thereupon Shah Zaman told him all he had seen, from commencement to conclusion, ending with these words: "When I beheld thy calamity and the treason of thy wife, O my brother, and I reflected that thou art in years my senior and in sovereignty my superior, mine own sorrow was belittled by the comparison, and my mind recovered tone and temper. So, throwing off melancholy and despondency, I was able to eat and drink and sleep, and thus I speedily regained health and strength. Such is the truth and the whole truth." When King Shahryar heard this he waxed wroth with exceeding wrath, and rage was like to strangle him. But presently he recovered himself and said, "O my brother, I would not give thee the lie in this matter, but I cannot credit it till I see it with mine own eyes." "And thou wouldst look upon thy calamity," quoth Shah Zaman, "rise at once and make ready again for hunting and coursing, and then hide thyself with me. So shalt thou witness it and thine eyes shall verify it." "True," quoth the King. Whereupon he let make proclamation of his intent to travel, and the troops and tents fared forth without the city, camping within sight, and Shahryar sallied out with them and took seat a-midmost his host, bidding the slaves admit no man to him. When night came on, he summoned his Wazir and said to him, "Sit thou in my stead, and let none wot of my absence till the term of three days."

Then the brothers disguised themselves and returned by night with all secrecy to the palace, where they passed the dark hours. And at dawn they seated themselves at the lattice overlooking the pleasure grounds, when presently the Queen and her handmaids came out as before, and passing under the windows, made for the fountain. Here they stripped, ten of them being men to ten women, and the King's wife cried out, "Where art thou, O Saeed?" The hideous blackamoor dropped from the tree straightway, and rushing into her arms without stay or delay, cried out, "I am Sa'ad al-Din Saood!" The lady laughed heartily, and all fell to satisfying their lusts, and remained so occupied for a couple of hours, when the white slaves rose up from the handmaidens' breasts and the blackamoor dismounted from the Queen's bosom. Then they went into the basin and after performing the ghusl, or complete ablution, donned their dresses and retired as they had done before.

When King Shahryar saw this infamy of his wife and concubines, he became as one distraught, and he cried out: "Only in utter solitude can man be safe from the doings of this vile world! By Allah, life is naught but one great wrong." Presently he added, "Do not thwart me, O my brother, in what I propose." And the other answered, "I will not." So he said: "Let us up as we are and depart forthright hence, for we have no concern with kingship, and let us overwander Allah's earth, worshiping the Almighty till we find someone to whom the like calamity hath happened. And if we find none then will death be more welcome to us than life."

So the two brothers issued from a second private postern of the palace, and they never stinted wayfaring by day and by night until they reached a tree a-middle of a meadow hard by a spring of sweet water on the shore of the salt sea. Both drank of it and sat down to take their rest. And when an hour of the day had gone by, lo! they heard a mighty roar and uproar in the middle of the main as though the heavens were falling upon the earth, and the sea brake with waves before them and from it towered a black pillar, which grew and grew till it rose skyward and began making for that meadow. Seeing it, they waxed fearful exceedingly and climbed to the top of the tree, which was a lofty, whence they gazed to see what might be the matter. And behold, it was a Jinni, huge of height and burly of breast and bulk, broad of brow and black of blee, bearing on his head a coffer of crystal. He strode to land, wading through the deep, and coming to the tree whereupon were the two Kings, seated himself beneath it. He then set down the coffer on its bottom and out of it drew a casket with seven padlocks of steel, which he unlocked with seven keys of steel he took from beside his thigh, and out of it a young lady to come was seen, whiteskinned and of winsomest mien, of stature fine and thin, and bright as though a moon of the fourteenth night she had been, or the sun raining lively sheen. Even so the poet Utayyah hath excellently said:—

> She rose like the morn as she shone through the night
> And she gilded the grove with her gracious sight.
> From her radiance the sun taketh increase when
> She unveileth and shameth the moonshine bright.
> Bow down all beings between her hands
> As she showeth charms with her veil undight.
> And she floodeth cities with torrent tears
> When she flasheth her look of levin light.

The Jinni seated her under the tree by his side and looking at her, said: "O choicest love of this heart of mine! O dame of noblest line, whom I snatched away on thy bride night that none might prevent me taking thy maidenhead or tumble thee before I did, and whom none save myself hath loved or hath enjoyed. O my sweetheart! I would lief sleep a little while." He then laid his head upon the lady's thighs, and, stretching out his legs, which extended down to the sea, slept and snored and snarked like the roll of thunder. Presently she raised her head toward the treetop and saw the two Kings perched near the summit. Then she softly lifted off her lap the Jinni's pate, which she was tired of supporting, and placed it upon the ground, then, standing upright under the tree, signed to the Kings, "Come ye down, ye two, and fear naught from this Ifrit." They were in a terrible fright when they found that she had seen them, and answered her in the same manner, "Allah upon thee and by thy modesty, O lady, excuse us from coming down!" But she rejoined by saying: "Allah upon you both that ye come down forthright. And if ye come not, I will rouse upon you my husband, this Ifrit, and he shall do you to die by the illest of deaths." And she continued making signals to them.

So, being afraid, they came down to her, and she rose before them and said, "Stroke me a strong stroke, without stay or delay, otherwise will I arouse and set upon you this Ifrit, who shall slay you straightway." They said to her: "O our lady, we conjure thee by Allah, let us off this work, for we are fugitives from such, and in extreme dread and terror of this thy husband. How then can we do it in such a way as thou desirest?" "Leave this talk. It needs must be so," quoth she, and she swore them by Him who raised the skies on high without prop or pillar that if they worked not her will, she would cause them to be slain and cast into the sea. Whereupon out of fear King Shahryar said to King Shah Zaman, "O my brother, do thou what she biddeth thee do." But he replied, "I will not do it till thou do it before I do." And they began disputing about futtering her.

Then quoth she to the twain: "How is it I see you disputing and demurring? If ye do not come forward like men and do the deed of kind, ye two, I will arouse upon you the Ifrit." At this, by reason of their sore dread of the Jinni, both did by her what she bade them do, and when they had dismounted from her, she said, "Well done!" She then took from her pocket a purse and drew out a knotted string whereon were strung five hundred and seventy seal rings, and asked, "Know ye what be these?" They answered her saying, "We know not!" Then quoth she: "These be the signets of five hundred and seventy men who have all futtered me upon the horns of this foul, this foolish, this filthy Ifrit. So give me also your two seal rings, ye pair of brothers."

When they had drawn their two rings from their hands and given them to her, she said to them: "Of a truth this Ifrit bore me off on my bride night, and put me into a casket and set the casket in a coffer, and to the coffer he affixed seven strong padlocks of steel and deposited me on the deep bottom of the sea that raves, dashing and clashing with waves, and guarded me so that I might remain chaste and honest, quotha! that none save himself might have connection with me. But I have lain under as many of my kind as I please, and this wretched Jinni wotteth not that Destiny may not be averted nor hindered by aught, and that whatso woman willeth, the same she fulfilleth however man nilleth. Even so saith one of them:

> "Rely not on women,
> Trust not to their hearts,
> Whose joys and whose sorrows
> Are hung to their parts!
> Lying love they will swear thee
> Whence guile ne'er departs.
> Take Yusuf for sample,
> 'Ware sleights and 'ware smarts!
> Iblis ousted Adam
> (See ye not?) thro' their arts."

Hearing these words, they marveled with exceeding marvel, and she went from them to the Ifrit, and taking up his head on her thigh as before, said to them softly, "Now wend your ways and bear yourselves beyond the bounds of his malice." So they fared forth saying either to other, "Allah! Allah!" and: "There be no Majesty and there be no Might save in Allah, the Glorious, the Great, and with Him we seek refuge from women's malice and sleight, for of a truth it hath no mate in might. Consider, O my brother, the ways of this marvelous lady with an Ifrit, who is so much more powerful than we are. Now since there hath happened to him a greater mishap than that which befell us and which should bear us abundant consolation, so return we to our countries and capitals, and let us decide never to intermarry with womankind, and presently we will show them what will be our action."

Thereupon they rode back to the tents of King Shahryar, which they reached on the morning of the third day. And having mustered the wazirs and emirs, the chamberlains and high officials, he gave a robe of honor to his Viceroy and issued orders for an immediate return to the city. There he sat him upon his throne and, sending for the Chief Minister, the father of the two damsels who (Inshallah!) will presently be mentioned, he said, "I command thee to take my wife and smite her to death, for she hath broken her plight and her faith." So he carried her to the place of execution and did her die. Then King

Shahryar took brand in hand and, repairing to the seraglio, slew all the concubines and their Mamelukes. He also sware himself by a binding oath that whatever wife he married he would abate her maidenhead at night and slay her next morning, to make sure of his honor. "For," said he, "there never was nor is there one chaste woman upon the face of earth."

Then Shah Zaman prayed for permission to fare homeward, and he went forth equipped and escorted and traveled till he reached his own country. Meanwhile Shahryar commanded his Wazir to bring him the bride of the night that he might go in to her. So he produced a most beautiful girl, the daughter of one of the emirs, and the King went in unto her at eventide. And when morning dawned, he bade his Minister strike off her head, and the Wazir did accordingly, for fear of the Sultan. On this wise he continued for the space of three years, marrying a maiden every night and killing her the next morning, till folk raised an outcry against him and cursed him, praying Allah utterly to destroy him and his rule. And women made an uproar and mothers wept and parents fled with their daughters till there remained not in the city a young person fit for carnal copulation.

Presently the King ordered his Chief Wazir, the same who was charged with the executions, to bring him a virgin, as was his wont, and the Minister went forth and searched and found none. So he returned home in sorrow and anxiety, fearing for his life from the King. Now he had two daughters, Scheherazade and Dunyazade, hight, of whom the elder had perused the books, annals, and legends of preceding kings, and the stories, examples, and instances of bygone men and things. Indeed it was said that she had collected a thousand books of histories relating to antique races and departed rulers. She had purused the works of the poets and knew them by heart, she had studied philosophy and the sciences, arts, and accomplishments. And she was pleasant and polite, wise and witty, well read and well bred. Now on that day she said to her father: "Why do I see thee thus changed and laden with cark and care? Concerning this matter quoth one of the poets:

> "Tell whoso hath sorrow
> Grief never shall last.
> E'en as joy hath no morrow
> So woe shall go past."

When the Wazir heard from his daughter these words, he related to her, from first to last, all that had happened between him and the King. Thereupon said she: "By Allah, O my father, how long shall this slaughter of women endure? Shall I tell thee what is in my mind in order to save both sides from destruction?" "Say on, O my daughter," quoth he, and quoth she: "I wish thou wouldst give me in marriage to this King Shahryar. Either I shall live or I shall be a ransom for the virgin daughters of Moslems and the cause of their deliverance from his hands and thine." "Allah upon thee!" cried he in wrath exceeding that lacked no feeding. "O scanty of wit, expose not thy life to such peril! How durst thou address me in words so wide from wisdom and unfar from foolishness? Know that one who lacketh experience in worldly matters readily falleth into misfortune, and whoso considereth not the end keepeth not the world to friend, and the vulgar say: 'I was lying at mine ease. Naught but my officiousness brought me unease'." "Needs must thou," she broke in, "make me a doer of this good deed, and let him kill me an he will. I shall only die a ransom for others." "O my daughter," asked he, "and how shall that profit thee when thou shalt have thrown away thy life?" And she answered, "O my father, it must be, come of it what will!" The Wazir was again moved to fury and blamed and reproached her, ending with, "In very deed I fear lest the same befall thee which befell the bull and the ass with the husbandman." "And what," asked she, "befell them, O my father?" Whereupon the Wazir began

THE TALE OF THE BULL AND THE ASS

KNOW, O my daughter, that there was once a merchant who owned much money and many men, and who was rich in cattle and camels. He had also a wife and family, and he dwelt in the country, being experienced in husbandry and devoted to agriculture. Now Allah Most High had endowed him with understanding the tongues of beasts and birds of every kind, but under pain of death if he divulged the gift to any. So he kept it secret for very fear. He had in his cow house a bull and an ass, each tethered in his own stall, one hard by the other. As the merchant was sitting near-hand one day with his servants and his children were playing about him, he heard and bull say to the ass:

"Hail and health to thee O Father of Waking! for that thou enjoyest rest and good ministering. All under thee is clean-swept and fresh-sprinkled. Men wait upon thee and feed thee, and thy provaunt is sifted barley and thy drink pure spring water, while I (unhappy creature!) am led forth in the middle of the night, when they set on my neck the plow and a something called yoke, and I tire at cleaving the earth from dawn of day till set of sun. I am forced to do more than I can and to bear all manner of ill-treatment from night to night. After which they take me back with my sides torn, my neck flayed, my legs aching, and mine eyelids sored with tears. Then they shut me up in the byre and throw me beans and crushed straw mixed with dirt and chaff, and I lie in dung and filth and foul stinks through the livelong night. But thou art ever in a place swept and sprinkled and cleansed, and thou art always lying at ease, save when it happens (and seldom enough!) that the master hath some business, when he mounts thee and rides thee to town and returns with thee forthright. So it happens that I am toiling and distrest while thou takest thine ease and thy rest. Thou sleepest while I am sleepless, I hunger still while thou eatest thy fill, and I win contempt while thou winnest goodwill."

When the bull ceased speaking, the ass turned toward him and said: "O Broad-o'-Brow, O thou lost one! He lied not who dubbed thee bullhead, for thou, O father of a bull, hast neither forethought nor contrivance. Thou art the simplest of simpletons, and thou knowest naught of good advisers. Hast thou not heard the saying of the wise?

>   "For others these hardships and labors I bear,
>   And theirs is the pleasure and mine is the care,
>   As the bleacher who blacketh his brow in the sun
>   To whiten the raiment which other men wear.

But thou, O fool, art full of zeal, and thou toilest and moilest before the master, and thou tearest and wearest and slayest thyself for the comfort of another. Hast thou never heard the saw that saith 'None to guide and from the way go wide'? Thou wendest forth at the call to dawn prayer and thou returnest not till sundown, and through the livelong day thou endurest all manner hardships: to wit, beating and belaboring and bad language.

"Now hearken to me, Sir Bull! When they tie thee to thy stinking manger, thou pawest the ground with thy forehand and lashest out with thy hind hoofs and pushest with thy horns and bellowest aloud, so they deem thee contented. And when they throw thee thy fodder, thou fallest on it with greed and hastenest to line thy fair fat paunch. But if thou accept any advice, it will be better for thee, and thou wilt lead an easier life even than mine. When thou goest a-field and they lay the thing called yoke on thy neck, lie down and rise not again, though haply they swinge thee. And if thou rise, lie down a second time. And when they bring thee home and offer thee thy beans, fall backward and only sniff at thy meat and withdraw thee and taste it not, and be satisfied with thy crushed straw and chaff. And on this wise feign thou art sick, and cease not doing thus for a day or two days or even three days; so shalt thou have rest from toil and moil."

When the Bull heard these words, he knew the ass to be his friend and thanked him, saying, "Right is thy rede," and prayed that all blessings might requite him, and cried: "O Father Wakener! Thou hast made up for my failings." (Now the merchant, O my daughter, understood all that passed between them.) Next day the driver took the bull and, settling the plow on his neck, made him work as wont. But the bull began to shirk his plowing, according to the advice of the ass, and the plowman drubbed him till he broke the yoke and made off. But the man caught him up and leathered him till he despaired of his life. Not the less, however, would he do nothing but stand still and drop down till the evening. Then the herd led him home and stabled him in his stall, but he drew back from his manger and neither stamped nor ramped nor butted nor bellowed as he was wont to do, whereat the man wondered. He brought him the beans and husks, but he sniffed at them and left them and lay down as far from them as he could and passed the whole night fasting. The peasant came next morning and, seeing the manger full of beans, the crushed straw untasted, and the ox lying on his back in sorriest plight, with legs outstretched and swollen belly, he was concerned for him, and said to himself, "By Allah, he hath assuredly sickened, and this is the cause why he would not plow yesterday."

Then he went to the merchant and reported: "O my master, the bull is ailing. He refused his fodder last night—nay, more, he hath not tasted a scrap of it this morning." Now the merchant-farmer understood what all this meant, because he had overheard the talk between the bull and the ass, so quoth he, "Take that rascal donkey, and set the yoke on his neck, and bind him to the plow and make him do bull's work." Thereupon the plowman took the ass, and worked him through the livelong day at the bull's task. And when he failed for weakness, he made him eat stick till his ribs were sore and his sides were sunken and his neck was flayed by the yoke. And when he came home in the evening he could hardly drag his limbs along, either forehand or hind legs. But as for the bull, he had passed the day lying at full length, and had eaten his fodder with an excellent appetite, and he ceased not calling down blessings on the ass for his good advice, unknowing what had come to him on his account.

So when night set in and the ass returned to the byre, the bull rose up before him in honor, and said: "May good tidings gladden thy heart, O Father Wakener! Through thee I have rested all this day, and I have eaten my meat in peace and quiet." But the ass returned no reply, for wrath and heartburning and fatigue and the beating he had gotten. And he repented with the most grievous of repentance, and quoth he to himself: "This cometh of my folly in giving good counsel. As the saw saith, I was in joy and gladness, naught save my officiousness brought me this sadness. And now I must take thought and put a trick upon him and return him to his place, else I die." Then he went aweary to his manger while the bull thanked him and blessed him.

And even so, O my daughter (said the Wazir) thou wilt die for lack of wits. Therefore sit thee still and say naught and expose not thy life to such stress, for, by Allah, I offer thee the best advice, which cometh of my affection and kindly solicitate for thee. "O my father," she answered, "needs must I go up to this King and be married to him." Quoth he, "Do not this deed," and quoth she, "Of a truth I will." Whereat he rejoined, "If thou be not silent and bide still, I will do with thee even what the merchant did with his wife." "And what did he?" asked she.

Know then (answered the Wazir) that after the return of the ass the merchant came out on the terrace roof with his wife and family, for it was a moonlit night and the moon at its full. Now the terrace overlooked the cow house, and presently as he sat there with his children playing about him, the trader heard the ass say to the bull, "Tell me, O father Broad-o'-Brow, what thou purposest to do tomorrow." The bull answered: "What but continue to follow thy counsel, O Aliboron? Indeed it was as good as good could be, and it hath given me rest and repose, nor will I now depart from it one tittle. So when they bring me my meat, I will refuse it and blow out my belly and counterfeit crank." The ass shook his head and said, "Beware of so doing, O Father of a Bull!" The bull asked, "Why?" and the ass answered, "Know that I am about to give thee the best of counsel, for verily I heard our owner say to the herd, 'If the bull rise not from his place to do his work this morning and if he retire from his fodder this day, make him over to the butcher that he may slaughter him and give his flesh to the poor, and fashion a bit of leather from his hide.' Now I fear for thee on account of this. So take my advice ere a calamity befall thee, and when they bring thee thy fodder, eat it and rise up and bellow and paw the ground, or our master will assuredly slay thee. And peace be with thee!"

Thereupon the bull arose and lowed aloud and thanked the ass, and said, "Tomorrow I will readily go forth with them." And he at once ate up all his meat and even licked the manger. (All this took place and the owner was listening to their talk.) Next morning the trader and his wife went to the bull's crib and sat down, and the driver came and led forth the bull, who, seeing his owner, whisked his tail and brake wind, and frisked about so lustily that the merchant laughed a loud laugh and kept laughing till he fell on his back. His wife asked him, "Whereat laughest thou with such loud laughter as this?" and he answered her, "I laughed at a secret something which I have heard and seen but cannot say lest I die my death." She returned, "Perforce thou must discover it to me, and disclose the cause of thy laughing even if thou come by thy death!" But he rejoined, "I cannot reveal what beasts and birds say in their lingo for fear I die." Then quoth she: "By Allah, thou liest! This is a mere pretext. Thou laughest at none save me, and now thou wouldest hide somewhat from me. But by the Lord of the Heaven, an thou disclose not the cause I will no longer cohabit with thee, I will leave thee at once." And she sat down and cried.

Whereupon quoth the merchant: "Woe betide thee! What means thy weeping? Fear Allah, and leave these words and query me no more questions." "Needs must thou tell me the cause of that laugh," said she, and he replied: "Thou wottest that when I prayed Allah to vouchsafe me understanding of the tongues of beasts and birds, I made a vow never to disclose the secret to any under pain of dying on the spot." "No matter!" cried she. "Tell me what secret passed between the bull and the ass and die this very hour an thou be so minded." And she ceased not to importune him till he was worn-out and clean distraught. So at last he said, "Summon thy father and thy mother and our kith and kin and sundry of our neighbors." Which she did, and he sent for the kazi[1] and his assessors, intending to make his will and reveal to her his secret and die the death; for he loved her with love exceeding because she was his cousin, the daughter of his father's brother, and the mother of his children, and he had lived with her a life of a hundred and twenty years.

Then, having assembled all the family and the folk of his neighborhood, he said to them, "By me there hangeth a strange story, and 'tis such that if I discover the secret to any, I am a dead man." Therefore quoth every one of those present to the woman, "Allah upon thee, leave this sinful obstinacy and recognize the right of this matter, lest haply thy husband and the father of thy children die." But she rejoined, "I will not turn from it till he tell me, even though he come by his death." So they ceased to urge her, and the trader rose from amongst them and repaired to an outhouse to perform the wuzu ablution, and he purposed thereafter to return and to tell them his secret and to die.

Now, Daughter Scheherazade, that merchant had in his outhouses some fifty hens under one cock, and whilst making ready to farewell his folk he heard one of his many farm dogs thus address in his own tongue the cock, who was flapping his wings and crowing lustily and jumping from one hen's back to another and treading all in turn, saying: "O Chanticleer! How mean is thy wit and how shameless is thy conduct! Be he disappointed who brought thee up. Art thou not ashamed of thy doings on such a day as this?" "And what," asked the rooster, "hath occurred this day?" when the dog answered; "Dost thou not know that our master is this day making ready for his death? His wife is resolved that he shall disclose the secret taught to him by Allah, and the moment he so doeth he shall surely die. We dogs are all a-mourning, but thou clappest thy wings and clarionest thy loudest and treadest hen after hen. Is this an hour for pastime and pleasuring? Art thou not ashamed of thyself?"

"Then by Allah," quoth the cock, "is our master a lackwit and a man scanty of sense. If he cannot manage matters with a single wife, his life is not worth prolonging. Now I have some fifty dame partlets, and I please this and provoke that and starve one and stuff another, and through my good governance they are all well under my control. This our master pretendeth to wit and wisdom, and he hath but one

[1] Judge.

wife and yet knoweth not how to manage her." Asked the dog, "What then, O Cock, should the master do to win clear of his strait?" "He should arise forthright," answered the cock, "and take some twigs from yon mulberry tree and give her a regular back-basting and ribroasting till she cry: 'I repent, O my lord! I will never ask thee a question as long as I live!' Then let him beat her once more and soundly, and when he shall have done this, he shall sleep free from care and enjoy life. But this master of ours owns neither sense nor judgment."

"Now, Daughter Scheherazade," continued the Wazir, "I will do to thee as did that husband to that wife." Said Scheherazade, "And what did he do?" He replied, "When the merchant heard the wise words spoken by his cock to his dog, he arose in haste and sought his wife's chamber, after cutting for her some mulberry twigs and hiding them there. And then he called to her, "Come into the closet, that I may tell thee the secret while no one seeth me, and then die." She entered with him and he locked the door and came down upon her with so sound a beating of back and shoulders, ribs, arms, and legs, saying the while "Wilt thou ever be asking questions about what concerneth thee not?" that she was well-nigh senseless. Presently she cried out: "I am of the repentant! By Allah, I will ask thee no more questions, and indeed I repent sincerely and wholesomely." Then she kissed his hand and feet and he led her out of the room submissive, as a wife should be. Her parents and all the company rejoiced and sadness and mourning were changed into joy and gladness.

Thus the merchant learnt family discipline from his cock and he and his wife lived together the happiest of lives until death. And thou also, O my daughter! continued the Wazir, unless thou turn from this matter I will do by thee what that trader did to his wife. But she answered him with much decision: "I will never desist, O my father, nor shall this tale change my purpose. Leave such talk and tattle. I will not listen to thy words and if thou deny me, I will marry myself to him despite the nose of thee. And first I will go up to the King myself and alone and I will say to him: 'I prayed my father to wive me with thee, but he refused, being resolved to disappoint his lord, grudging the like of me to the like of thee'." Her father asked, "Must this needs be?" and she answered, "Even so."

Hereupon the Wazir, being weary of lamenting and contending, persuading and dissuading her, all to no purpose, went up to King Shahryar and, after blessing him and kissing the ground before him, told him all about his dispute with his daughter from first to last and how he designed to bring her to him that night. The King wondered with exceeding wonder, for he had made an especial exception of the Wazir's daughter, and said to him: "O most faithful of counsellors, how is this? Thou wottest that I have sworn by the Raiser of the Heavens that after I have gone into her this night I shall say to thee on the morrow's morning, 'Take her and slay her!' And if thou slay her not, I will slay thee in her stead without fail." "Allah guide thee to glory and lengthen thy life, O King of the Age," answered the Wazir. "It is she that hath so determined. All this have I told her and more, but she will not hearken to me and she persisteth in passing this coming night with the King's Majesty." So Shahryar rejoiced greatly and said, " 'Tis well. Go get her ready, and this night bring her to me." The Wazir returned to his daughter and reported to her the command, saying, "Allah make not thy father desolate by thy loss!"

But Scheherazade rejoiced with exceeding joy and gat ready all she required and said to her younger sister, Dunyazade: "Note well what directions I entrust to thee! When I have gone into the King I will send for thee, and when thou comest to me and seest that he hath had his carnal will of me, do thou say to me: 'O my sister, an thou be not sleepy, relate to me some new story, delectable and delightsome, the better to speed our waking hours.' And I will tell thee a tale which shall be our deliverance, if so Allah please, and which shall turn the King from his bloodthirsty custom." Dunyazade answered "With love and gladness."

So when it was night, their father the Wazir carried Scheherazade to the King, who was gladdened at the sight and asked, "Hast thou brought me my need?" And he answered, "I have." But when the King took her to his bed and fell to toying with her and wished to go in to her, she wept, which made him ask, "What aileth thee?" She replied, "O King of the Age, I have a younger sister, and lief would I take leave of her this night before I see the dawn." So he sent at once for Dunyazade and she came and kissed the ground between his hands, when he permitted her to take her seat near the foot of the couch. Then the King arose and did away with his bride's maidenhead and the three fell asleep.

But when it was midnight Scheherazade awoke and signaled to her sister Dunyazade, who sat up and said, "Allah upon thee, O my sister, recite to us some new story, delightsome and delectable, wherewith to while away the waking hours of our latter night." "With joy and goodly gree," answered Scheherazade, "if this pious and auspicious King permit me." "Tell on," quoth the King, who chanced to be sleepless and restless and therefore was pleased with the prospect of hearing her story. So Scheherazade rejoiced, and thus, on the first night of the Thousand Nights and a Night, she began her recitations.

THE TALES OF SCHEHERAZADE

THE FISHERMAN AND THE JINNI

It hath reached me, O auspicious King, that there was a fisherman well stricken in years who had a wife and three children, and withal was of poor condition. Now it was his custom to cast his net every day four times, and no more. On a day he went forth about noontide to the seashore, where he laid down his basket and, tucking up his shirt and plunging into the water, made a cast with his net and waited till it settled to the bottom. Then he gathered the cords together and haled away at it, but found it weighty. And however much he drew it landward, he could not pull it up, so he carried the ends ashore and drove a stake into the ground and made the net fast to it. Then he stripped and dived into the water all about the net, and left not off working hard until he had brought it up.

He rejoiced thereat and, donning his clothes, went to the net, when he found in it a dead jackass which had torn the meshes. Now when he saw it, he exclaimed in his grief, "There is no Majesty and there is no Might save in Allah the Glorious, the Great!" Then quoth he, "This is a strange manner of daily bread," and he began reciting in extempore verse:

"O toiler through the glooms of night in peril and in pain,
  Thy toiling stint for daily bread comes not by might and main!
Seest thou not the fisher seek afloat upon the sea
  His bread, while glimmer stars of night as set in tangled skein?
Anon he plungeth in despite the buffet of the waves,
  The while to sight the bellying net his eager glances strain,
Till joying at the night's success, a fish he bringeth home
  Whose gullet by the hook of Fate was caught and cut in twain.
When buys that fish of him a man who spent the hours of night
  Reckless of cold and wet and gloom in ease and comfort fain,
Laud to the Lord who gives to this, to that denies, his wishes
  And dooms one toil and catch the prey and other eat the fishes."

Then quoth he, "Up and to it. I am sure of His beneficence, Inshallah!" So he continued:

> "When thou art seized of Evil Fate, assume
> The noble soul's long-suffering. 'Tis thy best.
> Complain not to the creature, this be 'plaint
> From one most Ruthful to the ruthlessest."

The fisherman, when he had looked at the dead ass, got it free of the toils and wrung out and spread his net. Then he plunged into the sea, saying, "In Allah's name!" and made a cast and pulled at it, but it grew heavy and settled down more firmly than the first time. Now he thought that there were fish in it, and he made it fast and, doffing his clothes, went into the water, and dived and haled until he drew it up upon dry land. Then found he in it a large earthern pitcher which was full of sand and mud, and seeing this, he was greatly troubled. So he prayed pardon of Allah and, throwing away the jar, wrung his net and cleansed it and returned to the sea the third time to cast his net, and waited till it had sunk. Then he pulled at it and found therein potsherds and broken glass. Then, raising his eyes heavenward, he said: "O my God! Verily Thou wottest that I cast not my net each day save four times. The third is done and as yet Thou hast vouchsafed me nothing. So this time, O my God, deign give me my daily bread."

Then, having called on Allah's name, he again threw his net and waited its sinking and settling, whereupon he haled at it but could not draw it in for that it was entangled at the bottom. He cried out in his vexation, "There is no Majesty and there is no Might save in Allah!" and he began reciting:

> "Fie on this wretched world, an so it be
> I must be whelmed by grief and misery.
> Tho' gladsome be man's lot when dawns the morn,
> He drains the cup of woe ere eve he see.
> Yet was I one of whom the world when asked
> 'Whose lot is happiest?' oft would say, ' 'Tis he!' "

Thereupon he stripped and, diving down to the net, busied himself with it till it came to land. Then he opened the meshes and found therein a cucumber-shaped jar of yellow copper, evidently full of something, whose mouth was made fast with a leaden cap stamped with the seal ring of our Lord Solomon, son of David (Allah accept the twain!). Seeing this, the fisherman rejoiced and said, "If I sell it in the brass bazaar, 'tis worth ten golden dinars." He shook it, and finding it heavy, continued: "Would to Heaven I knew what is herein. But I must and will open it and look to its contents and store it in my bag and sell it in the brass market." And taking out a knife, he worked at the lead till he had loosened it from the jar. Then he laid the cup on the ground and shook the vase to pour out whatever might be inside. He found nothing in it, whereat he marveled with an exceeding marvel. But presently there came forth from the jar a smoke which spired heavenward into ether (whereat he again marveled with mighty marvel), and which trailed along earth's surface till presently, having reached its full height, the thick vapor condensed, and became an Ifrit huge of bulk, whose crest touched the clouds while his feet were on the ground. His head was as a dome, his hands like pitchforks, his legs long as masts, and his mough big as a cave. His teeth were like large stones, his nostrils ewers, his eyes two lamps, and his look was fierce and lowering.

Now when the fisherman saw the Ifrit, his side muscles quivered, his teeth chattered, his spittle dried up, and he became blind about what to do. Upon this the Ifrit looked at him and cried, "there is no god but *the* God, and Solomon is the prophet of God," presently adding: "O Apostle of Allah, slay me not. Never again will I gainsay thee in word nor sin against thee in deed." Quoth the fisherman, "O Marid, diddest thou say Solomon the Apostle of Allah? And Solomon is dead some thousand and eight hundred years ago, and we are now in the last days of the world! What is thy story, and what is thy account of thyself, and what is the cause of thy entering into this cucurbit?"

Now when the Evil Spirit heard the words of the fisherman, quoth he: "There is no god but *the* God. Be of good cheer, O Fisherman!" Quoth the fisherman, "Why biddest thou me to be of good cheer?" And he replied, "Because of thy having to die an ill death in this very hour." Said the fisherman, "Thou deservest for thy good tidings the withdrawal of Heaven's protection, O thou distant one! Wherefore shouldest thou kill me, and what thing have I done to deserve death, I who freed thee from the jar, and saved thee from the depths of the sea, and brought thee up on the dry land?" Replied the Ifrit, "Ask of me only what mode of death thou wilt die, and by what manner of slaughter shall I slay thee." Rejoined the fisherman, "What is my crime, and wherefore such retribution?" Quoth the Ifrit, "Hear my story, O Fisherman!" And he answered, "Say on, and be brief in thy saying, for of very sooth my life breath is in my nostrils."

Thereupon quoth the Jinni: "Know that I am one among the heretical Jann, and I sinned against Solomon, David-son (on the twain be peace!), I together with the famous Sakhr al-Jinni, whereupon the Prophet sent his Minister, Asaf son of Barkhiya, to seize me. And this Wazir brought me against my will and led me in bonds to him (I being downcast despite my nose), and he placed me standing before him like a suppliant. When Solomon saw me, he took refuge with Allah and bade me embrace the True Faith and obey his behests. But I refused, so, sending for this cucurbit, he shut me up therein and stopped it over with lead, whereon he impressed the Most High Name, and gave his orders to the Jann, who carried me off and cast me into the midmost of the ocean. There I abode a hundred years, during which I said in my heart, 'Whoso shall release me, him will I enrich forever and ever.'

"But the full century went by and, when no one set me free, I entered upon the second fivescore saying, 'Whoso shall release me, for him I will open the hoards of the earth.' Still no one set me free, and thus four hundred years passed away. Then quoth I, 'Whoso shall release me, for him will I fulfill three wishes.' Yet no one set me free. Thereupon I waxed wroth with exceeding wrath and said to myself, 'Whoso shall release me from this time forth, him will I slay, and I will give him choice of what death he will die.' And now, as thou hast released me, I give thee full choice of deaths."

The fisherman, hearing the words of the Ifrit, said, "O Allah! The wonder of it that I have not come to free thee save in these days!" adding, "Spare my life, so Allah spare thine, and slay me not, lest Allah set one to slay thee." Replied the Contumacious One, "There is no help for it. Die thou must, so ask by way of boon what manner of death thou wilt die." Albeit thus certified, the fisherman again addressed the Ifrit, saying, "Forgive me this my death as a generous reward for having freed thee," and the Ifrit, "Surely I would not slay thee save on account of that same release." "O Chief of the Ifrits," said the fisherman, "I do thee good and thou requitest me with evil! In very sooth the old saw lieth not when it saith:

> "We wrought them weal, they met our weal with ill,
> Such, by my life! is every bad man's labor.
> To him who benefits unworthy wights
> Shall hap what hapt to Ummi-Amir's neighbor."[1]

Now when the Ifrit heard these words he answered: "No more of this talk. Needs must I kill thee." Upon this the fisherman said to himself: "This is a Jinni, and I am a man to whom Allah hath given a passably cunning wit, so I will now cast about to compass his destruction by my contrivance and by mine intelligence, even as he took counsel only of his malice and his frowardness." He began by asking the Ifrit, "Hast thou indeed resolved to kill me?" And, receiving for all answer "Even so," he cried, "Now in the Most Great Name, graven on the seal ring of Solomon the son of David (peace be with the holy twain!), an I question thee on a certain matter, wilt thou give me a true answer?" The Ifrit replied "Yea," but, hearing mention of the Most Great Name, his wits were troubled and he said with trembling, "Ask and be brief."

Quoth the fisherman: "How didst thou fit into this bottle which would not hold thy hand—no, nor even thy foot—and how came it to be large enough to contain the whole of thee?" Replied the Ifrit, "What! Dost not believe that I was all there?" And the fisherman rejoined, "Nay! I will never believe it until I see thee inside with my own eyes." The Evil Spirit on the instant shook and became a vapor, which condensed and entered the jar little and little, till all was well inside, when lo! the fisherman in hot haste took the leaden cap with the seal and stoppered therewith the mouth of the jar and called out to the Ifrit, saying: "Ask me by way of boon what death thou wilt die! By Allah, I will throw thee into the sea before us and here will I build me a lodge, and whoso cometh hither I will warn him against fishing and will say: 'In these waters abideth an Ifrit who giveth as a last favor a choice of deaths and fashion of slaughter to the man who saveth him!'"

Now when the Ifrit heard this from the fisherman and saw himself in limbo, he was minded to escape, but this was prevented by Solomon's seal. So he knew that the fisherman had cozened and outwitted him, and he waxed lowly and submissive and began humbly to say, "I did but jest with thee." But the other answered, "Thou liest, O vilest of the

---

[1] Ummi-Amir is the hyena, which bites the hand that feeds it.

Ifrits, and meanest and filthiest!" And he set off with the bottle for the seaside, the Ifrit calling out, "Nay! Nay!" and he calling out, "Aye! Aye!" Thereupon the Evil Spirit softened his voice and smoothed his speech and abased himself, saying, "What wouldest thou do with me, O Fisherman?" "I will throw thee back into the sea," he answered, "Where thou hast been housed and homed for a thousand and eight hundred years. And now I will leave thee therein till Judgment Day. Did I not say to thee, 'Spare me and Allah shall spare thee, and slay me not lest Allah slay thee'? yet thou spurnedst my supplication and hadst no intention save to deal ungraciously by me, and Allah hath now thrown thee into my hands, and I am cunninger that thou." Quoth the Ifrit, "Open for me that I may bring thee weal." Quoth the fisherman: "Thou liest, thou accursed! Nothing would satisfy thee save my death, so now I will do thee die by hurling thee into this sea." Then the Marid roared aloud and cried: "Allah upon thee, O Fisherman, don't! Spare me, and pardon my past doings, and as I have been tyrannous, so be thou generous, for it is said among sayings that go current: 'O thou who doest good to him who hath done thee evil, suffice for the ill-doer his ill deeds, and do not deal with me as did Umamah to 'Atikah.'"

Asked the fisherman, "And what was their case?" And the Ifrit answered, "This is not the time for storytelling and I in this prison, but set me free and I will tell thee the tale." Quoth the fisherman: "Leave this language. There is no help but that thou be thrown back into the sea, nor is there any way for thy getting out of it forever and ever. Vainly I placed myself under thy protection, and I humbled myself to thee with weeping, while thou soughtest only to slay me, who had done thee no injury deserving this at thy hands. Nay, so far from injuring thee by any evil act, I worked thee naught but weal in releasing thee from that jail of thine. Now I knew thee to be an evildoer when thou diddest to me what thou didst, and know that when I have cast thee back into this sea, I will warn whosoever may fish thee up of what hath befallen me with thee, and I will advise him to toss thee back again. So shalt thou abide here under these waters till The End of Time shall make an end of thee." But the Ifrit cried aloud: "Set me free. This is a noble occasion for generosity, and I make covenant with thee and vow never to do thee hurt and harm—nay, I will help thee to what shall put thee out of want."

The fisherman accepted his promises on both conditions, not to trouble him as before, but on the contrary to do him service, and after making firm the plight and swearing him a solemn oath by Allah Most Highest, he opened the cucurbit. Thereupon the pillar of smoke rose up till all of it was fully out, then it thickened and once more became an Ifrit of hideous presence, who forthright administered a kick to the bottle and sent it flying into the sea. The fisherman, seeing how the cucurbit was treated and making sure of his own death, piddled in his clothes and said to himself, "This promiseth badly," but he fortified his heart, and cried: "O Ifrit, Allah hath said: 'Perform your covenant, for the performance of your covenant shall be inquired into hereafter.' Thou hast made a vow to me and hast sworn an oath not to play me false lest Allah play thee false, for verily He is a jealous God who respiteth the sinner but letteth him not escape. I say to thee as said the Sage Duban to King Yunan, 'Spare me so Allah may spare thee!'" The Ifrit burst into laughter and stalked away, saying to the fisherman, "Follow me."

And the man paced after him at a safe distance (for he was not assured of escape) till they had passed round the suburbs of the city. Thence they struck into the uncultivated grounds and, crossing them, descended into a broad wilderness, and lo! in the midst of it stood a mountain tarn. The Ifrit waded in to the middle and again cried, "Follow me," and when this was done he took his stand in the center and bade the man cast his net and catch his fish. The fisherman looked into the water and was much astonished to see therein vari-colored fishes, white and red, blue and yellow. However, he cast his net and, hauling it in, saw that he had netted four fishes, one of each color. Thereat he rejoiced greatly, and more when the Ifrit said to him: "Carry these to the Sultan and set them in his presence, then he will give thee what shall make thee a wealthy man. And now accept my excuse, for by Allah, at this time I wot none other way of benefiting thee, inasmuch I have lain in this sea eighteen hundred years and have not seen the face of the world save within this hour. But I would not have thee fish here save once a day." The Ifrit then gave him Godspeed, saying, "Allah grant we meet again," and struck the earth with one foot, whereupon the ground clove asunder and swallowed him up.

The fisherman, much marveling at what had happened to him with the Ifrit, took the fish and made for the city, and as soon as he reached home he filled an earthen bowl with water and therein threw the fish, which began to struggle and wriggle about. Then he bore off the bowl upon his head and, repairing to the King's palace (even as the Ifrit had bidden him) laid the fish before the presence. And the King wondered with exceeding wonder at the sight, for never in his lifetime had he seen fishes like these in quality or in conformation. So he said, "Give those fish to the stranger slave girl who now cooketh for us," meaning the bondmaiden whom the King of Roum had sent to him only three days before, so that he had not yet made trial of her talents in the dressing of meat.

Thereupon the Wazir carried the fish to the cook and bade her fry them, saying: O damsel, the King sendeth this say to thee: 'I have not treasured thee, O tear o' me! save for stress time of me.' Approve, then, to us this day thy delicate handiwork and thy savory cooking, for this dish of fish is a present sent to the Sultan and evidently a rarity." The Wazir, after he had carefully charged her, returned to the King, who commanded him to give the fisherman four hundred dinars. He gave them accordingly, and the man took them to his bosom and ran off home stumbling and falling and rising again and deeming the whole thing to be a dream. However, he bought for his family all they wanted, and lastly he went to his wife in huge joy and gladness. So far concerning him.

But as regards the cookmaid, she took the fish and cleansed them and set them in the frying pan, basting them with oil till one side was dressed. Then she turned them over and behold, the kitchen wall clave asunder, and therefrom came a young lady, fair of form, oval of face, perfect in grace, with eyelids which kohl lines enchase. Her dress was a silken headkerchief fringed and tasseled with blue. A large ring hung from either ear, a pair of bracelets adorned her wrists, rings with bezels of priceless gems were on her fingers, and she hent in hand a long rod of rattan cane which she thrust into the frying pan, saying, "O fish! O fish! Be ye constant to your convenant?" When the cookmaiden saw this apparition she swooned away. The young lady repeated her words a second time and a third time, and at last the fishes raised their heads from the pan, and saying in articulate speech, "Yes! Yes!" began with one voice to recite:

> "Come back and so will I! Keep faith and so will I!
> And if ye fain forsake, I'll requite till quits we cry!"

After this the young lady upset the frying pan and went forth by the way she came in and the kitchen wall closed upon her. When the cookmaiden recovered from her fainting fit, she saw the four fishes charred black as charcoal, and crying out, "His staff brake in his first bout," she again fell swooning to the ground. Whilst she was in this case the Wazir came for the fish, and looking upon her as insensible she lay, not knowing Sunday from Thursday, shoved her with his foot and said, "Bring the fish for the Sultan!" Thereupon, recovering from her fainting fit, she wept and informed him of her case and all that had befallen her. The Wazir marveled greatly and exclaiming, "This is none other than a right strange matter!" he sent after the fisherman and said to him, "Thou, O Fisherman, must needs fetch us four fishes like those thou broughtest before."

Thereupon the man repaired to the tarn and cast his net, and when he landed it, lo! four fishes were therein exactly like the first. These he at once carried to the Wazir, who went in with them to the cookmaiden and said, "Up with thee and fry these in my presence, that I may see this business." The damsel arose and cleansed the fish, and set them in the frying pan over the fire. However, they remained there but a little while ere the wall clave asunder and the young lady appeared, clad as before and holding in hand the wand which she again thrust into the frying pan, saying, "O fish! O fish! Be ye constant to your olden convenant?" And behold, the fish lifted their heads and repeated "Yes! Yes!" and recited this couplet:

"Come back and so will I! Keep faith and so will I!
But if ye fain forsake, I'll requite till quits we cry!"

When the fishes spoke, and the young lady upset the frying pan with her rod and went forth by the way she came and the wall closed up, the Wazir cried out, "This is a thing not to be hidden from the King." So he went and told him what had happened, whereupon quoth the King, "There is no help for it but that I see this with mine own eyes." Then he sent for the fisherman and commanded him to bring four other fish like the first and to take with him three men as witnesses. The fisherman at once brought the fish, and the King, after ordering them to give him four hundred gold pieces, turned to the Wazir and said, "Up, and fry me the fishes here before me!" The Minister, replying, "To hear is to obey," bade bring the frying pan, threw therein the cleansed fish, and set it over the fire, when lo! the wall clave asunder, and out burst a black slave like a huge rock or a remnant of the tribe Ad, bearing in hand a branch of a green tree. And he cried in loud and terrible tones, "O fish! O fish! Be ye all constant to your antique convenant?" Whereupon the fishes lifted their heads from the frying pan and said, "Yes! Yes! We be true to our vow," and they again recited the couplet:

"Come back and so will I! Keep faith and so will I!
But if ye fain forsake, I'll requite till quits we cry!"

Then the huge blackamoor approached the frying pan and upset it with the branch and went forth by the way he came in. When he vanished from their sight, the King inspected the fish, and finding them all charred black as charcoal, was utterly bewildered, and said to the Wazir: "Verily this is a matter whereanent silence cannot be kept. And as for the fishes, assuredly some marvelous adventure connects with them." So he bade bring the fisherman and asked him, saying: "Fie on thee, fellow! Whence come these fishes?" And he answered, "From a tarn between four heights lying behind this mountain which is in sight of thy city." Quoth the King, "How many days' march?" Quoth he, "O our Lord the Sultan, a walk of half-hour." The King wondered, and straightway ordering his men to march and horsemen to mount, led off the fisherman, who went before as guide, privily damning the Ifrit.

They fared on till they had climbed the mountain and descended unto a great desert which they had never seen during all their lives. And the Sultan and his merry men marveled much at the wold set in the midst of four mountains, and the tarn and its fishes of four colors, red and white, yellow and blue. The King stood fixed to the spot in wonderment and asked his troops and all present, "Hath anyone among you ever seen this piece of water before now?" And all made answer, "O King of the Age, never did we set eyes upon it during all our days." They also questioned the oldest inhabitants they met, men well stricken in years, but they replied, each and every, "A lakelet like this we never saw in this place." Thereupon quoth the King, "By Allah, I will neither return to my capital nor sit upon the throne of my forebears till I learn the truth about this tarn and the fish therein."

He then ordered his men to dismount and bivouac all around the mountain, which they did, and summoning his Wazir, a Minister of much experience, sagacious, of penetrating wit and well versed in affairs, said to him: " 'Tis in my mind to do a certain thing, whereof I will inform thee. My heart telleth me to fare forth alone this night and root out the mystery of this tarn and its fishes. Do thou take thy seat at my tent door, and say to the emirs and wazirs, the nabobs and the chamberlains, in fine, to all who ask thee, 'The Sultan is ill at ease, and he hath ordered me to refuse all admittance.' And be careful thou let none know my design." And the Wazir could not oppose him. Then the King changed his dress and ornaments and, slinging his sword over his shoulder, took a path which led up one of the mountains and marched for the rest of the night till morning dawned, nor did he cease wayfaring till the heat was too much for him. After his long walk he rested for a while, and then resumed his march and fared on through the second night till dawn, when suddenly there appeared a black point in the far distance. Hereat he rejoiced and said to himself, "Haply someone here shall acquaint me with the mystery of the tarn and its fishes."

Presently, drawing near the dark object, he found it a palace built of swart stone plated with iron, and while one leaf of the gate stood wide-open, the other was shut. The King's spirits rose high as he stood before the gate and rapped a light rap, but hearing no answer, he knocked a second knock and a third, yet there came no sign. Then he knocked his loudest, but still no answer, so he said, "Doubtless 'tis empty." There upon he mustered up resolution and boldly walked through the main gate into the great hall, and there cried out aloud: "Holloa, ye people of the palace! I am a stranger and a wayfarer. Have you aught here of victual?" He repeated his cry a second time and a third, but still there came no reply.

So, strengthening his heart and making up his mind, he stalked through the vestibule into the very middle of the palace, and found no man in it. Yet it was furnished with silken stuffs gold-starred, and the hangings were let down over the doorways. In the midst was a spacious court off which sat four open saloons, each with its raised dais, saloon facing saloon. A canopy shaded the court, and in the center was a jetting fount with four figures of lions made of red gold, spouting from their mouths water clear as pearls and diaphanous gems. Round about the palace birds were let loose, and over it stretched a net of golden wire, hindering them from flying off. In brief, there was everything but human beings. The King marveled mightily thereat, yet felt he sad at heart for that he saw no one to give him an account of the waste and its tarn, the fishes, the mountains, and the palace itself. Presently as he sat between the doors in deep thought behold, there came a voice of lament, as from a heart grief-spent, and he heard the voice chanting these verses:

"I hid what I endured of him and yet it came to light,
  And nightly sleep mine eyelids fled and changed to sleepless night.
  O world! O Fate! Withhold thy hand and cease thy hurt and harm
  Look and behold my hapless sprite in dolor and affright.
  Wilt ne'er show ruth to highborn youth who lost him on the way
  Of Love, and fell from wealth and fame to lowest basest wight?
  Jealous of Zephyr's breath was I as on your form he breathed,
  But whenas Destiny descends she blindeth human sight.
  What shall the hapless archer do who when he fronts his foe
  And bends his bow to shoot the shaft shall find his string undight?
  When cark and care so heavy bear on youth of generous soul,
  How shall he 'scape his lot and where from Fate his place of flight?"

Now when the Sultan heard the mournful voice he sprang to his feet and following the sound, found a curtain let down over a chamber door. He raised it and saw behind it a young man sitting upon a couch about a cubit above the ground, and he fair to the sight, a well-shaped wight, with eloquence dight. His forehead was flower-white, his cheek rosy bright, and a mole on his cheek breadth like an ambergris mite, even as the poet doth indite:

> A youth slim-waisted from whose locks and brow
> The world in blackness and in light is set.
> Throughout Creation's round no fairer show
> No rarer sight thine eye hath ever met.
> A nut-brown mole sits throned upon a cheek
> Of rosiest red beneath an eye of jet.

The King rejoiced and saluted him, but he remained sitting in his caftan of silken stuff purfled with Egyptian gold and his crown studded with gems of sorts. But his face was sad with the traces of sorrow. He returned the royal salute in most courteous wise adding, "O my lord, thy dignity demandeth my rising to thee, and my sole excuse is to crave thy pardon." Quoth the King: "Thou art excused, O youth, so look upon me as thy guest come hither on an especial object. I would thou acquaint me with the secrets of this tarn and its fishes and of this palace and thy loneliness therein and the cause of thy groaning and wailing." When the young man heard these words he wept with sore weeping till his bosom was drenched with tears. The King marveled and asked him, "What maketh thee weep, O young man?" and he answered, "How should I not weep, when this is my case!" Thereupon he put out his hand and raised the skirt of his garment, when lo! the lower half of him appeared stone down to his feet while from his navel to the hair of his head he was man. The King, seeing this his plight, grieved with sore grief and of his compassion cried: "Alack and wellaway! In very sooth, O youth, thou heapest sorrow upon my sorrow. I was minded to ask thee the mystery of the fishes only, whereas now I am concerned to learn thy story as well as theirs. But there is no Majesty and there is no Might save in Allah, the Glorious, the Great! Lose no time, O youth, but tell me forthright thy whole tale." Quoth he, "Lend me thine ears, thy sight, and thine insight." And quoth the King, "All are at thy service!"

Thereupon the youth began, "Right wondrous and marvelous is my case and that of these fishes, and were it graven with gravers upon the eye corners it were a warner to whoso would be warned." "How is that?" asked the King, and the young man began to tell

THE TALE OF THE ENSORCELED PRINCE

KNOW then, O my lord, that whilom my sire was King of this city, and his name was Mahmud, entitled Lord of the Black Islands, and owner of what are now these four mountains. He ruled threescore and ten years, after which he went to the mercy of the Lord and I reigned as Sultan in his stead. I took to wife my cousin, the daughter of my paternal uncle, and she loved me with such abounding love that whenever I was absent she ate not and she drank not until she saw me again. She cohabited with me for five years till a certain day when she went forth to the hammam bath, and I bade the cook hasten to get ready all requisites for our supper. And I entered this palace and lay down on the bed where I was wont to sleep and bade two damsels to fan my face, one sitting by my head and the other at my feet.

But I was troubled and made restless by my wife's absence and could not sleep, for although my eyes were closed, my mind and thoughts were wide-awake. Presently I heard the slave girl at my head say to her at my feet: "O Mas'udah, how miserable is our master and how wasted in his youth, and oh! the pity of his being so betrayed by our mistress, the accursed whore!" The other replied: "Yes indeed. Allah curse all faithless women and adulterous! But the like of our master, with his fair gifts, deserveth something better than this harlot who lieth abroad every night." Then quoth she who sat by my head, "Is our lord dumb or fit only for bubbling that he questioneth her not!" and quoth the other: "Fie on thee! Doth our lord know her ways, or doth she allow him his choice? Nay, more, doth she not drug every night the cup she giveth him to drink before sleeptime, and put bhang into it? So he sleepeth and wotteth not whither she goeth, nor what she doeth, but we know that after giving him the drugged wine, she donneth her richest raiment and perfumeth herself and then she fareth out from him to be away till break of day. Then she cometh to him and burneth a pastille under his nose and he awaketh from his death-like sleep." When I heard the slave girls' words, the light became black before my sight and I thought night would never fall.

Presently the daughter of my uncle came from the baths, and they set the table for us and we ate and sat together a fair half-hour quaffing our wine, as was ever our wont. Then she called for the particular wine I used to drink before sleeping and reached me the cup, but, seeming to drink it according to my wont, I poured the contents into my bosom and, lying down, let her hear that I was asleep. Then, behold, she cried: "Sleep out the night, and never wake again! By Allah, I loathe thee and I loathe thy whole body, and my soul turneth in disgust from cohabiting with thee, and I see not the moment when Allah shall snatch away thy life!" Then she rose and donned her fairest dress and perfumed her person and slung my sword over her shoulder, and opening the gates of the palace, went her ill way.

I rose and followed her as she left the palace and she threaded the streets until she came to the city gate, where she spoke words I understood not and the padlocks dropped of themselves as if broken and the gate leaves opened. She went forth (and I after her without her noticing aught) till she came at last to the outlying mounds and a reed fence built about a round-roofed hut of mud bricks. As she entered the door, I climbed upon the roof, which commanded a view of the interior, And lo! my fair cousin had gone in to a hideous Negro slave with his upper lip like the cover of a pot and his lower like an open pot, lips which might sweep up sand from the gravel floor of the cot. He was to boot a leper and a paralytic, lying upon a strew of sugar-cane trash and wrapped in an old blanket and the foulest rags and tatters.

She kissed the earth before him, and he raised his head so as to see her and said: "Woe to thee! What call hadst thou to stay away all this time? Here have been with me sundry of the black brethren, who drank their wine and each had his young lady, and I was not content to drink because of thine absence." Then she: "O my lord, my heart's love and coolth of my eyes, knowest thou not that I am married to my cousin, whose very look I loathe, and hate myself when in his company? And did not I fear for thy sake, I would not let a single sun arise before making his city a ruined heap wherein raven should croak and howlet hoot, and jackal and wolf harbor and loot—nay, I had removed its very stones to the back side of Mount Kaf." Rejoined the slave: "Thou liest, damn thee! Now I swear an oath by the valor and honor of blackamoor men (and deem not our manliness to be the poor manliness of white men), from today forth if thou stay away till this hour, I will not keep company with thee nor will I glue my body with thy body. Dost play fast and loose with us, thou cracked pot, that we may satisfy thy dirty lusts, O vilest of the vile whites?"

When I heard his words, and saw with my own eyes what passed between these two wretches, the world waxed dark before my face and my soul knew not in what place it was. But my wife humbly stood up weeping before and wheedling the slave, and saying: "O my beloved, and very fruit of my heart, there is none left to cheer me but thy dear self, and, if thou cast me off, who shall take me in, O my beloved, O light of my eyes?" And she ceased not weeping and abasing herself to him until he deigned be reconciled with her. Then was she right glad and stood up and doffed her clothes, even to her petticoat trousers, and said, "O my master, what hast thou here for thy handmaiden to eat?" "Uncover the basin," he grumbled, "and thou shalt find at the bottom the broiled bones of some rats we dined on. Pick at them, and then go to that slop pot, where thou shalt find some leavings of beer which thou mayest drink." So she ate and drank and washed her hands, and went and lay down by the side of the slave upon the cane trash and crept in with him under his foul coverlet and his rags and tatters.

When I saw my wife, my cousin, the daughter of my uncle, do this deed, I clean lost my wits, and climbing down from the roof, I entered and took the sword which she had with her and drew it, determined to cut down the twain. I first struck at the slave's neck and thought that the death decree had fallen on him, for he groaned a loud hissing groan, but I had cut only the skin and flesh of the gullet and the two arteries! It awoke the daughter of my uncle, so I sheathed the sword and fared forth for the city, and entering the palace, lay upon my bed and slept till morning, when my wife aroused me and I saw that she had cut off her hair and had donned mourning garments. Quoth she: "O son of my uncle, blame me not for what I do. It hath just reached me that my mother is dead and my father hath been killed in holy war, and of my brothers one hath lost his life by a snake sting and the other by falling down some precipice, and I can and should do naught save weep and lament."

When I heard her words I refrained from all reproach and said only: "Do as thou list. I certainly will not thwart thee." She continued sorrowing, weeping and wailing one whole year from the beginning of its circle to the end, and when it was finished she said to me: "I wish to build me in thy palace a tomb with a cupola, which I will set apart for my mourning and will name the House of Lamentations." Quoth I again: "Do as thou list!" Then she built for herself a cenotaph wherein to mourn, and set on its center a dome under which showed a tomb like a santon's sepulcher. Thither she carried the slave and lodged him, but he was exceeding weak by reason of his wound, and unable to do her love service. He could only drink wine, and from the day of his hurt he spake not a word, yet he lived on because his appointed hour was not come. Every day, morning and evening, my wife went to him and wept and wailed over him and gave him wine and strong soups, and left not off doing after this manner a second year. And I bore with her patiently and paid no heed to her.

One day, however, I went in to her unawares, and I found her weeping and beating her face and crying: "Why art thou absent from my sight, O my heart's delight? Speak to me, O my life, talk with me, O my love." When she had ended for a time her words and her weeping I said to her, "O my cousin, let this thy mourning suffice, for in pouring forth tears there is little profit!" "Thwart me not," answered she, "in aught I do, or I will lay violent hands on myself!" So I held my peace and left her to go her own way, and she ceased not to cry and keen and indulge her affliction for yet another year. At the end of the third year I waxed aweary of this longsome mourning, and one day I happened to enter the cenotaph when vexed and angry with some matter which had thwarted me, and suddenly I heard her say: "O my lord, I never hear thee vouchsafe a single word to me! Why dost thou not answer me, O my master?" and she began reciting:

> "O thou tomb! O thou tomb! Be his beauty set in shade?
> Hast thou darkened that countenance all-sheeny as the noon?
> O thou tomb! Neither earth nor yet Heaven art to me,
> Then how cometh it in thee are conjoined my sun and moon?"

When I heard such verses as these rage was heaped upon my rage, I cried out: "Wellaway! How long is this sorrow to last?" and I began repeating:

> "O thou tomb! O thou tomb! Be his horrors set in blight?
> Hast thou darkened his countenance that sickeneth the soul?
> O thou tomb! Neither cesspool nor pipkin art to me,
> Then how cometh it in thee are conjoinèd soil and coal?"

When she heard my words she sprang to her feet crying: "Fie upon thee, thou cur! All this is of thy doings. Thou hast wounded my heart's darling and thereby worked me sore woe, and thou hast wasted his youth so that these three years he hath lain abed more dead than alive!" In my wrath I cried: "O thou foulest of harlots and filthiest of whores ever futtered by Negro slaves who are hired to have at thee! Yes, indeed it was I who did this good deed." And snatching up my sword, I drew it and made at her to cut her down. But she laughed my words and mine intent to scorn, crying: "To heel, hound that thou art! Alas for the past which shall no more come to pass, nor shall anyone avail the dead to raise. Allah hath indeed now given into my hand him who did to me this thing, a deed that hath burned my heart with a fire which died not a flame which might not be quenched!"

Then she stood up, and pronouncing some words to me unintelligible, she said, "By virtue of my egromancy become thou half stone and half man!" Whereupon I became what thou seest, unable to rise or to sit, and neither dead nor alive. Moreover, she ensorceled the city with all its streets and garths, and she turned by her gramarye the four islands into four mountains around the tarn whereof thou questionest me. And the citizens, who were of four different faiths, Moslem, Nazarene, Jew, and Magian, she transformed by her enchantments into fishes. The Moslems are the white, the Magians red, the Christians blue, and the Jews yellow. And every day she tortureth me and scourgeth me with a hundred stripes, each of which draweth floods of blood and cutteth the skin of my shoulders to strips. And lastly she clotheth my upper half with a haircloth and then throweth over them these robes. Hereupon the young man again shed tears and began reciting:

> "In patience, O my God, I endure my lot and fate,
> I will bear at will of Thee whatsoever be my state.
> They oppress me, they torture me, they make my life a woe,
> Yet haply Heaven's happiness shall compensate my strait.
> Yea, straitened is my life by the bane and hate o' foes,
> But Mustafa and Murtaza shall ope me Heaven's gate."

After this the Sultan turned toward the young Prince and said: "O youth, thou hast removed one grief only to add another grief. But now, O my friend, where is she, and where is the mausoleum wherein lieth the wounded slave?" "The slave lieth under yon dome," quoth the young man, "and she sitteth in the chamber fronting yonder door. And every day at sunrise she cometh forth, and first strippeth me, and whippeth me with a hundred strokes of the leathern scourge, and I weep and shriek, but there is no power of motion in my lower limbs to keep her off me. After ending her tormenting me she visiteth the slave, bringing him wine and boiled meats. And tomorrow at an early hour she will be here." Quoth the King: "By Allah, O youth, I will assuredly do thee a good deed which the world shall not willingly let die, and an act of derring-do which shall be chronicled long after I am dead and gone by."

Then the King sat him by the side of the young Prince and talked till nightfall, when he lay down and slept. But as soon as the false dawn showed, he arose and, doffing his outer garments, bared his blade and hastened to the place wherein lay the slave. Then was he ware of lighted candles and lamps, and the perfume of incenses and unguents, and directed by these, he made for the slave and struck him one stroke, killing him on the spot. After which he lifted him on his back and threw him into a well that was in the palace. Presently he returned and, donning the slave's gear, lay down at length within the mausoleum with the drawn sword laid close to and along his side. After an hour or so the accursed witch came, and first going to her husband, she stripped off his clothes and, taking a whip, flogged him cruelly while he cried out: "Ah! Enough for me the case I am in! Take pity on me, O my cousin!" But she replied, "Didst thou take pity on me and spare the life of my truelove on whom I doated?"

Then she drew the cilice over his raw and bleeding skin and threw the robe upon all and went down to the slave with a goblet of wine and a bowl of meat broth in her hands. She entered under the dome weeping and wailing, "Wellaway!" and crying: "O my lord! Speak a word to me! O my master! Talk awhile with me!" and began to recite these couplets:

> "How long this harshness, this unlove, shall bide?
> Suffice thee not tear floods thou hast espied?
> Thou dost prolong our parting purposely
> And if wouldst please my foe, thou'rt satisfied!"

Then she wept again and said: "O my lord! Speak to me, talk with me!" The King lowered his voice and, twisting his tongue, spoke after the fashion of the blackamoors and said " 'Lack, 'lack! There be no Ma'esty and there be no Might save in Allauh, the Gloriose, the Great!"

Now when she heard these words she shouted for joy, and fell to the ground fainting, and when her senses returned she asked, "O my lord, can it be true that thou hast power of speech?" And the King, making his voice small and faint, answered: "O my cuss! Dost thou deserve that I talk to thee and speak with thee?" "Why and wherefore?" rejoined she, and he replied: "The why is that all the livelong day thou tormentest thy hubby, and he keeps calling on 'eaven for aid until sleep is strange to me even from evenin' till mawnin', and he prays and damns, cussing us two, me and thee, causing me disquiet and much bother. Were this not so, I should long ago have got my health, and it is this which prevents my answering thee." Quoth she, "With thy leave I will release him from what spell is on him," and quoth the King, "Release him, and let's have some rest!" She cried, "To hear is to obey," and, going from the cenotaph to the palace, she took a metal bowl and filled it with water and spake over it certain words which made the contents bubble and boil as a caldron seetheth over the fire. With this she sprinkled her husband saying, "By virtue of the dread words I have spoken, if thou becamest thus by my spells, come forth out of that form into thine own former form."

And lo and behold! the young man shook and trembled, then he rose to his feet and, rejoicing at his deliverance, cried aloud, "I testify that there is no god but *the* God, and in very truth Mohammed is His Apostle, whom Allah bless and keep!" Then she said to him, "Go forth and return not hither, for if thou do I will surely slay thee," screaming these words in his face. So he went from between her hands, and she returned to the dome and, going down to the sepulcher, she said, "O my lord, come forth to me that I may look upon thee and thy goodliness!" The King replied in faint low words: "What thing hast thou done? Thou hast rid me of the branch, but not of the root." She asked: "O my darling! O my Negroling! What is the root?" And he answered: "Fie on thee, O my cuss! The people of this city and of the four islands every night when it's half-passed lift their heads from the tank in which thou hast turned them to fishes and cry to Heaven and call down its anger on me and thee, and this is the reason why my body's balked from health. Go at once and set them free, then come to me and take my hand, and raise me up, for a little strength is already back in me."

When she heard the King's words (and she still supposed him to be the slave) she cried joyously: "O my master, on my head and on my eyes be thy command. Bismillah!" So she sprang to her feet and, full of joy and gladness, ran down to the tarn and took a little of its water in the palm of her hand and spake over it words not to be understood, and the fishes lifted their heads and stood up on the instant like men, the spell on the people of the city having been removed. What was the lake again became a crowded capital. The bazaars were thronged with folk who bought and sold, each citizen was occupied with his own calling, and the four hills became islands as they were whilom.

Then the young woman, that wicked sorceress, returned to the King and (still thinking he was the Negro) said to him: "O my love! Stretch forth thy honored hand that I may assist thee to rise." "Nearer to me," quoth the King in a faint and feigned tone. She came close as to embrace him, when he took up the sword lying hid by his side and smote her across the breast, so that the point showed gleaming behind her back. Then he smote her a second time and cut her in twain and cast her to the ground in two halves. After which he fared forth and found the young man, now freed from the spell, awaiting him and gave him joy of his happy release while the Prince kissed his hand with abundant thanks.

Quoth the King, "Wilt thou abide in this city, or go with me to my capital?" Quoth the youth, "O King of the Age, wottest thou not what journey is between thee and thy city?" "Two days and a half," answered he, whereupon said the other: "An thou be sleeping, O King, awake! Between thee and thy city is a year's march for a well-girt walker, and thou haddest not come hither in two days and a half save that the city was under enchantment. And I, O King, will never part from thee—no, not even for the twinkling of an eye." The King rejoiced at his words and said: "Thanks be to Allah, Who hath bestowed thee upon me! From this hour thou art my son and my only son, for that in all my life I have never been blessed with issue." Thereupon they embraced and joyed with exceeding great joy. And, reaching the palace, the Prince who had been spellbound informed his lords and his grandees that he was about to visit the Holy Places as a pilgrim, and bade them get ready all things necessary for the occasion.

The preparations lasted ten days, after which he set out with the Sultan, whose heart burned in yearning for his city, whence he had been absent a whole twelvemonth. They journeyed with an escort of Mamelukes carrying all manners of precious gifts and rarities, nor stinted they wayfaring day and night for a full year until they approached the Sultan's capital, and sent on messengers to announce their coming. Then the Wazir and the whole army came out to meet him in joy and gladness, for they had given up all hope of ever seeing their King, and the troops kissed the ground before him and wished him joy of his safety. He entered and took seat upon his throne and the Minister came before him and, when acquainted with all that had befallen the young Prince, he congratulated him on his narrow escape.

When order was restored throughout the land, the King gave largess to many of his people, and said to the Wazir, "Hither the fisherman who brought us the fishes!" So he sent for the man who had been the first cause of the city and the citizens being delivered from enchantment, and when he came into the presence, the Sultan bestowed upon him a dress of honor, and questioned him of his condition and whether he had children. The fisherman gave him to know that he had two daughters and a son, so the King sent for them and, taking one daughter to wife, gave the other to the young Prince and made the son his head treasurer. Furthermore, he invested his Wazir with the Sultanate of the City in the Black Islands whilom belonging to the young Prince, and dispatched with him the escort of fifty armed slaves, together with dresses of honor for all the emirs and grandees. The Wazir kissed hands and fared forth on his way, while the Sultan and the Prince abode at home in all the solace and the delight of life, and the fisherman became the richest man of his age, and his daughters wived with the Kings until death came to them.

And yet, O King! this is not more wondrous than the story of

THE PORTER AND THE THREE LADIES OF BAGHDAD

ONCE upon a time there was a porter in Baghdad who was a bachelor and who would remain unmarried. It came to pass on a certain day, as he stood about the street leaning idly upon his crate, behold, there stood before him an honorable woman in a mantilla of Mosul silk broidered with gold and bordered with brocade. Her walking shoes were also purfled with gold, and her hair floated in long plaits. She raised her face veil and, showing two black eyes fringed with jetty lashes, whose glances were soft and languishing and whose perfect beauty was ever blandishing, she accosted the porter and said in the suavest tones and choicest language, "Take up thy crate and follow me."

The porter was so dazzled he could hardly believe that he heard her aright, but he shouldered his basket in hot haste, saying in himself, "O day of good luck! O day of Allah's grace!" and walked after her till she stopped at the door of a house. There she rapped, and presently came out to her an old man, a Nazarene, to whom she gave a gold piece, receiving from him in return what she required of strained wine clear as olive oil, and she set it safely in the hamper, saying, "Lift and follow." Quoth the porter, "This, by Allah, is indeed an auspicious day, a day propitious for the granting of all a man wisheth." He again hoisted up the crate and followed her till she stopped at a fruiterer's shop and bought from him Shami apples and Osmani quinces and Omani peaches, and cucumbers of Nile growth, and Egyptian limes and Sultani oranges and citrons, besides Aleppine jasmine, scented myrtle berries, Damascene nenuphars, flower of privet and camomile, blood-red anemones, violets, and pomegranate bloom, eglantine, and narcissus, and set the whole in the porter's crate, saying, "Up with it."

So he lifted and followed her till she stopped at a butcher's booth and said, "Cut me off ten pounds of mutton." She paid him his price and he wrapped it in a banana leaf, whereupon she laid it in the crate and said, "Hoist, O Porter." He hoisted accordingly, and followed her as she walked on till she stopped at a grocer's, where she bought dry fruits and pistachio kernels, Tihamah raisins, shelled almonds, and all wanted for dessert, and said to the porter, "Lift and follow me." So he up with his hamper and after her till she stayed at the confectioner's, and she bought an earthen platter, and piled it with all kinds of sweetmeats in his shop, open-worked tarts and fritters scented with musk, and "soap cakes," and lemon loaves, and melon preserves, and "Zaynab's combs," and "ladies' fingers," and "Kazi's titbits," and goodies of every description, and placed the platter in the porter's crate. Thereupon quoth he (being a merry man), "Thou shouldest have told me, and I would have brought with me a pony or a she-camel to carry all this market stuff." She smiled and gave him a little cuff on the nape, saying, "Step out and exceed not in words, for (Allah willing!) thy wage will not be wanting."

Then she stopped at a perfumer's and took from him ten sorts of waters, rose scented with musk, orange-flower, water-lily, willow-flower, violet and five others. And she also bought two loaves of sugar, a bottle for perfume-spraying, a lump of male incense, aloe wood, ambergris, and musk, with candles of Alexandria wax, and she put the whole into the basket, saying, "Up with thy crate and after me." He did so and followed until she stood before the greengrocer's, of whom she bought pickled safflower and olives, in brine and in oil, with tarragon and cream cheese and hard Syrian cheese, and she stowed them away in the crate, saying to the porter, "Take up thy basket and follow me." He did so and went after her till she came to a fair mansion fronted by a spacious court, a tall, fine place to which columns gave strength and grace. And the gate thereof had two leaves of ebony inlaid with plates of red gold. The lady stopped at the door and, turning her face veil sideways, knocked softly with her knuckles whilst the porter stood behind her, thinking of naught save her beauty and loveliness.

Presently the door swung back and both leaves were opened, whereupon he looked to see who had opened it, and behold, it was a lady of tall figure, some five feet high, a model of beauty and loveliness, brilliance and symmetry and perfect grace. Her forehead was flower-white, her cheeks like the anemone ruddy-bright. Her eyes were those of the wild heifer or the gazelle, with eyebrows like the crescent moon which ends Sha'aban and begins Ramazan. Her mouth was the ring of Solomon, her lips coral-red, and her teeth like a line of strung pearls or of camomile petals. Her throat recalled the antelope's, and her breasts, like two pomegranates of even size, stood at bay as it were. Her body rose and fell in waves below her dress like the rolls of a piece of brocade, and her navel would hold an ounce of benzoin ointment. In fine, she was like her of whom the poet said:

> On Sun and Moon of palace cast thy sight,
> Enjoy her flowerlike face, her fragrant light.
> Thine eyes shall never see in hair so black
> Beauty encase a brow so purely white.
> The ruddy rosy cheek proclaims her claim,
> Though fail her name whose beauties we indite.
> As sways her gait, I smile at hips so big
> And weep to see the waist they bear so slight.

When the porter looked upon her, his wits were waylaid and his senses were stormed so that his crate went nigh to fall from his head, and he said to himself, "Never have I in my life seen a day more blessed than this day!" Then quoth the lady portress to the lady cateress, "Come in from the gate and relieve this poor man of his load." So the provisioner went in, followed by the portress and the porter, and went on till they reached a spacious ground-floor hall, built with admirable skill and beautified with all manner colors and carvings, with upper balconies and groined arches and galleries and cupboards and recesses whose curtains hung before them. In the midst stood a great basin full of water surrounding a fine fountain, and at the upper end on the raised dais was a couch of juniper wood set with gems and pearls, with a canopy like mosquito curtains of red satin-silk looped up with pearls as big as filberts and bigger.

Thereupon sat a lady bright of blee, with brow beaming brilliancy, the dream of philosophy, whose eyes were fraught with Babel's gramarye and her eyebrows were arched as for archery. Her breath breathed ambergris and perfumery and her lips were sugar to taste and carnelian to see. Her stature was straight as the letter *l* and her face shamed the noon sun's radiancy; and she was even as a galaxy, or a dome with golden marquetry, or a bride displayed in choicest finery, or a noble maid of Araby. The third lady, rising from the couch, stepped forward with graceful swaying gait till she reached the middle of the saloon, when she said to her sisters: "Why stand ye here? Take it down from this poor man's head!" Then the cateress went and stood before him and the portress behind him while the third helped them, and they lifted the load from the porter's head, and, emptying it of all that was therein, set everything in its place. Lastly they gave him two gold pieces, saying, "Wend thy ways, O Porter."

But he went not, for he stood looking at the ladies and admiring what uncommon beauty was theirs, and their pleasant manners and kindly dispositions (never had he seen goodlier). And he gazed wistfully at that good store of wines and sweet-scented flowers and fruits and other matters. Also he marveled with exceeding marvel, especially to see no man in the place, and delayed his going, whereupon quoth the eldest lady: "What aileth thee that goest not? Haply thy wage be too little?" And, turning to her sister, the cateress, she said, "Give him another dinar!" But the porter answered: "By Allah, my lady, it is not for the wage, my hire is never more than two dirhams, but in very sooth my heart and my soul are taken up with you and your condition. I wonder to see you single with ne'er a man about you and not a soul to bear you company. And well you wot that the minaret toppleth o'er unless it stand upon four, and you want this same fourth, and women's pleasure without man is short of measure, even as the poet said:

> "Seest not we want for joy four things all told—
> The harp and lute, the flute and flageolet—
> And be they companied with scents fourfold,
> Rose, myrtle, anemone, and violet.
> Nor please all eight an four thou wouldst withhold—
> Good wine and youth and gold and pretty pet.

"You be three and want a fourth who shall be a person of good sense and prudence, smart-witted, and one apt to keep careful counsel." His words pleased and amused them much, and they laughed at him and said: "And who is to assure us of that? We are maidens, and we fear to entrust our secret where it may not be kept, for we have read in a certain chronicle the lines of one Ibn al-Sumam:

> "Hold fast thy secret and to none unfold,
> Lost is a secret when that secret's told.
> An fail thy breast thy secret to conceal,
> How canst thou hope another's breast shall hold?"

When the porter heard their words, he rejoined: "By your lives! I am a man of sense and a discreet, who hath read books and perused chronicles. I reveal the fair and conceal the foul and I act as the poet adviseth:

> "None but the good a secret keep,
> And good men keep it unrevealed.
> It is to me a well-shut house
> With keyless locks and door ensealed."

When the maidens heard his verse and its poetical application addressed to them, they said: "Thou knowest that we have laid out all our moneys on this place. Now say, hast thou aught to offer us in return for entertainment? For surely we will not suffer thee to sit in our company and be our cup companion, and gaze upon our faces so fair and so rare, without paying a round sum. Wottest thou not the saying:

> "Sans hope of gain
> Love's not worth a grain"?

Whereto the lady portress added, "If thou bring anything, thou art a something; if no thing, be off with thee, thou art a nothing." But the procuratrix interposed, saying: "Nay, O my sisters, leave teasing him, for by Allah he hath not failed us this day, and had he been other he never had kept patience with me, so whatever be his shot and scot I will take it upon myself."

The porter, overjoyed, kissed the ground before her and thanked her, saying, "By Allah, these moneys are the first fruits this day hath given me." Hearing this, they said, "Sit thee down and welcome to thee," and the eldest lady added: "By Allah, we may not suffer thee to join us save on one condition, and this it is, that no questions be asked as to what concerneth thee not, and frowardness shall be soundly flogged." Answered the porter: "I agree to this, O my lady. On my head and my eyes be it! Look ye, I am dumb, I have no tongue." Then arose the provisioneress and, tightening her girdle, set the table by the fountain and put the flowers and sweet herbs in their jars, and strained the wine and ranged the flasks in rows and made ready every requisite. Then sat she down, she and her sisters, placing amidst them the porter, who kept deeming himself in a dream. And she took up the wine flagon and poured out the first cup and drank it off, and likewise a second and a third. After this she filled a fourth cup, which she handed to one of her sisters, and lastly, she crowned a goblet and passed it to the porter, saying:

> "Drink the dear draught, drink free and fain
> What healeth every grief and pain."

He took the cup in his hand and, louting low, returned his best thanks and improvised:

> "Drain not the bowl save with a trusty friend,
> A man of worth whose good old blood all know.
> For wine, like wind, sucks sweetness from the sweet
> And stinks when over stench it haply blow."

Adding:

> "Drain not the bowl, save from dear hand like thine,
> The cup recalls thy gifts, thou, gifts of wine."

After repeating this couplet he kissed their hands and drank and was drunk and sat swaying from side to side and pursued:

> "All drinks wherein is blood the Law unclean
> Doth hold save one, the bloodshed of the vine.
> Fill! Fill! Take all my wealth bequeathed or won,
> Thou fawn! a willing ransome for those eyne."

Then the cateress crowned a cup and gave it to the portress, who took it from her hand and thanked her and drank. Thereupon she poured again and passed to the eldest lady, who sat on the couch, and filled yet another and handed it to the porter. He kissed the ground before them, and after drinking and thanking them, he again began to recite:

> "Here! Here! By Allah, here!
> Cups of the sweet, the dear!
> Fill me a brimming bowl,
> The Fount o' Life I speer."

Then the porter stood up before the mistress of the house and said, "O lady, I am thy slave, thy Mameluke, thy white thrall, thy very bondsman," and he began reciting:

> "A slave of slaves there standeth at thy door,
> Lauding thy generous boons and gifts galore.
> Beauty! May he come in awhile to 'joy
> Thy charms? For Love and I part nevermore!"

Then the lady took the cup and drank it off to her sisters' health, and they ceased not drinking (the porter being in the midst of them) and dancing and laughing and reciting verses and singing ballads and ritornellos. All this time the porter was carrying on with them, kissing, toying, biting, handling, groping, fingering whilst one thrust a dainty morsel in his mouth and another slapped him, and this cuffed his cheeks, and that threw sweet flowers at him. And he was in the very paradise of pleasure, as though he were sitting in the seventh sphere among the houris of Heaven. And they ceased not to be after this fashion till night began to fall. Thereupon said they to the porter, "Bismillah, O our master, up and on with those sorry old shoes of thine and turn thy face and show us the breadth of thy shoulders!" Said he: "By Allah, to part with my soul would be easier for me than departing from you. Come, let us join night to day, and tomorrow morning we will each wend our own way." "My life on you," said the procuratrix, "suffer him to tarry with us, that we may laugh at him. We may live out our lives and never meet with his like, for surely he is a right merry rogue and a witty." So they said: "Thou must not remain with us this night save on condition that thou submit to our commands, and that whatso thou seest, thou ask no questions thereanent, nor inquire of its cause." "All right," rejoined he, and they said, "Go read the writing over the door."

So he rose and went to the entrance and there found written in letters of gold wash: WHOSO SPEAKETH OF WHAT CONCERNETH HIM NOT SHALL HEAR WHAT PLEASETH HIM NOT! The porter said, "Be ye witnesses against me that I will not speak on whatso concerneth me not." Then the cateress arose and set food before them and they ate. After which they changed their drinking place for another, and she lighted the lamps and candles and burned ambergris and aloe wood, and set on fresh fruit and the wine service, when they fell to carousing and talking of their lovers. And they ceased not to eat and drink and chat, nibbling dry fruits and laughing and playing tricks for the space of a full hour, when lo! a knock was heard at the gate.

The knocking in no wise disturbed the séance, but one of them rose and went to see what it was and presently returned, saying, "Truly our pleasure for this night is to be perfect." "How is that?" asked they, and she answered: "At the gate be three Persian Kalandars[1] with their beards and heads and eyebrows shaven, and all three blind of the left eye—which is surely a strange chance. They are foreigners from Roumland with the mark of travel plain upon them. They have just entered Baghdad, this being their first visit to our city, and the cause of their knocking at our door is simply because they cannot find a lodging. Indeed one of them said to me: 'Haply the owner of this mansion will let us have the key of his stable or some old outhouse wherein we may pass this night.' For evening had surprised them and, being strangers in the land, they knew none who would give them shelter. And, O my sisters, each of them is a figure o' fun after his own fashion, and if we let them in we shall have matter to make sport of." She gave not over persuading them till they said to her: "Let them in, and make thou the usual condition with them that they speak not of what concerneth them not, lest they hear what pleased them not."

So she rejoiced and, going to the door, presently returned with the three monoculars whose beards and mustachios were clean-shaven. They salaamed and stood afar off by way of respect, but the three ladies rose up to them and welcomed them and wished them joy of their safe arrival and made them sit down. The Kalandars looked at the room and saw that it was a pleasant place, clean-swept and garnished with flowers, and the lamps were burning and the smoke of perfumes was spiring in air, and beside the dessert and fruits and wine, there were three fair girls who might be maidens. So they exclaimed with one voice, "By Allah, 'tis good!" Then they turned to the porter and saw that he was a merry-faced wight, albeit he was by no means sober and was sore after his slappings. So they thought that he was one of themselves and said, "A mendicant like us, whether Arab or foreigner!"

But when the porter heard these words, he rose up and, fixing his eyes fiercely upon them, said: "Sit ye here without exceeding in talk!

[1] Wandering dervishes.

Have you not read what is writ over the door? Surely it befitteth not fellows who come to us like paupers to wag your tongues at us." "We crave thy pardon, O Fakir," rejoined they, "and our heads are between thy hands." The ladies laughed consumedly at the squabble and, making peace between the Kalandars and the porter, seated the new guests before meat, and they ate. Then they sat together, and the portress served them with drink, and as the cup went round merrily, quoth the porter to the askers, "And you, O brothers mine, have ye no story or rare adventure to amuse us withal?"

Now the warmth of wine having mounted to their heads, they called for musical instruments, and the portress brought them a tambourine of Mosul, and a lute of Irak, and a Persian harp. And each mendicant took one and tuned it, this the tambourine and those the lute and the harp, and struck up a merry tune while the ladies sang so lustily that there was a great noise. And whilst they were carrying on, behold, someone knocked at the gate, and the portress went to see what was the matter there.

Now the cause of that knocking, O King (quoth Scheherazade) was this, the Caliph Harun al-Rashid had gone forth from the palace, as was his wont now and then, to solace himself in the city that night, and to see and hear what new thing was stirring. He was in merchant's gear, and he was attended by Ja'afar, his Wazir, and by Masrur, his Sworder of Vengeance. As they walked about the city, their way led them toward the house of the three ladies, where they heard the loud noise of musical instruments and singing and merriment. So quoth the Caliph to Ja'afar, "I long to enter this house and hear those songs and see who sing them." Quoth Ja'afar, "O Prince of the Faithful, these folk are surely drunken with wine, and I fear some mischief betide us if we get amongst them." "There is no help but that I go in there," replied the Caliph, "and I desire thee to contrive some pretext for our appearing among them." Ja'afar replied, "I hear and I obey," and knocked at the door, whereupon the portress came out and opened. Then Ja'afar came forward and, kissing the ground before her, said, "O my lady, we be merchants from Tiberias town. We arrived at Baghdad ten days ago and, alighting at the merchants' caravanserai, we sold all our merchandise. Now a certain trader invited us to an entertainment this night, so we went to his house and he set food before us and we ate. Then we sat at wine and wassail with him for an hour or so when he gave us leave to depart. And we went out from him in the shadow of the night and, being strangers, we could not find our way back to our khan. So haply of your kindness and courtesy you will suffer us to tarry with you this night, and Heaven will reward you!"

The portress looked upon them and, seeing them dressed like merchants and men of grave looks and solid, she returned to her sisters and repeated to them Ja'afar's story, and they took compassion upon the strangers and said to her, "Let them enter." She opened the door to them, when said they to her, "Have we thy leave to come in?" "Come in," quoth she, and the Caliph entered, followed by Ja'afar and Masrur. And when the girls saw them they stood up to them in respect and made them sit down and looked to their wants, saying, "Welcome, and well come and good cheer to the guests, but with one condition!" "What is that?" asked they, and one of the ladies answered, "Speak not of what concerneth you not, lest ye hear what pleaseth you not." "Even so," said they, and sat down to their wine and drank deep.

Presently the Caliph looked on the three Kalandars and, seeing them each and every blind of the left eye, wondered at the sight. Then he gazed upon the girls, and he was startled and he marveled with exceeding marvel at their beauty and loveliness. They continued to carouse and to converse, and said to the Caliph, "Drink!" But he replied, "I am vowed to pilgrimage," and drew back from the wine. Thereupon the portress rose and, spreading before him a tablecloth worked with gold, set thereon a porcelain bowl into which she poured willow-flower water with a lump of snow and a spoonful of sugar candy. The Caliph thanked her and said in himself, "By Allah, I will recompense her tomorrow for the kind deed she hath done." The others again addressed themselves to conversing and carousing, and when the wine gat the better of them, the eldest lady, who ruled the house, rose and, making obeisance to them, took the cateress by the hand and said, "Rise, O my sister, and let us do what is our devoir." Both answered "Even so!"

Then the portress stood up and proceeded to remove the table service and the remnants of the banquet, and renewed the pastilles and cleared the middle of the saloon. Then she made the Kalandars sit upon a sofa at the side of the estrade, and seated the Caliph and Ja'afar and Masrur on the other side of the saloon, after which she called the porter, and said: "How scant is thy courtesy! Now thou art no stranger—nay, thou art one of the household." So he stood up and, tightening his waistcloth, asked, "What would ye I do?" And she answered, "Stand in thy place." Then the procuratrix rose and set in the midst of the saloon a low chair and, opening a closet, cried to the porter, "Come help me."

So he went to help her and saw two black bitches with chains round their necks, and she said to him, "Take hold of them," and he took them and led them into the middle of the saloon. Then the lady of the house arose and tucked up her sleeves above her wrists and, seizing a scourge, said to the porter, "Bring forward one of the bitches." He brought her forward, dragging her by the chain, while the bitch wept and shook her head at the lady, who, however, came down upon her with blows on the sconce. And the bitch howled and the lady ceased not beating her till her forearm failed her. Then, casting the scourge from her hand, she pressed the bitch to her bosom and, wiping away her tears with her hands, kissed her head. Then said she to the porter, "Take her away and bring the second." And when he brought her, she did with her as she had done with the first.

Now the heart of the Caliph was touched at these cruel doings. His chest straitened and he lost all patience in his desire to know why the two bitches were so beaten. He threw a wink at Ja'afar, wishing him to ask, but the Minister, turning toward him, said by signs, "Be silent!" Then quoth the portress to the mistress of the house, "O my lady, arise and go to thy place, that I in turn may do my devoir." She answered, "Even so," and, taking her seat upon the couch of juniper wood, pargetted with gold and silver, said to the portress and cateress, "Now do ye what ye have to do." Thereupon the portress sat upon a low seat by the couch side, but the procuratrix, entering a closet, brought out of it a bag of satin with green fringes and two tassels of gold. She stood up before the lady of the house and, shaking the bag, drew out from it a lute which she tuned by tightening its pegs; and when it was in perfect order, she began to sing these quatrains:

> "Ye are the wish, the aim of me,
> And when, O love, thy sight I see,
> The heavenly mansion openeth,
> But Hell I see when lost thy sight.
> From thee comes madness, nor the less
> Comes highest joy, comes ecstasy.

Nor in my love for thee I fear
Or shame and blame, or hate and spite.
When Love was throned within my heart
I rent the veil of modesty,
And stints not Love to rend that veil,
Garring disgrace on grace to alight.
The robe of sickness then I donned,
But rent to rags was secrecy.
Wherefore my love and longing heart
Proclaim your high supremest might.
The teardrop railing adown my cheek
Telleth my tale of ignomy.
And all the hid was seen by all
And all my riddle ree'd aright.
Heal then my malady, for thou
Art malady and remedy!
But she whose cure is in thy hand
Shall ne'er be free of bane and blight.
Burn me those eyne that radiance rain,
Slay me the swords of phantasy.
How many hath the sword of Love
Laid low, their high degree despite?
Yet will I never cease to pine,
Nor to oblivion will I flee.
Love is my health, my faith, my joy,
Public and private, wrong or right.
O happy eyes that sight thy charms,
That gaze upon thee at their gree!
Yea, of my purest wish and will
The slave of Love I'll aye be hight."

When the damsel heard this elegy in quatrains, she cried out "Alas! Alas!" and rent her raiment, and fell to the ground fainting. And the Caliph saw scars of the palm rod on her back and welts of the whip, and marveled with exceeding wonder. Then the portress arose and sprinkled water on her and brought her a fresh and very fine dress and put it on her. But when the company beheld these doings, their minds were troubled, for they had no inkling of the case nor knew the story thereof. So the Caliph said to Ja'afar: "Didst thou not see the scars upon the damsel's body? I cannot keep silence or be at rest till I learn the truth of her condition and the story of this other maiden and the secret of the two black bitches." But Ja'afar answered: "O our lord, they made it a condition with us that we speak not of what concerneth us not, lest we come to hear what pleaseth us not."

Then said the portress, "By Allah, O my sister, come to me and complete this service for me." Replied the procuratrix, "With joy and goodly gree." So she took the lute and leaned it against her breasts and swept the strings with her finger tips, and began singing:

> "Give back mine eyes their sleep long ravishèd,
> And say me whither be my reason fled.
> I learnt that lending to thy love a place,
> Sleep to mine eyelids mortal foe was made.
> They said, 'We held thee righteous. Who waylaid
> Thy soul?' 'Go ask his glorious eyes,' I said.
> I pardon all my blood he pleased to spill,
> Owning his troubles drove him blood to shed.
> On my mind's mirror sunlike sheen he cast,
> Whose keen reflection fire in vitals bred.
> Waters of Life let Allah waste at will,
> Suffice my wage those lips of dewy red.
> And thou address my love thou'lt find a cause
> For plaint and tears or ruth or lustihed.
> In water pure his form shall greet your eyne,
> When fails the bowl nor need ye drink of wine."

Then she quoted from the same ode:

> "I drank, but the draught of his glance, not wine,
> And his swaying gait swayed to sleep these eyne.
> 'Twas not grape juice gript me but grasp of Past,
> 'Twas not bowl o'erbowled me but gifts divine.
> His coiling curllets my soul ennetted
> And his cruel will all my wits outwitted."

After a pause she resumed:

> "If we 'plain of absence, what shall we say?
> Or if pain afflict us, where wend our way?
> An I hire a truchman[1] to tell my tale,

---

[1] Interpreter.

> The lovers' plaint is not told for pay.
> If I put on patience, a lover's life
> After loss of love will not last a day.
> Naught is left me now but regret, repine,
> And tears flooding cheeks forever and aye.
> O thou who the babes of these eyes hast fled,
> Thou art homed in heart that shall never stray.
> Would Heaven I wot hast thou kept our pact
> Long as stream shall flow, to have firmest fay?
> Or hast forgotten the weeping slave,
> Whom groans afflict and whom griefs waylay?
> Ah, when severance ends and we side by side
> Couch, I'll blame thy rigors and chide thy pride!"

Now when the portress heard her second ode, she shrieked aloud and said: "By Allah! 'Tis right good!" and, laying hands on her garments, tore them as she did the first time, and fell to the ground fainting. Thereupon the procuratrix rose and brought her a second change of clothes after she had sprinkled water on her. She recovered and sat upright and said to her sister the cateress, "Onward, and help me in my duty, for there remains but this one song." So the provisioneress again brought out the lute and began to sing these verses:

> "How long shall last, how long this rigor rife of woe
> May not suffice thee all these tears thou seest flow?
> Our parting thus with purpose fell thou dost prolong
> Is't not enough to glad the heart of envious foe?
> Were but this lying world once true to lover heart,
> He had not watched the weary night in tears of woe.
> Oh, pity me whom overwhelmed thy cruel will,
> My lord, my king, 'tis time some ruth to me thou show.
> To whom reveal my wrongs, O thou who murdered me?
> Sad, who of broken troth the pangs must undergo!
> Increase wild love for thee and frenzy hour by hour,
> And days of exile minute by so long, so slow.
> O Moslems, claim vendetta for this slave of Love,
> Whose sleep Love ever wastes, whose patience Love lays low.
> Doth law of Love allow thee, O my wish! to lie
> Lapt in another's arms and unto me cry 'Go!'?
> Yet in thy presence, say, what joys shall I enjoy
> When he I love but works my love to overthrow?"

When the portress heard the third song, she cried aloud and, laying hands on her garments, rent them down to the very skirt and fell to the ground fainting a third time, again showing the scars of the scourge. Then said the three Kalandars, "Would Heaven we had never entered this house, but had rather nighted on the mounds and heaps outside the city! For verily our visit hath been troubled by sights which cut to the heart." The Caliph turned to them and asked, "Why so?" and they made answer, "Our minds are sore troubled by this matter." Quoth the Caliph, "Are ye not of the household?" and quoth they, "No, nor indeed did we ever set eyes on the place till within this hour." Hereat the Caliph marveled and rejoined, "This man who sitteth by you, would he not know the secret of the matter?" And so saying he winked and made signs at the porter. So they questioned the man, but he replied: "By the All-might of Allah, in love all are alike! I am the growth of Baghdad, yet never in my born days did I darken these doors till today, and my companying with them was a curious matter." "By Allah," they rejoined, "we took thee for one of them and now we see thou art one like ourselves."

Then said the Caliph: "We be seven men, and they only three women without even a fourth to help them, so let us question them of their case. And if they answer us not, fain we will be answered by force." All of them agreed to this except Ja'afar, who said, "This is not my recking. Let them be, for we are their guests and, as ye know, they made a compact and condition with us which we accepted and promised to keep. Wherefore it is better that we be silent concerning this matter, and as but little of the night remaineth, let each and every of us gang his own gait." Then he winked at the Caliph and whispered to him, "There is but one hour of darkness left and I can bring them before thee tomorrow, when thou canst freely question them all concerning their story." But the Caliph raised his head haughtily and cried out at him in wrath, saying: "I have no patience left for my longing to hear of them. Let the Kalandars question them forthright." Quoth Ja'afar, "This is not my rede."

Then words ran high and talk answered talk, and they disputed as to who should first put the question, but at last all fixed upon the porter. And as the jangle increased the house mistress could not but notice it and asked them, "O ye folk! On what matter are ye talking so loudly?" Then the porter stood up respectfully before her and said: "O my lady, this company earnestly desire that thou acquaint them with story of the two bitches and what maketh thee punish them so cruelly, and then thou fallest to weeping over them and kissing them. And lastly, they want to hear the tale of thy sister and why she hath been bastinadoed with palm sticks like a man. These are the questions they charge me to put, and peace be with thee." Thereupon quoth she who was the lady of the house to the guests, "Is this true that he saith on your part?" and all replied, "Yes!" save Ja'afar, who kept silence.

When she heard these words she cried: "By Allah, ye have wronged us, O our guests, with grievous wronging, for when you came before us we made compact and condition with you that whoso should speak of what concerneth him not should hear what pleaseth him not. Sufficeth ye not that we took you into our house and fed you with our best food? But the fault is not so much yours as hers who let you in." Then she tucked up her sleeves from her wrists and struck the floor thrice with her hand, crying, "Come ye quickly!" And lo! a closet door opened and out of it came seven Negro slaves with drawn swords in hand, to whom she said, "Pinion me those praters' elbows and bind them each to each." They did her bidding and asked her: "O veiled and virtuous! Is it thy high command that we strike off their heads?" But she answered, "Leave them awhile that I question them of their condition before their necks feel the sword." "By Allah, O my lady!" cried the porter, "slay me not for other's sin. All these men offended and deserve the penalty of crime save myself. Now, by Allah, our night had been charming had we escaped the mortification of those monocular Kalandars whose entrance into a populous city would convert it into a howling wilderness." Then he repeated these verses:

> "How fair is ruth the strong man deigns not smother!
> And fairest fair when shown to weakest brother.
> By Love's own holy tie between us twain,
> Let one not suffer for the sin of other."

When the porter ended his verse, the lady laughed despite her wrath, and came up to the party and spake thus: "Tell me who ye be, for ye have but an hour of life. And were ye not men of rank and perhaps notables of your tribes, you had not been so froward and I had hastened your doom." Then said the Caliph: "Woe to thee, O

Ja'afar, tell her who we are lest we be slain by mistake, and speak her fair before some horror befall us." " 'Tis part of thy deserts," replied he, whereupon the Caliph cried out at him, saying, "There is a time for witty words and there is a time for serious work." Then the lady accosted the three Kalandars and asked them, "Are ye brothers?" when they answered, "No, by Allah, we be naught but fakirs and foreigners." Then quoth she to one among them, "Wast thus born blind of one eye?" and quoth he, "No, by Allah, 'twas a marvelous matter and a wondrous mischance which caused my eye to be torn out, and mine is a tale which, if it were written upon the eye corners with needle gravers, were a warner to whoso would be warned." She questioned the second and third Kalandar, but all replied like the first, "By Allah, O our mistress, each one of us cometh from a different country, and we are all three the sons of kings, sovereign princes ruling over suzerains and capital cities."

Thereupon she turned toward them and said: "Let each and every of you tell me his tale in due order and explain the cause of his coming to our place, and if his story please us, let him stroke his head and wend his way." The first to come forward was the hammal, the porter, who said: "O my lady, I am a man and a porter. This dame, the cateress, hired me to carry a load and took me first to the shop of a vintner, then to the booth of a butcher, thence to the stall of a fruiterer, thence to a grocer who also sold dry fruits, thence to a confectioner and a perfumer-cum-druggist, and from him to this place, where there happened to me with you what happened. Such is my story, and peace be on us all!" At this the lady laughed and said, "Rub thy head and wend thy ways!" But he cried, "By Allah, I will not stump it till I hear the stories of my companions!" Then came forward one of the monoculars and began to tell her

THE FIRST KALANDAR'S TALE

KNOW, O my lady, that the cause of my beard being shorn and my eye being outtorn was as follows: My father was a king and he had a brother who was a king over another city; and it came to pass that I and my cousin, the son of my paternal uncle, were both born on one and the same day. And years and days rolled on and as we grew up I used to visit my uncle every now and then and to spend a certain number of months with him. Now my cousin and I were sworn friends, for he ever entreated me with exceeding kindness. He killed for me the fattest sheep and strained the best of his wines, and we enjoyed long conversing and carousing. One day when the wine had gotten the better of us, the son of my uncle said to me, "O my cousin, I have a great service to ask of thee, and I desire that thou stay me not in whatso I desire to do!" And I replied, "With joy and goodly will."

Then he made me swear the most binding oaths and left me, but after a little while he returned leading a lady veiled and richly appareled, with ornaments worth a large sum of money. Presently he turned to me (the woman being still behind him) and said, "Take this lady with thee and go before me to such a burial ground" (describing it, so that I knew the place) "and enter with her into such a sepulcher and there await my coming." The oaths I swore to him made me keep silence and suffered me not to oppose him, so I led the woman to the cemetery and both I and she took our seats in the sepulcher. And hardly had we sat down when in came my uncle's son, with a bowl of water, a bag of mortar, and an adze somewhat like a hoe. He went straight to the tomb in the midst of the sepulcher and, breaking it open with the adze, set the stones on one side. Then he fell to digging into the earth of the tomb till he came upon a large iron plate, the size of a wicket door, and on raising it there appeared below it a staircase vaulted and winding. Then he turned to the lady and said to her, "Come now and take thy final choice!"

She at once went down by the staircase and disappeared, then quoth he to me, "O son of my uncle, by way of completing thy kindness, when I shall have descended into this place, restore the trapdoor to where it was, and heap back the earth upon it as it lay before. And then of thy great goodness mix this unslaked lime which is in the bag with this water which is in the bowl and, after building up the stones, plaster the outside so that none looking upon it shall say: 'This is a new opening in an old tomb'. For a whole year have I worked at this place whereof none knoweth but Allah, and this is the need I have of thee," presently adding, "May Allah never bereave thy friends of thee nor make them desolate by thine absence, O son of my uncle, O my dear cousin!" And he went down the stairs and disappeared for ever.

When he was lost to sight, I replaced the iron plate and did all his bidding till the tomb became as it was before, and I worked almost unconsciously, for my head was heated with wine. Returning to the palace of my uncle, I was told that he had gone forth a-sporting and hunting, so I slept that night without seeing him. And when the morning dawned, I remembered the scenes of the past evening and what happened between me and my cousin. I repented of having obeyed him when penitence was of no avail. I still thought, however, that it was a dream. So I fell to asking for the son of my uncle, but there was none to answer me concerning him, and I went out to the graveyard and the sepulchers, and sought for the tomb under which he was, but could not find it. And I ceased not wandering about from sepulcher to sepulcher, and tomb to tomb, all without success, till night set in. So I returned to the city, yet I could neither eat nor drink, my thoughts being engrossed with my cousin, for that I knew not what was become of him. And I grieved with exceeding grief and passed another sorrowful night, watching until the morning. Then went I a second time to the cemetery, pondering over what the son of mine uncle had done and, sorely repenting my hearkening to him, went round among all the tombs, but could not find the tomb I sought. I mourned over the past, and remained in my mourning seven days, seeking the place and ever missing the path.

Then my torture of scruples grew upon me till I well-nigh went mad, and I found no way to dispel my grief save travel and return to my father. So I set out and journeyed homeward, but as I was entering my father's capital a crowd of rioters sprang upon me and pinioned me. I wondered thereat with all wonderment, seeing that I was the son of the Sultan, and these men were my father's subjects and amongst them were some of my own slaves. A great fear fell upon me, and I said to my soul, "Would Heaven I knew what hath happened to my father!" I questioned those that bound me of the cause of their so doing, but they returned me no answer. However, after a while one of them said to me (and he had been a hired servant of our house), "Fortune hath been false to thy father. His troops betrayed him, and the Wazir who slew him now reigneth in his stead, and we lay in wait to seize thee by the bidding of him." I was well-nigh distraught and felt ready to faint on hearing of my father's death, when they carried me off and placed me in presence of the usurper.

Now between me and him there was an olden grudge, the cause of which was this: I was fond of shooting with the stone bow, and it befell one day, as I was standing on the terrace roof of the palace, that a bird lighted on the top of the Wazir's house when he happened to be there. I shot at the bird and missed the mark, but I hit the Wazir's eye and knocked it out, as fate and fortune decreed. Now when I knocked out the Wazir's eye, he could not say a single word, for that my father was King of the city, but he hated me ever after, and dire was the grudge thus caused between us twain. So when I was set before him hand-bound and pinioned, he straightway gave orders for me to be beheaded. I asked, "For what crime wilt thou put me to death?" Whereupon he answered, "What crime is greater than this?" pointing the while to the place where his eye had been. Quoth I, "This I did by accident, not of malice prepense," and quoth he, "If thou didst it by accident, I will do the like by thee with intention." Then cried he, "Bring him forward," and they brought me up to him, when he thrust his finger into my left eye and gouged it out, whereupon I became one-eyed as ye see me.

Then he bade bind me hand and foot, and put me into a chest, and said to the sworder, "Take charge of this fellow, and go off with him to the wastelands about the city. Then draw thy scimitar and slay him, and leave him to feed the beasts and birds." So the headsman fared forth with me, and when he was in the midst of the desert, he took me out of the chest (and I with both hands pinioned and both feet fettered) and was about to bandage my eyes before striking off my head. But I wept with exceeding weeping until I made him weep with me and, looking at him I began to recite these couplets:

> "I deemed you coat o' mail that should withstand
> The foeman's shafts, and you proved foeman's brand.
> I hoped your aidance in mine every chance,
> Though fail my left to aid my dexter hand.
> Aloof you stand and hear the railer's gibe
> While rain their shafts on me the giber band.
> But an ye will not guard me from my foes,
> Stand clear, and succor neither these nor those!"

And I also quoted:

> "I deemed my brethren mail of strongest steel,
> And so they were—from foes to fend my dart!
> I deemed their arrows surest of their aim,
> And so they were—when aiming at my heart!"

When the headsman heard my lines (he had been sworder to my sire and he owed me a debt of gratitude), he cried, "O my lord, what can I do, being but a slave under orders?" presently adding, "Fly for thy life and nevermore return to this land, or they will slay thee and slay me with thee." Hardly believing in my escape, I kissed his hand and thought the loss of my eye a light matter in consideration of my escaping from being slain. I arrived at my uncle's capital, and going in to him, told him of what had befallen my father and myself, whereat he wept with sore weeping and said: "Verily thou addest grief to my grief, and woe to my woe, for thy cousin hath been missing these many days. I wot not what hath happened to him, and none can give me news of him." And he wept till he fainted. I sorrowed and condoled with him, and he would have applied certain medicaments to my eye, but he saw that it was become as a walnut with the shell empty. Then said he, "O my son, better to lose eye and keep life!"

After that I could no longer remain silent about my cousin, who was his only son and one dearly loved, so I told him all that had happened. He rejoiced with extreme joyance to hear news of his son and said, "Come now and show me the tomb." But I replied, "By Allah, O my uncle, I know not its place, though I sought it carefully full many times, yet could not find the site." However, I and my uncle went to the graveyard and looked right and left, till at last I recognized the tomb, and we both rejoiced with exceeding joy. We entered the sepulcher and loosened the earth about the grave, then, upraising the trapdoor, descended some fifty steps till we came to the foot of the staircase, when lo! we were stopped by a blinding smoke. Thereupon said my uncle that saying whose sayer shall never come to shame: "There is no Majesty and there is no Might save in Allah, the Glorious, the Great!" and we advanced till we suddenly came upon a saloon, whose floor was strewed with flour and grain and provisions and all manner necessaries, and in the midst of it stood a canopy sheltering a couch. Thereupon my uncle went up to the couch and, inspecting it, found his son and the lady who had gone down with him into the tomb, lying in each other's embrace.

But the twain had become black as charred wood. It was as if they had been cast into a pit of fire. When my uncle saw this spectacle, he spat in his son's face and said: "Thou hast thy deserts, O thou hog! This is thy judgment in the transitory world, and yet remaineth the judgment in the world to come, a durer and a more enduring." I marveled at his hardness of heart and, grieving for my cousin and the lady, said: "By Allah, O my uncle, calm thy wrath. Dost thou not see that all my thoughts are occupied with this misfortune, and how sorrowful I am for what hath befallen thy son, and how horrible it is that naught of him remaineth but a black heap of charcoal? And is not that enough, but thou must smite him with thy slipper?" Answered he: "O son of my brother, this youth from his boyhood was madly in love with his own sister, and often and often I forbade him from her, saying to myself, 'They are but little ones.' However, when they grew up sin befell between them, and although I could hardly believe it, I confined him and chided him and threatened him with the severest threats, and the eunuchs and servants said to him: 'Beware of so foul a thing which none before thee ever did, and which none after thee will ever do, and have a care lest thou be dishonored and disgraced among the kings of the day, even to the end of time.' And I added: 'Such a report as this will be spread abroad by caravans, and take heed not to give them cause to talk or I will assuredly curse thee and do thee to death.'

After that I lodged them apart and shut her up, but the accursed girl loved him with passionate love, for Satan had got the mastery of her as well as of him and made their foul sin seem fair in their sight. Now when my son saw that I separated them, he secretly built this souterrain and furnished it and transported to it victuals, even as thou seest, and when I had gone out a-sporting, came here with his sister and hid from me. Then His righteous judgment fell upon the twain and consumed them with fire from Heaven, and verily the Last Judgment will deal them durer pains and more enduring!" Then he wept and I wept with him, and he looked at me and said, "Thou art my son in his stead." And I bethought me awhile of the world and of its chances, how the Wazir had slain my father and had taken his place and had put out my eye, and how my cousin had come to his death by the strangest chance. And I wept again and my uncle wept with me.

Then we mounted the steps and let down the iron plate and heaped up the earth over it, and after restoring the tomb to its former condition, we returned to the palace. But hardly had we sat down ere we heard the tom-toming of the kettledrum and tantara of trumpets and clash of cymbals, and the rattling of war men's lances, and the clamors of assailants and the clanking of bits and the neighing of steeds, while the world was canopied with dense dust and sand clouds raised by the horses' hoofs. We were amazed at sight and sound, knowing not what could be the matter. So we asked, and were told us that the Wazir who had usurped my father's kingdom had marched his men, and that after levying his soldiery and taking a host of wild Arabs into service, he had come down upon us with armies like the sands of the sea. Their number none could tell, and against them none could prevail. They attacked the city unawares, and the citizens, being powerless to oppose them, surrendered the place. My uncle was slain and I made for the suburbs, saying to myself, "If thou fall into this villain's hands, he will assuredly kill thee."

On this wise all my troubles were renewed, and I pondered all that had betided my father and my uncle and I knew not what to do; for if the city people or my father's troops had recognized me, they would have done their best to win favor by destroying me. And I could think of no way to escape save by shaving off my beard and my eyebrows. So I shore them off and, changing my fine clothes for a Kalandar's rags, I fared forth from my uncle's capital and made for this city, hoping that peradventure someone would assist me to the presence of the Prince of the Faithful, and the Caliph who is the Viceregent of Allah upon earth. Thus have I come hither that I might tell him my tale and lay my case before him. I arrived here this very night, and was standing in doubt whither I should go when suddenly I saw this second Kalandar. So I salaamed to him, saying, 'I am a stranger' and he answered,—'I too am a stranger!' And as we were conversing, behold, up came our companion, this third Kalandar, and saluted us saying, 'I am a stranger!' And we answered, 'We too be strangers!'

Then we three walked on and together till darkness overtook us and Destiny drave us to your house. Such, then, is the cause of the shaving of my beard and mustachios and eyebrows, and the manner of my losing my left eye. They marveled much at this tale, and the Caliph said to Ja'afar, "By Allah, I have not seen nor have I heard the like of what hath happened to this Kalandar!" Quoth the lady of the house, "Rub thy head and wend thy ways." But he replied, "I will not go till I hear the history of the two others." Thereupon the second Kalander came forward and, kissing the ground, began to tell

THE SECOND KALANDAR'S TALE

KNOW, O my lady, that I was not born one-eyed, and mine is a strange story. And it were graven with needle graver on the eye corners, it were a warner to whoso would be warned. I am a king, son of a king, and was brought up like a prince. I learned intoning the Koran according the seven schools, and I read all manner books, and held disputations on their contents with the doctors and men of science. Moreover, I studied star lore and the fair sayings of poets, and I exercised myself in all branches of learning until I surpassed the people of my time. My skill in calligraphy exceeded that of all the scribes, and my fame was bruited abroad over all climes and cities, and all the kings learned to know my name.

Amongst others, the King of Hind heard of me and sent to my father to invite me to his court, with offerings and presents and rarities such as befit royalties. So my father fitted out six ships for me and my people, and we put to sea and sailed for the space of a full month till we made the land. Then we brought out the horses that were with us in the ships, and after loading the camels with our presents for the Prince, we set forth inland. But we had marched only a little way when behold, a dust cloud upflew, and grew until it walled the horizon from view. After an hour or so the veil lifted and discovered beneath it fifty horsemen, ravening lions to the sight, in steel armor dight. We observed them straightly and lo! they were cutters-off of the highway, wild as wild Arabs. When they saw that we were only four and had with us but the ten camels carrying the presents, they dashed down upon us with lances at rest. We signed to them with our fingers, as it were saying, "We be messengers of the great King of Hind, so harm us not!" But they answered on like wise, "We are not in his dominions to obey nor are we subject to his sway."

Then they set upon us and slew some of my slaves and put the lave to flight. And I also fled after I had gotten a wound, a grievous hurt, whilst the Arabs were taken up with the money and the presents which were with us. I went forth unknowing whither I went, having become mean as I was mighty, and I fared on until I came to the crest of a mountain, where I took shelter for the night in a cave. When day arose I set out again, nor ceased after this fashion till I arrived at a fair city and a well filled. Now it was the season when winter was turning away with his rime and to greet the world with his flowers came prime, and the young blooms were springing and the streams flowed ringing, and the birds were sweetly singing, as saith the poet concerning a certain city when describing it:

> A place secure from every thought of fear,
> Safety and peace forever lord it here.
> Its beauties seem to beautify its sons
> And as in Heaven its happy folk appear.

I was glad of my arrival, for I was wearied with the way, and yellow of face for weakness and want, but my plight was pitiable and I knew not whither to betake me. So I accosted a tailor sitting in his little shop and saluted him. He returned my salaam, and bade me kindly welcome and wished me well and entreated me gently and asked me of the cause of my strangerhood. I told him all my past from first to last, and he was concerned on my account and said: "O youth, disclose not thy secret to any. The King of this city is the greatest enemy thy father hath, and there is blood wite between them and thou hast cause to fear for thy life." Then he set meat and drink before me, and I ate and drank and he with me, and we conversed freely till nightfall, when he cleared me a place in a corner of his shop and brought me a carpet and a coverlet. I tarried with him three days, at the end of which time he said to me, "Knowest thou no calling whereby to win thy living, O my son?" "I am learned in the law," I replied, "and a doctor of doctrine, an adept in art and science, a mathematician, and a notable penman." He rejoined, "Thy calling is of no account in our city, where not a soul understandeth science or even writing, or aught save money-making." Then said I, "By Allah, I know nothing but what I have mentioned," and he answered, "Gird thy middle and take thee a hatchet and a cord, and go and hew wood in the wold for thy daily bread till Allah send thee relief, and tell none who thou art lest they slay thee."

Then he bought me an ax and a rope and gave me in charge to certain woodcutters, and with these guardians I went forth into the forest, where I cut fuel wood the whole of my day and came back in the evening bearing my bundle on my head. I sold it for half a dinar, with part of which I bought provision, and laid by the rest. In such work I spent a whole year, and when this was ended, I went out one day, as was my wont, into the wilderness and, wandering away from my companions, I chanced on a thickly grown lowland in which there was an abundance of wood. So I entered and I found the gnarled stump of a great tree and loosened the ground about it and shoveled away the earth. Presently my hatchet rang upon a copper ring, so I cleared away the soil and behold, the ring was attached to a wooden trapdoor. This I raised, and there appeared beneath it a staircase.

I descended the steps to the bottom and came to a door, which I opened and found myself in a noble hall strong of structure and beautifully built, where was a damsel like a pearl of great price, whose favor banished from my heart all grief and cark and care, and whose soft speech healed the soul in despair and captivated the wise and ware. Her figure measured five feet in height, her breasts were firm and upright, her cheek a very garden of delight, her color lively bright, her face gleamed like dawn through curly tresses which gloomed like night, and above the snows of her bosom glittered teeth of a pearly white. When I looked upon her I prostrated myself before Him who had created her, for the beauty and loveliness He had shaped in her, and she looked at me and said, "Art thou man or Jinni?" "I am a man," answered I, and she, "Now who brought thee to this place where I have abided five-and-twenty years without even yet seeing man in it?" Quoth I (and indeed I found her words wonder-sweet, and my heart was melted to the core by them), "O my lady, my good fortune led me hither for the dispelling of my cark and care."

Then I related to her all my mishap from first to last, and my case appeared to her exceeding grievous, so she wept and said: "I will tell thee my story in my turn. I am the daughter of the King Ifitamus, lord of the Islands of Abnus, who married me to my cousin, the son of my paternal uncle. But on my wedding night an Ifrit named Jirjis bin Rajmus, first cousin—this is, mother's sister's son—of Iblis, the Foul Fiend, snatched me up and, flying away with me like a bird, set me down in this place, wither he conveyed all I needed of fine stuffs, raiment and jewels and furniture, and meat and drink and other else. Once in every ten days he comes here and lies a single night with me, and then wends his way, for he took me without the consent of his family. And he hath agreed with me that if ever I need him by night or by day, I have only to pass my hand over yonder two lines engraved upon the alcove and he will appear to me before my fingers cease touching. Four days have now passed since he was here, and as there remain six days before he come again, say me, wilt thou abide with me five days, and go hence the day before his coming?" I replied "Yes, and yes again! O rare, if all this be not a dream!"

Hereat she was glad and, springing to her feet, seized my hand and carried me through an arched doorway to a hammam bath, a fair hall and richly decorate. I doffed my clothes, and she doffed hers, then we bathed and she washed me. And when this was done we left the bath, and she seated me by her side upon a high divan, and brought me sherbet scented with musk. When we felt cool after the bath, she set food before me and we ate and fell to talking, but presently she said to me, "Lay thee down and take thy rest, for surely thou must be weary." So I thanked her, my lady, and lay down and slept soundly, forgetting all that happened to me. When I awoke I found her rubbing and shampooing my feet, so I again thanked her and blessed her and we sat for a while talking. Said she, "By Allah, I was sad at heart, for that I have dwelt alone underground for these five-and-twenty years, and praise be to Allah Who hath sent me someone with whom I can converse!" Then she asked, "O youth, what sayest thou to wine?" and I answered, "Do as thou wilt." Whereupon she went to a cupboard and took out a sealed flask of right old wine and set off the table with flowers and scented herbs and began to sing these lines:

> "Had we known of thy coming we fain had dispread
> The cores of our hearts or the balls of our eyes,
> Our cheeks as a carpet to greet thee had thrown,
> And our eyelids had strown for thy feet to betread."

Now when she finished her verse I thanked her, for indeed love of her had gotten hold of my heart, and my grief and anguish were gone. We sat at converse and carousal till nightfall, and with her I spent the night—such night never spent I in all my life! On the morrow delight followed delight till midday, by which time I had drunken wine so freely that I had lost my wits, and stood up, staggering to the right and to the left, and said "Come, O my charmer, and I will carry thee up from this underground vault and deliver thee from the spell of thy Jinni." She laughed and replied: "Content thee and hold thy peace. Of every ten days one is for the Ifrit and the other nine are thine." Quoth I (and in good sooth drink had got the better of me), "This very instant will I break down the alcove whereon is graven the talisman and summon the Ifrit that I may slay him, for it is a practice of mine to slay Ifrits!" When she heard my words, her color waxed wan and she said, "By Allah, do not!" and she began repeating:

> "This is a thing wherein destruction lies.
> I rede thee shun it an thy wits be wise."

And these also:

> "O thou who seekest severance, draw the rein
> Of thy swift steed nor seek o'ermuch t' advance.
> Ah stay! for treachery is the rule of life,
> And sweets of meeting end in severance."

I heard her verse but paid no heed to her words—nay, I raised my foot and administered to the alcove a mighty kick, and behold, the air starkened and darkened and thundered and lightened, the earth trembled and quaked, and the world became invisible. At once the fumes of wine left my head. I cried to her, "What is the matter?" and she replied: "The Ifrit is upon us! Did I not warn thee of this? By Allah, thou hast brought ruin upon me, but fly for thy life and go up by the way thou camest down!" So I fled up the staircase, but in the excess of my fear I forgot sandals and hatchet. And when I had mounted two steps I turned to look for them, and lo! I saw the earth cleave asunder, and there arose from it an Ifrit, a monster of hideousness, who said to the damsel: "What trouble and pother be this wherewith thou disturbest me? What mishap hath betided thee?" "No mishap hath befallen me," she answered, "save that my breast was straitened and my heart heavy with sadness. So I drank a little wine to broaden it and to hearten myself, then I rose to obey a call of nature, but the wine had gotten into my head and I fell against the alcove." "Thou liest, like the whore thou art!" shrieked the Ifrit, and he looked around the hall right and left till he caught sight of my ax and sandals and said to her, "What be these but the belongings of some mortal who hath been in thy society?" She answered: "I never set eyes upon them till this moment. They must have been brought by thee hither cleaving to thy garments." Quoth the Ifrit, "These words are absurd, thou harlot! thou strumpet!"

Then he stripped her stark-naked and, stretching her upon the floor, bound her hands and feet to four stakes, like one crucified, and set about torturing and trying to make her confess. I could not bear to stand listening to her cries and groans, so I climbed the stair on the quake with fear, and when I reached the top I replaced the trapdoor and covered it with earth. Then repented I of what I had done with penitence exceeding, and thought of the lady and her beauty and loveliness, and the tortures she was suffering at the hands of the accursed Ifrit, after her quiet life of five-and-twenty years, and how all that had happened to her was for cause of me. I bethought me of my father and his kingly estate and how I had become a woodcutter, and how, after my time had been awhile serene, the world had again waxed turbid and troubled to me. So I wept bitterly and repeated this couplet:

> "What time Fate's tyranny shall most oppress thee
> Perpend! One day shall joy thee, one distress thee!"

Then I walked till I reached the home of my friend the tailor, whom I found most anxiously expecting me. Indeed he was, as the saying goes, on coals of fire for my account. And when he saw me he said: "All night long my heart hath been heavy, fearing for thee from wild beasts or other mischances. Now praise be to Allah for thy safety!" I thanked him for his friendly solicitude and, retiring to my corner, sat pondering and musing on what had befallen me, and I blamed and chided myself for my meddlesome folly and my frowardness in kicking the alcove. I was calling myself to account when behold, my friend the tailor came to me and said: "O youth, in the shop there is an old man, a Persian, who seeketh thee. He hath thy hatchet and thy sandals, which he had taken to the woodcutters, saying, I was going out at what time the muezzin began the call to dawn prayer, when I chanced upon these things and know not whose they are, so direct me to their owner. The woodcutters recognized thy hatchet and directed him to thee. He is sitting in my shop, so fare forth to him and thank him and take thine ax and sandals."

When I heard these words I turned yellow with fear and felt

stunned as by a blow, and before I could recover myself, lo! the floor of my private room clove asunder, and out of it rose the Persian, who was the Ifrit. He had tortured the lady with exceeding tortures, natheless she would not confess to him aught, so he took the hatchet and sandals and said to her, "As surely as I am Jirjis of the seed of Iblis, I will bring thee back the owner of this and these!" Then he went to the woodcutters with the pretense aforesaid and, being directed to me, after waiting a while in the shop till the fact was confirmed, he suddenly snatched me up as a hawk snatcheth a mouse and flew high in air, but presently descended and plunged with me under the earth (I being a-swoon the while), and lastly set me down in the subterranean palace wherein I had passed that blissful night.

And there I saw the lady stripped to the skin, her limbs bound to four stakes and blood welling from her sides. At the sight my eyes ran over with tears, but the Ifrit covered her person and said, "O wanton, is not this man thy lover?" She looked upon me and replied, "I wot him not, nor have I ever seen him before this hour!" Quoth the Ifrit, "What! This torture and yet no confessing?" And quoth she, "I never saw this man in my born days, and it is not lawful in Allah's sight to tell lies on him." "If thou know him not," said the Ifrit to her, "take this sword and strike off his head." She hent the sword in hand and came close up to me, and I signaled to her with my eyebrows, my tears the while flowing a-down my cheeks. She understood me and made answer, also by signs, "How couldest thou bring all this evil upon me?" And I rejoined after the same fashion, "This is the time for mercy and forgiveness." And the mute tongue of my case spake aloud saying:

> Mine eyes were dragomans for my tongue betied,
> And told full clear the love I fain would hide.
> When last we met and tears in torrents railed,
> For tongue struck dumb my glances testified.
> She signed with eye glance while her lips were mute,
> I signed with fingers and she kenned th' implied.
> Our eyebrows did all duty 'twixt us twain,
> And we being speechless, Love spake loud and plain.

Then, O my mistress, the lady threw away the sword and said: "How shall I strike the neck of one I wot not, and who hath done me no evil? Such deed were not lawful in my law!" and she held her hand.

Said the Ifrit: " 'Tis grievous to thee to slay thy lover, and, because he hath lain with thee, thou endurest these torments and obstinately refusest to confess. After this it is clear to me that only like loveth and pitieth like." Then he turned to me and asked me, "O man, haply thou also dost not know this woman," whereto I answered: "And pray who may she be? Assuredly I never saw her till this instant." "Then take the sword," said he, "and strike off her head and I will believe that thou wottest her not and will leave thee free to go, and will not deal hardly with thee." I replied, "That will I do," and, taking the sword, went forward sharply and raised my hand to smite. But she signed to me with her eyebrows, "Have I failed thee in aught of love, and is it thus that thou requitest me?" I understood what her looks implied and answered her with an eye glance, "I will sacrifice my soul for thee." And the tongue of the case wrote in our hearts these lines:

> How many a lover with his eyebrows speaketh
> To his beloved, as his passion pleadeth.
> With flashing eyne his passion he inspireth
> And well she seeth what his pleading needeth.
> How sweet the look when each on other gazeth,
> And with what swiftness and how sure it speedeth.
> And this with eyebrows all his passion writeth,
> And that with eyeballs all his passion readeth.

Then my eyes filled with tears to overflowing and I cast the sword from my hand, saying: "O mighty Ifrit and hero, if a woman lacking wits and faith deem it unlawful to strike off my head, how can it be lawful for me, a man, to smite her neck whom I never saw in my whole life? I cannot do such misdeed, though thou cause me drink the cup of death and perdition." Then said the Ifrit, "Ye twain show the good understanding between you, but I will let you see how such doings end." He took the sword and struck off the lady's hands first, with four strokes, and then her feet, whilst I looked on and made sure of death and she farewelled me with her dying eyes. So the Ifrit cried at her, "Thou whorest and makest me a wittol with thine eyes," and struck her so that her head went flying. Then turned he to me and said: "O mortal, we have it in our law that when the wife committeth advowtry, it is lawful for us to slay her. As for this damsel, I snatched her away on her bride night when she was a girl of twelve and she knew no one but myself. I used to come to her once in every ten days and lie with her the night, under the semblance of a man, a Persian, and when I was well assured that she had cuckolded me, I slew her. But as for thee, I am not well satisfied that thou hast wronged me in her. Nevertheless I must not let thee go unharmed, so ask a boon of me and I will grant it."

Then I rejoiced, O my lady, with exceeding joy and said, "What boon shall I crave of thee?" He replied, "Ask me this boon—into what shape I shall bewitch thee? Wilt thou be a dog, or an ass, or an ape?" I rejoined (and indeed I had hoped that mercy might be shown me), "By Allah, spare me, that Allah spare thee for sparing a Moslem and a man who never wronged thee." And I humbled myself before him with exceeding humility, and remained standing in his presence, saying, "I am sore oppressed by circumstance." Said the Ifrit: "Lengthen not thy words! As to my slaying thee, fear it not, and as to my pardoning thee, hope it not, but from my bewitching thee there is no escape." Then he tore me from the ground, which closed under my feet, and flew with me into the firmament till I saw the earth as a large white cloud or a saucer in the midst of the waters. Presently he set me down on a mountain, and taking a little dust, over which he muttered some magical words, sprinkled me therewith, saying, "Quit that shape and take thou the shape of an ape!" And on the instant I became an ape, a tailless baboon, the son of a century.

Now when he had left me and I saw myself in this ugly and hateful shape, I wept for myself, but resigned my soul to the tyranny of Time and Circumstance, well weeting that Fortune is fair and constant to no man. I descended the mountain and found at the foot a desert plain, long and broad, over which I traveled for the space of a month till my course brought me to the brink of the briny sea. After standing there awhile, I was ware of a ship in the offing which ran before a fair wind making for the shore. I hid myself behind a rock on the beach and waited till the ship drew near, when I leaped on board. I found her full of merchants and passengers, and one of them cried, "O Captain, this ill-omened brute will bring us ill luck!" And another said, "Turn this ill-omened beast out from among us." The Captain said, "Let us kill it!" Another said, "Slay it with the sword," a third, "Drown it," and a fourth, "Shoot it with an arrow."

But I sprang up and laid hold of the rais's[1] skirt, and shed tears which poured down my chops. The Captain took pity on me, and said, "O merchants, this ape hath appealed to me for protection and I will protect him. Henceforth he is under my charge, so let none do him aught hurt or harm, otherwise there will be bad blood between us." Then he entreated me kindly, and whatsoever he said I understood, and ministered to his every want and served him as a servant, albeit my tongue would not obey my wishes, so that he came to love me. The vessel sailed on, the wind being fair, for the space of fifty days, at the end of which we cast anchor under the walls of a great city wherein was a world of people, especially learned men. None could tell their number save Allah. No sooner had we arrived than we were visited by certain Mameluke officials from the King of that city, who, after boarding us, greeted the merchants and, giving them joy of safe arrival, said: "Our King welcometh you, and sendeth you this roll of paper, whereupon each and every of you must write a line. For ye shall know that the King's Minister, a calligrapher of renown, is dead, and the King hath sworn a solemn oath that he will make none Wazir in his stead who cannot write as well as he could."

He then gave us the scroll, which measured ten cubits long by a breadth of one, and each of the merchants who knew how to write wrote a line thereon, even to the last of them, after which I stood up (still in the shape of an ape) and snatched the roll out of their hands. They feared lest I should tear it or throw it overboard, so they tried to stay me and scare me, but I signed to them that I could write, whereat all marveled, saying, "We never yet saw an ape write." And the Captain cried: "Let him write, and if he scribble and scrabble we will kick him out and kill him. But if he write fair and scholarly, I will adopt him as my son, for surely I never yet saw a more intelligent and well-mannered monkey than he. Would Heaven my real son were his match in morals and manners!"

I took the reed and, stretching out my paw, dipped it in ink and wrote, in the hand used for letters, these two couplets:

> Time hath recorded gifts she gave the great,
> But none recorded thine, which be far higher.
> Allah ne'er orphan men by loss of thee
> Who be of Goodness mother, Bounty's sire.

[1] A rais is a chief of some sort, here the captain of the ship.

And I wrote in Rayhani or larger letters elegantly curved:

> Thou hast a reed of rede to every land,
> Whose driving causeth all the world to thrive.
> Nil is the Nile of Misraim by thy boons,
> Who makest misery smile with fingers five.

Then I wrote in the Suls character:

> There be no writer who from Death shall fleet
> But what his hand hath writ men shall repeat.
> Write, therefore, naught save what shall serve thee when
> Thou see't on Judgment Day an so thou see't!

Then I wrote in the character of Naskh:

> When to sore parting Fate our love shall doom,
> To distant life by Destiny decreed,
> We cause the inkhorn's lips to 'plain our pains,
> And tongue our utterance with the talking reed.

    Then I gave the scroll to the officials, and after we all had written our line, they carried it before the King. When he saw the paper, no writing pleased him save my writing, and he said to the assembled courtiers: "Go seek the writer of these lines and dress him in a splendid robe of honor. Then mount him on a she-mule, let a band of music precede him, and bring him to the presence." At these words they smiled and the King was wroth with them and cried "O accursed! I give you an order and you laugh at me?" "O King," replied they, "if we laugh 'tis not at thee and not without a cause." "And what is it?" asked he, and they answered, "O King, thou orderest us to bring to thy presence the man who wrote these lines. Now the truth is that he who wrote them is not of the sons of Adam, but an ape, a tailless baboon, belonging to the ship Captain." Quoth he, "Is this true that you say?" Quoth they, "Yea! by the rights of thy munificence!" The King marveled at their words and shook with mirth and said, "I am minded to buy this ape of the Captain."

    Then he sent messengers to the ship with the mule, the dress, the guard, and the state drums, saying, "Not the less do you clothe him in the robe of honor and mount him on the mule, and let him be surrounded by the guards and preceded by the band of music." They came to the ship and took me from the Captain and robed me in the robe of honor and, mounting me on the she-mule, carried me in state procession through the streets whilst the people were amazed and amused. And folk said to one another: "Halloo! Is our Sultan about to make an ape his Minister?" and came all agog crowding to gaze at me, and the town was astir and turned topsy-turvy on my account. When they brought me up to the King and set me in his presence, I kissed the ground before him three times, and once before the High Chamberlain and great officers, and he bade me be seated, and I sat respectfully on shins and knees, and all who were present marveled at my fine manners, and the King most of all.

Thereupon he ordered the lieges to retire, and when none remained save the King's Majesty, the eunuch on duty, and a little white slave, he bade them set before me the table of food, containing all manner of birds, whatever hoppeth and flieth and treadeth in nest, such as quail and sand grouse. Then he signed to me to eat with him, so I rose and kissed ground before him, then sat me down and ate with him. Presently they set before the King choice wines in flagons of glass and he drank. Then he passed on the cup to me, and I kissed the ground and drank and wrote on it:

> With fire they boilèd me to loose my tongue,
> And pain and patience gave for fellowship.
> Hence comes it hands of men upbear me high
> And honeydew from lips of maid I sip!

The King read my verse and said with a sigh, "Were these gifts in a man, he would excel all the folk of his time and age!" Then he called for the chessboard, and said, "Say, wilt thou play with me?" and I signed with my head, "Yes." Then I came forward and ordered the pieces and played with him two games, both of which I won. He was speechless with surprise, so I took the pen case and, drawing forth a reed, wrote on the board these two couplets:

> Two hosts fare fighting thro' the livelong day,
> Nor is their battling ever finishèd
> Until, when darkness girdeth them about,
> The twain go sleeping in a single bed.

The King read these lines with wonder and delight and said to his eunuch, "O Mukbil, go to thy mistress, Sitt al-Husn, and say her, 'Come, speak the King, who biddeth thee hither to take thy solace in seeing this right wondrous ape!'" So the eunuch went out, and presently returned with the lady, who when she saw me veiled her face and said: "O my father, hast thou lost all sense of honor? How cometh it thou art pleased to send for me and show me to strange men?" "O Sitt al-Husn," said he, "no man is here save this little foot page and the eunuch who reared thee and I, thy father. From whom, then, dost thou veil thy face?" She answered, "This whom thou deemest an ape is a young man, a clever and polite, a wise and learned, and the son of a king. But he is ensorceled, and the Ifrit Jirjaris, who is of the seed of Iblis, cast a spell upon him, after putting to death his own wife, the daughter of King Ifitamus lord of the Islands of Abnus." The King marveled at his daughter's words and, turning to me, said, "Is this true that she saith of thee?" and I signed by a nod of my head the answer "Yea, verily," and wept sore.

Then he asked his daughter, "Whence knewest thou that he is ensorceled?" and she answered: "O my dear Papa, there was with me in my childhood an old woman, a wily one and a wise and a witch to boot, and she taught me the theory of magic and its practice, and I took notes in writing and therein waxed perfect, and have committed to memory a hundred and seventy chapters of egromantic formulas, by the least of which I could transport the stones of thy city behind the Mountain Kaf and the Circumambient Main, or make its site an abyss of the sea and its people fishes swimming in the midst of it." "O my daughter," said her father, "I conjure thee, by my life, disenchant this young man, that I may make him my Wazir and marry thee to him, for indeed he is an ingenious youth and a deeply learned." "With joy and goodly gree," she replied and, hending in hand an iron knife whereon was inscribed the name of Allah in Hebrew characters she described a wide circle in the midst of the palace hall, and therein wrote in Kufic letters mysterious names and talismans. And she uttered words and muttered charms, some of which we understood and others we understood not.

Presently the world waxed dark before our sight till we thought that the sky was falling upon our heads, and lo! the Ifrit presented himself in his own shape and aspect. His hands were like many-pronged pitchforks, his legs like the masts of great ships, and his eyes like cressets of gleaming fire. We were in terrible fear of him, but the King's daughter cried at him, "No welcome to thee and no greeting, O dog!" Whereupon he changed to the form of a lion and said, "O traitress, how is it thou hast broken the oath we sware that neither should contraire other?" "O accursed one," answered she, "how could there be a compact between me and the like of thee?" Then said he, "Take what thou hast brought on thyself." And the lion open his jaws and rushed upon her, but she was too quick for him, and, plucking a hair from her head, waved it in the air muttering over it the while. And the hair straightway became a trenchant sword blade, wherewith she smote the lion and cut him in twain. Then the two halves flew away in air and the head changed to a scorpion and the Princess became a huge serpent and set upon the accursed scorpion, and the two fought, coiling and uncoiling, a stiff fight for an hour at least.

Then the scorpion changed to a vulture and the serpent became an eagle, which set upon the vulture and hunted him for an hour's time, till he became a black tomcat, which miauled and grinned and spat. Thereupon the eagle changed into a piebald wolf and these two battled in the palace for a long time, when the cat, seeing himself overcome, changed into a worm and crept into a huge red pomegranate which lay beside the jetting fountain in the midst of the palace hall. Whereupon the pomegranate swelled to the size of a watermelon in air and, falling upon the marble pavement of the palace, broke to pieces, and all the grains fell out and were scattered about till they covered the whole floor. Then the wolf shook himself and became a snow-white cock, which fell to picking up the grains, purposing not to leave one, but by doom of destiny one seed rolled to the fountain edge and there lay hid.

The cock fell to crowing and clapping his wings and signing to us with his beak as if to ask, "Are any grains left?" But we understood not what he meant, and he cried to us with so loud a cry that we thought the palace would fall upon us. Then he ran over all the floor till he saw the grain which had rolled to the fountain edge, and rushed eagerly to pick it up when behold, it sprang into the midst of the water and became a fish and dived to the bottom of the basin. Thereupon the cock changed to a big fish, and plunged in after the other, and the two disappeared for a while and lo! we heard loud shrieks and cries of pain which made us tremble. After this the Ifrit rose out of the water, and he was as a burning flame, casting fire and smoke from his mouth and eyes and nostrils. And immediately the Princess likewise came forth from the basin, and she was one live coal of flaming lowe, and these two, she and he, battled for the space of an hour, until their fires entirely compassed them about and their thick smoke filled the palace.

As for us, we panted for breath, being well-nigh suffocated, and we longed to plunge into the water, fearing lest we be burnt up and utterly destroyed. And the King said: "There is no Majesty and there is no Might save in Allah the Glorious, the Great! Verily we are Allah's and unto Him are we returning! Would Heaven I had not urged my daughter to attempt the disenchantment of this ape fellow, whereby I have imposed upon her the terrible task of fighing yon accursed Ifrit, against whom all the Ifrits in the world could not prevail. And would Heaven we had never seen this ape, Allah never assain nor bless the day of his coming! We thought to do a good deed by him before the face of Allah, and to release him from enchantment, and now we have brought this trouble and travail upon our heart." But I, O my lady, was tonguetied and powerless to say a word to him.

Suddenly, ere we were ware of aught, the Ifrit yelled out from under the flames and, coming up to us as we stood on the estrade, blew fire in our faces. The damsel overtook him and breathed blasts of fire at his face, and the sparks from her and from him rained down upon us, and her sparks did us no harm. But one of his sparks alighted upon my eye and destroyed it, making me a monocular ape. And another fell on the King's face, scorching the lower half, burning off his beard and mustachios and causing his underteeth to fall out, while a third lighted on the castrato's breast, killing him on the spot. So we despaired of life and made sure of death when lo! a voice repeated the saying: "Allah is Most Highest! Allah is Most Highest! Aidance and victory to all who the Truth believe, and disappointment and disgrace to all who the religion of Mohammed, the Moon of Faith, unbelieve." The speaker was the Princess, who had burnt the Ifrit, and he was become a heap of ashes. Then she came up to us and said, "Reach me a cup of water." They brought it to her and she spoke over it words we understood not and, sprinkling me with it, cried, "By virtue of the Truth, and by the Most Great Name of Allah, I charge thee return to thy former shape!" And behold, I shook and became a man as before, save that I had utterly lost an eye.

Then she cried out: "The fire! The fire! O my dear Papa, an arrow from the accursed hath wounded me to the death, for I am not used to fight with the Jann. Had he been a man, I had slain him in the beginning. I had no trouble till the time when the pomegranate burst and the grains scattered, but I overlooked the seed wherein was the very life of the Jinni. Had I picked it up, he had died on the spot, but as Fate and Fortune decreed, I saw it not, so he came upon me all unawares and there befell between him and me a sore struggle under the earth and high in air and in the water. And as often as I opened on him a gate, he opened on me another gate and a stronger, till at last he opened on me the gate of fire, and few are saved upon whom the door of fire openeth. But Destiny willed that my cunning prevail over his cunning, and I burned him to death after I vainly exhorted him to embrace the religion of Al-Islam. As for me, I am a dead woman. Allah supply my place to you!"

Then she called upon Heaven for help and ceased not to implore relief from the fire, when lo! a black spark shot up from her robed feet to her thighs, then it flew to her bosom and thence to her face. When it reached her face, she wept and said, "I testify that there is no god but *the* God and that Mohammed is the Apostle of God!" And we looked at her and saw naught but a heap of ashes by the side of the heap that had been the Ifrit. We mourned for her, and I wished I had been in her place, so had I not seen her lovely face who had worked me such weal become ashes, but there is no gainsaying the will of Allah.

When the King saw his daughter's terrible death, he plucked out what was left of his beard and beat his face and rent his raiment, and I did as he did and we both wept over her. Then came in the chamberlains and grandees, and were amazed to find two heaps of ashes and the Sultan in a fainting fit. So they stood round him till he revived and told them what had befallen his daughter from the Ifrit, whereat their grief was right grievous and the women and the slave girls shrieked and keened, and they continued their lamentations for the space of seven days. Moreover, the King bade build over his daughter's ashes a vast vaulted tomb, and burn therein wax tapers and sepulchral lamps. But as for the Ifrit's ashes, they scattered them on the winds, speeding them to the curse of Allah.

Then the Sultan fell sick of a sickness that well-nigh brought him to his death for a month's space, and when health returned to him and his beard grew again and he had been converted by the mercy of Allah to Al-Islam, he sent for me and said: "O youth, Fate had decreed for us the happiest of lives, safe from all the chances and changes of Time, till thou camest to us, when troubles fell upon us. Would to Heaven we had never seen thee and the foul face of thee! For we took pity on thee, and thereby we have lost our all. I have on thy account first lost my daughter, who to me was well worth a hundred men, secondly, I have suffered that which befell me by reason of the fire and the loss of my teeth, and my eunuch also was slain. I blame thee not, for it was out of thy power to prevent this. The doom of Allah was on thee as well as on us, and thanks be to the Almighty for that my daughter delivered thee, albeit thereby she lost her own life! Go forth now, O my son, from this my city, and suffice thee what hath befallen us through thee, even although 'twas decreed for us. Go forth in peace, and if I ever see thee again I will surely slay thee." And he cried out at me.

So I went forth from his presence, O my lady, weeping bitterly and hardly believing in my escape and knowing not whither I should wend. And I recalled all that had befallen me, my meeting the tailor, my love for the damsel in the palace beneath the earth, and my narrow escape from the Ifrit, even after he had determined to do me die, and how I had entered the city as an ape and was now leaving it a man once more. Then I gave thanks to Allah and said, "My eye and not my life!" And before leaving the place I entered the bath and shaved my poll and beard and mustachios and eyebrows, and cast ashes on my head and donned the coarse black woolen robe of a Kalandar.

Then I journeyed through many regions and saw many a city, intending for Baghdad, that I might seek audience in the House of Peace with the Commander of the Faithful, and tell him all that had befallen me. I arrived here this very night and found my brother in Allah, this first Kalandar, standing about as one perplexed, so I saluted him with "Peace be upon thee," and entered into discourse with him. Presently up came our brother, this third Kalandar, and said to us: "Peace be with you! I am a stranger," whereto we replied, "And we too be strangers, who have come hither this blessed night."

So we all three walked on together, none of us knowing the other's history, till Destiny drave us to this door and we came in to you. Such then is my story and my reason for shaving my beard and mustachios, and this is what caused the loss of my eye. Said the house mistress, "Thy tale is indeed a rare, so rub thy head and wend thy ways." But he replied, "I will not budge till I hear my companions' stories."

Then came forward the third Kalandar, and said, "O illustrious lady, my history is not like that of these my comrades, but more wondrous and far more marvelous. In their case Fate and Fortune came down on them unawares, but I drew down Destiny upon my own head and brought sorrow on mine own soul, and shaved my own beard and lost my own eye. Hear then

THE THIRD KALANDAR'S TALE

Know, O my lady, that I also am a king and the son of a king and my name is Ajib son of Khazib. When my father died I succeeded him, and I ruled and did justice and dealt fairly by all my lieges. I delighted in sea trips, for my capital stood on the shore, before which the ocean stretched far and wide, and near hand were many great islands with sconces and garrisons in the midst of the main. My fleet numbered fifty merchantmen, and as many yachts for pleasance, and a hundred and fifty sail ready fitted for holy war with the unbelievers.

It fortuned that I had a mind to enjoy myself on the islands aforesaid, so I took ship with my people in ten keel and, carrying with me a month's victual, I set out on a twenty days' voyage. But one night a head wind struck us, and the sea rose against us with huge waves. The billows sorely buffeted us and a dense darkness settled round us. We gave ourselves up for lost, and I said, "Whoso endangereth his days, e'en an he 'scape deserveth no praise." Then we prayed to Allah and besought Him, but the storm blasts ceased not to blow against us nor the surges to strike us till morning broke, when the gale fell, the seas sank to mirrory stillness, and the sun shone upon us kindly clear. Presently we made an island, where we landed and cooked somewhat of food, and ate heartily and took our rest for a couple of days. Then we set out again and sailed other twenty days, the seas broadening and the land shrinking.

Presently the current ran counter to us, and we found ourselves in strange waters, where the Captain had lost his reckoning, and was wholly bewildered in this sea, so said we to the lookout man, "Get thee to the masthead and keep thine eyes open." He swarmed up the mast and looked out and cried aloud, "O Rais, I espy to starboard something dark, very like a fish floating on the face of the sea, and to larboard there is a loom in the midst of the main, now black and now bright." When the Captain heard the lookout's words, he dashed his turban on the deck and plucked out his beard and beat his face, saying: "Good news indeed! We be all dead men, not one of us can be saved." And he fell to weeping and all of us wept for his weeping and also for our lives, and I said, "O Captain, tell us what it is the lookout saw."

"O my Prince," answered he, "know that we lost our course on the night of the storm, which was followed on the morrow by a two days' calm during which we made no way, and we have gone astray eleven days' reckoning from that night, with ne'er a wind to bring us back to our true course. Tomorrow by the end of the day we shall come to a mountain of black stone hight the Magnet Mountain, for thither the currents carry us willy-nilly. As soon as we are under its lea, the ship's sides will open and every nail in plank will fly out and cleave fast to the mountain, for that Almighty Allah hath gifted the loadstone with a mysterious virtue and a love for iron, by reason whereof all which is iron traveleth toward it. And on this mountain is much iron, how much none knoweth save the Most High, from the many vessels which have been lost there since the days of yore. The bright spot upon its summit is a dome of yellow laton from Andalusia, vaulted upon ten columns. And on its crown is a horseman who rideth a horse of brass and holdeth in hand a lance of laton, and there hangeth on his bosom a tablet of lead graven with names and talismans." And he presently added, "And, O King, none destroyeth folk save the rider on that steed, nor will the egromancy be dispelled till he fall from his horse."

Then, O my lady, the Captain wept with exceeding weeping and we all made sure of death doom and each and every one of us farewelled his friend and charged him with his last will and testament in case he might be saved. We slept not that night, and in the morning we found ourselves much nearer the Loadstone Mountain, whither the waters drave us with a violent send. When the ships were close under its lea, they opened and the nails flew out and all the iron in them sought the Magnet Mountain and clove to it like a network, so that by the end of the day we were all struggling in the waves round about the mountain. Some of us were saved, but more were drowned, and even those who had escaped knew not one another, so stupefied were they by the beating of the billows and the raving of the winds.

As for me, O my lady, Allah (be His name exalted!) preserved my life that I might suffer whatso He willed to me of hardship, misfortune, and calamity, for I scrambled upon a plank from one of the ships and the wind and waters threw it at the feet of the mountain. There I found a practicable path leading by steps carven out of the rock to the summit, and I called on the name of Allah Almighty and breasted the ascent, clinging to the steps and notches hewn in the stone, and mounted little by little. And the Lord stilled the wind and aided me in the ascent, so that I succeeded in reaching the summit. There I found no resting place save the dome, which I entered, joying with exceeding joy at my escape, and made the wudu ablution and prayed a two-bow prayer, a thanksgiving to God for my preservation.

Then I fell asleep under the dome, and heard in my dream a mysterious voice saying, "O son of Khazib! When thou wakest from thy sleep, dig under thy feet and thou shalt find a bow of brass and three leaden arrows inscribed with talismans and characts. Take the bow and shoot the arrows at the horseman on the dome top and free mankind from this sore calamity. When thou hast shot him he shall fall into the sea, and the horse will also drop at thy feet. Then bury it in the place of the bow. This done, the main will swell and rise till it is level with the mountain head, and there will appear on it a skiff carrying a man of laton (other than he thou shalt have shot) holding in his hand a pair of paddles. He will come to thee, and do thou embark with him, but beware of saying Bismillah or of otherwise naming Allah Almighty. He will row thee for a space of ten days, till he bring thee to certain islands called the Islands of Safety, and thence thou shalt easily reach a port and find those who will convey thee to thy native land. And all this shall be fulfilled to thee so thou call not on the name of Allah."

Then I started up from my sleep in joy and gladness and, hastening to do the bidding of the mysterious voice, found the bow and arrows and shot at the horseman and tumbled him into the main, whilst the horse dropped at my feet, so I took it and buried it. Presently the sea surged up and rose till it reached the top of the mountain, nor had I long to wait ere I saw a skiff in the offing coming toward me. I gave thanks to Allah, and when the skiff came up to me, I saw therein a man of brass with a tablet of lead on his breast inscribed with talismans and characts, and I embarked without uttering a word. The boatman rowed on with me through the first day and the second and the third, in all ten whole days, till I caught sight of the Islands of Safety, whereat I joyed with exceeding joy and for stress of gladness exclaimed, "Allah! Allah! In the name of Allah! There is no god but *the* God and Allah is Almighty." Thereupon the skiff forthwith upset and cast me upon the sea, then it righted and sank deep into the depths.

Now I am a fair swimmer, so I swam the whole day till nightfall, when my forearms and shoulders were numbed with fatigue and I felt like to die, so I testified to my faith, expecting naught but death. The sea was still surging under the violence of the winds, and presently there came a billow like a hillock and, bearing me up high in air, threw me with a long cast on dry land, that His will might be fulfilled. I crawled upon the beach and doffing my raiment, wrung it out to dry and spread it in the sunshine. Then I lay me down and slept the whole night. As soon as it was day, I donned my clothes and rose to look whither I should walk. Presently I came to a thicket of low trees and, making a cast round it, found that the spot whereon I stood was an islet, a mere holm, girt on all sides by the ocean, whereupon I said to myself, "Whatso freeth me from one great calamity casteth me into a greater!"

But while I was pondering my case and longing for death, behold, I saw afar off a ship making for the island, so I clomb a tree and hid myself among the branches. Presently the ship anchored and landed ten slaves, blackamoors, bearing iron hoes and baskets, who walked on till they reached the middle of the island. Here they dug deep into the ground until they uncovered a plate of metal, which they lifted, thereby opening a trapdoor. After this they returned to the ship and thence brought bread and flour, honey and fruits, clarified butter, leather bottles containing liquors, and many household stuffs; also furniture, table service, and mirrors; rugs, carpets, and in fact all needed to furnish a dwelling. And they kept going to and fro, and descending by the trapdoor, till they had transported into the dwelling all that was in the ship.

After this the slaves again went on board and brought back with them garments as rich as may be, and in the midst of them came an old old man, of whom very little was left, for Time had dealt hardly and harshly with him, and all that remained of him was a bone wrapped in a rag of blue stuff, through which the winds whistled west and east. As saith the poet of him:

> Time gars me tremble. Ah, how sore the balk!
> While Time in pride of strength doth ever stalk.
> Time was I walked nor ever felt I tired,
> Now am I tired albe' I never walk!

And the Sheikh held by the hand a youth cast in beauty's mold, all elegance and perfect grace, so fair that his comeliness deserved to be proverbial, for he was as a green bough or the tender young of the roe, ravishing every heart with his loveliness and subduing every soul with his coquetry and amorous ways. They stinted not their going, O my lady, till all went down by the trapdoor and did not reappear for an hour, or rather more; at the end of which time the slaves and the old man came up without the youth and, replacing the iron plate and carefully closing the door slab as it was before, they returned to the ship and made sail and were lost to my sight.

When they turned away to depart, I came down from the tree and, going to the place I had seen them fill up, scraped off and removed the earth, and in patience possessed my soul till I had cleared the whole of it away. Then appeared the trapdoor, which was of wood, in shape and size like a millstone, and when I lifted it up, it disclosed a winding staircase of stone. At this I marveled and, descending the steps till I reached the last, found a fair hall, spread with various kinds of carpets and silk stuffs, wherein was a youth sitting upon a raised couch and leaning back on a round cushion with a fan in his hand and nosegays and posies of sweet scented herbs and flowers before him. But he was alone and not a soul near him in the great vault. When he saw me he turned pale, but I saluted him courteously and said: "Set thy mind at ease and calm thy fears. No harm shall come near thee. I am a man like thyself and the son of a king to boot, whom the decrees of Destiny have sent to bear thee company and cheer thee in thy loneliness. But now tell me, what is thy story and what causeth thee to dwell thus in solitude under the ground?"

When he was assured that I was of his kind and no Jinni, he rejoiced and his fine color returned, and, making me draw near to him, he said: "O my brother, my story is a strange story and 'tis this. My father is a merchant jeweler possessed of great wealth, who hath white and black slaves traveling and trading on his account in ships and on camels, and trafficking with the most distant cities, but he was not blessed with a child, not even one. Now on a certain night he dreamed a dream that he should be favored with a son, who would be short-lived, so the morning dawned on my father, bringing him woe and weeping. On the following night my mother conceived and my father noted down the date of her becoming pregnant. Her time being fulfilled, she bare me, whereat my father rejoiced and made banquets and called together the neighbors and fed the fakirs and the poor, for that he had been blessed with issue near the end of his days. Then he assembled the astrologers and astronomers who knew the places of the planets, and the wizards and wise ones of the time, and men learned in horoscopes and nativities, and they drew out my birth scheme and said to my father: "Thy son shall live to fifteen years, but in his fifteenth there is a sinister aspect. An he safely tide it over, he shall attain a great age. And the cause that threateneth him with death is this. In the Sea of Peril standeth the Mountain Magnet hight, on whose summit is a horseman of yellow laton seated on a horse also of brass and bearing on his breast a tablet of lead. Fifty days after this rider shall fall from his steed thy son will die and his slayer will be he who shoots down the horseman, a Prince named Ajib son of King Khazib."

My father grieved with exceeding grief to hear these words, but reared me in tenderest fashion and educated me excellently well till my fifteenth year was told. Ten days ago news came to him that the horseman had fallen into the sea and he who shot him down was named Ajib son of King Khazib. My father thereupon wept bitter tears at the need of parting with me and became like one possessed of a Jinni. However, being in mortal fear for me, he built me this place under the earth, and stocking it with all required for the few days still remaining, he brought me hither in a ship and left me here. Ten are already past, and when the forty shall have gone by without danger to me, he will come and take me away, for he hath done all this only in fear of Prince Ajib. Such, then, is my story and the cause of my loneliness."

When I heard his history I marveled and said in my mind, "I am the Prince Ajib who hath done all this, but as Allah is with me I will surely not slay him!" So said I to him: "O my lord, far from thee be this hurt and harm and then, please Allah, thou shalt not suffer cark nor care nor aught disquietude, for I will tarry with thee and serve thee as a servant, and then wend my ways. And after having borne thee company during the forty days, I will go with thee to thy home, where thou shalt give me an escort of some of thy Mamelukes with whom I may journey back to my own city, and the Almighty shall requite thee for me." He was glad to hear these words, when I rose and lighted a large wax candle and trimmed the lamps and the three lanterns, and I set on meat and drink and sweetmeats. We ate and drank and sat talking over various matters till the greater part of the night was gone, when he lay down to rest and I covered him up and went to sleep myself.

Next morning I arose and warmed a little water, then lifted him gently so as to awake him and brought him the warm water, wherewith he washed his face, and said to me: "Heaven requite thee for me with every blessing, O youth! By Allah, if I get quit of this danger and am saved from him whose name is Ajib bin Khazib, I will make my father reward thee and send thee home healthy and wealthy. And if I die, then my blessing be upon thee." I answered, "May the day never dawn on which evil shall betide thee, and may Allah make my last day before thy last day!" Then I set before him somewhat of food and we ate, and I got ready perfumes for fumigating the hall, wherewith he was pleased. Moreover I made him a mankalah cloth; and we played and ate sweetmeats and we played again and took our pleasure till nightfall, when I rose and lighted the lamps, and set before him somewhat to eat, and sat telling him stories till the hours of darkness were far spent. Then he lay down to rest and I covered him up and rested also.

And thus I continued to do, O my lady, for days and nights, and affection for him took root in my heart and my sorrow was eased, and I said to myself: "The astrologers lied when they predicted that he should be slain by Ajib bin Khazib. By Allah, I will not slay him." I ceased not ministering to him and conversing and carousing with him and telling him all manner tales for thirty-nine days. On the fortieth night the youth rejoiced and said: "O my brother, Alhamdolillah!—praise be to Allah—who hath preserved me from death, and this is by thy blessing and the blessing of thy coming to me, and I prayed God that He restore thee to thy native land. But now, O my brother, I would thou warm me some water for the ghusl ablution and do thou kindly bathe me and change my clothes." I replied, "With love and gladness," and I heated water in plenty and carrying it in to him, washed his body all over, the washing of health, with meal of lupins, and rubbed him well and changed his clothes and spread him a high bed whereon he lay down to rest, being drowsy after bathing.

Then said he, "O my brother, cut me up a watermelon, and sweeten it with a little sugar candy." So I went to the storeroom and bringing out a fine watermelon, I found there, set it on a platter and laid it before him saying, "O my master, hast thou not a knife?" "Here it is," answered he, "over my head upon the high shelf." So I got up in haste and, taking the knife, drew it from its sheath, but my foot slipped in stepping down and I fell heavily upon the youth holding in my hand the knife, which hastened to fulfill what had been written on the Day that decided the destinies of man, and buried itself, as if planted, in the youth's heart. He died on the instant. When I saw that he was slain and knew that I had slain him, mauger myself I cried out with an exceeding loud and bitter cry and beat my face and rent my raiment and said: "Verily we be Allah's and unto Him we be returning, O Moslems! O folk fain of Allah! There remained for this youth but one day of the forty dangerous days which the astrologers and the learned had foretold for him, and the predestined death of this beautiful one was to be at my hand. Would Heaven I had not tried to cut the watermelon! What dire misfortune is this I must bear, lief or loath? What a disaster! What an affliction! O Allah mine, I implore thy pardon and declare to Thee my innocence of his death. But what God willeth, let that come to pass."

When I was certified that I had slain him, I arose and, ascending the stairs, replaced the trapdoor and covered it with earth as before. Then I looked out seaward and saw the ship cleaving the waters and making for the island, wherefore I was afeard and said, "The moment they come and see the youth done to death, they will know 'twas I who slew him and will slay me without respite." So I climbed up into a high tree and concealed myself among its leaves, and hardly had I done so when the ship anchored and the slaves landed with the ancient man, the youth's father, and made direct for the place, and when they removed the earth they were surprised to see it soft. Then they raised the trapdoor and went down and found the youth lying at full length, clothed in fair new garments, with a face beaming after the bath, and the knife deep in his heart. At the sight they shrieked and wept and beat their faces, loudly cursing the murderer, whilst a swoon came over the Sheikh so that the slaves deemed him dead, unable to survive his son. At last they wrapped the slain youth in his clothes and carried him up and laid him on the ground, covering him with a shroud of silk.

Whilst they were making for the ship the old man revived, and, gazing on his son who was stretched out, fell on the ground and strewed dust over his head and smote his face and plucked out his beard, and his weeping redoubled as he thought of his murdered son and he swooned away once more. After a while a slave went and fetched a strip of silk whereupon they lay the old man and sat down at his head. All this took place and I was on the tree above them watching everything that came to pass, and my heart became hoary before my head waxed gray, for the hard lot which was mine, and for the distress and anguish I had undergone, and I fell to reciting:

> "How many a joy by Allah's will hath fled
> With flight escaping sight of wisest head!
> How many a sadness shall begin the day,
> Yet grow right gladsome ere the day is sped!
> How many a weal trips on the heels of ill,
> Causing the mourner's heart with joy to thrill!"

But the old man, O my lady, ceased not from his swoon till near sunset, when he came to himself and, looking upon his dead son, he recalled what had happened, and how what he had dreaded had come to pass, and he beat his face and head. Then he sobbed a single sob and his soul fled his flesh. The slaves shrieked aloud, "Alas, our lord!" and showered dust on their heads and redoubled their weeping and wailing. Presently they carried their dead master to the ship side by side with his dead son and, having transported all the stuff from the dwelling to the vessel, set sail and disappeared from mine eyes. I descended from the tree and, raising the trapdoor, went down into the underground dwelling, where everything reminded me of the youth, and I looked upon the poor remains of him and began repeating these verses:

> "Their tracks I see, and pine with pain and pang,
> And on deserted hearths I weep and yearn.
> And Him I pray who doomèd them depart
> Some day vouchsafe the boon of safe return."

Then, O my lady, I went up again by the trapdoor, and every day I used to wander round about the island and every night I returned to the underground hall. Thus I lived for a month, till at last, looking at the western side of the island, I observed that every day the tide ebbed, leaving shallow water for which the flow did not compensate, and by the end of the month the sea showed dry land in that direction. At this I rejoiced, making certain of my safety, so I arose and, fording what little was left of the water, got me to the mainland, where I fell in with great heaps of loose sand in which even a camel's hoof would sink up to the knee. However, I emboldened my soul and, wading through the sand, behold, a fire shone from afar burning with a blazing light. So I made for it hoping haply to find succor and broke out into these verses:

> "Belike my Fortune may her bridle turn
> And Time bring weal although he's jealous hight,
> Forward my hopes, and further all my needs,
> And passèd ills with present weals requite."

And when I drew near the fire aforesaid, lo! it was a palace with gates of copper burnished red which, when the rising sun shone thereon, gleamed and glistened from afar, showing what had seemed to me a fire. I rejoiced in the sight, and sat down over against the gate, but I was hardly settled in my seat before there met me ten young men clothed in sumptuous gear, and all were blind of the left eye, which appeared as plucked out. They were accompanied by a Sheikh, an old, old man, and much I marveled at their appearance, and their all being blind in the same eye. When they saw me, they saluted me with the salaam and asked me of my case and my history, whereupon I related to them all what had befallen me and what full measure of misfortune was mine. Marveling at my tale, they took me to the mansion, where I saw ranged round the hall ten couches each with its blue bedding and coverlet of blue stuff and a-middlemost stood a smaller couch furnished like them with blue and nothing else.

As we entered each of the youths took his seat on his own couch and the old man seated himself upon the smaller one in the middle, saying to me, "O youth, sit thee down on the floor, and ask not of our case nor of the loss of our eyes." Presently he rose up and set before each young man some meat in a charger and drink in a larger mazer, treating me in like manner, and after that they sat questioning me concerning my adventures and what had betided me. And I kept telling them my tale till the night was far spent. Then said the young men: "O our Sheikh, wilt not thou set before us our ordinary? The time is come." He replied, "With love and gladness," and rose and, entering a closet, disappeared, but presently returned bearing on his head ten trays each covered with a strip of blue stuff. He set a tray before each youth and, lighting ten wax candles, he stuck one upon each tray, and drew off the covers and lo! under them was naught but ashes and powdered charcoal and kettle soot. Then all the young men tucked up their sleeves to the elbows and fell a-weeping and wailing and they blackened their faces and smeared their clothes and buffeted their brows and beat their breasts, continually exclaiming, "We were sitting at our ease, but our frowardness brought us unease!" They ceased not to do thus till dawn drew nigh, when the old man rose and heated water for them, and they washed their face and donned other and clean clothes.

Now when I saw this, O my lady, for very wonderment my senses left me and my wits went wild and heart and head were full of thought, till I forgot what had betided me and I could not keep silence, feeling I fain must speak out and question them of these strangenesses. So I said to them: "How come ye to do this after we have been so open-hearted and frolicsome? Thanks be to Allah, ye be all sound and sane, yet actions such as these befit none but madmen or those possessed of an evil spirit. I conjure you by all that is dearest to you, why stint ye to tell me your history, and the cause of your losing your eyes and your blackening your faces with ashes and soot?" Here-upon they turned to me and said, "O young man, hearken not to thy youthtide's suggestions, and question us no questions." Then they slept and I with them, and when they awoke the old man brought us some-what of food. And after we had eaten and the plates and goblets had been removed, they sat conversing till nightfall, when the old man rose and lit the wax candles and lamps and set meat and drink before us.

After we had eaten and drunken we sat conversing and carousing in companionage till the noon of night, when they said to the old man, "Bring us our ordinary, for the hour of sleep is at hand!" So he rose and brought them the trays of soot and ashes, and they did as they had done on the preceding night, nor more, nor less. I abode with them after this fashion for the space of a month, during which time they used to blacken their faces with ashes every night, and to wash and change their raiment when the morn was young, and I but marveled the more and my scruples and curiosity increased to such a point that I had to forgo even food and drink.

At last I lost command of myself, for my heart was aflame with fire unquenchable and lowe unconcealable, and I said, "O young men, will ye not relieve my trouble and acquaint me with the reason of thus blackening your faces and the meaning of your words, 'We were sitting at our ease, but our frowardness brought us unease'?" Quoth they, "'Twere better to keep these things secret." Still I was bewildered by their doings to the point of abstaining from eating and drinking and at last wholly losing patience, quoth I to them: "There is no help for it. Ye must acquaint me with what is the reason of these doings." They replied: "We kept our secret only for thy good. To gratify thee will bring down evil upon thee and thou wilt become a monocular even as we are." I repeated, "There is no help for it, and if ye will not, let me leave you and return to mine own people and be at rest from seeing these things, for the proverb saith:

"Better ye 'bide and I take my leave;
For what eye sees not heart shall never grieve."

Thereupon they said to me, "Remember, O youth, that should ill befall thee, we will not again harbor thee nor suffer thee to abide amongst us." And bringing a ram, they slaughtered it and skinned it. Lastly they gave me a knife, saying: "Take this skin and stretch thyself upon it and we will sew it around thee. Presently there shall come to thee a certain bird, hight roc, that will catch thee up in his pounces and tower high in air and then set thee down on a mountain. When thou feelest he is no longer flying, rip open the pelt with this blade and come out of it. The bird will be scared and will fly away and leave thee free. After this fare for half a day, and the march will place thee at a palace wondrous fair to behold, towering high in air and builded of khalanj, lign aloes and sandalwood, plated with red gold, and studded with all manner emeralds and costly gems fit for seal rings. Enter it and thou shalt win to thy wish, for we have all entered that palace, and such is the cause of our losing our eyes and of our blackening our faces. Were we now to tell thee our stories it would take too long a time, for each and every of us lost his left eye by an adventure of his own."

I rejoiced at their words, and they did with me as they said, and the bird roc bore me off and set me down on the mountain. Then I came out of the skin and walked on till I reached the palace. The door stood open as I entered and found myself in a spacious and goodly hall, wide exceedingly, even as a horse course. And around it were a hundred chambers with doors of sandal and aloe woods plated with red gold and furnished with silver rings by way of knockers. At the head or upper end of the hall I saw forty damsels, sumptuously dressed and ornamented and one and all bright as moons. None could ever tire of gazing upon them, and all so lovely that the most ascetic devotee on seeing them would become their slave and obey their will. When they saw me the whole bevy came up to me and said: "Welcome and well come and good cheer to thee, O our lord! This whole month have we been expecting thee. Praised be Allah Who hath sent us one who is worthy of us, even as we are worthy of him!"

Then they made me sit down upon a high divan and said to me, "This day thou art our lord and master, and we are thy servants and thy handmaids, so order us as thou wilt." And I marveled at their case. Presently one of them arose and set meat before me and I ate and they ate with me whilst others warmed water and washed my hands and feet and changed my clothes, and others made ready sherbets and gave us to drink, and all gathered around me, being full of joy and gladness at my coming. Then they sat down and conversed with me till nightfall, when five of them arose and laid the trays and spread them with flowers and fragrant herbs and fruits, fresh and dried, and confections in profusion. At last they brought out a fine wine service with rich old wine, and we sat down to drink and some sang songs and others played the lute and psaltery and recorders and other instruments, and the bowl went merrily round. Hereupon such gladness possessed me that I forgot the sorrows of the world one and all and said: "This is indeed life. O sad that 'tis fleeting!"

I enjoyed their company till the time came for rest, and our heads were all warm with wine, when they said, "O our lord, choose from amongst us her who shall be thy bedfellow this night and not lie with thee again till forty days be past." So I chose a girl fair of face and perfect in shape, with eyes kohl-edged by nature's hand, hair long and jet-black, with slightly parted teeth and joining brows. 'Twas as if she were some limber graceful branchlet or the slender stalk of sweet basil to amaze and to bewilder man's fancy. So I lay with her that night. None fairer I ever knew. And when it was morning, the damsels carried me to the hammam bath and bathed me and robed me in fairest apparel. Then they served up food, and we ate and drank and the cup went round till nightfall, when I chose from among them one fair of form and face, soft-sided and a model of grace, such a one as the poet described when he said:

> On her fair bosom caskets twain I scanned,
> Sealed fast with musk seals lovers to withstand.
> With arrowy glances stand on guard her eyes,
> Whose shafts would shoot who dares put forth a hand.

With her I spent a most goodly night, and, to be brief, O my mistress, I remained with them in all solace and delight of life, eating and drinking, conversing and carousing, and every night lying with one or other of them. But at the head of the New Year they came to me in tears and bade me farewell, weeping and crying out and clinging about me, whereat I wondered and said: "What may be the matter? Verily you break my heart!" They exclaimed, "Would Heaven we had never known thee, for though we have companied with many, yet never saw we a pleasanter than thou or a more courteous." And they wept again. "But tell me more clearly," asked I, "what causeth this weeping which maketh my gall bladder like to burst?" And they answered: "O lord and master, it is severance which maketh us weep, and thou, and thou only, art the cause of our tears. If thou hearken to us we need never be parted, and if thou hearken not we part forever, but our hearts tell us that thou wilt not listen to our words and this is the cause of our tears and cries." "Tell me how the case standeth."

"Know, O our lord, that we are the daughters of kings who have met here and have lived together for years, and once in every year we are perforce absent for forty days. And afterward we return and abide here for the rest of the twelvemonth eating and drinking and taking our pleasure and enjoying delights. We are about to depart according to our custom, and we fear lest after we be gone thou contraire our charge and disobey our injunctions. Here now we commit to thee the keys of the palace, which containeth forty chambers, and thou mayest open of these thirty and nine, but beware (and we conjure thee by Allah and by the lives of us!) lest thou open the fortieth door, for therein is that which shall separate us for ever." Quoth I, "Assuredly I will not open it if it contain the cause of severance from you." Then one among them came up to me and falling on my neck wept and recited these verses:

> "If Time unite us after absent-while,
> The world harsh-frowning on our lot shall smile,
> And if thy semblance deign adorn mine eyes,
> I'll pardon Time past wrongs and bygone guile."

And I recited the following:

> "When drew she near to bid adieu with her heart unstrung,
> While care and longing on that day her bosom wrung,
> Wet pearls she wept and mine like red carnelians rolled
> And, joined in sad rivière, around her neck they hung."

When I saw her weeping I said, "By Allah, I will never open that fortieth door, never and nowise!" and I bade her farewell. Thereupon all departed flying away like birds, signaling with their hands farewells as they went and leaving me alone in the palace. When evening drew near I opened the door of the first chamber and entering it found myself in a place like one of the pleasaunces of Paradise. It was a garden with trees of freshest green and ripe fruits of yellow sheen, and its birds were singing clear and keen and rills ran wimpling through the fair terrene. The sight and sounds brought solace to my sprite, and I walked among the trees, and I smelt the breath of the flowers on the breeze and heard the birdies sing their melodies hymning the One, the Almighty, in sweetest litanies, and I looked upon the apple whose hue is parcel red and parcel yellow, as said the poet:

> Apple whose hue combines in union mellow
> My fair's red cheek, her hapless lover's yellow.

Then I looked upon the pear whose taste surpasseth sherbet and sugar, and the apricot whose beauty striketh the eye with admiration, as if she were a polished ruby.

Then I went out of the place and locked the door as it was before.

When it was the morrow I opened the second door, and entering found myself in a spacious plain set with tall date palms and watered by a running stream whose banks were shrubbed with bushes of rose and jasmine, while privet and eglantine, oxeye, violet and lily, narcissus, origane, and the winter gilliflower carpeted the borders. And the breath of the breeze swept over these sweet-smelling growths diffusing their delicious odors right and left, perfuming the world and filling my soul with delight. After taking my pleasure there awhile I went from it and, having closed the door as it was before, opened the third door, wherein I saw a high open hall pargetted with particolored marbles and pietra dura of price and other precious stones, and hung with cages of sandalwood and eagle wood, full of birds which made sweet music, such as the "thousand-voiced," and the cushat, the merle, the turtledove, and the Nubian ringdove. My heart was filled with pleasure thereby, my grief was dispelled, and I slept in that aviary till dawn.

Then I unlocked the door of the fourth chamber, and therein found a grand saloon with forty smaller chambers giving upon it. All their doors stood open, so I entered and found them full of pearls and jacinths and beryls and emeralds and corals and carbuncles, and all manner precious gems and jewels, such as tongue of man may not describe. My thought was stunned at the sight and I said to myself, "These be things methinks united which could not be found save in the treasuries of a King of Kings, nor could the monarchs of the world have collected the like of these!" And my heart dilated and my sorrows ceased. "For," quoth I, "now verily am I the Monarch of the Age, since by Allah's grace this enormous wealth is mine, and I have forty damsels under my hand, nor is there any to claim them save myself." Then I gave not over opening place after place until nine and thirty days were passed, and in that time I had entered every chamber except that one whose door the Princesses had charged me not to open.

But my thoughts, O my mistress, ever ran on that forbidden fortieth, and Satan urged me to open it for my own undoing, nor had I patience to forbear, albeit there wanted of the trysting time but a single day. So I stood before the chamber aforesaid and, after a moment's hesitation, opened the door, which was plated with red gold, and entered. I was met by a perfume whose like I had never before smelt, and so sharp and subtle was the odor that it made my senses drunken as with strong wine, and I fell to the ground in a fainting fit which lasted a full hour. When I came to myself I strengthened my heart, and entering, found myself in a chamber whose floor was bespread with saffron and blazing with light from branched candelabra of gold and lamps fed with costly oils, which diffused the scent of musk and ambergris. I saw there also two great censers each big as a mazer bowl, flaming with lign aloes, nadd perfume, ambergris, and honeyed scents, and the place was full of their fragrance.

Presently, O my lady, I espied a noble steed, black as the murks of night when murkiest, standing ready saddled and bridled (and his saddle was of red gold) before two mangers, one of clear crystal wherein was husked sesame, and the other also of crystal containing water of the rose scented with musk. When I saw this I marveled and said to myself, "Doubtless in this animal must be some wondrous mystery." And Satan cozened me so I led him without the palace and mounted him, but he would not stir from his place. So I hammered his sides with my heels, but he moved not, and then I took the rein whip and struck him withal. When he felt the blow, he neighed a neigh with a sound like deafening thunder and, opening a pair of wings, flew up with me in the firmament of heaven far beyond the eyesight of man. After a full hour of flight he descended and alighted on a terrace roof and shaking me off his back, lashed me on the face with his tail and gouged out my left eye, causing it roll along my cheek.

Then he flew away. I went down from the terrace and found myself again amongst the ten one-eyed youths sitting upon their ten couches with blue covers, and they cried out when they saw me: "No welcome to thee, nor aught of good cheer! We all lived of lives the happiest and we ate and drank of the best. Upon brocades and cloths of gold we took our rest, and we slept with our heads on beauty's breast, but we could not await one day to gain the delights of a year!" Quoth I, "Behold, I have become one like unto you and now I would have you bring me a tray full of blackness, wherewith to blacken my face, and receive me into your society." "No, by Allah," quoth they, "thou shalt not sojourn with us, and now get thee hence!" So they drove me away.

Finding them reject me thus, I foresaw that matters would go hard with me, and I remembered the many miseries which Destiny had written upon my forehead, and I fared forth from among them heavy-hearted and tearful-eyed, repeating to myself these words: "I was sitting at mine ease, but my frowardness brought me to unease." Then I shaved beard and mustachios and eyebrows, renouncing the world, and wandered in Kalandar garb about Allah's earth, and the Almighty decreed safety for me till I arrived at Baghdad, which was on the evening of this very night. Here I met these two other Kalandars standing bewildered, so I saluted them saying, "I am a stranger!" and they answered, "And we likewise be strangers!" By the freak of Fortune we were like to like, three Kalandars and three monoculars all blind of the left eye.

Such, O my lady, is the cause of the shearing of my beard and the manner of my losing an eye. Said the lady to him, "Rub thy head and wend thy ways," but he answered, "By Allah, I will not go until I hear the stories of these others." Then the lady, turning toward the Caliph and Ja'afar and Masrur, said to them, "Do ye also give an account of yourselves, you men!" Whereupon Ja'afar stood forth and told her what he had told the portress as they were entering the house, and when she heard his story of their being merchants and Mosul men who had outrun the watch, she said, "I grant you your lives each for each sake, and now away with you all." So they all went out, and when they were in the street, quoth the Caliph to the Kalandars, "O company, whither go ye now, seeing that the morning hath not yet dawned?" Quoth they, "By Allah, O our lord, we know not where to go." "Come and pass the rest of the night with us," said the Caliph and, turning to Ja'afar, "Take them home with thee, and tomorrow bring them to my presence that we may chronicle their adventures."

Ja'afar did as the Caliph bade him and the Commander of the Faithful returned to his palace, but sleep gave no sign of visiting him that night and he lay awake pondering the mishaps of the three Kalandar Princes, and impatient to know the history of the ladies and the two black bitches. No sooner had morning dawned than he went forth and sat upon the throne of his sovereignty and, turning to Ja'afar, after all his grandees and officers of state were gathered together, he said, "Bring me the three ladies and the two bitches and the three Kalandars."

So Ja'afar fared forth and brought them all before him (and the ladies were veiled). Then the Minister turned to them and said in the Caliph's name: "We pardon you your maltreatment of us and your want of courtesy, in consideration of the kindness which forewent it, and for that ye knew us not. Now however I would have you to know that ye stand in presence of the fifth of the sons of Abbas, Harun al-Rashid, brother of Caliph Musa al-Hadi, son of Al-Mansur, son of Mohammed the brother of Al-Saffah bin Mohammed who was first of the royal house. Speak ye therefore before him the truth and the whole truth!" When the ladies heard Ja'afar's words touching the Commander of the Faithful, the eldest came forward and said, "O Prince of True Believers, my story is one which were it graven with needle gravers upon the eye corners, were a warner for whoso would be warned and an example for whoso can take profit from example." And she began to tell

THE ELDEST LADY'S TALE

VERILY a strange tale is mine and 'tis this: Yon two black bitches are my eldest sisters by one mother and father, and these two others she who beareth upon her the signs of stripes and the third our procuratrix, are my sisters by another mother. When my father died, each took her share of the heritage and after a while my mother also deceased, leaving me and my sisters german three thousand dinars, so each daughter received her portion of a thousand dinars and I the same, albe' the youngest. In due course of time my sisters married with the usual festivities and lived with their husbands, who bought merchandise with their wives' moneys and set out on their travels together. Thus they threw me off. My brothers-in-law were absent with their wives five years, during which period they spent all the money they had and, becoming bankrupt, deserted my sisters in foreign parts amid stranger folk.

After five years my eldest sister returned to me in beggar's gear with her clothes in rags and tatters and a dirty old mantilla, and truly she was in the foulest and sorriest plight. At first sight I did not know my own sister, but presently I recognized her and said, "What state is this?" "O our sister," she replied, "words cannot undo the done, and the reed of Destiny hath run through what Allah decreed." Then I sent her to the bath and dressed her in a suit of mine own, and boiled for her a bouillon and brought her some good wine, and said to her: "O my sister, thou art the eldest, who still standest to us in the stead of father and mother, and as for the inheritance which came to me as to you twain, Allah hath blessed it and prospered it to me with increase, and my circumstances are easy, for I have made much money by spinning and cleaning silk. And I and you will share my wealth alike."

I entreated her with all kindliness and she abode with me a whole year, during which our thoughts and fancies were always full of our other sister. Shortly after she too came home in yet fouler and sorrier plight than that of my eldest sister, and I dealt by her still more honorably than I had done by the first, and each of them had a share of my substance. After a time they said to me, "O our sister, we desire to marry again, for indeed we have not patience to drag on our days without husbands and to lead the lives of widows bewitched," and I replied: "O eyes of me! Ye have hitherto seen scanty weal in wedlock, for nowadays good men and true are become rareties and curiosities, nor do I deem your projects advisable, as ye have already made trial of matrimony and have failed." But they would not accept my advice, and married without my consent. Nevertheless I gave them outfit and dowries out of my money, and they fared forth with their mates.

In a mighty little time their husbands played them false and, taking whatever they could lay hands upon, levanted and left them in the lurch. Thereupon they came to me ashamed and in abject case and made their excuses to me, saying: "Pardon our fault and be not wroth with us, for although thou art younger in years yet art thou older in wit. Henceforth we will never make mention of marriage, so take us back as thy handmaidens that we may eat our mouthful." Quoth I, "Welcome to you, O my sisters, there is naught dearer to me than you." And I took them in and redoubled my kindness to them. We ceased not to live after this loving fashion for a full year, when I resolved to sell my wares abroad and first to fit me a conveyance for Bassorah. So I equipped a large ship, and loaded her with merchandise and valuable goods for traffic and with provaunt and all needful for a voyage, and said to my sisters, "Will ye abide at home whilst I travel, or would ye prefer to accompany me on the voyage?" "We will travel with thee," answered they, "for we cannot bear to be parted from thee." So I divided my moneys into two parts, one to accompany me and the other to be left in charge of a trusty person, for, as I said to myself, "Haply some accident may happen to the ship and yet we remain alive, in which case we shall find on our return what may stand us in good stead."

I took my two sisters and we went a-voyaging some days and nights, but the master was careless enough to miss his course, and the ship went astray with us and entered a sea other than the sea we sought. For a time we knew naught of this, and the wind blew fair for us ten days, after which the lookout man went aloft to see about him and cried, "Good news!" Then he came down rejoicing and said, "I have seen what seemeth to be a city as 'twere a pigeon." Hereat we rejoiced, and ere an hour of the day had passed, the buildings showed plain in the offing, and we asked the Captain, "What is the name of yonder city?" and he answered: "By Allah, I wot not, for I never saw it before and never sailed these seas in my life. But since our troubles have ended in safety, remains for you only to land where with your merchandise, and if you find selling profitable, sell and make your market of what is there, and if not, we will rest here two days and provision ourselves and fare away."

So we entered the port and the Captain went up town and was absent awhile, after which he returned to us and said, "Arise, go up into the city and marvel at the works of Allah with His creatures, and pray to be preserved from His righteous wrath!" So we landed, and going up into the city, saw at the gate men hending staves in hand, but when we drew near them, behold, they had been translated by the anger of Allah and had become stones. Then we entered the city and found all who therein woned into black stones enstoned. Not an inhabited house appeared to the espier, nor was there a blower of fire. We were awe-struck at the sight, and threaded the market streets, where we found the goods and gold and silver left lying in their places, and we were glad and said, "Doubtless there is some mystery in all this."

Then we dispersed about the thoroughfares and each busied himself with collecting the wealth and money and rich stuffs, taking scanty heed of friend or comrade.

As for myself, I went up to the castle, which was strongly fortified, and, entering the King's palace by its gate of red gold, found all the vaiselle of gold and silver, and the King himself seated in the midst of his chamberlains and nabobs and emirs and wazirs, all clad in raiment which confounded man's art. I drew nearer and saw him sitting on a throne encrusted and inlaid with pearls and gems, and his robes were of gold cloth adorned with jewels of every kind, each one flashing like a star. Around him stood fifty Mamelukes, white slaves, clothed in silks of divers sorts, holding their drawn swords in their hands. But when I drew near to them, lo! all were black stones. My understanding was confounded at the sight, but I walked on and entered the great hall of the harem, whose walls I found hung with tapestries of gold-striped silk, and spread with silken carpets embroidered with golden flowers. Here I saw the Queen lying at full length arrayed in robes purfled with fresh young pearls. On her head was a diadem set with many sorts of gems each fit for a ring, and around her neck hung collars and necklaces. All her raiment and her ornaments were in natural state, but she had been turned into a black stone by Allah's wrath.

Presently I espied an open door, for which I made straight, and found leading to it a flight of seven steps. So I walked up and came upon a place pargeted with marble and spread and hung with gold-worked carpets and tapestry, a-middlemost of which stood a throne of juniper wood inlaid with pearls and precious stones and set with bosses of emeralds. In the further wall was an alcove whose curtains, bestrung with pearls, were let down and I saw a light issuing therefrom, so I drew near and perceived that the light came from a precious stone as big as an ostrich egg, set at the upper end of the alcove upon a little chryselephantine couch of ivory and gold. And this jewel, blazing like the sun, cast its rays wide and side. The couch also was spread with all manner of silken stuffs amazing the gazer with their richness and beauty. I marveled much at all this, especially when seeing in that place candles ready lighted, and I said in my mind, "Needs must someone have lighted these candles." Then I went forth and came to the kitchen and thence to the buttery and the King's treasure chambers, and continued to explore the palace and to pace from place to place. I forgot myself in my awe and marvel at these matters and I was drowned in thought till the night came on.

Then I would have gone forth, but knowing not the gate, I lost my way, so I returned to the alcove whither the lighted candles directed me and sat down upon the couch, and wrapping myself in a coverlet, after I had repeated somewhat from the Koran, I would have slept but could not, for restlessness possessed me. When night was at its noon I heard a voice chanting the Koran in sweetest accents, but the tone thereof was weak. So I rose, glad to hear the silence broken, and followed the sound until I reached a closet whose door stood ajar. Then, peeping through a chink, I considered the place and lo! it was an oratory wherein was a prayer niche with two wax candles burning and lamps hanging from the ceiling. In it too was spread a prayer carpet whereupon sat a youth fair to see, and before him on its stand was a copy of the Koran, from which he was reading. I marveled to see him alone alive amongst the people of the city and entering, saluted him. Whereupon he raised his eyes and returned my salaam. Quoth I, "Now by the truth of what thou readest in Allah's Holy Book, I conjure thee to answer my question." He looked upon me with a smile and said: "O handmaid of Allah, first tell me the cause of thy coming hither, and I in turn will tell what hath befallen both me and the people of this city, and what was the reason of my escaping their doom." So I told him my story, whereat he wondered, and I questioned him of the people of the city, when he replied, "Have patience with me for awhile, O my sister!" and, reverently closing the Holy Book, he laid it up in a satin bag. Then he seated me by his side, and I looked at him and behold, he was as the moon at its full, fair of face and rare of form, soft-sided and slight, of well-proportioned height, and cheek smoothly bright and diffusing light. I glanced at him with one glance of eyes which caused me a thousand sighs, and my heart was at once taken captive-wise, so I asked him, "O my lord and my love, tell me that whereof I questioned thee," and he answered:

"Hearing is obeying! Know, O handmaid of Allah, that this city was the capital of my father who is the King thou sawest on the throne transfigured by Allah's wrath to a black stone, and the Queen thou foundest in the alcove is my mother. They and all the people of the city were Magians who fire adored in lieu of the Omnipotent Lord and were wont to swear by lowe and heat and shade and light, and the spheres revolving day and night. My father had ne'er a son till he was blest with me near the last of his days, and he reared me till I grew up and prosperity anticipated me in all things. Now it is fortuned there was with us an old woman well stricken in years, a Moslemah who, inwardly believing in Allah and His Apostle, conformed outwardly with the religion of my people. And my father placed thorough confidence in her for that he knew her to be trustworthy and virtuous, and he treated her with ever-increasing kindness, believing her to be of his own belief.

"So when I was well-nigh grown up my father committed me to her charge saying: 'Take him and educate him and teach him the rules of our faith. Let him have the best instructions and cease not thy fostering care of him.' So she took me and taught me the tenets of Al-Islam with the divine ordinances of the wuzu ablution and the five daily prayers and she made me learn the Koran by rote, often repeating, 'Serve none save Allah Almighty!' When I had mastered this much of knowledge, she said to me, 'O my son, keep this matter concealed from thy sire and reveal naught to him, lest he slay thee." So I hid it from him, and I abode on this wise for a term of days, when the old woman died, and the people of the city redoubled in their impiety and arrogance and the error of their ways.

"One day while they were as wont, behold, they heard a loud and terrible sound and a crier crying out with a voice like roaring thunder so every ear could hear, far and near: 'O folk of this city, leave ye your fire-worshiping and adore Allah the All-compassionate King!" At this, fear and terror fell upon the citizens and they crowded to my father (he being King of the city) and asked him: 'What is this awesome voice we have heard; for it hath confounded us with the excess of its terror?' And he answered: 'Let not a voice fright you nor shake your steadfast sprite nor turn you back from the faith which is right.' Their hearts inclined to his words and they ceased not to worship the fire and they persisted in rebellion for a full year from the time they heard the first voice. And on the anniversary came a second cry, and a third at the head of the third year, each year once.

Still they persisted in their malpractices till one day at break of dawn, judgment and the wrath of Heaven descended upon them with all suddenness, and by the visitation of Allah all were metamorphosed into black stones, they and their beasts and their cattle, and none was saved save myself, who at the time was engaged in my devotions. From that day to this I am in the case thou seest, constant in prayer and fasting and reading and reciting the Koran, but I am indeed grown weary by reason of my loneliness, having none to bear me company."

Then said I to him (for in very sooth he had won my heart and was the lord of my life and soul): "O youth, wilt thou fare with me to Baghdad city and visit the Ulema and men learned in the law and doctors of divinity and get thee increase of wisdom and understanding and theology? And know that she who standeth in thy presence will be thy handmaid, albeit she be head of her family and mistress over men and eunuchs and servants and slaves. Indeed my life was no life before it fell in with thy youth. I have here a ship laden with merchandise, and in very truth Destiny drove me to this city that I might come to the knowledge of these matters, for it was fated that we should meet." And I ceased not to persuade him and speak him fair and use every art till he consented. I slept that night at his feet and hardly knowing where I was for excess of joy.

As soon as the next morning dawned (she pursued, addressing the Caliph), I arose and we entered the treasuries and took thence whatever was light in weight and great in worth. Then we went down side by side from the castle to the city, where we were met by the Captain and my sisters and slaves, who had been seeking for me. When they saw me, they rejoiced and asked what had stayed me, and I told them all I had seen and related to them the story of the young Prince and the transformation wherewith the citizens had been justly visited. Hereat all marveled, but when my two sisters (these two bitches, O Commander of the Faithful!) saw me by the side of my young lover, they jaloused me on his account and were wroth and plotted mischief against me. We awaited a fair wind and went on board rejoicing and ready to fly for joy by reason of the goods we had gotten, but my own greatest joyance was in the youth. And we waited awhile till the wind blew fair for us and then we set sail and fared forth.

Now as we sat talking, my sisters asked me, "And what wilt thou do with this handsome young man?" and I answered, "I purpose to make him my husband!" Then I turned to him and said: "O my lord, I have that to propose to thee wherein thou must not cross me, and this it is that, when we reach Baghdad, my native city, I offer thee my life as thy handmaiden in holy matrimony, and thou shalt be to me baron and I will be femme to thee." He answered, "I hear and I obey! Thou art my lady and my mistress and whatso thou doest I will not gainsay." Then I turned to my sisters and said: "This is my gain. I content me with this youth and those who have gotten aught of my property, let them keep it as their gain with my goodwill." "Thou sayest and doest well," answered the twain, but they imagined mischief against me.

We ceased not spooning before a fair wind till we had exchanged the sea of peril for the seas of safety, and in a few days we made Bassorah city, whose buildings loomed clear before us as evening fell.

But after we had retired to rest and were sound asleep, my two sisters arose and took me up, bed and all, and threw me into the sea. They did the same with the young Prince, who, as he could not swim, sank and was drowned, and Allah enrolled him in the noble army of martyrs. As for me, would Heaven I had been drowned with him, but Allah deemed that I should be of the saved, so when I awoke and found myself in the sea and saw the ship making off like a flash of lightning, He threw in my way a piece of timber, which I bestrided, and the waves tossed me to and fro till they cast me upon an island coast, a high land and an uninhabited. I landed and walked about the island the rest of the night, and when morning dawned, I saw a rough track barely fit for child of Adam to tread, leading to what proved a shallow ford connecting island and mainland.

As soon as the sun had risen I spread my garments to dry in its rays, and ate of the fruits of the island and drank of its waters. Then I set out along the foot track and ceased not walking till I reached the mainland. Now when there remained between me and the city but a two hours' journey, behold, a great serpent, the bigness of a date palm, came fleeing toward me in all haste, gliding along now to the right, then to the left, till she was close upon me, whilst her tongue lolled groundward a span long and swept the dust as she went. She was pursued by a dragon who was not longer than two lances, and of slender build about the bulk of a spear, and although her terror lent her speed and she kept wriggling from side to side, he overtook her and seized her by the tail, whereat her tears streamed down and her tongue was thrust out in her agony. I took pity on her and, picking up a stone and calling upon Allah for aid, threw it at the dragon's head with such force that he died then and there, and the serpent, opening a pair of wings, flew into the lift and disappeared from before my eyes.

I sat down marveling over that adventure, but I was weary and, drowsiness overcoming me, I slept where I was for a while. When I awoke I found a jet-black damsel sitting at my feet shampooing them, and by her side stood two black bitches (my sisters, O Commander of the Faithful!). I was ashamed before her and, sitting up, asked her, "O my sister, who and what art thou?" and she answered: "How soon hast thou forgotten me! I am she for whom thou wroughtest a good deed and sowedest the seed of gratitude and slewest her foe, for I am the serpent whom by Allah's aidance thou didst just now deliver from the dragon. I am a Jinniyah and he was a Jinn who hated me, and none saved my life from him save thou. As soon as thou freedest me from him I flew on the wind to the ship whence thy sisters threw thee, and removed all that was therein to thy house. Then I ordered my attendant Marids to sink the ship, and I transformed thy two sisters into these black bitches, for I know all that hath passed between them and thee. But as for the youth, of a truth he is drowned."

So saying, she flew up with me and the bitches, and presently set us down on the terrace roof of my house, wherein I found ready stored the whole of what property was in my ship, nor was aught of it missing. "Now (continued the serpent that was), I swear by all engraven on the seal ring of Solomon (with whom be peace!) unless thou deal to each of these bitches three hundred stripes every day I will come and imprison thee forever under the earth." I answered, "Hearkening and obedience!" and away she flew. But before going she again charged me saying, "I again swear by Him who made the two seas flow (and this be my second oath), if thou gainsay me I will come and transform thee like thy sisters." Since then I have never failed, O Commander of the Faithful, to beat them with that number of blows till their blood flows with my tears, I pitying them the while, and well they wot that their being scourged is no fault of mine and they accept my excuses. And this is my tale and my history!

THE TALE OF THE THREE APPLES

THEY relate, O King of the Age and Lord of the Time and of these days, that the Caliph Harun al-Rashid summoned his Wazir Ja'afar one night and said to him: "I desire to go down into the city and question the common folk concerning the conduct of those charged with its governance, and those of whom they complain we will depose from office and those whom they commend we will promote." Quoth Ja'afar, "Hearkening and obedience!"

So the Caliph went down with Ja'afar and the eunuch Masrur to the town and walked about the streets and markets, and as they were threading a narrow alley, they came upon a very old man with a fishing net and crate to carry small fish on his head, and in his hands a staff, and as he walked at a leisurely pace, he repeated these lines:

> "They say me: 'Thou shinest a light to mankind
> With thy lore as the night which the Moon doth uplift!'
> I answer, 'A truce to your jests and your gibes.
> Without luck what is learning?—a poor-devil wight!
> If they take me to pawn with my lore in my pouch,
> With my volumes to read and my ink case to write,
> For one day's provision they never could pledge me,
> As likely on Doomsday to draw bill at sight.'
> How poorly, indeed, doth it fare wi' the poor,
> With his pauper existence and beggarly plight.
> In summer he faileth provision to find,
> In winter the fire pot's his only delight.
> The street dogs with bite and with bark to him rise,
> And each losel receives him with bark and with bite.
> If he lift up his voice and complain of his wrong,
> None pities or heeds him, however he's right,
> And when sorrows and evils like these he must brave,
> His happiest homestead were down in the grave."

When the Caliph heard his verses, he said to Ja'afar, "See this poor man and note his verses, for surely they point to his necessities."

Then he accosted him and asked, "O Sheikh, what be thine occupation?" And the poor man answered: "O my lord, I am a fisherman with a family to keep and I have been out between midday and this time, and not a thing hath Allah made my portion wherewithal to feed my family. I cannot even pawn myself to buy them a supper, and I hate and disgust my life and I hanker after death." Quoth the Caliph, "Say me, wilt thou return with us to Tigris' bank and cast thy net on my luck, and whatsoever turneth up I will buy of thee for a hundred gold pieces?" The man rejoiced when he heard these words and said: "On my head be it! I will go back with you," and, returning with them riverward, made a cast and waited a while.

Then he hauled in the rope and dragged the net ashore and there appeared in it a chest, padlocked and heavy. The Caliph examined it and lifted it, finding it weighty, so he gave the fisherman two hundred dinars and sent him about his business whilst Masrur, aided by the Caliph, carried the chest to the palace and set it down and lighted the candles. Ja'afar and Masrur then broke it open and found therein a basket of palm leaves corded with red worsted. This they cut open and saw within it a piece of carpet, which they lifted out, and under it was a woman's mantilla folded in four, which they pulled out, and at the bottom of the chest they came upon a young lady, fair as a silver ingot, slain and cut into nineteen pieces. When the Caliph looked upon her he cried, "Alas!" and tears ran down his cheeks and turning to Ja'afar, he said: "O dog of Wazirs, shall folk be murdered in our reign and be cast into the river to be a burden and a responsibility for us on the Day of Doom? By Allah, we must avenge this woman on her murderer, and he shall be made die the worst of deaths!"

And presently he added: "Now, as surely as we are descended from the Sons of Abbas, if thou bring us not him who slew her, that we do her justice on him, I will hang thee at the gate of my palace, thee and forty of thy kith and kin by thy side." And the Caliph was wroth with exceeding rage. Quoth Ja'afar, "Grant me three days' delay," and quoth the Caliph, "We grant thee this." So Ja'afar went out from before him and returned to his own house, full of sorrow and saying to himself: "How shall I find him who murdered this damsel, that I may bring him before the Caliph? If I bring other than the murderer, it will be laid to my charge by the Lord. In very sooth I wot not what to do." He kept his house three days, and on the fourth day the Caliph sent one of the chamberlains for him, and as he came into the presence, asked him, "Where is the murderer of the damsel?" To which answered Ja'afar, "O Commander of the Faithful, am I inspector of murdered folk that I should ken who killed her?" The Caliph was furious at his answer and bade hang him before the palace gate, and commanded that a crier cry through the streets of Baghdad: "Whoso would see the hanging of Ja'afar, the Barmaki, Wazir of the Caliph, with forty of the Barmecides, his cousins and kinsmen, before the palace gate, let him come and let him look!" The people flocked out from all the quarters of the city to witness the execution of Ja'afar and his kinsmen, not knowing the cause.

Then they set up the gallows and made Ja'afar and the others stand underneath in readiness for execution, but whilst every eye was looking for the Caliph's signal, and the crowd wept for Ja'afar and his cousins of the Barmecides, lo and behold! a young man fair of face and neat of dress and of favor like the moon raining light, with eyes black and bright, and brow flower-white, and cheeks red as rose and young down where the beard grows, and a mole like a grain of ambergris, pushed his way through the people till he stood immediately before the Wazir and said to him: "Safety to thee from this strait, O Prince of the Emirs and Asylum of the Poor! I am the man who slew the woman ye found in the chest, so hang me for her and do her justice on me!" When Ja'afar heard the youth's confession he rejoiced at his own deliverance, but grieved and sorrowed for the fair youth.

And whilst they were yet talking, behold, another man well stricken in years pressed forward through the people and thrust his way amid the populace till he came to Ja'afar and the youth, whom he saluted, saying: "Ho, thou the Wazir and Prince sans peer! Believe not the words of this youth. Of a surety none murdered the damsel but I. Take her wreak on me this moment, for an thou do not thus, I will require it of thee before Almighty Allah." Then quoth the young man: "O Wazir, this is an old man in his dotage who wotteth not whatso he saith ever, and I am he who murdered her, so do thou avenge her on me!" Quoth the old man: "O my son, thou art young and desirest the joys of the world and I am old and weary and surfeited with the world. I will offer my life as a ransom for thee and for the Wazir and his cousins. No one murdered the damsel but

I, so Allah upon thee, make haste to hang me, for no life is left in me now that hers is gone."

The Wazir marveled much at all this strangeness and taking the young man and the old man, carried them before the Caliph, where, after kissing the ground seven times between his hands, he said, "O Commander of the Faithful, I bring thee the murderer of the damsel!" "Where is he?" asked the Caliph, and Ja'afar answered: "This young man saith, 'I am the murderer,' and this old man, giving him the lie, saith, 'I am the murderer,' and behold, here are the twain standing before thee." The Caliph looked at the old man and the young man and asked, "Which of you killed the girl?" The young man replied, "No one slew her save I," and the old man answered, "Indeed none killed her but myself." Then said the Caliph to Ja'afar, "Take the twain and hang them both." But Ja'afar rejoined, "Since one of them was the murderer, to hang the other were mere injustice." "By Him who raised the firmament and dispread the earth like a carpet," cried the youth, "I am he who slew the damsel," and he went on to describe the manner of her murder and the basket, the mantilla, and the bit of carpet—in fact, all that the Caliph had found upon her.

So the Caliph was certified that the young man was the murderer, whereat he wondered and asked him: "What was the cause of thy wrongfully doing this damsel to die, and what made thee confess the murder without the bastinado, and what brought thee here to yield up thy life, and what made thee say 'Do her wreak upon me'?" The youth answered: "Know, O Commander of the Faithful, that this woman was my wife and the mother of my children, also my first cousin and the daughter of my paternal uncle, this old man, who is my father's own brother. When I married her she was a maid, and Allah blessed me with three male children by her. She loved me and served me and I saw no evil in her, for I also loved her with fondest love. Now on the first day of this month she fell ill with grievous sickness and I fetched in physicians to her, but recovery came to her little by little, and when I wished her to go to the hammam bath, she said, 'There is something I long for before I go to the bath, and I long for it with an exceeding longing.' 'To hear is to comply,' said I. 'And what is it?' Quoth she, 'I have a queasy craving for an apple, to smell it and bite a bit of it.' I replied, 'Hadst thou a thousand longings, I would try to satisfy them!' So I went on the instant into the city and sought for apples, but could find none, yet had they cost a gold piece each, would I have bought them. I was vexed at this and went home and said, 'O daughter of my uncle, by Allah I can find none!' She was distressed, being yet very weakly, and her weakness increased greatly on her that night and I felt anxious and alarmed on her account.

"As soon as morning dawned I went out again and made the round of the gardens, one by one, but found no apples anywhere. At last there met me an old gardener, of whom I asked about them and he answered, 'O my son, this fruit is a rarity with us and is not now to be found save in the garden of the Commander of the Faithful at Bassorah, where the gardener keepeth it for the Caliph's eating.' I returned to my house troubled by my ill success, and my love for my wife and my affection moved me to undertake the journey. So I gat me ready and set out and traveled fifteen days and nights, going and coming, and brought her three apples, which I bought from the gardener for three dinars. But when I went in to my wife and set them before her, she took no pleasure in them and let them lie by her side, for her weakness and fever had increased on her, and her malady lasted without abating ten days, after which she began to recover health.

"So I left my house and betaking me to my shop, sat there buying and selling. And about midday, behold, a great ugly black slave, long as a lance and broad as a bench, passed by my shop holding in hand one of the three apples, wherewith he was playing, Quoth I, 'O my good slave, tell me whence thou tookest that apple, that I may get the like of it?' He laughed and answered: 'I got it from my mistress, for I had been absent and on my return I found her lying ill with three apples by her side, and she said to me, "My horned wittol of a husband made a journey for them to Bassorah and bought them for three dinars." 'So I ate and drank with her and took this one from her.' When I heard such words from the slave, O Commander of the Faithful, the world grew black before my face, and I arose and locked up my shop and went home beside myself for excess of rage. I looked for the apples and finding only two of the three, asked my wife, 'O my cousin, where is the third apple?' And raising her head languidly, she answered, 'I wot not, O son of my uncle, where 'tis gone!' This convinced me that the slave had spoken the truth, so I took a knife and coming behind her, got upon her breast without a word said and cut her throat. Then I hewed off her head and her limbs in pieces and, wrapping her in her mantilla and a rag of carpet, hurriedly sewed up the whole, which I set in a chest and, locking it tight, loaded it on my he-mule and threw it into the Tigris with my own hands.

"So Allah upon thee, O Commander of the Faithful, make haste to hang me, as I fear lest she appeal for vengeance on Resurrection Day. For when I had thrown her into the river and one knew aught of it, as I went back home I found my eldest son crying, and yet he knew naught of what I had done with his mother. I asked him, 'What hath made thee weep, my boy?' and he answered, 'I took one of the three apples which were by my mammy and went down into the lane to play with my brethren when behold, a big long black slave snatched it from my hand and said, "Whence hadst thou this?" Quoth I, "My father traveled far for it, and brought it from Bassorah for my mother, who was ill, and two other apples for which he paid three ducats." 'He took no heed of my words and I asked for the apple a second and a third time, but he cuffed me and kicked me and went off with it. I was afraid lest my mother should swinge me on account of the apple, so for fear of her I went with my brother outside the city and stayed there till evening closed in upon us, and indeed I am in fear of her. And now, by Allah, O my father, say nothing to her of this or it may add to her ailment!"

"When I heard what my child said, I knew that the slave was he who had foully slandered my wife, the daughter of my uncle, and was certified that I had slain her wrongfully. So I wept with exceeding weeping and presently this old man, my paternal uncle and her father, came in, and I told him what had happened and he sat down by my side and wept, and we ceased not weeping till midnight. We have kept up mourning for her these last five days and we lamented her in the deepest sorrow for that she was unjustly done to die. This came from the gratuitous lying of the slave, the blackamoor, and this was the manner of my killing her. So I conjure thee, by the honor of thine ancestors, make haste to kill me and do her justice upon me, as there is no living for me after her!"

The Caliph marveled at his words and said: "By Allah, the young man is excusable. I will hang none but the accursed slave, and I will do a deed which shall comfort the ill-at-ease and suffering, and which shall please the All-glorious King." Then he turned to Ja'afar and said to him: "Bring before me this accursed slave who was the sole cause of this calamity, and if thou bring him not before me within three days, thou shalt be slain in his stead." So Ja'afar fared forth weeping and saying: "Two deaths have already beset me, nor shall the crock come off safe from every shock. In this matter craft and cunning are of no avail, but He who preserved my life the first time can preserve it a second time. By Allah, I will not leave my house during the three days of life which remain to me, and let the Truth (whose perfection be praised!) do e'en as He will." So he kept his house three days, and on the fourth day he summoned the kazis and legal witnesses and made his last will and testament, and took leave of his children weeping.

Presently in came a messenger from the Caliph and said to him: "The Commander of the Faithful is in the most violent rage that can be, and he sendeth to seek thee and he sweareth that the day shall certainly not pass without thy being hanged unless the slave be forthcoming." When Ja'afar heard this he wept, and his children and slaves and all who were in the house wept with him. After he had bidden adieu to everybody except this youngest daughter, he proceeded to farewell her, for he loved this wee one, who was a beautiful child, more than all his other children. And he pressed her to his breast and kissed her and wept bitterly at parting from her, when he felt something round inside the bosom of her dress and asked her, "O my little maid, what is in the bosom pocket?" "O my father," she replied, "it is an apple with the name of our Lord the Caliph written upon it. Rayhan our slave brought it to me four days ago, and would not let me have it till I gave him two dinars for it." When Ja'afar heard speak of the slave and the apple, he was glad and put his hand into his child's pocket and drew out the apple and knew it and rejoiced, saying, "O ready Dispeller of trouble!"

Then he bade them bring the slave and said to him, "Fie upon thee, Rayhan! Whence haddest thou this apple?" "By Allah, O my master," he replied, "though a lie may get a man once off, yet may truth get him off, and well off, again and again. I did not steal this apple from thy palace nor from the gardens of the Commander of the Faithful. The fact is that five days ago, as I was walking along one of the alleys of this city, I saw some little ones at play and this apple in hand of one of them. So I snatched it from him and beat him, and he cried and said, 'O youth, this apple is my mother's and she is ill. She told my father how she longed for an apple, so he traveled to Bassorah and bought her three apples for three gold pieces, and I took one of them to play withal.' He wept again, but I paid no heed to what he said and carried it off and brought it here, and my little lady bought it of me for two dinars of gold. And this is the whole story."

When Ja'afar heard his words he marveled that the murder of the damsel and all this misery should have been caused by his slave. He grieved for the relation of the slave to himself while rejoicing over his own deliverance, and he repeated these lines:

> "If ill betide thee through thy slave,
> Make him forthright thy sacrifice.
> A many serviles thou shalt find,
> But life comes once and never twice."

Then he took the slave's hand and, leading him to the Caliph, related the story from first to last, and the Caliph marveled with extreme astonishment, and laughed till he fell on his back, and ordered that the story be recorded and be made public amongst the people.

But Ja'afar said, "Marvel not, O Commander of the Faithful, at this adventure, for it is not more wondrous than the History of the Wazir Nur al-Din Ali of Egypt and his brother Shams al-Din Mohammed." Quoth the Caliph, "Out with it, but what can be stranger than this story?" And Ja'afar answered, "O Commander of the Faithful, I will not tell it thee save on condition that thou pardon my slave." And the Caliph rejoined, "If it be indeed more wondrous than that of the three apples, I grant thee his blood, and if not I will surely slay thy slave." So Ja'afar began in these words the

TALE OF NUR AL-DIN ALI AND HIS SON BADR AL-DIN HASAN

KNOW, O Commander of the Faithful, that in times of yore the land of Egypt was ruled by a Sultan endowed with justice and generosity, one who loved the pious poor and companied with the Ulema and learned men. And he had a Wazir, a wise and an experienced, well versed in affairs and in the art of government. This Minister, who was a very old man, had two sons, as they were two moons. Never man saw the like of them for beauty and grace—the elder called Shams al-Din Mohammed and the younger Nur al-Din Ali. But the younger excelled the elder in seemliness and pleasing semblance, so that folk heard his fame in far countries and men flocked to Egypt for the purpose of seeing him.

In course of time their father, the Wazir, died and was deeply regretted and mourned by the Sultan, who sent for his two sons and, investing them with dresses of honor, said to them, "Let not your hearts be troubled, for ye shall stand in your father's stead and be joint Ministers of Egypt." At this they rejoiced and kissed the ground before him and performed the ceremonial mourning for their father during a full month, after which time they entered upon the wazirate and the power passed into their hands as it had been in the hands of their father, each doing duty for a week at a time. They lived under the same roof and their word was one, and whenever the Sultan desired to travel they took it by turns to be in attendance on him.

It fortuned one night that the Sultan purposed setting out on a journey next morning, and the elder, whose turn it was to accompany him, was sitting conversing with his brother and said to him: "O my brother, it is my wish that we both marry, I and thou, two sisters, and go in to our wives on one and the same night." "Do, O my brother, as thou desirest," the younger replied, "for right is thy recking and surely I will comply with thee in whatso thou sayest." So they agreed upon this, and quoth Shams al-Din: "If Allah decree that we marry two damsels and go in to them on the same night, and they shall conceive on their bride nights and bear children to us on the same day, and by Allah's will thy wife bear thee a son and my wife bear me a daughter, let us wed them either to other, for they will be cousins." Quoth Nur al-Din: "O my brother, Shams al-Din, what dower wilt thou require from my son for thy daughter?" Quoth Shams al-Din: "I will take three thousand dinars and three pleasure gardens and three farms, and it would not be seemly that the youth make contract for less than this."

When Nur al-Din heard such demand, he said: "What manner of dower is this thou wouldest impose upon my son? Wottest thou not that we are brothers and both by Allah's grace Wazirs and equal in office? It behooveth thee to offer thy daughter to my son without marriage settlement, or, if one need be, it should represent a mere nominal value by way of show to the world. For thou knowest that the masculine is worthier than the feminine, and my son is a male and our memory will be preserved by him, not by thy daughter." "But what," said Shams al-Din, "is she to have?" And Nur al-Din continued, "Through her we shall not be remembered among the emirs of the earth, but I see thou wouldest do with me according to the saying, 'An thou wouldst bluff of a buyer, ask him high price and higher,' or as did a man who they say went to a friend and asked something of him being in necessity and was answered, 'Bismillah, in the name of Allah, I will do all what thou requirest, but come tomorrow!' Whereupon the other replied in this verse:

> 'When he who is asked a favor saith "Tomorrow,"
> The wise man wots 'tis vain to beg or borrow.'

Quoth Shams al-Din: "Basta! I see thee fail in respect to me by making thy son of more account than my daughter, and 'tis plain that thine understanding is of the meanest and that thou lackest manners. Thou remindest me of thy partnership in the wazirate, when I admitted thee to share with me only in pity for thee, and not wishing to mortify thee, and that thou mightest help me as a manner of assistant. But since thou talkest on this wise, by Allah, I will never marry my daughter to thy son—no, not for her weight in gold!" When Nur al-Din heard his brother's words, he waxed wroth and said: "And I too, I will never, never marry my son to thy daughter—no, not to keep from my lips the cup of death." Shams al-Din replied:

"I would not accept him as a husband for her, and he is not worth a paring of her nail. Were I not about to travel, I would make an example of thee. However, when I return thou shalt see, and I will show thee, how I can assert my dignity and vindicate my honor. But Allah doeth whatso He willeth."

When Nur al-Din heard this speech from his brother, he was filled with fury and lost his wits for rage, but he hid what he felt and held his peace; and each of the brothers passed the night in a place far apart, wild with wrath against the other.

As soon as morning dawned the Sultan fared forth in state and crossed over from Cairo to Jizah and made for the Pyramids, accompanied by the Wazir Shams al-Din, whose turn of duty it was, whilst his brother Nur al-Din, who passed the night in sore rage, rose with the light and prayed the dawn prayer. Then he betook himself to his treasury and, taking a small pair of saddlebags, filled them with gold. And he called to mind his brother's threats and the contempt wherewith he had treated him, and he repeated these couplets:

> "Travel! And thou shalt find new friends for old ones left behind.
> Toil! For the sweets of human life by toil and moil are found.
> The stay-at-home no honor wins, nor aught attains but want,
> So leave thy place of birth and wander all the world around!
> I've seen, and very oft I've seen, how standing water stinks,
> And only flowing sweetens it and trotting makes it sound.
> And were the moon forever full and ne'er to wax or wane,
> Man would not strain his watchful eyes to see its gladsome round.
> Except the lion leave his lair, he ne'er would fell his game,
> Except the arrow leave the bow, ne'er had it reached its bound.
> Gold dust is dust the while it lies untraveled in the mine,
> And aloes wood mere fuel is upon its native ground.
> And gold shall win his highest worth when from his goal ungoaled,
> And aloes sent to foreign parts grows costlier than gold."

When he ended his verse, he bade one of his pages saddle him his Nubian mare mule with her padded selle. Now she was a dapple-gray, with ears like reed pens and legs like columns and a back high and strong as a dome builded on pillars. Her saddle was of gold cloth and her stirrups of Indian steel, and her housing of Ispahan velvet. She had trappings which would serve the Chosroes, and she was like a bride adorned for her wedding night. Moreover, he bade lay on her back a piece of silk for a seat, and a prayer carpet under which were his saddlebags. When this was done, he said to his pages and slaves: "I purpose going forth a-pleasuring outside the city on the road to Kalyub town, and I shall lie three nights abroad, so let none of you follow me, for there is something straiteneth my breast." Then he mounted the mule in haste and, taking with him some provaunt for the way, set out from Cairo and faced the open and uncultivated country lying around it.

About noontide he entered Bilbays city, where he dismounted and stayed awhile to rest himself and his mule and ate some of his victual. He bought at Bilbays all he wanted for himself and forage for his mule and then fared on the way of the waste. Toward nightfall he entered a town called Sa'adiyah, where he alighted and took out somewhat of his viaticum and ate. Then he spread his strip of silk on the sand and set the saddlebags under his head and slept in the open air, for he was still overcome with anger. When morning dawned he mounted and rode onward till he reached the Holy City, Jerusalem, and thence he made Aleppo, where he dismounted at one of the caravanserais and abode three days to rest himself and the mule and to smell the air. Then, being determined to travel afar and Allah having written safety in his fate, he set out again, wending without wotting whither he was going. And having fallen in with certain couriers, he stinted not traveling till he had reached Bassorah city, albeit he knew not what the place was.

It was dark night when he alighted at the khan, so he spread out his prayer carpet and took down the saddlebags from the back of the mule and gave her with her furniture in charge of the doorkeeper that he might walk her about. The man took her and did as he was bid. Now it so happened that the Wazir of Bassorah, a man shot in years, was sitting at the lattice window of his palace opposite the khan and he saw the porter walking the mule up and down. He was struck by her trappings of price, and thought her a nice beast fit for the riding of wazirs or even of royalties, and the more he looked, the more was he perplexed, till at last he said to one of his pages, "Bring hither yon doorkeeper." The page went and returned to the Wazir with the porter, who kissed the ground between his hands, and the Minister asked him, "Who is the owner of yonder mule, and what manner of man is he?" and he answered, "O my lord, the owner of this mule is a comely young man of pleasant manners, withal grave and dignified, and doubtless one of the sons of the merchants."

When the Wazir heard the doorkeeper's words he arose forthright and, mounting his horse, rode to the khan and went in to Nur al-Din, who, seeing the Minister making toward him, rose to his feet and advanced to meet him and saluted him. The Wazir welcomed him to Bassorah and dismounting, embraced him and made him sit down by his side, and said, "O my son, whence comest thou, and what dost thou seek?" "O my lord," Nur al-Din replied, "I have come from Cairo city, of which my father was whilom Wazir, but he hath been removed to the grace of Allah." And he informed him of all that had befallen him from beginning to end, adding, "I am resolved never to return home before I have seen all the cities and countries of the world." When the Wazir heard this, he said to him: "O my son, hearken not to the voice of passion lest it cast thee into the pit, for indeed many regions be waste places, and I fear for thee the turns of Time." Then he let load the saddlebags and the silk and prayer carpets on the mule and carried Nur al-Din to his own house, where he lodged him in a pleasant place and entreated him honorably and made much of him, for he inclined to love him with exceeding love.

After a while he said to him: "O my son, here am I left a man in years and have no male children, but Allah hath blessed me with a daughter who eveneth thee in beauty, and I have rejected all her many suitors, men of rank and substance. But affection for thee hath entered into my heart. Say me, then, wilt thou be to her a husband? If thou accept this, I will go with thee to the Sultan of Bassorah and will tell him that thou art my nephew, the son of my brother, and bring thee to be appointed Wazir in my place that I may keep the house, for, by Allah, O my son, I am stricken in years and aweary." When Nur al-Din heard the Wazir's words, he bowed his head in modesty and said, "To hear is to obey!" At this the Wazir rejoiced and bade his servants prepare a feast and decorate the great assembly hall wherein they were wont to celebrate the marriages of emirs and grandees. Then he assembled his friends and the notables of the reign and the merchants of Bassorah, and when all stood before him he said to them: "I had a brother who was Wazir in the land of Egypt, and Allah Almighty blessed him with two sons, whilst to me, as well ye wot, He hath given a daughter. My brother charged me to marry my daughter to one of his sons, whereto I assented, and when my daughter was of age to marry, he sent me one of his sons, the young man now present, to whom I purpose marrying her, drawing up the contract and celebrating the night of unveiling with due ceremony. For he is nearer and dearer to me than a stranger, and after the wedding, if he please he shall abide with me, or if he desire to travel, I will forward him and his wife to his father's home." Hereat one and all replied, "Right is thy recking," and they looked at the bridegroom and were pleased with him.

So the Wazir sent for the kazi and legal witnesses and they wrote out the marriage contract, after which the slaves perfumed the guests with incense, and served them with sherbet of sugar and sprinkled rose-water on them, and all went their ways. Then the Wazir bade his servants take Nur al-Din to the hammam baths and sent him a suit of the best of his own especial raiment, and napkins and towelry and bowls and perfume-burners and all else that was required. And after the bath, when he came out and donned the dress, he was even as the full moon on the fourteenth night, and he mounted his mule and stayed not till he reached the Wazir's palace. There he dismounted and went in to the Minister and kissed his hands, and the Wazir bade him welcome, saying: "Arise and go in to thy wife this night, and on the morrow I will carry thee to the Sultan, and pray Allah bless thee with all manner of weal." So Nur al-Din left him and went in to his wife the Wazir's daughter.

Thus far concerning him, but as regards his elder brother, Shams al-Din, he was absent with the Sultan a long time, and when he returned from his journey he found not his brother, and he asked of his servants and slaves, who answered: "On the day of thy departure with the Sultan, thy brother mounted his mule fully caparisoned as for state procession saying, 'I am going towards Kalyub town, and I shall be absent one day or at most two days, for my breast is straitened, and let none of you follow me.' Then he fared forth, and from that time to this we have heard no tidings of him." Shams al-Din was greatly troubled at the sudden disappearance of his brother and grieved with exceeding grief at the loss, and said to himself: "This is only because I chided and upbraided him the night before my departure with the Sultan. Haply his feelings were hurt, and he fared forth a-traveling, but I must send after him." Then he went in to the Sultan and acquainted him with what had happened and wrote letters and dispatches, which he sent by running footmen to his deputies in every province. But during the twenty days of his brother's absence Nur al-Din had traveled far and had reached Bassorah, so after diligent search the messengers failed to come at any news of him and returned. Thereupon Shams al-Din despaired of finding his brother and said: "Indeed I went beyond all bounds in what I said to him with reference to the marriage of our children. Would that I had not done so! This all cometh of my lack of wit and want of caution."

Soon after this he sought in marriage the daughter of a Cairene merchant, and drew up the marriage contract, and went in to her. And it so chanced that on the very same night when Shams al-Din went in to his wife, Nur al-Din also went in to his wife, the daughter of the Wazir of Bassorah, this being in accordance with the will of Almighty Allah, that He might deal the decrees of Destiny to His creatures. Furthermore, it was as the two brothers had said, for their two wives became pregnant by them on the same night and both were brought to bed on the same day, the wife of Shams al-Din, Wazir of Egypt, of a daughter, never in Cairo was seen a fairer, and the wife of Nur al-Din of a son, none more beautiful was ever seen in his time, as one of the poets said concerning the like of him:

> That jetty hair, that glossy brow,
>   My slender waisted youth, of thine,
> Can darkness round creation throw,
>   Or make it brightly shine.
> The dusky mole that faintly shows
>   Upon his cheek, ah! blame it not.
> The tulip flower never blows
>   Undarkened by its spot.

They named the boy Badr al-Din Hasan and his grandfather, the Wazir of Bassorah, rejoiced in him, and on the seventh day after his birth made entertainments and spread banquets which would befit the birth of kings' sons and heirs. Then he took Nur al-Din and went up with him to the Sultan, and his son-in-law, when he came before the presence of the King, kissed the ground between his hands and repeated these verses, for he was ready of speech, firm of sprite and good in heart, as he was goodly in form:

> "The world's best joys long be thy lot, my lord!
> And last while darkness and the dawn o'erlap.
> O thou who makest, when we greet thy gifts,
> The world to dance and Time his palms to clap."

Then the Sultan rose up to honor them and, thanking Nur al-Din for his fine compliment, asked the Wazir, "Who may be this young man?" And the Minister answered, "This is my brother's son," and related his tale from first to last. Quoth the Sultan, "And how comes he to be thy nephew and we have never heard speak of him?" Quoth the Minister: "O our lord the Sultan, I had a brother who was Wazir in the land of Egypt and he died, leaving two sons, whereof the elder hath taken his father's place and the younger, whom thou seest, came to me. I had sworn I would not marry my daughter to any but him, so when he came I married him to her. Now he is young and I am old, my hearing is dulled and my judgment is easily fooled, wherefore I would solicit our lord the Sultan to set him in my stead, for he is my brother's son and my daughter's husband, and he is fit for the wazirate, being a man of good counsel and ready contrivance."

The Sultan looked at Nur al-Din and liked him, so he stablished him in office as the Wazir had requested and formally appointed him, presenting him with a splendid dress of honor and a she-mule from his private stud, and assigning to him solde, stipends, and supplies. Nur al-Din kissed the Sultan's hand and went home, he and his father-in-law, joying with exceeding joy and saying, "All this followeth on the heels of the boy Hasan's birth!" Next day he presented himself before the King and, kissing the ground, began repeating:

> "Grow thy weal and thy welfare day by day,
> And thy luck prevail o'er the envier's spite,
> And ne'er cease thy days to be white as day,
> And thy foeman's day to be black as night!"

The Sultan bade him be seated on the Wazir's seat, so he sat down and applied himself to the business of his office and went into the cases of the lieges and their suits, as is the wont of Ministers, while the Sultan watched him and wondered at his wit and good sense, judgment and insight. Wherefor he loved him and took him into intimacy. When the Divan was dismissed, Nur al-Din returned to his house and related what had passed to his father-in-law, who rejoiced.

And thenceforward Nur al-Din ceased not so to administer the wazirate that the Sultan would not be parted from him night or day, and increased his stipends and supplies till his means were ample and he became the owner of ships that made trading voyages at his command, as well as of Mamelukes and blackamoor slaves. And he laid out many estates and set up Persian wheels and planted gardens.

When his son Hasan was four years of age, the old Wazir deceased, and he made for his father-in-law a sumptuous funeral ceremony ere he was laid in the dust. Then he occupied himself with the education of this son, and when the boy waxed strong and came to the age of seven, he brought him a fakir, a doctor of law and religion, to teach him in his own house, and charged him to give him a good education and instruct him in politeness and good manners. So the tutor made the boy read and retain all varieties of useful knowledge, after he had spent some years in learning the Koran by heart, and he ceased not to grow in beauty and stature and symmetry. The professor brought him up in his father's palace, teaching him reading, writing and ciphering, theology, and belles lettres. His grandfather, the old Wazir, had bequeathed to him the whole of his property when he was but four years of age.

Now during all the time of his earliest youth he had never left the house till on a certain day his father, the Wazir Nur al-Din, clad him in his best clothes and, mounting him on a she-mule of the finest, went up with him to the Sultan. The King gazed at Badr al-Din Hasan and marveled at his comeliness and loved him. As for the city folk, when he first passed before them with his father, they marveled at his exceeding beauty and sat down on the road expecting his return, that they might look their fill on his beauty and loveliness and symmetry and perfect grace. And they blessed him aloud as he passed and called upon Almighty Allah to bless him. The Sultan entreated the lad with especial favor and said to his father, "O Wazir, thou must needs bring him daily to my presence." Whereupon he replied, "I hear and I obey."

Then the Wazir returned home with his son and ceased not to carry him to court till he reached the age of twenty. At that time the Minister sickened and, sending for Badr al-Din Hasan, said to him: "Know, O my son, that the world of the present is but a house of mortality, while that the future is a house of eternity. I wish, before I die, to bequeath thee certain charges, and do thou take heed of what I say and incline thy heart to my words." Then he gave him his last instructions as to the properest way of dealing with his neighbors and the due management of his affairs, after which he called to mind his brother and his home and his native land and wept over his separation from those he had first loved.

Then he wiped away his tears and, turning to his son, said to him: "Before I proceed, O my son, to my last charges and injunctions, know that I have a brother, and thou hast an uncle, Shams al-Din hight, the Wazir of Cairo, with whom I parted, leaving him against his will. Now take thee a sheet of paper and write upon it whatso I say to thee." Badr al-Din took a fair leaf and set about doing his father's bidding, and he wrote thereon a full account of what had happened to his sire first and last: the dates of his arrival at Bassorah and of his forgathering with the Wazir, of his marriage, of his going in to the Minister's daughter, and of the birth of his son—brief, his life of forty years from the day of his dispute with his brother, adding the words: "And this is written at my dictation, and may Almighty Allah be with him when I am gone!" Then he folded the paper and sealed it and said: "O Hasan, O my son, keep this paper with all care, for it will enable thee to establish thine origin and rank and lineage, and if anything contrary befall thee, set out for Cairo and ask for thine uncle and show him this paper, and say to him that I died a stranger far from mine own people and full of yearning to see him and them." So Badr al-Din Hasan took the document and folded it and, wrapping it up in a piece of waxed cloth, sewed it like a talisman between the inner and outer cloth of his skullcap and wound his light turban round it. And he fell to weeping over his father and at parting with him, and he but a boy.

Then Nur al-Din lapsed into a swoon, the forerunner of death, but presently recovering himself, he said: "O Hasan, O my son, I will now bequeath to thee five last behests. The FIRST BEHEST is: Be overintimate with none, nor frequent any, nor be familiar with any. So shalt thou be safe from his mischief, for security lieth in seclusion of thought and a certain retirement from the society of thy fellows, and I have heard it said by a poet:

> "In this world there is none thou mayst count upon
> To befriend thy case in the nick of need.
> So live for thyself nursing hope of none.
> Such counsel I give thee—enow, take heed!

"The SECOND BEHEST is, O my son: Deal harshly with none lest fortune with thee deal hardly, for the fortune of this world is one day with thee and another day against thee, and all worldly goods are but a loan to be repaid. And I have heard a poet say:

> "Take thought nor haste to win the thing thou wilt,
> Have ruth on man, for ruth thou may'st require.
> No hand is there but Allah's hand is higher,
> No tyrant but shall rue worse tyrant's ire!

"The THIRD BEHEST is: Learn to be silent in society and let thine own faults distract thine attention from the faults of other men, for it is said, 'In silence dwelleth safety,' and thereon I have heard the lines that tell us:

> "Reserve's a jewel, Silence safety is.
> Whenas thou speakest, many a word withhold,
> For an of Silence thou repent thee once,
> Of speech thou shalt repent times manifold.

"The FOURTH BEHEST, O my son, is: Beware of winebibbing, for wine is the head of all frowardness and a fine solvent of human wits. So shun, and again I say shun, mixing strong liquor, for I have heard a poet say:

> "From wine I turn and whoso wine cups swill,
> Becoming one of those who deem it ill.
> Wine driveth man to miss salvation way,
> And opes the gateway wide to sins that kill.

"The FIFTH BEHEST, O my son, is: Keep thy wealth and it will keep thee, guard thy money and it will guard thee, and waste not thy substance lest haply thou come to want and must fare a-begging from the meanest of mankind. Save thy dirhams and deem them the sovereignest salve for the wounds of the world. And here again I have heard that one of the poets said:

> "When fails my wealth no friend will deign befriend.
> When wealth abounds all friends their friendship tender.
> How many friends lent aid my wealth to spend,
> But friends to lack of wealth no friendship render."

On this wise Nur al-Din ceased not to counsel his son Badr al-Din Hasan till his hour came and, sighing one sobbing sigh, his life went forth. Then the voice of mourning and keening rose high in his house and the Sultan and all the grandees grieved for him and buried him. But his son ceased not lamenting his loss for two months, during which he never mounted horse, nor attended the Divan, nor presented himself before the Sultan. At last the King, being wroth with him, stablished in his stead one of his chamberlains and made him Wazir, giving orders to seize and set seals on all Nur al-Din's houses and goods and domains. So the new Wazir went forth with a mighty posse of chamberlains and people of the Divan, and watchmen and a host of idlers, to do this and to seize Badr al-Din Hasan and carry him before the King, who would deal with him as he deemed fit.

Now there was among the crowd of followers a Mameluke of the deceased Wazir who, when he had heard this order, urged his horse and rode at full speed to the house of Badr al-Din Hasan, for he could not endure to see the ruin of his old master's son. He found him sitting at the gate with head hung down and sorrowing, as was his wont, for the loss of his father, so he dismounted and, kissing his hand, said to him, "O my lord and son of my lord, haste ere ruin come and lay waste!" When Hasan heard this he trembled and asked, "What may be the matter?" and the man answered: "The Sultan is angered with thee and hath issued a warrant against thee, and evil cometh hard upon my track, so flee with thy life!" At these words Hasan's heart flamed with the fire of bale, and his rose-red cheek turned pale, and he said to the Mameluke: "O my brother, is there time for me to go in and get some worldly gear which may stand me in stead during my strangerhood?" But the slave replied, "O my lord, up at once and save thyself and leave this house while it is yet time." And he quoted these lines:

> "Escape with thy life, if oppression betide thee,
> And let the house tell of its builder's fate!
> Country for country thou'lt find, if thou seek it,
> Life for life never, early or late.
> It is strange men should dwell in the house of abjection
> When the plain of God's earth is so wide and so great!"

At these words of the Mameluke, Badr al-Din covered his head with the skirt of his garment and went forth on foot till he stood outside of the city, where he heard folk saying: "The Sultan hath sent his new Wazir to the house of the old Wazir, now no more, to seal his property and seize his son Badr al-Din Hasan and take him before the presence, that he may put him to death." And all cried, "Alas for his beauty and his loveliness!" When he heard this, he fled forth at hazard, knowing not whither he was going, and gave not over hurrying onward till Destiny drove him to his father's tomb. So he entered the cemetery and, threading his way through the graves, at last he reached the sepulcher, where he sat down and let fall from his head the skirt of his long robe, which was made of brocade with a gold-embroidered hem whereon were worked these couplets:

> O thou whose forehead, like the radiant East,
> Tells of the stars of Heaven and bounteous dews,
> Endure thine honor to the latest day,
> And Time thy growth of glory ne'er refuse!

While he was sitting by his father's tomb, behold, there came to him a Jew as he were a shroff, a money-changer, with a pair of saddlebags containing much gold, who accosted him and kissed his hand, saying: "Whither bound, O my lord? 'Tis late in the day, and thou art clad but lightly, and I read signs of trouble in thy face." "I was sleeping within this very hour," answered Hasan, "when my father appeared to me and chid me for not having visited his tomb. So I awoke trembling and came hither forthright lest the day should go by without my visiting him, which would have been grievous to me." "O my lord," rejoined the Jew, "thy father had many merchantmen at sea, and as some of them are now due, it is my wish to buy of thee the cargo of the first ship that cometh into port with this thousand dinars of gold." "I concent," quoth Hasan, whereupon the Jew took out a bag full of gold and counted out a thousand sequins, which he gave to Hasan, the son of the Wazir, saying, "Write me a letter of sale and seal it."

So Hasan took a pen and paper and wrote these words in duplicate: "The writer, Hasan Badr al-Din, son of Wazir Nur al-Din, hath sold to Isaac the Jew all the cargo of the first of his father's ships which cometh into port, for a thousand dinars, and he hath received the price in advance." And after he had taken one copy, the Jew put it into his pouch and went away, but Hasan fell a-weeping as he thought of the dignity and prosperity which had erst been his and night came upon him. So he leant his head against his father's grave and sleep overcame him—glory to Him who sleepeth not! He ceased not slumbering till the moon rose, when his head slipped from off the tomb and he lay on his back, with limbs outstretched, his face shining bright in the moonlight. Now the cemetery was haunted day and night by Jinns who were of the True Believers, and presently came out a Jinniyah who, seeing Hasan asleep, marveled at his beauty and loveliness and cried: "Glory to God! This youth can be none other than one of the Wuldan of Paradise." Then she flew firmamentward to circle it, as was her custom, and met an Ifrit on the wing, who saluted her, and said to him, "Whence comest thou?" "From Cairo," he replied. "Wilt thou come with me and look upon the beauty of a youth who sleepeth in yonder burial place?" she asked, and he answered, "I will."

So they flew till they lighted at the tomb and she showed him the youth and said, "Now diddest thou ever in thy born days see aught like this?" The Ifrit looked upon him and exclaimed: "Praise be to Him that hath no equal! But, O my sister, shall I tell thee what I have seen this day?" Asked she, "What is that?" and he answered: "I have seen the counterpart of this youth in the land of Egypt. She is the daughter of the Wazir Shams al-Din and she is a model of beauty and loveliness, of fairest favor and formous form, and dight with symmetry and perfect grace. When she had reached the age of nineteen, the Sultan of Egypt heard of her and, sending for the Wazir her father, said to him, 'Hear me, O Wazir. It hath reached mine ear that thou hast a daughter, and I wish to demand her of thee in marriage.' The Wazir replied:

"'O our lord the Sultan, deign accept my excuses and take compassion on my sorrows, for thou knowest that my brother, who was partner with me in the wazirate, disappeared from amongst us many years ago and we wot not where he is. Now the cause of his departure was that one night, as we were sitting together and talking of wives and children to come, we had words on the matter and he went off in high dudgeon. But I swore that I would marry my daughter to none save to the son of my brother on the day her mother gave her birth, which was nigh upon nineteen years ago. I have lately heard that my brother died at Bassorah, where he had married the daughter of the Wazir and that she bare him a son, and I will not marry my daughter but to him in honor of my brother's memory. I recorded the date of my marriage and the conception of my wife and the birth of my daughter, and from her horoscope I find that her name is conjoined with that of her cousin, and there are damsels in foison for our lord the Sultan.'

"The King, hearing his Minister's answer and refusal, waxed wroth with exceeding wrath and cried: 'When the like of me asketh a girl in marriage of the like of thee, he conferreth an honor, and thou rejectest me and puttest me off with cold excuses! Now, by the life of my head, I will marry her to the meanest of my men in spite of the nose of thee!' There was in the palace a horse groom which was a Gobbo with a bunch to his breast and a hunch to his back, and the Sultan sent for him and married him to the daughter of the Wazir, lief or loth, and hath ordered a pompous marriage procession for him and that he go in to his bride this very night. I have not just flown hither from Cairo, where I left the hunchback at the door of the hammam bath amidst the Sultan's white slaves, who were waving lighted flambeaux about him. As for the Minister's daughter, she sitteth among her nurses and tirewomen, weeping and wailing, for they have forbidden her father to come near her. Never have I seen, O my sister, more hideous being than this hunchback, whilst the young lady is the likest of all folk to this young man, albeit even fairer than he."

At this the Jinniyah cried at him: "Thou liest! This youth is handsomer than anyone of his day." The Ifrit gave her the lie again, adding: "By Allah, O my sister, the damsel I speak of is fairer than this. Yet none but he deserveth her, for they resemble each other like brother and sister, or at least cousins. And, wellaway, how she is wasted upon that hunchback!" Then said she, "O my brother, let us get under him and lift him up and carry him to Cairo, that we may compare him with the damsel of whom thou speakest and so determine whether of the twain is the fairer." "To hear is to obey!" replied he. "Thou speakest to the point, nor is there a righter recking than this of thine, and I myself will carry him." So he raised him from the ground and flew with him like a bird soaring in upper air, the Ifritah keeping close by his side at equal speed, till he alighted with him in the city of Cairo and set him down on a stone bench and woke him up. He roused himself and finding that he was no longer at his father's tomb in Bassorah city, he looked right and left and saw that he was in a strange place, and he would have cried out, but the Ifrit gave him a cuff which persuaded him to keep silence. Then he brought him rich raiment and clothed him therein and, giving him a lighted flambeau, said:

"Know that I have brought thee hither meaning to do thee a good turn for the love of Allah. So take this torch and mingle with the people at the hammam door and walk on with them without stopping till thou reach the house of the wedding festival. Then go boldly forward and enter the great saloon, and fear none, but take thy stand at the right hand of the hunchback bridegroom. And as often as any of the nurses and tirewomen and singing girls come up to thee, put thy hand into thy pocket, which thou wilt find filled with gold. Take it out and throw to them and spare not, for as often as thou thrustest fingers in pouch, thou shalt find it full of coin. Give largess by handfuls and fear nothing, but set thy trust upon Him who created thee, for this is not by thine own strength but by that of Allah Almighty, that His decrees may take effect upon His creatures."

When Badr al-Din Hasan heard these words from the Ifrit, he said to himself, "Would Heaven I knew what all this means and what is the cause of such kindness!" However, he mingled with the people and, lighting his flambeau, moved on with the bridal procession till he came to the bath, where he found the hunchback already on horseback. Then he pushed his way in among the crowd, a veritable beauty of a man in the finest apparel, wearing tarboosh and turban and a long-sleeved robe purfled with gold. And as often as the singing women stopped for the people to give him largess, he thrust his hand into his pocket and, finding it full of gold, took out a handful and threw it on the tambourine till he had filled it with gold pieces for the music girls and the tirewomen. The singers were amazed by his bounty and the people marveled at his beauty and loveliness and the splendor of his dress. He ceased not to do thus till he reached the mansion of the Wazir (who was his uncle), where the chamberlains drove back the people and forbade them to go forward, but the singing girls and the tirewomen said, "By Allah, we will not enter unless this young man enter with us, for he hath given us length o' life with his largess, and we will not display the bride unless he be present."

Therewith they carried him into the bridal hall and made him sit down, defying the evil glances of the hunchbacked bridegroom. The wives of the emirs and wazirs and chamberlains and courtiers all stood in double line, each holding a massy cierge ready lighted. All wore thin face veils, and the two rows right and left extended from the bride's throne to the head of the hall adjoining the chamber whence she was to come forth. When the ladies saw Badr al-Din Hasan and noted his beauty and loveliness and his face that shone like the new moon, their hearts inclined to him and the singing girls said to all that were present, "Know that this beauty crossed our hands with naught but red gold, so be not chary to do him womanly service and comply with all he says, no matter what he ask." So all the women crowded round Hasan with their torches and gazed on his loveliness and envied him his beauty, and one and all would gladly have lain on his bosom an hour, or rather a year. Their hearts were so troubled that they let fall their veils from before their faces and said, "Happy she who belongeth to this youth or to whom he belongeth!" And they called down curses on the crooked groom and on him who was the cause of his marriage to the girl beauty, and as often as they blessed Badr al-Din Hasan they damned the hunchback, saying, "Verily this youth and none else deserveth our bride. Ah, wellaway for such a lovely one with this hideous Quasimodo! Allah's curse light on his head and on the Sultan who commanded the marriage!"

Then the singing girls beat their tabrets and lullilooed with joy, announcing the appearing of the bride, and the Wazir's daughter came in surrounded by her tirewomen, who had made her goodly to look upon. For they had perfumed her and incensed her and adorned her hair, and they had robed her in raiment and ornaments befitting the mighty Chosroes kings. The most notable part of her dress was a loose robe worn over her other garments. It was diapered in red gold with figures of wild beasts, and birds whose eyes and beaks were of gems and claws of red rubies and green beryl. And her neck was graced with a necklace of Yamani work, worth thousands of gold pieces, whose bezels were great round jewels of sorts, the like of which was never owned by Kaysar or by Tobba king. And the bride was as the full moon when at fullest on fourteenth night, and as she paced into the hall she was like one of the houris of Heaven—praise be to Him who created her in such splendor of beauty! The ladies encompassed her as the white contains the black of the eye, they clustering like stars whilst she shone amongst them like the moon when it eats up the clouds.

Now Badr al-Din Hasan of Bassorah was sitting in full gaze of the folk when the bride came forward with her graceful swaying and swimming gait, and her hunchbacked bridegroom stood up to meet and receive her. She, however, turned away from the wight and walked forward till she stood before her cousin Hasan, the son of her uncle. Whereat the people laughed. But when the wedding guests saw her thus attracted toward Badr al-Din, they made a mighty clamor and the singing women shouted their loudest. Whereupon he put his hand into his pocket and, pulling out a handful of gold, cast it into their tambourines, and the girls rejoiced and said, "Could we win our wish, this bride were thine!" At this he smiled and the folk came round him, flambeaux in hand, like the eyeball round the pupil, while the Gobbo bridegroom was left sitting alone much like a tailless baboon. For every time they lighted a candle for him it went out willy-nilly, so he was left in darkness and silence and looking at naught but himself.

When Badr al-Din Hasan saw the bridegroom sitting lonesome in the dark, and all the wedding guests with their flambeaux and wax candles crowding about himself, he was bewildered and marveled much, but when he looked at his cousin, the daughter of his uncle, he rejoiced and felt an inward delight. He longed to greet her, and gazed intently on her face, which was radiant with light and brilliancy. Then the tirewomen took off her veil and displayed her in all her seven toilettes before Badr al-Din Hasan, wholly neglecting the Gobbo, who sat moping alone, and when she opened her eyes, she said, "O Allah, make this man my goodman and deliver me from the evil of this hunchbacked groom." As soon as they had made an end of this part of the ceremony they dismissed the wedding guests, who went forth, women, children and all, and none remained save Hasan and the hunchback, whilst the tirewomen led the bride into an inner room to change her garb and gear and get her ready for the bridegroom.

Thereupon Quasimodo came up to Badr al-Din Hasan and said: "O my lord, thou hast cheered us this night with thy good company and overwhelmed us with thy kindness and courtesy, but now why not get thee up and go?" "Bismillah," he answered. "In Allah's name, so be it!" And rising, he went forth by the door, where the Ifrit met him and said, "Stay in thy stead, O Badr al-Din, and when the hunchback goes out to the closet of ease, go in without losing time and seat thyself in the alcove, and when the bride comes say to her: "'Tis I am thy husband, for the King devised this trick only fearing for thee the evil eye, and he whom thou sawest is but a syce, a groom, one of our stablemen.' Then walk boldly up to her and unveil her face, for jealousy hath taken us of this matter."

While Hasan was still talking with the Ifrit, behold, the groom fared forth from the hall and entering the closet of ease, sat down on the stool. Hardly had he done this when the Ifrit came out of the tank, wherein the water was, in semblance of a mouse and squeaked out "Zeek!" Quoth the hunchback, "What ails thee?" And the mouse grew and grew till it became a coal-black cat and caterwauled "Miaow! Miaow!" Then it grew still more and more till it became a dog and barked out, "Owh! Owh!" When the bridegroom saw this, he was frightened and exclaimed "Out with thee, O unlucky one!" But the dog grew and swelled till it became an ass colt that brayed and snorted in his face, "Hauk! Hauk!" Whereupon the hunchback quaked and cried, "Come to my aid, O people of the house!" But behold, the ass colt grew and became big as a buffalo and walled the way before him and spake with the voice of the sons of Adam, saying, "Woe to thee, O thou hunchback, thou stinkard, O thou filthiest of grooms!"

Hearing this, the groom was seized with a colic and he sat down on the jakes in his clothes with teeth chattering and knocking together. Quoth the Ifrit, "Is the world so strait to thee thou findest none to marry save my ladylove?" But as he was silent the Ifrit continued, "Answer me or I will do thee dwell in the dust!" "By Allah," replied the Gobbo, "O King of the Buffaloes, this is no fault of mine, for they forced me to wed her, and verily I wot not that she had a lover amongst the buffaloes. But now I repent, first before Allah and then before thee." Said the Ifrit to him: "I swear to thee that if thou fare forth from this place, or thou utter a word before sunrise, I assuredly will wring thy neck. When the sun rises, wend thy went and never more return to this house." So saying, the Ifrit took up the Gobbo bridegroom and set him head downward and feet upward in the slit of the privy, and said to him: "I will leave thee here, but I shall be on the lookout for thee till sunrise, and if thou stir before then, I will seize thee by the feet and dash out thy brains against the wall. So look out for thy life!"

Thus far concerning the hunchback, but as regards Badr al-Din Hasan of Bassorah, he left the Gobbo and the Ifrit jangling and wrangling and, going into the house, sat him down in the very middle of the alcove. And behold, in came the bride attended by an old woman, who stood at the door and said, "O Father of Uprightness, arise and take what God giveth thee." Then the old woman went away and the bride, Sitt al-Husn or the Lady of Beauty hight, entered the inner part of the alcove brokenhearted and saying in herself, "By Allah, I will never yield my person to him—no, not even were he to take my life!"

But as she came to the further end she saw Badr al-Hasan and she said, "Dearling! Art thou still sitting here? By Allah, I was wishing that thou wert my bridegroom, or at least that thou and the hunchbacked horsegroom were partners in me." He replied, "O beautiful lady, how should the syce have access to thee, and how should he share in thee with me?" "Then," quoth she, "who *is* my husband, thou or he?" "Sitt al-Husn," rejoined Hasan, "we have not done this for mere fun, but only as a device to ward off the evil eye from thee. For when the tirewomen and singers and wedding guests saw thy beauty being displayed to me, they feared fascination, and thy father hired the horsegroom for ten dinars and a porringer of meat to take the evil eye off us, and now he hath received his hire and gone his gait."

When the Lady of Beauty heard these words she smiled and rejoiced and laughed a pleasant laugh. Then she whispered him: "By the Lord, thou hast quenched a fire which tortured me and now, by Allah, O my little dark-haired darling, take me to thee and press me to thy bosom!" Then she began singing:

> "By Allah, set thy foot upon my soul,
> Since long, long years for this alone I long.
> And whisper tale of love in ear of me,
> To me 'tis sweeter than the sweetest song!
> No other youth upon my heart shall lie,
> So do it often, dear, and do it long."

Then she stripped off her outer gear and she threw open her chemise from the neck downward and showed her person and all the rondure of her hips. When Badr al-Din saw the glorious sight, his desires were roused, and he arose and doffed his clothes, and wrapping up in his bag trousers the purse of gold which he had taken from the Jew and which contained the thousand dinars, he laid it under the edge of the bedding. Then he took off his turban and set it upon the settle atop of his other clothes, remaining in his skullcap and fine shirt of blue silk laced with gold. Whereupon the Lady of Beauty drew him to her and he did likewise. Then he took her to his embrace and found her a pearl unpierced, and he abaged her virginity and had joyance of her youth in his virility; and she conceived by him that very night. Then he laid his hand under her head and she did the same and they embraced and fell asleep in each other's arms, as a certain poet said of such lovers in these couplets:

> Visit thy lover, spurn what envy told,
> No envious churl shall smile on love ensouled.
> Merciful Allah made no fairer sight
> Than coupled lovers single couch doth hold,
> Breast pressing breast and robed in joys their own,
> With pillowed forearms cast in finest mold.
> And when heart speaks to heart with tongue of love,
> Folk who would part them hammer steel ice-cold.
> If a fair friend thou find who cleaves to thee,
> Live for that friend, that friend in heart enfold.
> O ye who blame for love us lover-kind,
> Say, can ye minister to diseasèd mind?

This much concerning Badr al-Din Hasan and Sitt al-Husn his cousin, but as regards the Ifrit, as soon as he saw the twain asleep, he said to the Ifritah: "Arise, slip thee under the youth, and let us carry him back to his place ere dawn overtake us, for the day is near-hand." Thereupon she came forward and getting under him as he lay asleep, took him up clad only in his fine blue shirt, leaving the rest of his garments, and ceased not flying (and the Ifrit vying with her in flight) till the dawn advised them that it had come upon them midway, and the muezzin began his call from the minaret: "Haste ye to salvation! Haste ye to salvation!" Then Allah suffered His angelic host to shoot down the Ifrit with a shooting star, so he was consumed, but the Ifritah escaped, and she descended with Badr al-Din at the place where the Ifrit was burnt, and did not carry him back to Bassorah, fearing lest he come to harm.

Now by the order of Him who predestineth all things, they alighted at Damascus of Syria, and the Ifritah set down her burden at one of the city gates and flew away. When day arose and the doors were opened, the folk who came forth saw a handsome youth, with no other raiment but his blue shirt of gold-embroidered silk and skullcap, lying upon the ground drowned in sleep after the hard labor of the night, which had not suffered him to take his rest. So the folk, looking at him, said: "Oh, her luck with whom this one spent the night! But would he had waited to don his garments!" Quoth another: "A sorry lot are the sons of great families! Haply he but now came forth of the tavern on some occasion of his own and his wine flew to his head, whereby he hath missed the place he was making for and strayed till he came to the gate of the city, and finding it shut, lay him down and went to by-by!"

As the people were bandying guesses about him, suddenly the morning breeze blew upon Badr al-Din and raising his shirt to his middle, showed a stomach and navel with something below it, and legs and thighs clear as crystal and smooth as cream. Cried the people, "By Allah, he is a pretty fellow!" and at the cry Badr al-Din awoke and found himself lying at a city gate with a crowd gathered around him. At this he greatly marveled and asked: "Where am I, O good folk, and what causeth you thus to gather round me, and what have I had to do with you?" and they answered: "We found thee lying here asleep during the call to dawn prayer, and this is all we know of the matter. But where diddest thou lie last night?" "By Allah, O good people," replied he, "I lay last night in Cairo." Said somebody, "Thou hast surely been eating hashish," and another, "He is a fool," and a third, "He is a *citrouille*," and a fourth asked him: "Art thou out of thy mind? Thou sleepest in Cairo and thou wakest in the morning at the gate of Damascus city!" Cried he: "By Allah, my good people, one and all, I lie not to you. Indeed I lay yesternight in the land of Egypt and yesternoon I was at Bassorah." Quoth one, "Well! well!" and quoth another, "Ho! ho!" and a third, "So! so!" and a fourth cried, "This youth is mad, is possessed of the Jinni!" So they clapped hands at him and said to one another: "Alas, the pity of it for his youth! By Allah, a madman! And madness is no respecter of persons."

Then said they to him: "Collect thy wits and return to thy reason! How couldest thou be in Bassorah yesterday and in Cairo yesternight and withal awake in Damascus this morning?" But he persisted, "Indeed I was a bridegroom in Cairo last night." "Belike thou hast been dreaming," rejoined they, "and sawest all this in thy sleep." So Hasan took thought for a while and said to them: "By Allah, this is no dream, nor visionlike doth it seem! I certainly was in Cairo, where they displayed the bride before me, in presence of a third person, the hunchback groom, who was sitting hard by. By Allah, O my brother, this be no dream, and if it were a dream, where is the bag of gold I bore with me, and where are my turban and my robe, and my trousers?"

Then he rose and entered the city, threading its highways and byways and bazaar streets, and the people pressed upon him and jeered at him, crying out "Madman! Madman!" till he, beside himself with rage, took refuge in a cook's shop. Now that cook had been a trifle too clever—that is, a rogue and thief—but Allah had made him repent and turn from his evil ways and open a cookshop, and all the people of Damascus stood in fear of his boldness and his mischief. So when the crowd saw the youth enter his shop, they dispersed, being afraid of him, and went their ways. The cook looked at Badr al-Din and, noting his beauty and loveliness, fell in love with him forthright and said: "Whence comest thou, O youth? Tell me at once thy tale, for thou art become dearer to me than my soul." So Hasan recounted to him all that had befallen him from beginning to end (but in repetition there is no fruition) and the cook said: "O my lord Badr al-Din, doubtless thou knowest that this case is wondrous and this story marvelous. Therefore, O my son, hide what hath betide thee, till Allah dispel what ills be thine, and tarry with me here the meanwhile, for I have no child and I will adopt thee." Badr al-Din replied, "Be it as thou wilt, O my uncle!" Whereupon the cook went to the bazaar and bought him a fine suit of clothes and made him don it, then fared with him to the kazi, and formally declared that he was his son. So Badr al-Din Hasan became known in Damascus city as the cook's son, and he sat with him in the shop to take the silver, and on this wise he sojourned there for a time.

Thus far concerning him, but as regards his cousin, the Lady of Beauty, when morning dawned she awoke and missed Badr al-Din Hasan from her side; but she thought that he had gone to the privy and she sat expecting him for an hour or so, when behold, entered her father Shams al-Din Mohammed, Wazir of Egypt. Now he was disconsolate by reason of what had befallen him through the Sultan, who had entreated him harshly and had married his daughter by force to the lowest of his menials and he too a lump of a groom hunchbacked withal, and he said to himself, "I will slay this daughter of mine if of her own free will she had yielded her person to this accursed carle." So he came to the door of the bride's private chamber, and said, "Ho! Sitt al-Husn." She answered him: "Here am I! Here am I! O my lord," and came out unsteady of gait after the pains and pleasures of the night. And she kissed his hand, her face showing redoubled brightness and beauty for having lain in the arms of that gazelle, her cousin.

When her father, the Wazir, saw her in such case, he asked her, "O thou accursed, art thou rejoicing because of this horse groom?" And Sitt al-Husn smiled sweetly and answered: "By Allah, don't ridicule me. Enough of what passed yesterday when folk laughed at me, and evened me with that groom fellow who is not worthy to bring my husband's shoes or slippers—nay, who is not worth the paring of my husband's nails! By the Lord, never in my life have I nighted a night so sweet as yesternight, so don't mock by reminding me of the Gobbo." When her parent heard her words he was filled with fury, and his eyes glared and stared, so that little of them showed save the whites and he cried: "Fie upon thee! What words are these? 'Twas the hunchbacked horse groom who passed the night with thee!" "Allah upon thee," replied the Lady of Beauty, "do not worry me about the Gobbo—Allah damn his father—and leave jesting with me, for this groom was only hired for ten dinars and a porringer of meat and he took his wage and went his way. As for me, I entered the bridal chamber, where I found my true bridegroom sitting, after the singer women had displayed me to him—the same who had crossed their hands with red gold till every pauper that was present waxed wealthy. And I passed the night on the breast of my bonny man, a most lively darling, with his black eyes and joined eyebrows."

When her parent heard these words, the light before his face became night, and he cried out at her, saying: "O thou whore! What is this thou tellest me? Where be thy wits?" "O my father," she rejoined, "thou breakest my heart. Enough for thee that thou hast been so hard upon me! Indeed my husband who took my virginity is but just now gone to the draught-house, and I feel that I have conceived by him." The Wazir rose in much marvel and entered the privy, where he found the hunchbacked horse groom with his head in the hole and his heels in the air. At this sight he was confounded and said, "This is none other than he, the rascal hunchback!" So he called to him, "Ho, Hunchback!" The Gobbo grunted out, *"Taghum! Taghum!"*

thinking it was the Ifrit spoke to him, so the Wazir shouted at him and said, "Speak out, or I'll strike off thy pate with this sword." Then quoth the hunchback, "By Allah, O Sheikh of the Ifrits, ever since thou settest me in this place I have not lifted my head, so Allah upon thee, take pity and entreat me kindly!"

When the Wazir heard this he asked: "What is this thou sayest? I'm the bride's father and no Ifrit." "Enough for thee that thou hast well-nigh done me die," answered Quasimodo. "Now go thy ways before he come upon thee who hath served me thus. Could ye not marry me to any save the ladylove of buffaloes and the beloved of Ifrits? Allah curse her, and curse him who married me to her and was the cause of this my case." Then said the Wazir to him, "Up and out of this place!" "Am I mad," cried the groom, "that I should go with thee without leave of the Ifrit whose last words to me were: 'When the sun rises, arise and go thy gait.' So hath the sun risen, or no? For I dare not budge from this place till then." Asked the Wazir, "Who brought thee hither?" And he answered, "I came here yesternight for a call of nature and to do what none can do for me, when lo! a mouse came out of the water, and squeaked at me and swelled and waxed gross till it was big as a buffalo, and spoke to me words that entered my ears. Then he left me here and went away. Allah curse the bride and him who married me to her!"

The Wazir walked up to him and lifted his head out of the cesspool hole, and he fared forth running for dear life and hardly crediting that the sun had risen, and repaired to the Sultan, to whom he told all that had befallen him with the Ifrit. But the Wazir returned to the bride's private chamber, sore troubled in spirit about her, and said to her, "O my daughter, explain this strange matter to me!" Quoth she: "'Tis simply this. The bridegroom to whom they displayed me yestereve lay with me all night, and took my virginity, and I am with child by him. He is my husband, and if thou believe me not, there are his turban twisted as it was, lying on the settle and his dagger and his trousers beneath the bed with a something, I wot not what, wrapped up in them."

When her father heard this, he entered the private chamber and found the turban which had been left there by Badr al-Din Hasan, his brother's son, and he took it in hand and turned it over, saying, "This is the turban worn by Wazirs, save that it is of Mosul stuff." So he opened it and, finding what seemed to be an amulet sewn up in the fez, he unsewed the lining and took it out. Then he lifted up the trousers, wherein was the purse of the thousand gold pieces and opening that also, found in it a written paper. This he read, and it was the sale receipt of the Jew in the name of Badr al-Din Hasan son of Nur al-Din Ali, the Egyptian, and the thousand dinars were also there.

No sooner had Shams al-Din read this than he cried out with a loud cry and fell to the ground fainting, and as soon as he revived and understood the gist of the matter he marveled and said: "There is no god but *the* God, whose All-might is over all things! Knowest thou, O my daughter, who it was that became the husband of thy virginity?" "No," answered she, and he said: "Verily he is the son of my brother, thy cousin, and this thousand dinars is thy dowry. Praise be to Allah! And would I wot how this matter came about!" Then opened he the amulet which was sewn up and found therein a paper in the handwriting of his deceased brother, Nur al-Din the Egyptian, father of Badr al-Din Hasan. And when he saw the handwriting, he kissed it again and again, and he wept and wailed over his dead brother. Then he read the scroll and found in it recorded the dates of his brother's marriage with the daughter of the Wazir of Bassorah, and of his going in to her, and her conception, and the birth of Badr al-Din Hasan, and all his brother's history and doings up to his dying day.

So he marveled much and shook with joy and, comparing the dates with his own marriage and going in unto his wife and the birth of his daughter, Sitt al-Husn, he found that they perfectly agreed. So he took the document and, repairing with it to the Sultan, acquainted him with what had passed, from first to last, whereat the King marveled and commanded the case to be at once recorded. The Wazir abode that day expecting to see his brother's son, but he came not, and he waited a second day, a third day, and so on to the seventh day without any tidings of him. So he said, "By Allah, I will do a deed such as none hath ever done before me!" And he took reed pen and ink and drew upon a sheet of paper the plan of the whole house, showing whereabouts was the private chamber with the curtain in such a place and the furniture in such another and so on with all that was in the room. Then he folded up the sketch and, causing all the furniture to be collected, he took Badr al-Din's garments and the turban and fez and robe and purse, and carried the whole to his house and locked them up, against the coming of his nephew, Badr al-Din Hasan, the son of his lost brother, with an iron padlock on which he set his seal.

As for the Wazir's daughter, when her tale of months was fulfilled, she bare a son like the full moon, the image of his father in beauty and loveliness and fair proportions and perfect grace. They cut his navel string and kohled his eyelids to strengthen his eyes, and gave him over to the nurses and nursery governesses, naming him Ajib, the Wonderful. His day was as a month and his month was as a year, and when seven years had passed over him, his grandfather sent him to school, enjoining the master to teach him Koran-reading, and to educate him well. He remained at the school four years, till he began to bully his schoolfellows and abuse them and bash them and thrash them and say: "Who among you is like me? I am the son of the Wazir of Egypt!"

At last the boys came in a body to complain to the monitor of what hard usage they were wont to have from Ajib, and he said to them: "I will tell you somewhat you may do to him so that he shall leave off coming to the school, and it is this. When he enters tomorrow, sit ye down about him and say some one of you to some other: 'By Allah, none shall play with us at this game except he tell us the names of his mamma and papa, for he who knows not the names of his mother and his father is a bastard, a son of adultery, and he shall not play with us.'" When morning dawned, the boys came to school, Ajib being one of them, and all flocked round him saying: "We will play a game wherein none shall join save he can tell the name of his mamma and his papa." And they all cried, "By Allah, good!" Then quoth one of them, "My name is Majid and my mammy's name is Alawiyah and my daddy's Izz al-Din." Another spoke in like guise and yet a third, till Ajib's turn came, and he said, "My name is Ajib, and my mother's is Sitt al-Husn, and my father's Shams al-Din, the Wazir of Cairo." "By Allah," cried they, "the Wazir is not thy true father." Ajib answered, "The Wazir is my father in very deed." Then the boys all laughed and clapped their hands at him, saying: "He does not know who is his papa. Get out from among us, for none shall play with us except he know his father's name."

Thereupon they dispersed from around him and laughed him to scorn, so his breast was straitened and he well-nigh choked with tears and hurt feelings. Then said the monitor to him: "We know that the

Wazir is thy grandfather, the father of thy mother, Sitt al-Husn, and not thy father. As for thy father, neither dost thou know him nor yet do we, for the Sultan married thy mother to the hunchbacked horse groom, but the Jinni came and slept with her and thou hast no known father. Leave, then, comparing thyself too advantageously with the littles ones of the school, till thou know that thou hast a lawful father, for until then thou wilt pass for a child of adultery amongst them. Seest thou not that even a huckster's son knoweth his own sire? Thy grandfather is the Wazir of Egypt, but as for thy father, we wot him not and we say indeed that thou hast none. So return to thy sound senses!"

When Ajib heard these insulting words from the monitor and the schoolboys and understood the reproach they put upon him, he went out at once and ran to his mother, Sitt al-Husn, to complain, but he was crying so bitterly that his tears prevented his speech for a while. When she heard his sobs and saw his tears, her heart burned as though with fire for him, and she said: "O my son, why dost thou weep? Allah keep the tears from thine eyes! Tell me what hath betided thee." So he told her all that he heard from the boys and from the monitor and ended with asking, "And who, O my mother, is my father?" She answered, "Thy father is the Wazir of Egypt." But he said: "Do not lie to me. The Wazir is thy father, not mine! Who then is my father? Except thou tell me the very truth I will kill myself with this hanger."

When his mother heard him speak of his father she wept, remembering her cousin and her bridal night with him and all that occurred there and then, and she repeated these couplets:

> "Love in my heart they lit and went their ways,
> And all I love to furthest lands withdrew,
> And when they left me sufferance also left,
> And when we parted Patience bade adieu.
> They fled and flying with my joys they fled,
> In very constancy my spirit flew.
> They made my eyelids flow with severance tears
> And to the parting pang these drops are due.
> And when I long to see reunion day,
> My groans prolonging sore for ruth I sue.
> Then in my heart of hearts their shapes I trace,
> And love and longing care and cark renew.

> O ye whose names cling round me like a cloak,
> Whose love yet closer than a shirt I drew,
> Beloved ones, how long this hard despite?
> How long this severance and this coy shy flight?"

Then she wailed and shrieked aloud and her son did the like, and behold, in came the Wazir, whose heart burnt within him at the sight of their lamentations and he said, "What makes you weep?" So the Lady of Beauty acquainted him with what happened between her son and the schoolboys, and he also wept, calling to mind his brother and what had past between them and what had betided his daughter and how he had failed to find out what mystery there was in the matter. Then he rose at once and, repairing to the audience hall, went straight to the King and told his tale and craved his permission to travel eastward to the city of Bassorah and ask after his brother's son. Furthermore, he besought the Sultan to write for him letters patent, authorizing him to seize upon Badr al-Din, his nephew and son-in-law, wheresoever he might find him. And he wept before the King, who had pity on him and wrote royal autographs to his deputies in all climes and countries and cities, whereat the Wazir rejoiced and prayed for blessings on him.

Then, taking leave of his sovereign, he returned to his house, where he equipped himself and his daughter and his adopted child Ajib with all things meet for a long march, and set out and traveled the first day and the second and the third and so forth till he arrived at Damascus city. The Wazir encamped on the open space called Al-Hasa, and after pitching tents, said to his servants, "A halt here for two days!" So they went into the city upon their several occasions, this to sell and that to buy, this to go to the hammam and that to visit the cathedral mosque of the Banu Umayyah, the Ommiades, whose like is not in this world. Ajib also went, with his attendant eunuch, for solace and diversion to the city, and the servant followed with a quarterstaff of almond wood so heavy that if he struck a camel therewith the beast would never rise again.

When the people of Damascus saw Ajib's beauty and brilliancy and perfect grace and symmetry (for he was a marvel of comeliness and winning loveliness, softer than the cool breeze of the North, sweeter than limpid waters to man in drought, and pleasanter than the health for which sick man sueth), a mighty many followed him, whilst others ran on before and sat down on the road until he should come up, that they might gaze on him, till, as Destiny had decreed, the eunuch stopped opposite the shop of Ajib's father, Badr al-Din Hasan. Now his beard had grown long and thick and his wits had ripened during the twelve years which had passed over him, and the cook and ex-rogue having died, the so-called Hasan of Bassorah had succeeded to his goods and shop, for that he had been formally adopted before the kazi and witnesses. When his son and the eunuch stepped before him, he gazed on Ajib and, seeing how very beautiful he was, his heart fluttered and throbbed, and blood drew to blood and natural affection spake out and his bowels yearned over him. He had just dressed a conserve of pomegranate grains with sugar, and Heaven-implanted love wrought within him, so he called to his son Ajib and said: "O my lord, O thou who hast gotten the mastery of my heart and my very vitals and to whom my bowels yearn, say me, wilt thou enter my house and solace my soul by eating of my meat?"

Then his eyes streamed with tears which he could not stay, for he bethought him of what he had been and what he had become. When Ajib heard his father's words, his heart also yearned himward, and he looked at the eunuch and said to him: "Of a truth, O my good guard, my heart yearns to this cook. He is as one that hath a son far away from him. So let us enter and gladden his heart by tasting of his hospitality. Perchance for our so doing Allah may reunite me with my father." When the eunuch heard these words, he cried: "A fine thing this, by Allah! Shall the sons of Wazirs be seen eating in a common cookshop? Indeed I keep off the folk from thee with this quarterstaff lest they even look upon thee, and I dare not suffer thee to enter this shop at all."

When Hasan of Bassorah heard his speech he marveled and turned to the eunuch with the tears pouring down his cheeks, and Ajib said, "Verily my heart loves him!" But he answered: "Leave this talk. Thou shalt not go in." Thereupon the father turned to the eunuch and said, "O worthy sir, why wilt thou not gladden my soul by entering my shop? O thou who art like a chestnut, dark without but white of heart within! O thou of the like of whom a certain poet said . . ." The eunuch burst out a-laughing and asked: "Said what? Speak out, by Allah, and be quick about it." So Hasan the Bassorite began reciting these couplets:

"If not master of manners or aught but discreet,
In the household of kings no trust could he take,
And then for the harem! What eunuch is he
Whom angels would serve for his service' sake?"

The eunuch marveled and was pleased at these words, so he took Ajib by the hand and went into the cook's shop; whereupon Hasan the Bassorite ladled into a saucer some conserve of pomegranate grains wonderfully good, dressed with almonds and sugar, saying: "You have honored me with your company. Eat, then, and health and happiness to you!" Thereupon Ajib said to his father, "Sit thee down and eat with us, so perchance Allah may unite us with him we long for." Quoth Hasan, "O my son, hast thou then been afflicted in thy tender years with parting from those thou lovest?" Quoth Ajib: "Even so, O nuncle mine. My heart burns for the loss of a beloved one who is none other than my father, and indeed I come forth, I and my grandfather, to circle and search the world for him. Oh, the pity of it, and how I long to meet him!" Then he wept with exceeding weeping, and his father also wept seeing him weep and for his own bereavement, which recalled to him his long separation from dear friends and from his mother, and the eunuch was moved to pity for him.

Then they ate together till they were satisfied, and Ajib and the slave rose and left the shop. Hereat Hasan the Bassorite felt as though his soul had departed his body and had gone with them, for he could not lose sight of the boy during the twinkling of an eye, albeit he knew not that Ajib was his son. So he locked up his shop and hastened after them, and he walked so fast that he came up with them before they had gone out of the western gate. The eunuch turned and asked him, "What ails thee?" and Badr al-Din answered, "When ye went from me, meseemed my soul had gone with you, and as I had business without the city gate, I purposed to bear you company till my matter was ordered, and so return." The eunuch was angered, and said to Ajib: "This is just what I feared! We ate that unlucky mouthful (which we are bound to respect), and here is the fellow following us from place to place, for the vulgar are ever the vulgar."

Ajib, turning and seeing the cook just behind him, was wroth, and his face reddened with rage and he said to the servant: "Let him walk the highway of the Moslems, but when we turn off it to our tents and find that he still follows us, we will send him about his business with a flea in his ear." Then he bowed his head and walked on, the eunuch walking behind him. But Hasan of Bassorah followed them to the plain Al-Hasa, and as they drew near to the tents, they turned round and saw him close on their heels, so Ajib was very angry, fearing that the eunuch might tell his grandfather what had happened. His indignation was the hotter for apprehension lest any say that after he had entered a cookshop the cook had followed him. So he turned and looked at Hasan of Bassorah and found his eyes fixed on his own, for the father had become a body without a soul, and it seemed to Ajib that his eye was a treacherous eye or that he was some lewd fellow.

So his rage redoubled and, stooping down, he took up a stone weighing half a pound and threw it at his father. It struck him on the forehead, cutting it open from eyebrow to eyebrow and causing the blood to stream down, and Hasan fell to the ground in a swoon whilst Ajib and the eunuch made for the tents. When the father came to himself, he wiped away the blood and tore off a strip from his turban and bound up his head, blaming himself the while, and saying, "I wronged the lad by shutting up my shop and following, so that he thought I was some evil-minded fellow." Then he returned to his place, where he busied himself with the sale of his sweetmeats, and he yearned after his mother at Bassorah, and wept over her and broke out repeating:

> "Unjust it were to bid the world be just
> And blame her not. She ne'er was made for justice.
> Take what she gives thee, leave all grief aside,
> For now to fair and then to foul her lust is."

So Hasan of Bassorah set himself steadily to sell his sweetmeats, but the Wazir, his uncle, halted in Damascus three days and then marched upon Emesa, and passing through that town, he made inquiry there, and at every place where he rested. Thence he fared on by way of Hamah and Aleppo and thence through Diyar Bakr and Maridin and Mosul, still inquiring, till he arrived at Bassorah city. Here, as soon as he had secured a lodging, he presented himself before the Sultan, who entreated him with high honor and the respect due to his rank, and asked the cause of his coming. The Wazir acquainted him with his history and told him that the Minister Nur al-Din was his brother, whereupon the Sultan exclaimed, "Allah have mercy upon him!" and added: "My good Sahib, he was my Wazir for fifteen years and I loved him exceedingly. Then he died leaving a son who abode only a single month after his father's death, since which time he has disappeared and we could gain no tidings of him. But his mother, who is the daughter of my former Minister, is still among us."

When the Wazir Shams al-Din heard that his nephew's mother was alive and well, he rejoiced and said, "O King, I much desire to meet her." The King on the instant gave him leave to visit her, so he betook himself to the mansion of his brother Nur al-Din and cast sorrowful glances on all things in and around it and kissed the threshold. Then he bethought him of his brother Nur al-Din Ali, and how he had died in a strange land far from kith and kin and friends, and he wept and repeated these lines:

> "I wander 'mid these walls, my Lavla's walls,
> And kissing this and other wall I roam.
> 'Tis not the walls or roof my heart so loves,
> But those who in this house had made their home."

Then he passed through the gate into a courtyard and found a vaulted doorway builded of hardest syenite inlaid with sundry kinds of multicolored marble. Into this he walked, and wandered about the house and, throwing many a glance around, saw the name of his brother Nur al-Din written in gold wash upon the walls. So he went up to the inscription and kissed it and wept and thought of how he had been separated from his brother and had now lost him forever.

Then he walked on till he came to the apartment of his brother's widow, the mother of Badr al-Din Hasan, the Egyptian. Now from the time of her son's disappearance she had never ceased weeping and wailing through the light hours and the dark, and when the years grew longsome with her, she built for him a tomb of marble in the midst of the saloon and there used to weep for him day and night, never sleeping save thereby. When the Wazir drew near her apartment, he heard her voice and stood behind the door while she addressed the sepulcher in verse and said:

"Answer, by Allah! Sepulcher, are all his beauties gone?
Hath change the power to blight his charms, that beauty's paragon?
Thou art not earth, O Sepulcher! Nor art thou sky to me.
How comes it, then, in thee I see conjoint the branch and moon?"

While she was bemoaning herself after this fashion, behold, the Wazir went in to her and saluted her and informed her that he was her husband's brother, and, telling her all that had passed beween them, laid open before her the whole story—how her son Badr al-Din Hasan had spent a whole night with his daughter full ten years ago, but had disappeared in the morning. And he ended with saying: "My daughter conceived by thy son and bare a male child who is now with me, and he is thy son and thy son's son by my daughter." When she heard the tidings that her boy Badr al-Din was still alive and saw her brother-in-law, she rose up to him and threw herself at his feet and kissed them. Then the Wazir sent for Ajib and his grandmother stood up and fell on his neck and wept, but Shams al-Din said to her: "This is no time for weeping. This is the time to get thee ready for traveling with us to the land of Egypt. Haply Allah will reunite me and thee with thy son and my nephew." Replied she, "Hearkening and obedience," and, rising at once, collected her baggage and treasures and her jewels, and equipped herself and her slave girls for the march, whilst the Wazir went to take his leave of the Sultan of Bassorah, who sent by him presents and rarities for the Sultan of Egypt.

Then he set out at once upon his homeward march and journeyed till he came to Damascus city, where he alighted in the usual place and pitched tents, and said to his suite, "We will halt a sennight here to buy presents and rare things for the Sultan." Now Ajib bethought him of the past, so he said to the eunuch: "O Laik, I want a little diversion. Come, let us go down to the great bazaar of Damascus and see what hath become of the cook whose sweetmeats we ate and whose head we broke, for indeed he was kind to us and we entreated him scurvily." The eunuch answered, "Hearing is obeying!" So they went forth from the tents, and the tie of blood drew Ajib toward his father, and forthwith they passed through the gateway, Bab al-Faradis hight, and entered the city and ceased not walking through the streets till they reached the cookshop, where they found Hasan of Bassorah standing at the door. It was near the time of midafternoon prayer, and it so fortuned that he had just dressed a confection of pomegranate grains.

When the twain drew near to him and Ajib saw him, his heart yearned toward him, and noticing the scar of the blow, which time had darkened on his brow, he said to him: "Peace be on thee, O man! Know that my heart is with thee." But when Badr al-Din looked upon his son, his vitals yearned and his heart fluttered, and he hung his head earthward and sought to make his tongue give utterance to his words, but he could not. Then he raised his head humbly and suppliant-wise toward his boy and repeated these couplets:

> "I longed for my beloved, but when I saw his face,
> Abashed I held my tongue and stood with downcast eye,
> And hung my head in dread and would have hid my love,
> But do whatso I would, hidden it would not lie.
> Volumes of plaints I had prepared, reproach and blame,
> But when we met, no single word remembered I."

And then said he to them: "Heal my broken heart and eat of my sweetmeats, for, by Allah, I cannot look at thee but my heart flutters. Indeed I should not have followed thee the other day but that I was beside myself." "By Allah," answered Ajib, "thou dost indeed love us! We ate in thy house a mouthful when we were here before and thou madest us repent for it, for that thou followedst us and wouldst have disgraced us, so now we will not eat aught with thee save on condition that thou make oath not to go out after us nor dog us. Otherwise we will not visit thee again during our present stay, for we shall halt a week here whilst my grandfather buys certain presents for the King." Quoth Hasan of Bassorah, "I promise you this."

So Ajib and the eunuch entered the shop, and his father set before them a saucerful of conserve of pomegranate grains. Said Ajib: "Sit thee down and eat with us. So haply shall Allah dispel our sorrows." Hasan the Bassorite was joyful and sat down and ate with them, but his eyes kept gazing fixedly on Ajib's face, for his very heart and vitals clove to him, and at last the boy said to him: "Did I not tell thee thou art a most noyous dotard? So do stint thy staring in my face!" Hasan kept putting morsels into Ajib's mouth at one time and at another time did the same by the eunuch, and they ate till they were satisfied and could no more. Then all rose up and the cook poured water on their hands, and loosing a silken waist shawl, dried them and sprinkled them with rose-water from a casting bottle he had by him. Then he went out and presently returned with a gugglet of sherbet flavored with rose-water, scented with musk, and cooled with snow, and he set this before them saying, "Complete your kindness to me!" So Ajib took the gugglet and drank and passed it to the eunuch, and it went round till their stomachs were full and they were surfeited with a meal larger than their wont.

Then they went away and made haste in walking till they reached the tents, and Ajib went in to his grandmother, who kissed him and, thinking of her son Badr al-Din Hasan, groaned aloud and wept. Then she asked Ajib: "O my son! Where hast thou been?" And he answered, "In Damascus city." Whereupon she rose and set before him a bit of scone and a saucer of conserve of pomegranate grains (which was too little sweetened), and she said to the eunuch, "Sit down with thy master!" Said the servant to himself: "By Allah, we have no mind to eat. I cannot bear the smell of bread." But he sat down, and so did Ajib, though his stomach was full of what he had eaten already and drunken. Nevertheless he took a bit of the bread and dipped it in the pomegranate conserve and made shift to eat it, but he found it too little sweetened, for he was cloyed and surfeited, so he said, "Faugh, what be this wild-beast stuff?" "O my son," cried his grandmother, "dost thou find fault with my cookery? I cooked this myself and none can cook it as nicely as I can, save thy father, Badr al-Din Hasan." "By Allah, O my lady," Ajib answered, "this dish is nasty stuff, for we saw but now in the city of Bassorah a cook who so dresseth pomegranate grains that the very smell openeth a way to the heart and the taste would make a full man long to eat. And as for this mess compared with his, 'tis not worth either much or little."

When his grandmother heard his words, she waxed wroth with exceeding wrath and looked at the servant and said: "Woe to thee! Dost thou spoil my son, and dost take him into common cookshops?" The eunuch was frightened and denied, saying, "We did not go into the shop, we only passed by it." "By Allah," cried Ajib, "but we *did* go in, and we ate till it came out of our nostrils, and the dish was better than thy dish!" Then his grandmother rose and went and told her brother-in-law, who was incensed against the eunuch, and sending for him, asked him, "Why didst thou take my son into a cookshop?" And the eunuch, being frightened, answered, "We did not go in."

But Ajib said, "We *did* go inside and ate conserve of pomegranate grains till we were full, and the cook gave us to drink of iced and sugared sherbet."

At this the Wazir's indignation redoubled and he questioned the castrato, but as he still denied, the Wazir said to him, "If thou speak sooth, sit down and eat before us." So he came forward and tried to eat, but could not, and threw away the mouthful crying: "O my lord! I am surfeited since yesterday." By this the Wazir was certified that he had eaten at the cook's, and bade the slaves throw him, which they did. Then they came down on him with a rib-basting which burned him till he cried for mercy and help from Allah, saying, "O my master, beat me no more and I will tell thee the truth." Whereupon the Wazir stopped the bastinado and said, "Now speak thou sooth." Quoth the eunuch, "Know then that we did enter the shop of a cook while he was dressing conserve of pomegranate grains, and he set some of it before us. By Allah! I never ate in my life its like, nor tasted aught nastier than this stuff which is now before us." Badr al-Din Hasan's mother was angry at this and said, "Needs must thou go back to the cook and bring me a saucer of conserved pomegranate grains from that which is in his shop and show it to thy master, that he may say which be the better and the nicer, mine or his." Said the unsexed, "I will."

So on the instant she gave him a saucer and a half-dinar and he returned to the shop and said to the cook, "O Sheikh of all Cooks, we have laid a wager concerning thy cookery in my lord's house, for they have conserve of pomegranate grains there also. So give me this half-dinar's worth and look to it, for I have eaten a full meal of stick on account of thy cookery, and so do not let me eat aught more thereof." Hasan of Bassorah laughed and answered: "By Allah, none can dress this dish as it should be dressed save myself and my mother, and she at this time is in a far country." Then he ladled out a saucerful and, finishing it off with musk and rose-water, put it in a cloth, which he sealed, and gave it to the eunuch, who hastened back with it. No sooner had Badr al-Din Hasan's mother tasted it and perceived its fine flavor and the excellence of the cookery then she knew who had dressed it, and she screamed and fell down fainting.

The Wazir, sorely startled, sprinkled rose-water upon her, and after a time she recovered and said: "If my son be yet of this world, none dressed this conserve of pomegranate grains but he, and this cook is my very son Badr al-Din Hasan. There is no doubt of it, nor can there be any mistake, for only I and he knew how to prepare it and I taught him." When the Wazir heard her words, he joyed with exceeding joy and said: "Oh, the longing of me for a sight of my brother's son! I wonder if the days will ever unite us with him! Yet it is to Almighty Allah alone that we look for bringing about this meeting." Then he rose without stay or delay and, going to his suite, said to them, "Be off, some fifty of you, with sticks and staves to the cook's shop and demolish it, then pinion his arms behind him with his own turban, saying, 'It was thou madest that foul mess of pomegranate grains!' And drag him here perforce, but without doing him a harm." And they replied, "It is well."

Then the Wazir rode off without losing an instant to the palace and, forgathering with the Viceroy of Damascus, showed him the Sultan's orders. After careful perusal he kissed the letter and placing it upon his head, said to his visitor, "Who is this offender of thine?" Quoth the Wazir, "A man which is a cook." So the Viceroy at once sent his apparitors to the shop, which they found demolished and everything in it broken to pieces, for whilst the Wazir was riding to the palace his men had done his bidding. Then they awaited his return from the audience, and Hasan of Bassorah, who was their prisoner, kept saying, "I wonder what they have found in the conserve of pomegranate grains to bring things to this pass!"

When the Wazir returned to them after his visit to the Viceroy, who had given him formal permission to take up his debtor and depart with him, on entering the tents he called for the cook. They brought him forward pinioned with his turban, and, when Badr al-Din Hasan saw his uncle, he wept with exceeding weeping and said, "O my lord, what is my offense against thee?" "Art thou the man who dressed that conserve of pomegranate grains?" asked the Wazir, and he answered "Yes! Didst thou find in it aught to call for the cutting off of my head?" Quoth the Wazir, "That were the least of thy deserts!" Quoth the cook, "O my lord, wilt thou not tell me my crime, and what aileth the conserve of pomegranate grains?" "Presently," replied the Wazir, and called aloud to his men, saying "Bring hither the camels."

So they struck the tents and by the Wazir's orders the servants took Badr al-Din Hasan and set him in a chest which they padlocked and put on a camel. Then they departed and stinted not journeying till nightfall, when they halted and ate some victual, and took Badr al-Din

Hasan out of his chest and gave him a meal and locked him up again. They set out once more and traveled till they reached Kimrah, where they took him out of the box and brought him before the Wazir, who asked him, "Art thou he who dressed that conserve of pomegranate grains?" He answered "Yes, O my lord!" and the Wazir said, "Fetter him!" So they fettered him and returned him to the chest and fared on again till they reached Cairo and lighted at the quarter called Al-Raydaniyah. Then the Wazir gave order to take Badr al-Din Hasan out of the chest and sent for a carpenter and said to him, "Make me a cross of wood for this fellow!" Cried Badr al-Din Hasan, "And what wilt thou do with it?" and the Wazir replied, "I mean to crucify thee thereon, and nail thee thereto and parade thee all about the city."

"And why wilt thou use me after this fashion?" "Because of thy villainous cookery of conserved pomegranate grains. How durst thou dress it and sell it lacking pepper?" "And for that it lacked pepper, wilt thou do all this to me? Is it not enough that thou hast broken my shop and smashed my gear and boxed me up in a chest and fed me only once a day?" "Too little pepper! Too little pepper! This is a crime which can be expiated only upon the cross!" Then Badr al-Din Hasan marveled and fell a-mourning for his life, whereupon the Wazir asked him, "Of what thinkest thou?" and he answered him, "Of maggoty heads like thine, for an thou had one ounce of sense, thou hadst not treated me thus." Quoth the Wazir, "It is our duty to punish thee, lest thou do the like again." Quoth Badr al-Din Hasan, "Of a truth my offense were overpunished by the least of what thou hast already done to me, and Allah damn all conserve of pomegranate grains and curse the hour when I cooked it, and would I had died ere this!" But the Wazir rejoined, "There is no help for it. I must crucify a man who sells conserve of pomegranate grains lacking pepper."

All this time the carpenter was shaping the wood and Badr al-Din looked on, and thus they did till night, when his uncle took him and clapped him into the chest, saying, "The thing shall be done tomorrow!" Then he waited till he knew Badr al-Din Hasan to be asleep, when he mounted and, taking the chest up before him, entered the city and rode on to his own house, where he alighted and said to his daughter, Sitt al-Husn, "Praised be Allah Who hath reunited thee with thy husband, the son of thine uncle! Up now, and order the house as it was on thy bridal night." So the servants arose and lit the candles, and the Wazir took out his plan of the nuptial chamber, and directed them what to do till they had set everything in its stead, so that whoever saw it would have no doubt but it was the very night of the marriage. Then he bade them put down Badr al-Din Hasan's turban on the settle, as he had deposited it with his own hand, and in like manner his bag trousers and the purse which were under the mattress, and told his daughter to undress herself and go to bed in the private chamber as on her wedding night, adding: "When the son of thine uncle comes in to thee say to him, 'Thou hast loitered while going to the privy,' and call him to lie by thy side and keep him in converse till daybreak, when we will explain the whole matter to him."

Then he bade take Badr al-Din Hasan out of the chest, after loosing the fetters from his feet and stripping off all that was on him save the fine shirt of blue silk in which he had slept on his wedding night, so that he was well-nigh naked, and trouserless. All this was done whilst he was sleeping on utterly unconscious. Then, by doom of Destiny, Badr al-Din Hasan turned over and awoke, and finding himself in a lighted vestibule, said to himself, "Surely I am in the mazes of some dream." So he rose and went on a little to an inner door and looked in, and lo! he was in the very chamber wherein the bride had been displayed to him, and there he saw the bridal alcove and the settle and his turban and all his clothes.

When he saw this, he was confounded, and kept advancing with one foot and retiring with the other, saying, "Am I sleeping or waking?" And he began rubbing his forehead and saying (for indeed he was thoroughly astounded): "By Allah, verily this is the chamber of the bride who was displayed before me! Where am I, then? I was surely but now in a box!" Whilst he was talking with himself, Sitt al-Husn suddenly lifted the corner of the chamber curtain and said, "O my lord, wilt thou not come in? Indeed thou hast loitered long in the watercloset." When he heard her words and saw her face, he burst out laughing and said, "Of a truth this is a very nightmare among dreams!" Then he went in sighing, and pondered what had come to pass with him and was perplexed about his case, and his affair became yet more obscure to him when he saw his turban and bag trousers and when, feeling the pocket, he found the purse containing the thousand gold pieces. So he stood still and muttered: "Allah is All-knowing! Assuredly I am dreaming a wild waking dream!"

Then said the Lady of Beauty to him, "What ails thee to look puzzled and perplexed?" adding, "Thou wast a very different man during the first of the night!" He laughed and asked her, "How long have I been away from thee?" and she answered him: "Allah preserve thee and His Holy Name be about thee! Thou didst but go out an hour ago for an occasion and return. Are thy wits clean gone?" When Badr al-Din Hasan heard this, he laughed and said: "Thou hast spoken truth, but when I went out from thee, I forgot myself awhile in the draughthouse and dreamed that I was a cook at Damascus and abode there ten years, and there came to me a boy who was of the sons of the great, and with him a eunuch." Here he passed his hand over his forehead and, feeling the scar, cried: "By Allah, O my lady, it must have been true, for he struck my forehead with a stone and cut it open from eyebrow to eyebrow, and here is the mark, so it must have been on wake." Then he added: "But perhaps I dreamt it when we fell asleep, I and thou, in each other's arms, for meseems it was as though I traveled to Damascus without tarboosh and trousers and set up as a cook there."

Then he was perplexed and considered for a while, and said: "By Allah, I also fancied that I dressed a conserve of pomegranate grains and put too little pepper in it. By Allah, I must have slept in the numero-cent and have seen the whole of this is a dream, but how long was that dream!" "Allah upon thee," said Sitt al-Husn, "and what more sawest thou?" So he related all to her, and presently said, "By Allah, had I not woke up, they would have nailed me to a cross of wood!" "Wherefore?" asked she, and he answered: "For putting too little pepper in the conserve of pomegranate grains, and meseemed they demolished my shop and dashed to pieces my pots and pans, destroyed all my stuff, and put me in a box. Then they sent for the carpenter to fashion a cross for me and would have crucified me thereon. Now Alhamdolillah! thanks be to Allah, for that all this happened to me in sleep, and not on wake." Sitt al-Husn laughed and clasped him to her bosom and he her to his.

Then he thought again and said: "By Allah, it could not be save while I was awake. Truly I know not what to think of it." Then he lay down, and all the night he was bewildered about his case, now saying, "I was dreaming!" and then saying, "I was awake!" till morning, when his uncle Shams al-Din, the Wazir, came too him and saluted him. When Badr al-Din Hasan saw him he said: "By Allah, art thou not he who bade bind my hands behind me and smash my shop and nail me to a cross on a matter of conserved pomegranate grains because the dish lacked a sufficiency of pepper?" Whereupon the Wazir said to him: "Know, O my son, that truth hath shown it soothfast and the concealed hath been revealed! Thou art the son of my brother, and I did all this with thee to certify myself that thou wast indeed he who went in unto my daughter that night. I could not be sure of this till I saw that thou knewest the chamber and thy turban and thy trousers and thy gold and the papers in thy writing and in that of thy father, my brother, for I had never seen thee afore that and knew thee not. And as to thy mother, I have prevailed upon her to come with me from Bassorah."

So saying, he threw himself on his nephew's breast and wept for joy, and Badr al-Din Hasan, hearing these words from his uncle, marveled with exceeding marvel and fell on his neck and also shed tears for excess of delight. Then said the Wazir to him, "O my son, the sole cause of all this is what passed between me and thy sire," and he told him the manner of his father wayfaring to Bassorah and all that had occurred to part them. Lastly the Wazir sent for Ajib, and when his father saw him he cried, "And this is he who struck me with the stone!" Quoth the Wazir, "This is thy son!" And Badr al-Din Hasan threw himself upon his boy and began repeating:

> "Long have I wept o'er severance' ban and bane,
> Long from mine eyelids tear rills rail and rain.
> And vowed I if Time reunion bring,
> My tongue from name of "Severance" I'll restrain.
> Joy hath o'ercome me to this stress that I
> From joy's revulsion to shed tears am fain.
> Ye are so trained to tears, O eyne of me!
> You weep with pleasure as you weep in pain."

When he had ended his verse his mother came in and threw herself upon him and began reciting:

> "When we met we complained,
> Our hearts were sore wrung.
> But plaint is not pleasant
> Fro' messenger's tongue."

Then she wept and related to him what had befallen her since his departure, and he told her what he had suffered, and they thanked Allah Almighty for their reunion.

Two days after his arrival the Wazir Shams al-Din went in to the Sultan and, kissing the ground between his hands, greeted him with the greeting due to kings. The Sultan rejoiced at his return and his face brightened and, placing him hard by his side, asked him to relate all he had seen in his wayfaring and whatso had betided him in his going and coming. So the Wazir told him all that had passed from first to last and the Sultan said: "Thanks be to Allah for thy victory and the winning of thy wish and thy safe return to thy children and thy people! And now I needs must see the son of thy brother, Hasan of Bassorah, so bring him to the audience hall tomorrow." Shams al-Din replied, "Thy slave shall stand in thy presence tomorrow, Inshallah, if it be God's will." Then he saluted him and, returning to his own house, informed his nephew of the Sultan's desire to see him, whereto replied Hasan, whilom the Bassorite, "The slave is obedient to the orders of his lord." And the result was that next day he accompanied his uncle, Shams al-Din, to the Divan, and after saluting the Sultan and doing him reverence in most ceremonious obeisance and with most courtly obsequiousness, he began improvising these verses:

> "The first in rank to kiss the ground shall deign
> Before you, and all ends and aims attain.
> You are Honor's fount, and all that hope of you,
> Shall gain more honor than Hope hoped to gain."

The Sultan smiled and signed to him to sit down. So he took a seat close to his uncle, Shams al-Din, and the King asked him his name. Quoth Badr al-Din Hasan, "The meanest of thy slaves is known as Hasan the Bassorite, who is instant in prayer for thee day and night." The Sultan was pleased at his words and, being minded to test his learning and prove his good breeding, asked him, "Dost thou remember any verses in praise of the mole on the cheek?" He answered, "I do," and began reciting:

> "When I think of my love and our parting smart,
> My groans go forth and my tears upstart.
> He's a mole that reminds me in color and charms
> O' the black o' the eye and the grain of the heart."

The King admired and praised the two couplets and said to him: "Quote something else. Allah bless thy sire, and may thy tongue never tire!" So he began:

> "That cheek mole's spot they evened with a grain
> Of Musk, nor did they here the simile strain.
> Nay, marvel at the face comprising all
> Beauty, nor falling short by single grain."

The King shook with pleasure and said to him: "Say more. Allah bless thy days!" So he began:

> "O you whose mole on cheek enthroned recalls
> A dot of musk upon a stone of ruby,
> Grant me your favors! Be not stone at heart!
> Core of my heart, whose only sustenance *you* be!"

Quoth the King: "Fair comparison, O Hasan! Thou hast spoken excellently well and hast proved thyself accomplished in every accomplishment! Now explain to me how many meanings be there in the Arabic language for the word *khal* or *mole*." He replied, "Allah keep the King! Seven and fifty, and some by tradition say fifty." Said the Sultan, "Thou sayest sooth," presently adding, "Hast thou knowledge as to the points of excellence in beauty?" "Yes," answered Badr al-Din Hasan. "Beauty consisteth in brightness of face, clearness of complexion, shapeliness of nose, gentleness of eyes, sweetness of mouth, cleverness of speech, slenderness of shape, and seemliness of all attributes. But the acme of beauty is in the hair and indeed al-Shihab the Hijazi hath brought together all these items in his doggrel verse of the meter Rajaz, and it is this:

> "Say thou to skin 'Be soft,' to face 'Be fair,'
> And gaze, nor shall they blame howso thou stare.
> Fine nose in Beauty's list is high esteemed,
> Nor less an eye full, bright and debonnair.
> Eke did they well to laud the lovely lips
> (Which e'en the sleep of me will never spare),
> A winning tongue, a stature tall and straight,
> A seemly union of gifts rarest rare.
> But Beauty's acme in the hair one views it,
> So hear my strain and with some few excuse it!"

The Sultan was captivated by his converse and, regarding him as a friend, asked, "What meaning is there in the saw 'Shurayh is foxier than the fox'?" And he answered, "Know, O King (whom Almighty Allah keep!), that the legist Shurayh was wont, during the days of the plague, to make a visitation to Al-Najaf, and whenever he stood up to pray, there came a fox which would plant himself facing him and which, by mimicking his movements, distracted him from his devotions. Now when this became longsome to him, one day he doffed his shirt and set it upon a cane and shook out the sleeves. Then, placing his turban on the top and girding its middle with a shawl, he stuck it up in the place where he used to pray. Presently up trotted the fox according to his custom and stood over against the figure, whereupon Shurayh came behind him, and took him. Hence the sayer saith, 'Shurayh is foxier than the fox.'" When the Sultan heard Badr al-Din Hasan's explanation he said to his uncle, Shams al-Din, "Truly this the son of thy brother is perfect in courtly breeding and I do not think that his like can be found in Cairo." At this Hasan arose and kissed the ground before him and sat down again as a Mameluke should sit before his master.

When the Sultan had thus assured himself of his courtly breeding and bearing and his knowledge of the liberal arts and belles-lettres, he joyed with exceeding joy and invested him with a splendid robe of honor and promoted him to an office whereby he might better his condition. Then Badr al-Din Hasan arose and, kissing the ground before the King, wished him continuance of glory and asked leave to retire with his uncle, the Wazir Shams al-Din. The Sultan gave him leave and he issued forth, and the two returned home, where food was set before them and they ate what Allah had given them. After finishing his meal Hasan repaired to the sitting chamber of his wife, the Lady of Beauty, and told her what had past between him and the Sultan, whereupon quoth she: "He cannot fail to make thee a cup companion and give thee largess in excess and load thee with favors and bounties. So shalt thou, by Allah's blessing, dispread, like the greater light, the rays of thy perfection wherever thou be, on shore or on sea." Said he to her, "I purpose to recite a Kasidah, an ode, in his praise, that he may redouble in affection for me." "Thou art right in thine intent," she answered, "so gather thy wits together and weigh thy words, and I shall surely see my husband favored with his highest favor." Thereupon Hasan shut himself up and composed these couplets on a solid base and abounding in inner grace and copied them out in a handwriting of the nicest taste. They are as follows:

> Mine is a Chief who reached most haught estate,
> Treading the pathways of the good and great.
> His justice makes all regions safe and sure,
> And against froward foes bars every gate.
> Bold lion, hero, saint, e'en if you call
> Seraph or Sovran he with all may rate!
> The poorest suppliant rich from him returns,
> All words to praise him were inadequate.
> He to the day of peace is saffron Morn,
> And murky Night in furious warfare's bate.
> Bow 'neath his gifts our necks, and by his deeds
> As King of freeborn souls he 'joys his state.
> Allah increase for us his term of years,
> And from his lot avert all risks and fears!

When he had finished transcribing the lines, he dispatched them in charge of one of his uncle's slaves to the Sultan, who perused them, and his fancy was pleased, so he read them to those present and all praised them with the highest praise. Thereupon he sent for the writer to his sitting chamber and said to him: "Thou art from this day forth my boon companion, and I appoint to thee a monthly solde of a thousand dirhams, over and above that I bestowed on thee aforetime." So Hasan rose and, kissing the ground before the King several times, prayed for the continuance of his greatness and glory and length of life and strength. Thus Badr al-Din Hasan the Bassorite waxed high in honor and his fame flew forth to many regions, and he abode in all comfort and solace and delight of life with his uncle and his own folk till death overtook him.

When the Caliph Harun al-Rashid heard this story from the mouth of his Wazir, Ja'afar the Barmecide, he marveled much and said, "It behooves that these stories be written in letters of liquid gold." Then he set the slaves at liberty and assigned to the youth who had slain his wife such a monthly stipend as sufficed to make his life easy. He also gave him a concubine from amongst his own slave girls, and the young man became one of his cup companions.

THE CITY OF MANY-COLUMNED IRAM AND ABDULLAH SON OF ABI KILABAH

IT is related that Abdullah bin Abi Kilabah went forth in quest of a she-camel which had strayed from him, and as he was wandering in the deserts of Al-Yaman and the district of Saba, behold, he came a great city girt by a vast castle around which were palaces and pavilions that rose high into middle air. He made for the place thinking to find there folk of whom he might ask concerning his she-camel. But when he reached it, he found it desolate, without a living soul in it. So (quoth he) I alighted and, hobbling my dromedary, and composing my mind, entered into the city.

Now when I came to the castle, I found it had two vast gates (never in the world was seen their like for size and height) inlaid with all manner jewels and jacinths, white and red, yellow and green. Beholding this, I marveled with great marvel and thought the case mighty wondrous. Then, entering the citadel in a flutter of fear and dazed with surprise and affright, I found it long and wide, about equaling Al-Medinah in point of size. And therein were lofty palaces laid out in pavilions all built of gold and silver and inlaid with many-colored jewels and jacinths and chrysolites and pearls. And the door leaves in the pavilions were like those of the castle for beauty, and their floors were strewn with great pearls and balls, no smaller than hazelnuts, of musk and ambergris and saffron.

Now when I came within the heart of the city and saw therein no created beings of the Sons of Adam, I was near swooning and dying for fear. Moreover, I looked down from the great roofs of the pavilion chambers and their balconies and saw rivers running under them, and in the main streets were fruit-laden trees and tall palms, and the manner of their building was one brick of gold and one of silver. So I said to myself, "Doubtless this is the Paradise promised for the world to come." Then I loaded me with the jewels of its gravel and the musk of its dust as much as I could carry, and returned to my own country, where I told the folk what I had seen.

After a time the news reached Mu'awiyah, son of Abu Sufyan, who was then Caliph in Al-Hijaz, so he wrote to his lieutenant in San'a of Al-Yaman to send for the teller of the story and question him of the truth of the case. Accordingly the lieutenant summoned me and questioned me of my adventure and of all appertaining to it, and I told him what I had seen, whereupon he dispatched me to Mu'awiyah, before whom I repeated the story of the strange sights, but he would not credit it. So I brought out to him some of the pearls and balls of musk and ambergris and saffron, in which latter there was still some sweet savor, but the pearls were grown yellow and had lost pearly color.

Now Mu'awiyah wondered at this and, sending for Ka'ab al-Ahbar, said to him, "O Ka'ab, I have sent for thee to ascertain the truth of a certain matter and hope that thou wilt be able to certify me thereof." Asked Ka'ab, "What is it, O Commander of the Faithful?" and Mu'awiyah answered, "Wottest thou of any city founded by man which is builded of gold and silver, the pillars whereof are of chrysolite and rubies and its gravel pearls and balls of musk and ambergris and saffron?" He replied, "Yes, O Commander of the Faithful, this is 'Iram with pillars decked and dight, the like of which was never made in the lands,' and the builder was Shaddad son of Ad the Greater." Quoth the Caliph, "Tell us something of its history," and Ka'ab said:

"Ad the Greater had two sons, Shadid and Shaddad, who when their father died ruled conjointly in his stead, and there was no King of the Kings of the earth but was subject to them. After awhile Shadid died and his brother Shaddad reigned over the earth alone. Now he was fond of reading in antique books, and happening upon the description of the world to come and of Paradise, with its pavilions and galleries and trees and fruits and so forth, his soul move him to build the like thereof in this world, after the fashion aforesaid. Now under his hand were a hundred thousand kings, each ruling over a hundred thousand chiefs, commanding each a hundred thousand warriors, so he called these all before him and said to them: 'I find in ancient books and annals a description of Paradise as it is to be in the next world, and I desire to build me its like in this world. Go ye forth therefore to the goodliest tract on earth and the most spacious, and build me there a city of gold and silver, whose gravel shall be chrysolite and rubies and pearls, and for support of its vaults make pillars of jasper. Fill it with palaces, whereon ye shall set galleries and balconies, and plant its lanes and thoroughfares with all manner trees bearing yellow-ripe fruits, and make rivers to run through it in channels of gold and silver.'

"Whereat said one and all, 'How are we able to do this thing thou hast commanded, and whence shall we get the chrysolites and rubies and pearls whereof thou speakest?' Quoth he, 'What! Weet ye not that the kings of the world are subject to me and under my hand and that none therein dare gainsay my word?' Answered they, 'Yes, we know that.' Whereupon the King rejoined, 'Fare ye then to the mines of chrysolites and rubies and pearls and gold and silver and collect their produce and gather together all of value that is in the world, and spare no pains and leave naught. And take also for me such of these things as be in men's hands and let nothing escape you. Be diligent and beware of disobedience.' And thereupon he wrote letters to all the kings of the world and bade them gather together whatso of these things was in their subjects' hands, and get them to the mines of precious stones and metals, and bring forth all that was therein, even from the abysses of the seas.

"This they accomplished in the space of twenty years, for the number of rulers then reigning over the earth was three hundred and sixty kings. And Shaddad presently assembled from all lands and countries architects and engineers and men of art and laborers and handicraftsmen, who dispersed over the world and explored all the wastes and wolds and tracts and holds. At last they came to an uninhabited spot, a vast and fair open plain clear of sand hills and mountains, with founts flushing and rivers rushing, and they said, 'This is the manner of place the King commanded us to seek and ordered us to find.' So they busied themselves in building the city even as bade them Shaddad, King of the whole earth in its length and breadth, leading the fountains in channels and laying the foundations after the prescribed fashion. Moreover, all the kings of earth's several reigns sent thither jewels and precious stones and pearls large and small and carnelian and refined gold and virgin silver upon camels by land, and in great ships over the waters, and there came to the builders' hands of all these materials so great a quantity as may neither be told nor counted nor conceived.

"So they labored at the work three hundred years, and when they had brought it to end, they went to King Shaddad and acquainted him therewith. Then said he: 'Depart and make thereon an impregnable castle, rising and towering high in air, and build around it a thousand pavilions, each upon a thousand columns of chrysolite and ruby and vaulted with gold, that in each pavilion a wazir may dwell.' So they returned forthwith and did this in other twenty years, after which they again presented themselves before King Shaddad and informed him of the accomplishment of his will. Then he commanded his wazirs, who were a thousand in number, and his chief officers and such of his troops and others as he put trust in, to prepare for departure and removal to Many-columned Iram, in the suite and at the stirrup of Shaddad, son of Ad, King of the world, and he bade also such as he would of his women and his harem and of his handmaids and eunuchs make them ready for the journey.

"They spent twenty years in preparing for departure, at the end of which time Shaddad set out with his host, rejoicing in the attainment of his desire till there remained but one day's journey between him and Iram of the Pillars. Then Allah sent down on him and on the stubborn unbelievers with him a mighty rushing sound from the Heavens of His power, which destroyed them all with its vehement clamor, and neither Shaddad nor any of his company set eyes on the city. Moreover, Allah blotted out the road which led to the city, and it stands in its stead unchanged until the Resurrection Day and the Hour of Judgment."

So Mu'awiyah wondered greatly at Ka'ab al-Ahbar's story, and said to him, "Hath any mortal ever made his way to that city?" He replied, "Yes, one of the companions of Mohammed (on whom be blessing and peace!) reached it, doubtless and for sure after the same fashion as this man here seated." And (quoth Al-Sha'abi) it is related, on the authority of learned men of Himyar in Al-Yaman that Shaddad, when destroyed with all his host by the sound, was succeeded in his kingship by his son Shaddad the Less, whom he left viceregent in Hazramaut and Saba when he and his marched upon Many-columned Iram. Now as soon as he heard of his father's death on the road, he caused his body to be brought back from the desert to Hazramaut and bade them hew him out a tomb in a cave, where he laid the body on a throne of gold and threw over the corpse threescore and ten robes of cloth of gold, purfled with precious stones. Lastly at his sire's head he set up a tablet of gold whereon were graven these verses:

> Take warning O proud,
> And in length o' life vain!
> I'm Shaddad son of Ad,
> Of the forts castellain,
> Lord of pillars and power,
> Lord of tried might and main,
> Whom all earth sons obeyed
> For my mischief and bane,
> And who held East and West
> In mine awfulest reign.
> He preached me salvation
> Whom God did assain,
> But we crossed him and asked,
> "Can no refuge be ta'en?"
> When a Cry on us cried
> From th' horizon plain,
> And we fell on the field
> Like the harvested grain,
> And the Fixt Day await
> We, in earth's bosom lain!

Al-Sa'alibi also relateth: It chanced that two men once entered this cave and found steps at its upper end, so they descended and came to an underground chamber, a hundred cubits long by forty wide and a hundred high. In the midst stood a throne of gold, whereon lay a man of huge bulk, filling the whole length and breadth of the throne. He was covered with jewels and raiment gold-and-silver-wrought, and at his head was a tablet of gold bearing an inscription. So they took the tablet and carried it off, together with as many bars of gold and silver and so forth as they could bear away.

And men also relate the tale of

THE SWEEP AND THE NOBLE LADY

DURING the season of the Meccan pilgrimage, whilst the people were making circuit about the Holy House and the place of compassing was crowded, behold, a man laid hold of the covering of the Kaaba and cried out from the bottom of his heart, saying, "I beseech thee, O Allah, that she may once again be wroth with her husband and that I may know her!" A company of the pilgrims heard him and seized him and carried him to the Emir of the pilgrims, after a sufficiency of blows, and, said they, "O Emir, we found this fellow in the Holy Places, saying thus and thus." So the Emir commanded to hang him, but he cried, "O Emir, I conjure thee, by the virtue of the Apostle (whom Allah bless and preserve!), hear my story and then do with me as thou wilt." Quoth the Emir, "Tell thy tale forthright."

"Know then, O Emir," quoth the man, "that I am a sweep who works in the sheep slaughterhouses and carries off the blood and the offal to the rubbish heaps outside the gates. And it came to pass as I went along one day with my ass loaded, I saw the people running away and one of them said to me, 'Enter this alley, lest haply they slay thee.' Quoth I, 'What aileth the folk running away?' and one of the eunuchs who were passing said to me, 'This is the harem of one of the notables, and her eunuchs drive the people out of her way and beat them all, without respect to persons.' So I turned aside with the donkey and stood still awaiting the dispersal of the crowd, and I saw a number of eunuchs with staves in their hands, followed by nigh thirty women slaves, and amongst them a lady as she were a willow wand or a thirsty gazelle, perfect in beauty and grace and amorous languor, and all were attending upon her.

"Now when she came to the mouth of the passage where I stood, she turned right and left and calling one of the castratos, whispered in his ear, and behold, he came up to me and laid hold of me, whilst another eunuch took my ass and made off with it. And when the spectators fled, the first eunuch bound me with a rope and dragged me after him, till I knew not what to do, and the people followed us and cried out, saying: 'This is not allowed of Allah! What hath this poor scavenger done that he should be bound with ropes?' and praying the eunuchs, 'Have pity on him and let him go, so Allah have pity on you!' And I the while said in my mind: 'Doubtless the eunuchry seized me because their mistress smelt the stink of the offal and it sickened her. Belike she is with child or ailing, but there is no Majesty and there is no Might save in Allah, the Glorious, the Great!"

"So I continued walking on behind them till they stopped at the door of a great house, and, entering before me, brought me into a big hall—I know not how I shall describe its magnificence—furnished with the finest furniture. And the women also entered the hall, and I bound and held by the eunuch and saying to myself, 'Doubtless they will torture me here till I die and none know of my death.' However, after a while they carried me into a neat bathroom leading out of the hall, and as I sat there, behold, in came three slave girls, who seated themselves round me and said to me, 'Strip off thy rags and tatters.' So I pulled off my threadbare clothes and one of them fell a-rubbing my legs and feet whilst another scrubbed my head and a third shampooed my body. When they had made an end of washing me, they brought me a parcel of clothes and said to me, 'Put these on,' and I answered, 'By Allah, I know not how!' So they came up to me and dressed me, laughing together at me the while. After which they brought casting bottles full of rose-water, and sprinkled me therewith.

"Then I went out with them into another saloon—by Allah, I know not how to praise its splendor for the wealth of paintings and furniture therein—and entering it, I saw a person seated on a couch of Indian rattan with ivory feet, and before her a number of damsels. When she saw me, she rose to me and called me, so I went up to her and she seated me by her side. Then she bade her slave girls bring food, and they brought all manner of rich meats, such as I never saw in all my life. I do not even know the names of the dishes, much less their nature. So I ate my fill, and when the dishes had been taken away and we had washed our hands, she called for fruits, which came without stay or delay, and ordered me eat of them. And when we had ended eating she bade one of the waiting women bring the wine furniture. So they set on flagons of divers kinds of wine and burned perfumes in all the censers, what while a damsel like the moon rose and served us with wine to the sound of the smitten strings. And I drank, and the lady drank, till we were swized with wine and the whole time I doubted not but that all this was an illusion of sleep.

"Presently, she signed to one of the damsels to spread us a bed in such a place, which being done, she rose and took me by the hand and led me thither, and lay down and I lay with her till the morning, and as often as I pressed her to my breast I smelt the delicious fragrance of musk and other perfumes that exaled from her, and could not think otherwise but that I was in Paradise, or in the vain phantasies of a dream. Now when it was day, she asked me where I lodged and I told her, 'In such a place,' whereupon she gave me leave to depart, handing to me a kerchief worked with gold and silver and containing somewhat tied in it, and took leave of me, saying, 'Go to the bath with this.' I rejoiced and said to myself, 'If there be but five coppers here, it will buy me this day my morning meal.'

"Then I left her, as though I were leaving Paradise, and returned to my poor crib, where I opened the kerchief and found in it fifty miskals of gold. So I buried them in the ground and, buying two farthings' worth of bread and "kitchen," seated me at the door and broke my fast. After which I sat pondering my case, and continued so doing till the time of afternoon prayer, when lo! a slave girl accosted me saying, 'My mistress calleth for thee.' I followed her to the house aforesaid and, after asking permission, she carried me into the lady, before whom I kissed the ground, and she commanded me to sit and called for meat and wine as on the previous day. After which I again lay with her all night. On the morrow, she gave me a second kerchief, with other fifty dinars therein, and I took it and, going home, buried this also. In such pleasant condition I continued eight days running, going in to her at the hour of afternoon prayer and leaving her at daybreak, but on the eighth night, as I lay with her, behold, one of her slave girls came running in and said to me, 'Arise, go up into yonder closet.'

"So I rose and went into the closet, which was over the gate, and presently I heard a great clamor and tramp of horse, and, looking out of the window which gave on the street in front of the house, I saw a young man as he were the rising moon on the night of fullness come riding up attended by a number of servants and soldiers who were about him on foot. He alighted at the door and entering the saloon, found the lady seated on the couch. So he kissed the ground between her hands, then came up to her and kissed her hands, but she would not speak to him. However, he continued patiently to humble himself, and soothe her and speak her fair, till he made his peace with her, and they lay together that night. Now when her husband had made his peace with the young lady, he lay with her that night, and next morning the soldiers came for him and he mounted and rode away, whereupon she drew near to me and said, 'Sawest thou yonder man?' I answered, 'Yes,' and she said, 'He is my husband, and I will tell thee what befell me with him.'

"It came to pass one day that we were sitting, he and I, in the garden within the house, and behold, he rose from my side and was absent a long while, till I grew tired of waiting and said to myself, 'Most like, he is in the privy.' So I arose and went to the watercloset, but not finding him there, went down to the kitchen, where I saw a slave girl, and when I enquired for him, she showed him to me lying with one of the cookmaids. Hereupon I swore a great oath that I assuredly would do adultery with the foulest and filthiest man in Baghdad, and the day the eunuch laid hands on thee, I had been four days going round about the city in quest of one who should answer to this description, but found none fouler nor filthier than thy good self. So I took thee and there passed between us that which Allah foreordained to us, and now I am quit of my oath.'

"Then she added, 'If, however, my husband return yet again to the cookmaid and lie with her, I will restore thee to thy lost place in my favors.' Now when I heard these words from her lips, what while she pierced my heart with the shafts of her glances, my tears streamed forth till my eyelids were chafed sore with weeping. Then she made them give me other fifty dinars (making in all four hundred gold pieces I had of her) and bade me depart. So I went out from her and came hither, that I might pray Allah (extolled and exalted be He!) to make her husband return to the cookmaid, that haply I might be again admitted to her favors."

When the Emir of the pilgrims heard the man's story, he set him free and said to the bystanders, "Allah upon you, pray for him, for indeed he is excusable."

THE MAN WHO STOLE THE DISH OF GOLD
WHEREIN THE DOG ATE

SOME time erst there was a man who had accumulated debts, and his case was straitened upon him so that he left his people and family and went forth in distraction, and he ceased not wandering on at random till he came after a time to a city tall of walls and firm of foundations. He entered it in a state of despondency and despair, harried by hunger and worn with the weariness of his way. As he passed through one of the main streets, he saw a company of the great going along, so he followed them till they reached a house like to a royal palace. He entered with them, and they stayed not faring forward till they came in presence of a person seated at the upper end of a saloon, a man of the most dignified and majestic aspect, surrounded by pages and eunuchs, as he were of the sons of the wazirs. When he saw the visitors, he rose to greet them and received them with honor, but the poor man aforesaid was confounded at his own boldness when beholding the goodliness of the place and the crowd of servants and attendants, so drawing back in perplexity and fear for his life, sat down apart in a place afar off, where none should see him.

Now it chanced that whilst he was sitting, behold, in came a man with four sporting dogs, whereon were various kinds of raw silk and brocade and wearing round their necks collars of gold with chains of silver, and tied up each dog in a place set privy for him. After which he went out and presently returned with four dishes of gold, full of rich meats, which he set severally before the dogs, one for each. Then he went away and left them, whilst the poor man began to eye the food for stress of hunger, and longed to go up to one of the dogs and eat with him. But fear of them withheld him. Presently, one of the dogs looked at him and Allah Almighty inspired the dog with a knowledge of his case, so he drew back from the platter and signed to the man, who came and ate till he was filled. Then he would have withdrawn, but the dog again signed to him to take for himself the dish and what food was left in it, and pushed it toward him with his forepaw. So the man took the dish and leaving the house, went his way, and none followed him.

Then he journeyed to another city, where he sold the dish and buying with the price a stock in trade, returned to his own town. There he sold his goods and paid his debts, and he throve and became affluent and rose to perfect prosperity. He abode in his own land, but after some years had passed he said to himself, "Needs must I repair to the city of the owner of the dish, and carry him a fit and handsome present and pay him the money value of that which his dog bestowed upon me." So he took the price of the dish and a suitable gift, and setting out, journeyed day and night till he came to that city. He entered it and sought the place where the man lived, but he found there naught save ruins moldering in row and croak of crow, and house and home desolate and all conditions in changed state. At this, his heart and soul were troubled, and he repeated the saying of him who saith:

> "Void are the private rooms of treasury.
> As void were hearts of fear and piety.
> Changed is the wady, nor are its gazelles
> Those fawns, nor sand hills those I wont to see."

Now when the man saw these moldering ruins and witnessed what the hand of time had manifestly done with the place, leaving but traces of the substantial things that erewhiles had been, a little reflection made it needless for him to inquire of the case, so he turned away. Presently, seeing a wretched man, in a plight which made him shudder and feel goose skin, and which would have moved the very rock to ruth, he said to him: "Ho, thou! What have time and fortune done with the lord of this place? Where are his lovely faces, his shining full moons and splendid stars? And what is the cause of the ruin that is come upon his abode, so that nothing save the walls thereof remain?" Quoth the other: "He is the miserable thou seest mourning that which hath left him naked. But knowest thou not the words of the Apostle (whom Allah bless and keep!), wherein is a lesson to him who will learn by it and a warning to whoso will be warned thereby and guided in the right way, 'Verily it is the way of

Allah Almighty to raise up nothing of this world, except He cast it down again'?

"If thou question of the cause of this accident, indeed it is no wonder, considering the chances and changes of Fortune. I was the lord of this place and I built it and founded it and owned it, and I was the proud possessor of its full moons lucent and its circumstance resplendent and its damsels radiant and its garniture magnificent, but Time turned and did away from me wealth and servants and took from me what it had lent (not given), and brought upon me calamities which it held in store hidden. But there must needs be some reason for this thy question, so tell it me and leave wondering."

Thereupon the man who had waxed wealthy, being sore concerned, told him the whole story, and added: "I have brought thee a present, such as souls desire, and the price of thy dish of gold which I took; for it was the cause of my affluence after poverty, and of the replenishment of my dwelling place after desolation, and of the dispersion of my trouble and straitness." But the man shook his head and weeping and groaning and complaining of his lot, answered: "Ho, thou! Methinks thou art mad, for this is not the way of a man of sense. How should a dog of mine make generous gift to thee of a dish of gold and I meanly take back the price of what a dog gave? This were indeed a strange thing! Were I in extremest unease and misery, by Allah, I would not accept of thee aught—no, not the worth of a nail paring! So return whence thou camest in health and safety." Whereupon the merchant kissed his feet and taking leave of him, returned whence he came, praising him and reciting this couplet:

> "Men and dogs together are all gone by,
> So peace be with all of them, dogs and men!"

And Allah is All-knowing!
    Again men tell the tale of

THE RUINED MAN WHO BECAME RICH AGAIN THROUGH A DREAM

THERE lived once in Baghdad a wealthy man and made of money, who lost all his substance and became so destitute that he could earn his living only by hard labor. One night he lay down to sleep dejected and heavyhearted, and saw in a dream a speaker who said to him, "Verily thy fortune is in Cairo. Go thither and seek it." So he set out for Cairo, but when he arrived there, evening overtook him and he lay down to sleep in a mosque. Presently, by decree of Allah Almighty, a band of bandits entered the mosque and made their way thence into an adjoining house, but the owners, being aroused by the noise of the thieves, awoke and cried out. Whereupon the Chief of Police came to their aid with his officers.

The robbers made off, but the Wali entered the mosque, and finding the man from Baghdad asleep there, laid hold of him and beat him with palm rods so grievous a beating that he was well-nigh dead. Then they cast him into jail, where he abode three days, after which the Chief of Police sent for him and asked him, "Whence art thou?" and he answered, "From Baghdad." Quoth the Wali, "And what brought thee to Cairo?" and quoth the Baghdadi, "I saw in a dream One who said to me, 'Thy fortune is in Cairo. Go thither to it.' But when I came to Cairo the fortune which he promised me proved to be the palm rods thou so generously gavest to me."

The Wali laughed till he showed his wisdom teeth and said, "O man of little wit, thrice have I seen in a dream one who said to me: 'There is in Baghdad a house in such a district and of such a fashion and its courtyard is laid out gardenwise, at the lower end whereof is a jetting fountain and under the same a great sum of money lieth buried. Go thither and take it.' Yet I went not, but thou, of the briefness of thy wit, hast journeyed from place to place on the faith of a dream, which was but an idle galimatias of sleep."

Then he gave him money, saying, "Help thee back herewith to thine own country," and he took the money and set out upon his homeward march. Now the house the Wali had described was the man's own house in Baghdad, so the wayfarer returned thither and, digging underneath the fountain in his garden, discovered a great treasure. And thus Allah gave him abundant fortune, and a marvelous coincidence occurred.

And a story is also current of

THE EBONY HORSE

THERE was once in times of yore and ages long gone before, a great and puissant King, of the kings of the Persians, Sabur by name, who was the richest of all the kings in store of wealth and dominion and surpassed each and every in wit and wisdom. He was generous, open-handed and beneficent, and he gave to those who sought him and repelled not those who resorted to him, and he comforted the broken-hearted and honorably entreated those who fled to him for refuge. Moreover, he loved the poor and was hospitable to strangers and did the oppressed justice upon the oppressor. He had three daughters, like full moons of shining light or flower gardens blooming bright, and a son as he were the moon. And it was his wont to keep two festivals in the twelvemonth, those of the Nau-Roz, or New Year, and Mihrgan, the Autumnal Equinox, on which occasions he threw open his palaces and gave largess and made proclamation of safety and security and promoted his chamberlains and viceroys. And the people of his realm came in to him and saluted him and gave him joy of the holy day, bringing him gifts and servants and eunuchs.

Now he loved science and geometry, and one festival day as he sat on his kingly throne there came in to him three wise men, cunning artificers and past masters in all manner of craft and inventions, skilled in making things curious and rare, such as confound the wit, and versed in the knowledge of occult truths and perfect in mysteries and subtleties. And they were of three different tongues and countries: the first a Hindi or Indian, the second a Roumi or Greek, and the third a Farsi or Persian. The Indian came forward and, prostrating himself before the King, wished him joy of the festival and laid before him a present befitting his dignity; that is to say, a man of gold, set with precious gems and jewels of price and hending in hand a golden trumpet. When Sabur saw this, he asked, "O sage, what is the virtue of this figure?" and the Indian answered: "O my lord, if this figure be set at the gate of thy city, it will be a guardian over it; for if an enemy enter the place, it will blow this clarion against him and he will be seized with a palsy and drop down dead." Much the King marveled at this and cried, "By Allah, O sage, an this thy word be true, I will grant thee thy wish and thy desire."

Then came forward the Greek and, prostrating himself before the King, presented him with a basin of silver in whose midst was a peacock of gold, surrounded by four and twenty chicks of the same metal. Sabur looked at them and turning to the Greek, said to him, "O sage, what is the virtue of this peacock?" "O my lord," answered he, "as often as an hour of the day or night passeth, it pecketh one of its young and crieth out and flappeth its wing, till the four and twenty hours are accomplished. And when the month cometh to an end, it will open its mouth and thou shalt see the crescent therein." And the King said, "An thou speak sooth, I will bring thee to thy wish and thy desire."

Then came forward the Persian sage and, prostrating himself before the King, presented him with a horse of the blackest ebony wood inlaid with gold and jewels, and ready harnessed with saddle, bridle, and stirrups such as befit kings, which when Sabur saw, he marveled with exceeding marvel and was confounded at the beauty of its form and the ingenuity of its fashion. So he asked, "What is the use of this horse of wood, and what is its virtue and what the secret of its movement?" and the Persian answered, "O my lord, the virtue of this horse is that if one mount him, it will carry him whither he will and fare with its rider through the air and cover the space of a year in a single day."

The King marveled and was amazed at these three wonders, following thus hard upon one another on the same day, and turning to the sage, said to him: "By Allah the Omnipotent, and our Lord the Beneficent, who created all creatures and feedeth them with meat and drink, an thy speech be veritable and the virtue of thy contrivance appear, I will assuredly give thee whatsoever thou lustest for and will bring thee to thy desire and thy wish!" Then he entertained the sages three days, that he might make trial of their gifts, after which they brought the figures before him and each took the creature he had wroughten and showed him the mystery of its movement. The trumpeter blew the trump, the peacock pecked its chicks, and the Persian sage mounted the ebony horse, whereupon it soared with him high in air and descended again. When King Sabur saw all this, he was amazed and perplexed and felt like to fly for joy and said to the three sages: "Now I am certified of the truth of your words and it behooveth me to quit me of my promise. Ask ye, therefore, what ye will, and I will give you that same."

Now the report of the King's daughters had reached the sages, so they answered: "If the King be content with us and accept of our gifts and allow us to prefer a request to him, we crave of him that he give us his three daughters in marriage, that we may be his sons-in-law, for that the stability of kings may not be gainsaid." Quoth the King, "I grant you that which you wish and you desire," and bade summon the kazi forthright, that he might marry each of the sages to one of his daughters. Now it fortuned that the Princesses were behind a curtain, looking on, and when they heard this, the youngest considered her husband-to-be and behold, he was an old man, a hundred years of age, with hair frosted, forehead drooping, eyebrows mangy, ears slitten, beard and mustachios stained and dyed, eyes red and goggle, cheeks bleached and hollow, flabby nose like a brinjall or eggplant, face like a cobbler's apron, teeth overlapping and lips like camel's kidneys, loose and pendulous—in brief, a terror, a horror, a monster, for he was of the folk of his time the unsightliest and of his age the frightfulest. Sundry of his grinders had been knocked out and his eyeteeth were like the tusks of the Jinni who frighteneth poultry in henhouses.

Now the girl was the fairest and most graceful of her time, more elegant than the gazelle, however tender, than the gentlest zephyr blander, and brighter than the moon at her full, for amorous fray right suitable, confounding in graceful sway the waving bough and outdoing in swimming gait the pacing roe,—in fine, she was fairer and sweeter by far than all her sisters. So when she saw her suitor, she went to her chamber and strewed dust on her head and tore her clothes and fell to buffeting her face and weeping and wailing. Now the Prince, her brother, Kamar al-Akmar, or the Moon of Moons hight, was then newly returned from a journey and, hearing her weeping and crying, came in to her (for he loved her with fond affection, more than his other sisters) and asked her: "What aileth thee? What hath befallen thee? Tell me, and conceal naught from me." So she smote her breast and answered: "O my brother and my dear one, I have nothing to hide. If the palace be straitened upon thy father, I will go out, and if he be resolved upon a foul thing, I will separate myself from him, though he consent not to make provision for me, and my Lord will provide." Quoth he, "Tell me what meaneth this talk and what hath straitened thy breast and troubled thy temper." "O my brother and my dear one," answered the Princess, "know that my father hath promised me in marriage to a wicked magician who brought him as a gift a horse of black wood, and hath bewitched him with his craft and his egromancy. But as for me, I will none of him, and would, because of him, I had never come into this world!"

Her brother soothed her and solaced her, then fared to his sire and said: "What be this wizard to whom thou hast given my youngest sister in marriage, and what is this present which he hast brought thee, so that thou hast killed my sister with chagrin? It is not right that this should be." Now the Persian was standing by, and when he heard the Prince's words, he was mortified and filled with fury, and the King said, "O my son, an thou sawest this horse, thy wit would be confounded and thou wouldst be amated with amazement." Then he bade the slaves bring the horse before him and they did so, and, when the Prince saw it, it pleased him. So (being an accomplished cavalier) he mounted it forthright and struck its sides with the shovel-shaped stirrup irons. But it stirred not, and the King said to the sage, "Go show him its movement, that he also may help thee to win thy wish."

Now the Persian bore the Prince a grudge because he willed not he should have his sister, so he showed him the pin of ascent on the right side of the horse and saying to him, "Trill this," left him. Thereupon the Prince trilled the pin and lo! the horse forthwith soared with him high in ether, as it were a bird, and gave not over flying till it disappeared from men's espying, whereat the King was troubled and perplexed about his case and said to the Persian, "O Sage, look how thou mayst make him descend." But he replied, "O my lord, I can do nothing, and thou wilt never see him again till Resurrection Day, for he, of his ignorance and pride, asked me not of the pin of descent, and I forgot to acquaint him therewith." When the King heard this, he was enraged with sore rage, and bade bastinado the sorcerer and clap him in jail, whilst he himself cast the crown from his head and beat his face and smote his breast. Moreover, he shut the doors of his palaces and gave himself up to weeping and keening, he and his wife and daughters and all the folk of the city, and thus their joy was turned to annoy and their gladness changed into sore affliction and sadness.

Thus far concerning them, but as regards the Prince, the horse gave not over soaring with him till he drew near the sun, whereat he gave himself up for lost and saw death in the skies, and was confounded at his case, repenting him of having mounted the horse and saying to himself: "Verily, this was a device of the sage to destroy me on account of my youngest sister. But there is no Majesty and there is no Might save in Allah, the Glorious, the Great! I am lost without recourse, but I wonder, did not he who made the ascent pin make also a descent pin?" Now he was a man of wit and knowledge and intelligence, so he fell to feeling all the parts of the horse, but saw nothing save a screw like a cock's head on its right shoulder and the like on the left, when quoth he to himself, "I see no sign save these things like button."

Presently he turned the right-hand pin, whereupon the horse flew heavenward with increased speed. So he left it, and looking at the sinister shoulder and finding another pin, he wound it up and immediately the steed's upward motion slowed and ceased and it began to descend, little by little, toward the face of the earth, while the rider became yet more cautious and careful of his life. And when he saw this and knew the uses of the horse, his heart was filled with joy and gladness and he thanked Almighty Allah for that He had deigned deliver him from destruction. Then he began to turn the horse's head whithersoever he would, making it rise and fall at pleasure, till he had gotten complete mastery over its every movement. He ceased not to descend the whole of that day, for that the steed's ascending flight had borne him afar from the earth, and as he descended, he diverted himself with viewing the various cities and countries over which he passed and which he knew not, never having seen them in his life.

Amongst the rest, he decried a city ordered after the fairest fashion in the midst of a verdant and riant land, rich in trees and streams, with gazelles pacing daintily over the plains, whereat he fell a-musing and said to himself, "Would I knew the name of yon town and in what land it is!" And he took to circling about it and observing it right and left. By this time, the day began to decline and the sun drew near to its downing, and he said in his mind, "Verily I find no goodlier place to night in than this city, so I will lodge here, and early on the morrow I will return to my kith and kin and my kingdom and tell my father and family what hath passed and acquaint him with what mine eyes have seen."

Then he addressed himself to seeking a place wherein he might safely bestow himself and his horse and where none should descry him, and presently, behold, he espied a-middlemost of the city a palace rising high in upper air surrounded by a great wall with lofty crenelles and battlements, guarded by forty black slaves clad in complete mail and armed with spears and swords, bows and arrows. Quoth he, "This is a goodly place," and turned the descent pin, whereupon the horse sank down with him like a weary bird, and alighted gently on the terrace roof of the palace. So the Prince dismounted and ejaculating "Alhamdolillah—praise be to Allah," he began to go round about the horse and examine it, saying: "By Allah, he who fashioned thee with these perfections was a cunning craftsman, and if the Almighty extend the term of my life and restore me to my country and kinsfolk in safety and reunite me with my father, I will assuredly bestow upon him all manner bounties and benefit him with the utmost beneficence."

By this time night had overtaken him and he sat on the roof till he was assured that all in the palace slept, and indeed hunger and thirst were sore upon him for that he had not tasted food nor drunk water since he parted from his sire. So he said within himself, "Surely the like of this palace will not lack of victual," and, leaving the horse above, went down in search of somewhat to eat. Presently he came to a staircase and, descending it to the bottom, found himself in a court paved with white marble and alabaster, which shone in the light of the moon. He marveled at the place and the goodliness of its fashion, but sensed no sound of speaker and saw no living soul and stood in perplexed surprise, looking right and left and knowing not whither he should wend. Then said he to himself, "I may not do better than return to where I left my horse and pass the night by it, and as soon as day shall dawn I will mount and ride away."

However, as he tarried talking to himself, he espied a light within the palace, and making toward it, found that it came from a candle that stood before a door of the harem, at the head of a sleeping eunuch, as he were one of the Ifrits of Solomon or a tribesman of the Jinn, longer than lumber and broader than a bench. He lay before the door, with the pommel of his sword gleaming in the flame of the candle, and at his head was a bag of leather hanging from a column of granite. When the Prince saw this, he was affrighted and said, "I crave help from Allah the Supreme! O mine Holy One, even as Thou hast already delivered me from destruction, so vouchsafe me strength to quit myself of the adventure of this palace!" So saying, he put out his hand to the budget and taking it, carried it aside and opened it and found in it food of the best.

He ate his fill and refreshed himself and drank water, after which he hung up the provision bag in its place and drawing the eunuch's sword from its sheath, took it, whilst the slave slept on, knowing not whence Destiny should come to him. Then the Prince fared forward into the palace and ceased not till he came to a second door, with a curtain drawn before it. So he raised the curtain and, behold, on entering he saw a couch of the whitest ivory inlaid with pearls and jacinths and jewels, and four slave girls sleeping about it. He went up to the couch, to see what was thereon, and found a young lady lying asleep, chemised with her hair as she were the full moon rising over the eastern horizon, with flower-white brow and shining hair parting and cheeks like blood-red anemones, and dainty moles thereon. He was amazed at her as she lay in her beauty and loveliness, her symmetry and grace, and he recked no more of death.

So he went up to her, trembling in every nerve, and, shuddering with pleasure, kissed her on the right cheek, whereupon she awoke forthright and opened her eyes, and seeing the Prince standing at her head, said to him, "Who art thou, and whence comest thou?" Quoth he, "I am thy slave and thy lover." Asked she, "And who brought thee hither?" and he answered, "My Lord and my fortune." Then said Shams al-Nahar (for such was her name). "Haply thou art he who demanded me yesterday of my father in marriage and he rejected thee, pretending that thou wast foul of favor. By Allah, my sire lied in his throat when he spoke this thing, for thou art not other than beautiful." Now the son of the King of Hind had sought her in marriage, but her father had rejected him for that he was ugly and uncouth, and she thought the Prince was he. So when she saw his beauty and grace (for indeed he was like the radiant moon) the syntheism of love gat hold of her heart as it were a flaming fire, and they fell to talk and converse.

Suddenly, her waiting women awoke and, seeing the Prince with their mistress, said to her, "O my lady, who is this with thee?" Quoth she: "I know not. I found him sitting by me when I woke up. Haply 'tis he who seeketh me in marriage of my sire." Quoth they, "O my lady, by Allah the All-Father, this is not he who seeketh thee in marriage, for he is hideous and this man is handsome and of high degree. Indeed, the other is not fit to be his servant." Then the handmaidens went out to the eunuch, and finding him slumbering, awoke him, and he started up in alarm. Said they, "How happeth it that thou art on guard at the palace and yet men come in to us whilst we are asleep?" When the black heard this, he sprang in haste to his sword, but found it not, and fear took him, and trembling. Then he went in, confounded, to his mistress and seeing the Prince sitting at talk with her, said to him, "O my lord, art thou man or Jinni?" Replied the Prince: "Woe to thee, O unluckiest of slaves. How darest thou even the sons of the royal Chosroes with one of the unbelieving Satans?" And he was as a raging lion.

Then he took the sword in his hand and said to the slave, "I am the King's son-in-law, and he hath married me to his daughter and bidden me go in to her." And when the eunuch heard these words he replied, "O my lord, if thou be indeed of kind a man as thou avouchest, she is fit for none but for thee, and thou art worthier of her than any other." Thereupon the eunuch ran to the King, shrieking loud and rending his raiment and heaving dust upon his head. And when the King heard his outcry, he said to him: "What hath befallen thee? Speak quickly and be brief, for thou hast fluttered my heart." Answered the eunuch, "O King, come to thy daughter's succor, for a devil of the Jinn, in the likeness of a King's son hath got possession of her, so up and at him!"

When the King heard this, he thought to kill him and said, "How camest thou to be careless of my daughter and let this demon come at her?" Then he betook himself to the Princess's palace, where he found her slave women standing to await him, and asked them, "What is come to my daughter?" "O King," answered they, "slumber overcame us and when we awoke, we found a young man sitting upon her couch in talk with her, as he were the full moon. Never saw we aught fairer of favor than he. So we questioned him of his case and he declared that thou hadst given him thy daughter in marriage. More than this we know not, nor do we know if he be a man or a Jinni, but he is modest and well-bred, and doth nothing unseemly or which leadeth to disgrace."

Now when the King heard these words, his wrath cooled, and he raised the curtain little by little and looking in, saw sitting at talk with his daughter a Prince of the goodliest, with a face like the full moon for sheen. At this sight he could not contain himself, of his jealousy for his daughter's honor, and putting aside the curtain, rushed in upon them drawn sword in hand like a furious Ghul. Now when the Prince saw him he asked the Princess, "Is this thy sire?" and she answered, "Yes." Whereupon he sprang to his feet and, seizing his sword, cried out at the King with so terrible a cry that he was confounded. Then the youth would have fallen on him with the sword, but the King, seeing that the Prince was doughtier than he, sheathed his scimitar and stood till the young man came up to him, when he accosted him courteously and said to him, "O youth, art thou a man or a Jinni?" Quoth the Prince: "Did I not respect thy right as mine host and thy daughter's honor, I would spill thy blood! How darest thou fellow me with devils, me that am a Prince of the sons of the royal Chosroes, who, had they wished to take thy kingdom, could shake thee like an earthquake from thy glory and thy dominions, and spoil thee of all thy possessions?"

Now when the King heard his words, he was confounded with awe and bodily fear of him and rejoined: "If thou indeed be of the sons of the Kings, as thou pretendest, how cometh it that thou enterest my palace without my permission, and smirchest mine honor, making thy way to my daughter and feigning that thou art her husband and claiming that I have given her to thee to wife, I that have slain kings and king's sons who sought her of me in marriage? And now who shall save thee from my might and majesty when, if I cried out to my slaves and servants and bade them put thee to the vilest of deaths, they would slay thee forthright? Who shall deliver thee out of my hand?"

When the Prince heard this speech of the King, he answered: "Verily, I wonder at thee and at the shortness and denseness of thy wit! Say me, canst covet for thy daughter a mate comelier than myself, and hast ever seen a stouter-hearted man or one better fitted for a Sultan or a more glorious in rank and dominion than I?" Rejoined the King: "Nay, by Allah! But I would have had thee, O youth, act after the custom of kings and demand her from me to wife before witnesses, that I might have married her to thee publicly. And now, even were I to marry her to thee privily, yet hast thou dishonored me in her person." Rejoined the Prince: "Thou sayest sooth, O King, but if thou summon thy slaves and thy soldiers and they fall upon me and slay me, as thou pretendest, thou wouldst but publish thine own disgrace, and the folk would be divided between belief in thee and disbelief in thee. Wherefore, O King, thou wilt do well, meseemeth, to turn from this thought to that which I shall counsel thee." Quoth the King, "Let me hear what thou hast to advise," and quoth the Prince:

"What I have to propose to thee is this: Either do thou meet me in combat singular, I and thou, and he who slayeth his adversary shall be held the worthier and having a better title to the kingdom; or else let me be this night, and whenas dawns the morn, draw out against me thy horsemen and footmen and servants, but first tell me their number." Said the King, "They are forty thousand horse, besides my own slaves and their followers, who are the like of them in number." Thereupon said the Prince: "When the day shall break, do thou array them against me and say to them: 'This man is a suitor to me for my daughter's hand, on condition that he shall do battle single-handed against you all; for he pretendeth that he will overcome you and put you to the rout, and indeed that ye cannot prevail against him.' After which, leave me to do battle with them. If they slay me, then is thy secret the surer guarded and thine honor the better warded, and if I overcome them and see their backs, then is it the like of me a king should covet to his son-in-law."

So the King approved of his opinion and accepted his proposition, despite his awe at the boldness of his speech and amaze at the pretensions of the Prince to meet in fight his whole host, such as he had described it to him, being at heart assured that he would perish in the fray and so he should be quit of him and freed from the fear of dishonor. Thereupon he called the eunuch and bade him go to his Wazir without stay and delay and command him to assemble the whole of the army and cause them don their arms and armor and mount their steeds. So the eunuch carried the King's order to the Minister, who straightway summoned the captains of the host and the lords of the realm and bade them don their harness of derring-do and mount horse and sally forth in battle array.

Such was their case, but as regards the King, he sat a long while conversing with the young Prince, being pleased with his wise speech and good sense and fine breeding. And when it was daybreak, he returned to his palace and, seating himself on his throne, commanded his merry men to mount, and bade them saddle one of the best of the royal steeds with handsome selle and housings and trappings and bring it to the Prince. But the youth said, "O King, I will not mount horse till I come in view of the troops and review them." "Be it as thou wilt," replied the King. Then the two repaired to the parade ground where the troops were drawn up, and the young Prince looked upon them and noted their great number. After which the King cried out to them, saying: "Ho, all ye men, there is come to me a youth who seeketh my daughter in marriage, and in very sooth never have I seen a goodlier than he—no, nor a stouter of heart nor a doughtier of arm, for he pretendeth that he can overcome you singlehanded, and force you to flight and that, were ye a hundred thousand in number, yet for him would ye be but few. Now when he chargeth down on you, do ye receive him upon point of pike and sharp of saber, for indeed he hath undertaken a mighty matter."

Then quoth the King to the Prince, "Up, O my son, and do thy devoir on them." Answered he: "O King, thou dealest not justly and fairly by me. How shall I go forth against them, seeing that I am afoot and the men be mounted?" The King retorted, "I bade thee mount, and thou refusedst, but choose thou which of my horses thou wilt." Then he said, "Not one of thy horses pleaseth me, and I will ride none but that on which I came." Asked the King, "And where is thy horse?" "Atop of thy palace." "In what part of my palace?" "On the roof." Now when the King heard these words, he cried: "Out on thee! This is the first sign thou hast given of madness. How can the horse be on the roof? But we shall at once see if thou speak truth or lies." Then he turned to one of his chief officers and said to him, "Go to my palace and bring me what thou findest on the roof." So all the people marveled at the young Prince's words, saying one to other, "How can a horse come down the steps from the roof? Verily this is a thing whose like we never heard."

In the meantime the King's messenger repaired to the palace and, mounting to the roof, found the horse standing there, and never had he looked on a handsomer. But when he drew near and examined it, he saw that it was made of ebony and ivory. Now the officer was accompanied by other high officers, who also looked on, and they laughed to one another, saying: "Was it of the like of this horse that the youth spake? We cannot deem him other than mad. However, we shall soon see the truth of his case. Peradventure herein is some mighty matter, and he is a man of high degree." Then they lifted up the horse bodily, carrying it to the King, set it down before him.

And all the lieges flocked round to look at it, marveling at the beauty of its proportions and the richness of its saddle and bridle. The King also admired it, and wondered at it with extreme wonder, and he asked the Prince, "O youth, is this thy horse?" He answered, "Yes, O King, this is my horse, and thou shalt soon see the marvel it showeth." Rejoined the King, "Then take and mount it," and the Prince retorted, "I will not mount till the troops withdraw afar from it."

So the King bade them retire a bowshot from the horse, whereupon quoth its owner: "O King, see thou, I am about to mount my horse and charge upon thy host and scatter them right and left and split their hearts asunder." Said the King, "Do as thou wilt, and spare not their lives, for they will not spare thine." Then the Prince mounted, whilst the troops ranged themselves in ranks before him, and one said to another, "When the youth cometh between the ranks, we will take him on the points of our pikes and the sharps of our sabers." Quoth another: "By Allah, this is a mere misfortune. How shall we slay a youth so comely of face and shapely of form?" And a third continued: "Ye will have hard work to get the better of him, for the youth had not done this but for what he knew of his own prowess and pre-eminence of valor."

Meanwhile, having settled himself in his saddle, the Prince turned the pin of ascent whilst all eyes were strained to see what he would do, whereupon the horse began to heave and rock and sway to and fro and make the strangest of movements steed ever made, till its belly was filled with air and it took flight with its rider and soared high into the sky. When the King saw this, he cried out to his men, saying: "Woe to you! Catch him, catch him, ere he 'scape you!" But his Wazirs and viceroys said to him: "O King, can a man overtake the flying bird? This is surely none but some mighty magician or Marid of the Jinn, or devil, and Allah save thee from him! So praise thou the Almighty for deliverance of thee and of all thy host from his hand."

Then the King returned to his palace after seeing the feat of the Prince, and going in to his daughter, acquainted her with what had befallen them both on the parade ground. He found her grievously afflicted for the Prince and bewailing her separation from him, wherefore she fell sick with violent sickness and took to her pillow. Now when her father saw her on this wise, he pressed her to his breast and kissing her between the eyes, said to her: "O my daughter, praise

Allah Almighty and thank Him for that He hath delivered us from this crafty enchanter, this villain, this low fellow, this thief who thought only of seducing thee!" And he repeated to her the story of the Prince and how he had disappeared in the firmament, and he abused him and cursed him, knowing not how dearly his daughter loved him. But she paid no heed to his words and did but redouble in her tears and wails, saying to herself, "By Allah, I will neither eat meat nor drain drink till Allah reunite me with him!" Her father was greatly concerned for her case and mourned much over her plight, but for all he could do to soothe her, love longing only increased on her.

Thus far concerning the King and Princess Shams al-Nahar, but as regards Prince Kamar al-Akmar, when he had risen high in air, he turned his horse's head toward his native land, and being alone, mused upon the beauty of the Princess and her loveliness. Now he had inquired of the King's people the name of the city and of its King and his daughter, and men had told him that it was the city of Sana'a. So he journeyed with all speed till he drew near his father's capital and, making an airy circuit about the city, alighted on the roof of the King's palace, where he left his horse whilst he descended into the palace, and seeing its threshold strewn with ashes, thought that one of his family was dead. Then he entered, as of wont, and found his father and mother and sisters clad in mourning raiment of black, all pale of faces and lean of frames. When his sire descried him and was assured that it was indeed his son, he cried out with a great cry and fell down in a fit, but after a time, coming to himself, threw himself upon him and embraced him, clipping him to his bosom and rejoicing in him with exceeding joy and extreme gladness. His mother and sisters heard this, so they came in, and seeing the Prince, fell upon him, kissing him and weeping and joying with exceeding joyance.

Then they questioned him of his case, so he told them all that had past from first to last, and his father said to him, "Praised be Allah for thy safety, O coolth of my eyes and core of my heart!" Then the King bade hold high festival, and the glad tidings flew through the city. So they beat drums and cymbals and, doffing the weed of mourning, they donned the gay garb of gladness and decorated the streets and markets, whilst the folk vied with one another who should be the first to give the King joy, and the King proclaimed a general pardon, and opening the prisons, released those who were therein prisoned. Moreover, he made banquets for the people, with great abundance of eating and drinking, for seven days and nights, and all creatures were gladsomest. And he took horse with his son and rode out with him, that the folk might see him and rejoice.

After a while the Prince asked about the maker of the horse, saying, "O my father, what hath fortune done with him?" and the King answered: "Allah never bless him nor the hour wherein I set eyes on him! For he was the cause of thy separation from us, O my son, and he hath lain in jail since the day of thy disappearance." Then the King bade release him from prison and, sending for him, invested him in a dress of satisfaction and entreated him with the utmost favor and munificence, save that he would not give him his daughter to wife. Whereat the sage raged with sore rage and repented of that which he had done, knowing that the Prince had secured the secret of the steed and the manner of its motion. Moreover, the King said to his son: "I reck thou wilt do well not to go near the horse henceforth, and more especially not to mount it after this day; for thou knowest not its properties, and belike thou art in error about it."

Now the Prince had told his father of his adventure with the King of Sana'a and his daughter, and he said, "Had the King intended to kill thee, he had done so, but thine hour was not yet come." When the rejoicings were at an end, the people returned to their places and the King and his son to the palace, where they sat down and fell to eating, drinking, and making merry. Now the King had a handsome handmaiden who was skilled in playing the lute, so she took it and began to sweep the strings and sing thereto before the King and his son of separation of lovers, and she chanted the following verses:

> "Deem not that absence breeds in me aught of forgetfulness.
> What should remember I did you fro' my remembrance wane?
> Time dies but never dies the fondest love for you we bear,
> And in your love I'll die and in your love I'll arise again."

When the Prince heard these verses, the fires of longing flamed up in his heart, and pine and passion redoubled upon him. Grief and regret were sore upon him and his bowels yearned in him for love of the King's daughter of Sana'a. So he rose forthright and, escaping his father's notice, went forth the palace to the horse and mounting it, turned the pin of ascent, whereupon birdlike it flew with him high in air and soared toward the upper regions of the sky. In early morning his father missed him, and going up to the pinnacle of the palace in great concern, saw his son rising into the firmament, whereat he was sore afflicted and repented in all penitence that he had not taken the horse and hidden it. And he said to himself, "By Allah, if but my son returned to me, I will destroy the horse, that my heart may be at rest concerning my son." And he fell again to weeping and bewailing himself.

Such was his case, but as regards the Prince, he ceased not flying on through air till he came to the city of Sana'a and alighted on the roof as before. Then he crept down stealthily and, finding the eunuch asleep, as of wont, raised the curtain and went on little by little till he came to the door of the Princess's alcove chamber and stopped to listen, when lo! he heard her shedding plenteous tears and reciting verses, whilst her women slept round her. Presently, overhearing her weeping and wailing, quoth they, "O our mistress, why wilt thou mourn for one who mourneth not for thee?" Quoth she, "O ye little of wit, is he for whom I mourn of those who forget or who are forgotten?" And she fell again to wailing and weeping, till sleep overcame her.

Hereat the Prince's heart melted for her and his gall bladder was like to burst, so he entered and, seeing her lying asleep without covering, touched her with his hand, whereupon she opened her eyes and espied him standing by her. Said he, "Why all this crying and mourning?" And when she knew him, she threw herself upon him and took him around the neck and kissed him and answered, "For thy sake and because of my separation from thee." Said he, "O my lady, I have been made desolate by thee all this long time!" But she replied, "'Tis thou who hast desolated *me,* and hadst thou tarried longer, I had surely died!" Rejoined he: "O my lady, what thinkest thou of my case with thy father, and how he dealt with me? Were it not for my love of thee, O temptation and seduction of the Three Worlds, I had certainly slain him and made him a warning to all beholders, but even as I love thee, so I love him for thy sake." Quoth she: "How couldst thou leave me? Can my life be sweet to me after thee?" Quoth he: "Let what hath happened suffice. I am now hungry, and thirsty." So she bade her maidens make ready meat and drink, and they sat eating and drinking and conversing till night was well-nigh ended;

and when day broke he rose to take leave of her and depart ere the eunuch should awake.

Shams al-Nahar asked him, "Whither goest thou?" and he answered, "To my father's house, and I plight thee my troth that I will come to thee once in every week." But she wept and said: "I conjure thee, by Allah the Almighty, take me with thee whereso thou wendest and make me not taste anew the bitter gourd of separation from thee." Quoth he, "Wilt thou indeed go with me?" and quoth she, "Yes." "Then," said he, "arise, that we depart." So she rose forthright and going to a chest, arrayed herself in what was richest and dearest to her of her trinkets of gold and jewels of price, and she fared forth, her handmaids recking naught. So he carried her up to the roof of the palace and, mounting the ebony horse, took her up behind him and made her fast to himself, binding her with strong bonds. After which he turned the shoulder pin of ascent and the horse rose with him high in air.

When her slave women saw this, they shrieked aloud and told her father and mother, who in hot haste ran to the palace roof and looking up, saw the magical horse flying away with the Prince and Princess. At this the King was troubled with ever-increasing trouble and cried out, saying, "O King's son, I conjure thee, by Allah, have ruth on me and my wife and bereave us not of our daughter!" The Prince made him no reply, but, thinking in himself that the maiden repented of leaving father and mother, asked her, "O ravishment of the age, say me, wilt thou that I restore thee to thy mother and father?" Whereupon she answered: "By Allah, O my lord, that is not my desire. My only wish is to be with thee, wherever thou art, for I am distracted by the love of thee from all else, even from my father and mother." Hearing these words, the Prince joyed with great joy, and made the horse fly and fare softly with them, so as not to disquiet her. Nor did they stay their flight till they came in sight of a green meadow, wherein was a spring of running water. Here they alighted and ate and drank, after which the Prince took horse again and set her behind him, binding her in his fear for her safety, after which they fared on till they came in sight of his father's capital.

At this, the Prince was filled with joy and bethought himself to show his beloved the seat of his dominion and his father's power and dignity and give her to know that it was greater than that of her sire. So he set her down in one of his father's gardens without the city where his parent was wont to take his pleasure, and carrying her into a domed summerhouse prepared there for the King, left the ebony horse at the door and charged the damsel keep watch over it, saying, "Sit here till my messenger come to thee, for I go now to my father to make ready a palace for thee and show thee my royal estate." She was delighted when she heard these words and said to him, "Do as thou wilt," for she thereby understood that she should not enter the city but with due honor and worship, as became her rank.

Then the Prince left her and betook himself to the palace of the King his father, who rejoiced in his return and met him and welcomed him, and the Prince said to him: "Know that I have brought with me the King's daughter of whom I told thee, and have left her without the city in such a garden and come to tell thee, that thou mayest make ready the procession of estate and go forth to meet her and show her the royal dignity and troops and guards." Answered the King, "With joy and gladness," and straightway bade decorate the town with the goodliest adornment. Then he took horse and rode out in all magnificence and majesty, he and his host, high officers, and household, with drums and kettledrums, fifes and clarions and all manner instruments, whilst the Prince drew forth of his treasuries jewelry and apparel and what else of the things which kings hoard and made a rare display of wealth and splendor. Moreover he got ready for the Princess a canopied litter of brocades, green, red, and yellow, wherein he set Indian and Greek and Abyssinian slave girls. Then he left the litter and those who were therein and preceded them to the pavilion where he had set her down, and searched but found naught, neither Princess nor horse.

When he saw this, he beat his face and rent his raiment and began to wander round about the garden as he had lost his wits, after which he came to his senses and said to himself: "How could she have come at the secret of this horse, seeing I told her nothing of it? Maybe the Persian sage who made the horse hath chanced upon her and stolen her away, in revenge for my father's treatment of him." Then he sought the guardians of the garden and asked them if they had seen any pass the precincts, and said: "Hath anyone come in here? Tell me the truth and the whole truth, or I will at once strike off your heads." They were terrified by his threats, but they answered with one voice, "We have seen no man enter save the Persian sage, who came to gather healing herbs." So the Prince was certified that it was indeed he that had taken away the maiden, and abode confounded and perplexed concerning his case. And he was abashed before the folk and, turning to his sire, told him what had happened and said to him: "Take the troops and march them back to the city. As for me, I will never return till I have cleared up this affair."

When the King heard this, he wept and beat his breast and said to him: "O my son, calm thy choler and master thy chagrin and come home with us and look what king's daughter thou wouldst fain have, that I may marry thee to her." But the Prince paid no heed to his words and farewelling him, departed, whilst the King returned to the city, and their joy was changed into sore annoy. Now, as Destiny issued her decree, when the Prince left the Princess in the garden house and betook himself to his father's palace for the ordering of his affair, the Persian entered the garden to pluck certain simples and, scenting the sweet savor of musk and perfumes that exhaled from the Princess and impregnated the whole place, followed it till he came to the pavilion and saw standing at the door the horse which he had made with his own hands. His heart was filled with joy and gladness, for he had bemourned its loss much since it had gone out of his hand. So he went up to it and, examining its every part, found it whole and sound, whereupon he was about to mount and ride away when he bethought himself and said, "Needs must I first look what the Prince hath brought and left here with the horse." So he entered the pavilion and seeing the Princess sitting there, as she were the sun shining sheen in the sky serene, knew her at the first glance to be some highborn lady, and doubted not but the Prince had brought her thither on the horse and left her in the pavilion whilst he went to the city to make ready for her entry in state procession with all splendor.

Then he went up to her and kissed the earth between her hands, whereupon she raised her eyes to him and, finding him exceedingly foul of face and favor, asked, "Who art thou?" and he answered, "O my lady, I am a messenger sent by the Prince, who hath bidden me bring thee to another pleasance nearer the city, for that my lady the Queen cannot walk so far and is unwilling, of her joy in thee, that another should forestall her with thee." Quoth she, "Where is the Prince?" and quoth the Persian, "He is in the city, with his sire, and forthwith he shall come for thee in great state." Said she: "O thou! Say me, could he find none handsomer to send to me?" Whereat loud laughed the sage and said: "Yea verily, he hath not a Mameluke as ugly as I am, but, O my lady, let not the ill favor of my face and the foulness of my form deceive thee. Hadst thou profited of me as hath the Prince, verily thou wouldst praise my affair. Indeed, he chose me as his messenger to thee because of my uncomeliness and loathsomeness in his jealous love of thee. Else hath he Mamelukes and Negro slaves, pages, eunuchs, and attendants out of number, each goodlier than other."

Whenas she heard this, it commended itself to her reason and she believed him, so she rose forthright and, putting her hand in his, said, "O my father, what hast thou brought me to ride?" He replied, "O my lady thou shalt ride the horse thou camest on," and she, "I cannot ride it by myself." Whereupon he smiled and knew that he was her master and said, "I will ride with thee myself." So he mounted and, taking her up behind him, bound her to himself with firm bonds, while she knew not what he would with her. Then he turned the ascent pin, whereupon the belly of the horse became full of wind and it swayed to and fro like a wave of the sea, and rose with them high in air, nor slackened in its flight till it was out of sight of the city. Now when Shams al-Nahar saw this, she asked him: "Ho, thou! What is become of that thou toldest me of my Prince, making me believe that he sent thee to me?" Answered the Persian, "Allah damn the Prince! He is a mean and skinflint knave." She cried: "Woe to thee! How darest thou disobey thy lord's commandment?" Whereto the Persian replied: "He is no lord of mine. Knowest thou who I am?" Rejoined the Princess, "I know nothing of thee save what thou toldest me," and retorted he: "What I told thee was a trick of mine against thee and the King's son. I have long lamented the loss of this horse which is under us, for I constructed it and made myself master of it. But now I have gotten firm hold of it and of thee too, and I will burn his heart even as he hath burnt mine, nor shall he ever have the horse again—no, never! So be of good cheer and keep thine eyes cool and clear, for I can be of more use to thee than he. And I am generous as I am wealthy. My servants and slaves shall obey thee as their mistress. I will robe thee in finest raiment and thine every wish shall be at thy will."

When she heard this, she buffeted her face and cried out, saying: "Ah, wellaway! I have not won my beloved and I have lost my father and mother!" And she wept bitter tears over what had befallen her, whilst the sage fared on with her, without ceasing, till he came to the land of the Greeks and alighted in a verdant mead, abounding in streams and trees. Now this meadow lay near a city wherein was a King of high puissance, and it chanced that he went forth that day to hunt and divert himself. As he passed by the meadow, he saw the Persian standing there, with the damsel and the horse by his side, and before the sage was ware, the King's slaves fell upon him and carried him and the lady and the horse to their master, who, noting the foulness of the man's favor and his loathsomeness and the beauty of the girl and her loveliness, said, "O my lady, what kin is this oldster to thee?" The Persian made haste to reply, saying, "She is my wife and the daughter of my father's brother." But the lady at once gave him the lie and said: "O King, by Allah, I know him not, nor is he my husband. Nay, he is a wicked magician who hath stolen me away by force and fraud." Thereupon the King bade bastinado the Persian, and they beat him till he was well-nigh dead, after which the King commanded to carry him to the city and cast him into jail; and, taking from him the damsel and the ebony horse (though he knew not its properties nor the secret of its motion), set the girl in his seraglio and the horse amongst his hoards.

Such was the case with the sage and the lady, but as regards Prince Kamar al-Akmar, he garbed himself in traveling gear and taking what he needed of money, set out tracking their trail in very sorry plight, and journeyed from the country to country and city to city seeking the Princess and inquiring after the ebony horse, whilst all who heard him marveled at him and deemed his talk extravagant. Thus he continued doing a long while, but for all his inquiry and quest, he could hit on no news of her. At last he came to her father's city of Sana'a and there asked for her, but could get no tidings of her and found her father mourning her loss. So he turned back and made for the land of the Greeks, continuing to inquire concerning the twain as he went till, as chance would have it, he alighted at a certain khan and saw a company of merchants sitting at talk. So he sat down near them and heard one say, "O my friends, I lately witnessed a wonder of wonders." They asked, "What was that?" and he answered: "I was visiting such a district in such a city (naming the city wherein was the Princess), and I heard its people chatting of a strange thing which had lately befallen. It was that their King went out one day hunting and coursing with a company of his courtiers and the lords of his realm, and issuing from the city, they came to a green meadow where they espied an old man standing, with a woman sitting hard by a horse of ebony. The man was foulest foul of face and loathly of form, but the woman was a marvel of beauty and loveliness and elegance and perfect grace, and as for the wooden horse, it was a miracle—never saw eyes aught goodlier than it nor more gracious than its make." Asked the others, "And what did the King with them?" and the merchant answered: "As for the man, the King seized him and questioned him of the damsel and he pretended that she was his wife and the daughter of his paternal uncle, but she gave him the lie forthright and declared that he was a sorcerer and a villain. So the King took her from the old man and bade beat him and cast him into the trunk house. As for the ebony horse, I know not what became of it."

When the Prince heard these words, he drew near to the merchant and began questioning him discreetly and courteously touching the name of the city and of its King, which when he knew, he passed the night full of joy. And as soon as dawned the day he set out and traveled sans surcease till he reached that city. But when he would have entered, the gatekeepers laid hands on him, that they might bring him before the King to question him of his condition and the craft in which he skilled and the cause of his coming thither—such being the usage and custom of their ruler. Now it was suppertime when he entered the city, and it was then impossible to go in to the King or take counsel with him respecting the stranger. So the guards carried him to the jail, thinking to lay him by the heels there for the night. But when the warders saw his beauty and loveliness, they could not find it in their hearts to imprison him. They made him sit with them without the walls, and when food came to them, he ate with them what sufficed him.

As soon as they had made an end of eating, they turned to the Prince and said, "What countryman art thou?" "I come from Fars," answered he, "the land of the Chosroes." When they heard this, they laughed and one of them said: "O Chosroan, I have heard the talk of men and their histories and I have looked into their conditions, but never saw I or heard I a bigger liar than the Chosroan which is with us in the jail." Quoth another, "And never did I see aught fouler than his favor or more hideous than his visnomy." Asked the Prince, "What have ye seen of his lying?" and they answered: "He pretendeth that he is one of the wise! Now the King came upon him as he went a-hunting, and found with him a most beautiful woman and a horse of the blackest ebony—never saw I a handsomer. As for the damsel, she is with the King, who is enamored of her and would fain marry her. But she is mad, and were this man a leech, as he claimeth to be, he would have healed her, for the King doth his utmost to discover a cure for her case and a remedy for her disease, and this whole year past hath he spent treasures upon physicians and astrologers on her account, but none can avail to cure her. As for the horse, it is in the royal hoard house, and the ugly man is here with us in prison, and as soon as night falleth, he weepeth and bemoaneth himself and will not let us sleep."

When the warders had recounted the case of the Persian egromancer they held in prison and his weeping and wailing, the Prince at once devised a device whereby he might compass his desire, and presently the guards of the gate, being minded to sleep, led him into the jail and locked the door. So he overheard the Persian weeping and bemoaning himself in his own tongue, and saying: "Alack, and alas for my sin, that I sinned against myself and against the King's son, in that which I did with the damsel, for I neither left her nor won my will of her! All this cometh of my lack of sense, in that I sought for myself that which I deserved not and which befitted not the like of me. For whoso seeketh what suiteth him not at all, falleth with the like of my fall." Now when the King's son heard this, he accosted him in Persian, saying: "How long will this weeping and wailing last? Say me, thinkest thou that hath befallen thee that which never befell other than thou?"

Now when the Persian heard this, he made friends with him and began to complain to him of his case and misfortunes. And as soon as the morning morrowed, the warders took the Prince and carried him before their King, informing him that he had entered the city on the previous night, at a time when audience was impossible. Quoth the King to the Prince, "Whence comest thou, and what is thy name and trade, and why hast thou traveled hither?" He replied: "As to my name, I am called in Persian Harjah. As to my country, I come from the land of Fars, and I am of the men of art and especially of the art of medicine and healing the sick and those whom the Jinns drive mad. For this I go round about all countries and cities, to profit by adding knowledge to my knowledge, and whenever

I see a patient I heal him, and this is my craft." Now when the King heard this, he rejoiced with exceeding joy and said, "O excellent sage, thou hast indeed come to us at a time when we need thee." Then he acquainted him with the case of the Princess, adding, "If thou cure her and recover her from her madness, thou shalt have of me everything thou seekest." Replied the Prince, "Allah save and favor the King. Describe to me all thou hast seen of her insanity, and tell me how long it is since the access attacked her, also how thou camest by her and the horse and the sage."

So the King told him the whole story, from first to last, adding, "The sage is in jail." Quoth the Prince, "O auspicious King, and what hast thou done with the horse?" Quoth the King, "O youth, it is with me yet, laid up in one of my treasure chambers." Whereupon said the Prince within himself: "The best thing I can do is first to see the horse and assure myself of its condition. If it be whole and sound, all will be well and end well. But if its motor works be destroyed, I must find some other way of delivering my beloved." Thereupon he turned to the King and said to him: "O King, I must see the horse in question. Haply I may find in it somewhat that will serve me for the recovery of the damsel." "With all my heart," replied the King, and taking him by the hand, showed him into the place where the horse was. The Prince went round about it, examining its condition, and found it whole and sound, whereat he rejoiced greatly and said to the King: "Allah save and exalt the King! I would fain go in to the damsel, that I may see how it is with her, for I hope in Allah to heal her by my healing hand through means of the horse." Then he bade them take care of the horse and the King carried him to the Princess's apartment, where her lover found her wringing her hands and writhing and beating herself against the ground, and tearing her garments to tatters as was her wont. But there was no madness of Jinn in her, and she did this but that none might approach her.

When the Prince saw her thus, he said to her, "No harm shall betide thee, O ravishment of the Three Worlds," and went on to soothe her and speak her fair, till he managed to whisper, "I am Kamar al-Akmar," whereupon she cried out with a loud cry and fell down fainting for excess of joy. But the King thought this was epilepsy brought on by her fear of him, and by her suddenly being startled. Then the Prince put his mouth to her ear and said to her: "O Shams al-Nahar, O seduction of the universe, have a care for thy life and mine and be patient and constant; for this our position needeth sufferance and skillful contrivance to make shift for our delivery from this tyrannical King. My first move will be now to go out to him and tell him that thou art possessed of a Jinn and hence thy madness, but that I will engage to heal thee and drive away the evil spirit if he will at once unbind thy bonds. So when he cometh in to thee, do thou speak him smooth words, that he may think I have cured thee, and all will be done for us as we desire." Quoth she, "Hearkening and obedience," and he went out to the King in joy and gladness, and said to him: "O august King, I have, by thy good fortune, discovered her disease and its remedy, and have cured her for thee. So now do thou go in to her and speak her softly and treat her kindly, and promise her what may please her. So shall all thou desirest of her be accomplished to thee."

Thereupon the King went in to her, and when she saw him, she rose and kissing the ground before him, bade him welcome and said, "I admire how thou hast come to visit thy handmaid this day." Whereat he was ready to fly for joy and bade the waiting women and the eunuchs attend her and carry her to the hammam and make ready for her dresses and adornment. So they went in to her and saluted her, and she returned their salaams with the goodliest language and after the pleasantest fashion. Whereupon they clad her in royal apparel and, clasping a collar of jewels about her neck, carried her to the bath and served her there. Then they brought her forth as she were the full moon, and when she came into the King's presence, she saluted him and kissed ground before him. Whereupon he joyed in her with joy exceeding and said to the Prince: "O Sage, O Philosopher, all this is of thy blessing. Allah increase to us the benefit of thy healing breath!" The Prince replied: "O King, for the completion of her cure it behooveth that thou go forth, thou and all thy troops and guards, to the place where thou foundest her, not forgetting the beast of black wood which was with her. For therein is a devil, and unless I exorcise him, he will return to her and afflict her at the head of every month." "With love and gladness," cried the King, "O thou Prince of all philosophers and most learned of all who see the light of day."

Then he brought out the ebony horse to the meadow in question and rode thither with all his troops and the Princess, little weeting the purpose of the Prince. Now when they came to the appointed place, the Prince, still habited as a leech, bade them set the Princess and the steed as far as eye could reach from the King and his troops, and said to him: "With thy leave, and at thy word, I will now proceed to the fumigations and conjurations, and here imprison the adversary of mankind, that he may never more return to her. After this, I shall mount this wooden horse, which seemeth to be made of ebony, and take the damsel up behind me, whereupon it will shake and sway to and fro and fare forward till it come to thee, when the affair will be at an end. And after this thou mayest do with her as thou wilt." When the King heard his words, he rejoiced with extreme joy, so the Prince mounted the horse, and taking the damsel up behind him, whilst the King and his troops watched him, bound her fast to him. Then he turned the ascending pin and the horse took flight and soared with them high in air, till they disappeared from every eye.

After this the King abode half the day expecting their return, but they returned not. So when he despaired of them, repenting him greatly of that which he had done and grieving sore for the loss of the damsel, he went back to the city with his troops. He then sent for the Persian who was in prison and said to him: "O thou traitor, O thou villain, why didst thou hide from me the mystery of the ebony horse? And now a sharper hath come to me and hath carried it off, together with a slave girl whose ornaments are worth a mint of money, and I shall never see anyone or anything of them again!" So the Persian related to him all his past, first and last, and the King was seized with a fit of fury which well-nigh ended his life. He shut himself up in his palace for a while, mourning and afflicted. But at last his Wazirs came in to him and applied themselves to comfort him, saying: "Verily, he who took the damsel is an enchanter, and praised be Allah who hath delivered thee from his craft and sorcery!" And they ceased not from him till he was comforted for her loss.

Thus far concerning the King, but as for the Prince, he continued his career toward his father's capital in joy and cheer, and stayed not till he alighted on his own palace, where he set the lady in safety. After which he went in to his father and mother and saluted them and acquainted them with her coming, whereat they were filled with solace and gladness. Then he spread great banquets for the townsfolk and they held high festival a whole month, at the end of which time he went in to the Princess and they took their joy of each other with exceeding joy. But his father brake the ebony horse in pieces and destroyed its mechanism for flight.

Moreover, the Prince wrote a letter to the Princess's father, advising him of all that had befallen her and informing him how she was now married to him and in all health and happiness, and sent it by a messenger, together with costly presents and curious rarities. And when the messenger arrived at the city which was Sana'a and delivered the letter and the presents to the King, he read the missive and rejoiced greatly thereat and accepted the presents, honoring and rewarding the bearer handsomely. Moreover, he forwarded rich gifts to his son-in-law by the same messenger, who returned to his master and acquainted him with what had passed, whereat he was much cheered. And after this the Prince wrote a letter every year to his father-in-law and sent him presents till, in course of time, his sire King Sabur deceased and he reigned in his stead, ruling justly over his lieges and conducting himself well and righteously toward them, so that the land submitted to him and his subjects did him loyal service. And Kamar al-Akmar and his wife Shams al-Nahar abode in the enjoyment of all satisfaction and solace of life till there came to them the Destroyer of delights and Sunderer of societies, the Plunderer of palaces, the Caterer for cemeteries, and the Garnerer of graves. And now glory be to the Living One who dieth not and in whose hand is the dominion of the worlds visible and invisible!

Moreover I have heard tell the tale of

THE ANGEL OF DEATH WITH THE PROUD KING AND THE DEVOUT MAN

IT is related, O auspicious King, that one of the olden monarchs was once minded to ride out in state with the officers of his realm and the grandees of his retinue and display to the folk the marvels of his magnificence. So he ordered his lords and emirs equip them therefor and commanded his keeper of the wardrobe to bring him of the richest of raiment, such as befitted the King in his state, and he bade them bring his steeds of the finest breeds and pedigrees every man heeds. Which being done, he chose out of the raiment what rejoiced him most and of the horses that which he deemed best, and donning the clothes, together with a collar set with margarites and rubies and all manner jewels, mounted and set forth in state, making his destrier prance and curvet among his troops and glorying in his pride and despotic power.

And Iblis came to him and, laying his hand upon his nose, blew into his nostrils the breath of hauteur and conceit, so that he magnified and glorified himself and said in his heart, "Who among men is like unto me?" And he became so puffed up with arrogance and self-sufficiency, and so taken up with the thought of his own splendor and magnificence, that he would not vouchsafe a glance to any man. Presently there stood before him one clad in tattered clothes and saluted him, but he returned not his salaam, whereupon the stranger laid hold of his horse's bridle. "Lift thy hand!" cried the King. "Thou knowest not whose bridle rein it is whereof thou takest hold." Quoth the other, "I have a need of thee." Quoth the King, "Wait till I alight, and then name thy need." Rejoined the stranger, "It is a secret and I will not tell it but in thine ear." So the King bowed his head to him and he said, "I am the Angel of Death and I purpose to take thy soul." Replied the King, "Have patience with me a little, whilst I return to my house and take leave of my people and children and neighbors and wife." "By no means so," answered the Angel. "Thou shalt never return nor look on them again, for the fated term of thy life is past."

So saying, he took the soul of the King (who fell off his horse's back dead) and departed thence. Presently the Death Angel met a devout man, of whom Almighty Allah had accepted, and saluted him. He returned the salute, and the Angel said to him, "O pious man, I have a need of thee which must be kept secret." "Tell it in my ear," quoth the devotee, and quoth the other, "I am the Angel of Death." Replied the man: "Welcome to thee! And praised be Allah for thy coming! I am aweary of awaiting thine arrival, for indeed long hath been thine absence from the lover which longeth for thee." Said the Angel, "If thou have any business, make an end of it," but the other answered, saying, "There is nothing so urgent to me as the meeting with my Lord, to whom be honor and glory!" And the Angel said, "How wouldst thou fain have me take thy soul? I am bidden to take it as thou willest and choosest." He replied, "Tarry till I make the wuzu ablution and pray, and when I prostrate myself, then take my soul while my body is on the ground." Quoth the Angel, "Verily, my Lord (be He extolled and exalted!) commanded me not to take thy soul but with thy consent and as thou shouldst wish, so I will do thy will." Then the devout man made the minor ablution and prayed, and the Angel of Death took his soul in the act of prostration and Almighty Allah transported it to the place of mercy and acceptance and forgiveness.

And they tell another tale of the adventures of

SINDBAD THE SEAMAN AND SINDBAD THE LANDSMAN

THERE lived in the city of Baghdad during the reign of the Commander of the Faithful, Harun al-Rashid, a man named Sindbad the Hammal, one in poor case who bore burdens on his head for hire. It happened to him one day of great heat that whilst he was carrying a heavy load, he became exceeding weary and sweated profusely, the heat and the weight alike oppressing him. Presently, as he was passing the gate of a merchant's house before which the ground was swept and watered, and there the air was temperate, he sighted a broad bench beside the door, so he set his load thereon, to take rest and smell the air. He sat down on the edge of the bench, and at once heard from within the melodious sound of lutes and other stringed instruments, and mirth-exciting voices singing and reciting, together with the song of birds warbling and glorifying Almighty Allah in various tunes and tongues,—turtles, mocking birds, merles, nightingales, cushats, and stone curlews—whereat he marveled in himself and was moved to mighty joy and solace.

Then he went up to the gate and saw within a great flower garden wherein were pages and black slaves and such a train of servants and attendants and so forth as is found only with kings and sultans. And his nostrils were greeted with the savory odours of all manner meats rich and delicate, and delicious and generous wines. So he raised his eyes heavenward and said, "Glory to Thee, O Lord, O Creator and Provider, Who providest whomso Thou wilt without count or stint! O mine Holy One, I cry Thee pardon for all sins and turn to Thee repenting of all offenses!

> "How many by my labors, that evermore endure,
> All goods of life enjoy and in cooly shade recline?
> Each morn that dawns I wake in travail and in woe,
> And strange is my condition and my burden gars me pine.
> Many others are in luck and from miseries are free,
> And Fortune never load them with loads the like o' mine.

> They live their happy days in all solace and delight,
> Eat, drink, and dwell in honor 'mid the noble and the digne.
> All living things were made of a little drop of sperm,
> Thine origin is mine and my provenance is thine,
> Yet the difference and distance 'twixt the twain of us are far
> As the difference of savor 'twixt vinegar and wine.
> But at Thee, O God All-wise! I venture not to rail,
> Whose ordinance is just and whose justice cannot fail."

When Sindbad the Porter had made an end of reciting his verses, he bore up his burden and was about to fare on when there came forth to him from the gate a little foot page, fair of face and shapely of shape and dainty of dress, who caught him by the hand saying, "Come in and speak with my lord, for he calleth for thee." The porter would have excused himself to the page, but the lad would take no refusal, so he left his load with the doorkeeper in the vestibule and followed the boy into the house, which he found to be a goodly mansion, radiant and full of majesty, till he brought him to a grand sitting room wherein he saw a company of nobles and great lords seated at tables garnished with all manner of flowers and sweet-scented herbs, besides great plenty of dainty viands and fruits dried and fresh and confections and wines of the choicest vintages. There also were instruments of music and mirth and lovely slave girls playing and singing. All the company was ranged according to rank, and in the highest place sat a man of worshipful and noble aspect whose beard sides hoariness had stricken, and he was stately of stature and fair of favor, agreeable of aspect and full of gravity and dignity and majesty. So Sindbad the Porter was confounded at that which he beheld and said in himself, "By Allah, this must be either a piece of Paradise or some king's palace!"

Then he saluted the company with much respect, praying for their prosperity, and kissing the ground before them, stood with his head bowed down in humble attitude. The master of the house bade him draw near and be seated and bespoke him kindly, bidding him welcome. Then he set before him various kinds of viands, rich and delicate and delicious, and the porter, after saying his Bismillah, fell to and ate his fill, after which he exclaimed, "Praised be Allah, whatso be our case!" and, washing his hands, returned thanks to the company for his entertainment. Quoth the host: "Thou art welcome, and thy day is a blessed. But what is thy name and calling?" Quoth the other, "O my lord, my name is Sindbad the Hammal, and I carry folk's goods on my head for hire." The housemaster smiled and rejoined: "Know, O Porter, that thy name is even as mine, for I am Sindbad the Seaman. And now, O Porter, I would have thee let me hear the couplets thou recitedst at the gate anon." The porter was abashed and replied: "Allah upon thee! Excuse me, for toil and travail and lack of luck when the hand is empty teach a man ill manners and boorish ways." Said the host: "Be not ashamed. Thou art become my brother. But repeat to me the verses, for they pleased me whenas I heard thee recite them at the gate."

Hereupon the Porter repeated the couplets and they delighted the merchant, who said to him: "Know, O Hammal, that my story is a wonderful one, and thou shalt hear all that befell me and all I underwent ere I rose to this state of prosperity and became the lord of this place wherein thou seest me. For I came not to this high estate save after travail sore and perils galore, and how much toil and trouble have I not suffered in days of yore! I have made seven voyages, by each of which hangeth a marvelous tale, such as confoundeth the reason, and all this came to pass by doom of Fortune and Fate. For from what Destiny doth write there is neither refuge nor flight. Know, then, good my lords," continued he, "that I am about to relate the

FIRST VOYAGE OF SINDBAD HIGHT THE SEAMAN

My father was a merchant, one of the notables of my native place, a moneyed man and ample of means, who died whilst I was yet a child, leaving me much wealth in money and lands and farmhouses. When I grew up, I laid hands on the whole and ate of the best and drank freely and wore rich clothes and lived lavishly, companioning and consorting with youths of my own age, and considering that this course of life would continue forever and ken no change. Thus did I for a long time, but at last I awoke from my heedlessness and, returning to my senses, I found my wealth had become unwealth and my condition ill-conditioned, and all I once hent had left my hand. And recovering my reason, I was stricken with dismay and confusion and bethought me of a saying of our lord Solomon, son of David (on whom be peace!), which I had heard aforetime from my father: "Three things are better than other three. The day of death is better than the day of birth, a live dog is better than a dead lion, and the grave is better than want." Then I got together my remains of estates and property and sold all, even my clothes, for three thousand dirhams, with which I resolved to travel to foreign parts, remembering the saying of the poet:

> By means of toil man shall scale the height,
> Who to fame aspires mustn't sleep o' night.
> Who seeketh pearl in the deep must dive,
> Winning weal and wealth by his main and might.
> And who seeketh Fame without toil and strife
> Th' impossible seeketh and wasteth life.

So, taking heart, I bought me goods, merchandise and all needed for a voyage, and impatient to be at sea, I embarked, with a company of merchants, on board a ship bound for Bassorah. There we again embarked and sailed many days and nights, and we passed from isle to isle and sea to sea and shore to shore, buying and selling and bartering everywhere the ship touched, and continued our course till we came to an island as it were a garth of the gardens of Paradise. Here the captain cast anchor and, making fast to the shore, put out the landing planks. So all on board landed and made furnaces, and lighting fires therein, busied themselves in various ways, some cooking and some washing, whilst other some walked about the island for solace, and the crew fell to eating and drinking and playing and sporting. I was one of the walkers, but as we were thus engaged, behold the master, who was standing on the gunwale, cried out to us at the top of his voice, saying: "Ho there! Passengers, run for your lives and hasten back to the ship and leave your gear and save yourselves from destruction, Allah preserve you! For this island whereon ye stand is no true island, but a great fish stationary a-middle-most of the sea, whereon the sand hath settled and trees have sprung up of old time, so that it is become like unto an island. But when ye lighted fires on it, it felt the heat and moved, and in a moment it will sink with you into the sea and ye will all be drowned. So leave your gear and seek your safety ere ye die!"

All who heard him left gear and goods, clothes washed and unwashed, fire pots and brass cooking pots, and fled back to the ship for their lives, and some reached it while others (amongst whom was I) did not, for suddenly the island shook and sank into the abysses of the deep, with all that were thereon, and the dashing sea surged over it with clashing waves. I sank with the others down, down into the deep, but Almighty Allah preserved me from drowning and threw in my way a great wooden tub of those that had served the ship's company for tubbing. I gripped it for the sweetness of life and, bestriding it like one riding, paddled with my feet like oars, whilst the waves tossed me as in sport right and left. Meanwhile the captain made sail and departed with those who had reached the ship, regardless of the drowning and the drowned. And I ceased not following the vessel with my eyes till she was hid from sight and I made sure of death.

Darkness closed in upon me while in this plight, and the winds and waves bore me on all that night and the next day, till the tub brought to with me under the lee of a lofty island with trees overhanging the tide. I caught hold of a branch and by its aid clambered up onto the land, after coming nigh upon death. But when I reached the shore, I found my legs cramped and numbed and my feet bore traces of the nibbling of fish upon their soles, withal I had felt nothing for excess of anguish and fatigue. I threw myself down on the island ground like a dead man, and drowned in desolation, swooned away, nor did I return to my senses till next morning, when the sun rose and revived me. But I found my feet swollen, so made shift to move by shuffling on my breech and crawling on my knees, for in that island were found store of fruits and springs of sweet water. I ate of the fruits, which strengthened me. And thus I abode days and nights till my life seemed to return and my spirits began to revive and I was better able to move about. So, after due consideration, I fell to exploring the island and diverting myself with gazing upon all things that Allah Almighty had created there, and rested under the trees, from one of which I cut me a staff to lean upon.

One day as I walked along the marge I caught sight of some object in the distance and thought it a wild beast or one of the monster creatures of the sea, but as I drew near it, looking hard the while, I saw that it was a noble mare, tethered on the beach. Presently I went up to her, but she cried out against me with a great cry, so that I trembled for fear and turned to go away, when there came forth a man from under the earth and followed me, crying out and saying, "Who and whence art thou, and what caused thee to come hither?" "O my lord," answered I, "I am in very sooth a waif, a stranger, and was left to drown with sundry others by the ship we voyaged in.

But Allah graciously sent me a wooden tub, so I saved myself thereon and it floated with me, till the waves cast me up on this island." When he heard this, he took my hand and saying, "Come with me," carried me into a great sardab, or underground chamber, which was spacious as a saloon.

He made me sit down at its upper end, then he brought me somewhat of food and, being a-hungered, I ate till I was satisfied and refreshed. And when he had put me at mine ease, he questioned me of myself, and I told him all that had befallen me from first to last. And as he wondered at my adventure, I said: "By Allah, O my lord, excuse me, I have told thee the truth of my case and the accident which betided me, and now I desire that thou tell me who thou art and why thou abidest here under the earth and why thou hast tethered yonder mare on the brink of the sea." Answered he: "Know that I am one of the several who are stationed in different parts of this island, and we are of the grooms of King Mihrjan, and under our hand are all his horses. Every month about new-moon tide we bring hither our best mares which have never been covered, and picket them on the seashore and hide ourselves in this place under the ground, so that none may espy us. Presently the stallions of the sea scent the mares and come up out of the water and, seeing no one, leap the mares and do their will of them. When they have covered them, they try to drag them away with them, but cannot, by reason of the leg ropes. So they cry out at them and butt at them and kick them, which we hearing, know that the stallions have dismounted, so we run out and shout at them, whereupon they are startled and return in fear to the sea. Then the mares conceive by them and bear colts and fillies worth a mint of money, nor is their like to be found on earth's face.

This is the time of the coming forth of the sea stallions, and Inshallah! I will bear thee to King Mihrjan and show thee our country. And know that hadst thou not happened on us, thou hadst perished miserably and none had known of thee. But I will be the means of the saving of thy life and of thy return to thine own land." I called down blessings on him and thanked him for his kindness and courtesy. And while we were yet talking, behold, the stallion came up out of the sea, and giving a great cry, sprang upon the mare and covered her. When he had done his will of her, he dismounted and would have carried her away with him, but could not by reason of the tether.

She kicked and cried out at him, whereupon the groom took a sword and target and ran out of the underground saloon, smiting the buckler with the blade and calling to his company, who came up shouting and brandishing spears. And the stallion took fright at them and plunging into the sea like a buffalo, disappeared under the waves.

After this we sat awhile till the rest of the grooms came up, each leading a mare, and seeing me with their fellow syce, questioned me of my case, and I repeated my story to them. Thereupon they drew near me and spreading the table, ate and invited me to eat. So I ate with them, after which they took horse and mounting me on one of the mares, set out with me and fared on without ceasing till we came to the capital city of King Mihrjan, and going in to him, acquainted him with my story. Then he sent for me, and when they set me before him and salaams had been exchanged, he gave me a cordial welcome and wishing me long life, bade me tell him my tale. So I related to him all that I had seen and all that had befallen me from first to last, whereat he marveled and said to me: "By Allah, O my son, thou hast indeed been miraculously preserved! Were not the term of thy life a long one, thou hadst not escaped from these straits. But praised be Allah for safety!" Then he spoke cheerily to me and entreated me with kindness and consideration. Moreover, he made me his agent for the port and registrar of all ships that entered the harbor. I attended him regularly, to receive his commandments, and he favored me and did me all manner of kindness and invested me with costly and splendid robes. Indeed, I was high in credit with him as an intercessor for the folk and an intermediary between them and him when they wanted aught of him.

I abode thus a great while, and as often as I passed through the city to the port, I questioned the merchants and travelers and sailors of the city of Baghdad, so haply I might hear of an occasion to return to my native land, but could find none who knew it or knew any who resorted thither. At this I was chagrined, for I was weary of long strangerhood, and my disappointment endured for a time till one day, going in to King Mihrjan, I found with him a company of Indians. I saluted them and they returned my salaam, and politely welcomed me and asked me of my country. When they asked me of my country, I questioned them of theirs and they told me that they were of various castes, some being called shakiriyah, who are the noblest of their casts and neither oppress nor offer violence to any, and others Brahmans, a folk who abstain from wine but live in delight and solace and merriment and own camels and horses and cattle. Moreover, they told me that the people of India are divided into two and seventy castes, and I marveled at this with exceeding marvel.

Amongst other things that I saw in King Mihrijan's dominions was an island called Kasil, wherein all night is heard the beating of drums and tabrets, but we were told by the neighboring islanders and by travelers that the inhabitants are people of diligence and judgment. In this sea I saw also a fish two hundred cubits long and the fishermen fear it, so they strike together pieces of wood and put it to flight. I also saw another fish with a head like that of an owl, besides many other wonders and rarities, which it would be tedious to recount. I occupied myself thus in visiting the islands till one day as I stood in the port with a staff in my hand, according to my custom, behold, a great ship, wherein were many merchants, came sailing for the harbor. When it reached the small inner port where ships anchor under the city, the master furled his sails and making fast to the shore, put out the landing planks, whereupon the crew fell to breaking bulk and landing cargo whilst I stood by, taking written note of them.

They were long in bringing the goods ashore, so I asked the master, "Is there aught left in thy ship?" and he answered: "O my lord, there are divers bales of merchandise in the hold, whose owner was drowned from amongst us at one of the islands on our course; so his goods remained in our charge by way of trust, and we purpose to sell them and note their price, that we may convey it to his people in the city of Baghdad, the Home of Peace." "What was the merchant's name?" quoth I, and quoth he, "Sindbad the Seaman," whereupon I straitly considered him and knowing him, cried out to him with a great cry, saying: "O Captain, I am that Sindbad the Seaman who traveled with other merchants, and when the fish heaved and thou calledst to us, some saved themselves and others sank, I being one of them. But Allah Almighty threw in my way a great tub of wood, of those the crew had used to wash withal, and the winds and waves carried me to this island, where by Allah's grace I fell in with King Mihrjan's grooms and they brought me hither to the King their master. When I told him my story, he entreated me with favor and made me his harbor-master, and I have prospered in his service and found acceptance with him. These bales therefore are mine, the goods which God hath given me."

The other exclaimed: "There is no Majesty and there is no Might save in Allah, the Glorious, the Great! Verily, there is neither conscience nor good faith left among men!" Said I, "O Rais, what mean these words, seeing that I have told thee my case?" And he answered, "Because thou heardest me say that I had with me goods whose owner was drowned, thou thinkest to take them without right. But this is forbidden by law to thee, for we saw him drown before our eyes, together with many other passengers, nor was one of them saved. So how canst thou pretend that thou art the owner of the goods?" "O Captain," said I, "listen to my story and give heed to my words, and my truth will be manifest to thee, for lying and leasing are the letter marks of the hypocrites." Then I recounted to him all that had befallen me since I sailed from Baghdad with him to the time when we came to the fish island where we were nearly drowned, and I reminded him of certain matters which had passed between us. Whereupon both he and the merchants were certified of the truth of my story and recognized me and gave me joy of my deliverance, saying: "By Allah, we thought not that thou hadst escaped drowning! But the Lord hath granted thee new life."

Then they delivered my bales to me, and I found my name written thereon, nor was aught thereof lacking. So I opened them and making up a present for King Mihrjan of the finest and costliest of the contents, caused the sailors carry it up to the palace, where I went in to the King and laid my present at his feet, acquainting him with what had happened, especially concerning the ship and my goods, whereat he wondered with exceeding wonder, and the truth of all that I had told him was made manifest to him. His affection for me redoubled after that and he showed me exceeding honor and bestowed on me a great present in return for mine. Then I sold my bales and what other matters I owned, making a great profit on them, and bought me other goods and gear of the growth and fashion of the island city.

When the merchants were about to start on their homeward voyage, I embarked on board the ship all that I possessed, and going in to the King, thanked him for all his favors and friendship and craved his leave to return to my own land and friends. He farewelled me and bestowed on me great store of the country stuffs and produce, and I took leave of him and embarked. Then we set sail and fared on nights and days, by the permission of Allah Almighty, and Fortune served us and Fate favored us, so that we arrived in safety at Bassorah city, where I landed rejoiced at my safe return to my natal soil. After a short stay, I set out for Baghdad, the House of Peace, with store of goods and commodities of great price. Reaching the city in due time, I went straight to my own quarter and entered my house, where all my friends and kinsfolk came to greet me.

Then I bought me eunuchs and concubines, servants and Negro slaves, till I had a large establishment, and I bought me houses, and lands and gardens, till I was richer and in better case than before, and returned to enjoy the society of my friends and familiars more assiduously than ever, forgetting all I had suffered of fatigue and hardship and strangerhood and every peril of travel. And I applied myself to all manner joys and solaces and delights, eating the daintiest viands and drinking the deliciousest wines, and my wealth allowed this state of things to endure.

This, then, is the story of my first voyage, and tomorrow, Inshallah! I will tell you the tale of the second of my seven voyages. (Saith he who telleth the tale): Then Sindbad the Seaman made Sindbad the Landsman sup with him and bade give him a hundred gold pieces, saying, "Thou hast cheered us with thy company this day." The porter thanked him and, taking the gift, went his way, pondering that which he had heard and marveling mightily at what things betide mankind. He passed the night in his own place and with early morning repaired to the abode of Sindbad the Seaman, who received him with honor and seated him by his side. As soon as the rest of the company was assembled, he set meat and drink before them, and when they had well eaten and drunken and were merry and in cheerful case, he took up his discourse and recounted to them in these words the narrative of

THE SECOND VOYAGE OF SINDBAD THE SEAMAN

KNOW, O my brother, that I was living a most comfortable and enjoyable life, in all solace and delight, as I told you yesterday, until one day my mind became possessed with the thought of traveling about the world of men and seeing their cities and islands, and a longing seized me to traffic and to make money by trade. Upon this resolve I took a great store of cash and buying goods and gear fit for travel, bound them up in bales. Then I went down to the riverbank, where I found a noble ship and brand-new about to sail, equipped with sails of fine cloth and well manned and provided. So I took passage in her, with a number of other merchants, and after embarking our goods, we weighed anchor the same day. Right fair was our voyage, and we sailed from place to place and from isle to isle, and whenever we anchored we met a crowd of merchants and notables and customers, and we took to buying and selling and bartering.

At last Destiny brought us to an island, fair and verdant, in trees abundant, with yellow-ripe fruits luxuriant, and flowers fragrant and birds warbling soft descant, and streams crystalline and radiant. But no sign of man showed to the descrier—no, not a blower of the fire. The captain made fast with us to this island, and the merchants and sailors landed and walked about, enjoying the shade of the trees and the song of the birds, that chanted the praises of the One, the Victorious, and marveling at the works of the Omnipotent King. I landed with the rest, and, sitting down by a spring of sweet water that welled up among the trees, took out some vivers I had with me and ate of that which Allah Almighty had allotted unto me. And so sweet was the zephyr and so fragrant were the flowers that presently I waxed drowsy and, lying down in that place, was soon drowned in sleep.

When I awoke, I found myself alone, for the ship had sailed and left me behind, nor had one of the merchants or sailors bethought himself of me. I searched the island right and left, but found neither man nor Jinn, whereat I was beyond measure troubled, and my gall was like to burst for stress of chagrin and anguish and concern, because I was left quite alone, without aught of worldly gear or meat or drink, weary and heartbroken. So I gave myself up for lost and said: "Not always doth the crock escape the shock. I was saved the first time by finding one who brought me from the desert island to an inhabited place, but now there is no hope for me." Then I fell to weeping and wailing and gave myself up to an access of rage, blaming myself for having again ventured upon the perils and hardships of voyage, whenas I was at my ease in mine own house in mine own land, taking my pleasure with good meat and good drink and good clothes and lacking nothing, neither money nor goods. And I repented me of having left Baghdad, and this the more after all the travails and dangers I had undergone in my first voyage, wherein I had so narrowly escaped destruction, and exclaimed, "Verily we are Allah's, and unto Him we are returning!"

I was indeed even as one mad and Jinn-struck, and presently I rose and walked about the island, right and left and every whither, unable for trouble to sit or tarry in any one place. Then I climbed a tall tree and looked in all directions, but saw nothing save sky and sea and trees and birds and isles and sands. However, after a while my eager glances fell upon some great white thing, afar off in the interior of the island. So I came down from the tree and made for that which I had seen, and behold, it was a huge white dome rising high in air and of vast compass. I walked all around it, but found no door thereto, nor could I muster strength or nimbleness by reason of its exceeding smoothness and slipperiness. So I marked the spot where I stood and went round about the dome to measure its circumference, which I found fifty good paces. And as I stood casting about how to gain an entrance, the day being near its fall and the sun being near the horizon, behold, the sun was suddenly hidden from me and the air became dull and dark. Methought a cloud had come over the sun, but it was the season of summer, so I marveled at this and, lifting my head, looked steadfastly at the sky, when I saw that the cloud was none other than an enormous bird, of gigantic girth and inordinately wide of wing, which as it flew through the air veiled the sun and hid it from the island.

At this sight my wonder redoubled and I remembered a story I had heard aforetime of pilgrims and travelers, how in a certain island dwelleth a huge bird, called the "roc," which feedeth its young on elephants, and I was certified that the dome which caught my sight was none other than a roc's egg. As I looked and wondered at the marvelous works of the Almighty, the bird alighted on the dome and brooded over it with its wings covering it and its legs stretched out behind it on the ground, and in this posture it fell asleep, glory be to Him who sleepeth not! When I saw this, I arose and, unwinding my turban from my head, doubled it and twisted it into a rope, with which I girt my middle and bound my waist fast to the legs of the roc, saying in myself, "Peradventure this bird may carry me to a land of cities and inhabitants, and that will be better than abiding in this desert island." I passed the night watching and fearing to sleep, lest the bird should fly away with me unawares, and as soon as the dawn broke and morn shone, the roc rose off its egg and spreading its wings with a great cry, flew up into the air dragging me with it, nor ceased it to soar and to tower till I thought it had reached the limit of the firmament. After which it descended earthward, little by little, till it lighted on the top of a high hill.

As soon as I found myself on the hard ground, I made haste to unbind myself, quaking for fear of the bird, though it took no heed of me nor even felt me, and loosing my turban from its feet, I made off with my best speed. Presently I saw it catch up in its huge claws something from the earth and rise with it high in air, and observing it narrowly, I saw it to be a serpent big of bulk and gigantic of girth, wherewith it flew away clean out of sight. I marveled at this, and faring forward, found myself on a peak overlooking a valley, exceeding great and wide and deep and bounded by vast mountains that spired high in air. None could descry their summits for the excess of their height, nor was any able to climb up thereto. When I saw this, I blamed myself for that which I had done and said: "Would Heaven I had tarried in the island! It was better than this wild desert, for there I had at least fruits to eat and water to drink, and here are neither trees nor fruits nor streams. But there is no Majesty and there is no Might save in Allah, the Glorious, the Great! Verily, as often as I am quit of one peril, I fall into a worse danger and a more grievous."

However, I took courage and walking along the wady, found that its soil was of diamond, the stone wherewith they pierce minerals and precious stones and porcelain and the onyx, for that it is a dense stone and a dure, whereon neither iron nor hardhed hath effect, neither can we cut off aught therefrom nor break it, save by means of loadstone. Moreover, the valley swarmed with snakes and vipers, each big as a palm tree, that would have made but one gulp of an elephant. And they came out by night, hiding during the day lest the rocs and eagles pounce on them and tear them to pieces, as was their wont, why I wot not. And I repented of what I had done and said, "By Allah, I have made haste to bring destruction upon myself!" The day began to wane as I went along, and I looked about for a place where I might pass the night, being in fear of the serpents, and I took no thought of meat and drink in my concern for my life. Presently, I caught sight of a cave near-hand, with a narrow doorway, so I entered, and seeing a great stone close to the mouth, I rolled it up and stopped the entrance, saying to myself, "I am safe here for the night, and as soon as it is day, I will go forth and see what Destiny will do." Then I looked within the cave and saw at the upper end a great serpent brooding on her eggs, at which my flesh quaked and my hair stood on end, but I raised my eyes to Heaven and, committing my case to fate and lot, abode all that night without sleep till daybreak, when I rolled back the stone from the mouth of the cave and went forth, staggering like a drunken man and giddy with watching and fear and hunger.

As in this sore case I walked along the valley, behold, there fell down before me a slaughtered beast. But I saw no one, whereat I marveled with great marvel and presently remembered a story I had heard aforetime of traders and pilgrims and travelers—how the mountains where are the diamonds are full of perils and terrors, nor can any fare through them, but the merchants who traffic in diamonds have a device by which they obtain them; that is to say, they take a sheep and slaughter and skin it and cut it in pieces and cast them down from the mountaintops into the valley sole, where, the meat being fresh and sticky with blood, some of the gems cleave to it. There they leave it till midday, when the eagles and vultures swoop down upon it and carry it in their claws to the mountain summits, whereupon the merchants come and shout at them and scare them away from the meat. Then they come, and taking the diamonds which they find sticking to it, go their ways with them and leave the meat to the birds and beasts, nor can any come at the diamonds but by this device.

So when I saw the slaughtered beast fall (he pursued) and bethought me of the story, I went up to it and filled my pockets and shawl girdle and turban and the folds of my clothes with the choicest diamonds, and as I was thus engaged, down fell before me another great piece of meat. Then with my unrolled turban and lying on my back, I set the bit on my breast so that I was hidden by the meat, which was thus raised above the ground. Hardly had I gripped it when an eagle swooped down upon the flesh and, seizing it with his talons, flew up with it high in air and me clinging thereto, and ceased not its flight till it alighted on the head of one of the mountains, where, dropping the carcass he fell to rending it. But, behold, there arose behind him a great noise of shouting and clattering of wood, whereat the bird took fright and flew away. Then I loosed off myself the meat, with clothes daubed with blood therefrom, and stood up by its side. Whereupon up came the merchant who had cried out at the eagle, and seeing me standing there, bespoke me not, but was affrighted at me and shook with fear.

However, he went up to the carcass and, turning it over, found no diamonds sticking to it, whereat he gave a great cry and exclaimed: "Harrow, my disappointment! There is no Majesty and there is no Might save in Allah with Whom we seek refuge from Satan the stoned!" And he bemoaned himself and beat hand upon hand, saying: "Alas, the pity of it! How cometh this?" Then I went up to him and he said to me, "Who art thou, and what causeth thee to come hither?" And I: "Fear not, I am a man and a good man and a merchant. My story is a wondrous and my adventures marvelous and the manner of my coming hither is prodigious. So be of good cheer. Thou shalt receive of me what shall rejoice thee, for I have with me great plenty of diamonds and I will give thee thereof what shall suffice thee, for each is better than aught thou couldst get otherwise. So fear nothing." The man rejoiced thereat and thanked and blessed me. Then we talked together till the other merchants, hearing me in discourse with their fellow, came up and saluted me, for each of them had thrown down his piece of meat.

And as I went off with them and told them my whole story, how I had suffered hardships at sea and the fashion of my reaching the valley. But I gave the owner of the meat a number of the stones I had by me, so they all wished me joy of my escape, saying: "By Allah, a new life hath been decreed to thee, for none ever reached yonder valley and came off thence alive before thee, but praised be Allah for thy safety!" We passed the night together in a safe and pleasant place, beyond measure rejoiced at my deliverance from the Valley of Serpents and my arrival in an inhabited land. And on the morrow we set out and journeyed over the mighty range of mountains, seeing many serpents in the valley, till we came to a fair great island wherein was a garden of huge champhor trees under each of which a hundred men might take shelter. When the folk have a mind to get camphor, they bore into the upper part of the bole with a long iron, whereupon the liquid camphor, which is the sap of the tree, floweth out and they catch it in vessels, where it concreteth like gum; but after this the tree dieth and becometh firewood.

Moreover, there is in this island a kind of wild beast, called rhinoceros, that pastureth as do steers and buffaloes with us; but it is a huge brute, bigger of body than the camel, and like it feedeth upon the leaves and twigs of trees. It is a remarkable animal with a great and thick horn, ten cubits long, a-middleward its head, wherein, when cleft in twain, is the likeness of a man. Voyagers and pilgrims and travelers declare that this beast called *karkadan* will carry off a great elephant on its horn and graze about the island and the seacoast therewith and take no heed of it till the elephant dieth and its fat, melting in the sun, runneth down into the rhinoceros's eyes and blindeth him, so that he lieth down on the shore. Then comes the bird roc and carrieth off both the rhinoceros and that which is on its horn, to feed its young withal. Moreover, I saw in this island many kinds of oxen and buffaloes, whose like are not found in our country.

Here I sold some of the diamonds which I had by me for gold dinars and silver dirhams and bartered others for the produce of the country, and loading them upon beasts of burden, fared on with the merchants from valley to valley and town to town, buying and selling and viewing foreign countries and the works and creatures of Allah till we came to Bassorah city, where we abode a few days, after which I continued my journey to Baghdad. I arrived at home with great store of diamonds and money and goods, and forgathered with my friends and relations and gave alms and largess and bestowed curious gifts and made presents to all my friends and companions. Then I betook myself to eating well and drinking well and wearing fine clothes and making merry with my fellows, and forgot all my sufferings in the pleasures of return to the solace and delight of life, with light heart and broadened breast. And everyone who heard of my return came and questioned me of my adventures and of foreign countries, and I related to them all that had befallen me, and the much I had suffered, whereat they wondered and gave me joy of my safe return.

This, then, is the end of the story of my second voyage, and tomorrow, Inshallah! I will tell you what befell me in my third voyage. The company marveled at his story and supped with him, after which he ordered a hundred dinars of gold to be given to the porter, who took the sum with many thanks and blessings (which he stinted not even when he reached home) and went his way, wondering at what he had heard. Next morning as soon as day came in its sheen and shone, he rose and, praying the dawn prayer, repaired to the house of Sindbad the Seaman, even as he had bidden him, and went in and gave him good morrow. The merchant welcomed him and made him sit with him till the rest of the company arrived, and when they had well eaten and drunken and were merry with joy and jollity, their host began by saying: Hearken, O my brothers, to what I am about to tell you, for it is even more wondrous than what you have already heard. But Allah alone kenneth what things His Omniscience concealed from man! And listen to

THE THIRD VOYAGE OF SINDBAD THE SEAMAN

As I told you yesterday, I returned from my second voyage overjoyed at my safety and with great increase of wealth, Allah having requited me all that I had wasted and lost, and I abode awhile in Baghdad city savoring the utmost ease and prosperity and comfort and happiness, till the carnal man was once more seized with longing for travel and diversion and adventure, and yearned after traffic and lucre and emolument, for that the human heart is naturally prone to evil. So, making up my mind, I laid in great plenty of goods suitable for a sea voyage and repairing to Bassorah, went down to the shore and found there a fine ship ready to sail, with a full crew and a numerous company of merchants, men of worth and substance, faith, piety, and consideration. I embarked with them and we set sail on the blessing of Allah Almighty and on His aidance and His favor to bring our voyage to a safe and prosperous issue, and already we congratulated one another on our good fortune and boon voyage.

We fared on from sea to sea and from island to island and city to city, in all delight and contentment, buying and selling wherever we touched, and taking our solace and our pleasure, till one day when as we sailed athwart the dashing sea swollen with clashing billows, behold, the master (who stood on the gunwale examining the ocean in all directions) cried out with a great cry, and buffeted his face and pluckt out his beard and rent his raiment, and bade furl the sail and cast the anchors. So we said to him, "O Rais, what is the matter?" "Know, O my brethren (Allah preserve you!) that the wind hath gotten the better of us and hath driven us out of our course into midocean, and Destiny, for our ill luck, hath brought us to the Mountain of the Zughb, a hairy folk like apes, among whom no man ever fell and came forth alive. And my heart presageth that we all be dead men."

Hardly had the master made an end of his speech when the apes were upon us. They surrounded the ship on all sides, swarming like locusts and crowding the shore. They were the most frightful of wild creatures, covered with black hair like felt, foul of favor and small of stature, being but four spans high, yellow-eyed and black-faced. None knoweth their language nor what they are, and they shun the company of men. We feared to slay them or strike them or drive them away, because of their inconceivable multitude, lest if we hurt one, the rest fall on us and slay us, for numbers prevail over courage. So we let them do their will, albeit we feared they would plunder our goods and gear. They swarmed up the cables and gnawed them asunder, and on like wise they did with all the ropes of the ship, so that if fell off from the wind and stranded upon their mountainous coast. Then they laid hands on all the merchants and crew, and landing us on the island, made off with the ship and its cargo and went their ways, we wot not whither.

We were thus left on the island, eating of its fruits and potherbs and drinking of its streams till one day we espied in its midst what seemed an inhabited house. So we made for it as fast as our feet could carry us and, behold, it was a castle strong and tall, compassed about with a lofty wall, and having a two-leaved gate of ebony wood, both of which leaves open stood. We entered and found within a space wide and bare like a great square, round which stood many high doors open thrown, and at the farther end a long bench of stone and braziers, with cooking gear hanging thereon and about it great plenty of bones. But we saw no one and marveled thereat with exceeding wonder. Then we sat down in the courtyard a little while, and presently falling asleep, slept from the forenoon till sundown, when lo! the earth trembled under our feet and the air rumbled with a terrible tone.

Then there came down upon us, from the top of the castle, a huge creature in the likeness of a man, black of color, tall and big of bulk, as he were a great date tree, with eyes like coals of fire and eyeteeth like boar's tusks and a vast big gape like the mouth of a well. Moreover, he had long loose lips like camel's hanging down upon his breast, and ears like two jarms falling over his shoulder blades, and the nails of his hands were like the claws of a lion. When we saw this frightful giant, we were like to faint and every moment increased our fear and terror, and we became as dead men for excess of horror and affright. And after trampling upon the earth, he sat awhile on the bench. Then he arose and coming to us, seized me by the arm, choosing me out from among my comrades the merchants. He took me up in his hand and turning me over, felt me as a butcher feeleth a sheep he is about to slaughter, and I but a little mouthful in his hands. But finding me lean and fleshless for stress of toil and trouble and weariness, let me go and took up another, whom in like manner he turned over and felt and let go. Nor did he cease to feel and turn over the rest of us, one after another, till he came to the master of the ship.

Now he was a sturdy, stout, broad-shouldered wight, fat and in full vigor, so he pleased the giant, who seized him as a butcher seizeth a beast, and throwing him down, set his foot on his neck and brake it, after which he fetched a long spit and thrusting it up his backside, brought it forth of the crown of his head. Then, lighting a fierce fire, he set over it the spit with the rais thereon, and turned it over the coals till the flesh was roasted, when he took the spit off the fire and set it like a kobab stick before him. Then he tare the body, limb from limb, as one jointeth a chicken and, rending the flesh with his nails, fell to eating of it and gnawing the bones, till there was nothing left but some of these, which he threw on one side of the wall. This done, he sat for a while, then he lay down on the stone bench and fell asleep, snarking and snoring like the gurgling of a lamb or a cow with its throat cut, nor did he awake till morning, when he rose and fared forth and went his ways.

As soon as we were certified that he was gone, we began to talk with one another, weeping and bemoaning ourselves for the risk we ran, and saying: "Would Heaven we had been drowned in the sea or that the apes had eaten us! That were better than to be roasted over the coals. By Allah, this is a vile, foul death! But whatso the Lord willeth must come to pass, and there is no Majesty and there is no Might save in Him, the Glorious, the Great! We shall assuredly perish miserably and none will know of us, as there is no escape for us from this place." Then we arose and roamed about the island, hoping that haply we might find a place to hide us in or a means of flight, for indeed death was a light matter to us, provided we were not roasted over the fire and eaten. However, we could find no hiding place, and the evening overtook us, so, of the excess of our terror, we returned to the castle and sat down awhile.

Presently, the earth trembled under our feet and the black ogre came up to us and turning us over, felt one after other till he found a man to his liking, whom he took and served as he had done the captain, killing and roasting and eating him. After which he lay down on the bench and slept all night, snarking and snoring like a beast with its throat cut, till daybreak, when he arose and went out as before. Then we drew together and conversed and said one to other, "By Allah, we had better throw ourselves into the sea and be drowned than die roasted, for this is an abominable death!" Quoth one of us: "Hear ye my words! Let us cast about to kill him, and be at peace from the grief of him and rid the Moslems of his barbarity and tyranny." Then said I: "Hear me, O my brothers. If there is nothing for it but to slay him, let us carry some of this firewood and planks down to the seashore and make us a boat wherein, if we succeed in slaughtering him, we may either embark and let the waters carry us whither Allah willeth, or else abide here till some ship pass, when we will take passage in it. If we fail to kill him, we will embark in the boat and put out to sea. And if we be drowned, we shall at least escape being roasted over a kitchen fire with sliced weasands, whilst if we escape, we escape, and if we be drowned, we die martyrs." "By Allah," said they all, "this rede is a right," and we agreed upon this, and set about carrying it out. So we haled down to the beach the pieces of wood which lay about the bench, and making a boat, moored it to the strand, after which we stowed therein somewhat of victual and returned to the castle.

As soon as evening fell the earth trembled under our feet and in came the blackamoor upon us, snarling like a dog about to bite. He came up to us, and feeling us and turning us over one by one, took one of us and did with him as he had done before and ate him, after which he lay down on the bench and snored and snorted like thunder. As soon as we were assured that he slept, we arose and taking two iron spits of those standing there, heated them in the fiercest of the fire till they were red-hot, like burning coals, when we gripped fast hold of them, and going up to the giant as he lay snoring on the bench, thrust them into his eyes and pressed upon them, all of us, with our united might, so that his eyeballs burst and he became stone-blind. Thereupon he cried with a great cry, whereat our hearts trembled, and springing up from the bench, he fell a-groping after us, blindfold. We fled from him right and left and he saw us not, for his sight was altogether blent, but we were in terrible fear of him and made sure we were dead men despairing of escape. Then he found the door, feeling for it with his hands, and went out roaring aloud, and behold, the earth shook under us for the noise of his roaring, and we quaked for fear. As he quitted the castle we followed him and betook ourselves to the place where we had moored our boat, saying to one another: "If this accursed abide absent till the going down of the sun and come not to the castle, we shall know that he is dead; and if he come back, we will embark in the boat and paddle till we escape, committing our affair to Allah."

But as we spoke, behold, up came the blackamoor with other two as they were Ghuls, fouler and more frightful than he, with eyes like red-hot coals, which when we saw, we hurried into the boat and casting off the moorings, paddled away, and pushed out to sea. As soon as the ogres caught sight of us, they cried out at us, and running down to the seashore, fell a-pelting us with rocks, whereof some fell amongst us and others fell into the sea. We paddled with all our might till we were beyond their reach, but the most part of us were slain by the rock-throwing, and the winds and waves sported with us and carried us into the midst of the dashing sea, swollen with billows clashing. We knew not whither we went, and my fellows died one after another till there remained but three, myself and two others, for as often as one died, we threw him into the sea. We were sore exhausted for stress of hunger, but we took courage and heartened one another and worked for dear life, and paddled with main and might till the winds cast us upon an island, as we were dead men for fatigue and fear and famine.

We landed on the island and walked about it for a while, finding that it abounded in trees and streams and birds, and we ate of the fruits and rejoiced in our escape from the black and our deliverance from the perils of the sea. And thus we did till nightfall, when we lay down and fell asleep for excess of fatigue. But we had hardly closed our eyes before we were aroused by a hissing sound, like the sough of wind, and awakening, saw a serpent like a dragon, a seldseen sight, of monstrous make and belly of enormous bulk, which lay in a circle around us. Presently it reared its head, and seizing one of my companions, swallowed him up to his shoulders. Then it gulped down the rest of him, and we heard his ribs crack in its belly. Presently it went its way, and we abode in sore amazement and grief for our comrade and mortal fear for ourselves, saying: "By Allah, this is a marvelous thing! Each kind of death that threateneth us is more terrible than the last. We were rejoicing in our escape from the black ogre and our deliverance from the perils of the sea, but now we have fallen into that which is worse. There is no Majesty and there is no Might save in Allah! By the Almighty, we have escaped from the blackamoor and from drowning, but how shall we escape from this abominable and viperish monster?" Then we walked about the island, eating of its fruits and drinking of its streams till dusk, when we climbed up into a high tree and went to sleep there, I being on the topmost bough.

As soon as it was dark night, up came the serpent, looking right and left, and making for the tree whereon we were, climbed up to my comrade and swallowed him down to his shoulders. Then it coiled about the bole with him, whilst I, who could not take my eyes off the sight, heard his bones crack in its belly, and it swallowed him whole, after which it slid down from the tree. When the day broke and the light showed me that the serpent was gone, I came down, as I were a dead man for stress of fear and anguish, and thought to cast myself into the sea and be at rest from the woes of the world, but could not bring myself to this, for verily life is dear. So I took five pieces of wood, broad and long, and bound one crosswise to the soles of my feet and others in like fashion on my right and left sides and over my breast, and the broadest and largest I bound across my head and made them fast with ropes. Then I lay down on the ground on my back, so that I was completely fenced in by the pieces of wood, which enclosed me like a bier.

So as soon as it was dark, up came the serpent as usual, and made toward me, but could not get at me to swallow me for the wood that fenced me in. So it wriggled round me on every side whilst I looked on like one dead by reason of my terror, and every now and then it would glide away, and come back. But as often as it tried to come at me, it was hindered by the pieces of wood wherewith I had bound myself on every side. It ceased not to beset me thus from sundown till dawn, but when the light of day shone upon the beast it made off, in the utmost fury and extreme disappointment. Then I put out my hand and unbound myself, well-nigh down among the dead men for fear and suffering, and went down to the island shore, whence a ship afar off in the midst of the waves suddenly struck my sight. So I tore off a great branch of a tree and made signs with it to the crew, shouting out the while, which when the ship's company saw they said to one another: "We must stand in and see what this is. Peradventure 'tis a man." So they made for the island and presently heard my cries, whereupon they took me on board and questioned me of my case. I told them all my adventures from first to last, whereat they marveled mightily and covered my shame with some of their clothes. Moreover, they set before me somewhat of food and I ate my fill and I drank cold sweet water and was mightily refreshed, and Allah Almighty quickened me after I was virtually dead. So I praised the Most Highest and thanked Him for His favors and exceeding mercies, and my heart revived in me after utter despair, till meseemed as if all I had suffered were but a dream I had dreamed.

We sailed on with a fair wind the Almighty sent us till we came to an island called Al-Salahitah, which aboundeth in sandalwood, when the captain cast anchor. And when we had cast anchor, the merchants and the sailors landed with their goods to sell and to buy. Then the captain turned to me and said: "Hark'ee, thou art a stranger and a pauper and tellest us that thou hast undergone frightful hardships, wherefore I have a mind to benefit thee with somewhat that may further thee to thy native land, so thou wilt ever bless me and pray for me." "So be it," answered I. "Thou shalt have my prayers." Quoth he: "Know then that there was with us a man, a traveler, whom we lost, and we know not if he be alive or dead, for we had no news of him. So I purpose to commit his bales of goods to thy charge, that thou mayst sell them in this island. A part of the proceeds we will give thee as an equivalent for thy pains and service, and the rest we will keep till we return to Baghdad, where we will inquire for his family and deliver it to them, together with the unsold goods. Say me then, wilt thou undertake the charge and land and sell them as other merchants do?" I replied, "Hearkening and obedience to thee, O my lord, and great is thy kindness to me," and thanked him. Whereupon he bade the sailors and porters bear the bales in question ashore and commit them to my charge.

The ship's scribe asked him, "O master, what bales are these, and what merchant's name shall I write upon them?" and he answered: "Write on them the name of Sindbad the Seaman, him who was with us in the ship and whom we lost at the roc's island, and of whom we have no tidings. For we mean this stranger to sell them, and we will give him a part of the price for his pains and keep the rest till we return to

Baghdad, where if we find the owner we will make it over to him, and if not, to his family." And the clerk said, "Thy words are apposite and thy rede is right." Now when I heard the captain give orders for the bales to be inscribed with my name, I said to myself, "By Allah, I am Sindbad the Seaman!" So I armed myself with courage and patience and waited till all the merchants had landed and were gathered together, talking and chaffering about buying and selling. Then I went up to the captain and asked him, "O my lord, knowest thou what manner of man was this Sindbad whose goods thou hast committed to me for sale?" and he answered, "I know of him naught save that he was a man from Baghdad city, Sindbad hight the Seaman, who was drowned with many others when we lay anchored at such an island, and I have heard nothing of him since then."

At this I cried out with a great cry and said: "O Captain, whom Allah keep! know that I am that Sindbad the Seaman and that I was not drowned, but when thou castest anchor at the island, I landed with the rest of the merchants and crew. And I sat down in a pleasant place by myself and ate somewhat of food I had with me and enjoyed myself till I became drowsy and was drowned in sleep. And when I awoke, I found no ship, and none near me. These goods are my goods and these bales are my bales, and all the merchants who fetch jewels from the Valley of Diamonds saw me there and will bear me witness that I am the very Sindbad the Seaman; for I related to them everything that had befallen me and told them how you forgot me and left me sleeping on the island, and that betided me which betided me." When the passengers and crew heard my words, they gathered about me and some of them believed me and others disbelieved, but presently, behold, one of the merchants, hearing me mention the Valley of Diamonds, came up to me and said to them: "Hear what I say, good people! When I related to you the most wonderful thing in my travels, and I told you that at the time we cast down our slaughtered animals into the Valley of Serpents (I casting with the rest as was my wont), there came up a man hanging to mine, ye believed me not and gave me the lie." "Yes," quoth they, "thou didst tell us some such tale, but we had no call to credit thee." He resumed: "Now this is the very man, by token that he gave me diamonds of great value and high price whose like are not to be found, requiting me more than would have come up sticking to my quarter of meat. And I companied with him to Bassorah city, where he took leave of us and went on to his native stead whilst we returned to our own land. This is he, and he told us his name, Sindbad the Seaman, and how the ship left him on the desert island. And know ye that Allah hath sent him hither, so might the truth of my story be made manifest to you. Moreover, these are his goods, for when he first forgathered with us, he told us of them; and the truth of his words is patent."

Hearing the merchant's speech, the captain came up to me and considered me straitly awhile, after which he said, "What was the mark on thy bales?" "Thus and thus," answered I, and reminded him of somewhat that had passed between him and me when I shipped with him from Bassorah. Thereupon he was convinced that I was indeed Sindbad the Seaman and took me round the neck and gave me joy of my safety, saying: "By Allah, O my lord, thy case is indeed wondrous and thy tale marvelous. But lauded be Allah Who hath brought thee and me together again, and Who hath restored to thee thy goods and gear!" Then I disposed of my merchandise to the best of my skill, and profited largely on them, whereat I rejoiced with exceeding joy and congratulated myself on my safety and the recovery of my goods. We ceased not to buy and sell at the several islands till we came to the land of Hind, where we bought cloves and ginger and all manner spices. And thence we fared on to the land of Sind, where also we bought and sold.

In these Indian seas I saw wonders without number or count, amongst others a fish like a cow which bringeth forth its young and suckleth them like human beings, and of its skin bucklers are made. There were eke fishes like asses and camels and tortoises twenty cubits wide. And I saw also a bird that cometh out of a sea shell and layeth eggs and hatcheth her chicks on the surface of the water, never coming up from the sea to the land. Then we set sail again with a fair wind and the blessing of Almighty Allah, and after a prosperous voyage, arrived safe and sound at Bassorah. Here I abode a few days, and presently returned to Baghdad, where I went at once to my quarter and my house and saluted my family and familiars and friends. I had gained on this voyage what was beyond count and reckoning, so I gave alms and largess and clad the widow and orphan, by way of thanksgiving for my happy return, and fell to feasting and making merry with my companions and intimates and forgot while eating well and drinking well and dressing well everything that had befallen me and all the perils and hardships I had suffered.

These, then, are the most admirable things I sighted on my third voyage, and tomorrow, an it be the will of Allah, you shall come to me and I will relate the adventures of my fourth voyage, which is still more wonderful than those you have already heard. (Saith he who telleth the tale): Then Sindbad the Seaman bade give Sindbad the Landsman a hundred golden dinars as of wont, and called for food. So they spread the tables and the company ate the night meal and went their ways, marveling at the tale they had heard. The porter after taking his gold passed the night in his own house, also wondering at what his namesake the seaman had told him, and as soon as day broke and the morning showed with its sheen and shone, he rose and praying the dawn prayer, betook himself to Sindbad the Seaman, who returned his salute and received him with an open breast and cheerful favor and made him sit with him till the rest of the company arrived, when he caused set on food and they ate and drank and made merry. Then Sindbad the Seaman bespake them and related to them the narrative of

THE FOURTH VOYAGE OF SINDBAD THE SEAMAN

KNOW, O my brethren, that after my return from my third voyage and forgathering with my friends, and forgetting all my perils and hardships in the enjoyment of ease and comfort and repose, I was visited one day by a company of merchants who sat down with me and talked of foreign travel and traffic till the old bad man within me yearned to go with them and enjoy the sight of strange countries, and I longed for the society of the various races of mankind and for traffic and profit. So I resolved to travel with them and, buying the necessaries for a long voyage and great store of costly goods, more than ever before, transported them from Baghdad to Bassorah, where I took ship with the merchants in question, who were of the chief of the town. We set out, trusting in the blessing of Almighty Allah, and with a favoring breeze and the best conditions we sailed from island to island and sea to sea till one day there arose against us a contrary wind and the captain cast out his anchors and brought the ship to a standstill, fearing lest she should founder in midocean.

Then we all fell to prayer and humbling ourselves before the Most

High, but as we were thus engaged there smote us a furious squall which tore the sails to rags and tatters. The anchor cable parted and, the ship foundering, we were cast into the sea, goods and all. I kept myself afloat by swimming half the day till, when I had given myself up for lost, the Almighty threw in my way one of the planks of the ship, whereon I and some others of the merchants scrambled and, mounting it as we would a horse, paddled with our feet in the sea. We abode thus a day and a night, the wind and waves helping us on, and on the second day shortly before the midtime between sunrise and noon the breeze freshened and the sea wrought and the rising waves cast us upon an island, well-nigh dead bodies for weariness and want of sleep, cold and hunger and fear and thirst. We walked about the shore and found abundance of herbs, whereof we ate enough to keep breath in body and to stay our failing spirits, then lay down and slept till morning hard by the sea. And when morning came with its sheen and shone, we arose and walked about the island to the right and left till we came in sight of an inhabited house afar off. So we made toward it, and ceased not walking till we reached the door thereof when lo! a number of naked men issued from it, and without saluting us or a word said, laid hold of us masterfully and carried us to their King, who signed us to sit. So we sat down and they set food before us such as we knew not and whose like we had never seen in all our lives. My companions ate of it, for stress of hunger, but my stomach revolted from it and I would not eat, and my refraining from it was, by Allah's favor, the cause of my being alive till now. For no sooner had my comrades tasted of it than their reason fled and their condition changed and they began to devour it like madmen possessed of an evil spirit. Then the savages give them to drink of coconut oil and anointed them therewith, and straightway after drinking thereof their eyes turned into their heads and they fell to eating greedily, against their wont.

When I saw this, I was confounded, and concerned for them, nor was I less anxious about myself, for fear of the naked folk. So I watched them narrowly, and it was not long before I discovered them to be a tribe of Magian cannibals whose King was a Ghul. All who came to their country or whoso they caught in their valleys or on their roads they brought to this King and fed them upon that food and anointed them with that oil, whereupon their stomachs dilated that they might eat largely, wilst their reason fled and they lost the power of thought and became idiots. Then they stuffed them with coconut oil and the aforesaid food till they became fat and gross, when they slaughtered them by cutting their throats and roasted them for the King's eating, but as for the savages themselves, they ate human flesh raw. When I saw this, I was sore dismayed for myself and my comrades, who were now become so stupefied that they knew not what was done with them. And the naked folk committed them to one who used every day to lead them out and pasture them on the island like cattle. And they wandered amongst the trees and rested at will, thus waxing very fat.

As for me, I wasted away and became sickly for fear and hunger and my flesh shriveled on my bones, which when the savages saw, they left me alone and took no thought of me and so far forgot me that one day I gave them the slip and walking out of their place, made for the beach, which was distant, and there espied a very old man seated on a high place girt by the waters. I looked at him and knew him for the herdsman who had charge of pasturing my fellows, and with him were many others in like case. As soon as he saw me, he knew me to be in possession of my reason and not afflicted like the rest whom he was pasturing, so signed to me from afar, as who should say, "Turn back and take the right-hand road, for that will lead thee into the King's highway." So I turned back, as he bade me, and followed the right-hand road, now running for fear and then walking leisurely to rest me, till I was out of the old man's sight. By this time the sun had gone down and the darkness set in, so I sat down to rest and would have slept, but sleep came not to me that night for stress of fear and famine and fatigue.

When the night was half spent, I rose and walked on till the day broke in all its beauty and the sun rose over the heads of the lofty hills and athwart the low gravelly plains. Now I was weary and hungry and thirsty, so I ate my fill of herbs and grasses that grew in the island and kept life in body and stayed my stomach, after which I set out again and fared on all that day and the next night, staying my greed with roots and herbs. Nor did I cease walking for seven days and their nights, till the morn of the eighth day, when I caught sight of a faint object in the distance. So I made toward it, though my heart quaked for all I had suffered first and last, and, behold, it was a company of men gathering pepper grains. As soon as they saw me, they hastened up to me and surrounding me on all sides, said to me, "Who art thou, and whence come?" I replied, "Know, O folk, that I am a poor stranger," and acquainted them with my case and all the hardships and perils I had suffered, whereat they marveled and gave me joy of my safety, saying: "By Allah, this is wonderful! But how didst thou escape from these blacks who swarm in the island and devour all who fall in with them, nor is any safe from them, nor can any get out of their clutches?"

And after I had told them the fate of my companions, they made me sit by them till they got quit of their work, and fetched me somewhat of good food, which I ate, for I was hungry, and rested awhile. After which they took ship with me and carrying me to their island home, brought me before their King, who returned my salute and received me honorably and questioned me of my case. I told him all that had befallen me from the day of my leaving Baghdad city, whereupon he wondered with great wonder at my adventures, he and his courtiers, and bade me sit by him. Then he called for food and I ate with him what sufficed me and washed my hands and returned thanks to Almighty Allah for all His favors, praising Him and glorifying Him. Then I left the King and walked for solace about the city, which I found wealthy and populous, abounding in market streets well stocked with food and merchandise and full of buyers and sellers. So I rejoiced at having reached so pleasant a place and took my ease there after my fatigues, and I made friends with the townsfolk, nor was it long before I became more in honor and favor with them and their King than any of the chief men of the realm.

Now I saw that all the citizens, great and small, rode fine horses, high-priced and thoroughbred, without saddles or housings, whereat I wondered and said to the King: "Wherefore, O my lord, dost thou not ride with a saddle? Therein is ease for the rider and increase of power." "What is a saddle?" asked he. "I never saw nor used such a thing in all my life." And I answered, "With thy permission I will make thee a saddle, that thou mayst ride on it and see the comfort thereof." And quoth he, "Do so." So quoth I to him, "Furnish me with some woods." which being brought, I sought me a clever carpenter and sitting by him, showed him how to make the saddletree, portraying for him the fashion thereof in ink on the wood. Then I took wool and teased it and made felt of it, and, covering the saddletree with leather, stuffed it, and polished it, and attached the girth and stirrup leathers. After which I fetched a blacksmith and described to him the fashion of the stirrups and bridle bit. So he forged a fine pair of stirrups and a bit, and filed them smooth and tinned them. Moreover, I made fast to them fringes of silk and fitted bridle leathers to the bit. Then I fetched one of the best of the royal horses and saddling and bridling him, hung the stirrups to the saddle and led him to the King. The thing took his fancy and he thanked me, then he mounted and rejoiced greatly in the saddle and rewarded me handsomely for my work.

When the King's Wazir saw the saddle, he asked of me one like it, and I made it for him. Furthermore, all the grandees and officers of state came for saddles to me, so I fell to making saddles (having taught the craft to the carpenter and blacksmith) and selling them to all who sought, till I amassed great wealth and became in high honor and great favor with the King and his household and grandees. I abode thus till one day, as I was sitting with the King in all respect and contentment, he said to me: "Know thou, O such a one, thou art become one of us, dear as a brother, and we hold thee in such regard and affection that we cannot part with thee nor suffer thee to leave our city. Wherefore I desire of thee obedience in a certain matter, and I will not have thee gainsay me." Answered I: "O King, what is it thou desirest of me? Far be it from me to gainsay thee in aught, for I am indebted to thee for many favors and bounties and much kindness, and (praised be Allah!) I am become one of thy servants." Quoth he: "I have a mind to marry thee to a fair, clever, and agreeable wife who is wealthy as she is beautiful, so thou mayest be naturalized and domiciled with us. I will lodge thee with me in my palace, wherefore oppose me not neither cross me in this." When I heard these words I was ashamed and held my peace nor could make him any answer, by reason of my much bashfulness before him. Asked he, "Why dost thou not reply to me, O my son?" and I answered, saying, "O my master, it is thine to command, O King of the Age!" So he summoned the kazi and the witnesses and married me straightway to a lady of a noble tree and high pedigree, wealthy in moneys and means, the flower of an ancient race, of surpassing beauty and grace, and the owner of farms and estates and many a dwelling place.

Now after the King my master had married me to this choice wife, he also gave me a great and goodly house standing alone, together with slaves and officers, and assigned me pay and allowances. So I became in all ease and contentment and delight and forgot everything which had befallen me of weariness and trouble and hardship. For I loved my wife with fondest love and she loved me no less, and we were as one, and abode in the utmost comfort of life and in its happiness. And I said in myself, "When I return to my native land, I will carry her with me." But whatso is predestined to a man, that needs must be, and none knoweth what shall befall him. We lived thus a great while, till Almighty Allah bereft one of my neighbors of his wife. Now he was a gossip of mine, so hearing the cry of the keeners, I went in to condole him on his loss and found him in very ill plight, full of trouble and weary of soul and mind. I condoled with him and conforted him, saying: "Mourn not for thy wife, who hath now found the mercy of Allah. The Lord will surely give thee a better in her stead, and thy name shall be great and thy life shall be long in the land, Inshallah!"

But he wept bitter tears and replied: "O my friend, how can I marry another wife, and how shall Allah replace her to me with a better than she, whenas I have but one day left to live?" "O my brother," said I, "return to thy senses and announce not glad tidings of thine own death, for thou art well, sound, and in good case." "By thy life, O my friend," rejoined he, "tomorrow thou wilt lose me, and wilt never see me again till the Day of Resurrection." I asked, "How so?" and he answered: "This very day they bury my wife, and they bury me with her in one tomb. For it is the custom with us, if the wife die first, to bury the husband alive with her, and in like manner the wife if the husband die first, so that neither may enjoy life after losing his or her mate." "By Allah," cried I, "this is a most vile, lewd custom, and not to be endured of any!" Meanwhile, behold, the most part of the townsfolk came in and fell to condoling with my gossip for his wife and for himself.

Presently they laid the dead woman out, as was their wont, and setting her on a bier, carried her and her husband without the city till they came to a place in the side of a mountain at the end of the island by the sea. And here they raised a great rock and discovered the mouth of a stone-riveted pit or well, leading down into a vast underground cavern that ran beneath the mountain. Into this pit they threw the corpse, then, tying a rope of palm fibers under the husband's armpits, they let him down into the cavern, and with him a great pitcher of fresh water and seven scones by way of viaticum. When he came to the bottom, he loosed himself from the rope and they drew it up, and stopping the mouth of the pit with the great stone, they returned to the city, leaving my friend in the cavern with his dead wife. When I saw this, I said to myself, "By Allah, this fashion of death is more grievous than the first!" And I went in to the King and said to him, "O my lord, why do ye bury the quick with the dead?" Quoth he: "It hath been the custom, thou must know, of our forebears and our olden kings from time immemorial, if the husband die first, to bury his wife with him, and the like with the wife, so we may not sever them, alive or dead." I asked, "O King of the Age, if the wife of a foreigner like myself die among you, deal ye with him as with yonder man?" and he answered, "Assuredly we do with him even as thou hast seen." When I heard this, my gall bladder was like to burst, for the violence of my dismay and concern for myself. My wit became dazed, I felt as if in a vile dungeon, and hated their society, for I went about in fear lest my wife should die before me and they bury me alive with her. However, after a while I comforted myself, saying, "Haply I shall predecease her, or shall have returned to my own land before she die, for none knoweth which shall go first and which shall go last."

Then I applied myself to diverting my mind from this thought with various occupations, but it was not long before my wife sickened and complained and took to her pillow and fared after a few days to the mercy of Allah. And the King and the rest of the folk came, as was their wont, to condole with me and her family and to console us for her loss, and not less to condole with me for myself. Then the women washed her, and arraying her in her richest raiment and golden ornaments, necklaces, and jewelry, laid her on the bier and bore her to the mountain aforesaid, where they lifted the cover of the pit and cast her in. After which all my intimates and acquaintances and my wife's kith and kin came round me, to farewell me in my lifetime and console me for my own death, whilst I cried out among them, saying: "Almighty Allah never made it lawful to bury the quick with the dead! I am a stranger, not one of your kind, and I cannot abear your custom, and had I known it I never would have wedded among you!" They heard me not and paid no heed to my words, but laying hold of me, bound me by force and let me down into the cavern, with a large gugglet of sweet water and seven cakes of bread, according to their custom. When I came to the bottom, they called out to me to cast myself loose from the cords, but I refused to do so, so they threw them down on me and, closing the mouth of the pit with the stones aforesaid, went their ways.

I looked about me and found myself in a vast cave full of dead bodies that exhaled a fulsome and loathsome smell, and the air was heavy with the groans of the dying. Thereupon I fell to blaming myself for what I had done, saying: "By Allah, I deserve all that hath befallen me and all that shall befall me! What curse was upon me to take a wife in this city? There is no Majesty and there is no Might save in Allah, the Glorious, the Great! As often as I say I have escaped from one calamity, I fall into a worse. By Allah, this is an abominable death to die! Would Heaven I had died a decent death and been washed and shrouded like a man and a Moslem. Would I had been drowned at sea, or perished in the mountains! It were better than to die this miserable death!" And on such wise I kept blaming my own folly and greed of gain in that black hole, knowing not night from day, and I ceased not to ban the Foul Fiend and to bless the Almighty Friend. Then I threw myself down on the bones of the dead and lay there, imploring Allah's help, and in the violence of my despair invoking death, which came not to me, till the fire of hunger burned my stomach and thirst set my throat aflame, when I sat up and feeling for the bread, ate a morsel and upon it swallowed a mouthful of water.

After this, the worst night I ever knew, I arose, and exploring the cavern, found that it extended a long way with hollows in its sides, and its floor was strewn with dead bodies and rotten bones that had lain there from olden time. So I made myself a place in a cavity of the cavern, afar from the corpses lately thrown down, and there slept. I abode thus a long while, till my provision was like to give out, and yet I ate not save once every day or second day, nor did I drink more than an occasional draught, for fear my victual should fail me before my death. And I said to myself: "Eat little and drink little. Belike the Lord shall vouchsafe deliverance to thee!" One day as I sat thus, pondering my case and bethinking me how I should do when my bread and water should be exhausted, behold, the stone that covered the opening was suddenly rolled away and the light streamed down upon me. Quoth I: "I wonder what is the matter. Haply they have brought another corpse." Then I espied folk standing about the mouth of the pit, who presently let down a dead man and a live woman, weeping and bemoaning herself, and with her an ampler supply of bread and water than usual. I saw her and she was a beautiful woman, but she saw me not. And they closed up the opening and went away. Then I took the leg bone of a dead man and, going up to the woman, smote her on the crown of the head, and she cried one cry and fell down in a swoon. I smote her a second and a third time, till she was dead, when I laid hands on her bread and water and found on her great plenty of ornaments and rich apparel, necklaces, jewels and gold trinkets, for it was their custom to bury women in all their finery. I carried the vivers to my sleeping place in the cavern side and ate and drank of them sparingly, no more than sufficed to keep the life in me, lest the provaunt come speedily to an end and I perish of hunger and thirst.

Yet did I never wholly lose hope in Almighty Allah. I abode thus a great while, killing all the live folk they let down into the cavern and taking their provisions of meat and drink, till one day, as I slept, I was awakened by something scratching and burrowing among the bodies in a corner of the cave and said, "What can this be?" fearing wolves or hyenas. So I sprang up, and seizing the leg bone aforesaid, made for the noise. As soon as the thing was ware of me, it fled from me into the inward of the cavern, and lo! it was a wild beast. However, I followed it to the further end, till I saw afar off a point of light not bigger than a star, now appearing and then disappearing. So I made for it, and as I drew near, it grew larger and brighter, till I was certified that it was a crevice in the rock, leading to the open country, and I said to myself: "There must be some reason for this opening. Either it is the mouth of a second pit such as that by which they let me down, or else it is a natural fissure in the stonery." So I bethought me awhile, and nearing the light, found that it came from a breach in the back side of the mountain, which the wild beasts had enlarged by burrowing, that they might enter and devour the dead and freely go to and fro. When I saw this, my spirits revived and hope came back to me and I made sure of life, after having died a death. So I went on, as in a dream, and making shift to scramble through the breach, found myself on the slope of a high mountain overlooking the salt sea and cutting off all access thereto from the island, so that none could come at that part of the beach from the city. I praised my Lord and thanked Him, rejoicing greatly and heartening myself with the prospect of deliverance.

Then I returned through the crack to the cavern and brought out all the food and water I had saved up, and donned some of the dead folk's clothes over my own. After which I gathered together all the collars and necklaces of pearls and jewels and trinkets of gold and silver set with precious stones and other ornaments and valuables I could find upon the corpses, and making them into bundles with the graveclothes and raiment of the dead, carried them out to the back of the mountain facing the seashore, where I established myself, purposing to wait there till it should please Almighty Allah to send me relief by means of some passing ship. I visited the cavern daily, and as often as I found folk buried alive there, I killed them all indifferently, men and women, and took their victual and valuables and transported them to my seat on the seashore.

Thus I abode a long while till one day I caught sight of a ship passing in the midst of the clashing sea swollen with dashing billows. So I took a piece of a white shroud I had with me, and tying it to a staff, ran along the seashore making signals therewith and calling to the people in the ship, till they espied me, and hearing my shouts, sent a boat to fetch me off. When it drew near, the crew called out to me, saying, "Who art thou, and how camest thou to be on this mountain, whereon never saw we any in our born days?" I answered: "I am a gentleman and a merchant who hath been wrecked and saved myself on one of the planks of the ship, with some of my goods. And by the blessing of the Almighty and the decrees of Destiny and my own strength and skill, after much toil and moil I have landed with my gear in this place, where I awaited some passing ship to take me off." So they took me in their boat, together with the bundles I had made of the jewels and valuables from the cavern, tied up in clothes and shrouds, and rowed back with me to the ship, where the captain said to me: "How camest thou, O man, to yonder place on yonder mountain behind which lieth a great city? All my life I have sailed these seas and passed to and fro hard by these heights, yet never saw I here any living thing save wild beasts and birds." I repeated to him the story I had told the sailors, but acquainted him with nothing of that which had befallen me in the city and the cavern, lest there should be any of the islandry in the ship.

Then I took out some of the best pearls I had with me and offered them to the captain, saying: "O my lord, thou hast been the means of saving me off this mountain. I have no ready money, but take this from me in requital of thy kindness and good offices." But he refused to accept it of me, saying: "When we find a shipwrecked man on the seashore or on an island, we take him up and give him meat and drink, and if he be naked we clothe him, nor take we aught from him —nay, when we reach a port of safety, we set him ashore with a present of our own money and entreat him kindly and charitably, for the love of Allah the Most High." So I prayed that his life be long in the land and rejoiced in my escape, trusting to be delivered from my stress and to forget my past mishaps, for every time I remembered being let down into the cave with my dead wife I shuddered in horror.

Then we pursued our voyage and sailed from island to island and sea to sea till we arrived at the Island of the Bell, which containeth a city two days' journey in extent, whence after a six days' run we reached the Island Kala, hard by the land of Hind. This place is governed by a potent and puissant King, and it produceth excellent camphor and an abundance of the Indian rattan. Here also is a lead mine. At last by the decree of Allah we arrived in safety at Bassorah town, where I tarried a few days, then went on to Baghdad city, and finding my quarter, entered my house with lively pleasure. There I forgathered with my family and friends, who rejoiced in my happy return and gave me joy of my safety. I laid up in my storehouses all the goods I had brought with me, and gave alms and largess to fakirs and beggars and clothed the widow and the orphan. Then I gave myself up to pleasure and enjoyment, returning to my old merry mode of life.

Such, then, be the most marvelous adventures of my fourth voyage, but tomorrow, if you will kindly come to me, I will tell you that which befell me in my fifth voyage, which was yet rarer and more marvelous than those which forewent it. And thou, O my brother Sindbad the Landsman, shalt sup with me as thou art wont. (Saith he who telleth the tale): When Sindbad the Seaman had made an end of his story, he called for supper, so they spread the table and the guests ate the evening meal, after which he gave the porter a hundred dinars as usual, and he and the rest of the company went their ways, glad at heart and marveling at the tales they had heard, for that each story was more extraordinary than that which forewent it. The porter Sindbad passed the night in his own house, in all joy and cheer and wonderment, and as soon as morning came with its sheen and shone, he prayed the dawn prayer and repaired to the house of Sindbad the Seaman, who welcomed him and bade him sit with him till the rest of the company arrived, when they ate and drank and made merry and the talk went round amongst them. Presently, their host began the narrative of

THE FIFTH VOYAGE OF SINDBAD THE SEAMAN

KNOW, O my brothers, that when I had been awhile on shore after my fourth voyage, and when, in my comfort and pleasures and merrymakings and in my rejoicing over my large gains and profits, I had forgotten all I had endured of perils and sufferings, the carnal man was again seized with the longing to travel and to see foreign countries and islands. Accordingly I bought costly merchandise suited to my purpose and, making it up into bales, repaired to Bassorah, where I walked about the river quay till I found a fine tall ship, newly builded, with gear unused and fitted ready for sea. She pleased me, so I bought her and, embarking my goods in her, hired a master and crew, over whom I set certain of my slaves and servants as inspectors. A number of merchants also brought their outfits and paid me freight and passage money. Then, after reciting the fatihah, we set sail over Allah's pool in all joy and cheer, promising ourselves a prosperous voyage and much profit.

We sailed from city to city and from island to island and from sea to sea viewing the cities and countries by which we passed, and selling and buying in not a few, till one day we came to a great uninhabited island, deserted and desolate, whereon was a white dome of biggest bulk half buried in the sands. The merchants landed to examine this dome, leaving me in the ship, and when they drew near, behold, it was a huge roc's egg. They fell a-beating it with stones, knowing not what it was, and presently broke it open, whereupon much water ran out of it and the young roc appeared within. So they pulled it forth of the shell and cut its throat and took of it great store of meat. Now I was in the ship and knew not what they did, but presently one of the passengers came up to me and said, "O my lord, come and look at the egg that we thought to be a dome." So I looked, and seeing the merchants beating it with stones, called out to them: "Stop, stop! Do not meddle with that egg, or the bird roc will come out and break our ship and destroy us." But they paid no heed to me and gave not over smiting upon the egg, when behold, the day grew dark and dun and the sun was hidden from us, as if some great cloud had passed over the firmament. So we raised our eyes and saw that what we took for a cloud was the roc poised between us and the sun, and it was his wings that darkened the day. When he came and saw his egg broken, he cried a loud cry, whereupon his mate came flying up and they both began circling about the ship, crying out at us with voices louder than thunder. I called to the rais and crew, "Put out to sea and seek safety in flight, before we be all destroyed!" So the merchants came on board and we cast off and made haste from the island to gain the open sea.

When the rocs saw this, they flew off, and we crowded all sail on the ship, thinking to get out of their country, but presently the two reappeared and flew after us and stood over us, each carrying in its claws a huge boulder which it had brought from the mountains. As soon as the he-roc came up with us, he let fall upon us the rock he held in his pounces, but the master put about ship, so that the rock missed her by some small matter and plunged into the waves with such violence that the ship pitched high and then sank into the trough of the sea, and the bottom the ocean appeared to us. Then the she-roc let fall her rock, which was bigger than that of her mate, and as Destiny had decreed, it fell on the poop of the ship and crushed it, the rudder flying into twenty pieces. Whereupon the vessel foundered and all and everything on board were cast into the main. As for me, I struggled for sweet life till Almighty Allah threw in my way one of the planks of the ship, to which I clung and bestriding it, fell a-paddling with my feet.

Now the ship had gone down hard by an island in the midst of the main, and the winds and waves bore me on till, by permission of the Most High, they cast me up on the shore of the island, at the last gasp for toil and distress and half-dead with hunger and thirst. So I landed more like a corpse than a live man, and throwing myself down on the beach, lay there awhile till I began to revive and recover spirits, when I walked about the island, and found it as it were one of the garths and gardens of Paradise. Its trees, in abundance dight, bore ripe-yellow fruit for freight, its streams ran clear and bright, its flowers were fair to scent and to sight, and its birds warbled with delight the praises of Him to whom belong Permanence and All-might. So I ate my fill of the fruits and slaked my thirst with the water of the streams till I could no more, and I returned thanks to the Most High and glorified Him, after which I sat till nightfall hearing no voice and seeing none inhabitant. Then I lay down, well-nigh dead for travail and trouble and terror, and slept without surcease till morning, when I arose and walked about under the trees till I came to the channel of a draw well fed by a spring of running water, by which well sat an old man of venerable aspect, girt about with a waistcloth made of the fiber of palm fronds. Quoth I to myself. "Haply this Sheikh is of those who were wrecked in the ship and hath made his way to this island."

So I drew near to him and saluted him, and he returned my salaam by signs, but spoke not, and I said to him, "O nuncle mine, what causeth thee to sit here?" He shook his head and moaned and signed to me with his hand as who should say, "Take me on thy shoulders and carry me to the other side of the well channel." And quoth I in my mind: "I will deal kindly with him and do what he desireth. It may be I shall win me a reward in Heaven, for he may be a paralytic." So I took him on my back, and carrying him to the place whereat he pointed, said to him, "Dismount at thy leisure." But he would not get off my back, and wound his legs about my neck. I looked at them, and seeing that they were like a buffalo's hide for blackness and roughness, was affrighted and would have cast him off, but he clung to me and gripped my neck with his legs till I was well-nigh choked, the world grew black in my sight and I fell senseless to the ground like one dead.

But he still kept his seat and raising his legs, drummed with his heels and beat harder than palm rods my back and shoulders, till he forced me to rise for excess of pain. Then he signed to me with his hand to carry him hither and thither among the trees which bore the best fruits, and if ever I refused to do his bidding or loitered or took my leisure, he beat me with his feet more grievously than if I had been beaten with whips. He ceased not to signal with his hand wherever he was minded to go, so I carried him about the island, like a captive slave, and he dismounted not night or day. And whenas he wished to sleep, he wound his legs about my neck and leaned back and slept awhile, then arose and beat me, whereupon I sprang up in haste, unable to gainsay him because of the pain he inflicted on me. And indeed I blamed myself and sore repented me of having taken compassion on him, and continued in this condition, suffering fatigue not to be described, till I said to myself: "I wrought him a weal and he requited me with my ill. By Allah, never more will I do any man a service so long as I live!" And again and again I besought the Most High that I might die, for stress of weariness and misery.

And thus I abode a long while till one day I came with him to a place wherein was abundance of gourds, many of them dry. So I took a great dry gourd and cutting open the head, scooped out the inside and cleaned it, after which I gathered grapes from a vine which grew hard by and squeezed them into the gourd till it was full of the juice. Then I stopped up the mouth and set it in the sun, where I left it for some days until it became strong wine, and every day I used to drink of it, to comfort and sustain me under my fatigues with that froward and obstinate fiend. And as often as I drank myself drunk, I forgot my troubles and took new heart. One day he saw me drinking and signed to me with his hand, as who should say, "What is that?" Quoth I, "It is an excellent cordial, which cheereth the heart and reviveth the spirits." Then, being heated with wine, I ran and danced with him among the trees, clapping my hands and singing and making merry, and I staggered under him by design.

When he saw this, he signed to me to give him the gourd that he might drink, and I feared him and gave it him. So he took it, and draining it to the dregs, cast it on the ground, whereupon he grew frolicsome and began to clap hands and jig to and fro on my shoulders, and he made water upon me so copiously that all my dress was drenched. But presently, the fumes of the wine rising to his head, he became helplessly drunk and his side muscles and limbs relaxed and he swayed to and fro on my back. When I saw that he had lost his senses for drunkenness, I put my hand to his legs and, loosing them from my neck, stooped down well-nigh to the ground and threw him at full length. Then I took up a great stone from among the trees and coming up to him, smote him therewith on the head with all my might and crushed in his skull as he lay dead-drunk. Thereupon his flesh and fat and blood being in a pulp, he died and went to his deserts, The Fire, no mercy of Allah be upon him!

I then returned, with a heart at ease, to my former station on the shore, and abode in that island many days, eating of its fruits and drinking of its waters and keeping a lookout for passing ships, till one day, as I sat on the beach recalling all that had befallen me and saying, "I wonder if Allah will save me alive and restore me to my home and family and friends!" behold, a ship was making for the island through the dashing sea and clashing waves. Presently it cast anchor and the passengers landed, so I made for them, and when they saw me all hastened up to me and gathering round me, questioned me of my case and how I came thither. I told them all that had betided me, whereat they marveled with exceeding marvel and said: "He who rode on thy shoulder is called the Sheikh-al-Bahr or Old Man of the Sea, and none ever felt his legs on neck and came off alive but thou, and those who die under him he eateth. So praised be Allah for thy safety!" Then they set somewhat of food before me, whereof I ate my fill, and gave me somewhat of clothes, wherewith I clad myself anew and covered my nakedness. After which they took me up into the ship and we sailed days and nights till Fate brought us to a place called the City of Apes, built with lofty houses, all of which gave upon the sea, and it had a single gate studded and strengthened with iron nails.

Now every night as soon as it is dusk the dwellers in this city used to come forth of the gates and, putting out to sea in boats and ships, pass the night upon the waters in their fear lest the apes should come down on them from the mountains. Hearing this, I was sore troubled, remembering what I had before suffered from the ape kind. Presently I landed to solace myself in the city, but meanwhile the ship set sail without me, and I repented of having gone ashore, and calling to mind my companions and what had befallen me with the apes, first and after, sat down and fell aweeping and lamenting. Presently one of the townsfolk accosted me and said to me, "O my lord, meseemeth thou art a stranger to these parts?" "Yes," answered I, "I am indeed a stranger and a poor one, who came hither in a ship which cast anchor here, and I landed to visit the town. But when I would have gone on board again, I found they had sailed without me." Quoth he, "Come and embark with us, for if thou lie the night in the city, the apes will destroy thee." "Hearkening and obedience," replied I, and rising, straightway embarked with him in one of the boats, whereupon they pushed off from shore, and anchoring a mile or so from the land, there passed the night. At daybreak they rowed back to the city, and landing, went each about his business. Thus they did every night, for if any tarried in the town by night the apes came down on him and slew him. As soon as it was day, the apes left the place and ate of the fruits of the gardens, then went back to the mountains and slept there till nightfall, when they again came down upon the city.

Now this place was in the farthest part of the country of the blacks, and one of the strangest things that befell me during my sojourn in the city was on this wise. One of the company with whom I passed the night in the boat asked me: "O my lord, thou art apparently a stranger in these parts. Hast thou any craft whereat thou canst work?" and I answered: "By Allah, O my brother, I have no trade nor know I any handicraft, for I was a merchant and a man of money and substance and had a ship of my own, laden with great store of goods and merchandise. But it foundered at sea and all were drowned excepting me, who saved myself on a piece of plank which Allah vouchsafed to me of His favor."

Upon this he brought me a cotton bag and giving it to me, said: "Take this bag and fill it with pebbles from the beach and go forth with a company of the townsfolk to whom I will give a charge respecting thee. Do as they do and belike thou shalt gain what may further thy return voyage to thy native land." Then he carried me to the beach, where I filled my bag with pebbles large and small, and presently we saw a company of folk issue from the town, each bearing a bag like mine, filled with pebbles. To these he committed me, commending me to their care, and saying: "This man is a stranger, so take him with you and teach him how to gather, that he may get his daily bread, and you will earn your reward and recompense in Heaven." "On our head and eyes be it!" answered they, and bidding me welcome, fared on with me till we came to a spacious wady, full of lofty trees with trunks so smooth that none might climb them.

Now sleeping under these trees were many apes, which when they saw us rose and fled from us and swarmed up among the branches, whereupon my companions began to pelt them with what they had in their bags, and the apes fell to plucking of the fruit of the trees and casting them at the folk. I looked at the fruits they cast at us and found them to be Indian or coconuts, so I chose out a great tree full of apes, and going up to it, began to pelt them with stones, and they in return pelted me with nuts, which I collected, as did the rest. So that even before I had made an end of my bagful of pebbles, I had gotten great plenty of nuts. And as soon as my companions had in like manner gotten as many nuts as they could carry, we returned to the city, where we arrived at the fag end of day. Then I went in to the kindly man who had brought me in company with the nut-gatherers and gave him all I had gotten, thanking him for his kindness, but he would not accept them, saying, "Sell them and make profit by the price," and presently he added (giving me the key of a closet in his house): "Store thy nuts in this safe place and go thou forth every morning and gather them as thou hast done today, and choose out the worst for sale and supplying thyself; but lay up the rest here, so haply thou mayst collect enough to serve thee for thy return home." "Allah requite thee!" answered I, and did as he advised me, going out daily with the coconut gatherers, who commended me to one another and showed me the best-stocked trees. Thus did I for some time, till I had laid up great store of excellent nuts, besides a large sum of money, the price of those I had sold. I became thus at my ease and bought all I saw and had a mind to, and passed my time pleasantly, greatly enjoying my stay in the city, till as I stood on the beach one day a great ship steering through the heart of the sea presently cast anchor by the shore and landed a company of merchants, who proceeded to sell and buy and barter their goods for coconuts and other commodities.

Then I went to my friend and told him of the coming of the ship and how I had a mind to return to my own country, and he said, "'Tis for thee to decide." So I thanked him for his bounties and took leave of him. Then, going to the captain of the ship, I agreed with him for my passage and embarked my coconuts and what else I possessed. We weighed anchor the same day and sailed from island to island and sea to sea, and whenever we stopped, I sold and traded with my coconuts, and the Lord requited me more than I erst had and lost.

Amongst other places, we came to an island abounding in cloves and cinnamon and pepper, and the country people told me that by the side of each pepper bunch groweth a great leaf which shadeth it from the sun and casteth the water off it in the wet season; but when the rain ceaseth, the leaf turneth over and droopeth down by the side of the bunch. Here I took in great store of pepper and cloves and cinnamon, in exchange for coconuts, and we passed thence to the Island of Al-Usirat, whence cometh the Comorin aloes wood, and thence to another island, five days' journey in length, where grows the Chinese lign aloes, which is better than the Comorin. But the people of this island are fouler of condition and religion than those of the other, for that they love fornication and wine bibbing, and know not prayer nor call to prayer.

Thence we came to the pearl fisheries, and I gave the divers some of my coconuts and said to them, "Dive for my luck and lot!" They did so and brought up from the deep bight great store of large and priceless pearls, and they said to me, "By Allah, O my master, thy luck is a lucky!" Then we sailed on, with the blessing of Allah (Whose name be exalted!), and ceased not sailing till we arrived safely at Bassorah. There I abode a little and then went on to Baghdad, where I entered my quarter and found my house and forgathered with my family and saluted my friends, who gave me joy of my safe return, and I laid up all my goods and valuables in my storehouses. Then I distributed alms and largess and clothed the widow and the orphan and made presents to my relations and comrades, for the Lord had requited me fourfold that I had lost. After which I returned to my old merry way of life and forgot all I had suffered in the great profit and gain I had made.

Such, then, is the history of my fifth voyage and its wonderments, and now to supper, and tomorrow, come again and I will tell you what befell me in my sixth voyage, for it was still more wonderful than this. (Saith he who telleth the tale): Then he called for food, and the servants spread the table, and when they had eaten the evening meal, he bade give Sindbad the Porter a hundred golden dinars and the landsman returned home and lay him down to sleep, much marveling at all he had heard. Next morning, as soon as it was light, he prayed the dawn prayer, and, after blessing Mohammed the Cream of all creatures, betook himself to the house of Sindbad the Seaman and wished him a good day. The merchant bade him sit, and talked with him till the rest of the company arrived. Then the servants spread the table, and when they had well eaten and drunken and were mirthful and merry, Sindbad the Seaman began in these words the narrative of

THE SIXTH VOYAGE OF SINDBAD THE SEAMAN

KNOW, O my brothers and friends and companions all, that I abode some time, after my return from my fifth voyage, in great solace and satisfaction and mirth and merriment, joyance and enjoyment, and I forgot what I had suffered, seeing the great gain and profit I had made, till one day as I sat making merry and enjoying myself with my friends, there came in to me a company of merchants whose case told tales of travel, and talked with me of voyage and adventure and greatness of pelf and lucre. Hereupon I remembered the days of my return from abroad, and my joy at once more seeing my native land and forgathering with my family and friends, and my soul yearned for travel and traffic. So, compelled by Fate and Fortune, I resolved to undertake another voyage, and, buying me fine and costly merchandise meet for foreign trade, made it up into bales, with which I journeyed from Baghdad to Bassorah.

Here I found a great ship ready for sea and full of merchants and notables, who had with them goods of price, so I embarked my bales therein. And we left Bassorah in safety and good spirits under the safeguard of the King, the Preserver, and continued our voyage from place to place and from city to city, buying and selling and profiting and diverting ourselves with the sight of countries where strange folk dwell. And Fortune and the voyage smiled upon us till one day, as we went along, behold, the captain suddenly cried with a great cry and cast his turban on the deck. Then he buffeted his face like a woman and plucked out his beard and fell down in the waist of the ship well-nigh fainting for stress of grief and rage, and crying, "Oh, and alas for the ruin of my house and the orphanship of my poor children!" So all the merchants and sailors came round about him and asked him, "O master, what is the matter?" For the light had become night before their sight. And he answered, saying: "Know, O folk, that we have wandered from our course and left the sea whose ways we wot, and come into a sea whose ways I know not, and unless Allah vouchsafe us a means of escape, we are all dead men. Wherefore pray ye to the Most High that He deliver us from this strait. Haply amongst you is one righteous whose prayers the Lord will accept." Then he arose and clomb the mast to see an there were any escape from that strait. And he would have loosed the sails, but the wind redoubled upon the ship and whirled her round thrice and drave her backward, whereupon her rudder brake and she fell off toward a high mountain.

With this the captain came down from the mast, saying: "There is no Majesty and there is no Might save in Allah, the Glorious, the Great, nor can man prevent that which is foreordained of Fate! By Allah, we are fallen on a place of sure destruction, and there is no way of escape for us, nor can any of us be saved!" Then we all fell a-weeping over ourselves and bidding one another farewell for that our days were come to an end, and we had lost all hopes of life. Presently the ship struck the mountain and broke up, and all and everything on board of her were plunged into the sea. Some of the merchants were drowned and others made shift to reach the shore and save themselves upon the mountain, I amongst the number. And when we got ashore, we found a great island, or rather peninsula, whose base was strewn with wreckage and crafts and goods and gear cast up by the sea from broken ships whose passengers had been drowned, and the quantity confounded count and calculation. So I climbed the cliffs into the inward of the isle and walked on inland till I came to a stream of sweet water that welled up at the nearest foot of the mountains and disappeared in the earth under the range of hills on the opposite side. But all the other passengers went over the mountains to the inner tracts, and, dispersing hither and thither, were confounded at what they saw and became like madmen at the sight of the wealth and treasures wherewith the shores were strewn.

As for me, I looked into the bed of the stream aforesaid and saw therein great plenty of rubies, and great royal pearls and all kinds of jewels and precious stones, which were as gravel in the bed of the rivulets that ran through the fields, and the sands sparkled and glittered with gems and precious ores. Moreover, we found in the island abundance of the finest lign aloes, both Chinese and Comorin. And there also is a spring of crude ambergris, which floweth like wax or gum over the stream banks, for the great heat of the sun, and runneth down to the seashore, where the monsters of the deep come up and, swallowing it, return into the sea. But it burneth in their bellies, so they cast it up again and it congealeth on the surface of the water, whereby its color and quantities are changed, and at last the waves cast it ashore, and the travelers and merchants who know it collect it and sell it. But as to the raw ambergris which is not swallowed, it floweth over the channel and congealeth on the banks, and when the sun shineth on it, it melteth and scenteth the whole valley with a musk-like fragrance. Then when the sun ceaseth from it, it congealeth again. But none can get to this place where is the crude ambergris, because of the mountains which enclose the island on all sides and which foot of man cannot ascend.

We continued thus to explore the island, marveling at the wonderful works of Allah and the riches we found there, but sore troubled for our own case, and dismayed at our prospects. Now we had picked up on the beach some small matter of victual from the wreck and husbanded it carefully, eating but once every day or two, in our fear lest it should fail us and we die miserably of famine and affright. Moreover, we were weak for colic brought on by seasickness and low diet, and my companions deceased, one after other, till there was but a small company of us left. Each that died we washed and shrouded in some of the clothes and linen cast ashore by the tides, and after a little, the rest of my fellows perished one by one, till I had buried the last of the party and abode alone on the island, with but a little provision left, I who was wont to have so much. And I wept over myself, saying: "Would Heaven I had died before my companions and they had washed me and buried me! It had been better than I should perish and none wash me and shroud me and bury me. But there is no Majesty and there is no Might save in Allah, the glorious, the Great!" Now after I had buried the last of my party and abode alone on the island, I arose and dug me a deep grave on the seashore, saying to myself: "Whenas I grow weak and know that death cometh to me, I will cast myself into the grave and die there, so the wind may drift the sand over me and cover me and I be buried therein."

Then I fell to reproaching myself for my little wit in leaving my native land and betaking me again to travel, after all I had suffered during my first five voyages, and when I had not made a single one without suffering more horrible perils and more terrible hardships than in its forerunners, and having no hope of escape from my present stress. And I repented me of my folly and bemoaned myself, especially as I had no need of money, seeing that I had enough and could not spend what I had—no, nor a half of it in all my life. However, after a while Allah sent me a thought, and I said to myself: "By God, needs must this stream have an end as well as a beginning, ergo an issue somewhere, and belike its course may lead to some inhabited place. So my best plan is to make me a little boat big enough to sit in, and carry it and, launching it on the river, embark therein and drop down the stream. If I escape, I escape, by God's leave, and if I perish, better die in the river than here." Then, sighing for myself, I set to work collecting a number of pieces of Chinese and Comorin aloes wood and I bound them together with ropes from the wreckage. Then I chose out from the broken-up ships straight planks of even size and fixed them firmly upon the aloes wood, making me a boat raft a little narrower than the channel of the stream, and I tied it tightly and firmly as though it were nailed. Then I loaded it with the goods, precious ores and jewels, and the union pearls which were like gravel, and the best of the ambergris crude and pure, together with what I had collected on the island and what was left me of victual and wild herbs. Lastly I lashed a piece of wood on either side, to serve me as oars, and launched it, and embarking, did according to the saying of the poet:

> Fly, fly with life whenas evils threat,
> Leave the house to tell of its builder's fate!
> Land after land shalt thou seek and find,
> But no other life on thy wish shall wait.
> Fret not thy soul in thy thoughts o' night,
> All woes shall end or sooner or late.
> Whoso is born in one land to die,
> There and only there shall gang his gait.
> Nor trust great things to another wight,
> Soul hath only soul for confederate.

My boat raft drifted with the stream, I pondering the issue of my affair, and the drifting ceased not till I came to the place where it disappeared beneath the mountain. I rowed my conveyance into the place, which was intensely dark, and the current carried the raft with it down the underground channel. The thin stream bore me on through a narrow tunnel where the raft touched either side and my head rubbed against the roof, return therefrom being impossible. Then I blamed myself for having thus risked my life, and said, "If this passage grow any straiter, the raft will hardly pass, and I cannot turn back, so I shall inevitably perish miserably in this place." And I threw myself down upon my face on the raft, by reason of the narrowness of the channel, whilst the stream ceased not to carry me along, knowing not night from day for the excess of the gloom which encompassed me about and my terror and concern for myself lest I should perish. And in such condition my course continued down the channel, which now grew wider and then straiter. Sore a-weary by reason of the darkness which could be felt, I feel asleep as I lay prone on the craft, and I slept knowing not an the time were long or short.

When I awoke at last, I found myself in the light of Heaven

and opening my eyes, I saw myself in a broad of the stream and the raft moored to an island in the midst of a number of Indians and Abyssinians. As soon as these blackamoors saw that I was awake, they came up to me and bespoke me in their speech. But I understood not what they said and thought that this was a dream and a vision which had betided me for stress of concern and chagrin. But I was delighted at my escape from the river. When they saw I understood them not and made them no answer, one of them came forward and said to me in Arabic: "Peace be with thee, O my brother! Who art thou, and whence faredst thou hither? How camest thou into this river, and what manner of land lies behind yonder mountains, for never knew we anyone make his way thence to us?" Quoth I: "And upon thee be peace and the ruth of Allah and His blessing! Who are ye, and what country is this?" "O my brother," answered he, "we are husbandmen and tillers of the soil, who came out to water our fields and plantations, and finding thee asleep on this raft, laid hold of it and made it fast by us, against thou shouldst awake at thy leisure. So tell us how thou camest hither." I answered, "For Allah's sake, O my lord, ere I speak give me somewhat to eat, for I am starving, and after ask me what thou wilt."

So he hastened to fetch me food and I ate my fill, till I was refreshed and my fear was calmed by a good bellyful and my life returned to me. Then I rendered thanks to the Most High for mercies great and small, glad to be out of the river and rejoicing to be amongst them, and I told them all my adventures from first to last, especially my troubles in the narrow channel. They consulted among themselves and said to one another, "There is no help for it but we carry him with us and present him to our King, that he may acquaint him with his adventures." So they took me, together with raft boat and its lading of moneys and merchandise, jewels, minerals, and golden gear, and brought me to their King, who was King of Sarandib, telling him what had happened. Whereupon he saluted me and bade me welcome. Then he questioned me of my condition and adventures through the man who had spoken Arabic, and I repeated to him my story from beginning to end, whereat he marveled exceedingly and gave me joy of my deliverance. After which I arose and fetched from the raft great store of precious ores and jewels and ambergris and lign aloes and presented them to the King, who accepted them and entreated me with the utmost honor, appointing me a lodging in his own palace. So I consorted with the chief of the islanders, and they paid me the utmost respect. And I quitted not the royal palace.

Now the Island Sarandib lieth under the equinoctial line, its night and day both numbering twelve hours. It measureth eighty leagues long by a breadth of thirty and its width is bounded by a lofty mountain and a deep valley. The mountain is conspicuous from a distance of three days, and it containeth many kinds of rubies and other minerals, and spice trees of all sorts. The surface is covered with emery, wherewith gems are cut and fashioned; diamonds are in its rivers and pearls are in its valleys. I ascended that mountain and solaced myself with a view of its marvels, which are indescribable, and afterward I returned to the King. Thereupon all the travelers and merchants who came to the place questioned me of the affairs of my native land and of the Caliph Harun al-Rashid and his rule, and I told them of him and of that wherefor he was renowned, and they praised him because of this, whilst I in turn questioned them of the manners and customs of their own countries and got the knowledge I desired.

One day the King himself asked me of the fashions and form of government of my country, and I acquainted him with the circumstance of the Caliph's sway in the city of Baghdad and the justice of his rule. The King marveled at my account of his appointments and said: "By Allah, the Caliph's ordinances are indeed wise and his fashions of praiseworthy guise, and thou hast made me love him by what thou tellest me. Wherefore I have a mind to make him a present and send it by thee." Quoth I: "Hearkening and obedience, O my lord. I will bear thy gift to him and inform him that thou art his sincere lover and true friend." Then I abode with the King in great honor and regard and consideration for a long while till one day, as I sat in his palace, I heard news of a company of merchants that were fitting out a ship for Bassorah, and said to myself, "I cannot do better than voyage with these men." So I rose without stay or delay and kissed the King's hand and acquainted him with my longing to set out with the merchants, for that I pined after my people and mine own land. Quoth he, "Thou art thine own master, yet if it be thy will to abide with us, on our head and eyes be it, for thou gladdenest us with thy company." "By Allah, O my lord," answered I, "thou hast indeed overwhelmed me with thy favors and well-doings, but I weary for a sight of my friends and family and native country."

When he heard this, he summoned the merchants in question and commended me to their care, paying my freight and passage money. Then he bestowed on me great riches from his treasuries and charged me with a magnificent present for the Caliph Harun al-Rashid. Moreover, he gave me a sealed letter, saying, "Carry this with thine own hand to the Commander of the Faithful, and give him many salutations from us!" "Hearing and obedience," I replied. The missive was written on the skin of the khawi (which is finer than lamb parchment and of yellow color), with ink of ultramarine, and the contents were as follows: "Peace be with thee from the King of Al-Hind, before whom are a thousand elephants and upon whose palace crenelles are a thousand jewels. But after (laud to the Lord and praises to His Prophet!) we send thee a trifling gift, which be thou pleased to accept. Thou art to us a brother and a sincere friend, and great is the love we bear for thee in heart. Favor us therefore with a reply. The gift besitteth not thy dignity, but we beg of thee, O our brother, graciously to accept it, and peace be with thee." And the present was a cup of ruby a span high, the inside of which was adorned with precious pearls; and a bed covered with the skin of the serpent which swalloweth the elephant, which skin hath spots each like a dinar and whoso sitteth upon it never sickeneth; and a hundred thousand miskals of Indian lign aloes and a slave girl like a shining moon.

Then I took leave of him and of all my intimates and acquaintances in the island, and embarked with the merchants aforesaid. We sailed with a fair wind, committing ourselves to the care of Allah (be He extolled and exalted!), and by His permission arrived at Bassorah, where I passed a few days and nights equipping myself and packing up my bales. Then I went on to Baghdad city, the House of Peace, where I sought an audience of the Caliph and laid the King's presents before him. He asked me whence they came, and I said to him, "By Allah, O Commander of the Faithful, I know not the name of the city nor the way thither!" He then asked me, "O Sindbad, is this true which the King writeth?" and I answered, after kissing the ground: "O my lord, I saw in his kingdom much more than he hath written in his letter. For state processions a throne is set for him upon a huge elephant eleven cubits high, and upon this he sitteth having his great lords and officers and guests standing in two ranks, on his right hand and on his left. At his head is a man hending in hand a golden javelin and behind him another with a great mace of gold whose head is an emerald a span long and as thick as a man's thumb. And when he mounteth horse there mount with him a thousand horsemen clad in gold brocade and silk, and as the King proceedeth a man precedeth him, crying, 'This is the King of great dignity, of high authority!' And he continueth to repeat his praises in words I remember not, saying at the end of his panegyric, 'This is the King owning the crown whose like nor Solomon nor the Mihraj ever possessed.' Then he is silent and one behind him proclaimeth, saying, 'He will die! Again I say he will die!' and the other addeth, 'Extolled be the perfection of the Living who dieth not!' Moreover, by reason of his justice and ordinance and intelligence, there is no kazi in his city, and all his lieges distinguish between truth and falsehood." Quoth the Caliph: "How great is this King! His letter hath shown me this, and as for the mightiness of his dominion thou hast told us what thou hast eyewitnessed. By Allah, he hath been endowed with wisdom, as with wide rule."

Then I related to the Commander of the Faithful all that had befallen me in my last voyage, at which he wondered exceedingly and bade his historians record my story and store it up in his treasuries, for the edification of all who might see it. Then he conferred on me exceeding great favors, and I repaired to my quarter and entered my home, where I warehoused all my goods and possessions. Presently my friends came to me and I distributed presents among my family and gave alms and largess, after which I yielded myself to joyance and enjoyment, mirth and merrymaking, and forgot all that I had suffered.

Such, then, O my brothers, is the history of what befell me in my sixth voyage, and tomorrow, Inshallah! I will tell you the story of my seventh and last voyage, which is still more wondrous and marvelous than that of the first six. (Saith he who telleth the tale): Then he bade lay the table, and the company supped with him, after which he gave the porter a hundred dinars, as of wont, and they all went their ways, marveling beyond measure at that which they had heard. Sindbad the Landsman went home and slept as of wont. Next day he rose and prayed the dawn prayer and repaired to his namesake's house, where, after the company was all assembled, the host began to relate

THE SEVENTH VOYAGE OF SINDBAD THE SEAMAN

Know, O company, that after my return from my sixth voyage, which brought me abundant profit, I resumed my former life in all possible joyance and enjoyment and mirth and making merry day and night. And I tarried sometime in this solace and satisfaction, till my soul began once more to long to sail the seas and see foreign countries and company with merchants and hear new things. So, having made up my mind, I packed up in bales a quantity of precious stuffs suited for sea trade and repaired with them from Baghdad city to Bassorah town, where I found a ship ready for sea, and in her a company of considerable merchants. I shipped with them and, becoming friends, we set forth on our venture in health and safety, and sailed with a fair wind till we came to a city called Madinat-al-Sin.

But after we had left it, as we fared on in all cheer and confidence, devising of traffic and travel, behold, there sprang up a violent head wind and a tempest of rain fell on us and drenched us and our goods. So we covered the bales with our cloaks and garments and drugget and canvas, lest they be spoiled by the rain, and betook ourselves to prayer and supplication to Almighty Allah, and humbled ourselves before Him for deliverance from the peril that was upon us. But the captain arose and, tightening his girdle, tucked up his skirts, and after taking refuge with Allah from Satan the Stoned, clomb to the masthead, whence he looked out right and left, and gazing at the passengers and crew, fell to buffeting his face and plucking out his beard. So we cried to him, "O Rais, what is the matter?" and he replied, saying: "Seek ye deliverance of the Most High from the strait into which we have fallen, and bemoan yourselves and take leave of one another. For know that the wind hath gotten the mastery of us, and hath driven us into the uttermost of the seas of the world." Then he came down from the masthead and opening his sea chest, pulled out a bag of blue cotton, from which he took a powder like ashes. This he set in a saucer wetted with a little water, and after waiting a short time, smelt and tasted it. And then he took out of the chest a booklet, wherein he read awhile, and said, weeping:

"Know, O ye passengers, that in this book is a marvelous matter, denoting that whoso cometh hither shall surely die, without hope of escape. For that this ocean is called the Sea of the Clime of the King, wherein is the sepulcher of our lord Solomon, son of David (on both be peace!), and therein are serpents of vast bulk and fearsome aspect. And what ship soever cometh to these climes, there riseth to her a great fish out of the sea and swalloweth her up with all and everything on board her." Hearing these words from the captain, great was our wonder, but hardly had he made an end of speaking when the ship was lifted out of the water and let fall again, and we applied to praying the death prayer and committing our souls to Allah.

Presently we heard a terrible great cry like the loud-pealing thunder whereat we were terror-struck and became as dead men, giving ourselves up for lost. Then, behold, there came up to us a huge fish, as big as a tall mountain, at whose sight we became wild for affright and, weeping sore, made ready for death, marveling at its vast size and gruesome semblance. When lo! a second fish made its appearance, than which we had seen naught more monstrous. So we bemoaned ourselves of our lives and farewelled one another. But suddenly up came a third fish bigger than the two first, whereupon we lost the power of thought and reason and were stupefied for the excess of our fear and horror. Then the three fish began circling round about the ship and the third and biggest opened his mouth to swallow it, and we looked into its mouth and, behold, it was wider than the gate of a city and its throat was like a long valley. So we besought the Almighty and called for succor upon His Apostle (on whom be blessing and peace!), when suddenly a violent squall of wind arose and smote the ship, which rose out of the water and settled upon a great reef, the haunt of sea monsters, where it broke up and fell asunder into planks, and all and everything on board were plunged into the sea.

As for me, I tore off all my clothes but my gown, and swam a little way, till I happened upon one of the ship's planks, whereto I clung and bestrode it like a horse, whilst the winds and the waters sported with me and the waves carried me up and cast me down. And I was in most piteous plight for fear and distress and hunger and thirst. Then I reproached myself for what I had done and my soul was weary after a life of ease and comfort, and I said to myself: "O Sindbad, O Seaman, thou repentest not and yet thou art ever suffering hardships and travails, yet wilt thou not renounce sea travel, or an thou say, 'I renounce,' thou liest in thy renouncement. Endure then with patience that which thou sufferest, for verily thou deservest all that betideth thee!" And I ceased not to humble myself before Almighty Allah and weep and bewail myself, recalling my former estate of solace and satisfaction and mirth and merriment and joyance. And thus I abode two days, at the end of which time I came to a great island abounding in trees and streams. There I landed and ate of the fruits of the island and drank of its waters, till I was refreshed and my life returned to me and my strength and spirits were restored and I recited:

> "Oft when thy case shows knotty and tangled skein,
> Fate downs from Heaven and straightens every ply.
> In patience keep thy soul till clear thy lot,
> For He who ties the knot can eke untie."

Then I walked about till I found on the further side a great river of sweet water, running with a strong current, whereupon I called to mind the boat raft I had made aforetime and said to myself: "Needs must I make another. Haply I may free me from this strait. If I escape, I have my desire and I vow to Allah Almighty to foreswear travel. And if I perish, I shall be at peace and shall rest from toil and moil." So I rose up and gathered together great store of pieces of wood from the trees (which were all of the finest sandalwood, whose like is not albe' I knew it not), and made shift to twist creepers and tree twigs into a kind of rope, with which I bound the billets together and so contrived a raft. Then saying, "An I be saved, 'tis of God's grace," I embarked thereon and committed myself to the current, and it bore me on for the first day and the second and the third after leaving the island whilst I lay in the raft, eating not and drinking, when I was athirst, of the water of the river, till I was weak and giddy as a chicken for stress of fatigue and famine and fear.

At the end of this time I came to a high mountain, whereunder ran the river, which when I saw, I feared for my life by reason of the straitness I had suffered in my former journey, and I would fain have stayed the raft and landed on the mountainside. But the current overpowered me and drew it into the subterranean passage like an archway, whereupon I gave myself up for lost and said, "There is no Majesty and there is no Might save in Allah, the Glorious, the Great!" However, after a little the raft glided into open air and I saw before me a wide valley, whereinto the river fell with a noise like the rolling of thunder and a swiftness as the rushing of the wind. I held onto the raft, for fear of falling off it, whilst the waves tossed me right and left, and the craft continued to descend with the current, nor could I avail to stop it nor turn it shoreward till it stopped with me at a great and goodly city, grandly edified and containing much people. And when the townsfolk saw me on the raft, dropping down with the current, they threw me out ropes, which I had not strength enough to hold. Then they tossed a net over the craft and drew it ashore with me, whereupon I fell to the ground amidst them, as I were a dead man, for stress of fear and hunger and lack of sleep.

After a while, there came up to me out of the crowd an old man of reverend aspect, well stricken in years, who welcomed me and threw over me abundance of handsome clothes, wherewith I covered my nakedness. Then he carried me to the hammam bath and brought me cordial sherbets and delicious perfumes. Moreover, when I came out, he bore me to his house, where his people made much of me and, seating me in a pleasant place, set rich food before me, whereof I ate my fill and returned thanks to God the Most High for my deliverance. Thereupon his pages fetched me hot water, and I washed my hands, and his handmaids brought me silken napkins, with which I dried them and wiped my mouth. Also the Sheikh set apart for me an apartment in a part of his house, and charged his pages and slave girls to wait upon me and do my will and supply my wants. They were assiduous in my service, and I abode with him in the guest chamber three days, taking my ease of good eating and good drinking and good scents till life returned to me and my terrors subsided and my heart was calmed and my mind was eased.

On the fourth day the Sheikh, my host, came in to me and said: "Thou cheerest us with thy company, O my son, and praised be Allah for thy safety! Say, wilt thou now come down with me to the beach and the bazaar and sell thy goods and take their price? Belike thou mayest buy thee wherewithal to traffic. I have ordered my servants to remove thy stock in trade from the sea, and they have piled it on the shore." I was silent awhile and said to myself, "What mean these words, and what goods have I?" Then said he: "O my son, be not troubled nor careful, but come with me to the market, and if any offer for thy goods what price contenteth thee, take it. But an thou be not satisfied, I will lay them up for thee in my warehouse, against a fitting occasion for sale." So I bethought me of my case and said to myself, "Do his bidding and see what are these goods!" and I said to him: "O my nuncle the Sheikh I hear and obey. I may not gainsay thee in aught, for Allah's blessing is on all thou dost."

Accordingly he guided me to the market street, where I found that he had taken in pieces the raft which carried me and which was of sandalwood, and I heard the broker crying it for sale. Then the merchants came and opened the gate of bidding for the wood and bid against one another till its price reached a thousand dinars, when they left bidding and my host said to me: "Hear, O my son, this is the current price of thy goods in hard times like these. Wilt thou sell them for this, or shall I lay them up for thee in my storehouses till such time as prices rise?" "O my lord," answered I, "the business is in thy hands. Do as thou wilt." Then asked he: "Wilt thou sell the wood to me, O my son, for a hundred gold pieces over and above what the merchants have bidden for it?" and I answered, "Yes, I have sold it to thee for monies received." So he bade his servants transport the wood to his storehouses, and, carrying me back to his house, seated me, and counted out to me the purchase money. After which he laid it in bags and, setting them in a privy place, locked them up with an iron padlock and gave me its key.

Some days after this the Sheikh said to me, "O my son, I have somewhat to propose to thee, wherein I trust thou wilt do my bidding." Quoth I, "What is it?" Quoth he: "I am a very old man, and have no son, but I have a daughter who is young in years and fair of favor and endowed with abounding wealth and beauty. Now I have a mind to marry her to thee, that thou mayest abide with her in this our country. And I will make thee master of all I have in hand, for I am an old man and thou shalt stand in my stead." I was silent for shame and made him no answer, whereupon he continued: "Do my desire in this, O my son, for I wish but thy weal. And if thou wilt but do as I say, thou shalt have her at once and be as my son, and all that is under my hand or that cometh to me shall be thine. If thou have a mind to traffic and travel to thy native land, none shall hinder thee, and thy property will be at thy sole disposal. So do as thou wilt." "By Allah, O my uncle," replied I, "thou art become to me even as my father, and I am a stranger and have undergone many hardships, while for stress of that which I have suffered naught of judgment or knowledge is left to me. It is for thee, therefore, to decide what I shall do."

Hereupon he sent his servants for the kazi and the witnesses and married me to his daughter, making for us a noble marriage feast and high festival. When I went in to her, I found her perfect in beauty and loveliness and symmetry and grace, clad in rich raiment and covered with a profusion of ornaments and necklaces and other trinkets of gold and silver and precious stones, worth a mint of money, a price none could pay. She pleased me, and we loved each other, and I abode with her in all solace and delight of life till her father was taken to the mercy of Allah Almighty. So we shrouded him and buried him, and I laid hands on the whole of his property and all his servants and slaves became mine. Moreover, the merchants installed me in his office, for he was their sheikh and their chief, and none of them purchased aught but with his knowledge and by his leave. And now his rank passed on to me.

When I became acquainted with the townsfolk, I found that at the beginning of each month they were transformed, in that their faces changed and they became like unto birds and they put forth wings wherewith they flew unto the upper regions of the firmament; and none remained in the city save the women and children. And I said in my mind, "When the first of the month cometh, I will ask one of them to carry me with them, whither they go." So when the time came and their complexion changed and their forms altered, I went in to one of the townsfolk and said to him: "Allah upon thee! Carry me with thee, that I might divert myself with the rest and return with you." "This may not be," answered he. But I ceased not to solicit him, and I importuned him till he consented. Then I went out in his company, without telling any of my family or servants or friends, and he took me on his back and flew up with me so high in air that I heard the angels glorifying God in the heavenly dome, whereat I wondered and exclaimed: "Praised be Allah! Extolled be the perfection of Allah!"

Hardly had I made an end of pronouncing the tasbih—praised be Allah!—when there came out a fire from Heaven and all but consumed the company. Whereupon they fled from it and descended with curses upon me and, casting me down on a high mountain, went away exceeding wroth with me, and left me there alone. As I found myself in this plight, I repented of what I had done and reproached myself for having undertaken that for which I was unable, saying: "There is no Majesty and there is no Might save in Allah, the Glorious, the Great! No sooner am I delivered from one affliction than I fall into a worse." And I continued in this case, knowing not whither I should go, when lo! there came up two young men, as they were moons, each using as a staff a rod of red gold. So I approached them and saluted them; and when they returned my salaam, I said to them: "Allah upon you twain. Who are ye, and what are ye?" Quoth they, "We are of the servants of the Most High Allah, abiding in this mountain," and giving me a rod of red gold they had with them, went their ways and left me.

I walked on along the mountain ridge, staying my steps with the staff and pondering the case of the two youths, when behold, a serpent came forth from under the mountain, with a man in her jaws whom she had swallowed even to below his navel, and he was crying out and saying, "Whoso delivereth me, Allah will deliver him from all adversity!" So I went up to the serpent and smote her on the head with the golden staff, whereupon she cast the man forth of her mouth. Then I smote her a second time, and she turned and fled, whereupon he came up to me and said, "Since my deliverance from yonder serpent hath been at thy hands I will never leave thee, and thou shalt be my comrade on this mountain." "And welcome," answered I. So we fared on along the mountain till we fell in with a company of folk, and I looked and saw amongst them the very man who had carried me and cast me down there. I went up to him and spake him fair, excusing myself to him and saying, "O my comrade, it is not thus that friend should deal with friend." Quoth he, "It was thou who well-nigh destroyed us by thy tasbih and thy glorifying God on my back." Quoth I, "Pardon me, for I had no knowledge of this matter, but if thou wilt take me with thee, I swear not to say a word."

So he relented and consented to carry me with him, but he made an express condition that so long as I abode on his back, I should abstain from pronouncing the tasbih or otherwise glorifying God. Then I gave the wand of gold to him whom I had delivered from the serpent and bade him farewell, and my friend took me on his back and flew with me as before, till he brought me to the city and set me down in my own house. My wife came to meet me and, saluting me, gave me joy of my safety and then said: "Beware of going forth hereafter with yonder folk, neither consort with them, for they are brethren of the devils, and know not how to mention the name of Allah Almighty, neither worship they Him." "And how did thy father with them?" asked I, and she answered: "My father was not of them, neither did he as they. And as now he is dead, methinks thou hadst better sell all we have and with the price buy merchandise and journey to thine own country and people, and I with thee; for I care not to tarry in this city, my father and my mother being dead." So I sold all the Sheikh's property piecemeal, and looked for one who should be journeying thence to Bassorah that I might join myself to him.

And while thus doing I heard of a company of townsfolk who had a mind to make the voyage but could not find them a ship, so they bought wood and built them a great ship, wherein I took passage with them, and paid them all the hire. Then we embarked, I and my wife, with all our movables, leaving our houses and domains and so forth, and set sail, and ceased not sailing from island to island and from sea to sea, with a fair wind and a favoring, till we arrived at Bassorah safe and sound. I made no stay there, but freighted another vessel and, transferring my goods to her, set out forthright for Baghdad city, where I arrived in safety, and entering my quarter and repairing to my house, forgathered with my family and friends and familiars and laid up my goods in my warehouses.

When my people, who, reckoning the period of my absence on this my seventh voyage, had found it to be seven and twenty years and had given up all hope of me, heard of my return, they came to welcome me and to give me joy of my safety. And I related to them all that had befallen me, whereat they marveled with exceeding marvel. Then I foreswore travel and vowed to Allah the Most High I would venture no more by land or sea, for that this seventh and last voyage had surfeited me of travel and adventure, and I thanked the Lord (be He praised and glorified!), and blessed Him for having restored me to my kith and kin and country and home. "Consider, therefore, O Sindbad, O Landsman," continued Sindbad the Seaman, "what sufferings I have undergone and what perils and hardships I have endured before coming to my present state." "Allah upon thee, O my Lord!" answered Sindbad the Landsman. "Pardon me the wrong I did thee." And they ceased not from friendship and fellowship, abiding in all cheer and pleasures and solace of life till there came to them the

Destroyer of delights and the Sunderer of Societies, and the Shatterer of palaces and the Caterer for Cemeteries; to wit, the Cup of Death, and glory be to the Living One who dieth not!

And there is a tale touching

THE LADY AND HER FIVE SUITORS

A WOMAN of the daughters of the merchants was married to a man who was a great traveler. It chanced once that he set out for a far country and was absent so long that his wife, for pure ennui, fell in love with a handsome young man of the sons of the merchants, and they loved each other with exceeding love. One day the youth quarreled with another man, who lodged a complaint against him with the Chief of Police, and he cast him into prison. When the news came to the merchant's wife his mistress, she well-nigh lost her wits. Then she arose and donning her richest clothes, repaired to the house of the Chief of Police. She saluted him and presented a written petition to this purport: "He thou hast clapped in jail is my brother Such-and-such, who fell out with Such-a-one, and those who testified against him bore false witness. He hath been wrongfully imprisoned, and I have none other to come in to me nor to provide for my support, therefore I beseech thee of thy grace to release him." When the magistrate had read the paper, he cast his eyes on her and fell in love with her forthright, so he said to her: "Go into the houses till I bring him before me. Then I will send for thee and thou shalt take him." "O my lord," replied she, "I have none to protect me save Almighty Allah! I am a stranger and may not enter any man's abode." Quoth the Wali, "I will not let him go except thou come to my home and I take my will of thee." Rejoined she, "If it must be so, thou must needs come to my lodging and sit and sleep the siesta and rest the whole day there." "And where is thy abode?" asked he, and she answered, "In such a place," and appointed him for such a time.

Then she went out from him, leaving his heart taken with love of her, and she repaired to the Kazi of the city, to whom she said, "O our lord the Kazi!" He exclaimed, "Yes!" and she continued, "Look into my case, and thy reward be with Allah the Most High!" Quoth he, "Who hath wronged thee?" and quoth she, "O my lord, I have a brother and I have none but that one, and it is on his account that I come to thee, because the Wali hath imprisoned him for a criminal and men have borne false witness against him that he is a wrongdoer, and I beseech thee to intercede for him with the Chief of Police."

When the Kazi looked on her, he fell in love with her forthright and said to her: "Enter the house and rest awhile with my handmaids whilst I send to the Wali to release thy brother. If I knew the money fine which is upon him, I would pay it out of my own purse, so I may have my desire of thee, for thou pleaseth me with thy sweet speech." Quoth she, "If thou, O my lord, do thus, we must not blame others." Quoth he, "An thou wilt not come in, wend thy ways." Then said she, "An thou wilt have it so, O our lord, it will be privier and better in my place than in thine, for here are slave girls and eunuchs and goers-in and comers-out, and indeed I am a woman who wotteth naught of this fashion, but need compelleth." Asked the Kazi, "And where is thy house?" and she answered, "In such a place," and appointed him for the same day and time as the Chief of Police.

Then she went out from him to the Wazir, to whom she preferred her petition for the release from prison of her brother, who was absolutely necessary to her. But he also required her of herself, saying, "Suffer me to have my will of thee and I will set thy brother free." Quoth she: "An thou wilt have it so, be it in my house, for there it will be privier both for me and for thee. It is not far distant, and thou knowest that which behooveth us women of cleanliness and adornment." Asked he, "Where is thy house?" "In such a place," answered she, and appointed him for the same time as the two others.

Then she went out from him to the King of the city and told him her story and sought of him her brother's release. "Who imprisoned him?" enquired he, and she replied, "'Twas thy Chief of Police." When the King heard her speech, it transpierced his heart with the arrows of love and he bade her enter the palace with him, that he might send to the Kazi and release her brother. Quoth she: "O King, this thing is easy to thee, whether I will or nill, and if the King will indeed have this of me, it is of my good fortune. But if he come to my house, he will do me the more honor by setting step therein, even as saith the poet:

"O my friends, have ye seen or have ye heard
Of his visit whose virtues I hold so high?"

Quoth the King, "We will not cross thee in this." So she appointed him for the same time as the three others, and told him where her house was.

Then she left him, and betaking herself to a man which was a carpenter, said to him: "I would have thee make me a cabinet with four compartments one above other, each with its door for locking up. Let me know thy hire and I will give it thee." Replied he: "My price will be four dinars. But, O noble lady and well-protected, if thou wilt vouchsafe me thy favors, I will ask nothing of thee." Rejoined she, "An there be no help but that thou have it so, then make thou five compartments with their padlocks." And she appointed him to bring it exactly on the day required. Said he, "It is well. Sit down, O my lady, and I will make it for thee forthright, and after I will come to thee at my leisure." So she sat down by him whilst he fell to work on the cabinet, and when he had made an end of it, she chose to see it at once carried home and set up in the sitting chamber. Then she took four gowns and carried them to the dyer, who dyed them each of a different color, after which she applied herself to making ready meat and drink, fruits, flowers, and perfumes.

Now when the appointed trysting day came, she donned her costliest dress and adorned herself and scented herself, then spread the sitting room with various kinds of rich carpets, and sat down to await who should come. And behold, the Kazi was the first to appear, devancing the rest, and when she saw him, she rose to her feet and kissed the ground before him, then, taking him by the hand, made him sit down by her on the couch and lay with him and fell to jesting and toying with him. By and by he would have her do his desire, but she said, "O my lord, doff thy clothes and turban and assume this yellow cassock and this headkerchief, whilst I bring thee meat and drink, and after thou shalt win thy will." So saying, she took his clothes and turban and clad him in the cassock and the kerchief. But hardly had she done this when lo! there came a knocking at the door. Asked he, "Who is that rapping at the door?" and she answered, "My husband." Quoth the Kazi, "What is to be done, and where shall I go?" Quoth she, "Fear nothing. I will hide thee in this cabinet," and he, "Do as seemeth good to thee."

So she took him by the hand and pushing him into the lowest compartment, locked the door upon him. Then she went to the house door, where she found the Wali, so she bussed ground before him and taking his hand, brought him into the saloon, where she made him sit down and said to him: "O my lord, this house is thy house, this place is thy place, and I am thy handmaid. Thou shalt pass all this day with me, wherefore do thou doff thy clothes and don this red gown, for it is a sleeping gown." So she took away his clothes and made him assume the red gown and set on his head an old patched rag she had by her. After which she sat by him on the divan and she sported with him while he toyed with her awhile, till he put out his hand to her. Whereupon she said to him: "O our lord, this day is thy day and none shall share in it with thee. But first, of thy favor and benevolence, write me an order for my brother's release from gaol, that my heart may be at ease." Quoth he, "Hearkening and obedience. On my head and eyes be it!" and wrote a letter to his treasurer, saying: "As soon as this communication shall reach thee, do thou set Such-a-one free, without stay or delay, neither answer the bearer a word." Then he sealed it and she took it from him, after which she began to toy again with him on the divan when, behold, someone knocked at the door. He asked, "Who is that?" and she answered, "My husband." "What shall I do?" said he, and she, "Enter this cabinet, till I send him away and return to thee." So she clapped him into the second compartment from the bottom and padlocked the door on him, and meanwhile the Kazi heard all they said.

Then she went to the house door and opened it, whereupon lo! the Wazir entered. She bussed the ground before him and received him with all honor and worship, saying: "O my lord, thou exaltest us by thy coming to our house. Allah never deprive us of the light of thy countenance!" Then she seated him on the divan and said to him, "O my lord, doff thy heavy dress and turban and don these lighter vestments." So he put off his clothes and turban and she clad him in a blue cassock and a tall red bonnet, and said to him: "Erst thy garb was that of the wazirate, so leave it to its own time and don this light gown, which is better fitted for carousing and making merry and sleep." Thereupon she began to play with him and he with her, and he would have done his desire of her, but she put him off, saying, "O my lord, this shall not fail us." As they were talking there came a knocking at the door, and the Wazir asked her, "Who is that?" to which she answered, "My husband." Quoth he, "What is to be done?" Quoth she, "Enter this cabinet, till I get rid of him and come back to thee, and fear thou nothing."

So she put him in the third compartment and locked the door on him, after which she went out and opened the house door when lo and behold! in came the King. As soon as she saw him she kissed ground before him, and taking him by the hand, led him into the saloon and seated him on the divan at the upper end. Then said she to him, "Verily, O King, thou dost us high honor, and if we brought thee to gift the world and all that therein is, it would not be worth a single one of thy steps usward." And when he had taken his seat upon the divan she said, "Give me leave to speak one word." "Say what thou wilt." answered he, and she said, "O my lord, take thine ease and doff thy dress and turban." Now his clothes were worth a thousand dinars, and when he put them off she clad him in a patched gown, worth at the very most ten dirhams, and fell to talking and jesting with him, all this while the folk in the cabinet hearing everything that passed, but not daring to say a word. Presently the King put his hand to her neck and sought to do his desire of her, when she said, "This thing shall not fail us, but I had first promised myself to entertain thee in this sitting chamber, and I have that which shall content thee." Now as they were speaking, someone knocked at the door and he asked her, "Who is that?" "My husband," answered she, and he, "Make him go away of his own goodwill, or I will fare forth to him and send him away perforce." Replied she, "Nay, O my lord, have patience till I send him away by my skillful contrivance." "And I, how shall I do!" inquired the King. Whereupon she took him by the hand and making him enter the fourth compartment of the cabinet, locked it upon him.

Then she went out and opened the house door, when behold, the carpenter entered and saluted her. Quoth she, "What manner of thing is this cabinet thou hast made me?" "What aileth it, O my lady?" asked he, and she answered, "The top compartment is too strait." Rejoined he, "Not so," and she, "Go in thyself and see. It is not wide enough for thee." Quoth he, "It is wide enough for four." and entered the fifth compartment, whereupon she locked the door on him. Then she took the letter of the Chief of Police and carried it to the Treasurer, who, having read and understood it, kissed it and delivered her lover to her. She told him all she had done and he said, "And how shall we act now?" She answered, "We will remove hence to another city, for after this work there is no tarrying for us here."

So the twain packed up what goods they had and, loading them on camels, set out forthright for another city. Meanwhile, the five abode each in his compartment of the cabinet without eating or drinking three whole days, during which time they held their water until at last the carpenter could retain his no longer, so he staled on the King's head, and the King urinated on the Wazir's head, and the Wazir piddled on the Wali, and the Wali pissed on the head of the Kazi. Whereupon the Judge cried out and said: "What nastiness is this? Doth not what strait we are in suffice us, but you must make water upon us?" The Chief of Police recognized the Kazi's voice and answered, saying aloud, "Allah increase thy reward, O Kazi!" And when the Kazi heard him, he knew him for the Wali. Then the Chief of Police lifted up his voice and said, "What means this nastiness?" and the Wazir answered, saying, "Allah increase thy reward, O Wali!" whereupon he knew him to be the Minister. Then the Wazir lifted up his voice and said, "What means this nastiness?" But when the King heard and recognized his Minister's voice, he held his peace and concealed his affair.

Then said the Wazir: "May Allah damn this woman for her dealing with us! She hath brought hither all the chief officers of the state, except the King. Quoth the King, "Hold your peace, for I was the first to fall into the toils of this lewd strumpet." Whereat cried the carpenter: "And I, what have I done? I made her a cabinet for four gold pieces, and when I came to seek my hire, she tricked me into entering this compartment and locked the door on me." And they fell to talking with one another, diverting the King and doing away his chagrin. Presently the neighbors came up to the house and, seeing it deserted, said one to other: "But yesterday our neighbor, the wife of Such-a-one, was in it, but now no sound is to be heard therein nor is soul to be seen. Let us break open the doors and see how the case stands, lest it come to the ears of the Wali or the King and we be cast into prison and regret not doing this thing before."

So they broke open the doors and entered the saloon, where they saw a large wooden cabinet and heard men within groaning for hunger and thirst. Then said one of them, "Is there a Jinni in this cabinet?" and his fellow, "Let us heap fuel about it and burn it with fire." When the Kazi heard this, he bawled out to them, "Do it not!"

And they said to one another, "Verily the Jinn make believe to be mortals and speak with men's voices." Thereupon the Kazi repeated somewhat of the Sublime Koran and said to the neighbors, "Draw near to the cabinet wherein we are." So they drew near, and he said, "I am So-and-so the Kazi, and ye are Such-a-one and Such-a-one, and we are here a company." Quoth the neighbors, "Who brought you here?" And he told them the whole case from beginning to end. Then they fetched a carpenter, who opened the five doors and let out Kazi, Wazir, Wali, King, and carpenter in their queer disguises; and each, when he saw how the others were accoutered, fell a-laughing at them. Now she had taken away all their clothes, so every one of them sent to his people for fresh clothes and put them on and went out, covering himself therewith from the sight of the folk. Consider, therefore, what a trick this woman played off upon the folk!

And I have heard tell also a tale of

KHALIFAH THE FISHERMAN OF BAGHDAD

THERE was once in tides of yore and in ages and times long gone before in the city of Baghdad a fisherman, Khalifah hight, a pauper wight, who had never once been married in all his days. It chanced one morning that he took his net and went with it to the river as was his wont, with the view of fishing before the others came. When he reached the bank, he girt himself and tucked up his skirts. Then stepping into the water, he spread his net and cast it a first cast and a second, but it brought up naught. He ceased not to throw it till he had made ten casts, and still naught came up therein, wherefore his breast was straitened and his mind perplexed concerning his case and he said: "I crave pardon of God the Great, there is no god but He, the Living, the Eternal, and unto Him I repent. There is no Majesty and there is no Might save in Allah, the Glorious, the Great! Whatso He willeth is and whatso He nilleth is not! Upon Allah (to Whom belong Honor and Glory!) dependeth daily bread! When as He giveth to His servant, none denieth him; and when as He denieth a servant, none giveth to him." And of the excess of his distress, he recited these two couplets:

> "An Fate afflict thee, with grief manifest,
> Prepare thy patience and make broad thy breast;
> For of His grace the Lord of all the worlds
> Shall send to wait upon unrest sweet Rest."

Then he said in his mind, "I will make this one more cast, trusting in Allah, so haply He may not disappoint my hope." And he rose, and casting into the river the net as far as his arm availed, gathered the cords in his hands and waited a full hour, after which he pulled at it and, finding it heavy, handled it gently and drew it in, little by little, till he got it ashore, when lo and behold! he saw in it a one-eyed, lame-legged ape. Seeing this, quoth Khalifah: "There is no Majesty and there is no Might save in Allah! Verily, we are Allah's and to Him we are returning! What meaneth this heartbreaking, miserable ill luck and hapless fortune? What is come to me this blessed day? But all this is of the destinies of Almighty Allah!" Then he took the ape and tied him with a cord to a tree which grew on the riverbank, and grasping a whip he had with him, raised his arm in the air, thinking to bring down the scourge upon the quarry, when Allah made the ape speak with a fluent tongue, saying: "O Khalifah, hold thy hand and beat me not, but leave me bounden to this tree and go down to the river and cast thy net, confiding in Allah; for He will give thee thy daily bread."

Hearing this, Khalifah went down to the river, and casting his net, let the cords run out. Then he pulled it in and found it heavier than before, so he ceased not to tug at it till he brought it to land, when, behold, there was another ape in it, with front teeth wide apart, kohl-darkened eyes, and hands stained with henna dyes; and he was laughing, and wore a tattered waistcloth about his middle. Quoth Khalifah, "Praised be Allah Who hath changed the fish of the river into apes!" Then, going up to the first ape, who was still tied to the tree, he said to him: "See, O unlucky, how fulsome was the counsel thou gavest me! None but thou made me light on this second ape; and for that thou gavest me good morrow with thy one eye and thy lameness, I am become distressed and weary, without dirham or dinar."

So saying, he hent in hand a stick and flourishing it thrice in the air, was about to come down with it upon the lame ape, when the creature cried out for mercy and said to him: "I conjure thee, by Allah, spare me for the sake of this my fellow, and seek of him thy need; for he will guide thee to thy desire!" So he held his hand from him, and throwing down the stick, went up to and stood by the second ape, who said to him: "O Khalifah, this my speech will profit thee naught except thou hearken to what I say to thee; but an thou do my bidding and cross me not, I will be the cause of thine enrichment." Asked Khalifah, "And what hast thou to say to me that I may obey thee therein?" The ape answered, "Leave me bound on the bank and hie thee down to the river, then cast thy net a third time, and after I will tell thee what to do."

So he took his net, and going down to the river, cast it once more and waited awhile. Then he drew it in, and finding it heavy, labored at it and ceased not his travail till he got it ashore, when he found in it yet another ape. But this one was red, with a blue waistcloth about his middle; his hands and feet were stained with henna and his eyes blackened with kohl. When Khalifah saw this, he exclaimed: "Glory to God the Great! Extolled be the perfection of the Lord of Dominion! Verily, this is a blessed day from first to last. Its ascendant was fortunate in the countenance of the first ape, and the scroll is known by its superscription! Verily, today is a day of apes. There is not a single fish left in the river, and we are come out today but to catch monkeys!"

Then he turned to the third ape and said, "And what thing art thou also, O unlucky?" Quoth the ape, "Dost thou not know me, O Khalifah!" and quoth he, "Not I!" The ape cried, "I am the ape of Abu al-Sa'adat the Jew, the shroff." Asked Khalifah, "And what dost thou for him?" and the ape answered, "I give him good morrow at the first of the day, and he gaineth five ducats; and again at the end of the day, I give him good even, and he gaineth other five ducats." Whereupon Khalifah turned to the first ape and said to him: "See, O unlucky, what fine apes other folk have! As for thee, thou givest me good morrow with thy one eye and thy lameness and thy ill-omened phiz, and I become poor and bankrupt and hungry!" So saying, he took the cattle stick, and flourishing it thrice in the air, was about to come down with it on the first ape, when Abu al-Sa'adat's ape said to him: "Let him be, O Khalifah. Hold thy hand and come hither to me, that I may tell thee what to do."

So Khalifah threw down the stick, and walking up to him, cried, "And what hast thou to say to me, O monarch of all monkeys?" Replied the ape: "Leave me and the other two apes here, and take thy net and cast it into the river; and whatever cometh up, bring it to me, and I will tell thee what shall gladden thee." He replied, "I hear and obey," and took the net and gathered it on his shoulder, reciting these couplets:

> "When straitened is my breast I will of my Creator pray,
> Who may and can the heaviest weight lighten in easiest way;
> For ere man's glance can turn or close his eye by God His grace
> Waxeth the broken whole and yieldeth jail its prison prey.
> Therefore with Allah one and all of thy concerns commit,
> Whose grace and favor men of wit shall nevermore gainsay."

Now when Khalifah had made an end of his verse, he went down to the river, and casting his net, waited awhile. After which he drew it up and found therein a fine young fish, with a big head, a tail like a ladle, and eyes like two gold pieces. When Khalifah saw this fish, he rejoiced, for he had never in his life caught its like, so he took it, marveling, and carried it to the ape of Abu al-Sa'adat the Jew, as 'twere he had gotten possession of the universal world. Quoth the ape, "O Khalifah, what wilt thou do with this, and with thine ape?" and quoth the fisherman: "I will tell thee, O monarch of monkeys, all I am about to do. Know then that first, I will cast about to make away with yonder accursed, my ape, and take thee in his stead, and give thee every day to eat of whatso thou wilt." Rejoined the ape: "Since thou hast made choice of me, I will tell thee how thou shalt do wherein, if it please Allah Almighty, shall be the mending of thy fortune. Lend thy mind, then, to what I say to thee and 'tis this! Take another cord and tie me also to a tree, where leave me and go to the midst of the dike and cast thy net into the Tigris. Then after waiting awhile, draw it up and thou shalt find therein a fish than which thou never sawest a finer in thy whole life. Bring it to me and I will tell thee how thou shalt do after this."

So Khalifah rose forthright, and casting his net into the Tigris, drew up a great catfish the bigness of a lamb. Never had he set eyes on its like, for it was larger than the first fish. He carried it to the ape, who said to him: "Gather thee some green grass and set half of it in a basket; lay the fish therein and cover it with the other moiety. Then, leaving us here tied, shoulder the basket and betake thee to Baghdad. If any bespeak thee or question thee by the way, answer him not, but fare on till thou comest to the market street of the money-changers, at the upper end whereof thou wilt find the shop of Master Abu al-Sa'adat the Jew, Sheikh of the shroffs, and wilt see him sitting on a mattress, with a cushion behind him and two coffers, one for gold and one for silver, before him, while around him stand his Mamelukes and Negro slaves and servant lads. Go up to him and set the basket before him, saying: 'O Abu al-Sa'adat, verily I went out today to fish and cast my net in thy name, and Allah Almighty sent me this fish.' He will ask, 'Hast thou shown it to any but me?' and do thou answer, 'No, by Allah!' Then will he take it of thee and give thee a dinar. Give it him back and he will give thee two dinars; but do thou return them also, and so do with everything he may offer thee; and take naught from him, though he give thee the fish's weight in gold.

Then will he say to thee, 'Tell me what thou wouldst have, and do thou reply, 'By Allah, I will not sell the fish save for two words!' He will ask, 'What are they?' And do thou answer, 'Stand up and say, "Bear witness, O ye who are present in the market, that I give Khalifah the fisherman my ape in exchange for his ape, and that I barter for his lot my lot and luck for his luck." This is the price of the fish, and I have no need of gold.' If he do this, I will every day give thee good morrow and good even, and every day thou shalt gain ten dinars of good gold; whilst this one-eyed, lame-legged ape shall daily give the Jew good morrow, and Allah shall afflict him every day with an avanie which he must needs pay, nor will he cease to be thus afflicted till he is reduced to beggary and hath naught. Hearken then to my words, so shalt thou prosper and be guided aright."

Quoth Khalifah: "I accept thy counsel, O monarch of all the monkeys! But as for this unlucky, may Allah never bless him! I know not what to do with him." Quoth the ape, "Let him go into the water, and let me go also." "I hear and obey," answered Khalifah, and unbound the three apes, and they went down into the river. Then he took up the catfish, which he washed, then laid it in the basket upon some green grass, and covered it with other, and lastly, shouldering his load, set out with the basket upon his shoulder and ceased not faring till he entered the city of Baghdad. And as he threaded the streets the folk knew him and cried out to him, saying, "What hast thou there, O Khalifah?" But he paid no heed to them and passed on till he came to the market street of the money-changers and fared between the shops, as the ape had charged him, till he found the Jew seated at the upper end, with his servants in attendance upon him, as he were a King of the Kings of Khorasan. He knew him at first sight; so he went up to him and stood before him, whereupon Abu al-Sa'adat raised his eyes and recognizing him, said: "Welcome, O Khalifah! What wantest thou, and what is thy need? If any have missaid thee or spited thee, tell me and I will go with thee to the Chief of Police, who shall do thee justice on him." Replied Khalifah: "Nay, as thy head liveth, O chief of the Jews, none hath missaid me. But I went forth this morning to the river and, casting my net into the Tigris on thy luck, brought up this fish."

Therewith he opened the basket and threw the fish before the Jew, who admired it and said, "By the Pentateuch and the Ten Commandments, I dreamt last night that the Virgin came to me and said, 'Know, O Abu al-Sa'adat, that I have sent thee a pretty present!' And doubtless 'tis this fish." Then he turned to Khalifah and said to him, "By thy faith, hath any seen it but I?" Khalifah replied, "No, by Allah, and by Abu Bakr the Veridical, none hath seen it save thou, O chief of the Jews!" Whereupon the Jew turned to one of his lads and said to him: "Come, carry this fish to my house and bid Sa'adah dress it and fry and broil it, against I make an end of my business and hie me home." And Khalifah said, "Go, O my lad, let the master's wife fry some of it and broil the rest." Answered the boy, "I hear and I obey, O my lord," and, taking the fish, went away with it to the house.

Then the Jew put out his hand and gave Khalifah the fisherman a dinar, saying, "Take this for thyself, O Khalifah, and spend it on thy family." When Khalifah saw the dinar on his palm, he took it, saying, "Laud to the Lord of Dominion!" as if he had never seen aught of gold in his life, and went somewhat away. But before he had gone far, he was minded of the ape's charge and turning back, threw down the ducat, saying: "Take thy gold and give folk back their fish! Dost thou make a laughingstock of folk?" The Jew, hearing this, thought he was jesting, and offered him two dinars upon the other, but Khalifah said: "Give me the fish, and no nonsense. How knewest thou I would sell it at this price?" Whereupon the Jew gave him two more dinars and said, "Take these five ducats for thy fish and leave greed." So Khalifah hent the five dinars in hand and went away, rejoicing, and gazing and marveling at the gold and saying: "Glory be to God! There is not with the Caliph of Baghdad what is with me this day!"

Then he ceased not faring on till he came to the end of the market street, when he remembered the words of the ape and his charge, and returning to the Jew, threw him back the gold. Quoth he: "What aileth thee, O Khalifah? Dost thou want silver in exchange for gold?" Khalifah replied: "I want nor dirhams nor dinars. I only want thee to give me back folk's fish." With this the Jew waxed wroth and shouted out at him, saying: "O Fisherman, thou bringest me a fish not worth a sequin and I give thee five for it, yet art thou not content! Art thou Jinn-mad? Tell me for how much thou wilt sell it."

Answered Khalifah, "I will not sell it for silver nor for gold, only for two sayings thou shalt say me."

When the Jew heard speak of the "two sayings," his eyes sank into his head, he breathed hard and ground his teeth for rage, and said to him, "O nail paring of the Moslems, wilt thou have me throw off my faith for the sake of thy fish, and wilt thou debauch me from my religion and stultify my belief and my conviction which I inherited of old from my forebears?" Then he cried out to the servants who were in waiting and said: "Out on you! Bash me this unlucky rogue's neck and bastinado him soundly!" So they came down upon him with blows and ceased not beating him till he fell beneath the shop, and the Jew said to them, "Leave him and let him rise." Whereupon Khalifah jumped up as if naught ailed him, and the Jew said to him: "Tell me what price thou asketh for this fish and I will give it thee; for thou hast gotten but scant good of us this day." Answered the fisherman, "Have no fear for me, O master, because of the beating, for I can eat ten donkeys' rations of stick."

The Jew laughed at his words and said, "Allah upon thee, tell me what thou wilt have and by the right of my faith, I will give it thee!" The fisherman replied, "Naught from thee will remunerate me for this fish save the two words whereof I spake." And the Jew said, "Meseemeth thou wouldst have me become a Moslem." Khalifah rejoined: "By Allah, O Jew, an thou Islamize, 'twill nor advantage the Moslems nor damage the Jews. And in like manner, an thou hold to thy misbelief 'twill nor damage the Moslems nor advantage the Jews. But what I desire of thee is that thou rise to thy feet and say: 'Bear witness against me, O people of the market, that I barter my ape for the ape of Khalifah the fisherman and my lot in the world for his lot and my luck for his luck'." Quoth the Jew, "If this be all thou desirest, 'twill sit lightly upon me." So he rose without stay or delay and standing on his feet, repeated the required words. After which he turned to the fisherman and asked him, "Hast thou aught else to ask of me?" "No," answered he, and the Jew said, "Go in peace!"

Hearing this Khalifah sprung to his feet forthright, took up his basket and net, and returned straight to the Tigris, where he threw his net and pulled it in. He found it heavy and brought it not ashore but with travail, when he found it full of fish of all kinds. Presently up came a woman with a dish, who gave him a dinar, and he gave her fish for it, and after her a eunuch, who also bought a dinar's worth of fish, and so forth till he had sold ten dinars' worth. And he continued to sell ten dinars' worth of fish daily for ten days, till he had gotten a hundred dinars.

Now Khalifah the fisherman had quarters in the Passage of the Merchants, and as he lay one night in his lodging much bemused with hashish, he said to himself: "O Khalifah, the folk all know thee for a poor fisherman, and now thou hast gotten a hundred golden dinars. Needs must the Commander of the Faithful, Harun al-Rashid, hear of this from someone, and haply he will be wanting money and will send for thee and say to thee: 'I need a sum of money and it hath reached me that thou hast an hundred dinars, so do thou lend them to me those same.' I shall answer, 'O Commander of the Faithful, I am a poor man, and whoso told thee that I had a hundred dinars lied against me, for I have naught of this.' Thereupon he will commit me to the Chief of Police, saying, 'Strip him of his clothes and torment him with the bastinado till he confess and give up the hundred dinars in his possession.' Wherefore, meseemeth to provide against this predicament, the best thing I can do is to rise forthright and bash myself with the whip, so to use myself to beating." And his hashish said to him, "Rise, doff thy dress."

So he stood up, and putting off his clothes, took a whip he had by him and set handy a leather pillow. Then he fell to lashing himself, laying every other blow upon the pillow and roaring out the while: "Alas! Alas! By Allah, 'tis a false saying, O my lord, and they have lied against me, for I am a poor fisherman and have naught of the goods of the world!" The noise of the whip falling on the pillow and on his person resounded in the still of night and the folk heard it, and amongst others the merchants, and they said: "Whatever can ail the poor fellow, that he crieth and we hear the noise of blows falling on him? 'Twould seem robbers have broken in upon him and are tormenting him." Presently they all came forth of their lodgings at the noise of the blows and the crying, and repaired to Khalifah's room, but they found the door locked and said one to other: "Belike the robbers have come in upon him from the back of the adjoining saloon. It behooveth us to climb over by the roofs."

So they clomb over the roofs, and coming down through the skylight, saw him naked and flogging himself, and asked him, "What aileth thee, O Khalifah?" He answered: "Know, O folk, that I have gained some dinars and fear lest my case be carried up to the Prince of True Believers, Harun al-Rashid, and he send for me and demand of me those same gold pieces; whereupon I should deny, and I fear that if I deny, he will torture me, so I am torturing myself, by way of accustoming me to what may come." The merchants laughed at him and said: "Leave this fooling. May Allah not bless thee and the dinars thou hast gotten! Verily thou hast disturbed us this night and hast troubled our hearts."

So Khalifah left flogging himself and slept till the morning, when he rose and would have gone about his business, but bethought him of his hundred dinars and said in his mind: "An I leave them at home, thieves will steal them, and if I put them in a belt about my waist, peradventure someone will see me and lay in wait for me till he come upon me in some lonely place and slay me and take the money. But I have a device that should serve me well, right well." So he jumped up forthright and made him a pocket in the collar of his gabardine, and tying the hundred dinars up in a purse, laid them in the collar pocket. Then he took his net and basket and staff and went down to the Tigris, where he made a cast, but brought up naught. So he removed from that place to another and threw again, but once more the net came up empty. And he went on removing from place to place till he had gone half a day's journey from the city, ever casting the net, which kept bringing up naught. So he said to himself, "By Allah, I will throw my net a-stream but this once more, whether ill come of it or weal!"

Then he hurled the net with all his force, of the excess of his wrath, and the purse with the hundred dinars flew out of his collar pocket and, lighting in midstream, was carried away by the strong current. Whereupon he threw down the net, and doffing his clothes, left them on the bank and plunged into the water after the purse. He dived for it nigh a hundred times, till his strength was exhausted and he came up for sheer fatigue, without chancing on it. When he despaired of finding the purse, he returned to the shore, where he saw nothing but staff, net, and basket and sought for his clothes but could light on no trace of them. So he said in himself: "O vilest of those wherefor was made the byword: 'The pilgrimage is not perfected save by copulation with the camel!'" Then he wrapped the net about him, and taking staff in one hand and basket in other, went trotting about like a camel in rut, running right and left and backward and forward, disheveled and dusty, as he were a rebel Marid let loose from Solomon's prison.

So far for what concerns the fisherman Khalifah; but as regards the Caliph Harun al-Rashid, he had a friend, a jeweler called Ibn al-Kirnas, and all the traders, brokers, and middlemen knew him for the Caliph's merchant. Wherefore there was naught sold in Baghdad by way of rarities and things of price or Mamelukes or handmaidens but was first shown to him. As he sat one day in his shop, behold, there came up to him the Sheikh of the brokers, with a slave girl whose like seers never saw, for she was of passing beauty and loveliness, symmetry and perfect grace, and among her gifts that she knew all arts and sciences and could make verses and play upon all manner musical instruments. So Ibn al-Kirnas bought her for five thousand golden dinars and clothed her with other thousand. After which he carried her to the Prince of True Believers, with whom she lay the night, and who made trial of her in every kind of knowledge and accomplishment and found her versed in all sorts of arts and sciences, having no equal in her time. Her name was Kut al-Kulub and she was even as saith the poet:

> I fix my glance on her, whene'er she wends,
> And nonacceptance of my glance breeds pain.
> She favors graceful-necked gazelle at gaze,
> And "Graceful as gazelle" to say we're fain.

On the morrow the Caliph sent for Ibn al-Kirnas, the jeweler, and bade him receive ten thousand dinars to her price. And his heart was taken up with the slave girl Kut al-Kulub and he forsook the Lady Zubaydah bint al-Kasim, for all she was the daughter of his father's brother, and he abandoned all his favorite concubines and abode a whole month without stirring from Kut al-Kulub's side save to go to the Friday prayers and return to her all in haste. This was grievous to the lords of the realm and they complained thereof to the Wazir Ja'afar the Barmecide, who bore with the Commander of the Faithful and waited till the next Friday, when he entered the cathedral mosque and, forgathering with the Caliph, related to him all that occurred to him of extraordinary stories anent seld-seen love and lovers, with intent to draw out what was in his mind.

Quoth the Caliph, "By Allah, O Ja'afar, this is not of my choice, but my heart is caught in the snare of love and wot I not what is to be done!" The Wazir Ja'afar replied: "O Commander of the Faithful, thou knowest how this girl Kut al-Kulub is become at thy disposal and of the number of thy servants, and that which hand possesseth soul coveteth not. Moreover, I will tell thee another thing, which is that the highest boast of kings and princes is in hunting and the pursuit of sport and victory; and if thou apply thyself to this, perchance it will divert thee from her, and it may be thou wilt forget her." Rejoined the Caliph: "Thou sayest well, O Ja'afar. Come let us go a-hunting forthright, without stay or delay." So soon as Friday prayers were prayed, they left the mosque, and at once mounting their she-mules, rode forth to the chase, occupied with talk, and their attendants outwent them.

Presently the heat became overhot and Al-Rashid said to his Wazir, "O Ja'afar, I am sore athirst." Then he looked around, and espying a figure in the distance on a high mound, asked Ja'afar, "Seest thou what I see?" Answered the Wazir: "Yes, O Commander of the Faithful. I see a dim figure on a high mound. Belike he is the keeper of a garden or of a cucumber plot, and in whatso wise water will not be lacking in his neighborhood," presently adding, "I will go to him and fetch thee some." But Al-Rashid said: "My mule is swifter than thy mule, so do thou abide here, on account of the troops, whilst I go myself to him and get of this person drink and return." So saying, he urged his she-mule, which started off like racing wind or railing water, and in the twinkling of an eye made the mound, where he found the figure he had seen to be none other than Khalifah the fisherman, naked and wrapped in the net.

And indeed he was horrible to behold, as to and fro he rolled with eyes for very redness like cresset gleam and dusty hair in disheveled trim, as he were an Ifrit or a lion grim. Al-Rashid saluted him and he returned his salutation, but he was wroth, and fires might have been lit at his breath. Quoth the Caliph, "O man, hast thou any water?" and quote Khalifah: "How, thou, art thou blind, or Jinn-mad? Get thee to the river Tigris, for 'tis behind this mound." So Al-Rashid went around the mound, and going down to the river, drank and watered his mule. Then without a moment's delay he returned to Khalifah and said to him, "What aileth thee, O man, to stand here, and what is thy calling?" The fisherman cried: "This is a stranger and sillier question than that about the water! Seest thou not the gear of my craft on my shoulder?" Said the Caliph, "Belike thou art a fisherman?" and he replied, "Yes." Asked Al-Rashid, "Where is thy gabardine, and where are thy waistcloth and girdle, and where be the rest of thy raiment?"

Now these were the very things which had been taken from Khalifah, like for like, so when he heard the Caliph name them, he got into his head that it was he who had stolen his clothes from the riverbank, and coming down from the top of the mound, swiftlier than the blinding levin, laid hold of the mule's bridle, saying, "Hark ye, man, bring me back my things and leave jesting and joking." Al-Rashid replied, "By Allah, I have not seen thy clothes, nor know aught of them!" Now the Caliph had large cheeks and a small mouth, so Khalifah said to him: "Belike thou art by trade a singer, or a piper on pipes? But bring me back my clothes fairly and without more ado, or I will bash thee with this my staff till thou bepiss thyself and befoul thy clothes." When Al-Rashid saw the staff in the fisherman's hand and that he had the vantage of him, he said to himself, "By Allah, I cannot brook from this mad beggar half a blow of that staff!" Now he had on a satin gown, so he pulled it off and gave it to Khalifah, saying, "O man, take this in place of thy clothes." The fisherman took it and turned it about and said, "My clothes are worth ten of this painted aba cloak," and rejoined the Caliph, "Put it on till I bring thee thy gear."

So Khalifah donned the gown, but finding it too long for him, took a knife he had with him tied to the handle of his basket, and cut off nigh a third of the skirt, so that it fell only beneath his knees. Then he turned to Al-Rashid and said to him, "Allah upon thee, O piper, tell me what wage thou gettest every month from thy master, for thy craft of piping." Replied the Caliph, "My wage is ten dinars a month," and Khalifah continued: "By Allah, my poor fellow, thou makest me sorry for thee! Why, I make thy ten dinars every day! Hast thou a mind to take service with me, and I will teach thee the art of fishing and share my gain with thee? So shalt thou make five dinars a day and be my slavey and I will protect thee against thy master with this staff." Quoth Al-Rashid, "I will well," and quoth Khalifah: "Then get off thy she-ass and tie her up, so she may serve us to carry the fish hereafter, and come hither, that I may teach thee to fish forthright."

So Al-Rashid alighted, and hobbling his mule, tucked his skirts into his girdle, and Khalifah said to him, "O piper, lay hold of the net thus and put it over thy forearm thus and cast it into the Tigris thus." Accordingly the Caliph took heart of grace and, doing as the fisherman showed him, threw the net and pulled at it, but could not draw it up. So Khalifah came to his aid and tugged at it with him, but the two together could not hale it up. Whereupon said the fisherman: "O piper of ill-omen, for the first time I took thy gown in place of my clothes, but this second time I will have thine ass and will beat thee to boot till thou bepiss and beskit thyself, an I find my net torn." Quoth Al-Rashid, "Let the twain of us pull at once." So they both pulled together, and succeeded with difficulty in hauling that net ashore, when they found it full of fish of all kinds and colors, and Khalifah said to Al-Rashid: "By Allah, O piper, thou art foul of favor but an thou apply thyself to fishing, thou wilt make a mighty fine fisherman. But now 'twere best thou bestraddle thine ass and make for the market and fetch me a pair of frails, and I will look after the fish till thou return, when I and thou will load it on thine ass's back. I have scales and weights and all we want, so we can take them with us, and thou wilt have nothing to do but to hold the scales and punch the price. For here we have fish worth twenty dinars. So be fast with the frails and loiter not."

Answered the Caliph, "I hear and obey" and mounting, left him with his fish, and spurred his mule, in high good humor, and ceased not laughing over his adventure with the fisherman till he came up to Ja'afar, who said to him, "O Commander of the Faithful, belike when thou wentest down to drink, thou foundest a pleasant flower garden and enteredst and tookest thy pleasure therein alone?" At this Al-Rashid fell a laughing again and all the Barmecides rose and kissed the ground before him, saying: "O Commander of the Faithful, Allah make joy to endure for thee and do away annoy from thee! What was the cause of thy delaying when thou faredst to drink, and what hath befallen thee?" Quoth the Caliph, "Verily, a right wondrous tale and a joyous adventure and a wondrous hath befallen me."

And he repeated to them what had passed between himself and the fisherman and his words, "Thou stolest my clothes!" and how he had given him his gown and how he had cut off a part of it, finding it too long for him. Said Ja'afar, "By Allah, O Commander of the Faithful, I had it in mind to beg the gown of thee, but now I will go straight to the fisherman and buy it of him." The Caliph replied, "By Allah, he hath cut off a third part of the skirt and spoilt it! But, O Ja'afar, I am tired with fishing in the river, for I have caught great store of fish, which I left on the bank with my master Khalifah, and he is watching them and waiting for me to return to him with a couple of frails and a matchet. Then we are to go, I and he, to the market and sell the fish and share the price." Ja'afar rejoined, "O Commander of the Faithful, I will bring you a purchaser for your fish." And Al-Rashid retorted: "O Ja'afar, by the virtue of my holy forefathers, whoso bringeth me one of the fish that are before Khalifah, who taught me angling, I will give him for it a gold dinar!" So the crier proclaimed among the troops that they should go forth and buy fish for the Caliph, and they all arose and made for the riverside.

Now while Khalifah was expecting the Caliph's return with the two frails, behold, the Mamelukes swooped down upon him like vultures and took the fish and wrapped them in gold-embroidered kerchiefs, beating one another in their eagerness to get at the fisherman. Whereupon quoth Khalifah, "Doubtless these are the fish of Paradise!" and hending two fish in right hand and left, plunged into the water up to his neck and fell a-saying, "O Allah, by the virtue of these fish, let Thy servant the piper, my partner, came to me at this very moment." And suddenly up to him came a black slave which was the chief of the Caliph's Negro eunuchs. He had tarried behind the rest, by reason of his horse having stopped to make water by the way, and finding that naught remained of the fish, little or much, looked right and left till he espied Khalifah standing in the stream with a fish in either hand, and said to him, "Come hither, O Fisherman!" But Khalifah replied, "Begone and none of your impudence!" So the eunuch went up to him and said, "Give me the fish and I will pay thee their price." Replied the fisherman: "Art thou little of wit? I will not sell them." Therewith the eunuch drew his mace upon him, and Khalifah cried out, saying: "Strike not, O loon! Better largess than the mace."

So saying, he threw the two fishes to the eunuch, who took them and laid them in his kerchief. Then he put hand in pouch, but found not a single dirham, and said to Khalifah: "O fisherman, verily thou art out of luck for, by Allah, I have not a silver about me! But come tomorrow to the palace of the Caliphate and ask for the eunuch Sandal, whereupon the castratos will direct thee to me, and by coming thither thou shalt get what falleth to thy lot and therewith wend thy ways." Quoth Khalifah, "Indeed, this is a blessed day, and its blessedness was manifest from the first of it!"

Then he shouldered his net and returned to Baghdad, and as he passed through the streets, the folk saw the Caliph's gown on him and stared at him till he came to the gate of his quarter, by which was the shop of the Caliph's tailor. When the man saw him wearing a dress of the apparel of the Caliph, worth a thousand dinars, he said to him, "O Khalifah, whence hadst thou that gown?" Replied the fisherman: "What aileth thee to be impudent? I had it of one whom I taught to fish and who is become my apprentice. I forgave him the cutting off of his hand[1] for that he stole my clothes and gave me this cape in their place." So the tailor knew that the Caliph had come upon him as he was fishing and jested with him and given him the gown.

Such was his case, but as regards Harun al-Rashid, he had gone out a-hunting and a-fishing only to divert his thoughts from the damsel Kut al-Kulub. But when Zubaydah heard of her and of the Caliph's devotion to her, the lady was fired with the jealousy which the more especially fireth women, so that she refused meat and drink and rejected the delights of sleep, and awaited the Caliph's going forth on a journey or what not, that she might set a snare for the damsel. So when she learnt that he was gone hunting and fishing, she bade her women furnish the palace fairly and decorate it splendidly and serve up viands and confections. And amongst the rest she made a China dish of the daintiest sweetmeats that can be made, wherein she had put bhang.

Then she ordered one of her eunuchs go to the damsel Kut al-Kulub and bid her to the banquet, saying: "The Lady Zubaydah bint al-Kasim, the wife of the Commander of the Faithful, hath drunken medicine today, and having heard tell of the sweetness of thy singing, longeth to divert herself with somewhat of thine art." Kut al-Kulub replied, "Hearing and obedience are due to Allah and the Lady Zubaydah," and rose without stay or delay, unknowing what was hidden for her in the secret purpose. Then she took with her what

[1] The punishment for theft.

instruments she needed and, accompanying the eunuch, ceased not faring till she stood in the presence of the Princess. When she entered she kissed the ground before her again and again, then rising to her feet, said: "Peace be on the Lady of the exalted seat and the presence whereto none may avail, daughter of the house Abbasi and scion of the Prophet's family! May Allah fulfill thee of peace and prosperity in the days and the years!"

Then she stood with the rest of the women and eunuchs, and presently the Lady Zubaydah raised her eyes and considered her beauty and loveliness. She saw a damsel with cheeks smooth as rose and breasts like granado, a face moon-bright, a brow flower-white, and great eyes black as night. Her eyelids were languor-dight and her face beamed with light, as if the sun from her forehead arose and the murks of the night from the locks of her brow. And the fragrance of musk from her breath strayed, and flowers bloomed in her lovely face inlaid. The moon beamed from her forehead and in her slender shape the branches swayed. She was like the full moon shining in the nightly shade. Her eyes wantoned, her eyebrows were like a bow arched, and her lips of coral molded. Her beauty amazed all who espied her and her glances amated all who eyed her. Glory be to Him Who formed her and fashioned her and perfected her!

Quoth the Lady Zubaydah: "Well come, and welcome and fair cheer to thee, O Kut al-Kulub! Sit and divert us with thine art and the goodliness of thine accomplishments." Quoth the damsel, "I hear and I obey," and rose and exhibited tricks of sleight of hand and legerdemain and all manner pleasing arts, till the Princess came near to fall in love with her and said to herself, "Verily, my cousin Al-Rashid is not to blame for loving her!" Then the damsel kissed ground before Zubaydah and sat down, whereupon they set food before her. Presently they brought her the drugged dish of sweetmeats and she ate thereof, and hardly had it settled in her stomach when her head fell backward and she sank on the ground sleeping. With this, the lady said to her women, "Carry her up to one of the chambers, till I summon her," and they replied, "We hear and we obey." Then said she to one of her eunuchs, "Fashion me a chest and bring it hitherto to me!" And shortly afterward she bade make the semblance of a tomb and spread the report that Kut al-Kulub had choked and died, threatening her familiars that she would smite the neck of whoever should say, "She is alive."

Now, behold, the Caliph suddenly returned from the chase, and the first inquiry he made was for the damsel. So there came to him one of his eunuchs, whom the Lady Zubaydah had charged to declare she was dead if the Caliph should ask for her and, kissing ground before him, said: "May thy head live, O my lord! Be certified that Kut al-Kulub choked in eating and is dead." Whereupon cried Al-Rashid, "God never gladden thee with good news, O thou bad slave!" and entered the palace, where he heard of her death from everyone and asked, "Where is her tomb?" So they brought him to the sepulcher and showed him the pretended tomb, saying, "This is her burial place." The Caliph, weeping sore for her, abode by the tomb a full hour, after which he arose and went away, in the utmost distress and the deepest melancholy.

So the Lady Zubaydah saw that her plot had succeeded, and forthright sent for the eunuch and said, "Hither with the chest!" He set it before her, when she bade bring the damsel, and locking her up therein, said to the eunuch: "Take all pains to sell this chest, and make it a condition with the purchaser that he buy it locked. Then give alms with its price." So he took it and went forth to do her bidding.

Thus fared it with these, but as for Khalifah the fisherman, when morning morrowed and shone with its light and sheen, he said to himself, "I cannot do aught better today than visit the eunuch who bought the fish of me, for he appointed me to come to him in the palace of the Caliphate." So he went forth of his lodging, intending for the palace, and when he came thither, he found Mamelukes, Negro slaves, and eunuchs standing and sitting, and looking at them, behold, seated amongst them was the eunuch who had taken the fish of him, with the white slaves waiting on him. Presently, one of the Mameluke lads called out to him, whereupon the eunuch turned to see who he was and lo! it was the fisherman. Now when Khalifah was ware that he saw him and recognized him, he said to him: "I have not failed thee, O my little Tulip! On this wise are men of their word." Hearing his address, Sandal the eunuch laughed and replied, "By Allah, thou art right, O Fisherman," and put his hand to his pouch, to give him somewhat. But at that moment there arose a great clamor. So he raised his head to see what was to do, and finding that it was the Wazir Ja'afar the Barmecide coming forth from the Caliph's presence, he rose to him and forewent him, and they walked about conversing for a longsome time.

Khalifah the fisherman waited awhile, then, growing weary of standing, and finding that the eunuch took no heed of him, he set himself in his way and beckoned to him from afar, saying, "O my lord Tulip, give me my due and let me go!" The eunuch heard him, but was ashamed to answer him because of the Minister's presence, so he went on talking with Ja'afar and took no notice whatever of the fisherman. Whereupon quoth Khalifah: "O slow o' pay! May Allah put to shame all churls and all who take folk's goods and are niggardly with them! I put myself under thy protection, O my lord Bran-belly, to give me my due and let me go!" The eunuch heard him, but was ashamed to answer him before Ja'afar, and the Minister saw the fisherman beckoning and talking to him, though he knew not what he was saying. So he said to Sandal, misliking his behavior, "O Eunuch, what would yonder beggar with thee?" Sandal replied, "Dost thou not know him, O my lord the Wazir?" and Ja'afar answered: "By Allah, I know him not! How should I know a man I have never seen but at this moment?"

Rejoined the Eunuch: "O my lord, this is the fisherman whose fish we seized on the banks of the Tigris. I came too late to get any and was ashamed to return to the Prince of True Believers empty-handed when all the Mamelukes had some. Presently I espied the fisherman standing in midstream, calling on Allah, with four fishes in his hands, and said to him, 'Give me what thou hast there and take their worth.' He handed me the fish and I put my hand into my pocket, purposing to gift him with somewhat, but found naught therein and said, 'Come to me in the palace, and I will give thee wherewithal to aid thee in thy poverty.' So he came to me today and I was putting hand to pouch, that I might give him somewhat, when thou camest forth and I rose to wait on thee and was diverted with thee from him, till he grew tired of waiting. And this is the whole story how he cometh to be standing here."

The Wazir, hearing this account, smiled and said: "O Eunuch, how is it that this fisherman cometh in his hour of need and thou satisfiest him not? Dost thou not know him, O chief of the eunuchs?" "No," answered Sandal, and Ja'afar said: "This is the master of the Commander of the Faithful, and his partner and our lord the Caliph hath arisen this morning strait of breast, heavy of heart, and troubled in thought, nor is there aught will broaden his breast save this fisherman. So let him not go till I crave the Caliph's pleasure concerning him and bring him before him. Perchance Allah will relieve him of his oppression and console him for the loss of Kut al-Kulub by means of the fisherman's presence, and he will give him wherewithal to better himself, and thou wilt be the cause of this." Replied Sandal: "O my lord, do as thou wilt, and may Allah Almighty long continue thee a pillar of the dynasty of the Commander of the Faithful, whose shadow Allah perpetuate and prosper it, root and branch!"

Then the Wazir Ja'afar rose up and went in to the Caliph, and Sandal ordered the Mamelukes not to leave the fisherman, whereupon Khalifah cried: "How goodly is thy bounty, O Tulip! The seeker is become the sought. I come to seek my due, and they imprison me for debts in arrears!" When Ja'afar came into the presence of the Caliph, he found him sitting with his head bowed earthward, breast straitened and mind melancholy, humming the verses of the poet:

> My blamers instant bid that I for her become consoled,
> But I, what can I do, whose heart declines to be controlled?
> And how can I in patience bear the loss of lovely maid
> When fails me patience for a love that holds with firmest hold!
> Ne'er I'll forget her nor the bowl that 'twixt us both went round
> And wine of glances maddened me with drunkenness ensouled.

Whenas Ja'afar stood in the presence, he said: "Peace be upon thee, O Commander of the Faithful, Defender of the honor of the Faith and descendant of the uncle of the Prince of the Apostles, Allah assain him and save him and his family one and all!" The Caliph raised his head and answered, "And on thee be peace and the mercy of Allah and His blessings!" Quoth Ja'afar, "With leave of the Prince of True Believers, his servant would speak without restraint." Asked the Caliph: "And when was restraint put upon thee in speech, and thou the Prince of Wazirs? Say what thou wilt." Answered Ja'afar: "When I went out, O my lord, from before thee, intending for my house, I saw standing at the door thy master and teacher and partner, Khalifah the fisherman, who was aggrieved at thee and complained of thee, saying: 'Glory be to God! I taught him to fish and he went away to fetch me a pair of frails, but never came back. And this is not the way of a good partner or of a good apprentice.' So, if thou hast a mind to partnership, well and good; and if not, tell him, that he may take to partner another."

Now when the Caliph heard these words, he smiled and his straitness of breast was done away with and he said, "My life on thee, is this the truth thou sayest, that the fisherman standeth at the door?" and Ja'afar replied, "By thy life, O Commander of the Faithful, he standeth at the door." Quoth the Caliph: "O Ja'afar, by Allah, I will assuredly do my best to give him his due! If Allah at my hands send him misery, he shall have it, and if prosperity, he shall have it." Then he took a piece of paper, and cutting it in pieces, said to the Wazir: "O Ja'afar, write down with thine own hand twenty sums of money, from one dinar to a thousand, and the names of all kinds of offices and dignities from the least appointment to the Caliphate; also twenty kinds of punishment, from the lightest beating to death." "I hear and I obey, O Commander of the Faithful," answered Ja'afar, and did as he was bidden.

Then said the Caliph: "O Ja'afar, I swear by my holy forefathers and by my kinship to Hamzah and Akil, that I mean to summon the fisherman and bid him take one of these papers, whose contents none knoweth save thou and I. And whatsoever is written in the paper which he shall choose, I will give it to him. Though it be the Caliphate, I will divest myself thereof and invest him therewith and grudge it not to him. And on the other hand, if there be written therein hanging or mutilation or death, I will execute it upon him. Now go and fetch him to me." When Ja'afar heard this, he said to himself: "There is no Majesty and there is no Might save in Allah, the Glorious, the Great! It may be somewhat will fall to this poor wretch's lot that will bring about his destruction, and I shall be the cause. But the Caliph hath sworn, so nothing remains now but to bring him in, and naught will happen save whatso Allah willeth." Accordingly he went out to Khalifah the fisherman and laid hold of his hand, to carry him in to the Caliph, whereupon his reason fled and he said in himself: "What a stupid I was to come after yonder ill-omened slave, Tulip, whereby he hath brought me in company with Bran-belly!" Ja'afar fared on with him, with Mamelukes before and behind, whilst he said, "Doth not arrest suffice, but these must go behind and before me, to hinder my making off?" till they had traversed seven vestibules, when the Wazir said to him: "Mark my words, O Fisherman! Thou standest before the Commander of the Faithful and Defender of the Faith!"

Then he raised the great curtain and Khalifah's eyes fell on the Caliph, who was seated on his couch, with the lords of the realm standing in attendance upon him. As soon as he knew him, he went up to him and said: "Well come, and welcome to thee, O piper! 'Twas not right of thee to make thyself a fisherman and go away, leaving me sitting to guard the fish, and never to return! For, before I was aware, there came up Mamelukes on beasts of all manner colors, and snatched away the fish from me, I standing alone. And this was all of thy fault, for hadst thou returned with the frails forthright, we had sold a hundred dinars' worth of fish. And now I come to seek my due, and they have arrested me. But thou, who hath imprisoned thee also in this place?" The Caliph smiled, and raising a corner of the curtain, put forth his head and said to the fisherman, "Come hither and take thee one of these papers." Quoth Khalifah the fisherman: "Yesterday thou wast a fisherman, and today thou hast become an astrologer, but the more trades a man hath, the poorer he waxeth." Thereupon Ja'afar said: "Take the paper at once, and do as the Commander of the Faithful biddeth thee, without prating."

So he came forward and put forth his hand saying, "Far be it from me that this piper should ever again be my knave and fish with me!" Then, taking the paper, he handed it to the Caliph, saying: "O piper, what hath come out for me therein? Hide naught thereof." So Al-Rashid received it and passed it on to Ja'afar and said to him, "Read what is therein." He looked at it and said, "There is no Majesty and there is no Might save in Allah, the Glorious, the Great!" Said the Caliph: "Good news, O Ja'afar? What seest thou therein?" Answered the Wazir: "O Commander of the Faithful, there came up from the paper, 'Let the Fisherman receive a hundred blows with a stick.'" So the Caliph commanded to beat the Fisherman and they gave him a hundred sticks, after which he rose, saying: "Allah damn this, O Branbelly! Are jail and sticks part of the game?"

Then said Ja'afar: "O Commander of the Faithful, this poor devil is come to the river, and how shall he go away thirsting? We hope that among the alms deeds of the Commander of the Faithful he may have leave to take another paper, so haply somewhat may come out wherewithal he may succor his poverty." Said the Caliph: "By Allah, O Ja'afar, if he take another paper and death be written therein, I will assuredly kill him, and thou wilt be the cause." Answered Ja'afar, "If he die he will be at rest." But Khalifah the fisherman said to him: "Allah ne'er gladden thee with good news! Have I made Baghdad strait upon you, that ye seek to slay me?" Quoth Ja'afar, "Take thee a paper, and crave the blessing of Allah Almighty!"

So he put out his hand, and taking a paper, gave it to Ja'afar, who read it and was silent. The Caliph asked, "Why art thou silent, O son of Yahya?" and he answered: "O Commander of the Faithful, there hath come out on this paper, 'Naught shall be given to the fisherman.'" Then said the Caliph: "His daily bread will not come from us. Bid him fare forth from before our face." Quoth Ja'afar: "By the claims of thy pious forefathers, let him take a third paper. It may be it will bring him alimony," and quoth the Caliph, "Let him take one and no more."

So he put out his hand and took a third paper, and behold, therein was written, "Let the Fisherman be given one dinar." Ja'afar cried to him, "I sought good fortune for thee, but Allah willed not to thee aught save this dinar." And Khalifah answered: "Verily, a dinar for every hundred sticks were rare good luck. May Allah not send thy body health!" The Caliph laughed at him and Ja'afar took him by the hand and led him out. When he reached the door, Sandal the eunuch saw him and said to him: "Hither, O Fisherman! Give us portion of that which the Commander of the Faithful hath bestowed on thee whilst jesting with thee." Replied Khalifah: "By Allah, O Tulip, thou art right! Wilt thou share with me, O nigger? Indeed, I have eaten stick to the tune of a hundred blows and have earned one dinar, and thou art but too welcome to it." So saying, he threw him the dinar and went out, with the tears flowing down the plain of his cheeks.

When the eunuch saw him in this plight, he knew that he had spoken sooth and called to the lads to fetch him back. So they brought him back and Sandal, putting his hand to his pouch, pulled out a red purse, whence he emptied a hundred golden dinars into the fisherman's hand, saying, "Take this gold in payment of thy fish, and wend thy ways." So Khalifah, in high good humor, took the hundred ducats and the Caliph's one dinar and went his way, and forgot the beating.

Now as Allah willed it for the furthering of that which He had decreed, he passed by the mart of the handmaidens, and seeing there a mighty ring where many folks were forgathering, said to himself,

"What is this crowd?" So he brake through the merchants and others, who said, "Make wide the way for Skipper Rapscallion, and let him pass." Then he looked, and behold, he saw a chest, with a eunuch seated thereon and an old man standing by it, and the Sheikh was crying: "O merchants, O men of money, who will hasten and hazard his coin for this chest of unknown contents from the palace of the Lady Zubaydah bint al-Kasim, wife of the Commander of the Faithful? How much shall I say for you? Allah bless you all!" Quoth one of the merchants: "By Allah, this is a risk! But I will say one word, and no blame to me. Be it mine for twenty dinars." Quoth another, "Fifty," and they went on bidding, one against other, till the price reached a hundred ducats.

Then said the crier, "Will any of you bid more, O merchants?" And Khalifah the fisherman said, "Be it mine for a hundred dinars and one dinar." The merchants, hearing these words, thought he was jesting and laughed at him, saying, "O Eunuch, sell it to Khalifah for a hundred dinars and one dinar!" Quoth the eunuch: "By Allah, I will sell it to none but him! Take it, O Fisherman. The Lord bless thee in it, and here with thy gold." So Khalifah pulled out the ducats and gave them to the eunuch, who, the bargain being duly made, delivered to him the chest and bestowed the price in alms on the spot, after which he returned to the palace and acquainted the Lady Zubaydah with what he had done, whereat she rejoiced. Meanwhile the fisherman hove the chest on shoulder, but could not carry it on this wise for the excess of its weight, so he lifted it onto his head and thus bore it to the quarter where he lived. Here he set it down, and being weary, sat awhile bemusing what had befallen him and saying in himself, "Would Heaven I knew what is in this chest!"

Then he opened the door of his lodging and haled the chest till he got it into his closet, after which he strove to open it, but failed. Quoth he: "What folly possessed me to buy this chest? There is no help for it but to break it open and see what is herein." So he applied himself to the lock, but could not open it, and said to himself, "I will leave it till tomorrow." Then he would have stretched him out to sleep, but could find no room, for the chest filled the whole closet. So he got upon it and lay him down. But when he had lain awhile, behold, he felt something stir under him, whereat sleep forsook him and his reason fled. So he arose and cried: "Meseems there be Jinns in the chest. Praise to Allah Who suffered me not to open it! For had I done so, they had risen against me in the dark and slain me, and from them would have befallen me naught of good."

Then he lay down again, when lo! the chest moved a second time, more than before, whereupon he sprang to his feet and said: "There it goes again. But this is terrible!" And he hastened to look for the lamp, but could not find it and had not the wherewithal to buy another. So he went forth and cried out, "Ho, people of the quarter!" Now the most part of the folk were asleep, but they awoke at his crying and asked, "What aileth thee, O Khalifah?" He answered, "Bring me a lamp, for the Jinn are upon me." They laughed at him and gave him a lamp, wherewith he returned to his closet. Then he smote the lock of the chest with a stone and broke it, and opening it, saw a damsel like a houri lying asleep within. Now she had been drugged with bhang, but at that moment she threw up the stuff and awoke. Then she opened her eyes, and feeling herself confined and cramped, moved. At this sight quoth Khalifah, "By Allah, O my lady, whence art thou?" and quoth she, "Bring me jessamine, and narcissus." And Khalifah answered, "There is naught here but henna flowers."

Thereupon she came to herself, and considering Khalifah, said to him, "What art thou?" presently adding, "And where am I?" He said, "Thou art in my lodging." Asked she, "Am I not in the palace of the Caliph Harun al-Rashid?" And quoth he: "What manner of thing is Al-Rashid? O madwoman, Thou art naught but my slave girl. I bought thee this very day for a hundred dinars and one dinar, and brought thee home, and thou wast asleep in this here chest." When she heard these words she said to him, "What is thy name?" Said he: "My name is Khalifah. How comes my star to have grown propitious, when I know my ascendant to have been otherwise?" She laughed and cried: "Spare me this talk! Hast thou anything to eat?" Replied he: "No, by Allah, nor yet to drink! I have not eaten these two days, and am now in want of a morsel." She asked, "Hast thou no money?" and he said: "Allah keep this chest which hath beggared me. I gave all I had for it and am become bankrupt."

The damsel laughed at him and said: "Up with thee and seek of thy neighbors somewhat for me to eat, for I am hungry." So he went forth and cried out, "Ho, people of the quarter!" Now the folk were asleep, but they awoke and asked, "What aileth thee, O

Khalifah?" Answered he, "O my neighbors, I am hungry and have nothing to eat." So one came down to him with a bannock and another with broken meats and a third with a bittock of cheese and a fourth with a cucumber, and so on till his lap was full and he returned to his closet and laid the whole between her hands, saying, "Eat." But she laughed at him, saying: "How can I eat of this when I have not a mug of water whereof to drink? I fear to choke with a mouthful and die." Quoth he, "I will fill thee this pitcher." So he took the pitcher, and going forth, stood in the midst of the street and cried out, saying, "Ho, people of the quarter!" Quoth they, "What calamity is upon thee tonight, O Khalifah!" And he said, "Ye gave me food and I ate, but now I am athirst, so give me to drink."

Thereupon one came down to him with a mug and another with an ewer and a third with a gugglet, and he filled his pitcher, and bearing it back, said to the damsel, "O my lady, thou lackest nothing now." Answered she, "True, I want nothing more at this present." Quoth he, "Speak to me and say me thy story." And quoth she: "Fie upon thee! An thou knowest me not, I will tell thee who I am. I am Kut al-Kulub, the Caliph's handmaiden, and the Lady Zubaydah was jealous of me, so she drugged me with bhang and set me in this chest," presently adding: "Alhamdolillah—praised be God—for that the matter hath come to easy issue and no worse! But this befell me not save for thy good luck, for thou wilt certainly get of the Caliph Al-Rashid money galore, that will be the means of thine enrichment." Quoth Khalifah, "Is not Al-Rashid he in whose palace I was imprisoned?" "Yes," answered she, and he said: "By Allah, never saw I more niggardly wight than he, that piper little of good and wit! He gave me a hundred blows with a stick yesterday and but one dinar, for all I taught him to fish and made him my partner, but he played me false." Replied she: "Leave this unseemly talk, and open thine eyes and look thou bear thyself respectfully whenas thou seest him after this, and thou shalt win thy wish."

When he heard her words, it was if he had been asleep and awoke, and Allah removed the veil from his judgment, because of his good luck, and he answered, "O my head and eyes!" Then said he to her, "Sleep, in the name of Allah." So she lay down and fell asleep (and he afar from her) till the morning, when she sought of him ink case and paper, and when they were brought, wrote to Ibn al-Kirnas, the Caliph's friend, acquainting him with her case and how at the end of all that had befallen her she was with Khalifah the fisherman, who had bought her. Then she gave him the scroll, saying: "Take this and hie thee to the jewel market and ask for the shop of Ibn al-Kirnas the Jeweler and give him this paper, and speak not." "I hear and I obey," answered Khalifah, and going with the scroll to the market, inquired for the shop of Ibn al-Kirnas. They directed him thither, and on entering it he saluted the merchant, who returned his salaam with contempt and said to him, "What dost thou want?" Thereupon he gave him the letter and he took it, but read it not, thinking the fisherman a beggar who sought an alms of him, and said to one of his lads, "Give him half a dirham." Quoth Khalifah: "I want no alms. Read the paper."

So Ibn al-Kirnas took the letter and read it, and no sooner knew its import than he kissed it and laid it on his head. Then he arose and said to Khalifah, "O my brother, where is thy house?" Asked Khalifah: "What wantest thou with my house? Wilt thou go thither and steal my slave girl?" Then Ibn al-Kirnas answered: "Not so. On the contrary, I will buy thee somewhat whereof you may eat, thou and she." So he said, "My house is in such a quarter," and the merchant rejoined: "Thou hast done well. May Allah not give thee health, O unlucky one!" Then he called out to two of his slaves and said to them: "Carry this man to the shop of Mohsin the shroff and say to him, 'O Mohsin, give this man a thousand dinars of gold,' then bring him back to me in haste."

So they carried him to the money-changer, who paid him the money, and returned with him to their master, whom they found mounted on a dapple she-mule worth a thousand dinars, with Mamelukes and pages about him, and by his side another mule like his own, saddled and bridled. Quoth the jeweler to Khalifah, "Bismillah, mount this mule." Replied he, "I won't, for by Allah, I fear she throw me," and quoth Ibn al-Kirnas, "By God, needs must thou mount." So he came up, and mounting her, face to crupper, caught hold of her tail and cried out, whereupon she threw him on the ground and they laughed at him. But he rose and said, "Did I not tell thee I would not mount this great jenny-ass?" Thereupon Ibn al-Kirnas left him in the market, and repairing to the Caliph, told him of the damsel, after which he returned and removed her to his own house.

Meanwhile Khalifah went home to look after the handmaid and found the people of the quarter forgathering and saying: "Verily, Khalifah is today in a terrible pickle! Would we knew whence he can have gotten this damsel!" Quoth one of them: "He is a mad pimp. Haply he found her lying on the road drunken, and carried her to his own house, and his absence showeth that he knoweth his offense." As they were talking, behold, up came Khalifah, and they said to him: "What a plight is thine, O unhappy! Knowest thou not what is come to thee?" He replied, "No, by Allah!" and they said: "But just now there came Mamelukes and took away thy slave girl whom thou stolest, and sought for thee, but found thee not." Asked Khalifah, "And how came they to take my slave girl?" and quoth one, "Had he fallen in their way, they had slain him."

But he, so far from heeding them, returned running to the shop of Ibn al-Kirnas, whom he met riding, and said to him: "By Allah, 'twas not right of thee to wheedle me and meanwhile send thy Mamelukes to take my slave girl!" Replied the jeweler, "O idiot, come with me, and hold thy tongue." So he took him and carried him into a house handsomely builded, where he found the damsel seated on a couch of gold, with ten slave girls like moons round her. Sighting her, Ibn al-Kirnas kissed ground before her, and she said, "What hast thou done with my new master, who bought me with all he owned?" He replied, "O my lady, I gave him a thousand golden dinars," and related to her Khalifah's history from first to last, whereat she laughed and said: "Blame him not, for he is but a common wight. These other thousand dinars are a gift from me to him, and Almighty Allah willing, he shall win of the Caliph what shall enrich him."

As they were talking, there came a eunuch from the Commander of the Faithful in quest of Kut al-Kulub, for when he knew that she was in the house of Ibn al-Kirnas, he could not endure the severance, but bade bring her forthwith. So she repaired to the Palace, taking Khalifah with her, and going into the presence, kissed ground before the Caliph, who rose to her, saluting and welcoming her, and asked her how she had fared with him who had brought her. She replied: "He is a man, Khalifah the fisherman hight, and there he standeth at the door. He telleth me that he hath an account to settle with the Commander of the Faithful, by reason of a partnership between him and the Caliph in fishing." Asked Al-Rashid, "Is he at the door?" and she answered, "Yes." So the Caliph sent for him and he kissed ground before him and wished him endurance of glory and prosperity. The Caliph marveled at him and laughed at him, and said to him, "O Fisherman, wast thou in very deed my partner yesterday?" Khalifah took his meaning, and heartening his heart and summoning spirit, replied: "By Him who bestowed upon thee the succession to thy cousin, I know her not in anywise and have had no commerce with her save by way of sight and speech!"

Then he repeated to him all that had befallen him since he last saw him, whereat the Caliph laughed and his breast broadened and he said to Khalifah, "Ask of us what thou wilt, O thou who bringest to owners their own!" But he was silent, so the Caliph ordered him fifty thousand dinars of gold and a costly dress of honor such as great sovereigns don, and a she-mule, and gave him black slaves of the Sudan to serve him, so that he became as he were one of the kings of that time. The Caliph was rejoiced at the recovery of his favorite and knew that all this was the doing of his cousin-wife, the Lady Zubaydah, wherefore he was sore enraged against her and held aloof from her a great while, visiting her not, neither inclining to pardon her. When she was certified of this, she was sore concerned for his wrath, and her face, that was wont to be rosy, waxed pale and wan till, when her patience was exhausted, she sent a letter to her cousin, the Commander of the Faithful, making her excuses to him and confessing her offenses, and ending with these verses:

> I long once more the love that was between us to regain,
> That I may quench the fire of grief and bate the force of bane.
> O lord of me, have ruth upon the stress my passion deals,
> Enough to me is what you doled of sorrow and of pain.
> 'Tis life to me an deign you keep the troth you deigned to plight,
> 'Tis death to me an troth you break and fondest vows profane.
> Given I've sinned a sorry sin, yet grant me ruth, for naught,
> By Allah, sweeter is than friend who is of pardon fain.

When the Lady Zubaydah's letter reached the Caliph, and reading it, he saw that she confessed her offense and sent her excuses to him therefor, he said to himself, "Verily, all sins doth Allah forgive—aye, Gracious, Merciful is He!" And he returned her an answer expressing satisfaction and pardon and forgiveness for what was past, whereat she rejoiced greatly.

As for Khalifah the fisherman, the Caliph assigned him a monthly solde of fifty dinars, and took him into especial favor, which would lead to rank and dignity, honor and worship. Then he kissed ground before the Commander of the Faithful and went forth with stately gait. When he came to the door, the eunuch Sandal, who had given him the hundred dinars, saw him, and knowing him, said to him, "O Fisherman, whence all this?" So he told him all that had befallen him, first and last, whereat Sandal rejoiced, because he had been the cause of his enrichment, and said to him, "Wilt thou not give me largess of this wealth which is now become thine?" So Khalifah put hand to pouch and taking out a purse containing a thousand dinars, gave it to the eunuch, who said, "Keep thy coins, and Allah bless thee therein!" and marveled at his manliness and at the liberality of his soul, for all his late poverty.

Then, leaving the eunuch, Khalifah mounted his she-mule and rode, with the slaves' hands on her crupper, till he came to his lodging at the khan, whilst the folk stared at him in surprise for that which had betided him of advancement. When he alighted from his beast, they accosted him and inquired the cause of his change from poverty to prosperity, and he told them all that had happened to him from incept to conclusion. Then he bought a fine mansion and laid out thereon much money, till it was perfect in all points. And he took up his abode therein and was wont to recite thereon these two couplets:

> Behold a house that's like the Dwelling of Delight,
> Its aspect heals the sick and banishes despite.
> Its sojourn for the great and wise appointed is,
> And Fortune fair therein abideth day and night.

Then, as soon as he was settled in his house, he sought him in marriage the daughter of one of the chief men of the city, a handsome girl, and went in unto her and led a life of solace and satisfaction, joyaunce and enjoyment; and he rose to passing affluence and exceeding prosperity. So when he found himself in this fortunate condition, he offered up thanks to Allah (extolled and excelled be He!) for what He had bestowed on him of wealth exceeding and of favors ever succeeding, praising his Lord with the praise of the grateful. And thereafter Khalifah continued to pay frequent visits to the Caliph Harun al-Rashid, with whom he found acceptance and who ceased not to overwhelm him with boons and bounty. And he abode in the enjoyment of the utmost honor and happiness and joy and gladness, and in riches more than sufficing and in rank ever rising—brief, a sweet life and a savory, pure as pleasurable, till there came to him the Destroyer of delights and the Sunderer of societies. And extolled be the perfection of Him to whom belong glory and permanence and He is the Living, the Eternal, who shall never die!

And amongst the tales they tell is one of

ABU KIR THE DYER AND ABU SIR THE BARBER

THERE dwelt once, in Alexander city, two men, of whom one was a dyer, by name of Abu Kir, and the other a barber, Abu Sir, and they were neighbors in the market street, where their shops stood side by side. The dyer was a swindler and a liar, an exceeding wicked wight, as if indeed his head temples were hewn out of a boulder rock or fashioned of the threshold of a Jewish synagogue, nor was he ashamed of any shameful work he wrought amongst the folk. It was his wont, when any brought him cloth for staining, first to require of him payment under pretense of buying dyestuffs therewith. So the customer would give him the wage in advance and wend his ways, and the dyer would spend all he received on meat and drink, after which he would sell the cloth itself as soon as ever its owner turned his back and waste its worth in eating and drinking and what not else, for he ate not but of the daintiest and most delicate viands nor drank but of the best of that which doth away the wit of man. And when the owner of the cloth came to him, he would say to him, "Return to me tomorrow before sunrise and thou shalt find thy stuff dyed."

So the customer would go away, saying to himself, "One day is near another day," and return next day at the appointed time, when the dyer would say to him: "Come tomorrow. Yesterday I was not at work, for I had with me guests and was occupied with doing what their wants required till they went, but tomorrow before sunrise come and take thy cloth dyed." So he would fare forth and return on the third day, when Abu Kir would say to him: "Indeed yesterday I was excusable, for my wife was brought to bed in the night, and all day I was busy with manifold matters, but tomorrow, without fail, come and take thy cloth dyed." When the man came again at the appointed time, he would put him off with some other pretense, it mattered little what, and would swear to him, as often as he came, till the customer lost patience and said, "How often wilt thou say to me, 'Tomorrow?' Give me my stuff, I will not have it dyed." Whereupon the dyer would make answer: "By Allah, O my brother, I am abashed at thee, but

I must tell the truth and may Allah harm all who harm folk in their goods!" The other would exclaim, "Tell me what hath happened," and Abu Kir would reply: "As for thy stuff, I dyed that same on matchless wise and hung it on the drying rope, but 'twas stolen and I know not who stole it." If the owner of the stuff were of the kindly he would say, "Allah will compensate me," and if he were of the ill-conditioned, he would haunt him with exposure and insult, but would get nothing of him, though he complained of him to the judge.

He ceased not doing thus till his report was noised abroad among the folk and each used to warn other against Abu Kir, who became a byword amongst them. So they all held aloof from him and none would be entrapped by him save those who were ignorant of his character; but for all this, he failed not daily to suffer insult and exposure from Allah's creatures. By reason of this his trade became slack, and he used to go to the shop of his neighbor the barber Abu Sir and sit there, facing the dyery and with his eyes on the door. Whenever he espied anyone who knew him not standing at the dyery door with a piece of stuff in his hand, he would leave the barber's booth and go up to him saying, "What seekest thou, O thou?" and the man would reply, "Take and dye me this thing." So the dyer would ask, "What color wilt thou have it?" For, with all his knavish tricks, his hand was in all manner of dyes. But he was never true to anyone, wherefore poverty had gotten the better of him. Then he would take the stuff and say, "Give me my wage in advance, and come tomorrow and take the stuff." So the stranger would advance him the money and wend his way, whereupon Abu Kir would carry the cloth to the market street and sell it and with its price buy meat and vegetables and tobacco and fruit and what not else he needed. But whenever he saw anyone who had given him stuff to dye standing at the door of his shop, he would not come forth to him or even show himself to him.

On this wise he abode years and years, till it fortuned one day that he received cloth to dye from a man of wrath, and sold it and spent the proceeds. The owner came to him every day, but found him not in his shop; for whenever he espied anyone who had claim against him, he would flee from him into the shop of the barber, Abu Sir. At last that angry man, finding that he was not to be seen and growing weary of such work, repaired to the kazi, and bringing one of his sergeants to the shop, nailed up the door, in presence of a number of

Moslems, and sealed it, for that he saw therein naught save some broken pans of earthenware to stand him instead of his stuff. After which the sergeant took the key, saying to the neighbors, "Tell him to bring back this man's cloth, then come to me and take his shop-key," and went his way, he and the man.

Then said Abu Sir to Abu Kir: "What ill business is this? Whoever bringeth thee aught, thou losest it for him. What hath become of this angry man's stuff?" Answered the dyer, "O my neighbor, 'twas stolen from me." "Prodigious!" exclaimed the barber. "Whenever anyone giveth thee aught, a thief stealeth it from thee! Art thou then the meeting place of every rogue upon town? But I doubt me thou liest, so tell me the truth." Replied Abu Kir, "O my neighbor, none hath stolen aught from me." Asked Abu Sir, "What then dost thou with the people's property?" and the dyer answered, "Whenever anyone giveth me aught to dye, I sell it and spend the price." Quoth Abu Sir, "Is this permitted thee of Allah?" and quoth Abu Kir, "I do this only out of poverty, because business is slack with me and I am poor and have nothing." And he went on to complain to him of the dullness of his trade and his lack of means.

Abu Sir in like manner lamented the little profit of his own calling, saying: "I am a master of my craft and have not my equal in this city, but no one cometh to me to be polled, because I am a pauper. And I loathe this art and mystery, O my brother." Abu Kir replied: "And I also loathe my own craft, by reason of its slackness. But, O my brother, what call is there for our abiding in this town? Let us depart from it, I and thou, and solace ourselves in the lands of mankind, carrying in our hands our crafts which are in demand all the world over. So shall we breathe the air, and rest from this grievous trouble." And he ceased not to command travel to Abu Sir till the barber became wishful to set out, so they agreed upon their route. When they agreed to travel together, Abu Kir said to Abu Sir: "O my neighbor, we are become brethren and there is no difference between us, so it behooveth us to recite the fatihah that he of us who gets work shall of his gain feed him who is out of work, and whatever is left, we will lay in a chest. And when we return to Alexandria, we will divide it fairly and equally." "So be it," replied Abu Sir, and they repeated the opening chapter of the Koran on this understanding.

Then Abu Sir locked up his shop and gave the key to its owner, whilst Abu Kir left his door locked and sealed and let the key lie with the kazi's sergeant. After which they took their baggage and embarked on the morrow in a galleon upon the salt sea. They set sail the same day and fortune attended them, for, of Abu Sir's great good luck, there was not a barber in the ship, albeit it carried a hundred and twenty men, besides captain and crew. So when they loosed the sails, the barber said to the dyer: "O my brother, this is the sea, and we shall need meat and drink. We have but little provaunt with us and haply the voyage will be long upon us, wherefore methinks I will shoulder my budget and pass among the passengers, and maybe someone will say to me, 'Come hither, O barber, and shave me,' and I will shave him for a scone or a silver bit or a draught of water. So shall we profit by this, I and thou too." "There's no harm in that," replied the dyer, and laid down his head and slept, whilst the barber took his gear and water tasse, and throwing over his shoulder a rag to serve as napkin (because he was poor), passed among the passengers.

Quoth one of them, "Ho, master, come and shave me." So he shaved him, and the man gave him a half-dirham, whereupon quoth Abu Sir: "O my brother, I have no use for this bit. Hadst thou given me a scone, 'twere more blessed to me in this sea, for I have a shipmate, and we are short of provision." So he gave him a loaf and a slice of cheese and filled him the tasse with sweet water. The barber carried all this to Abu Kir and said, "Eat the bread and cheese and drink the water." Accordingly he ate and drank, whilst Abu Sir again took up his shaving gear and, tasse in hand and rag on shoulder, went round about the deck among the passengers. One man he shaved for two scones and another for a bittock of cheese, and he was in demand, because there was no other barber on board. Also he bargained with everyone who said to him, "Ho, master, shave me!" for two loaves and a half-dirham, and they gave him whatever he sought, so that by sundown he had collected thirty loaves and thirty silvers with store of cheese and olives and botargos. And besides these he got from the passengers whatever he asked for and was soon in possession of things galore.

Amongst the rest, he shaved the captain, to whom he complained of his lack of victual for the voyage, and the skipper said to him, "That art welcome to bring thy comrade every night and sup with me, and have no care for that so long as ye sail with us." Then he returned to the dyer, whom he found asleep. So he roused him, and when Abu Kir awoke, he saw at his head an abundance of bread and cheese and olives and botargos and said, "Whence gottest thou all this?" "From the bounty of Allah Almighty," replied Abu Sir. Then Abu Kir would have fallen to, but the barber said to him: "Eat not of this, O my brother, but leave it to serve us another time. For know that I shaved the captain and complained to him of our lack of victual, whereupon quoth he: 'Welcome to thee! Bring thy comrade and sup both of ye with me every night.' And this night we sup with him for the first time."

But Abu Kir replied, "My head goeth round with seasickness and I cannot rise from my stead, so let me sup off these things and fare thou alone to the captain." Abu Sir replied, "There is no harm in that," and sat looking at the other as he ate, and saw him hew off gobbets as the quarryman heweth stone from the hill quarries and gulp them down with the gulp of an elephant which hath not eaten for days, bolting another mouthful ere he had swallowed the previous one and glaring the while at that which was before him with the glowering of a Ghul, and blowing as bloweth the hungry bull over his beans and bruised straw. Presently up came a sailor and said to the barber, "O craftsmaster, the captain biddeth thee come to supper and bring thy comrade." Quoth the barber to the dyer, "Wilt thou come with us?" but quoth he, "I cannot walk." So the barber went by himself and found the captain sitting before a tray whereon were a score or more of dishes, and all the company were awaiting him and his mate.

When the captain saw him, he asked, "Where is thy friend?" and Abu Sir answered, "O my lord, he is seasick." Said the skipper, "That will do him no harm, his sickness will soon pass off, but do thou carry him his supper and come back, for we tarry for thee." Then he set apart a porringer of kababs and putting therein some of each dish, till there was enough for ten, gave it to Abu Sir, saying, "Take this to thy chum." He took it and carried it to the dyer, whom he found grinding away with his dog teeth at the food which was before him, as he were a camel, and heaping mouthful on mouthful in his hurry. Quoth Abu Sir, "Did I not say to thee, 'Eat not of this'? Indeed the captain is a kindly man. See what he hath sent thee, for that I told him thou wast seasick." "Give it here," cried the dyer. So the barber gave him the platter, and he snatched it from him and fell upon his food, ravening for it and resembling a grinning dog or a raging lion or a roc pouncing on a pigeon or one well-nigh dead for hunger who, seeing meat, falls ravenously to eat.

Then Abu Sir left him, and going back to the captain, supped and enjoyed himself and drank coffee with him, after which he returned to Abu Kir and found that he had eaten all that was in the porringer and thrown it aside, empty. So he took it up and gave it to one of the captain's servants, then went back to Abu Kir and slept till the morning. On the morrow he continued to shave, and all he got by way of meat and drink he gave to his shipmate, who ate and drank and sat still, rising not save to do what none could do for him, and every night the barber brought him a full porringer from the captain's table.

They fared thus twenty days until the galleon cast anchor in the harbor of a city, whereupon they took leave of the skipper, and landing, entered the town and hired them a closet in a khan. Abu Sir furnished it, and buying a cooking pot and a platter and spoons and what else they needed, fetched meat and cooked it. But Abu Kir fell asleep the moment he entered the caravanserai and awoke not till Abu Sir aroused him and set the tray of food before him. When he awoke, he ate, and saying to Abu Sir, "Blame me not, for I am giddy," fell asleep again. Thus he did forty days, whilst every day the barber took his gear, and making the round of the city, wrought for that which fell to his lot, and returning, found the dyer asleep and aroused him. The moment he awoke he fell ravenously upon the food, eating as one who cannot have his fill nor be satisfied, after which he went asleep again.

On this wise he passed other forty days, and whenever the barber said to him, "Sit up and be comfortable and go forth and take an airing in the city, for 'tis a gay place and a pleasant and hath not its equal among the cities," he would reply, "Blame me not, for I am giddy." Abu Sir cared not to hurt his feelings nor give him hard words, but on the forty-first day, he himself fell sick and could not go abroad, so he engaged the porter of the khan to serve them both, and he did the needful for them and brought them meat and drink whilst Abu Kir would do nothing but eat and sleep. The man ceased not to wait upon them on this wise for four days, at the end of which time the barber's malady redoubled on him, till he lost his senses for stress of sickness; and Abu Kir, feeling the sharp pangs of hunger, arose and sought in his comrade's clothes, where he found a thousand silver bits.

He took them and, shutting the door of the closet upon Abu Sir, fared forth without telling any, and the doorkeeper was then at market and thus saw him not go out.

Presently Abu Kir betook himself to the bazaar and clad himself in costly clothes, at a price of five hundred half-dirhams. Then he proceeded to walk about the streets and divert himself by viewing the city, which he found to be one whose like was not among cities. But he noted that all its citizens were clad in clothes of white and blue, without other color. Presently he came to a dyer's, and seeing naught but blue in his shop, pulled out to him a kerchief and said, "O master, take this and dye it and win thy wage." Quoth the dyer, "The cost of dyeing this will be twenty dirhams," and quoth Abu Kir, "In our country we dye it for two." "Then go and dye it in your own country! As for me, my price is twenty dirhams and I will not bate a tittle thereof." "What color wilt thou dye it?" "I will dye it blue." "But I want it dyed red." "I know not how to dye red." "Then dye it green." "I know not how to dye it green." "Yellow." "Nor yet yellow." Thereupon Abu Kir went on to name the different tints to him, one after other, till the dyer said: "We are here in this city forty master dyers, not one more nor one less, and when one of us dieth, we teach his son the craft. If he leave no son, we abide lacking one, and if he leave two sons, we teach one of them the craft, and if he die, we teach his brother. This our craft is strictly ordered, and we know how to dye but blue and no other tint whatsoever."

Then said Abu Kir: "Know that I too am a dyer, and wot how to dye all colors, and I would have thee take me into thy service on hire, and I will teach thee everything of my art, so thou mayst glory therein over all the company of dyers." But the dyer answered, "We never admit a stranger into our craft." Asked Abu Kir, "And what if I open a dyery for myself?" whereto the other answered, "We will not suffer thee to do that on any wise." Whereupon he left him, and going to a second dyer, made him the like proposal, but he returned him the same answer as the first. And he ceased not to go from one to other till he had made the round of the whole forty masters, but they would not accept him either to master or apprentice. Then he repaired to the Sheikh of the dyers and told what had passed, and he said, "We admit no strangers into our craft."

Hereupon Abu Kir became exceeding wroth, and going up to the King of that city, made complaint to him, saying, "O King of the

Age, I am a stranger and a dyer by trade," and he told him whatso had passed between himself and the dyers of the town, adding: "I can dye various kinds of red, such as rose-color and jujubel-color and various kinds of green, such as grass-green and pistachio-green and olive and parrot's wing, and various kinds of black, such as coal-black and kohl-black, and various shades of yellow, such as orange and lemon-color," and went on to name to him the rest of the colors. Then said he, "O King of the Age, all the dyers in thy city cannot turn out of hand any one of these tints, for they know not how to dye aught but blue. Yet they will not admit me amongst them, either to master or apprentice." Answered the King: "Thou sayst sooth for that matter, but I will open to thee a dyery and give thee capital, and have thou no care anent them; for whoso offereth to do thee let or hindrance, I will hang him over his shop door."

Then he sent for builders and said to them, "Go round about the city with this master dyer, and whatsoever place pleaseth him, be it shop or khan or what not, turn out its occupier and build him a dyery after his wish. Whatsoever he biddeth you, that do ye, and oppose him not in aught." And he clad him in a handsome suit and gave him two white slaves to serve him, and a horse with housings of brocade and a thousand dinars, saying, "Expend this upon thyself against the building be completed." Accordingly Abu Kir donned the dress, and mounting the horse, became as he were an emir. Moreover the King assigned him a house, and bade furnish it, so they furnished it for him and he took up his abode therein. On the morrow he mounted and rode through the city, whilst the architects went before him, and he looked about him till he saw a place which pleased him and said, "This stead is seemly," whereupon they turned out the owner and carried him to the King, who gave him as the price of his holding, what contented him and more.

Then the builders fell to work, whilst Abu Kir said to them, "Build thus and thus and do this and that," till they built him a dyery that had not its like. Whereupon he presented himself before the King and informed him that they had done building the dyery and that there needed but the price of the dyestuffs and gear to set it going. Quoth the King, "Take these four thousand dinars to thy capital and let me see the first fruits of thy dyery." So he took the money and went to the market where, finding dyestuffs plentiful and well-nigh worthless, he bought all he needed of materials for dyeing; and the

King sent him five hundred pieces of stuff, which he set himself to dye of all colors, and then he spread them before the door of his dyery.

When the folk passed by the shop, they saw a wonder sight whose like they had never in their lives seen, so they crowded about the entrance, enjoying the spectacle and questioning the dyer and saying, "O master, what are the names of these colors?" Quoth he, "This is red and that yellow and the other green," and so on, naming the rest of the colors. And they fell to bringing him longcloth and saying to him, "Dye it for us like this and that, and take what hire thou seekest." When he had made an end of dyeing the King's stuffs, he took them and went up with them to the Divan, and when the King saw them he rejoiced in them and bestowed abundant bounty on the dyer. Furthermore, all the troops brought him stuffs, saying, "Dye for us thus and thus," and he dyed for them to their liking, and they threw him gold and silver. After this his fame spread abroad, and his shop was called the Sultan's Dyery. Good came in to him at every door and none of the other dyers could say a word to him, but they used to come to him kissing his hands and excusing themselves to him for past affronts they had offered him and saying, "Take us to thine apprentices." But he would none of them, for he had become the owner of black slaves and handmaids and had amassed store of wealth.

On this wise fared it with Abu Kir, but as regards Abu Sir, after closet door had been locked on him and his money had been stolen, he abode prostrate and unconscious for three successive days, at the end of which the concierge of the khan, chancing to look at the door, observed that it was locked, and bethought himself that he had not seen and heard aught of the two companions for some time. So he said in his mind: "Haply they have made off without paying rent, or perhaps they are dead, or what is to do with them?" And he waited till sunset, when he went up to the door and heard the barber groaning within. He saw the key in the lock, so he opened the door, and entering, found Abu Sir lying groaning, and said to him: "No harm to thee. Where is thy friend?" Replied Abu Sir: "By Allah, I came to my senses only this day and called out, but none answered my call. Allah upon thee, O my brother, look for the purse under my head and take from it five half-dirhams and buy me somewhat nourishing, for I am sore a-hungered." The porter put out his hand, and taking the purse, found it empty and said to the barber, "The purse is empty, there is nothing in it." Whereupon Abu Sir knew that Abu Kir had taken that which was therein and had fled, and he asked the porter, "Hast thou not seen my friend?" Answered the doorkeeper, "I have not seen him for these three days, and indeed methought you had departed, thou and he." The barber cried, "Not so, but he coveted my money and took it and fled, seeing me sick."

Then he fell a-weeping and a-wailing, but the doorkeeper said to him, "No harm shall befall thee, and Allah will requite him his deed." So he went away and cooked him some broth, whereof he ladled out a plateful and brought it to him. Nor did he cease to tend him and maintain him with his own moneys for two months' space, when the barber sweated and the Almighty made him whole of his sickness. Then he stood up and said to the porter: "An ever the Most High Lord enable me, I will surely requite thee thy kindness to me. But none requiteth save the Lord of His bounty!" Answered the porter: "Praised be He for thy recovery! I dealt not thus with thee but of desire for the face of Allah the Bountiful."

Then the barber went forth of the khan and threaded the market streets of the town till Destiny brought him to the bazaar wherein was Abu Kir's dyery, and he saw the varicolored stuffs dispread before the shop and a jostle of folk crowding to look upon them. So he questioned one of the townsmen and asked him, "What place is this, and how cometh it that I see the folk crowding together?" whereto the man answered, saying: "This is the Sultan's Dyery, which he set up for a foreigner, Abu Kir hight. And whenever he dyeth new stuff, we all flock to him and divert ourselves by gazing upon his handiwork, for we have no dyers in our land who know how to stain with these colors. And indeed there befell him with the dyers who are in the city that which befell." And he went on to tell him all that had passed between Abu Kir and the master dyers and how he had complained of them to the Sultan, who took him by the hand and built him that dyery and gave him this and that—brief, he recounted to him all that had occurred.

At this the barber rejoiced and said in himself: "Praised be Allah Who hath prospered him, so that he is become a master of his craft! And the man is excusable, for of a surety he hath been diverted from thee by his work and hath forgotten thee; but thou actedst kindly by him and entreatedst him generously what time he was out of work, so when he seeth thee, he will rejoice in thee and entreat thee generously, even as thou entreatedst him." According he made for the door of the dyery, and saw Abu Kir seated on a high mattress spread upon a bench beside the doorway, clad in royal apparel and attended by four blackamoor slaves and four white Mamelukes all robed in the richest of raiment. Moreover, he saw the workmen, ten Negro slaves, standing at work; for when Abu Kir bought them, he taught them the craft of dyeing, and he himself sat amongst his cushions as he were a grand wazir or a mighty monarch, putting his hand to naught but only saying to the men, "Do this and do that." So the barber went up to him and stood before him, deeming he would rejoice in him when he saw him and salute him and entreat him with honor and make much of him. But when eye fell upon eye, the dyer said to him: "O scoundrel, how many a time have I bidden thee stand not at the door of the workshop? Hast thou a mind to disgrace me with the folk, thief that thou art? Seize him."

So the blackamoors ran at him and laid hold of him, and the dyer rose up from his seat and said, "Throw him." Accordingly they threw him down and Abu Kir took a stick and dealt him a hundred strokes on the back, after which they turned him over and he beat him other hundred blows on his belly. Then he said to him: "O scoundrel, O villain, if ever again I see thee standing at the door of this dyery, I will forthwith send thee to the King, and he will commit thee to the Chief of Police, that he may strike thy neck. Begone, may Allah not bless thee!" So Abu Sir departed from him, brokenhearted by reason of the beating and shame that had betided him, whilst the bystanders asked Abu Kir, "What hath this man done?" He answered: "The fellow is a thief, who stealeth the stuffs of folk. He hath robbed me of cloth, how many a time! And I still said to myself, 'Allah forgive him!' He is a poor man, and I cared not to deal roughly with him, so I used to give my customers the worth of their goods and forbid him gently, but he would not be forbidden. And if he come again, I will send him to the King, who will put him to death and rid the people of his mischief." And the bystanders fell to abusing the barber after his back was turned.

Such was the behavior of Abu Kir, but as regards Abu Sir, he returned to the khan, where he sat pondering that which the dyer had done by him, and he remained seated till the burning of the beating subsided, when he went out and walked about the markets of the city. Presently he bethought him to go to the hammam bath, so he said to one of the townsfolk, "O my brother, which is the way to the baths?" Quoth the man, "And what manner of thing may the baths be?" and quoth Abu Sir, "'Tis a place where people wash themselves and do away their dirt and defilements, and it is of the best of the good things of the world." Replied the townsman, "Get thee to the sea," but the barber rejoined, "I want the hammam baths." Cried the other: "We know not what manner of thing is the hammam, for we all resort to the sea. Even the King, when he would wash, betaketh himself to the sea."

When Abu Sir was assured that there was no bath in the city and that the folk knew not the baths nor the fashion thereof, he betook himself to the King's Divan and, kissing ground between his hands, called down blessings on him and said: "I am a stranger and a bathman by trade, and I entered thy city and thought to go to the hammam, but found not one therein. How cometh a city of this comely quality to lack a hammam, seeing that the bath is of the highest of the delights of this world?" Quoth the King, "What manner of thing is the hammam?" So Abu Sir proceeded to set forth to him the quality of the bath, saying, "Thy capital will not be a perfect city till there be a hammam therein." "Welcome to thee!" said the King and clad him in a dress that had not its like and gave him a horse and two blackamoor slaves, presently adding four handmaids and as many white Mamelukes. He also appointed him a furnished house and honored him yet more abundantly than he had honored the dyer.

After this he sent builders with him, saying to them, "Build him a hammam in what place soever shall please him." So he took them and went with them through the midst of the city till he saw a stead that suited him. He pointed it out to the builders and they set to work, whilst he directed them, and they wrought till they built him a hammam that had not its like. Then he bade them paint it, and they painted it rarely, so that it was a delight to the beholders. After which Abu Sir went up to the King and told him that they had made an end of building and decorating the hammam, adding, "There lacketh naught save the furniture." The King gave him ten thousand dinars wherewith he furnished the bath and ranged the napkins on the ropes, and all who passed by the door stared at it and their mind was confounded at its decorations. So the people crowded to this spectacle, whose like they had never in their lives seen, and solaced themselves by staring at it and saying, "What is this thing?" To which Abu Sir replied, "This is a hammam," and they marveled thereat. Then he heated water and set the bath a-working, and he made a jetting fountain in the great basin, which ravished the wit of all who saw it of the people of the city.

Furthermore, he sought of the King ten Mamelukes not yet come to manhood, and he gave him ten boys like moons, whereupon Abu Sir proceeded to shampoo them, saying, "Do in this wise with the bathers." Then he burnt perfumes and sent out a crier to cry aloud in the city, saying, "O creatures of Allah, get ye to the baths which be called the Sultan's Hammam!" So the lieges came thither and Abu Sir bade the slave boys wash their bodies. The folk went down into the tank and coming forth, seated themselves on the raised pavement whilst the boys shampooed them, even as Abu Sir had taught them. And they continued to enter the hammam and do their need therein gratis and go out, without paying, for the space of three days.

On the fourth day the barber invited the King, who took horse with his grandees and rode to the baths, where he put off his clothes and entered. Then Abu Sir came in to him and rubbed his body with the bag gloves, peeling from his skin dirt rolls like lampwicks and showing them to the King, who rejoiced therein, and clapping his hand upon his limbs, heard them ring again for very smoothness and cleanliness. After which thorough washing Abu Sir mingled rose-water with the water of the tank and the King went down therein. When he came forth, his body was refreshed and he felt a lightness and liveliness such as he had never known in his life. Then the barber made him sit on the dais and the boys proceeded to shampoo him, whilst the censers fumed with the finest lign aloes.

Then said the King, "O master, is this the hammam?" and Abu Sir said, "Yes." Quoth the King, "As my head liveth, my city is not become a city indeed but by this bath," presently adding, "But what pay takest thou for each person?" Quoth Abu Sir, "That which thou biddest will I take," whereupon the King cried, "Take a thousand gold pieces for everyone who washeth in thy hammam." Abu Sir, however, said: "Pardon, O King of the Age! All men are not alike, but there are amongst them rich and poor, and if I take of each a thousand dinars, the hammam will stand empty, for the poor man cannot pay this price." Asked the King, "How then wilt thou do for the price?" and the barber answered: "I will leave it to their generosity.

Each who can afford aught shall pay that which his soul grudgeth not to give, and we will take from every man after the measure of his means. On this wise will the folk come to us, and he who is wealthy shall give according to his station and he who is wealthless shall give what he can afford. Under such condition the hammam will still be at work and prosper exceedingly. But a thousand dinars is a monarch's gift, and not every man can avail to this."

The lords of the realm confirmed Abu Sir's words, saying: "This is the truth, O King of the Age! Thinkest thou that all folk are like unto thee, O glorious King?" The King replied: "Ye say sooth, but this man is a stranger and poor, and 'tis incumbent on us to deal generously with him, for that he hath made in our city this hammam whose like we have never in our lives seen and without which our city were not adorned nor hath gotten importance. Wherefore, an we favor him with increase of fee, 'twill not be much." But the grandees said: "An thou wilt guerdon him, be generous with thine own moneys, and let the King's bounty be extended to the poor by means of the low price of the hammam, so the lieges may bless thee. But as for the thousand dinars, we are the lords of thy land, yet do our souls grudge to pay it, and how then should the poor be pleased to afford it?" Quoth the King: "O my Grandees, for this time let each of you give him a hundred dinars and a Mameluke, a slave girl, and a blackamoor," and quoth they: "'Tis well. We will give it, but after today whoso entereth shall give him only what he can afford, without grudging." "No harm in that," said the King, and they gave him the thousand gold pieces and three chattels.

Now the number of the nobles who were washed with the King that day was four hundred souls, so that the total of that which they gave him was forty thousand dinars, besides four hundred Mamelukes and a like number of Negroes and slave girls. Moreover, the King gave him ten thousand dinars, besides ten white slaves and ten handmaidens and a like number of blackamoors, whereupon, coming forward, Abu Sir kissed the ground before him and said: "O auspicious Sovereign, lord of justice, what place will contain me all these women and slaves?" Quoth the King: "O weak o' wit, I bade not my nobles deal thus with thee but that we might gather together unto thee wealth galore; for maybe thou wilt bethink thee of thy country and family and repine for them and be minded to return to thy mother land—so shalt thou take from our country muchel of money to maintain thyself withal, what while thou livest in thine own country." And quoth Abu Sir: "O King of the Age (Allah advance thee!), these white slaves and women and Negroes befit only kings, and hadst thou ordered me ready money, it were more profitable to me than this army; for they must eat and drink and dress, and whatever betideth me of wealth, it will not suffice for their support."

The King laughed and said: "By Allah, thou speaketh sooth! They are indeed a mighty host, and thou hast not the wherewithal to maintain them; but wilt thou sell them to me for a hundred dinars a head?" Said Abu Sir, "I sell them to thee at that price." So the King sent to his treasurer for the coin and he brought it and gave Abu Sir the whole of the price without abatement and in full tale, after which the King restored the slaves to their owners, saying, "Let each of you who knoweth his slaves take them, for they are a gift from me to you." So they obeyed his bidding and took each what belonged to him, whilst Abu Sir said to the King: "Allah ease thee, O King of the Age, even as thou hast eased me of these Ghuls, whose bellies none may fill save Allah!" The King laughed, and said he spake sooth. Then, taking the grandees of his realm from the hammam, returned to his palace. But the barber passed the night in counting out his gold and laying it up in bags and sealing them, and he had with him twenty black slaves and a like number of Mamelukes and four slave girls to serve him.

Now when morning morrowed, he opened the hammam and sent out a crier to cry, saying: "Whoso entereth the baths and washeth shall give that which he can afford and which his generosity requireth him to give." Then he seated himself by the pay chest and customers flocked in upon him, each putting down that which was easy to him, nor had eventide evened ere the chest was full of the good gifts of Allah the Most High. Presently the Queen desired to go to the hammam, and when this came to Abu Sir's knowledge, he divided the day on her account into two parts, appointing that between dawn and noon to men and that between midday and sundown to women. As soon as the Queen came, he stationed a handmaid behind the pay chest, for he had taught four slave girls the service of the hammam, so that they were become expert bathwomen and tirewomen. When the Queen entered, this pleased her, and her breast waxed broad, and she laid down a thousand dinars.

Thus his report was noised abroad in the city, and all who entered the bath he entreated with honor, were they rich or poor. Good came in upon him at every door, and he made acquaintance with the royal guards and got him friends and intimates. The King himself used to come to him one day in every week, leaving with him a thousand dinars, and the other days were for rich and poor alike; and he was wont to deal courteously with the folk and use them with the utmost respect. It chanced that the King's sea captain came in to him one day in the bath, so Abu Sir did off his dress and going in with him, proceeded to shampoo him, and entreated him with exceeding courtesy. When he came forth, he made him sherbet and coffee, and when he would have given him somewhat, he swore that he would not accept from him aught. So the captain was under obligation to him, by reason of his exceeding kindness and courtesy, and was perplexed how to requite the bathman his generous dealing.

Thus fared it with Abu Sir, but as regards Abu Kir, hearing all the people recounting wonders of the baths and saying, "Verily, this hammam is the Paradise of this world! Inshallah, O Such-a-one, thou shalt go with us tomorrow to this delightful bath," he said to himself, "Needs must I fare like the rest of the world, and see this bath that hath taken folk's wits." So he donned his richest dress, and mounting a she-mule and bidding the attendance of four white slaves and four blacks, walking before and behind him, he rode to the hammam. When he alighted at the door, he smelt the scent of burning aloes wood and found people going in and out and the benches full of great and small. So he entered the vestibule, and saw Abu Sir, who rose to him and rejoiced in him, but the dyer said to him: "Is this the way of well-born men? I have opened me a dyery and am become master dyer of the city and acquainted with the King and have risen to prosperity and authority, yet camest thou not to me nor askest of me nor saidst, 'Where's my comrade?' For my part, I sought thee in vain and sent my slaves and servants to make search for thee in all the khans and other places, but they knew not whither thou hadst gone, nor could anyone give me tidings of thee."

Said Abu Sir, "Did I not come to thee, and didst thou not make me out a thief and bastinado me and dishonor me before the world?" At this Abu Kir made a show of concern and asked: "What manner of talk is this? Was it thou whom I beat?" and Abu Sir answered, "Yes, 'twas I." Whereupon Abu Kir swore to him a thousand oaths that he knew him not and said: "There was a fellow like thee, who used to come every day and steal the people's stuff, and I took thee for him." And he went on to pretend penitence, beating hand upon hand and saying: "There is no Majesty and there is no Might save in Allah, the Glorious, the Great. Indeed we have sinned against thee, but would that thou hadst discovered thyself to me and said, 'I am Such-a-one!' Indeed the fault is with thee, for that thou madest not thyself known unto me, more especially seeing that I was distracted for much business." Replied Abu Sir: "Allah pardon thee, O my comrade! This was foreordained in the secret purpose, and reparation is with Allah. Enter and put off thy clothes and bathe at thine ease." Said the dyer, "I conjure thee, by Allah, O my brother, forgive me!" and said Abu Sir: "Allah acquit thee of blame and forgive thee! Indeed this thing was decreed to me from all eternity."

Then asked Abu Kir, "Whence gottest thou this high degree?" and answered Abu Sir: "He who prospered thee prospered me, for I went up to the King and described to him the fashion of the hammam, and he bade me build one." And the dyer said: "Even as thou art beknown of the King, so also am I, and, Inshallah—God willing— I will make him love and favor thee more than ever, for my sake. He knoweth not that thou art my comrade, but I will acquaint him of this and commend thee to him." But Abu Sir said: "There needeth no commendation, for He who moveth man's heart to love still liveth, and indeed the King and all his Court affect me and have given me this and that." And he told him the whole tale, and said to him: "Put off thy clothes behind the chest and enter the hammam, and I will go in with thee and rub thee down with the glove." So he doffed his dress, and Abu Sir, entering the bath with him, soaped him and gloved him and then dressed him and busied himself with his service till he came forth, when he brought him dinner and sherbets, whilst all the folk marveled at the honor he did him.

Then Abu Kir would have given him somewhat, but he swore that he would not accept aught from him, and said to him: "Shame upon such doing! Thou art my comrade, and there is no difference between us." Then Abu Kir observed: "By Allah, O my comrade, this is a mighty fine hammam of thine, but there lacketh somewhat in its ordinance." Asked Abu Sir, "And what is that?" and Abu Kir answered: "It is the depilatory, to wit, the paste compounded of yellow arsenic and quicklime which removeth the hair with comfort. Do thou prepare it, and next time the King cometh, present it to him, teaching him how he shall cause the hair to fall off by such means, and he will love thee with exceeding love and honor thee." Quoth Abu Sir, "Thou speaketh sooth, and Inshallah, I will at once make it."

Then Abu Kir left him and mounted his mule, and going to the King, said to him, "I have a warning to give thee, O King of the Age!" "And what is thy warning?" asked the King, and Abu Kir answered, "I hear that thou hast built a hammam." Quoth the King: "Yes. There came to me a stranger and I built the baths for him, even as I built the dyery for thee, and indeed 'tis a mighty fine hammam and an ornament to my city," and he went on to describe to him the virtues of the bath. Quoth the dyer, "Hast thou entered therein?" and quoth the King, "Yes." Thereupon cried Abu Kir: "Alhamdolillah—praised be God—who saved thee from the mischief of yonder villain and foe of the Faith—I mean the bathkeeper!" The King inquired, "And what of him?" and Abu Kir replied: "Know, O King of the Age, that an thou enter the hammam again after this day, thou wilt surely perish." "How so?" said the King, and the dyer said: "This bathkeeper is thy foe and the foe of the Faith, and he induced thee not to stablish this bath but because he designed therein to poison thee. He hath made for thee somewhat, and he will present it to thee when thou enterest the hammam, saying, 'This is a drug which, if one apply to his parts below the waist, will remove the hair with comfort." Now it is no drug, but a drastic dreg and a deadly poison, for the Sultan of the Christians hath promised this obscene fellow to release to him his wife and children an he will kill thee. For they are prisoners in the hands of that Sultan. I myself was captive with him in their land, but I opened a dyery and dyed for them various colors, so that they conciliated the King's heart to me and he bade me ask a boon of him. I sought of him freedom and he set me at liberty, whereupon I made my way to this city, and seeing yonder man in the hammam, said to him, 'How didst thou effect thine escape and win free with thy wife and children?' Quoth he: 'We ceased not to be in captivity, I and my wife and children, till one day the King of the Nazarenes held a Court whereat I was present, amongst a number of others. And as I stood amongst the folk, I heard them open out on the kings and name them, one after other, till they came to the name of the King of this city, whereupon the King of the Christians cried out "Alas!" and said, "None vexeth me in the world, but the King of such a city! Whosoever will contrive me his slaughter I will give him all he shall ask." So I went up to him and said, "An I compass for thee his slaughter, wilt thou set me free, me and my wife and my children?" The King replied, "Yes, and I will give thee to boot whatso thou shalt desire." So we agreed upon this, and he sent me in a galleon to this city, where I presented myself to the King and he built me this hammam.

"'Now, therefore, I have naught to do but to slay him and return to the King of the Nazarenes, that I may redeem my children and my wife and ask a boon of him.' Quoth I: 'And how wilt thou go about to kill him?' and quoth he, 'By the simplest of all devices, for I have compounded him somewhat wherein is poison, so when he cometh to the bath, I shall say to him "Take this paste and anoint therewith thy parts below the waist for it will cause the hair to drop off." So he will take it and apply it to himself, and the poison will work in him a day and a night, till it reacheth his heart and destroyeth him. And meanwhile I shall have made off and none will know that it was I slew him.' When I heard this," added Abu Kir, "I feared for thee, my benefactor, wherefore I have told thee of what is doing."

As soon as the King heard the dyer's story, he was wroth with exceeding wrath and said to him, "Keep this secret." Then he resolved to visit the hammam, that he might dispel doubt by supplying certainty, and when he entered, Abu Sir doffed his dress, and betaking himself as of wont to the service of the King, proceeded to glove him, after which he said to him, "O King of the Age, I have made a drug which assisteth in plucking out the lower hair." Cried the King, "Bring it to me." So the barber brought it to him and the King, finding it nauseous of smell, was assured that it was poison, wherefore he was incensed and called out to his guards, saying, "Seize him!" Accordingly they seized him, and the King donned his dress and returned to his palace; boiling with fury, whilst none knew the cause of his indignation, for, of the excess of his wrath he had acquainted no one therewith and none dared ask him.

Then he repaired to the audience chamber, and causing Abu Sir to be brought before him with his elbows pinioned, sent for his sea captain and said to him: "Take this villain and set him in a sack with two quintals of lime unslaked and tie its mouth over his head. Then lay him in a cockboat and row out with him in front of my palace, where thou wilt see me sitting at the lattice.

Do thou say to me, 'Shall I cast him in?' and if I answer, 'Cast him!' throw the sack into the sea, so the quicklime may be slacked on him to the intent that he shall die drowned and burnt." "Hearkening and obeying," quoth the captain, and taking Abu Sir from the presence, carried him to an island facing the King's palace, where he said to him: "Ho, thou, I once visited thy hammam and thou entreatedst me with honor and accomplishedst all my needs and I had great pleasure of thee. Moreover, thou swarest that thou wouldst take no pay of me, and I love thee with a great love. So tell me how the case standeth between thee and the King, and what abominable deed thou hast done with him that he is wroth with thee and hath commanded me that thou shouldst die this foul death."

Answered Abu Sir, "I have done nothing, nor weet I of any crime I have committed against him which merited this!" Rejoined the captain: "Verily, thou wast high in rank with the King, such as none ever won before thee, and all who are prosperous are envied. Haply someone was jealous of thy good fortune and threw out certain hints concerning thee to the King, by reason whereof he is become enraged against thee with rage so violent. But be of good cheer, no harm shall befall thee. For even as thou entreatedst me generously, without acquaintanceship between me and thee, so now I will deliver thee. But an I release thee, thou must abide with me on this island till some galleon sail from our city to thy native land, when I will send thee thither therein."

Abu Sir kissed his hand and thanked him for that, after which the captain fetched the quicklime and set it in a sack, together with a great stone, the size of a man, saying, "I put my trust in Allah!" Then he gave the barber a net, saying: "Cast this net into the sea, so haply thou mayest take somewhat of fish. For I am bound to supply the King's kitchen with fish every day, but today I have been distracted from fishing by this calamity which hath befallen thee, and I fear lest the cook's boys come to me in quest of fish and find none. So, an thou take aught, they will find it and thou wilt veil my face, whilst I go and play off my practice in front of the palace and feign to cast thee into the sea." Answered Abu Sir: "I will fish the while. Go thou, and God help thee!" So the captain set the sack in the boat and paddled till it came under the palace, where he saw the King seated at the lattice and said to him, "O King of the Age, shall I cast him in?" "Cast him!" cried the King, and signed to him with his hand, when lo and behold! something flashed like levin and fell into the sea. Now that which had fallen into the water was the King's seal ring, and the same was enchanted in such way that when the King was wroth with anyone and was minded to slay him, he had but to sign to him with his right hand, whereon was the signet ring, and therefrom issued a flash of lightning, which smote the object, and thereupon his head fell from between his shoulders. And the troops obeyed him not, nor did he overcome the men of might, save by means of the ring. So when it dropped from his finger, he concealed the matter and kept silence, for that he dared not say, "My ring is fallen into the sea," for fear of the troops, lest they rise against him and slay him.

On this wise it befell the King. But as regards Abu Sir, after the captain had left him on the island he took the net and casting it into the sea, presently drew it up full of fish, nor did he cease to throw it and pull it up full till there was a great mound of fish before him. So he said in himself, "By Allah, this long while I have not eaten fish!" and chose himself a large fat fish, saying, "When the captain cometh back, I will bid him fry it for me, so I may dine on it." Then he cut its throat with a knife he had with him, but the knife stuck in its gills, and there he saw the King's signet ring, for the fish had swallowed it and Destiny had driven it to that island, where it had fallen into the net. He took the ring and drew it on his little finger, not knowing its peculiar properties. Presently up came two of the cook's boys in quest of fish, and seeing Abu Sir, said to him, "O man, whither is the captain gone?" "I know not," said he, and signed to them with his right hand, when, behold, the heads of both underlings dropped off from between their shoulders. At this Abu Sir was amazed and said, "Would I wot who slew them!"

And their case was grievous to him, and he was still pondering it when the captain suddenly returned, and seeing the mound of fishes and two man lying dead and the seal ring on Abu Sir's finger, said to him: "O my brother, move not thy hand whereon is the signet ring, else thou wilt kill me." Abu Sir wondered at this speech and kept his hand motionless, whereupon the captain came up to him and said, "Who slew these two men?" "By Allah, O my brother, I wot not!" "Thou sayest sooth, but tell me, whence hadst thou that ring?" "I found it in this fish's gills." "True," said the captain, "for I saw it fall flashing from the King's palace and disappear in the sea, what time he signed toward thee, saying, 'Cast him in.' So I cast the sack into the water, and it was then that the ring slipped from his finger and fell into the sea, where this fish swallowed it, and Allah drave it to thee, so that thou madest it thy prey, for this ring was thy lot. But kennest thou its property?"

Said Abu Sir, "I knew not that it had any properties peculiar to it," and the captain said: "Learn, then, that the King's troops obey him not save for fear of this signet ring, because it is spelled, and when he was wroth with anyone and had a mind to kill him, he would sign at him therewith and his head would drop from between his shoulders, for there issued a flash of lightning from the ring and its ray smote the object of his wrath, who died forthright." At this, Abu Sir rejoiced with exceeding joy and said to the captain, "Carry me back to the city," and he said, "That will I, now that I no longer fear for thee from the King, for wert thou to sign at him with thy hand, purposing to kill him, his head would fall down between thy hands. And if thou be minded to slay him and all his host, thou mayst slaughter them without let or hindrance."

So saying, he embarked him in the boat and bore him back to the city, so Abu Sir landed, and going up to the palace, entered the council chamber, where he found the King seated facing his officers, in sore cark and care by reason of the seal ring and daring not tell any of his folk anent its loss. When he saw Abu Sir, he said to him: "Did we not cast thee into the sea? How hast thou contrived to come forth of it?" Abu Sir replied: "O King of the Age, whenas thou badest throw me into the sea, thy captain carried me to an island and asked me of the cause of thy wrath against me, saying, 'What hast thou done with the King, that he should decree thy death?' I answered, 'By Allah, I know not that I have wrought him any wrong!' Quoth he: 'Thou wast high in rank with the King, and haply someone envied thee and threw out certain hints concerning thee to him, so that he is become incensed against thee. But when I visited thee in thy hammam, thou entreatedst me honorably, and I will requite thee thy hospitality to me by setting thee free and sending thee back to thine own land.' Then he set a great stone in the sack in my stead and cast it into the seat, but when thou signedst to him to throw me in, thy seal ring dropped from thy finger into the main, and a fish swallowed it.

"Now I was on the island a-fishing, and this fish came up in the net with others, whereupon I took it, intending to broil it. But when I opened its belly, I found the signet ring therein, so I took it and put it on my finger. Presently up came two of the servants of the kitchen, questing fish, and I signed to them with my hand, knowing not the property of the seal ring, and their heads fell off. Then the captain came back, and seeing the ring on my finger, acquainted me with its spell. And, behold, I have brought it back to thee, for that thou dealtest kindly by me and entreatedst me with the utmost honor, nor is that which thou hast done me of kindness lost upon me. Here is thy ring, take it! But an I have done with thee aught deserving of death, tell me my crime and slay me and thou shalt be absolved of sin in shedding my blood."

So saying, he pulled the ring from his finger and gave it to the King, who, seeing Abu Sir's noble conduct, took the ring and put it on and felt life return to him afresh. Then he rose to his feet, and embracing the barber, said to him: "O man, thou art indeed of the flower of the well-born! Blame me not, but forgive me the wrong I have done thee. Had any but thou gotten hold of this ring, he had never restored it to me." Answered Abu Sir: "O King of the Age, an thou wouldst have me forgive thee, tell me what was my fault which drew down thine anger upon me, so that thou commandedst to do me die." Rejoined the King: "By Allah, 'tis clear to me that thou art free and guiltless in all things of offense, since thou hast done this good deed. Only the dyer denounced thee to me in such and such words," and he told him all that Abu Kir had said. Abu Sir replied: "By Allah, O King of the Age, I know no King of the Nazarenes, nor during my days have ever journeyed to a Christian country, nor did it ever come into my mind to kill thee. But this dyer was my comrade and neighbor in the city of Alexandria, where life was straitened upon us. Therefore we departed thence, to seek our fortunes, by reason of the narrowness of our means at home, after we had recited the opening chapter of the Koran together, pledging ourselves that he who got work should feed him who lacked work. And there befell me with him such-and-such things."

Then he went on to relate to the King all that had betided him with Abu Kir the dyer: how he had robbed him of his dirhams and had left him alone and sick in the khan closet, and how the door keeper had fed him of his own moneys till Allah recovered him of his sickness, when he went forth and walked about the city with his budget, as was his wont, till his espied a dyery, about which the folk were crowding; so he looked at the door, and seeing Abu Kir seated on a bench there, went in to salute him, whereupon he accused him of being a thief and beat him a grievous beating—brief, he told him his whole tale, from first to last, and added: "O King of the Age, 'twas he who counseled me to make the depilatory and present it to thee, saying: 'The hammam is perfect in all things but that it lacketh this.' And know, O King of the Age, that this drug is harmless and we use it in our land, where 'tis one of the requisites of the bath, but I had forgotten it. So when the dyer visited the hammam, I entreated him with honor and he reminded me of it, and enjoined me to make it forthwith. But do thou send after the porter of such a khan and the workmen of the dyery and question them all of that which I have told thee."

Accordingly the King sent for them and questioned them one and all and they acquainted him with the truth of the matter. Then he summoned the dyer, saying, "Bring him barefooted, bareheaded, and with elbows pinioned!" Now he was sitting in his house, rejoicing in Abu Sir's death, but ere he could be ware, the King's guards rushed in upon him and cuffed him on the nape, after which they bound him and bore him into the presence, where he saw Abu Sir seated by the King's side and the doorkeeper of the khan and workmen of the dyery standing before him. Quoth the doorkeeper to him: "Is not this thy comrade whom thou robbedst of his silvers and leftest with me sick in the closet doing such-and-such by him?" And the workmen said to him, "Is not this he whom thou badest us seize and beat?" Therewith Abu Kir's baseness was made manifest to the King, and he was certified that he merited torture yet sorer than the torments of Munkar and Nakir. So he said to his guards: "Take him and parade him about the city and the markets; then set him in a sack and cast him into the sea." Whereupon quoth Abu Sir: "O King of the Age, accept my intercession for him, for I pardon him all he hath done with me." But quoth the King: "An thou pardon him all his offenses against thee, I cannot pardon him his offenses against me." And he cried out, saying, "Take him."

So they took him and paraded him about the city, after which they set him in a sack with quicklime and cast him into the sea, and he died, drowned and burnt. Then said the King to the barber, "O Abu Sir, ask of me what thou wilt and it shall be given thee."

And he answered, saying, "I ask of thee to send me back to my own country, for I care no longer to tarry here." Then the King gifted him great store of gifts, over and above that which he had whilom bestowed on him, and amongst the rest a galleon freighted with goods. And the crew of this galleon were Mamelukes, so he gave him these also, after offering to make him his Wazir, whereto the barber consented not. Presently he farewelled the King and set sail in his own ship manned by his own crew, nor did he cast anchor till he reached Alexandria and made fast to the shore there. They they landed, and one of his Mamelukes, seeing a sack on the beach, said to Abu Sir: "O my lord, there is a great heavy sack on the seashore, with the mouth tied up, and I know not what therein."

So Abu Sir came up, and opening the sack, found therein the remains of Abu Kir, which the sea had borne thither. He took it forth, and burying it near Alexandria, built over the grave a place of visitation. After this Abu Sir abode awhile, till Allah took him to Himself, and they buried him hard by the tomb of his comrade Abu Kir, wherefore that place was called Abu Kir and Abu Sir, but it is now known as Abu Kir only. This, then, is that which hath reached us of their history, and glory be to Him Who endureth forever and aye and by Whose will enterchange the night and the day.

And of the stories they tell is one anent

THE SLEEPER AND THE WAKER

It hath reached me, O auspicious King, that there was once at Baghdad, in the caliphate of Harun al-Rashid, a man and a merchant who had a son Abu al-Hasan al-Khali'a by name. The merchant died leaving great store of wealth to his heir, who divided it into two equal parts, whereof he laid up one and spent of the other half. And he fell to companying with Persians and with the sons of the merchants, and he gave himself up to good drinking and good eating till all the wealth he had with him was wasted and wantoned. Whereupon he betook himself to his friends and comrades and cup companions and expounded to them his case, discovering to them the failure of that which was in his hand of wealth. But not one of them took heed of him or even deigned answer him.

So he returned to his mother (and indeed his spirit was broken) and related to her that which had happened to him and what had befallen him from his friends, how they had neither shared with him nor requited him with speech. Quoth she: "O Abu al-Hasan, on this wise are the sons of this time: And thou have aught, they draw thee near to them, and if thou have naught, they put thee away from them." And she went on to condole with him, what while he bewailed himself and his tears flowed and he repeated these lines:

> "An wane my wealth, no man will succor me,
> When my wealth waxeth all men friendly show.
> How many a friend for wealth showed friendliness
> Who, when my wealth departed, turned to foe!"

Then he sprang up, and going to the place wherein was the other half of his goods, took it and lived with it well. And he sware that he would never again consort with a single one of those he had known, but would company only with the stranger, nor entertain even him but one night, and that when it morrowed, he would never know him more. Accordingly he fell to sitting every eventide on the bridge over Tigris and looking at each one who passed by him. And if he saw him to be a stranger, he made friends with him and carried him to his house, where he conversed and caroused with him all night till morning. Then he dismissed him, and would never more salute him with the salaam nor ever more drew near unto him, neither invited him again.

Thus he continued to do for the space of a full year, till one day while he sat on the bridge, as was his wont, expecting who should come to him so he might take him and pass the night with him, behold, up came the Caliph and Masrur, the Sworder of his vengeance, disguised in merchants' dress, according to their custom. So Abu al-Hasan looked at them, and rising, because he knew them not, asked them: "What say ye? Will ye go with me to my dwelling place, so ye may eat what is ready and drink what is at hand; to wit, platter bread and meat cooked and wine strained?" The Caliph refused this, but he conjured him and said to him: "Allah upon thee, O my lord. Go with me, for thou art my guest this night, and balk not my hopes of thee!" And he ceased not to press him till he consented, whereat Abu al-Hasan rejoiced, and walking on before him, gave not over talking with him till they came to his house and he carried the Caliph into the saloon.

Al-Rashid entered a hall such as an thou sawest it and gazedst upon its walls, thou hadst beheld marvels, and hadst thou looked narrowly at its water conduits, thou wouldst have seen a fountain cased with gold. The Caliph made his man abide at the door, and as soon as he was seated, the host brought him somewhat to eat. So he ate, and Abu al-Hasan ate with him, that eating might be grateful to him. Then he removed the tray and they washed their hands and the Commander of the Faithful sat down again. Whereupon Abu al-Hasan set on the drinking vessels, and seating himself by his side, fell to filling and giving him to drink and entertaining him with discourse. And when they had drunk their sufficiency the host called for a slave girl like a branch of ban, who took a lute and sang to it these two couplets:

> "O thou aye dwelling in my heart,
> Whileas thy form is far from sight,
> Thou art my sprite by me unseen,
> Yet nearest near art thou, my sprite."

His hospitality pleased the Caliph, and the goodliness of his manners, and he said to him: "O youth, who art thou? Make me acquainted with thyself, so I may requite thee thy kindness." But Abu al-Hasan smiled and said: 'O my lord, far be it, alas! that what is past should again come to pass and that I company with thee at other time than this time!" The Prince of True Believers asked: "Why so? And why wilt thou not acquaint me with thy case?" and Abu al-Hasan answered, "Know, O my lord, that my story is strange and that there is a cause for this affair." Quoth Al-Rashid, "And what is the cause?" and quoth he, "The cause hath a tail." The Caliph laughed at his words and Abu al-Hasan said, "I will explain to thee this saying by the tale of the larrikin and the cook. So hear thou, O my lord, the

STORY OF THE LARRIKIN AND THE COOK"

ONE of the ne'er do-wells found himself one fine morning without aught, and the world was straitened upon him and patience failed him. So he lay down to sleep, and ceased not slumbering till the sun stang him and the foam came out upon his mouth, whereupon he arose, and he was penniless and had not even so much as a single dirham. Presently he arrived at the shop of a cook, who had set his pots and pans over the fire and washed his saucers and wiped his scales and swept his shop and sprinkled it. And indeed his fats and oils were clear and clarified and his spices fragrant, and he himself stood behind his cooking pots ready to serve customers. So the larrikin, whose wits had been sharpened by hunger, went in to him and saluting him, said to him, "Weigh me half a dirham's worth of meat and a quarter of a dirham's worth of boiled grain, and the like of bread." So the kitchener weighed it out to him and the good-for-naught entered the shop, whereupon the man set the food before him and he ate till he had gobbled up the whole and licked the saucers and sat perplexed, knowing not how he should do with the cook concerning the price of that he had eaten, and turning his eyes about upon everything in the shop.

And as he looked, behold, he caught sight of an earthen pan lying arsy-versy upon its mouth, so he raised it from the ground and found under it a horse's tail, freshly cut off and the blood oozing from it, whereby he knew that the cook adulterated his meat with horse-flesh. When he discovered this default, he rejoiced therein, and washing his hands, bowed his head and went out. And when the kitchener saw that he went and gave him naught, he cried out, saying, "Stay, O pest, O burglar!" So the larrikin stopped and said to him, "Dost thou cry out upon me and call to me with these words, O cornute?" Whereat the cook was angry, and coming down from the shop, cried: "What meanest thou by thy speech, O low fellow, thou that devourest meat and millet and bread and kitchen and goest forth with 'the peace be on thee!' as it were the thing had not been, and payest down naught for it?" Quoth the lackpenny, "Thou liest, O accursed son of a cuckold!" Whereupon the cook cried out, and laying hold of his debtor's collar, said, "O Moslems, this fellow is my first customer this day, and he hath eaten my food and given me naught."

So the folk gathered about them and blamed the ne'er-do-well and said to him, "Give him the price of that which thou hast eaten." Quoth he, "I gave him a dirham before I entered the shop," and quoth the cook: "Be everything I sell this day forbidden to me, if he gave me so much as the name of a coin! By Allah, he gave me naught, but ate my food and went out and would have made off, without aught said." Answered the larrikin, "I gave thee a dirham," and he reviled the kitchener, who returned his abuse, whereupon he dealt him a buffet and they gripped and grappled and throttled each other. When the folk saw them fighting, they came up to them and asked them, "What is this strife between you, and no cause for it?" and the lackpenny answered, "Ay, by Allah, but there is a cause for it, and the cause hath a tail!" Whereupon cried the cook: "Yea, by Allah, now thou mindest me of thyself and thy dirham! Yes, he gave me a dirham, and but a quarter of the coin is spent. Come back and take the rest of the price of thy dirham." For he understood what was to do, at the mention of the tail.

"And I, O my brother," added Abu al-Hasan, "my story hath a cause, which I will tell thee." The Caliph laughed at his speech and said: "By Allah, this is none other than a pleasant tale! Tell me thy story and the cause."

Replied the host: "With love and goodly gree! Know, O my lord, that my name is Abu al-Hasan al-Khali'a and that my father died and left me abundant wealth, of which I made two parts. One I laid up, and with the other I betook myself to enjoying the pleasures of friendship and conviviality and consorting with intimates and boon companions and the sons of the merchants, nor did I leave one but I caroused with him and he with me. And I lavished all my money on comrades and good cheer, till there remained with me naught. Whereupon I betook myself to the friends and fellow topers upon whom I wasted my wealth, so perhaps they might provide for my case, but when I visited them and went round about to them all, I found no vantage in one of them, nor would any so much as break a bittock of bread in my face. So I wept for myself, and repairing to my mother, complained to her of my case. Quoth she: 'Such are friends. An thou have aught, they frequent thee and devour thee, but an thou have naught, they cast thee off and chase thee away.' Then I brought out the other half of my money and bound myself by an oath that I would never more entertain any save one single night, after which I would never again salute him nor notice him. Hence my saying to thee: 'Far be it, alas! that what is past should again come to pass, for I will never again company with thee after this night.'"

When the Commander of the Faithful heard this, he laughed a loud laugh and said: "By Allah, O my brother, thou art indeed excused in this matter, now that I know the cause and that the cause hath a tail. Nevertheless, Inshallah, I will not sever myself from thee." Replied Abu al-Hasan: "O my guest, did I not say to thee, 'Far be it, alas! that what is past should again come to pass?' For indeed I will never again forgather with any!" Then the Caliph rose and the host set before him a dish of roast goose and a bannock of first bread, and sitting down, fell to cutting off morsels and morseling the Caliph therewith. They gave not over eating till they were filled, when Abu al-Hasan brought basin and ewer and potash and they washed their hands. Then he lighted three wax candles and three lamps, and spreading the drinking cloth, brought strained wine, clear, old, and fragrant, whose scent was as that of virgin musk. He filled the first cup and saying, "O my boon companion, be ceremony laid aside between us by thy leave! Thy slave is by thee, may I not be afflicted with thy loss!" drank if off and filled a second cup, which he handed to the Caliph with due reverence.

His fashion pleased the Commander of the Faithful, and the goodliness of his speech, and he said to himself, "By Allah, I will assuredly requite him for this!" Then Abu al-Hasan filled the cup again and handed it to the Caliph, reciting these two couplets:

THE ARABIAN NIGHTS

"Had we thy coming known, we would for sacrifice
Have poured thee out heart's blood or blackness of the eyes.
Ay, and we would have spread our bosoms in thy way,
That so thy feet might fare on eyelids, carpet-wise."

When the Caliph heard his verses, he took the cup from his hand and kissed it and drank it off and returned it to Abu al-Hasan, who made him an obeisance and filled and drank. Then he filled again, and kissing the cup thrice, recited these lines:

"Your presence honoreth the base,
And we confess the deed of grace.
An you absent yourself from us,
No freke we find to fill your place."

Then he gave the cup to the Caliph, saying: "Drink it in health and soundness! It doeth away malady and bringeth remedy and setteth the runnels of health to flow free." So they ceased not carousing and conversing till middle night, when the Caliph said to his host, "O my brother, hast thou in thy heart a concupiscence thou wouldst have accomplished, or a contingency thou wouldst avert?" Said he: "By Allah, there is no regret in my heart save that I am not empowered with bidding and forbidding, so I might manage what is in my mind!" Quoth the Commander of the Faithful, "By Allah, and again by Allah, O my brother, tell me what is in thy mind!" And quoth Abu al-Hasan: "Would Heaven I might be Caliph for one day and avenge myself on my neighbors, for that in my vicinity is a mosque, and therein four sheikhs, who hold it a grievance when there cometh a guest to me, and they trouble me with talk and worry me in words and menace me that they will complain of me to the Prince of True Believers, and indeed they oppress me exceedingly. And I crave of Allah the Most High power for one day, that I may beat each and every of them with four hundred lashes, as well as the imam of the mosque, and parade them round about the city of Baghdad and bid cry before them: 'This is the reward and the least of the reward of whoso exceedeth in talk and vexeth the folk and turneth their joy to annoy.' This is what I wish, and no more."

Said the Caliph: "Allah grant thee that thou seekest! Let us crack one last cup and rise ere the dawn draw near, and tomorrow night I will be with thee again." Said Abu al-Hasan, "Far be it!" Then the Caliph crowned a cup, and putting therein a piece of Cretan bhang, gave it to his host and said to him, "My life on thee, O my brother, drink this cup from my hand!" and Abu al-Hasan answered, "Ay, by thy life, I will drink it from thy hand." So he took it and drank it off, but hardly had it settled in his stomach when his head forewent his heels and he fell to the ground like one slain. Whereupon the Caliph went out and said to his slave Masrur: "Go in to yonder young man, the housemaster, and take him up and bring him to me at the palace. And when thou goest out, shut the door." So saying, he went away, whilst Masrur entered, and taking up Abu al-Hasan, shut the door behind him, and made after his master till he reached with him the palace what while the night drew to an end and the cocks began crowing, and set him down before the Commander of the Faithful, who laughed at him.

Then he sent for Ja'afar the Barmecide and when he came before him, said to him, "Note thou yonder young man," pointing to Abu al-Hasan, "and when thou shalt see him tomorrow seated in my place of estate and on the throne of my caliphate and clad in my royal clothing, stand thou in attendance upon him, and enjoin the emirs and grandees and the folk of my household and the officers of my realm to be upon their feet, as in his service, and obey him in whatso he shall bid them do. And thou, if he speak to thee of aught, do it, and hearken unto his say and gainsay him not in anything during this coming day." Ja'afar acknowledged the order with "Hearkening and obedience" and withdrew, whilst the Prince of True Believers went in to the palace women, who came up to him, and he said to them: "When this sleeper shall awake tomorrow, kiss ye the ground between his hands, and do ye wait upon him and gather round about him and clothe him in the royal clothing and serve him with the service of the caliphate, and deny not aught of his estate, but say to him, 'Thou art the Caliph.'" Then he taught them what they should say to him and how they should do with him, and withdrawing to a retired room, let down a curtain before himself and slept.

Thus fared it with the Caliph, but as regards Abu al-Hasan, he gave not over snoring in his sleep till the day brake clear and the rising of the sun drew near, when a woman in waiting came up to him and said to him, "O our lord, the morning prayer!" Hearing these words, he laughed, and opening his eyes, turned them about the palace and found himself in an apartment whose walls were painted with gold and lapis lazuli and its ceiling dotted and starred with red gold. Around it were sleeping chambers with curtains of gold-embroidered silk let down over their doors, and all about vessels of gold and porcelain and crystal and furniture and carpets dispread and lamps burning before the niche wherein men prayed, and slave girls and eunuchs and Mamelukes and black slaves and boys and pages and attendants.

When he saw this, he was bewildered in his wit and said: "By Allah, either I am dreaming a dream, or this is Paradise and the Abode of Peace!" And he shut his eyes and would have slept again. Quoth one of the eunuchs, "O my lord, this is not of thy wont, O Commander of the Faithful!" Then the rest of the handmaids of the palace came up to him and lifted him into a sitting posture, when he found himself upon a mattress raised a cubit's height from the ground and all stuffed with floss silk. So they seated him upon it and propped his elbow with a pillow, and he looked at the apartment and its vastness and saw those eunuchs and slave girls in attendance upon him and standing about his head, whereupon he laughed at himself and said, "By Allah, 'tis not as I were on wake, yet I am not asleep!" And in his perplexity he bowed his chin upon his bosom, and then opened his eyes, little by little, smiling, and saying, "What is this state wherein I find myself?" Then he arose and sat up, whilst the damsels laughed at him privily, and he was bewildered in his wit, and bit his finger, and as the bite pained him, he cried "Oh!" and was vexed. And the Caliph watched him whence he saw him not, and laughed.

Presently Abu al-Hasan turned to a damsel and called to her, whereupon she answered, "At thy service, O Prince of True Believers!" Quoth he, "What is thy name?" and quoth she, "Shajarat al-Durr." Then he said to her, "By the protection of Allah, O damsel, am I Commander of the Faithful?" She replied, "Yes, indeed, by the protection of Allah thou in this time art Commander of the Faithful." Quoth he, "By Allah, thou liest, O thousandfold whore!" Then he glanced at the chief eunuch and called to him, whereupon he came to him and kissing the ground before him, said, "Yes, O Commander of the Faithful." Asked Abu al-Hasan, "Who is Commander of the Faithful?" and the eunuch answered "Thou." And Abu al-Hasan said, "Thou liest, thousandfold he-whore that thou art!" Then he turned to another eunuch and said to him, "O my chief, by the protection of Allah, am I Prince of the True Believers?" Said he: "Ay, by Allah, O my lord, thou art in this time Commander of the Faithful and Viceregent of the Lord of the Three Worlds."

Abu al-Hasan laughed at himself and doubted of his reason and was bewildered at what he beheld, and said: "In one night do I become Caliph? Yesterday I was Abu al-Hasan the Wag, and today I am Commander of the Faithful." Then the Chief Eunuch came up to him and said: "O Prince of True Believers (the name of Allah encompass thee!), thou art indeed Commander of the Faithful and Viceregent of the Lord of the Three Worlds!" And the slave girls and eunuchs flocked round about him, till he arose and abode wondering at his case. Hereupon the eunuch brought him a pair of sandals wrought with raw silk and green silk and purfled with red gold, and he took them and after examining them, set them in his sleeve. Whereat the castrato cried out and said: "Allah! Allah! O my lord, these are sandals for the treading of thy feet, so thou mayst wend to the wardrobe." Abu al-Hasan was confounded, and shaking the sandals from his sleeve, put them on his feet, whilst the Caliph died of laughter at him. The slave forewent him to the chapel of ease, where he entered, and doing his job, came out into the chamber, whereupon the slave girls brought him a basin of gold and a ewer of silver and poured water on his hands, and he made the wuzu ablution. Then they spread him a prayer carpet and he prayed.

Now he knew not how to pray, and gave not over bowing and prostrating for twenty inclinations, pondering in himself the while and saying: "By Allah, I am none other than the Commander of the Faithful in very truth! This is assuredly no dream, for all these things happen not in a dream." And he was convinced and determined in himself that he was Prince of True Believers, so he pronounced the salaam and finished his prayers, whereupon the Mamelukes and slave girls came round about him with bundled suits of silken and linen stuffs and clad him in the costume of the caliphate and gave the royal dagger in his hand.

Then the chief eunuch came in and said, "O Prince of True Believers, the Chamberlain is at the door craving permission to enter." Said he, "Let him enter!" whereupon he came in, and after kissing ground, offered the salutation, "Peace be upon thee, O Commander of the Faithful!" At this Abu al-Hasan rose and descended from the couch to the floor, whereupon the official exclaimed: "Allah! Allah! O Prince of True Believers, wottest thou not that all men are thy lieges and under thy rule and that it is not meet for the Caliph to rise to any man?" Presently the eunuch went out before him, and the little white slaves behind him, and they ceased not going till they raised the curtain and brought him into the hall of judgment and the throne room of the caliphate. There he saw all curtains and the forty doors and Al-'Ijli and Al-Rakashi the poet, and 'Ibdan and Jadim and Abu Ishak the cup companion, and beheld swords drawn and the lions compassing the throne as the white of the eye encircleth the black, and gilded glaives and death-dealing bows and Ajams and Arabs and Turks and Daylamites and folk and peoples and emirs and wazirs and captains and grandees and lords of the land and men of war in band, and in very sooth there appeared the might of the House of Abbas and the majesty of the Prophet's family.

So he sat down upon the throne of the caliphate and set the dagger on his lap, whereupon all present came up to kiss ground between his hands and called down on him length of life and continuance of weal. Then came forward Ja'afar the Barmecide and, kissing the ground, said: "Be the wide world of Allah the treading of thy feet, and may Paradise be thy dwelling place and the fire the home of thy foes! Never may neighbor defy thee, nor the lights of fire die out for thee, O Caliph of all cities and ruler of all countries!" Therewithal Abu al-Hasan cried out at him and said, "O dog of the sons of Barmak, go down forthright, thou and the chief of the city police, to such a place in such a street, and deliver a hundred dinars of gold to the mother of Abu al-Hasan the Wag, and bear her my salutation. Then go to such a mosque and take the four Sheikhs and the imam and scourge each of them with a thousand lashes and mount them on beasts, face to tail, and parade them round about all the city and banish them to a place other than this city. And bid the crier make cry before them, saying: 'This is the reward and the least of the reward of whoso multiplieth words and molesteth his neighbors and damageth their delights and stinteth their eating and drinking!'"

Ja'afar received the command and answered "With obedience," after which he went down from before Abu al-Hasan to the city and did all he had ordered him to do. Meanwhile, Abu al-Hasan abode in the caliphate, taking and giving, bidding and forbidding and carrying out his command till the end of the day, when he gave leave and permission to withdraw, and the emirs and officers of state departed to their several occupations and he looked toward the Chamberlain and the rest of the attendants and said, "Begone!" Then the eunuchs came to him, and calling down on him length of life and continuance of weal, walked in attendance upon him and raised the curtain, and he entered the pavilion of the harem, where he found candles lighted and lamps burning and singing women smiting on instruments, and ten slave girls, high-bosomed maids. When he saw this, he was confounded in his wit and said to himself, "By Allah, I am in truth Commander of the Faithful!" presently adding: "Or haply these are of the Jann, and he who was my guest yesternight was one of their kings who saw no way to requite my favors save by commanding his Ifrits to address me as Prince of True Believers. But an these be of the Jann, may Allah deliver me in safety from their mischief!"

As soon as he appeared, the slave girls rose to him, and carrying him up on to the dais, brought him a great tray bespread with the richest viands. So he ate thereof with all his might and main, till he had gotten his fill, when he called one of the handmaids and said to her, "What is thy name?" Replied she, "My name is Miskah," and he said to another, "What is thy name?" Quoth she, "My name is Tarkah." Then he asked a third, "What is thy name?" who answered, "My name is Tohfah." And he went on to question the damsels of their names, one after other, till he had learned the ten, when he rose from that place and removed to the wine chamber. He found it every way complete, and saw therein ten great trays, covered with all fruits and cates and every sort of sweetmeats. So he sat down and ate thereof after the measure of his competency, and finding there three troops of singing girls, was amazed, and made the girls eat.

Then he sat and the singers also seated themselves, whilst the black slaves and the white slaves and the eunuchs and pages and boys stood, and of the slave girls some sat and others stood. The damsels sang and warbled all varieties of melodies and the place rang with the sweetness of the songs, whilst the pipes cried out and the lutes with them wailed, till it seemed to Abu al-Hasan that he was in Paradise, and his heart was heartened and his breast broadened. So he sported, and joyaunce grew on him and he bestowed robes of honor on the damsels and gave and bestowed, challenging this girl and kissing that and toying with a third, plying one with wine and morseling another with meat, till nightfall.

All this while the Commander of the Faithful was diverting himself with watching him and laughing, and when night fell he bade one of the slave girls drop a piece of bhang in the cup and give it to Abu al-Hasan to drink. So she did his bidding and gave him the cup, which no sooner had he drunk than his head forewent his feet. Therewith the Caliph came forth from behind the curtain laughing, and calling to the attendant who had brought Abu al-Hasan to the palace, said to him, "Carry this man to his own place." So Masrur took him up, and carrying him to his own house, set him down in the saloon. Then he went forth from him, and shutting the saloon door upon him, returned to the Caliph, who slept till the morrow.

As for Abu al-Hasan, he gave not over slumbering till Almighty Allah brought on the morning, when he recovered from the drug and awoke, crying out and saying: "Ho, Tuffahah! Ho, Rahat al-Kulub! Ho, Miskah! Ho, Tohfah!" And he ceased not calling upon the palace handmaids till his mother heard him summoning strange damsels, and rising, came to him and said: "Allah's name encompass thee! Up with thee, O my son, O Abu al-Hasan! Thou dreamest." So he opened his eyes, and finding an old woman at his head, raised his eyes and said to her, "Who art thou?" Quoth she, "I am thy mother," and quoth he: "Thou liest! I am the Commander of the Faithful the Viceregent of Allah." Whereupon his mother shrieked aloud and said to him: "Heaven preserve thy reason! Be silent, O my son, and cause not the loss of our lives and the wasting of thy wealth, which will assuredly befall us if any hear this talk and carry it to the Caliph."

So he rose from his sleep, and finding himself in his own saloon and his mother by him, had doubts of his wit, and said to her: "By Allah, O my mother, I saw myself in a dream in a palace, with slave girls and Mamelukes about me and in attendance upon me, and I sat upon the throne of the Caliphate and ruled. By Allah, O my mother, this is what I saw, and in very sooth it was no dream!" Then he bethought himself awhile and said: "Assuredly, I am Abu al-Hasan al-Khali'a, and this that I saw was only a dream when I was made Caliph and bade and forbade." Then he bethought himself again and said: "Nay, but 'twas not a dream, and I am none other than the Caliph, and indeed I gave gifts and bestowed honor robes." Quoth his mother to him: "O my son, thou sportest with thy reason. Thou wilt go to the madhouse and become a gazingstock. Indeed, that which thou hast seen is only from the Foul Fiend, and it was an imbroglio of dreams, for at times Satan sporteth with men's wits in all manner of ways."

Then said she to him, "O my son, was there anyone with thee yesternight?" And he reflected and said: "Yes, one lay the night with me and I acquainted him with my case and told him my tale. Doubtless, he was of the devils, and I, O my mother, even as thou sayst truly, am Abu al-Hasan al-Khali'a." She rejoined: "O my son, rejoice in tidings of all good, for yesterday's record is that there came the Wazir Ja'afar the Barmecide and his many, and beat the Sheikhs of the mosque and the imam, each a thousand lashes, after which they paraded them round about the city, making proclamation before them and saying, 'This is the reward and the least of the reward of whoso faileth in goodwill to his neighbors and troubleth on them their lives!' And he banished them from Baghdad. Moreover, the Caliph sent me a hundred dinars and sent to salute me."

Whereupon Abu al-Hasan cried out and said to her: "O ill-omened crone, wilt thou contradict me and tell me that I am not the Prince of True Believers? 'Twas I who commanded Ja'afar the Barmecide to beat the Sheikhs and parade them about the city and make proclamation before them, and 'twas I, very I, who sent thee the hundred dinars and sent to salute thee, and I, O beldam of ill luck, am in very deed the Commander of the Faithful, and thou art a liar, who would make me out an idiot." So saying, he rose up and fell upon her and beat her with a staff of almond wood, till she cried out, "Help, O Moslems!" And he increased the beating upon her till the folk heard her cries, and coming to her, found Abu al-Hasan bashing his mother and saying to her: "Old woman of ill omen, am I not the Commander of the Faithful? Thou hast ensorceled me!" When the folk heard his words, they said, "This man raveth," and doubted not of his madness.

So they came in upon him, and seizing him, pinioned his elbows, and bore him to the bedlam. Quoth the superintendant, "What aileth this youth?" and quoth they, "This is a madman, afflicted of the Jinn." "By Allah," cried Abu al-Hasan, "they lie against me! I am no madman, but the Commander of the Faithful." And the superintendent answered him, saying, "None lieth but thou, O foulest of the Jinn-maddened!" Then he stripped him of his clothes, and clapping on his neck a heavy chain, bound him to a high lattice and fell to beating him two bouts a day and two a-nights, and he ceased not abiding on this wise the space of ten days. Then his mother came to him and said: "O my son, O Abu al-Hasan, return to thy right reason, for this is the Devil's doing." Quoth he: "Thou sayest sooth, O my mother, and bear thou witness of me that I repeat me of that talk and turn me from my madness. So do thou deliver me, for I am nigh upon death." Accordingly his mother went out to the superintendent and procured his release, and he returned to his own house.

Now this was at the beginning of the month, and when it ended, Abu al-Hasan longed to drink liquor and, returning to his former habit, furnished his saloon and made ready food and bade bring wine. Then, going forth to the bridge, he sat there, expecting one whom he should converse and carouse with, according to his custom. As he sat thus, behold, up came the Caliph and Masrur to him, but Abu al-Hasan saluted them not and said to Al-Rashid, "No friendly welcome to thee, O King of the Jann!" Quoth Al-Rashid, "What have I done to thee?" and quoth Abu al-Hasan, "What more couldst thou do than what thou hast done to me, O foulest of the Jann? I have been beaten and thrown into bedlam, where all said I was Jinn-mad, and this was caused by none save thyself. I brought thee to my house and fed thee with my best, after which thou dist empower thy Satans and Marids to disport themselves with my wits from morning to evening. So avaunt and aroynt thee and wend thy ways!"

The Caliph smiled and, seating himself by his side, said to him, "O my brother, did I not tell thee that I would return to thee?" Quoth Abu al-Hasan, "I have no need of thee, and as the byword sayeth in verse:

> "Fro' my friend, 'twere meeter and wiser to part,
> For what eye sees not born shall ne'er sorrow heart."

And indeed, O my brother, the night thou camest to me and we conversed and caroused together, I and thou, 'twas as if the Devil came to me and troubled me that night." Asked the Caliph, "And who is he, the Devil?" and answered Abu al-Hasan, "He is none other than thou." Whereat the Caliph laughed and coaxed him and spake him fair, saying: "O my brother, when I went out from thee,

I forgot the door and left it open, and perhaps Satan came in to thee." Quoth Abu al-Hasan: "Ask me not of that which hath betided me. What possessed thee to leave the door open, so that the Devil came in to me and there befell me with him this and that?" And he related to him all that had betided him, first and last (and in repetition is no fruition), what while the Caliph laughed and hid his laughter.

Then said he to Abu al-Hasan: "Praised be Allah who hath done away from thee whatso irked thee, and that I see thee once more in weal!" And Abu al-Hasan said: "Never again will I take thee to cup companion or sitting comrade, for the proverb saith, 'Whoso stumbleth on a stone and thereto returneth, upon him be blame and reproach.' And thou, O my brother, nevermore will I entertain thee nor company with thee, for that I have not found thy heel propitious to me." But the Caliph coaxed him and said, "I have been the means of thy winning to thy wish anent the imam and the Sheikhs." Abu al-Hasan replied, "Thou hast," and Al-Rashid continued, "And haply somewhat may betide which shall gladden thy heart yet more." Abu al-Hasan asked, "What dost thou require of me?" and the Commander of the Faithful answered: "Verily, I am thy guest. Reject not the guest." Quoth Abu al-Hasan: "On condition that thou swear to me by the characts on the seal of Solomon, David's son (on the twain be the peace!) that thou wilt not suffer thine Ifrits to make fun of me." He replied, "To hear is to obey!"

Whereupon the wag took him and brought him into the saloon and set food before him and entreated him with friendly speech. Then he told him all that had befallen him, whilst the Caliph was like to die of stifled laughter. After which Abu al-Hasan removed the tray of food, and bringing the wine service, filled a cup and cracked it three times, then gave it to the Caliph, saying: "O boon companion mine, I am thy slave, and let not that which I am about to say offend thee, and be thou not vexed, neither do thou vex me." And he recited these verses:

> "Hear one that wills thee well! Lips none shall bless
> Save those who drink for drunk and all transgress.
> Ne'er will I cease to swill while night falls dark
> Till lout my forehead low upon my tass.
> In wine like liquid sun is my delight
> Which clears all care and gladdens allegresse."

When the Caliph heard these his verses and saw how apt he was at couplets, he was delighted with exceeding delight, and taking the cup, drank it off, and the twain ceased not to converse and carouse till the wine rose to their heads. Then quoth Abu al-Hasan to the Caliph: "O boon companion mine, of a truth I am perplexed concerning my affair, for meseemed I was Commander of the Faithful and ruled and gave gifts and largess, and in very deed, O my brother, it was not a dream." Quoth the Caliph, "These were the imbroglios of sleep," and crumbling a bit of bhang into the cup, said to him, "By my life, do thou drink this cup," and said Abu al-Hasan, "Surely I will drink it from thy hand." Then he took the cup and drank it off, and no sooner had it settled in his stomach than his head fell to the ground before his feet. Now his manners and fashions pleased the Caliph, and the excellence of his composition and his frankness, and he said in himself, "I will assuredly make him my cup companion and sitting comrade." So he rose forthright, and saying to Masrur, "Take him up," returned to the palace.

Accordingly, the eunuch took up Abu al-Hasan, and carrying him to the palace of the caliphate, set him down before Al-Rashid, who bade the slaves and slave girls compass him about, whilst he himself hid in a place where Abu al-Hasan could not see him. Then he commanded one of the handmaidens to take the lute and strike it over the wag's head, whilst the rest smote upon their instruments. So they played and sang, till Abu al-Hasan awoke at the last of the night and heard the symphony of lutes and tambourines and the sound of the flutes and the singing of the slave girls, whereupon he opened eyes, and finding himself in the palace, with the handmaids and eunuchs about him, exclaimed: "There is no Majesty and there is no Might save in Allah, the Glorious, the Great! Come to my help this night, which meseems more unlucky than the former! Verily, I am fearful of the madhouse and of that which I suffered therein the first time, and I doubt not but the Devil is come to me again, as before. O Allah, my Lord, put thou Satan to shame!" Then he shut his eyes and laid his head in his sleeve, and fell to laughing softly and raising his head betimes, but still found the apartment lighted and the girls singing.

Presently one of the eunuchs sat down at his head and said to him, "Sit up, O Prince of True Believers, and look on thy palace and thy slave girls." Said Abu al-Hasan: "Under the veil of Allah, am I in truth Commander of the Faithful, and dost thou not lie? Yesterday I rode not forth, neither ruled, but drank and slept, and this eunuch cometh to make me rise." Then he sat up and recalled to thought that which had betided him with his mother and how he had beaten her and entered the bedlam, and he saw the marks of the beating wherewith the superintendant had beaten him, and was perplexed concerning his affair and pondered in himself, saying, "By Allah, I know not how my case is nor what is this that betideth me!" Then, gazing at the scene around him, he said privily, "All these are of the Jann in human shape, and I commit my case to Allah."

Presently he turned to one of the damsels and said to her, "Who am I?" Quoth she, "Thou art the Commander of the Faithful," and quoth he: "Thou liest, O calamity! If I be indeed the Commander of the Faithful, bite my finger." So she came to him and bit it with all her might, and he said to her, "It doth suffice." Then he asked the chief eunuch, "Who am I?" and he answered, "Thou art the Commander of the Faithful." So he left him and returned to his wonderment. Then, turning to a little white slave, said to him, "Bite my ear," and he bent his head low down to him and put his ear to his mouth. Now the Mameluke was young and lacked sense, so he closed his teeth upon Abu al-Hasan's ear with all his might, till he came near to sever it. And he knew not Arabic, so as often as the wag said to him, "It doth suffice," he concluded that he said, "Bite like a vice," and redoubled his bite and made his teeth meet in the ear, whilst the damsels were diverted from him with hearkening to the singing girls, and Abu al-Hasan cried out for succor from the boy and the Caliph lost his senses for laughter.

Then he dealt the boy a cuff, and he let go his ear, whereupon all present fell down with laughter and said to the little Mameluke, "Art mad that thou bitest the Caliph's ear on this wise?" And Abu al-Hasan cried to them: "Sufficeth ye not, O ye wretched Jinns, that which hath befallen me? But the fault is not yours. The fault is of your chief, who transmewed you from Jinn shape to mortal shape. I seek refuge against you this night by the Throne Verse and the Chapter of Sincerity and the Two Preventives!" So saying, the wag put off his clothes till he was naked, with prickle and breech exposed, and danced among the slave girls. They bound his hands and he wantoned among them, while they died of laughing at him and the Caliph swooned away for excess of laughter.

Then he came to himself, and going forth the curtain to Abu al-Hasan, said to him: "Out on thee, O Abu al-Hasan! Thou slayest me with laughter." So he turned to him, and knowing him, said to him, "By Allah, 'tis thou slayest me and slayest my mother and slewest the Sheikhs and the imam of the mosque!" After which he kissed ground before him and prayed for the permanence of his prosperity and the endurance of his days. The Caliph at once robed him in a rich robe and gave him a thousand dinars, and presently he took the wag into especial favor and married him and bestowed largess on him and lodged him with himself in the palace and made him of the chief of his cup companions, and indeed he was preferred with him above them, and the Caliph advanced him over them all, so that he sat with him and the Lady Zubaydah bint al-Kasim, whose treasuress, Nuzhat al-Fuad hight, was given to him in marriage.

After this Abu al-Hasan the wag abode with his wife in eating and drinking and all delight of life, till whatso was with them went the way of money, when he said to her, "Harkye, O Nuzhat al-Fuad!" Said she, "At thy service," and he continued, "I have it in mind to play a trick on the Caliph, and thou shalt do the like with the Lady Zubaydah, and we will take of them at once, to begin with, two hundred dinars and two pieces of silk." She rejoined, "As thou willest, but what thinkest thou to do?" And he said: "We will feign ourselves dead, and this is the trick. I will die before thee and lay myself out, and do thou spread over me a silken napkin and loose my turban over me and tie my toes and lay on my stomach a knife and a little salt. Then let down thy hair and betake thyself to thy mistress Zubaydah, tearing thy dress and slapping thy face and crying out. She will ask thee, 'What aileth thee?' and do thou answer her, 'May thy head outlive Abu al-Hasan the wag, for he is dead.' She will mourn for me and weep and bid her new treasuress give thee a hundred dinars and a piece of silk and will say to thee, 'Go, lay him out and carry him forth.' So do thou take of her the hundred dinars and the piece of silk and come back, and when thou returnest to me, I will rise up and thou shalt lie down in my place, and I will go to the Caliph and say to him, 'May thy head outlive Nuzhat al-Fuad,' and rend my raiment and pluck out my beard. He will mourn for thee and say to his treasurer, 'Give Abu al-Hasan a hundred dinars and a piece of silk.' Then he will say to me, 'Go, lay her out and carry her forth,' and I will come back to thee."

Therewith Nuzhat al-Fuad rejoiced and said, "Indeed, this is an excellent device." Then Abu al-Hasan stretched himself out forthright and she shut his eyes and tied his feet and covered him with the napkin and did whatso her lord had bidden her. After which she tare her gear and bared her head and letting down her hair, went in to the Lady Zubaydah, crying out and weeping. When the Princess saw her in this state, she cried: "What plight is this? What is thy story, and what maketh thee weep?" And Nuzhatal-Fuad answered, weeping and loud-wailing the while: "O my lady, may thy head live and mayst thou survive Abu al-Hasan al-Khali'a, for he is dead!" The Lady Zubaydah mourned for him and said, "Alas, poor Abu al-Hasan the wag!" and she shed tears for him awhile. Then she bade her treasuress give Nuzhat al-Fuad a hundred dinars and a piece of silk and said to her, "O Nuzhat al-Fuad, go, lay him out and carry him forth."

So she took the hundred dinars and the piece of silk and returned to her dwelling, rejoicing, and went in to her spouse and acquainted him what had befallen, whereupon he arose and rejoiced and girdled his middle and danced and took the hundred dinars and the piece of silk and laid them up. Then he laid out Nuzhat al-Fuad and did with her as she had done with him, after which he rent his raiment and plucked out his beard and disordered his turban and ran out, nor ceased running till he came in to the Caliph, who was sitting in the judgment hall, and he in this plight, beating his breast. The Caliph asked him, "What aileth thee, O Abu al-Hasan?" and he wept and answered, "Would Heaven thy cup companion had never been, and would his hour had never come!" Quoth the Caliph, "Tell me thy case," and quoth Abu al-Hasan, "O my lord, may thy head outlive Nuzhat al-Fuad!" The Caliph exclaimed, "There is no god but God," and smote hand upon hand. Then he comforted Abu al-Hasan and said to him, "Grieve not, for we will bestow upon thee a bedfellow other than she." And he ordered the treasurer to give him a hundred dinars and a piece of silk. Accordingly the treasurer did what the Caliph bade him, and Al-Rashid said to him, "Go, lay her out and carry her forth and make her a handsome funeral."

So Abu al-Hasan took that which he had given him and returning to his house, rejoicing, went in to Nuzhat al-Fuad and said to her, "Arise, for our wish is won." Hereat she arose and he laid before her the hundred ducats and the piece of silk, whereat she rejoiced, and they added the gold to the gold and the silk to the silk and sat talking and laughing each to other.

Meanwhile, when Abu al-Hasan fared forth the presence of the Caliph and went to lay out Nuzhat al-Fuad, the Commander of the Faithful mourned for her, and dismissing the Divan, arose and betook himself, leaning upon Masrur, the Sworder of his vengeance, to the Lady Zubaydah, that he might condole with her for her handmaid. He found her sitting weeping and awaiting his coming, so she might condole with him for his boon companion Abu al-Hasan the wag. So he said to her, "May thy head outlive thy slave girl Nuzhat al-Fuad!" and said she: "O my lord, Allah preserve my slave girl! Mayst thou live and long survive thy boon companion Abu al-Hasan al-Khali'a, for he is dead." The Caliph smiled and said to his eunuch: "O Masrur, verily women are little of wit. Allah upon thee, say, was not Abu al-Hasan with me but now?" Quoth the Lady Zubaydah, laughing from a heart full of wrath: "Wilt thou not leave thy jesting? Sufficeth thee not that Abu al-Hasan is dead, but thou must put to death my slave girl also and bereave us of the twain, and style me little of wit?" The Caliph answered, "Indeed, 'tis Nuzhat al-Fuad who is dead." And the Lady Zubaydah said: "Indeed he hath not been with thee, nor hast thou seen him, and none was with me but now save Nuzhat al-Fuad, and she sorrowful, weeping, with her clothes torn to tatters. I exhorted her to patience and gave her a hundred dinars and a piece of silk, and indeed I was awaiting thy coming, so I might console thee for thy cup companion Abu al-Hasan al-Khali'a, and was about to send for thee." The Caliph laughed and said, "None is dead save Nuzhat al-Fuad," and she, "No, no, good my lord; none is dead but Abu al-Hasan the wag."

With this the Caliph waxed wroth, and the hashimi vein started out from between his eyes and throbbed, and he cried out to Masrur and said to him, "Fare thee forth to the house of Abu al-Hasan the wag, and see which of them is dead." So Masrur went out, running, and the Caliph said to the Lady Zubaydah, "Wilt thou lay me a wager?" And said she, "Yes, I will wager, and I say that Abu al-Hasan is dead." Rejoined the Caliph: "And I wager and say that none is dead save Nuzhat al-Fuad, and the stake between me and thee shall be the Garden of Pleasaunce against thy palace and the Pavilion of Pictures." So they agreed upon this and sat awaiting Masrur's return with the news.

As for the eunuch, he ceased not running till he came to the by-street wherein was the stead of Abu al-Hasan al-Khali'a. Now the wag was comfortably seated and leaning back against the lattice, and chancing to look round, saw Masrur running along the street and said to Nuzhat al-Fuad, "Meseemeth the Caliph, when I went forth from him, dismissed the Divan and went in to the Lady Zubaydah to condole with her, whereupon she arose and condoled with him, saying, 'Allah increase thy recompense for the loss of Abu al-Hasan al-Khali'a!' And he said to her, 'None is dead save Nuzhat al-Fuad, may thy head outlive her!' Quoth she, ''Tis not she who is dead, but Abu al-Hasan al-Khali'a, thy boon companion.' And quoth he, 'None is dead save Nuzhat al-Fuad.' And they waxed so obstinate that the Caliph became wroth and they laid a wager, and he hath sent Masrur the Sworder to see who is dead. Now, therefore, 'twere best that thou lie down, so he may sight thee and go and acquaint the Caliph and confirm my saying."

So Nuzhat al-Fuad stretched herself out and Abu al-Hasan covered her with her mantilla and sat weeping at her head. Presently, Masrur, the eunuch, suddenly came in to him and saluted him, and seeing Nuzhat al-Fuad stretched out, uncovered her face and said: "There is no god but God! Our sister Nuzhat al-Fuad is dead indeed. How sudden was the stroke of Destiny! Allah have ruth on thee and acquit thee of all charge!" Then he returned and related what had passed before the Caliph and the Lady Zubaydah, and he laughing as he spoke. "O accursed one," cried the Caliph: "this is no time for laughter! Tell us which is dead of them." Masrur replied: "By Allah, O my lord, Abu al-Hasan is well, and none is dead but Nuzhat al-Fuad." Quoth the Caliph to Zubaydah, "Thou hast lost thy pavilion in thy play," and he jeered at her and said, "O Masrur, tell her what thou sawest."

Quoth the eunuch: "Verily, O my lady, I ran without ceasing till I came in to Abu al-Hasan in his house, and found Nuzhat al-Fuad lying dead and Abu al-Hasan sitting tearful at her head. I saluted him and condoled with him and sat down by his side and uncovered the face of Nuzhat al-Fuad and saw her dead and her face swollen. So I said to him, 'Carry her out forthwith, so we may pray over her.' He replied, ''Tis well,' and I left him to lay her out and came hither, that I might tell you the news." The Prince of True Believers laughed and said, "Tell it again and again to thy lady Little-wits." When the

Lady Zubaydah heard Masrur's words and those of the Caliph she was wroth and said, "None is little of wit save he who believeth a black slave." And she abused Masrur, whilst the Commander of the Faithful laughed; and the eunuch, vexed at this, said to the Caliph, "He spake sooth who said, 'Women are little of wits and lack religion.'"

Then said the Lady Zubaydah to the Caliph: "O Commander of the Faithful, thou sportest and jestest with me, and this slave hoodwinketh me, the better to please thee. But I will send and see which of them be dead." And he answered, saying, "Send one who shall see which of them is dead." So the Lady Zubaydah cried out to an old duenna, and said to her: "Hie thee to the house of Nuzhat al-Fuad in haste and see who is dead, and loiter not." And she used hard words to her. So the old woman went out running, whilst the Prince of True Believers and Masrur laughed, and she ceased not running till she came into the street. Abu al-Hasan saw her, and knowing her, said to his wife: "O Nuzhat al-Fuad, meseemeth the Lady Zubaydah hath sent to us to see who is dead and hath not given credit to Masrur's report of thy death. Accordingly she hath dispatched the old crone, her duenna, to discover the truth. So it behooveth me to be dead in my turn for the sake of thy credit with the Lady Zubaydah."

Hereat he lay down and stretched himself out, and she covered him and bound his eyes and feet and sat in tears at his head. Presently the old woman came in to her and saw her sitting at Abu al-Hasan's head, weeping and recounting his fine qualities; and when she saw the old trot, she cried out and said to her: "See what hath befallen me! Indeed Abu al-Hasan is dead and hath left me lone and lorn!" Then she shrieked out and rent her raiment and said to the crone, "O my mother, how very good he was to me!" Quoth the other, "Indeed thou art excused, for thou wast used to him and he to thee."

Then she considered what Masrur had reported to the Caliph and the Lady Zubaydah and said to her, "Indeed, Masrur goeth about to cast discord between the Caliph and the Lady Zubaydah." Asked Nuzhat al-Fuad, "And what is the cause of discord, O my mother?" and the other replied: "O my daughter, Masrur came to the Caliph and the Lady Zubaydah and gave them news of thee that thou wast dead and that Abu al-Hasan was well." Nuzhat al-Fuad said to her: "O naunty mine, I was with my lady just now and she gave me a hundred dinars and a piece of silk, and now see my case and that which hath befallen me! Indeed I am bewildered, and how shall I do, and I lone and lorn? Would Heaven I had died and he had lived!" Then she wept and with her wept the old woman, who, going up to Abu al-Hasan and uncovering his face, saw his eyes bound and swollen for the swathing. So she covered him again and said, "Indeed, O Nuzhat al-Fuad, thou art afflicted in Abu al-Hasan!"

Then she condoled with her, and going out from her, ran along the street till she came into the Lady Zubaydah and related to her the story, and the Princess said to her, laughing: "Tell it over again to the Caliph, who maketh me out little of wit, and lacking of religion, and who made this ill-omened liar of a slave presume to contradict me." Quoth Masrur, "This old woman lieth, for I saw Abu al-Hasan well and Nuzhat al-Fuad it was who lay dead." Quoth the duenna, " 'Tis thou that liest, and wouldst fain cast discord between the Caliph and the Lady Zubaydah." And Masrur cried, "None lieth but thou, O old woman of ill omen, and thy lady believeth thee, and she must be in her dotage." Whereupon the Lady Zubaydah cried out at him, and in very sooth she was enraged with him and with his speech and shed tears.

Then said the Caliph to her: "I lie and my eunuch lieth, and thou liest and thy waiting-woman lieth, so 'tis my rede we go, all four of us together, that we may see which of us telleth the truth." Masrur said: "Come, let us go, that I may do to this ill-omened old woman evil deeds and deal her a sound drubbing for her lying." And the duenna answered him: "O dotard, is thy wit like into my wit? Indeed thy wit is as the hen's wit." Masrur was incensed at her words and would have laid violent hands on her, but the Lady Zubaydah pushed him away from her and said to him, "Her truth-speaking will presently be distinguished from thy truth-speaking and her leasing from thy leasing." Then they all four arose, laying wagers one with other, and went forth afoot from the palace gate and hied on till they came in at the gate of the street where Abu al-Hasan al-Khali'a dwelt.

He saw them, and said to his wife, Nuzhat al-Fuad: "Verily, all that is sticky is not a pancake they cook, nor every time shall the crock escape the shock. It seemeth the old woman hath gone and told her lady and acquainted her with our case and she hath disputed with Masrur, the eunuch, and they have laid wagers each with other about our death and are come to us, all four, the Caliph and the eunuch and the Lady Zubaydah and the old trot." When Nuzhat al-Fuad heard this, she started up from her outstretched posture and asked, "How shall we do?" whereto he answered, "We will both feign ourselves dead together and stretch ourselves out and hold out breath." So she hearkened unto him and they both lay down on the place where they usually slept the siesta and bound their feet and shut their eyes and covered themselves with the veil and held their breath.

Presently up came the Caliph, Zubaydah, Masrur, and the old woman, and entering, found Abu al-Hasan the wag and wife both stretched out as dead, which when the Lady saw, she wept and said: "They ceased not to bring ill news of my slave girl till she died. Methinketh Abu al-Hasan's death was grievous to her and that she died after him." Quoth the Caliph: "Thou shalt not prevent me with thy prattle and prate. She certainly died before Abu al-Hasan, for he came to me with his raiment rent and his beard plucked out, beating his breast with two bits of unbaked brick, and I gave him a hundred dinars and a piece of silk and said too him, 'Go, bear her forth, and I will give thee a bedfellow other than she and handsomer, and she shall be instead of her.' But it would appear that her death was no light matter to him and he died after her, so it is I who have beaten thee and gotten thy stake." The Lady Zubaydah answered him in words galore, and the dispute between them waxed sore.

At last the Caliph sat down at the heads of the pair and said: "By the tomb of the Apostle of Allah (whom may He save and assain!) and the sepulchers of my fathers and forefathers, whoso will tell me which of them died before the other, I will willingly give him a thousand dinars!" When Abu al-Hasan heard the Caliph's words, he sprang up in haste and said: "I died first, O Commander of the Faithful! Here with the thousand dinars, and acquit thee of thine oath and the swear thou sworest." Nuzhat al-Fuad rose also and stood up before the Caliph and the Lady Zubaydah, who both rejoiced in this and in their safety, and the Princess chid her slave girl. Then the Caliph and Zubaydah gave them joy of their well-being and knew that this death was a trick to get the gold, and the Lady said to Nuzhat al-Fuad: "Thou shouldst have sought of me that which thou needest, without this fashion, and not have burned my heart for thee." And she, "Verily, I was ashamed, O my lady."

As for the Caliph, he swooned away for laughing and said, "O Abu al-Hasan, thou wilt never cease to be a wag and do peregrine things and prodigious!" Quoth he: "O Commander of the Faithful, this trick I played off for that the money which thou gavest me was exhausted, and I was ashamed to ask of thee again. When I was single, I could never keep money in hand, but since thou marriedst me to this damsel, if I possessed even thy wealth, I should lay it waste. Wherefore when all that was in my hand was spent, I wrought this sleight so I might get of thee the hundred dinars and the piece of silk, and all this is an alms from our lord. But now make haste to give me the thousand dinars and acquit thee of thine oath." The Caliph and the Lady Zubaydah laughed and returned to the palace, and he gave Abu al-Hasan the thousand dinars saying, "Take them as a douceur for thy perservation from death," whilst her mistress did the like with Nuzhat al-Fuad, honoring her with the same words. Moreover, the Caliph increased the wag in his solde and supplies, and he and his wife ceased not to live in joy and contentment till there came to them the Destroyer of delights and Severer of societies, the Plunderer of palaces, and the Garnerer of graves.

And among tales they tell is one touching

ALADDIN; OR, THE WONDERFUL LAMP

It hath reached me, O King of the Age, that there dwelt in a city of the cities of China a man which was a tailor, withal a pauper, and he had one son, Aladdin hight. Now this boy had been from his babyhood a ne'er-do-well, a scapegrace. And when he reached his tenth year, his father inclined to teach him his own trade, and, for that he was overindigent to expend money upon his learning other work or craft or apprenticeship, he took the lad into his shop that he might be taught tailoring. But, as Aladdin was a scapegrace and a ne'er-do-well and wont to play at all times with the gutter boys of the quarter, he would not sit in the shop for a single day. Nay, he would await his father's leaving it for some purpose, such as to meet a creditor, when he would run off at once and fare forth to the gardens with the other scapegraces and low companions, his fellows. Such was his case—counsel and castigation were of no avail, nor would he obey either parent in aught or learn any trade. And presently, for his sadness and sorrowing because of his son's vicious indolence, the tailor sickened and died.

Aladdin continued in his former ill courses, and when his mother saw that her spouse had deceased and that her son was a scapegrace and good for nothing at all, she sold the shop and whatso was to be found therein and fell to spinning cotton yarn. By this toilsome industry she fed herself and found food for her son Aladdin the scapegrace, who, seeing himself freed from bearing the severities of his sire, increased in idleness and low habits. Nor would he ever stay at home save at meal hours while his miserable wretched mother lived only by what her hands could spin until the youth had reached his fifteenth year. It befell one day of the days that as he was sitting about the quarter at play with the vagabond boys, behold, a dervish from the Maghrib, the Land of the Setting Sun, came up and stood gazing for solace upon the lads. And he looked hard at Aladdin and carefully considered his semblance, scarcely noticing his companions the while. Now this dervish was a Moorman from Inner Morocco, and he was a magician who could upheap by his magic hill upon hill, and he was also an adept in astrology. So after narrowly considering Aladdin, he said in himself, "Verily, this is the lad I need and to find whom I have left my natal land." Presently he led one of the children apart and questioned him anent the scapegrace saying, "Whose son is he?" And he sought all information concerning his condition and whatso related to him.

After this he walked up to Aladdin, and drawing him aside, asked, "O my son, haply thou art the child of Such-a-one the tailor?" and the lad answered, "Yes, O my lord, but 'tis long since he died." The Maghrabi, the magician, hearing these words, threw himself upon Aladdin and wound his arms around his neck and fell to bussing him, weeping the while with tears trickling a-down his cheeks. But when the lad saw the Moorman's case, he was seized with surprise thereat and questioned him, saying, "What causeth thee weep, O my lord, and how camest thou to know my father?" "How canst thou, O my son," replied the Moorman, in a soft voice saddened by emotion, "question me with such query after informing me that thy father and my brother is deceased? For that he was my brother german, and now I come from my adopted country and after long exile I rejoiced with exceeding joy in the hope of looking upon him once more and condoling with him over the past. And now thou hast announced to me his demise. But blood hideth not from blood, and it hath revealed to me that thou art my nephew, son of my brother, and I knew thee amongst all the lads, albeit thy father, when I parted from him, was yet unmarried."

Then he again clasped Aladdin to his bosom, crying: "O my son, I have none to condole with now save thyself. And thou standest in stead of thy sire, thou being his issue and representative and 'whoso leaveth issue dieth not,' O my child!" So saying, the magician put hand to purse, and pulling out ten gold pieces, gave them to the lad, asking, "O my son, where is your house and where dwelleth she, thy mother and my brother's widow?" Presently Aladdin arose with him and showed him the way to their home, and meanwhile quoth the wizard: "O my son, take these moneys and give them to thy mother, greeting her from me, and let her know that thine uncle, thy father's brother, hath reappeared from his exile and that Inshallah—God willing—on the morrow I will visit her to salute her with the salaam and see the house wherein my brother was homed and look upon the place where he lieth buried." Thereupon Aladdin kissed the Maghrabi's hand, and after running in his joy at fullest speed to his mother's dwelling, entered to her clean contrariwise to his custom, inasmuch as he never came near her save at mealtimes only.

And when he found her, the lad exclaimed in his delight: "O my mother, I give thee glad tidings of mine uncle who hath returned from his exile, and who now sendeth me to salute thee." "O my son," she replied, "meseemeth thou mockest me! Who is this uncle, and how canst thou have an uncle in the bonds of life?" He rejoined: "How sayest thou, O my mother, that I have no living uncles nor kinsmen, when this man is my father's own brother? Indeed he embraced me and bussed me, shedding tears the while, and bade me acquaint thee herewith." She retorted, "O my son, well I wot thou haddest an uncle, but he is now dead, nor am I ware that thou hast other eme."

The Moroccan magician fared forth next morning and fell to finding out Aladdin, for his heart no longer permitted him to part from the lad. And as he was to-ing and fro-ing about the city highways, he came face to face with him disporting himself, as was his wont, amongst the vagabonds and the scapegraces. So he drew near to him, and taking his hand, embraced him and bussed him. Then pulled out of his poke two dinars and said: "Hie thee to thy mother and give her these couple of ducats and tell her that thine uncle would eat the evening meal with you. So do thou take these two gold pieces and prepare for us a succulent supper. But before all things, show me once more the way to your home." "On my head and mine eyes be it, O my uncle," replied the lad and forewent him, pointing out the street leading to the house. Then the Moorman left him and went his ways and Aladdin ran home and, giving the news and the two sequins to his parent, said, "My uncle would sup with us."

So she arose straightway and, going to the market street, bought all she required. Then, returning to her dwelling, she borrowed from the neighbors whatever was needed of pans and platters and so forth, and when the meal was cooked and suppertime came she said to Aladdin: "O my child, the meat is ready, but peradventure thine uncle wotteth not the way to our dwelling. So do thou fare forth and meet him on the road." He replied, "To hear is to obey," and before the twain ended talking a knock was heard at the door. Aladdin went out and opened, when, behold, the Maghrabi, the magician, together with a eunuch carrying the wine and the dessert fruits. So the lad led them in and the slave went about his business. The Moorman on entering saluted his sister-in-law with the salaam, then began to shed tears and to question her, saying, "Where be the place whereon my brother went to sit?" She showed it to him, whereat he went up to it and prostrated himself in prayer and kissed the floor, crying: "Ah, how scant is my satisfaction and how luckless is my lot, for that I have lost thee, O my brother, O vein of my eye!" And after such fashion he continued weeping and wailing till he swooned away for excess of sobbing and lamentation, wherefor Aladdin's mother was certified of his soothfastness. So, coming up to him, she raised him from the floor and said, "What gain is there in slaying thyself?"

As soon as he was seated at his ease, and before the food trays were served up, he fell to talking with her and saying: "O wife of my brother, it must be a wonder to thee how in all thy days thou never sawest me nor learnst thou aught of me during the lifetime of my brother who hath found mercy. Now the reason is that forty years ago I left this town and exiled myself from my birthplace and wandered forth over all the lands of Al-Hind and Al-Sind and entered Egypt and settled for a long time in its magnificent city, which is one of the world wonders, till at last I fared to the regions of the setting sun and abode for a space of thirty years in the Moroccan interior. Now one day of the days, O wife of my brother, as I was sitting alone at home, I fell to thinking of mine own country and of my birthplace and of my brother (who hath found mercy). And my yearning to see him waxed excessive and I bewept and bewailed my strangerhood and distance from him. And at last my longings drave me homeward until I resolved upon traveling to the region which was the falling place of my head and my homestead, to the end that I might again see my brother. Then quoth I to myself: 'O man, how long wilt thou wander like a wild Arab from thy place of birth and native stead? Moreover, thou hast one brother and no more, so up with thee and travel and look upon him ere thou die, for who wotteth the woes of the world and the changes of the days? 'Twould be saddest regret an thou lie down to die without beholding thy brother. And Allah (laud be to the Lord!) hath vouchsafed thee ample wealth, and belike he may be straitened and in poor case, when thou wilt aid thy brother as well as see him.'

"So I arose at once and equipped me for wayfare and recited the fatihah. Then, whenas Friday prayers ended, I mounted and traveled to this town, after suffering manifold toils and travails which I patiently endured whilst the Lord (to Whom be honor and glory!) veiled me with the veil of His protection. So I entered, and whilst wandering about the streets the day before yesterday I beheld my brother's son Aladdin disporting himself with the boys and, by God the Great, O wife of my brother, the moment I saw him this heart of mine went forth to him (for blood yearneth unto blood!), and my soul felt and informed me that he was my very nephew. So I forgot all my travails and troubles at once on sighting him, and I was like to fly for joy. But when he told me of the dear one's departure to the ruth of Allah Almighty, I fainted for stress of distress and disappointment. Perchance, however, my nephew hath informed thee of the pains which prevailed upon me. But after a fashion I am consoled by the sight of Aladdin, the legacy bequeathed to us by him who hath found mercy for that 'whoso leaveth issue is not wholly dead.'"

And when he looked at his sister-in-law, she wept at these his words, so he turned to the lad, that he might cause her to forget the mention of her mate, as a means of comforting her and also of completing his deceit, and asked him, saying: "O my son Aladdin, what hast thou learned in the way of work, and what is thy business? Say me, hast thou mastered any craft whereby to earn a livelihood for thyself and for thy mother?" The lad was abashed and put to shame and he hung down his head and bowed his brow groundward. But his parent spake out: "How, forsooth? By Allah, he knoweth nothing at all, a child so ungracious as this I never yet saw—no, never! All the day long he idleth away his time with the sons of the quarter, vagabonds like himself, and his father (O regret of me!) died not save of dolor for him. And I also am now in piteous plight. I spin cotton and toil at my distaff night and day, that I may earn me a couple of scones of bread which we eat together. This is his condition, O my brother-in-law, and, by the life of thee, he cometh not near me save at mealtimes, and none other. Indeed, I am thinking to lock the house door, nor ever open to him again, but leave him to go and seek a livelihood whereby he can live, for that I am now grown a woman in years and have no longer strength to toil and go about for a maintenance after this fashion. O Allah, I am compelled to provide him with daily bread when I require to be provided!"

Hereat the Moorman turned to Aladdin and said: "Why is this, O son of my brother, thou goest about in such ungraciousness? 'Tis a disgrace to thee and unsuitable for men like thyself. Thou art a youth of sense, O my son, and the child of honest folk, so 'tis for thee a shame that thy mother, a woman in years, should struggle to support thee. And now that thou hast grown to man's estate, it becometh thee to devise thee some device whereby thou canst live, O my child. Look around thee and Alhamdolillah—praise be to Allah—in this our town are many teachers of all manner of crafts, and nowhere are they more numerous. So choose thee some calling which may please thee to the end that I stablish thee therein, and when thou growest up, O my son, thou shalt have some business whereby to live. Haply thy father's industry may not be to thy liking, and if so it be, choose thee some other handicraft which suiteth thy fancy. Then let me know and I will aid thee with all I can, O my son." But when the Maghrabi saw that Aladdin kept silence and made him no reply, he knew that the lad wanted none other occupation than a scapegrace life, so he said to him: "O son of my brother, let not my words seem hard and harsh to thee, for if despite all I say thou still dislike to learn a craft, I will open thee a merchant's store furnished with costliest stuffs and thou shalt become famous amongst the folk and take and give and buy and sell and be well known in the city."

Now when Aladdin heard the words of his uncle the Moorman, and the design of making him a khwajah—merchant and gentleman —he joyed exceedingly, knowing that such folk dress handsomely and fare delicately. So he looked at the Maghrabi smiling and drooping his head groundward and saying with the tongue of the case that he was content. The Maghrabi, the magician, looked at Aladdin and saw him smiling, whereby he understood that the lad was satisfied to become a trader. So he said to him: "Since thou art content that I open thee a merchant's store and make thee a gentleman, do thou, O son of my brother, prove thyself a man and Inshallah— God willing—tomorrow I will take thee to the bazaar in the first place will have a fine suit of clothes cut out for thee, such gear as merchants wear; and secondly, I will look after a store for thee and keep my word."

Now Aladdin's mother had somewhat doubted the Moroccan being her brother-in-law, but as soon as she heard his promise of opening a merchant's store for her son and setting him up with stuffs and capital and so forth, the woman decided and determined in her mind that this Maghrabi was in very sooth her husband's brother, seeing that no stranger man would do such goodly deed by her son. So she began directing the lad to the right road and teaching him to cast ignorance from out his head and to prove himself a man. Moreover, she bade him ever obey his excellent uncle as though he were his son, and to make up for the time he had wasted in frowardness with his fellows. After this she arose and spread the table, then served up supper, so all sat down and fell to eating and drinking while the Maghrabi conversed with Aladdin upon matters of business and the like, rejoicing him to such degree that he enjoyed no sleep that night. But when the Moorman saw that the dark hours were passing by, and the wine was drunken, he arose and sped to his own stead. But ere going he agreed to return next morning and take Aladdin and look to his suit of merchant's clothes being cut out for him.

And as soon as it was dawn, behold, the Maghrabi rapped at the door, which was opened by Aladdin's mother. The Moorman, however, would not enter, but asked to take the lad with him to the market street. Accordingly Aladdin went forth to his uncle and, wishing him good morning, kissed his hand, and the Moroccan took him by the hand and fared with him to the bazaar. There he entered a clothier's shop containing all kinds of clothes, and called for a suit of the most sumptuous, whereat the merchant brought him out his need, all wholly fashioned and ready sewn, and the Moorman said to the lad, "Choose, O my child, whatso pleaseth thee." Aladdin rejoiced exceedingly, seeing that his uncle had given him his choice, so he picked out the suit most to his own liking and the Moroccan paid to the merchant the price thereof in ready money. Presently he led the lad to the hammam baths, where they bathed. Then they came out and drank sherbets, after which Aladdin arose and, donning his new dress in huge joy and delight, went up to his uncle and kissed his hand and thanked him for his favors.

The Maghrabi, the magician, after leaving the hammam with Aladdin, took him and trudged with him to the merchants' bazaar, and having diverted him by showing the market and its sellings and buyings, and to him: "O my son, it besitteth thee to become familiar with the folk, especially with the merchants, so thou mayest learn of them merchant craft, seeing that the same hath now become thy calling." Then he led him forth and showed him the city and its cathedral mosques, together with all the pleasant sights therein, and lastly made him enter a cook's shop. Here dinner was served to them on platters of silver and they dined well and ate and drank their sufficiency, after which they went their ways. Presently the Moorman pointed out to Aladdin the pleasaunces and noble buildings, and went in with him to the Sultan's palace and diverted him with displaying all the apartments, which were mighty fine and grand, and led him finally to the khan of stranger merchants, where he himself had his abode. Then the Moroccan invited sundry traders which were in the caravanserai, and they came and sat down to supper, when he notified to them that the youth was his nephew, Aladdin by name. And after they had eaten and drunken and night had fallen, he rose up, and taking the lad with him, led him back to his mother, who no sooner saw her boy as he were one of the merchants than her wits took flight and she waxed sad for very gladness.

Then she fell to thanking her false connection, the Moorman, for all his benefits and said to him: "O my brother-in-law, I can never say enough though I expressed my gratitude to thee during the rest of thy days and praised thee for the good deeds thou hast done by this my child." Thereupon quoth the Moroccan: "O wife of my brother, deem this not mere kindness of me, for that the lad is mine own son, and 'tis incumbent on me to stand in the stead of my brother, his sire. So be thou fully satisfied!" And quoth she: "I pray Allah by the honor of the Hallows, the ancients and the moderns, that He preserve thee and cause thee continue, O my brother-in-law, and prolong for me thy life. So shalt thou be a wing overshadowing this orphan lad, and he shall ever be obedient to thine orders, nor shall he do aught save whatso thou biddest him thereunto."

The Maghrabi replied: "O wife of my brother, Aladdin is now a man of sense and the son of goodly folk, and I hope to Allah that he will follow in the footsteps of his sire and cool thine eyes. But I regret that, tomorrow being Friday, I shall not be able to open his shop, as 'tis meeting day when all the merchants, after congregational prayer, go forth to the gardens and pleasaunces. On the Sabbath, however, Inshallah!—an it please the Creator—we will do our business. Meanwhile tomorrow I will come to thee betimes and take Aladdin for a pleasant stroll to the gardens and pleasaunces without the city, which haply he may hitherto not have beheld. There also he shall see the merchants and notables who go forth to amuse themselves, so shall he become acquainted with them and they with him."

The Maghrabi went away and lay that night in his quarters, and early next morning he came to the tailor's house and rapped at the door. Now Aladdin (for stress of his delight in the new dress he had donned and for the past day's enjoyment in the hammam and in eating and drinking and gazing at the folk, expecting futhermore his uncle to come at dawn and carry him off on pleasuring to the gardens) had not slept a wink that night, nor closed his eyelids, and would hardly believe it when day broke. But hearing the knock at the door, he went out at once in hot haste, like a spark of fire, and opened and saw his uncle, the magician, who embraced him and kissed him. Then, taking his hand, the Moorman said to him as they fared forth together, "O son of my brother, this day will I show thee a sight thou never sawest in all thy life," and he began to make the lad laugh and cheer him with pleasant talk. So doing, they left the city gate, and the Moroccan took to promenading with Aladdin amongst the gardens and to pointing out for his pleasure the mighty fine pleasances and the marvelous high-builded pavilions. And whenever they stood to stare at a garth or a mansion or a palace, the Maghrabi would say to his companion, "Doth this please thee, O son of my brother?"

Aladdin was nigh to fly with delight at seeing sights he had never seen in all his born days, and they ceased not to stroll about and solace themselves until they waxed a-weary, then they entered a mighty grand garden which was near-hand, a place that the heart delighted and the sight belighted, for that its swift-running rills flowed amidst the flowers and the waters jetted from the jaws of lions molded in yellow brass like unto gold. So they took seat over against a lakelet and rested a little while, and Aladdin enjoyed himself with joy exceeding and fell to jesting with his uncle and making merry with him as though the magician were really his father's brother.

Presently the Maghrabi arose, and loosing his girdle, drew forth from thereunder a bag full of victual, dried fruits and so forth, saying to Aladdin: "O my nephew, haply thou art become a-hungered, so come forward and eat what thou needest." Accordingly the lad fell upon the food and the Moorman ate with him, and they were gladdened and cheered by rest and good cheer. Then quoth the magician: "Arise, O son of my brother, an thou be reposed, and let us stroll onward a little and reach the end of our walk." Thereupon Aladdin arose and the Moroccan paced with him from garden to garden until they left all behind them and reached the base of a high and naked hill, when the lad, who during all his days had never issued from the city gate and never in his life had walked such a walk as this, said to the Maghrabi: "O uncle mine, whither are we wending? We have left the gardens behind us one and all and have reached the barren hill country. And if the way be still long, I have no strength left for walking. Indeed I am ready to fall with fatigue. There are no gardens before us, so let us hark back and return to town." Said the magician: "No, O my son. This is the right road, nor are the gardens ended, for we are going to look at one which hath ne'er its like amongst those of the kings, and all thou hast beheld are naught in comparison therewith. Then gird thy courage to walk. Thou art now a man, Alhamdolillah—praise be to Allah!"

Then the Maghrabi fell to soothing Aladdin with soft words and telling him wondrous tales, lies as well as truth, until they reached the site intended by the African magician, who had traveled from the sunset land to the regions of China for the sake thereof. And when they made the place, the Moorman said to Aladdin: "O son of my brother, sit thee down and take thy rest, for this is the spot we are now seeking and, Inshallah, soon will I divert thee by displaying marvel matters whose like not one in the world ever saw, nor hath any solaced himself with gazing upon that which thou art about to behold. But when thou art rested, arise and seek some wood chips and fuel sticks which be small and dry, wherewith we may kindle a fire. Then will I show thee, O son of my brother, matters beyond the range of matter." Now when the lad heard these words, he longed to look upon what his uncle was about to do and, forgetting his fatigue, he rose forthright and fell to gathering small wood chips and dry sticks, and continued until the Moorman cried to him, "Enough, O son of my brother!"

Presently the magician brought out from his breast pocker a casket, which he opened, and drew from it all he needed of incense. Then he fumigated and conjured and adjured, muttering words none might understand. And the ground straightway clave asunder after thick gloom and quake of earth and bellowings of thunder. Hereat Aladdin was startled and so affrighted that he tried to fly, but when the African magician saw his design, he waxed wroth with exceeding wrath, for that without the lad his work would profit him naught, the hidden hoard which he sought to open being not to be opened save by means of Aladdin. So, noting this attempt to run away, the magician arose, and raising his hand, smote Aladdin on the head a buffet so sore that well-nigh his back teeth were knocked out, and he fell swooning to the ground. But after a time he revived by the magic of the magician, and cried, weeping the while: "O my uncle, what have I done that deserveth from thee such a blow as this?" Hereat the Maghrabi fell to soothing him, and said: "O my son, 'tis my intent to make thee a man. Therefore do thou not gainsay me, for that I am thine uncle and like unto thy father. Obey me, therefore, in all I bid thee, and shortly thou shalt forget all this travail and toil whenas thou shalt look upon the marvel matters I am about to show thee."

And soon after the ground had cloven asunder before the Moroccan, it displayed a marble slab wherein was fixed a copper ring. The Maghrabi, striking a geomantic table, turned to Aladdin and said to him: "An thou do all I shall bid thee, indeed thou shalt become wealthier than any of the kings. And for this reason, O my son, I struck thee, because here lieth a hoard which is stored in thy name, and yet thou designedst to leave it and to levant. But now collect thy thoughts, and behold how I opened earth by my spells and adjurations. Under yon stone wherein the ring is set lieth the treasure wherewith I acquainted thee. So set thy hand upon the ring and raise the slab, for that none other amongst the folk, thyself excepted, hath power to open it, nor may any of mortal birth save thyself set foot within this enchanted treasury which hath been kept for thee. But 'tis needful that thou learn of me all wherewith I would charge thee, nor gainsay e'en a single syllable of my words. All this, O my child, is for thy good, the hoard being of immense value, whose like the kings of the world never accumulated, and do thou remember that 'tis for thee and me."

So poor Aladdin forgot his fatigue and buffet and tear-shedding, and he was dumbed and dazed at the Maghrabi's words and rejoiced that he was fated to become rich in such measure that not even the sultans would be richer than himself. Accordingly he cried: "O my uncle, bid me do all thou pleasest, for I will be obedient unto thy bidding." The Maghrabi replied: "O my nephew, thou art to me as my own child and even dearer, for being my brother's son and for my having none other kith and kin except thyself. And thou, O my child, art my heir and successor." So saying, he went up to Aladdin and kissed him and said: "For whom do I intend these my labors? Indeed, each and every are for thy sake, O my son, to the end that I may leave thee a rich man and one of the very greatest. So gainsay me not in all I shall say to thee, and now go up to yonder ring and uplift it as I bade thee." Aladdin answered: "O uncle mine, this ring is overheavy for me. I cannot raise it single-handed, so do thou also come forward and lend me strength and aidance toward uplifting it, for indeed I am young in years." The Moorman replied: "O son of my brother, we shall find it impossible to do aught if I assist thee, and all our efforts would be in vain. But do thou set thy hand upon the ring and pull it up, and thou shalt raise the slab forthright, and in very sooth I told thee that none can touch it save thyself. But whilst haling at it cease not to pronounce thy name and the names of thy father and mother, so 'twill rise at once to thee, nor shalt thou feel its weight."

Thereupon the lad mustered up strength and girt the loins of resolution and did as the Moroccan had bidden him, and hove up the slab with all ease when he pronounced his name and the names of his parents, even as the magician had bidden him. And as soon as the stone was raised he threw it aside, and there appeared before him a sardab, a souterrain, whereunto led a case of some twelve stairs, and the Maghrabi said: "O Aladdin, collect thy thoughts and do whatso I bid thee to the minutest detail, nor fail in aught thereof. Go down with all care into yonder vault until thou reach the bottom, and there shalt thou find a space divided into four halls, and in each of these thou shalt see four golden jars and others of virgin or and silver. Beware, however, lest thou take aught therefrom or touch them, nor allow thy gown or its skirts even to brush the jars or the walls. Leave them and fare forward until thou reach the fourth hall, without lingering for a single moment on the way. And if thou do aught contrary thereto, thou wilt at once be transformed and become a black stone. When reaching the fourth hall, thou wilt find therein a door, which do thou open, and pronouncing the names thou spakest over the slab, enter therethrough into a garden adorned everywhere with fruit-bearing trees. This thou must traverse by a path thou wilt see in front of thee measuring some fifty cubits long beyond which thou wilt come upon an open saloon, and herein a ladder of some thirty rungs. Thou shalt there find a lamp hanging from its ceiling, so mount the ladder and take that lamp and place it in thy breast pocket after pouring out its contents. Nor fear evil from it for thy clothes, because its contents are not common oil. And on return thou art allowed to pluck from the trees whoso thou pleasest, for all is thine so long as the lamp is in thy hand."

Now when the Moorman ended his charge to Aladdin, he drew off a seal ring and put it upon the lad's forefinger, saying: "O my son, verily this signet shall free thee from all hurt and fear which may threaten thee, but only on condition that thou bear in mind all I have told thee. So arise straightway and go down the stairs, strengthening thy purpose and girding the loins of resolution. Moreover, fear not, for thou art now a man and no longer a child. And in shortest time, O my son, thou shalt win thee immense riches and thou shalt become the wealthiest of the world."

Accordingly, Aladdin arose and descended into the souterrain, where he found the four halls, each containing four jars of gold, and these he passed by as the Moroccan had bidden him, with the utmost care and caution. Thence he fared into the garden and walked along its length until he entered the saloon, where he mounted the ladder and took the lamp, which he extinguished, pouring out the oil which was therein, and placed it in his breast pocket. Presently, descending the ladder, he returned to the garden, where he fell to gazing at the trees, whereupon sat birds glorifying with loud voices their Great Creator. Now he had not observed them as he went in, but all these trees bare for fruitage costly gems. Moreover, each had its own kind of growth and jewels of its peculiar sort, and these were of every color, green and white, yellow, red, and other such brilliant hues, and the radiance flashing from these gems paled the rays of the sun in forenoon sheen. Furthermore the size of each stone so far surpassed description that no King of the Kings of the World owned a single gem equal to the larger sort, nor could boast of even one half the size of the smaller kind of them. Aladdin walked amongst the trees and gazed upon them and other things which surprised the sight and bewildered the wits, and as he considered them, he saw that in lieu of common fruits the produce was of mighty fine jewels and precious stones, such as emeralds and diamonds, rubies, spinels, and balases, pearls and similar gems, astounding the mental vision of man.

And forasmuch as the lad had never beheld things like these during his born days, nor had reached those years of discretion which would teach him the worth of such valuables (he being still but a little lad), he fancied that all these jewels were of glass or crystal. So he collected them until he had filled his breast pockets, and began to certify himself if they were or were not common fruits, such as grapes, figs, and suchlike edibles. But seeing them of glassy substance, he, in his ignorance of precious stones and their prices, gathered into his breast pockets every kind of growth the trees afforded, and having failed of his purpose in finding them food, he said in his mind, "I will collect a portion of these glass fruits for playthings at home." So he fell to plucking them in quantities and cramming them in his pokes and breast pockets till these were stuffed full. After which he picked others which he placed in his waist shawl and then, girding himself therewith, carried off all he availed to, purposing to place them in the house by way of ornaments and, as hath been mentioned, never imagining that they were other than glass.

Then he hurried his pace in fear of his uncle, the Maghrabi, until he had passed through the four halls and lastly on his return reached the souterrain, where he cast not a look at the jars of gold, albeit he was able and allowed to take of the contents on his way back. But when he came to the souterrain stairs and clomb the steps till naught remained but the last, and finding this higher than all the others, he was unable alone and unassisted, burthened moreover as he was, to mount it. So he said to the Maghrabi, "O my uncle, lend me thy hand and aid me to climb." But the Moorman answered: "O my son, give me the lamp and lighten thy load. Belike 'tis that weighteth thee down." The lad rejoined: "O my uncle, 'tis not the lamp downweigheth me at all, but do thou lend me a hand, and as soon as I reached ground I will give it to thee." Hereat the Moroccan, the magician, whose only object was the lamp and none other, began to insist upon Aladdin giving it to him at once. But the lad (forasmuch as he had placed it at the bottom of his breast pocket and his other pouches, being full of gems, bulged outward) could not reach it with his fingers to hand it over, so the wizard after much vain persistency in requiring what his nephew was unable to give fell to raging with furious rage and to demanding the lamp, whilst Aladdin could not get at it. Yet had the lad promised truthfully that he would give it up as soon as he might reach ground, without lying thought or ill intent. But when the Moorman saw that he would not hand it over, he waxed wroth with wrath exceeding and cut off all his hopes of winning it. So he conjured and adjured and cast incense a-middlemost the fire, when forthright the slab made a cover of itself, and by the might of magic lidded the entrance. The earth buried the stone as it was aforetime, and Aladdin, unable to issue forth, remained underground.

Now the sorcerer was a stranger and, as we have mentioned, no uncle of Aladdin's, and he had misrepresented himself and preferred a lying claim, to the end that he might obtain the lamp by means of the lad for whom this hoard had been upstored. So the accursed heaped the earth over him and left him to die of hunger. For this Maghrabi was an African of Afrikiyah proper, born in the inner Sunset Land, and from his earliest age upward he had been addicted to witchcraft and had studied and practiced every manner of occult science, for which unholy lore the city of Africa is notorious. And he ceased not to read and hear lectures until he had become a past master in all such knowledge. And of the abounding skill in spells and conjurations which he had acquired by the perusing and the lessoning of forty years, one day of the days he discovered by devilish inspiration that there lay in an extreme city of the cities of China, named Al-Kal'as, an immense hoard, the like whereof none of the kings in this world had ever accumulated. Moreover, that the most marvelous article in this enchanted treasure was a wonderful lamp, which whoso possessed could not possibly be surpassed by any man upon earth, either in high degree or in wealth and opulence, nor could the mightiest monarch of the universe attain to the all-sufficiency of this lamp with its might of magical means. When the Maghrabi assured himself by his science and saw that this hoard could be opened only by the presence of a lad named Aladdin, of pauper family and abiding in that very city, and learnt how taking it would be easy and without hardships, he straightway and without stay or delay equipped himself for a voyage to China (as we have already told), and he did what he did with Aladdin fancying that he would become Lord of the Lamp. But his attempt and his hopes were baffled and his work was clean wasted. Whereupon, determining to do the lad die, he heaped up the earth over him by gramarye to the end that the unfortunate might perish, reflecting that "The live man hath no murtherer." Secondly, he did so with the design that, as Aladdin could not come forth from underground, he would also be impotent to bring out the lamp from the souterrain. So presently he wended his ways and retired to his own land, Africa, a sadder man and disappointed of all his expectations.

Such was the case with the wizard, but as regards Aladdin, when the earth was heaped over him, he began shouting to the Moorman, whom he believed to be his uncle, and praying him to lend a hand that he might issue from the souterrain and return to earth's surface. But however loudly he cried, none was found to reply. At that moment he comprehended the sleight which the Moroccan had played upon him, and that the man was no uncle, but a liar and a wizard. Then the unhappy despaired of life, and learned to his sorrow that there was no escape for him, so he fell to beweeping with sore weeping the calamity had befallen him. And after a little while he stood up and descended the stairs to see if Allah Almighty had lightened his grief load by leaving a door of issue. So he turned him to the right and to the left, but he saw naught save darkness and four walls closed upon him, for that the magician had by his magic locked all the doors and had shut up even the garden wherethrough the lad erst had passed, lest it offer him the means of issuing out upon earth's surface, and that he might surely die. Then Aladdin's weeping waxed sorer and his wailing louder whenas he found all the doors fast shut, for he had thought to solace himself awhile in the garden. But when he felt that all were locked, he fell to shedding tears and lamenting like unto one who hath lost his every hope, and he returned to sit upon the stairs of the flight whereby he had entered the souterrain.

But it is a light matter for Allah (be He exalted and extolled!) whenas He designeth aught to say, "Be," and it becometh, for that He createth joy in the midst of annoy. And on this wise it was with Aladdin. Whilst the Maghrabi, the magician, was sending him down into the souterrain, he set upon his finger by way of gift a seal ring and said: "Verily this signet shall save thee from every strait an thou fall into calamity and ill shifts of time, and it shall remove from thee all hurt and harm, and aid thee with a strong arm whereso thou mayest be set." Now this was by Destiny of God the Great, that it might be the means of Aladdin's escape. For whilst he sat wailing and weeping over his case and cast away all hope of life, and utter misery overwhelmed him, he rubbed his hands together for excess of sorrow, as is the wont of the woeful. Then, raising them in supplication to Allah, he cried, "I testify that there is no God save Thou alone, the Most Great, the Omnipotent, the All-conquering, Quickener of the dead, Creator of man's need and Granter thereof, Resolver of his difficulties and duress and Bringer of joy, not of annoy. Thou art my sufficiency and Thou art the Truest of Trustees. And I bear my witness that Mohammed is Thy servant and Thine Apostle, and I supplicate Thee, O my God, by his favor with Thee to free me from this my foul plight."

And whilst he implored the Lord and was chafing his hands in the soreness of his sorrow for that had befallen him of calamity, his fingers chanced to rub the ring, when, lo and behold! forthright its familiar rose upright before him and cried: "Adsum! Thy slave between thy hands is come! Ask whatso thou wantest, for that I am the thrall of him on whose hand is the ring, the signet of my lord and master." Hereat the lad looked at him and saw standing before him a Marid like unto an Ifrit of our lord Solomon's Jinns. He trembled at the terrible sight, but, hearing the Slave of the Ring say, "Ask whatso thou wantest. Verily, I am thy thrall, seeing that the signet of my lord be upon thy finger," he recovered his spirits and remembered the Moorman's saying when giving him the ring. So he rejoiced exceedingly and became brave and cried, "Ho, thou slave of the Lord of the Ring, I desire thee to set me upon the face of the earth." And hardly had he spoken this speech when suddenly the ground clave asunder and he found himself at the door of the hoard and outside it in full view of the world. Now for three whole days he had been sitting in the darkness of the treasury underground, and when the sheen of day and the shine of sun smote his face he found himself unable to keep his eyes open; so he began to unclose the lids a little and to close them a little until his eyeballs regained force and got used to the light and were purged of the noisome murk. Withal he was astounded at finding himself without the hoard door whereby he had passed in when it was opened by the Maghrabi, the magician, especially as the adit had been lidded and the ground had been smoothed, showing no sign whatever of entrance.

Thereat his surprise increased until he fancied himself in another place, nor was his mind convinced that the stead was the same until he saw the spot whereupon they had kindled the fire of wood chips and dried sticks, and where the African wizard had conjured over the incense. Then he turned him rightward and leftward and sighted the gardens from afar and his eyes recognized the road whereby he had come. So he returned thanks to Allah Almighty, Who had restored him to the face of earth and had freed him from death after he had cut off all hopes of life. Presently he arose and walked along the way to the town, which now he knew well, until he entered the streets and passed on to his own home. Then he went in to his mother, and on seeing her, of the overwhelming stress of joy at his escape and the memory of past affright and the hardships he had borne and the pangs of hunger, he fell to the ground before his parent in a fainting fit. Now his mother had been passing sad since the time of his leaving her, and he found her moaning and crying about him. However, on sighting him enter the house she joyed with exceeding joy, but soon was overwhelmed with woe when he sank upon the ground swooning before her eyes. Still, she did not neglect the matter or treat it lightly, but at once hastened to sprinkle water upon his face, and after she asked of the neighbors some scents which she made him snuff up. And when he came round a little, he prayed her to bring him somewhat of food saying, "O my mother, 'tis now three days since I ate anything at all." Thereupon she arose and brought him what she had by her, then, setting it before him, said: "Come forward, O my son. Eat and be cheered, and when thou shalt have rested, tell me what hath betided and affected thee, O my child. At this present I will not question thee, for thou art aweary in very deed." Aladdin ate and drank and was cheered, and after he had rested and had recovered spirits he cried:

"Ah, O my mother, I have a sore grievance against thee for leaving me to that accursed wight who strave to compass my destruction and designed to take my life. Know thou that I beheld death with mine own eyes at the hand of this damned wretch, whom thou didst certify to be my uncle, and had not Almighty Allah rescued me from him, I and thou, O my mother, had been cozened by the excess of this accursed's promises to work my welfare, and by the great show of affection which he manifested to us. Learn, O my mother, that this fellow is a sorcerer, a Moorman, an accursed, a liar, a traitor, a hypocrite, nor deem I that the devils under the earth are damnable as he. Allah abase him in his every book! Hear then, O my mother, what this abominable one did, and all that I shall tell thee will be soothfast and certain. See how the damned villain brake every promise he made, certifying that he would soon work all good with me. And do thou consider the fondness which he displayed to me and the deeds which he did by me, and all this only to win his wish, for his design was to destroy me. And Alhamdolillah—laud to the Lord —for my deliverance. Listen and learn, O my mother, how this accursed entreated me."

Then Aladdin informed his mother of all that had befallen him, weeping the while for stress of gladness—how the Maghrabi had led him to a hill wherein was hidden the hoard and how he had conjured and fumigated, adding: "After which, O my mother, mighty fear gat hold of me when the hill split and the earth gaped before me by his wizardry. And I trembled with terror at the rolling of thunder in mine ears and the murk which fell upon us when he fumigated and muttered spells. Seeing these horrors, I in mine affright designed to fly, but when he understood mine intent, he reviled me and smote me a buffet so sore that it caused me swoon. However, inasmuch as the treasury was to be opened only by means of me, O my mother, he could not descend therein himself, it being in my name and not in his. And for that he is an ill-omened magician, he understood that I was necessary to him and this was his need of me." Aladdin acquainted his mother with all that had befallen him from the Maghrabi, the magician, and said:

"After he had buffeted me, he judged it advisable to soothe me in order that he might send me down into the enchanted treasury, and first he drew from his finger a ring, which he placed upon mine. So I descended and found four halls all full of gold and silver, which counted as naught, and the accursed had charged me not to touch aught thereof. Then I entered a mighty fine flower garden everywhere bedecked with tall trees whose foilage and fruitage bewildered the wits, for all, O my mother, were of varicolored glass, and lastly I reached the hall wherein hung this lamp. So I took it straightway and put it out and poured forth its contents." And so saying, Aladdin drew the lamp from his breast pocket and showed it to his mother, together with the gems and jewels which he had brought from the garden. And there were two large bag pockets full of precious stones, whereof not one was to be found amongst the kings of the world. But the lad knew naught anent their worth, deeming them glass or crystal. And presently he resumed:

"After this, O mother mine, I reached the hoard door carrying the lamp and shouted to the accursed sorcerer which called himself my uncle to lend me a hand and hale me up, I being unable to mount of myself the last step for the overweight of my burthen. But he would not and said only, 'First hand me the lamp!' As, however, I had placed it at the bottom of my breast pocket and the other pouches bulged out beyond it, I was unable to get at it and said, 'O my uncle, I cannot reach thee the lamp, but I will give it to thee when outside the treasury.' His only need was the lamp, and he designed, O my mother, to snatch it from me and after that slay me, as indeed he did his best to do by heaping the earth over my head. Such then is what befell me from this foul sorcerer." Hereupon Aladdin fell to abusing the magician in hot wrath and with a burning heart, and crying: "Wellaway! I take refuge from this damned wight, the illomened, the wrongdoer, the forswearer, the lost to all humanity, the archtraitor, the hypocrite, the annihilator of ruth and mercy." When Aladdin's mother heard his words and what had befallen him from the Maghrabi, the magician, she said: "Yea, verily, O my son, he is a miscreant, a hypocrite who murthereth the folk by his magic. But 'twas the grace of Allah Almighty, O my child, that saved thee from the tricks and the treachery of this accursed sorcerer whom I deemed to be truly thine uncle."

Then, as the lad had not slept a wink for three days and found himself nodding, he sought his natural rest, his mother doing on like wise, nor did he awake till about noon on the second day. As soon as he shook off slumber he called for somewhat of food, being sore a-hungered, but said his mother: "O my son, I have no victual for thee, inasmuch as yesterday thou atest all that was in the house. But wait patiently a while. I have spun a trifle of yarn which I will carry to the market street and sell it and buy with what it may be worth some victual for thee." "O my mother," said he, "keep your yarn and sell it not, but fetch me the lamp I brought hither that I may go vend it, and with its price purchase provuant, for that I deem 'twill bring more money than the spinnings." So Aladdin's mother arose and fetched the lamp for her son, but while so doing she saw that it was dirty exceedingly, so that said: "O my son, here is the lamp, but 'tis very foul. After we shall have washed it and polished it 'twill sell better." Then, taking a handful of sand, she began to rub therewith, but she had only begun when appeared to her one of the Jann, whose favor was frightful and whose bulk was horrible big, and he was gigantic as one of the Jababirah. And forthright he cried to her: "Say whatso thou wantest of me. Here am I, thy slave and slave to whoso holdeth the lamp, and not I alone, but all the Slaves of the Wonderful Lamp which thou hendest in hand."

She quaked and terror was sore upon her when she looked at that frightful form, and her tongue being tied, she could not return aught reply, never having been accustomed to espy similar semblances. Now her son was standing afar off, and he had already seen the Jinni of the ring which he had rubbed within the treasury, so when he heard the slave speaking to his parent, he hastened forward, and snatching the lamp from her hand, said: "O Slave of the Lamp, I am a-hungered, and 'tis my desire that thou fetch me somewhat to eat, and let it be something toothsome beyond our means." The Jinni disappeared for an eye twinkle and returned with a mighty fine tray and precious of price, for that 'twas all in virginal silver, and upon it stood twelve golden platters of meats manifold and dainties delicate, with bread snowier than snow; also two silvern cups and as many black jacks full of wine clear-strained and long-stored. And after setting all these before Aladdin, he vanished from vision.

Thereupon the lad went and sprinkled rose-water upon his mother's face and caused her snuff up perfumes pure and pungent, and said to her when she revived: "Rise, O mother mine, and let us eat of these meats wherewith Almighty Allah hath eased our poverty." But when she saw that mighty fine silvern tray she fell to marveling at the matter, and quoth she: "O my son, who be this generous, this beneficent one who hath abated our hunger pains and our penury? We are indeed under obligation to him, and meseemeth 'tis the Sultan who, hearing of our mean condition and our misery, hath sent us this food tray." Quoth he: "O my mother, this be no time for questioning. Arouse thee and let us eat, for we are both a-famished." Accordingly they sat down to the tray and fell to feeding, when Aladdin's mother tasted meats whose like in all her time she had never touched. So they devoured them with sharpened appetites and all the capacity engendered by stress of hunger. And secondly, the food was such that marked the tables of the kings. But neither of them knew whether the tray was or was not valuable, for never in their born days had they looked upon aught like it.

As soon as they had finished the meal (withal leaving victual enough for supper and eke for the next day), they arose and washed their hands and sat at chat, when the mother turned to her son and said: "Tell me, O my child, what befell thee from the slave, the Jinni, now that Alhamdolillah—laud to the Lord!—we have eaten our full of the good things wherewith He hath favored us and thou hast no pretext for saying to me, 'I am a-hungered.'" So Aladdin related to her all that took place between him and the slave what while she had sunk upon the ground a-swoon for sore terror, and at this she, being seized with mighty great surprise, said: "'Tis true, for the Jinns do present themselves before the sons of Adam, but I, O my son, never saw them in all my life, and meseemeth that this be the same who saved thee when thou wast within the enchanted hoard." "This is not he, O my mother. This who appeared before thee is the Slave of the Lamp!" "Who may this be, O my son?" "This be a slave of sort and shape other than he. That was the familiar of the ring, and this his fellow thou sawest was the Slave of the Lamp thou hendest in hand." And when his parent heard these words she cried: "There! there! So this accursed, who showed himself to me and went nigh unto killing me with affright, is attached to the lamp." "Yes," he replied, and she rejoined: "Now I conjure thee, O my son, by the milk wherewith I suckled thee, to throw away from thee this lamp and this ring, because they can cause us only extreme terror, and I especially can never a-bear a second glance at them. Moreover, all intercourse with them is unlawful, for that the Prophet (whom Allah save and assain!) warned us against them with threats."

He replied: "Thy commands, O my mother, be upon my head and mine eyes, but as regards this saying thou saidest, 'tis impossible that I part or with lamp or with ring. Thou thyself hast seen what good the slave wrought us whenas we were famishing, and know, O my mother, that the Maghrabi, the liar, the magician, when sending me down into the hoard, sought nor the silver nor the gold wherewith the four halls were fulfilled, but charged me to bring him only the lamp (naught else), because in very deed he had learned its priceless value. And had he not been certified of it, he had never endured such toil and trouble, nor had he traveled from his own land to our land in search thereof, neither had he shut me up in the treasury when he despaired of the lamp which I would not hand to him. Therefore it besitteth us, O my mother, to keep this lamp and take all care thereof, nor disclose its mysteries to any, for this is now our means of livelihood and this it is shall enrich us. And likewise as regards the ring, I will never withdraw it from my finger, inasmuch as but for this thou hadst nevermore seen me on life—nay, I should have died within the hoard underground. How then can I possibly remove it from my finger? And who wotteth that which may betide me by the lapse of time, what trippings or calamities or injurious mishaps wherefrom this ring may deliver me? However, for regard to thy feelings I will stow away the lamp, nor ever suffer it to be seen of thee hereafter." Now when his mother heard his words and pondered them, she knew they were true and said to him: "Do, O my son, whatso thou willest. For my part, I wish never to see them nor ever sight that frightful spectacle I erst saw."

Aladdin and his mother continued eating of the meats brought them by the Jinni for two full told days till they were finished. But when he learned that nothing of food remained for them, he arose and took a platter of the platters which the slave had brought upon the tray. Now they were all of the finest gold, but the lad knew naught thereof, so he bore it to the bazaar and there, seeing a man which was a Jew, a viler than the Satans, offered it to him for sale. When the Jew espied it, he took the lad aside that none might see him, and he looked at the platter and considered it till he was certified that it was of gold refined. But he knew not whether Aladdin was acquainted with its value or he was in such matters a raw laddie, so he asked him, "For how much, O my lord, this platter?" and the other answered, "Thou wottest what be its worth." The Jew debated with himself as to how much he should offer, because Aladdin had returned him a craftsmanlike reply, and he thought of the smallest valuation. At the same time he feared lest the lad, haply knowing its worth, should expect a considerable sum. So he said in his mind, "Belike the fellow is an ignoramus in such matters, nor is ware of the price of the platter." Whereupon he pulled out of his pocket a dinar, and Aladdin eyed the gold piece lying in his palm and, hastily taking it, went his way, whereby the Jew was certified of his customer's innocence of all such knowledge, and repented with entire repentance that he had given him a golden dinar in lieu of a copper carat, a bright-polished groat.

However, Aladdin made no delay, but went at once to the baker's, where he bought him bread and changed the ducat. Then, going to his mother, he gave her the scones and the remaining small coin and said, "O my mother, hie thee and buy thee all we require." So she arose and walked to the bazaar and laid in the necessary stock, after which they ate and were cheered. And whenever the price of the platter was expended, Aladdin would take another and carry it to the accursed Jew, who brought each and every at a pitiful price; and even this he would have minished but, seeing how he had paid a dinar for the first, he feared to offer a lesser sum, lest the lad go and sell to some rival in trade and thus he lose his usurious gains. Now when all the golden platters were sold, there remained only the silver tray whereupon they stood, and for that it was large and weighty, Aladdin brought the Jew to his house and produced the article, when the buyer, seeing its size, gave him ten dinars, and these being accepted, went his ways.

Aladdin and his mother lived upon the sequins until they were spent, then he brought out the lamp and rubbed it, and straightway appeared the slave who had shown himself aforetime. And said the lad: "I desire that thou bring me a tray of food like unto that thou broughtest me erewhiles, for indeed I am famisht." Accordingly, in the glance of an eye the slave produced a similar tray supporting twelve platters of the most sumptuous, furnished with requisite cates, and thereon stood clean bread and sundry glass bottles of strained wine. Now Aladdin's mother had gone out when she knew he was about to rub the lamp, that she might not again look upon the Jinni; but after a while she returned, and when she sighted the tray covered with silvern platters and smelt the savor of the rich meats diffused over the house, she marveled and rejoiced. Thereupon quoth he: "Look, O my mother! Thou badest me throw away the lamp. See now its virtues," and quoth she, "O my son, Allah increase his weal, but I would not look upon him." Then the lad sat down with his parent to the tray and they ate and drank until they were satisfied, after which they removed what remained for use on the morrow.

As soon as the meats had been consumed, Aladdin arose and stowed away under his clothes a platter of the platters and went forth to find the Jew, purposing to sell it to him, but by fiat of Fate he passed by the shop of an ancient jeweler, an honest man and a pious who feared Allah. When the Sheikh saw the lad, he asked him, saying: "O my son, what dost thou want? For that times manifold have I seen thee passing hereby and having dealings with a Jewish man, and I have espied thee handing over to him sundry articles. Now also I fancy thou hast somewhat for sale and thou seekest him as a buyer thereof. But thou wottest not, O my child, that the Jews ever hold lawful to them the good of Moslems, the confessors of Allah Almighty's unity, and always defraud them, especially this accursed Jew with whom thou hast relations and into whose hands thou hast fallen. If then, O my son, thou have aught thou wouldest sell, show the same to me and never fear, for I will give thee its full price, by the truth of Almighty Allah."

Thereupon Aladdin brought out the platter, which when the ancient goldsmith saw, he took and weighed it in his scales and asked the lad, saying, "Was it the fellow of this thou soldest to the Jew?" "Yes, its fellow and its brother," he answered, and quoth the old man, "What price did he pay thee?" Quoth the lad, "One dinar." The ancient goldsmith, hearing from Aladdin how the Jew used to give only one dinar as the price of the platter, cried, "Ah! I take refuge from this accursed who cozeneth the servants of Allah Almighty!" Then, looking at the lad, he exclaimed: "O my son, verily yon tricksy Jew hath cheated thee and laughed at thee, this platter being pure silver and virginal. I have weighed it and found it worth seventy dinars, and, if thou please to take its value, take it." Thereupon the Sheikh counted out to him seventy gold pieces, which he accepted, and presently thanked him for his kindness in exposing the Jew's rascality.

And after this, whenever the price of a platter was expended, he would bring another, and on such wise he and his mother were soon in better circumstances. Yet they ceased not to live after their olden fashion as middle-class folk, without spending on diet overmuch or squandering money. But Aladdin had now thrown off the ungraciousness of his boyhood. He shunned the society of scapegraces and he began to frequent good men and true, repairing daily to the market street of the merchants and there companying with the great and small of them, asking about matters of merchandise and learning the price of investments and so forth. He likewise frequented the bazaars of the goldsmiths and the jewelers, where he would sit and divert himself by inspecting their precious stones and by noting how jewels were sold and bought therein. Accordingly, he presently became ware that the tree truits wherewith he had filled his pockets what time he entered the enchanged treasury were neither glass nor crystal, but gems rich and rare, and he understood that he had acquired immense wealth such as the kings never can possess. He then considered all the precious stones which were in the jewelers' quarter, but found that their biggest was not worth his smallest.

On this wise he ceased not every day repairing to the bazaar and making himself familiar with the folk and winning their loving will, and inquiring anent selling and buying, giving and taking, the dear and the cheap, until one day of the days when, after rising at dawn and donning his dress he went forth, as was his wont, to the jewelers' bazaar and as he passed along it he heard the crier crying as follows: "By command of our magnificent master, the King of the Time and the Lord of the Age and the Tide, let all the folk lock up their shops and stores and retire within their houses, for that the Lady Badr al-Budur, daughter of the Sultan, designeth to visit the hammam. And whoso gainsayeth the order shall be punished with death penalty, and be his blood upon his own neck!" But when Aladdin heard the proclamation, he longed to look upon the King's daughter and said in his mind, "Indeed all the lieges talk of her beauty and loveliness, and the end of my desires is to see her." Then Aladdin fell to contriving some means whereby he might look upon the Princess Badr al-Budur, and at last judged best to take his station behind the hammam door, whence he might see her face as she entered. Accordingly, without stay or delay he repaired to the baths before she was expected and stood a-rear of the entrance, a place whereat none of the folk happened to be looking.

Now when the Sultan's daughter had gone the rounds of the city and its main streets and had solaced herself by sight-seeing, she finally reached the hammam, and whilst entering she raised her veil and Aladdin saw her favor, he said: "In very truth her fashion magnifieth her Almighty Fashioner, and glory be to Him Who created her and adorned her with this beauty and loveliness." His strength was struck down from the moment he saw her and his thoughts were distraught. His gaze was dazed, the love of her gat hold of the whole of his heart, and when he returned home to his mother, he was as one in ecstasy. His parent addressed him, but he neither replied nor denied, and, when she set before him the morning meal he continued in like case, so quoth she: "O my son, what is't may have befallen thee? Say me, doth aught ail thee? Let me know what ill hath betided thee, for, unlike thy custom, thou speakest not when I bespeak thee." Thereupon Aladdin (who used to think that all women resembled his mother and who, albeit he had heard of the charms of Badr al-Budur, daughter of the Sultan, yet knew not what "beauty" and "loveliness" might signify) turned to his parent and exclaimed, "Let me be!" However, she persisted in praying him to come forward and eat, so he did her bidding, but hardly touched food. After which he lay at full length on his bed all the night through in cogitation deep until morning morrowed.

The same was his condition during the next day, when his mother was perplexed for the case of her son and unable to learn what had happened to him. So, thinking that belike he might be ailing, she drew near him and asked him, saying: "O my son, an thou sense aught of pain or suchlike, let me know, that I may fare forth and fetch thee the physician. And today there be in this our city a leech from the land of the Arabs whom the Sultan hath sent to summon, and the bruit abroad reporteth him to be skillful exceedingly. So, an be thou ill, let me go and bring him to thee." Aladdin, hearing his parent's offer to summon the mediciner, said: "O my mother, I am well in body and on no wise ill. But I ever thought that all women resembled thee until yesterday, when I beheld the Lady Badr al-Budur, daughter of the Sultan, as she was faring for the baths."

Then he related to her all and everything that had happened to him, adding: "Haply thou also hast heard the crier a-crying: 'Let no man open shop or stand in street that the Lady Badr al-Budur may repair to the hammam without eye seeing her.' But I have looked upon her even as she is, for she raised her veil at the door, and when I viewed her favor and beheld that noble work of the Creator, a sore fit of ecstasy, O my mother, fell upon me for love of her, and firm resolve to win her hath opened its way into every limb of me, nor is repose possible for me except I win her. Wherefor I purpose asking her to wife from the Sultan, her sire, in lawful wedlock." When Aladdin's mother heard her son's words, she belittled his wits and cried: "O my child, the name of Allah upon thee! Meseemeth thou hast lost thy senses. But be thou rightly guided, O my son, nor be thou as the men Jinn-maddened!" He replied: "Nay, O mother of mine, I am not out of my mind, nor am I of the maniacs, nor shall this thy saying alter one jot of what is in my thoughts. For rest is impossible to me until I shall have won the dearling of my heart's core, the beautiful Lady Badr al-Budur. And now I am resolved to ask her of her sire the Sultan."

She rejoined: "O my son, by my life upon thee, speak not such speech, lest any overhear thee and say thou be insane. So cast away from thee such nonsense! Who shall undertake a matter like this, or make such request to the King? Indeed, I know not how, supposing thy speech to be soothfast, thou shalt manage to crave such grace of the Sultan, or through whom thou desirest to propose it." He retorted: "Through whom shall I ask it, O my mother, when thou art present? And who is there fonder and more faithful to me than thyself? So my design is that thou thyself shalt proffer this my petition." Quoth she: "O my son, Allah remove me far therefrom! What! Have I lost my wits, like thyself? Cast the thought away, and a long way, from thy heart. Remember whose son thou art, O my child, the orphan boy of a tailor, the poorest and meanest of the tailors toiling in this city; and I, thy mother, am also come of pauper folk and indigent. How then durst thou ask to wife the daughter of the Sultan, whose sire would not deign marry her with the sons of the kings and the sovereigns, except they were his peers in honor and grandeur and majesty, and were they but one degree lower, he would refuse his daughter to them." Aladdin took patience until his parent had said her say, when quoth he: "O my mother, everything thou hast called to mind is known to me. Moreover, 'tis thoroughly well known to me that I am the child of pauper parents, withal do not these words of thee divert me from my design at all, at all. Nor the less do I hope of thee, an I be thy son and thou truly love me, that thou grant me this favor. Otherwise thou wilt destroy me, and present death hovereth over my head except I win my will of heart's dearling. And I, O my mother, am in every case thy child."

Hearing these words, his parent wept of her sorrow for him and said: "O my child! Yes, in very deed I am thy mother, nor have I any son or life's blood of my liver except thyself, and the end of my wishes is to give thee a wife and rejoice in thee. But suppose that I would seek a bride of our likes and equals, her people will at once ask an thou have any land or garden, merchandise or handicraft, wherewith thou canst support her, and what is the reply I can return? Then, if I cannot possibly answer the poor like ourselves, how shall I be bold enough, O my son, to ask for the daughter of the Sultan of China land, who hath no peer or behind or before him? Therefore do thou weigh this matter in thy mind. Also who shall ask her to wife for the son of a snip? Well indeed I wot that my saying aught of this kind will but increase our misfortunes, for that it may be the cause of our incurring mortal danger from the Sultan—peradventure even death for thee and me.

"And, as concerneth myself, how shall I venture upon such rash deed and perilous, O my son? And in what way shall I ask the Sultan for his daughter to be thy wife, and indeed how ever shall I even get access to him? And should I succeed therein, what is to be my answer an they ask me touching thy means? Haply the King will hold me to be a madwoman. And lastly, suppose that I obtain audience of the Sultan, what offering is there I can submit to the King's majesty? 'Tis true, O my child, that the Sultan is mild and merciful, never rejecting any who approach him to require justice or ruth or protection, nor any who pray him for a present, for he is liberal and lavisheth favor upon near and far. But he dealeth his boons to those deserving them, to men who have done some derring-do in battle under his eyes or have rendered as civilians great service to his estate. But thou! Do thou tell me what feat thou hast performed in his presence or before the public that thou meritest from him such grace? And secondly, this boon thou ambitionest is not for one of our condition, nor is it possible that the King grant to thee the bourne of thine aspiration. For whoso goeth to the Sultan and craveth of him a favor, him it besitteth to take in hand somewhat that suiteth the royal majesty, as indeed I warned thee aforetime. How, then, shalt thou risk thyself to stand before the Sultan and ask his daughter in marriage when thou hast with thee naught to offer him of that which beseemeth his exalted station?"

Hereto Aladdin replied: "O my mother, thou speakest to the point and hast reminded me aright, and 'tis meet that I revolve in mind the whole of thy remindings. But, O my mother, the love of Princess Badr al-Budur hath entered into the core of my heart, nor can I rest without I win her. However, thou hast also recalled to me a matter which I forgot, and 'tis this emboldeneth me to ask his daughter of the King. Albeit thou, O my mother, declarest that I have no gift which I can submit to the Sultan, as is the wont of the world, yet in very sooth I have an offering and a present whose equal, O my mother, I hold none of the kings to possess—no, even aught like it. Because verily that which I deemed glass or crystal was nothing but precious stones, and I hold that all the kings of the world have never possessed anything like one of the smallest thereof. For by frequenting the jeweler folk I have learned that they are the costliest gems, and these are what I brought in my pockets from the hoard, whereupon, an thou please, compose thy mind.

"We have in our house a bowl of China porcelain, so arise thou and fetch it, that I may fill it with these jewels, which thou shalt carry as a gift to the King, and thou shalt stand in his presence and solicit him for my requirement. I am certified that by such means the matter will become easy to thee, and if thou be unwilling, O my mother, to strive for the winning of my wish as regards the Lady Badr al-Budur, know thou that surely I shall die. Nor do thou imagine that this gift is of aught save the costliest of stones, and be assured, O my mother, that in my many visits to the jewelers' bazaar I have observed the merchants selling for sums man's judgment may not determine jewels whose beauty is not worth one quarter-carat of what we possess, seeing which I was certified that ours are beyond all price. So arise, O my mother, as I bade thee, and bring me the porcelain bowl aforesaid, that I may arrange therein some of these gems, and we will see what semblance they show."

So she brought him the china bowl, saying in herself, "I shall know what to do when I find out if the words of my child concerning these jewels be soothfast or not." And she set it before her son, who pulled the stones out of his pockets and disposed them in the bowl, and ceased not arranging therein gems of sorts till such time as he had filled it. And when it was brimful, she could not fix her eyes firmly upon it; on the contrary, she winked and blinked for the dazzle of the stones and their radiance and excess of lightninglike glance, and her wits were bewildered thereat. Only she was not certified of their value being really of the enormous extent she had been told. Withal she reflected that possibly her son might have spoken aright when he declared that their like was not to be found with the kings. Then Aladdin turned to her and said: "Thou hast seen, O my mother, that this present intended for the Sultan is magnificent, and I am certified that it will procure for thee high honor with him, and that he will receive thee with all respect. And now, O my mother, thou hast no excuse, so compose thy thoughts and arise. Take thou this bowl, and away with it to the palace."

His mother rejoined: "O my son, 'tis true that the present is high-priced exceedingly and the costliest of the costly, also that according to thy word none owneth its like. But who would have the boldness to go and ask the Sultan for his daughter, the Lady Badr al-Budur? I indeed dare not say to him, 'I want thy daughter!' when he shall ask me, 'What is thy want?' For know thou, O my son, that my tongue will be tied. And granting that Allah assist me and I embolden myself to say to him, 'My wish is to become a connection of thine through the marriage of thy daughter the Lady Badr al-Budur, to my son Aladdin,' they will surely decide at once that I am demented and will thrust me forth in disgrace and despised. I will not tell thee that I shall thereby fall into danger of death, for 'twill not be I only, but thou likewise. However, O my son, of my regard for thine inclination I needs must embolden myself and hie thither. Yet, O my child, if the King receive me and honor me on account of the gift and inquire of me what thou desirest, and in reply I ask of him that which thou desirest in the matter of thy marriage with his daughter, how shall I answer him and he ask me, as is man's wont, 'What estates hast thou, and what income?' And perchance, O my son, he will question me of this before questioning me of thee."

Aladdin replied: " 'Tis not possible that the Sultan should make such demand what time he considereth the jewels and their magnificence, nor is it meet to think of such things as these, which may never occur. Now do thou but arise and set before him this present of precious stones and ask of him his daughter for me, and sit not yonder making much of the difficulty in thy fancy. Ere this thou hast learned, O mother mine, that the lamp which we possess hath become to us a stable income, and that whatso I want of it the same is supplied to me. And my hope is that by means thereof I shall learn how to answer the Sultan should he ask me of that thou sayest." Then Aladdin and his mother fell to talking over the subject all that night long, and when morning morrowed, the dame arose and heartened her heart, especially as her son had expounded to her some little of the powers of the lamp and the virtues thereof; to wit, that it would supply all they required of it. Aladdin, however, seeing his parent take courage when he explained to her the workings of the lamp, feared lest she might tattle to the folk thereof, so he said to her: "O my mother, beware how thou talk to any of the properties of the lamp and its profit, as this is our one great good. Guard thy thoughts lest thou speak overmuch concerning it before others, whoso they be. Haply we shall lose it and lose the boon fortune we possess and the benefits we expect, for that 'tis of him." His mother replied, "Fear not therefor, O my son," and she arose and took the bowl full of jewels, which she wrapped up in a fine kerchief, and went forth betimes that she might reach the Divan ere it became crowded.

When she passed into the palace, the levee not being fully attended, she saw the wazirs and sundry of the lords of the land going into the presence room, and after a short time, when the Divan was made complete by the Ministers and high officials and chieftains and emirs and grandees, the Sultan appeared, and the wazirs made their obeisance and likewise did the nobles and the notables. The King seated himself upon the throne of his kingship, and all present at the levee stood before him with crossed arms awaiting his commandment to sit, and when they received it, each took his place according to his degree. Then the claimants came before the Sultan, who delivered sentence, after his wonted way, until the Divan was ended, when the King arose and withdrew into the palace and the others all went their ways. And when Aladdin's mother saw the throne empty and the King passing into his harem, she also wended her ways and returned home. But as soon as her son espied her, bowl in hand, he thought that haply something untoward had befallen her, but he would not ask of aught until such time as she had set down the bowl, when she acquainted him with that had occurred and ended by adding: "Alhamdolillah—laud to the Lord!—O my child, that I found courage enough and secured for myself standing place in the levee this day. And, albe' I dreaded to bespeak the King yet (Inshallah!) on the morrow I will address him. Even today were many who, like myself, could not get audience of the Sultan. But be of good cheer, O my son, and tomorrow needs must I bespeak him for thy sake, and what happened not may happen." When Aladdin heard his parent's words, he joyed with excessive joy, and, although he expected the matter to be managed hour by hour, for excess of his love and longing to the Lady Badr al-Budur, yet he possessed his soul in patience.

They slept well that night, and betimes next morning the mother of Aladdin arose and went with her bowl to the King's Court, which she found closed. So she asked the people and they told her that the Sultan did not hold a levee every day, but only thrice in the sennight, wherefor she determined to return home. And after this, whenever she saw the Court open she would stand before the King until the reception ended, and when it was shut she would go to make sure thereof, and this was the case for the whole month. The Sultan was wont to remark her presence at every levee, but on the last day when she took her station, as was her wont, before the Council, she allowed it to close, and lacked boldness to come forward and speak even a syllable. Now as the King, having risen, was making for his harem accompanied by the Grand Wazir, he turned to him and said: "O Wazir, during the last six or seven levee days I see yonder old woman present herself at every reception, and I also note that she always carrieth a something under her mantilla. Say me, hast thou, O Wazir, any knowledge of her and her intention?" "O my lord the Sultan," said the other, "verily women be weakly of wits, and haply this goodwife cometh hither to complain before thee against her goodman or some of her people." But this reply was far from satisfying the Sultan—nay, he bade the Wazir, in case she should come again, set her before him, and forthright the Minister placed hand on head and exclaimed, "To hear is to obey, O our lord the Sultan!"

Now one day of the days, when she did according to her custom, the Sultan cast his eyes upon her as she stood before him and said to his Grand Wazir: "This be the very woman whereof I spake to thee yesterday, so do thou straightway bring her before me, that I may see what be her suit and fulfill her need." Accordingly the Minister at once introduced her, and when in the presence she saluted the King by kissing her finger tips and raising them to her brow, and, praying for the Sultan's glory and continuance and the permanence of his prosperity, bussed ground before him. Thereupon quoth he: "O woman, for sundry days I have seen thee attend the levee sans a word said, so tell me an thou have any requirement I may grant." She kissed ground a second time and after blessing him, answered: "Yea, verily, as thy head liveth, O King of the Age, I have a want. But first of all, do thou deign grant me a promise of safety, that I may prefer my suit to the ears of our lord the Sultan, for haply thy Highness may find it a singular." The King, wishing to know her need, and being a man of unusual mildness and clemency, gave his word for her immunity and bade forthwith dismiss all about him, remaining without other but the Grand Wazir. Then he turned toward his suppliant and said: "Inform me of thy suit. Thou hast the safeguard of Allah Almighty." "O King of the Age," replied she, "I also require of thee pardon," and quoth he, "Allah pardon thee even as I do."

Then quoth she: "O our lord the Sultan, I have a son, Aladdin hight, and he, one day of the days, having heard the crier commanding all men to shut shop and shun the streets for that the Lady Badr al-Budur, daughter of the Sultan, was going to the hammam, felt an uncontrollable longing to look upon her, and hid himself in a stead whence he could sight her right well, and that place was behind the door of the baths. When she entered, he beheld her and considered her as he wished, and but too well, for since the time he looked upon her, O King of the Age, unto this hour, life hath not been pleasant to him. And he hath required of me that I ask her to wife for him from thy Highness, nor could I drive this fancy from his mind, because love of her hath mastered his vitals and to such degree that he said to me, 'Know thou, O mother mine, that an I win not my wish surely I shall die.' Accordingly I hope that thy Highness will deign be mild and merciful and pardon this boldness on the part of me and my child and refrain to punish us therefor."

When the Sultan heard her tale, he regarded her with kindness and, laughing aloud, asked her, "What may be that thou carriest, and what be in yonder kerchief?" And she, seeing the Sultan laugh in lieu of waxing wroth at her words, forthright opened the wrapper and set before him the bowl of jewels, whereby the audience hall was illumined as it were by lusters and candelabra. And he was dazed and amazed at the radiance of the rare gems, and he fell to marveling at their size and beauty and excellence and cried: "Never at all until this day saw I anything like these jewels for size and beauty and excellence, nor deem I that there be found in my Treasury a single one like them." Then he turned to his Minister and asked: "What sayest thou, O Wazir? Tell me, hast thou seen in thy time such mighty fine jewels as these?" The other answered: "Never saw I such, O our lord the Sultan, nor do I think that there be in the treasures of my lord the Sultan the fellow of the least thereof." The King resumed: "Now indeed whoso hath presented to me such jewels meriteth to become bridegroom to my daughter, Badr al-Budur, because, as far as I see, none is more deserving of her than he." When the Wazir heard the Sultan's words, he was tongue-tied with concern, and he grieved with sore grief, for the King had promised to give the Princess in marriage to his son. So after a little while he said: "O King of the Age, thy Highness deigned promise me that the Lady Badr al-Budur should be spouse to my son, so 'tis but right that thine

Exalted Highness vouchsafe us a delay of three months, during which time, Inshallah! my child may obtain and present an offering yet costlier than this." Accordingly the King, albeit he knew that such a thing could not be done, or by the Wazir or by the greatest of his grandees, yet of his grace and kindness granted him the required delay.

Then he turned to the old woman, Aladdin's mother, and said: "Go to thy son and tell him I have pledged my word that my daughter shall be in his name. Only 'tis needful that I make the requisite preparations of nuptial furniture for her use, and 'tis only meet that he take patience for the next three months." Receiving this reply, Aladdin's mother thanked the Sultan and blessed him, then, going forth in hottest haste, as one flying for joy, she went home. And when her son saw her entering with a smiling face, he was gladdened at the sign of good news, especially because she had returned without delay, as on the past days, and had not brought back the bowl. Presently he asked her saying: "Inshallah, thou bearest me, O my mother, glad tidings, and peradventure the jewels and their value have wrought their work, and belike thou hast been kindly received by the King and he hath shown thee grace and hath given ear to thy request?" So she told him the whole tale, how the Sultan had entreated her well and had marveled at the extraordinary size of the gems and their surpassing water, as did also the Wazir, adding: "And he promised that his daughter should be thine. Only, O my child, the Wazir spake of a secret contract made with him by the Sultan before he pledged himself to me and, after speaking privily, the King put me off to the end of three months. Therefore I have become fearful lest the Wazir be evilly disposed to thee, and perchance he may attempt to change the Sultan's mind."

When Aladdin heard his mother's words and how the Sultan had promised him his daughter, deferring, however, the wedding until after the third month, his mind was gladdened and he rejoiced exceedingly and said: "Inasmuch as the King hath given his word after three months (well, it *is* a long time!), at all events my gladness is mighty great." Then he thanked his parent, showing her how her good work had exceeded her toil and travail, and said to her: "By Allah, O my mother, hitherto I was as 'twere in my grave and therefrom thou hast withdrawn me. And I praise Allah Almighty because I am at this moment certified that no man in the world is happier than I, or more fortunate." Then he took patience until two of the three months had gone by.

Now one day of the days his mother fared forth about sundown to the bazaar that she might buy somewhat of oil, and she found all the market shops fast shut and the whole city decorated, and the folk placing waxen tapers and flowers at their casements. And she beheld the soldiers and household troops and agas riding in procession, and flambeaux and lusters flaming and flaring, and she wondered at the marvelous sight and the glamour of the scene. So she went in to an oilman's store which stood open still and bought her need of him and said: "By thy life, O uncle, tell me what be the tidings in town this day, that people have made all these decorations and every house and market street are adorned and the troops all stand on guard?" The oilman asked her, "O woman, I suppose thou art a stranger, and not one of this city?" and she answered, "Nay, I am thy townswoman." He rejoined: "Thou a townswoman, and yet wottest not that this very night the son of the Grand Wazir goeth in to the Lady Badr al-Budur, daughter of the Sultan! He is now in the hammam, and all this power of soldiery is on guard and standing under arms to await his coming forth, when they will bear him in bridal procession to the palace, where the Princess expecteth him."

As the mother of Aladdin heard these words, she grieved and was distraught in thought and perplexed how to inform her son of this sorrowful event, well knowing that the poor youth was looking, hour by hour, to the end of the three months. But she returned straightway home to him, and when she entered she said, "O my son, I would give thee certain tidings, yet hard to me will be the sorrow they shall occasion thee." He cried, "Let me know what be thy news," and she replied: "Verily the Sultan hath broken his promise to thee in the matter of the Lady Badr al-Budur, and this very night the Grand Wazir's son goeth in to her. And for some time, O my son, I have suspected that the Minister would change the King's mind, even as I told thee how he had spoken privily to him before me." Aladdin asked: "How learnedst thou that the Wazir's son is this night to pay his first visit to the Princess?" So she told him the whole tale, how when going to buy oil she had found the city decorated and the eunuch officials and lords of the land with the troops under arms awaiting the bridegroom from the baths, and that the first visit was appointed for that very night.

Hearing this, Aladdin was seized with a fever of jealousy brought on by his grief. However, after a short while he remembered the lamp and, recovering his spirits, said: "By thy life, O my mother, do thou believe that the Wazir's son will not enjoy her as thou thinkest. But now leave we this discourse, and arise thou and serve up supper, and after eating let me retire to my own chamber and all will be well and happy." After he had supped Aladdin retired to his chamber and, locking the door, brought out the lamp and rubbed it, whenas forthright appeared to him its familiar, who said: "Ask whatso thou wantest, for I am thy slave and slave to him who holdeth the lamp in hand, I and all the Slaves of the Lamp." He replied: "Hear me! I prayed the Sultan for his daughter to wife and he plighted her to me after three months, but he hath not kept his word—nay, he hath given her to the son of the Wazir, and this very night the bridegroom will go in to her. Therefore I command thee (an thou be a trusty servitor to the lamp), when thou shalt see bride and bridegroom bedded together this night, at once take them up and bear them hither abed. And this be what I want of thee." The Marid replied, "Hearing and obeying, and if thou have other service but this, do thou demand of me all thou desirest." Aladdin rejoined, "At the present time I require naught save that I bade thee do."

Hereupon the slave disappeared and Aladdin returned to pass the rest of the evening with his mother. But at the hour when he knew that the servitor would be coming, he arose and retired to his chamber, and after a little while, behold, the Marid came, bring to him the newly wedded couple upon their bridal bed. Aladdin rejoiced to see them with exceeding joy, then he cried to the slave, "Carry yonder gallowsbird hence and lay him at full length in the privy." His bidding was done straightway, but before leaving him, the slave blew upon the bridegroom a blast so cold that it shriveled him, and the plight of the Wazir's son became piteous. Then the servitor, returning to Aladdin, said to him, "An thou require aught else, inform me thereof," and said the other, "Return a-morn, that thou mayest restore them to their stead," whereto, "I hear and obey," quoth the Marid, and evanished.

Presently Aladdin arose, hardly believing that the affair had been such a success for him, but whenas he looked upon the Lady Badr al-Budur lying under his own roof, albeit he had long burned with her love, yet he preserved respect for her and said: "O Princess of fair ones, think not that I brought thee hither to minish thy honor. Heaven forfend! Nay, 'twas only to prevent the wrong man enjoying thee, for that thy sire, the Sultan, promised thee to me. So do thou rest in peace." When the Lady Badr al-Budur, daughter of the Sultan, saw herself in that mean and darksome lodging, and heard Aladdin's words, she was seized with fear and trembling and waxed clean distraught, nor could she return aught of reply. Presently the youth arose, and stripping off his outer dress, placed a scimitar between them and lay upon the bed beside the Princess. And he did no villain deed, for it sufficed him to prevent the consummation of her nuptials with the Wazir's son. On the other hand, the Lady Badr al-Budur passed a night the evilest of all nights, nor in her born days had she seen a worse. And the same was the case with the Minister's son, who lay in the chapel of ease and who dared not stir for the fear of the Jinni which overwhelmed him.

As soon as it was morning the slave appeared before Aladdin without the lamp being rubbed, and said to him: "O my lord, an thou require aught, command me therefor, that I may do it upon my head and mine eyes." Said the other: "Go, take up and carry the bride and bridegroom to their own apartment." So the servitor did his bidding in an eye glance and bore away the pair and placed them in the palace as whilom they were and without their seeing anyone. But both died of affright when they found themselves being transported from stead to stead. And the Marid had barely time to set them down and wend his ways ere the Sultan came on a visit of congratulation to his daughter. And when the Wazir's son heard the doors thrown open, he sprang straightway from his couch and donned his dress, for he knew that none save the King could enter at that hour. Yet it was exceedingly hard for him to leave his bed, wherein he wished to warm himself a trifle after his cold night in the watercloset which he had lately left. The Sultan went in to his daughter, Badr al-Budur, and, kissing her between the eyes, gave her good morning and asked her of her bridegroom and whether she was pleased and satisfied with him. But she returned no reply whatever and looked at him with the eye of anger, and although he repeated his words again and again, she held her peace, nor bespake him with a single syllable.

So the King quitted her and, going to the Queen, informed her of what had taken place between him and his daughter, and the mother, unwilling to leave the Sultan angered with their child, said to him: "O King of the Age, this be the custom of most newly married couples, at least during their first days of marriage, for that they are bashful and somewhat coy. So deign thou excuse her, and after a little while she will again become herself and speak with the folk as before, whereas now her shame, O King of the Age, keepeth her silent. However, 'tis my wish to fare forth and see her." Thereupon the Queen arose and donned her dress, then, going to her daughter, wished her good morning and kissed her between the eyes. Yet would the Princess make no answer at all, whereat quoth the Queen to herself: "Doubtless some strange matter hath occurred to trouble her with such trouble as this." So she asked her, saying: "O my daughter, what hath caused this thy case? Let me know what hath betided thee that when I come and give thee good morning, thou hast not a word to say to me." Thereat the Lady Badr al-Budur raised her head and said: "Pardon me, O my mother, 'twas my duty to meet thee with all respect and worship, seeing that thou hast honored me by this visit. However, I pray thee to hear the cause of this my condition and see how the night I have just spent hath been to me the evilest of the nights. Hardly had we lain down, O my mother, than one whose form I wot not uplifted our bed and transported it to a darksome place, fulsome and mean."

Then the Princess related to the Queen Mother all that had befallen her that night—how they had taken away her bridegroom, leaving her lone and lonesome, and how after a while came another youth who lay beside her in lieu of her bridegroom, after placing his scimitar between her and himself. "And in the morning," she continued, "he who carried us off returned and bore us straight back to our own stead. But at once when he arrived hither he left us, and suddenly my sire, the Sultan, entered at the hour and moment of our coming and I had nor heart nor tongue to speak him withal, for the stress of the terror and trembling which came upon me. Haply such lack of duty may have proved sore to him, so I hope, O my mother, that thou wilt acquaint him with the cause of this my condition, and that he will pardon me for not answering him and blame me not, but rather accept my excuses."

When the Queen heard these words of Princess Badr al-Budur,

she said to her: "O my child, compose thy thoughts. An thou tell such tale before any, haply shall he say, 'Verily, the Sultan's daughter hath lost her wits.' And thou hast done right well in not choosing to recount thine adventure to thy father, and beware, and again I say beware, O my daughter, lest thou inform him thereof." The Princess replied: "O my mother, I have spoken to thee like one sound in senses, nor have I lost my wits. This be what befell me, and if thou believe it not because coming from me, ask my bridegroom." To which the Queen replied: "Rise up straightway, O my daughter, and banish from thy thoughts such fancies as these. And robe thyself and come forth to glance at the bridal feasts and festivities they are making in the city for the sake of thee and thy nuptials, and listen to the drumming and the singing and look at the decorations all intended to honor thy marriage, O my daughter."

So saying, the Queen at once summoned the tirewoman, who dressed and prepared the Lady Badr al-Budur, and presently she went in to the Sultan and assured him that their daughter had suffered during all her wedding night from swevens and nightmare, and said to him, "Be not severe with her for not answering thee." Then the Queen sent privily for the Wazir's son and asked of the matter, saying, "Tell me, are these words of the Lady Badr al-Budur soothfast or not?" But he, in his fear of losing his bride out of hand, answered, "O my lady, I have no knowledge of that whereof thou speakest." Accordingly the mother made sure that her daughter had seen visions and dreams. The marriage feasts lasted throughout that day with almes and singers and the smiting of all manner instruments of mirth and merriment, while the Queen and the Wazir and his son strave right strenuously to enhance the festivities that the Princess might enjoy herself. And that day they left nothing of what exciteth to pleasure unrepresented in her presence, to the end that she might forget what was in her thoughts and derive increase of joyance.

Yet did naught of this take any effect upon her—nay, she sat in silence, sad of thought, sore perplexed at what had befallen her during the last night. It is true that the Wazir's son had suffered even more because he had passed his sleeping hours lying in the watercloset. He, however, had falsed the story and had cast out remembrance of the night, in the first place for his fear of losing his bride and with her the honor of a connection which brought him such excess of consideration and for which men envied him so much, and secondly, on account of the wondrous loveliness of the Lady Badr al-Budur and her marvelous beauty.

Aladdin also went forth that day and looked at the merrymakings, which extended throughout the city as well as the palace, and he fell a-laughing, especially when he heard the folk prating of the high honor which had accrued to the son of the Wazir and the prosperity of his fortunes in having become son-in-law to the Sultan, and the high consideration shown by the wedding fêtes. And he said in his mind: "Indeed ye wot not, O ye miserables, what befell him last night, that ye envy him!" But after darkness fell and it was time for sleep, Aladdin arose and, retiring to his chamber, rubbed the lamp, whereupon the slave incontinently appeared and was bidden to bring him the Sultan's daughter, together with her bridegroom, as on the past night, ere the Wazir's son could abate her maidenhead. So the Marid without stay or delay evanished for a little while until the appointed time, when he returned carrying the bed whereon lay the Lady Badr al-Budur and the Wazir's son. And he did with the bridegroom as he had done before; to wit, he took him and laid him at full length in the jakes and there left him dried-up for excess of fear and trembling. Then Aladdin arose and, placing the scimitar between himself and the Princess, lay down beside her, and when day broke the slave restored the pair to their own place, leaving Aladdin filled with delight at the state of the Minister's son.

Now when the Sultan woke up a-morn, he resolved to visit his daughter and see if she would treat him as on the past day. So, shaking off his sleep, he sprang up and arrayed himself in his raiment, and going to the apartment of the Princess, bade open the door. Thereat the son of the Wazir arose forthright and came down from his bed and began donning his dress whilst his ribs were wrung with cold. For when the King entered the slave had but just brought him back. The Sultan, raising the arras, drew near his daughter as she lay abed and gave her good morning. Then, kissing her between the eyes, he asked her of her case. But he saw her looking sour and sad, and she answered him not at all, only glowering at him as one in anger, and her plight was pitiable. Hereat the Sultan waxed wroth with her for that she would not reply, and he suspected that something evil had befallen her, whereupon he bared his blade and cried to her, brand in hand, saying: "What be this hath betided thee? Either acquaint me with what happened or this very moment I will take thy life! Is such conduct the token of honor and respect I expect of thee, that I address thee and thou answerest me not a word?"

When the Lady Badr al-Budur saw her sire in high dudgeon and the naked glaive in his grip, she was freed from her fear of the past, so she raised her head and said to him: "O my beloved father, be not wroth with me, nor be hasty in thy hot passion, for I am excusable in what thou shalt see of my case. So do thou lend an ear to what occurred to me, and well I wot that after hearing my account of what befell to me during these two last nights, thou wilt pardon me, and thy Highness will be softened to pitying me even as I claim of thee affection for thy child." Then the Princess informed her father of all that had betided her, adding: "O my sire, an thou believe me not, ask my bridegroom and he will recount to thy Highness the whole adventure. Nor did I know either what they would do with him when they bore him away from my side or where they would place him." When the Sultan heard his daughter's words, he was saddened and his eyes brimmed with tears, then he sheathed his saber and kissed her, saying: "O my daughter, wherefore didst thou not tell me what happened on the past night, that I might have guarded thee from this torture and terror which visited thee a second time? But now 'tis no matter. Rise and cast out all such care, and tonight I will set a watch to ward thee, nor shall any mishap again make thee miserable."

Then the Sultan returned to his palace and straightway bade summon the Grand Wazir and asked him as he stood before him in his service: "O Wazir, how dost thou look upon this matter? Haply thy son hath informed thee of what occurred to him and to my daughter." The Minister replied, "O King of the Age, I have not seen my son or yesterday or today." Hereat the Sultan told him all that had afflicted the Princess, adding: "'Tis my desire that thou at once seek tidings of thy son concerning the facts of the case. Peradventure of her fear my daughter may not be fully aware of what really befell her, withal I hold all her words to be truthful." So the Grand Wazir arose, and going forth, bade summon his son and asked him anent all his lord had told him whether it be true or untrue. The youth replied: "O my father the Wazir, Heaven forbid that the Lady Badr al-Budur speak falsely. Indeed all she said was sooth, and these two nights proved to us the evilest of our nights instead of being nights of pleasure and marriage joys. But what befell me was the greater evil, because instead of sleeping abed with my bride, I lay in the wardrobe, a black hole, frightful, noisome of stench, truly damnable, and my ribs were bursten with cold." In fine, the young man told his father the whole tale, adding as he ended it: "O dear father mine, I implore thee to speak with the Sultan that he may set me free from this marriage. Yes, indeed 'tis a high honor for me to be the Sultan's son-in-law, and especially the love of the Princess hath gotten hold of my vitals, but I have no strength left to endure a single night like unto these two last."

The Wazir, hearing the words of his son, was saddened and sorrowful exceedingly, for it was his design to advance and promote his child by making him son-in-law to the Sultan. So he became thoughtful and perplexed about the affair and the device whereby to manage it, and it was sore grievous for him to break off the marriage, it having been a rare enjoyment to him that he had fallen upon such high good fortune. Accordingly he said: "Take patience, O my son, until we see what may happen this night, when we will set watchmen to ward you. Nor do thou give up the exalted distinction which hath fallen to none save to thyself." Then the Wazir left him and, returning to the sovereign, reported that all told to him by the Lady Badr al-Budur was a true tale. Whereupon quoth the Sultan, "Since the affair is on this wise, we require no delay," and he at once ordered all the rejoicings to cease and the marriage to be broken off. This caused the folk and the citizens to marvel at the matter, especially when they saw the Grand Wazir and his son leaving the palace in pitiable plight for grief and stress of passion, and the people fell to asking, "What hath happened, and what is the cause of the wedding being made null and void?"

Nor did any know aught of the truth save Aladdin, the lover who claimed the Princess's hand, and he laughed in his sleeve. But even after the marriage was dissolved, the Sultan forgot nor even recalled to mind his promise made to Aladdin's mother, and the same was the case with the Grand Wazir, while neither had any inkling of whence befell them that which had befallen. So Aladdin patiently awaited the lapse of the three months after which the Sultan had pledged himself to give him to wife his daughter. But soon as ever the term came, he sent his mother to the Sultan for the purpose of requiring him to keep his covenant. So she went to the palace, and when the King appeared in the Divan and saw the old woman standing before him, he remembered his promise to her concerning the marriage after a term of three months, and he turned to the Minister and said: "O Wazir, this be the ancient dame who presented me with the jewels and to whom we pledged our word that when the three months had elapsed we would summon her to our presence before all others." So the Minister went forth and fetched her, and when she went in to the Sultan's presence she saluted him and prayed for his glory and permanence of prosperity. Hereat the King asked her if she needed aught, and she answered: "O King of the Age, the three months' term thou assignedst to me is finished, and this is thy time to marry my son Aladdin with thy daughter, the Lady Badr al-Budur."

The Sultan was distraught at this demand, especially when he saw the old woman's pauper condition, one of the meanest of her kind, and yet the offering she had brought to him was of the most magnificent, far beyond his power to pay the price. Accordingly he turned to the Grand Wazir and said: "What device is there with thee? In very sooth I did pass my word, yet meseemeth that they be pauper folk, and not persons of high condition." The Grand Wazir, who was dying of envy and who was especially saddened by what had befallen his son, said to himself, "How shall one like this wed the King's daughter and my son lose this highmost honor?" Accordingly he answered his sovereign, speaking privily: "O my lord, 'tis an easy matter to keep off a poor devil such as this, for he is not worthy that thy Highness give his daughter to a fellow whom none knoweth what he may be." "By what means," inquired the Sultan, "shall we put off the man when I pledged my promise, and the word of the kings is their bond?" Replied the Wazir: "O my lord, my rede is that thou demand of him forty platters made of pure sand gold and full of gems (such as the woman brought thee aforetime), with forty white slave girls to carry the platters and forty black eunuch slaves." The King rejoined: "By Allah, O Wazir, thou hast spoken to the purpose, seeing that such thing is not possible, and by this way we shall be freed."

Then quoth he to Aladdin's mother: "Do thou go and tell thy son that I am a man of my word even as I plighted it to him, but on condition that he have power to pay the dower of my daughter. And that which I require of him is a settlement consisting of twoscore platters of virgin gold, all brimming with gems the like of those thou broughtest to me, and as many white handmaids to carry them and twoscore black eunuch slaves to serve and escort the bearers. An thy son avail hereto, I will marry him with my daughter." Thereupon she returned home wagging her head and saying in her mind: "Whence can my poor boy procure these platters and such jewels? And granted that he return to the enchanted treasury and pluck them from the trees—which, however, I hold impossible—yet given that he bring them, whence shall he come by the girls and the blacks?" Nor did she leave communing with herself till she reached her home, where she found Aladdin awaiting her, and she lost no time in saying: "O my son, did I not tell thee never to fancy that thy power would extend to the Lady Badr al-Budur, and that such a matter is not possible to folk like ourselves?"

"Recount to me the news," quoth he, so quoth she: "O my child, verily the Sultan received me with all honor according to his custom, and meseemeth his intentions toward us be friendly. But thine enemy is that accursed Wazir, for after I addressed the King in thy name as thou badest me say, 'In very sooth the promised term is past,' adding, ' 'Twere well an thy Highness would deign issue commandment for the espousals of thy daughter the Lady Badr al-Budur to my son Aladdin,' he turned to and addressed the Minister, who answered privily, after which the Sultan gave me his reply." Then she enumerated the King's demand and said: "O my son, he indeed expecteth of thee an instant reply, but I fancy that we have no answer for him." When Aladdin heard these words, he laughed and said: "O my mother, thou affirmest that we have no answer and thou deemest the case difficult exceedingly, but compose thy thoughts and arise and bring me somewhat we may eat. And after we have dined, an the Compassionate be willing, thou shalt see my reply. Also the Sultan thinketh like thyself that he hath demanded a prodigious dower in order to divert me from his daughter, whereas the fact is that he hath required of me a matter far less than I expected. But do thou fare forth at once and purchase the provision and leave me to procure thee a reply."

So she went out to fetch her needful from the bazaar and Aladdin retired to his chamber and, taking the lamp, rubbed it, when forthright appeared to him its slave and said, "Ask, O my lord, whatso thou wantest." The other replied: "I have demanded of the Sultan his daughter to wife, and he hath required of me forty bowls of purest gold each weighing ten pounds and all to be filled with gems such as we find in the gardens of the hoard; furthermore, that they be borne on the heads of as many white handmaids, each attended by her black eunuch slave, also forty in full rate. So I desire that thou bring all these into my presence." "Hearkening and obeying, O my lord," quoth the slave and, disappearing for the space of an hour or so, presently returned bringing the platters and jewels, handmaids and eunuchs. Then, setting them before him, the Marid cried: "This be what thou demandest of me. Declare now an thou want any matter or service other than this." Aladdin rejoined: "I have need of naught else, but an I do, I will summon thee and let thee know."

The slave now disappeared, and after a little while, Aladdin's mother returned home, and on entering the house, saw the blacks and the handmaids. Hereat she wondered and exclaimed, "All this proceedeth from the lamp which Allah perpetuate to my son!" But ere she doffed her mantilla Aladdin said to her: "O my mother, this be thy time. Before the Sultan enter his seraglio palace do thou carry to him what he required, and wend thou with it at once, so may he know that I avail to supply all he wanteth and yet more. Also that he is beguiled by his Grand wazir, and the twain imagined vainly that they would baffle me." Then he arose forthright and opened the house door, when the handmaids and blackamoors paced forth in pairs, each girl with her eunuch besider her, until they crowded the quarter, Aladdin's mother foregoing them. And when the folk of that ward sighted such mighty fine sight and marvelous spectacle, all stood at gaze and they considered the forms and figures of the handmaids, marveling at their beauty and loveliness, for each and every wore robes inwrought with gold and studded with jewels, no dress being worth less than a thousand dinars. They stared as intently at the bowls, and albeit these were covered with pieces of brocade, also orfrayed and dubbed with precious stones, yet the sheen outshot from them dulled the shine of sun.

Then Aladdin's mother walked forward and all the handmaids and eunuchs paced behind her in the best of ordinance and disposition, and the citizens gathered to gaze at the beauty of the damsels, glorifying God the Most Great, until the train reached the palace and entered it accompanied by the tailor's widow. Now when the agas and chamberlains and army officers beheld them, all were seized with surprise, notably by seeing the handmaids, who each and every would ravish the reason of an anchorite. And albeit the royal chamberlains and officials were men of family, the sons of grandees and emirs, yet they could not but especially wonder at the costly dresses of the girls and the platters borne upon their heads, nor could they gaze at them open-eyed by reason of the exceeding brilliance and radiance. Then the nabobs went in and reported to the King, who forthright bade admit them to the presence chamber, and Aladdin's mother went in with them.

When they stood before the Sultan, all saluted him with every sign of respect and worship and prayed for his glory and prosperity. Then they set down from their heads the bowls at his feet and, having removed the brocade covers, rested with arms crossed behind them. The Sultan wondered with exceeding wonder, and was distraught by the beauty of the handmaids and their loveliness, which passed praise. And his wits were wildered when he considered the golden bowls brimful of gems which captured man's vision, and he was perplexed at the marvel until he became like the dumb, unable to utter a syllable for the excess of his wonder. Also his sense was stupefied the more when he bethought him that within an hour or so all these treasures had been collected. Presently he commanded the slave girls to enter, with what loads they bore, the dower of the Princess, and when they had done his bidding, Aladdin's mother came forward and said to the Sultan: "O my lord, this be not much wherewith to honor the Lady Badr al-Budur, for that she meriteth these things multiplied times manifold."

Hereat the sovereign turned to the Minister and asked: "What sayest thou, O Wazir? Is not he who could produce such wealth in a time so brief, is he not, I say, worthy to become the Sultan's son-in-law and take the King's daughter to wife?" Then the Minister (although he marveled at these riches even more than did the Sultan), whose envy was killing him and growing greater hour by hour, seeing his liege lord satisfied with the moneys and the dower and yet being unable to fight against fact, made answer, " 'Tis not worthy of her." Withal he fell to devising a device against the King, that he might withhold the Lady Badr al-Budur from Aladdin, and accordingly he continued: "O my liege, the treasures of the universe all of them are not worth a nail paring of thy daughter. Indeed thy Highness hath prized these things overmuch in comparison with her."

When the King heard the words of his Grand Wazir, he knew that the speech was prompted by excess of envy, so, turning to the mother of Aladdin, he said: "O woman, go to thy son and tell him that I have accepted of him the dower and stand to my bargain, and that my daughter be his bride and he my son-in-law. Furthermore, bid him at once make act of presence that I may become familiar with him. He shall see naught from me save all honor and consideration, and this night shall be the beginning of the marriage festivities. Only, as I said to thee, let him come to me and tarry not." Thereupon Aladdin's mother returned home with the speed of the storm winds that she might hasten her utmost to congratulate her son, and she flew with joy at the thought that her boy was about to become son-in-law to the Sultan.

After her departure the King dismissed the Divan and, entering the palace of the Princess, bade them bring the bowls and the handmaids before him and before her, that she also might inspect them. But when the Lady Badr al-Budur considered the jewels, she waxed distraught and cried: "Meseemeth that in the treasuries of the world there be not found one jewel rivaling these jewels." Then she looked at the handmaids and marveled at their beauty and loveliness, and knew that all this came from her new bridegroom, who had sent them in her service. So she was gladdened, albeit she had been grieved and saddened on account of her former husband, the Wazir's son, and she rejoiced with exceeding joy when she gazed upon the damsels and their charms. Nor was her sire, the Sultan, less pleased and inspirited when he saw his daughter relieved of all her mourning and melancholy, and his own vanished at the sight of her enjoyment. Then he asked her: "O my daughter, do these things divert thee? Indeed I deem that this suitor of thine be more suitable to thee than the son of the Wazir, and right soon, Inshallah! O my daughter, thou shalt have fuller joy with him."

Such was the case with the King, but as regards Aladdin, as soon as he saw his mother entering the house with face laughing for stress of joy he rejoiced at the sign of glad tidings and cried: "To Allah alone be lauds! Perfected is all I desired." Rejoined his mother: "Be gladdened at my good news, O my son, and hearten thy heart and cool thine eyes for the winning of thy wish. The Sultan hath accepted thine offering—I mean the moneys and the dower of the Lady Badr al-Budur, who is now thine affianced bride. And this very night, O my child, is your marriage and thy first visit to her, for the King, that he might assure me of his word, hath proclaimed to the world thou art his son-in-law, and promised this night to be the night of going in. But he also said to me, 'Let thy son come hither forthright that I may become familiar with him and receive him with all honor and worship.' And now here am I, O my son, at the end of my labors. Happen whatso may happen, the rest is upon thy shoulders."

Thereupon Aladdin arose and kissed his mother's hand and thanked her, enhancing her kindly service. Then he left her and, entering his chamber, took the lamp and rubbed it, when, lo and behold! its slave appeared and cried: "Adsum! Ask whatso thou wantest." The young man replied: "'Tis my desire that thou take me to a hammam whose like is not in the world. Then fetch me a dress so costly and kingly that no royalty ever owned its fellow." The Marid replied, "I hear and I obey," and carried him to baths such as were never seen by the Kings of the Chosroes, for the building was all of alabaster and carnelian, and it contained marvelous limnings which captured the sight, and the great hall was studded with precious stones. Not a soul was therein, but when Aladdin entered, one of the Jann in human shape washed him and bathed him to the best of his desire. Aladdin, after having been washed and bathed, left the baths and went into the great hall, where he found that his old dress had been removed and replaced by a suit of the most precious and princely. Then he was served with sherbets and ambergrised coffee, and after drinking he arose and a party of black slaves came forward and clad him in the costliest of clothing, then perfumed and fumigated him. It is known that Aladdin was the son of a tailor, a pauper, yet now would none deem him to be such—nay, all would say: "This be the greatest that is of the progeny of the kings. Praise be to Him Who changeth and Who is not changed!"

Presently came the Jinni and, lifting him up, bore him to his home, and asked, "O my lord, tell me, hast thou aught of need?" He answered: "Yes, 'tis my desire that thou bring me eight and forty Mamelukes, of whom two dozen shall forego me and the rest follow me, the whole number with their war chargers and clothing and accouterments. And all upon them and their steeds must be of naught save of highest worth and the costliest, such as may not be found in treasuries of the kings. Then fetch me a stallion fit for the riding of the Chosroes and let his furniture, all thereof, be of gold crusted with the finest gems. Fetch me also eight and forty thousand dinars, that each white slave may carry a thousand gold pieces. 'Tis now my intent to fare to the Sultan, so delay thou not, for that without all these requisites whereof I bespake thee I may no visit him. Moreover, set before me a dozen slave girls unique in beauty and dight with the most magnificent dresses, that they wend with my mother to the royal palace, and let every handmaid be robed in raiment that befitteth Queen's wearing." The slave replied, "To hear is to obey," and, disappearing for an eye twinkling, brought all he was bidden bring, and led by hand a stallion whose rival was not amongst the Arabian Arabs, and its saddlecloth was of splendid brocade gold-inwrought.

Thereupon, without stay or delay, Aladdin sent for his mother and gave her the garments she should wear and committed to her charge the twelve slave girls forming her suite to the palace. Then he sent one of the Mamelukes whom the Jinni had brought to see if the Sultan had left the seraglio or not. The white slave went forth lighter than the lightning and, returning in like haste, said, "O my lord, the Sultan awaiteth thee!" Hereat Aladdin arose and took horse, his Mamelukes riding a-van and arear of him, and they were such that all must cry, "Laud to the Lord Who created them and clothed them with such beauty and loveliness!" And they scattered gold amongst the crowd in front of their master, who surpassed them all in comeliness and seemlihed, nor needest thou ask concerning the sons of the kings— praise be to the Bountiful, the Eternal! All this was of the virtues of the wonderful lamp, which whoso possessed, him it gifted with fairest favor and finest figure, with wealth and with wisdom. The folk admired Aladdin's liberality and exceeding generosity, and all were distraught seeing his charms and elegance, his gravity and his good manners. They glorified the Creator for this noble creation, they blessed him each and every, and albeit they knew him for the son of Such-a-one, the tailor, yet no man envied him—nay, all owned that he deserved his great good fortune.

Now the Sultan had assembled the lords of the land and, informing them of the promise he had passed to Aladdin touching the marriage of his daughter, had bidden them await his approach and then go forth, one and all, to meet him and greet him. Hereupon the emirs and wazirs, the chamberlains, the nabobs and the army officers, took their stations expecting him at the palace gate. Aladdin would fain have dismounted at the outer entrance, but one of the nobles, whom the King had deputed for such duty, approached him and said,

"O my lord, 'tis the royal command that thou enter riding thy steed, nor dismount except at the Divan door." Then they all forewent him in a body and conducted him to the appointed place, where they crowded about him, these to hold his stirrup and those supporting him on either side whilst others took him by the hands and helped him dismount. After which all the emirs and nobles preceded him into the Divan and led him close up to the royal throne.

Thereupon the Sultan came down forthright from his seat of estate and, forbidding him to buss the carpet, embraced and kissed and seated him to the right of and beside himself. Aladdin did whatso is suitable in the case of the kings of salutation and offering of blessings, and said: "O our lord the Sultan, indeed the generosity of thy Highness demanded that thou deign vouchsafe to me the hand of thy daughter, the Lady Badr al-Budur, albeit I undeserve the greatness of such gift, I being but the humblest of thy slaves. I pray Allah grant thee prosperity and perpetuance, but in very sooth, O King, my tongue is helpless to thank thee for the fullness of the favor, passing all measure, which thou hast bestowed upon me. And I hope of thy Highness that thou wilt give me a piece of ground fitted for a pavilion which shall besit thy daughter, the Lady Badr al-Budur." The Sultan was struck with admiration when he saw Aladdin in his princely suit and looked upon him and considered his beauty and loveliness, and noted the Mamelukes standing to serve him in their comeliness and seemlihed. And still his marvel grew when the mother of Aladdin approached him in costly raiment and sumptuous, clad as though she were a queen, and when he gazed upon the twelve handmaids standing before her with crossed arms and with all worship and reverence doing her service. He also considered the eloquence of Aladdin and his delicacy of speech, and he was astounded thereat, he and all his who were present at the levee.

Thereupon fire was kindled in the Grand Wazir's heart for envy of Aladdin until he was like to die. And it was worse when the Sultan, after hearing the youth's succession of prayers and seeing his high dignity of demeanor, respectful withal, and his eloquence and elegance of language, clasped him to his bosom and kissed him and cried, "Alas, O my son, that I have not enjoyed thy converse before this day!" He rejoiced in him with mighty great joy and straightway bade the music and the bands strike up. Then he arose and taking the youth, led him into the palace, where supper had been prepared, and the eunuchs at once laid the tables. So the sovereign sat down and seated his son-in-law on his right side, and the wazirs and high officials and lords of the land took places each according to his degree, whereupon the bands played and a mighty fine marriage feast was dispread in the palace. The King now applied himself to making friendship with Aladdin and conversed with the youth, who answered him with all courtesy and eloquence, as though he had been bred in the palaces of the kings or he had lived with them his daily life. And the more the talk was prolonged between them, the more did the Sultan's pleasure and delight increase, hearing his son-in-law's readiness of reply and his sweet flow of language.

But after they had eaten and drunken and the trays were removed, the King bade summon the kazis and witnesses, who presently attended and knitted the knot and wrote out the contract writ between Aladdin and the Lady Badr al-Budur. And presently the bridegroom arose and would have fared forth, when his father-in-law withheld him and asked: "Whither away, O my child? The bride fêtes have begun and the marriage is made and the tie is tied and the writ is written." He replied: "O my lord the King, 'tis my desire to edify, for the Lady Badr al-Budur, a pavilion befitting her station and high degree, nor can I visit her before so doing. But, Inshallah! the building shall be finished within the shortest time, by the utmost endeavor of thy slave and by the kindly regard of thy Highness. And although I do (yes indeed!) long to enjoy the society of the Lady Badr al-Budur, yet 'tis incumbent of me first to serve her, and it becometh me to set about the work forthright." "Look around thee, O my son," replied the Sultan, "for what ground thou deemest suitable to thy design, and do thou take all things into thy hands. But I deem the best for thee will be yonder broad plain facing my palace, and if it please thee, build thy pavilion thereupon." "And this," answered Aladdin, "is the sum of my wishes, that I may be near-hand to thy Highness."

So saying, he farewelled the King and took horse, with his Mamelukes riding before him and behind him, and all the world blessed him and cried, "By Allah he is deserving," until such time as he reached his home. Then he alighted from his stallion and repairing to his chamber, rubbed the lamp and behold, the slave stood before him and said, "Ask, O my lord, whatso thou wantest," and Aladdin rejoined: "I require thee of a service grave and important which thou must do for me, and 'tis that thou build me with all urgency a pavilion fronting the palace of the Sultan. And it must be a marvel for it shall be provided with every requisite, such as royal furniture and so forth." The slave replied, "To hear is to obey," and evanished, and before the next dawn brake returned to Aladdin and said: "O my lord, the pavilion is finished to the fullest of thy fancy, and if thou wouldst inspect it, arise forthright and fare with me."

Accordingly he rose up, and the slave carried him in the space of an eye glance to the pavilion, which when Aladdin looked upon it struck him with surprise at such building, all its stones being of jasper and alabaster, Sumaki marble and mosaicwork. Then the slave led him into the treasury, which was full of all manner of gold and silver and costly gems, not to be counted or computed, priced or estimated. Thence to another place, where Aladdin saw all requisites for the table, plates and dishes, spoons and ladles, basins and covers, cups and tasses, the whole of precious metal. Thence to the kitchen, where they found the kitcheners provided with their needs and cooking batteries, likewise golden and silvern. Thence to a warehouse piled up with chests full-packed of royal raiment, stuffs that captured the reason, such as gold-wrought brocades from India and China and kimcobs or orfrayed cloths. Thence to many apartments replete with appointments which beggar description. Thence to the stables containing coursers whose like was not to be met with amongst the kings of the universe. And lastly they went to the harness rooms all hung with housings, costly saddles, and other furniture, everywhere studded with pearls and precious stones. And all this was the work of one night.

Aladdin was wonder-struck and astounded by that magnificent display of wealth, which not even the mightiest monarch on earth could produce, and more so to see his pavilion fully provided with eunuchs and handmaids whose beauty would seduce a saint. Yet the prime marvel of the pavilion was an upper kiosque or belvedere of four and twenty windows all made of emeralds and rubies and other gems, and one window remained unfinished at the requirement of Aladdin, that the Sultan might prove him impotent to complete it. When the youth had inspected the whole edifice, he was pleased and gladdened exceedingly. Then, turning to the slave, he said: "I require of thee still one thing which is yet wanting and whereof I had forgotten to tell thee." "Ask, O my lord, thy want," quoth the servitor, and quoth the other: "I demand of thee a carpet of the primest brocade all gold-inwrought which, when unrolled and outstretched, shall extend hence to the Sultan's palace, in order that the Lady Badr al-Budur may, when coming hither, pace upon it and not tread common earth." The slave departed for a short while and said on his return, "O my lord, verily that which thou demandest is here." Then he took him and showed him a carpet, which wildered the wits, and it extended from palace to pavilion. And after this the servitor bore off Aladdin and set him down in his own home.

Now day was brightening, so the Sultan rose from his sleep and throwing open the casement, looked out and espied opposite his palace a palatial pavilion ready edified. Thereupon he fell to rubbing his eyes and opening them their widest and considering the scene, and he soon was certified that the new edifice was mighty fine, and grand enough to bewilder the wits. Moreover, with amazement as great he saw the carpet dispread between palace and pavilion. Like their lord, also the royal doorkeepers and the household, one and all, were dazed and amazed at the spectacle. Meanwhile the Wazir came in, and as he entered, espied the newly built pavilion and the carpet, whereat he also wondered. And when he went in to the Sultan, the twain fell to talking on this marvelous matter with great surprise at a sight which distracted the gazer and attracted the heart. They said finally, "In very truth, of this pavilion we deem that none of the royalties could build its fellow," and the King, turning to the Minister, asked him: "Hast thou seen now that Aladdin is worthy to be the husband of the Princess, my daughter? Hast thou looked upon and considered this right royal building, this magnificence of opulence, which thought of man cannot contain?" But the Wazir in his envy of Aladdin replied: "O King of the Age, indeed this foundation and this building and this opulence may not be save by means of magic, nor can any man in the world, be he the richest in good or the greatest in governance, avail to found and finish in a single night such edifice as this." The Sultan rejoined: "I am surprised to see in thee how thou dost continually harp on evil opinion of Aladdin, but I hold that 'tis caused by thine envy and jealousy. Thou wast present when I gave him the ground at his own prayer for a place whereon he might build a pavilion wherein to lodge my daughter, and I myself favored him with a site for the same, and that too before thy very face. But however that be, shall one who could send me as dower for the Princess such store of such stones whereof the kings never obtained even a few, shall he, I say, be unable to edify an edifice like this?" When the Wazir heard the Sultan's words, he knew that his lord loved Aladdin exceedingly, so his envy and malice increased. Only, as he could do nothing against the youth, he sat silent, and impotent to return a reply.

But Aladdin, seeing that it was broad day and the appointed time had come for his repairing to the palace (where his wedding was being celebrated and the emirs and wazirs and grandees were gathered together about the Sultan to be present at the ceremony), arose and rubbed the lamp, and when its slave appeared and said, "O my lord, ask whatso thou wantest, for I stand before thee and at thy service," said he: "I mean forthright to seek the palace, this day being my wedding festival, and I want thee to supply me with ten thousand dinars." The slave evanished for an eye twinkling and returned bringing the moneys, when Aladdin took horse with his Mamelukes a-van and arear and passed on his way, scattering as he went gold pieces upon the lieges until all were fondly affected toward him and his dignity was enhanced. But when he drew near the palace, and the emirs and agas and army officers who were standing to await him noted his approach, they hastened straightway to the King and gave him the tidings thereof, whereupon the Sultan rose and met his son-in-law and, after embracing and kissing him, led him, still holding his hand, into his own apartment, where he sat down and seated him by his right side.

The city was all decorated and music rang through the palace and the singers sang until the King bade bring the noon meal, when the eunuchs and Mamelukes hastened to spread the tables and trays which are such as are served to the kings. Then the Sultan and Aladdin and the lords of the land and the grandees of the realm took their seats and ate and drank until they were satisfied. And it was a mighty fine wedding in city and palace, and the high nobles all rejoiced therein and the commons of the kingdom were equally gladdened, while the governors of provinces and nabobs of districts flocked from far regions to witness Aladdin's marriage and its processions and festivities. The Sultan also marveled in his mind to look at Aladdin's mother and recall to mind how she was wont to visit him in pauper plight while her son could command all this opulence and magnificence. And when the spectators who crowded the royal palace to enjoy the wedding feasts looked upon Aladdin's pavilion and the beauties of the building, they were seized with an immense surprise that so vast an edifice as this could be reared on high during a single night, and they blessed the youth and cried: "Allah gladden him: By Allah, he deserveth all this! Allah bless his days!"

When dinner was done, Aladdin rose and, farewelling the Sultan, took horse with his Mamelukes and rode to his own pavilion, that he might prepare to receive therein his bride, the Lady Badr al-Budur. And as he passed, all the folk shouted their good wishes with one voice and their words were: "Allah gladden thee! Allah increase thy glory! Allah grant thee length of life!" while immense crowds of people gathered to swell the marriage procession, and they conducted him to his new home, he showering gold upon them during the whole time. When he reached his pavilion, he dismounted and walked in and sat him down on the divan, whilst his Mamelukes stood before him with arms afolded. Also after a short delay they brought him sherbets, and when these were drunk, he ordered his white slaves and handmaids and eunuchs and all who were in the pavilion to make ready for meeting the Lady Badr al-Budur. Moreover, as soon as midafternoon came and the air had cooled and the great heat of the sun was abated, the Sultan bade his army officers and emirs and wazirs go down into the maydan plain, whither he likewise rode. And Aladdin also took horse with his Mamelukes, he mounting a stallion whose like was not among the steeds of the Arab al-Arba, and he showed his horsemanship in the hippodrome, and so played with the jarid that none could withstand him, while his bride sat gazing upon him from the latticed balcony of her bower and, seeing in him such beauty and cavalarice, she fell headlong in love of him and was like to fly for joy. And after they had ringed their horses on the maydan and each had displayed whatso he could of horsemanship, Aladdin proving himself the best man of all, they rode in a body to the Sultan's palace and the youth also returned to his own pavilion.

But when it was evening, the wazirs and nobles took the bridegroom and, falling in, escorted him to the royal hammam (known as the Sultani), when he was bathed and perfumed. As soon as he came out he donned a dress more magnificent than the former and took horse with the emirs and the soldier officers riding before him and forming a grand cortège, wherein four of the wazirs bore naked swords round about him. All the citizens and the strangers and the troops marched before him in ordered throng carrying wax candles and kettledrums and pipes and other instruments of mirth and merriment, until they conducted him to his pavilion. Here he alighted and, walking in, took his seat and seated the wazirs and emirs who had escorted him, and the Mamelukes brought sherbets and sugared drinks, which they also passed to the people who had followed in his train. It was a world of folk whose tale might not be told. Withal Aladdin bade his Mamelukes stand without the pavilion doors and shower gold upon the crowd.

When the Sultan returned from the maydan plain to his palace, he ordered the household, men as well as women, straightway to form a cavalcade for his daughter, with all ceremony, and bear her to her bridegroom's pavilion. So the nobles and soldier officers who had followed and escorted the bridegroom at once mounted, and the handmaids and eunuchs went forth with wax candles and made a mighty fine procession for the Lady Badr al-Budur, and they paced on preceding her till they entered the pavilion of Aladdin, whose mother walked beside the bride. In front of the Princess also fared the wives of the wazirs and emirs, grandees and notables, and in attendance on her were the eight and forty slave girls presented to her aforetime by her bridegroom, each hending in hand a huge cierge scented with camphor and ambergris and set in a candlestick of gem-studded gold. And reaching Aladdin's pavilion, they led her to her bower in the upper story and changed her robes and enthroned her. Then, as soon as the displaying was ended, they accompanied her to Aladdin's apartments, and presently he paid her the first visit. Now his mother was with the bride, and when the bridegroom came up and did off her veil, the ancient dame fell to considering the beauty of the Princess and her loveliness, and she looked around at the pavilion, which was all litten up by gold and gems besides the manifold candelabra of precious metals encrusted with emeralds and jacinths, so she said in her mind: "Once upon a time I thought the Sultan's palace mighty fine, but this pavilion is a thing apart. Nor do I deem that any of the greatest kings of Chosroes attained in his day to aught like thereof. Also am I certified that all the world could not build anything evening it." Nor less did the Lady Badr al-Budur fall to gazing at the pavilion and marveling for its magnificence.

Then the tables were spread and they all ate and drank and were gladdened, after which fourscore damsels came before them, each holding in hand an instrument of mirth and merriment. Then they deftly moved their finger tips and touched the strings, smiting them into song most musical, most melancholy, till they rent the hearts of the hearers. Hereat the Princess increased in marvel, and quoth she to herself, "In all my life ne'er heard I songs like these," till she forsook food, the better to listen. And at last Aladdin poured out for her wine and passed it to her with his own hand. So great joy and jubilee went round amongst them, and it was a notable night, such a one as Iskandar, Lord of the Two Horns, had never spent in his time. When they had finished eating and drinking and the tables were removed from before them, Aladdin arose and went in to his bride.

As soon as morning morrowed he left his bed, and the treasurer brought him a costly suit and a mighty fine, of the most sumptuous robes worn by the kings. Then, after drinking coffee flavored with ambergris, he ordered the horses be saddled and, mounting with his Mamelukes before and behind him, rode to the Sultan's palace, and on his entering its court the eunuchs went in and reported his coming to their lord. When the Sultan heard of Aladdin's approach, he rose up forthright to receive him and embraced and kissed him as though he were his own son. Then, seating him on his right, he blessed and prayed for him, as did the wazirs and emirs, the lords of the land and the grandees of the realm. Presently the King commanded bring the morning meal, which the attendants served up, and all broke their fast together, and when they had eaten and drunken their sufficiency and the tables were removed by the eunuchs, Aladdin turned to the Sultan and said: "O my lord, would thy Highness deign honor me this day at dinner in the house of the Lady Badr al-Budur, thy beloved daughter, and come accompanied by all thy Ministers and grandees of the reign?" The King replied (and he was delighted with his son-in-law), "Thou art surpassing in liberality, O my son!"

Then he gave orders to all invited and rode forth with them (Aladdin also riding beside him) till they reached the pavilion, and as he entered it and considered its construction, its architecture and its stonery, all jasper and carnelian, his sight was dazed and his wits were amazed at such grandeur and magnificence of opulence. Then, turning to the Minister, he thus addressed him: "What sayest thou? Tell me, hast thou seen in all thy time aught like this amongst the mighties of earth's monarchs for the abundance of gold and gems we are now beholding?" The Grand Wazir replied: "O my lord the King, this be a feat which cannot be accomplished by might of monarch amongst Adam's sons, nor could the collected peoples of the universal world build a palace like unto this,—nay, even builders could not be found to make aught resembling it, save (as I said to thy Highness) by force of sorcery." These words certified the King that his Minister spake not except in envy and jealousy of Aladdin, and would stablish in the royal mind that all this splendor was not made of man, but by means of magic and with the aid of the black art. So quoth he to him: "Suffice thee so much, O Wazir. Thou hast none other word to speak, and well I know what cause urgeth thee to say this say."

Then Aladdin preceded the Sultan till he conducted him to the upper kiosque, where he saw its skylights, windows, and latticed casements and jalousies wholly made of emeralds and rubies and other costly gems, whereat his mind was perplexed and his wits were bewildered and his thoughts were distraught. Presently he took to strolling round the kiosque and solacing himself with these sights which captured the vision, till he chanced to cast a glance at the window which Aladdin by design had left unwrought and not finished like the rest. And when he noted its lack of completion, he cried, "Woe and wellaway for thee, O window, because of thine imperfection," and, turning to his Minister, he asked, "Knowest thou the reason of leaving incomplete this window and its framework?" The Wazir said: "O my lord, I conceive that the want of finish in this window resulteth from thy Highness having pushed on Aladdin's marriage, and he lacked the leisure to complete it." Now at that time Aladdin had gone in to his bride, the Lady Badr al-Budur, to inform her of her father's presence, and when he returned, the King asked him: "O my son, what is the reason why the window of this kiosque was not made perfect?" "O King of the Age, seeing the suddenness of my wedding," answered he, "I failed to find artists for finishing it." Quoth the Sultan, "I have a mind to complete it myself," and quoth Aladdin: "Allah perpetuate thy glory, O thou the King. So shall thy memory endure in thy daughter's pavilion."

The Sultan forthright bade summon jewelers and goldsmiths, and ordered them be supplied from the treasury with all their needs of gold and gems and noble ores, and when they were gathered together, he commanded them to complete the work still wanting in the kiosque window. Meanwhile the Princess came forth to meet her sire, the Sultan, who noticed as she drew near her smiling face, so he embraced her and kissed her, then led her to the pavilion, and all entered in a body. Now this was the time of the noonday meal and one table had been spread for the sovereign, his daughter, and his son-in-law and a second for the wazirs, the lords of the land, the grandees of the realm, the chief officers of the host, the chamberlains and the nabobs. The King took seat between the Princess and her husband, and when he put forth his hand to the food and tasted it, he was struck with surprise by the flavor of the dishes and their savory and sumptuous cooking. Moreover, there stood before him the fourscore damsels, each and every saying to the full moon, "Rise that I may seat myself in thy stead!" All held instruments of mirth and merriment, and they tuned the same and deftly moved their finger tips and smote the srings into song most musical, most melodious, which expanded the mourner's heart. Hereby the Sultan was gladdened, and time was good to him, and for high enjoyment he exclaimed, "In very sooth the thing is beyond the compass of King and Caesar."

Then they fell to eating and drinking, and the cup went round until they had drunken enough, when sweetmeats and fruits of sorts and other such edibles were served, the dessert being laid out in a different salon, whither they removed and enjoyed of these pleasures their sufficiency. Presently the Sultan arose that he might see if the produce of his jewelers and goldsmiths favored that of the pavilion. So he went upstairs to them and inspected their work and how they had wrought, but he noted a mighty great difference, and his men were far from being able to make anything like the rest of Aladdin's pavilion. They informed him how all the gems stored in the lesser Treasury had been brought to them and used by them, but that the whole had proved insufficient. Wherefor he bade open the greater Treasury, and gave the workmen all they wanted of him. Moreover, he allowed them, an it sufficed not, to take the jewels wherewith Aladdin had gifted him. They carried off the whole and pushed on their labors, but they found the gems fail them, albeit had they not finished half the part wanting to the kiosque window. Herewith the King commanded them to seize all the precious stones owned by the wazirs and grandees of the realm, but although they did his bidding, the supply still fell short of their requirements.

Next morning Aladdin arose to look at the jewelers' work and remarked that they had not finished a moiety of what was wanting to the kiosque window. So he at once ordered them to undo all they had done and restore the jewels to their owners. Accordingly they pulled out the precious stones and sent the Sultan's to the Sultan and the wazirs' to the wazirs. Then the jewelers went to the King and told him of what

Aladdin had bidden, so he asked them: "What said he to you, and what was his reason, and wherefore was he not content that the window be finished, and why did he undo the work ye wrought?" They answered, "O our lord, we know not at all, but he bade us deface whatso we had done." Hereupon the Sultan at once called for his horse, and mounting, took the way pavilionward, when Aladdin, after dismissing the goldsmiths and jewelers had retired into his closet and had rubbed the lamp. Hereat straightway its servitor appeared to him and said: "Ask whatso thou wantest. Thy slave is between thy hands," and said Aladdin, " 'Tis my desire that thou finish the window which was left unfinished." The Marid replied, "On my head be it, and also upon mine eyes!" Then he vanished, and after a little while returned, saying, "O my lord, verily that thou commandedst me do is completed." So Aladdin went upstairs to the kiosque and found the whole window in wholly finished state, and whilst he was still considering it, behold, a castrato came in to him and said: "O my lord, the Sultan hath ridden forth to visit thee and is passing through the pavilion gate."

So Aladdin at once went down and received his father-in-law. The Sultan, on sighting his son-in-law, cried to him: "Wherefore, O my child, hast thou wrought on this wise and sufferedst not the jewelers to complete the kiosque window, leaving in the pavilion an unfinished place?" Aladdin replied: "O King of the Age, I left it not imperfect save for a design of mine own, nor was I incapable of perfecting it, nor could I purpose that thy Highness should honor me with visiting a pavilion wherein was aught of deficiency. And that thou mayest know I am not unable to make it perfect, let thy Highness deign walk upstairs with me and see if anything remain to be done therewith or not." So the Sultan went up with him and, entering the kiosque, fell to looking right and left, but he saw no default at all in any of the windows—nay, he noted that all were perfect. So he marveled at the sight and embraced Aladdin and kissed him, saying: "O my son, what be this singular feat? Thou canst work in a single night what in months the jewelers could not do. By Allah, I deem thou hast nor brother nor rival in this world." Quoth Aladdin: "Allah prolong thy life and preserve thee to perpetuity! Thy slave deserveth not this encomium." And quoth the King: "By Allah, O my child, thou meritest all praise for a feat whereof all the artists of the world were incapable." Then the Sultan came down and entered the apartments of his daughter, the Lady Badr al-Budur, to take rest beside her, and he saw her joyous exceedingly at the glory and grandeur wherein she was. Then, after reposing awhile, he returned to his palace.

Now Aladdin was wont every day to thread the city streets with his Mamelukes riding a-van and arear of him showering rightward and leftward gold upon the folk, and all the world, stranger and neighbor, far and near, were fulfilled of his love for the excess of his liberality and generosity. Moreover, he increased the pensions of the poor Religious and the paupers, and he would distribute alms to them with his own hand, by which good deed he won high renown throughout the realm and most of the lords of the land and emirs would eat at his table, and men swore not at all save by his precious life. Nor did he leave faring to the chase and the maydan plain and the riding of horses and playing at javelin play in presence of the Sultan. And whenever the Lady Badr al-Budur beheld him disporting himself on the backs of steeds, she loved him much the more, and thought to herself that Allah had wrought her abundant good by causing to happen whatso happened with the son of the Wazir and by preserving her virginity intact for her true bridegroom, Aladdin. Aladdin won for himself day by day a fairer fame and a rarer report, while affection for him increased in the hearts of all the lieges and he waxed greater in the eyes of men.

Moreover, it chanced that in those days certain enemies took horse and attacked the Sultan, who armed and accoutered an army to repel them and made Aladdin commander thereof. So he marched with his men, nor ceased marching until he drew near the foe, whose forces were exceeding many, and presently when the action began, he bared his brand and charged home upon the enemy. Then battle and slaughter befell and violent was the hurly-burly, but at last Aladdin broke the hostile host and put all to flight, slaying the best part of them and pillaging their coin and cattle, property and possessions, and he despoiled them of spoils that could not be counted nor computed. Then he returned victorious after a noble victory and entered the capital, which had decorated herself in his honor, of her delight in him. And the Sultan went forth to meet him and giving him joy, embraced him and kissed him. And throughout the kingdom was held high festival with great joy and gladness. Presently the sovereign and his son-in-law repaired to the pavilion, where they were met by the Princess Badr al-Budur, who rejoiced in her husband and, after kissing him between the eyes, led him to her apartments. After a time the Sultan also came and they sat down while the slave girls brought them sherbets and confections, which they ate and drank. Then the Sultan commanded that the whole kingdom be decorated for the triumph of his son-in-law and his victory over the invader, and the subjects and soldiery and all the people knew only Allah in Heaven and Aladdin on earth, for that their love, won by his liberality, was increased by his noble horsemanship and his successful battling for the country and putting to flight the foe.

Such then was the high fortune of Aladdin, but as regards the Maghrabi, the magician, after returning to his native country he passed all this space of time in bewailing what he had borne of toil and travail to win the lamp, and mostly that his trouble had gone vain and that the morsel when almost touching his lips had flown from his grasp. He pondered all this and mourned and reviled Aladdin for the excess of his rage against him, and at times he would exclaim: "For this bastard's death underground I am well satisfied, and hope only that some time or other I may obtain the lamp, seeing how 'tis yet safe." Now one day of the days he struck a table of sand and dotted down the figures and carefully considered their consequence, then he transferred them to paper that he might study them and make sure of Aladdin's destruction and the safety of the lamp preserved beneath the earth. Presently he firmly stablished the sequence of the figures, mothers as well as daughters, but still he saw not the lamp. Thereupon rage overrode him and he made another trial to be assured of Aladdin's death, but he saw him not in the enchanted treasure.

Hereat his wrath still grew, and it waxed greater when he ascertained that the youth had issued from underground and was now upon earth's surface alive and alert. Furthermore, that he had become owner of the lamp, for which he had himself endured such toil and travail and troubles as man may not bear save for so great an object. Accordingly quoth he to himself: "I have suffered sore pains and penalties which none else could have endured for the lamp's sake in order that other than that I may carry it off, and this accursed hath taken it without difficulty. And who knoweth an he wot the virtues of the lamp, than whose owner none in the world should be wealthier? There is no help but that I work for his destruction." He then struck another geomantic table and, examining the figures, saw that the lad had won for himself unmeasurable riches and had wedded the daughter of his King, so of his envy and jealousy he was fired with the flame of wrath, and rising without let or stay, he equipped himself and set forth for China land, where he arrived in due season.

Now when he had reached the King's capital wherein was Aladdin, he alighted at one of the khans, and when he had rested from the weariness of wayfare, he donned his dress and went down to wander about the streets, where he never passed a group without hearing them prate about the pavilion and its grandeur and vaunt the beauty of Aladdin and his lovesomeness, his liberality and generosity, his fine manners and his good morals. Presently he entered an establishment wherein men were drinking a certain warm beverage, and going up to one of those who were loud in their lauds, he said to him, "O fair youth, who may be the man ye describe and commend?" "Apparently thou art a foreigner, O man," answered the other, "and thou comest from a far country. But even this granted, how happeneth it thou hast not heard of the Emir Aladdin, whose renown, I fancy, hath filled the universe, and whose pavilion, known by report to far and near, is one of the wonders of the world? How, then, never came to thine ears aught of this or the name of Aladdin (whose glory and enjoyment Our Lord increase!) and his fame?" The Moorman replied: "The sum of my wishes is to look upon this pavilion, and if thou wouldest do me a favor, prithee guide me thereunto, for I am a foreigner." The man rejoined, "To hear is to obey," and, foregoing him, pointed out Aladdin's pavilion, whereupon the Moroccan fell to considering it, and at once understood that it was the work of the lamp. So he cried: "Ah! Ah! needs must I dig a pit for this accursed, this son of a snip, who could not earn for himself even an evening meal. And if the Fates abet me, I will assuredly destroy his life and send his mother back to spinning at her wheel, e'en as she was wont erewhiles to do."

So saying, he returned to his caravanserai in a sore state of grief and melancholy and regret bred by his envy and hate of Aladdin. He took his astrological gear and geomantic table to discover where might be the lamp, and he found that it was in the pavilion and not upon Aladdin's person. So he rejoiced thereat with joy exceeding and exclaimed: "Now indeed 'twill be an easy task to take the life of this accursed and I see my way to getting the lamp." Then he went to a coppersmith and said to him: "Do thou make me a set of lamps, and take from me their full price and more, only I would have thee hasten to finish them." Replied the smith, "Hearing and obeying," and fell a-working to keep his word. And when they were ready, the Moorman paid him what price he required, then, taking them, he carried them to the khan and set them in a basket. Presently he began wandering about the highways and market streets of the capital crying aloud: "Ho! Who will exchange old lamps for new lamps?" But when the folk heard him cry on this wise, they derided him and said, "Doubtless this man is Jinnmad, for that he goeth about offering new for old." And a world followed him, and the children of the quarter caught him up from place to place, laughing at him the while, nor did he forbid them or care for their maltreatment. And he ceased not strolling about the streets till he came under Aladdin's pavilion, where he shouted with his loudest voice, and the boys screamed at him: "A madman! A madman!"

Now Destiny had decreed that the Lady Badr al-Budur be sitting in her kiosque, whence she heard one crying like a crier, and the children bawling at him. Only she understood not what was going on, so she gave orders to one of her slave girls, saying, "Go thou and see who 'tis that crieth, and what be his cry." The girl fared forth and looked on, when she beheld a man crying, "Ho! Who will exchange old lamps for new lamps?" and the little ones pursuing and laughing at him. And as loudly laughed the Princess when this strange case was told to her. Now Aladdin had carelessly left the lamp in his pavilion without hiding it and locking it up in his strongbox, and one of the slave girls who had seen it said: "O my lady, I think to have noticed in the apartment of my lord Aladdin an old lamp, so let us give it in change for a new lamp to this man, and see if his cry be truth or lie." Whereupon the Princess said to the slave girl, "Bring the old lamp which thou saidst to have seen in thy lord's apartment."

Now the Lady Badr al-Budur knew naught of the lamp and of the specialities thereof which had raised Aladdin, her spouse, to such high degree and grandeur, and her only end and aim was to understand by experiment the mind of a man who would give in exchange the new for the old. So the handmaid fared forth and went up to Aladdin's apartment and returned with the lamp to her lady, who, like all the others, knew nothing of the Maghrabi's cunning tricks and his crafty device. Then the Princess bade an aga of the eunuchry go down and barter the old lamp for a new lamp. So he obeyed her bidding and, after taking a new lamp from the man, he returned and laid it before his lady, who looking at it and seeing that it was brand-new, fell to laughing at the Moorman's wits.

But the Moroccan, when he held the article in hand and recognized it for the lamp of the enchanted treasury, at once placed it in his breast pocket and left all the other lamps to the folk who were bartering of him. Then he went forth running till he was clear of the city, when he walked leisurely over the level grounds, and he took patience until night fell on him in desert ground, where was none other but himself. There he brought out the lamp, when suddenly appeared to him the Marid, who said: "Adsum! Thy slave between thy hands is come. Ask of me whatso thou wantest." " 'Tis my desire," the Moorman replied, "that thou upraise from its present place Aladdin's pavilion, with its inmates and all that be therein, not forgetting myself, and set it down upon my own land, Africa. Thou knowest my town, and I want the building placed in the gardens hard by it." The Marid slave replied: "Hearkening and obedience. Close thine eyes and open thine eyes, whenas thou shalt find thyself together with the pavilion in thine own country." This was done, and in an eye twinkling the Moroccan and the pavilion, with all therein, were transported to the African land.

Such then was the work of the Maghrabi, the magician, but now let us return to the Sultan and his son-in-law. It was the custom of the King, because of his attachment to and his affection for his daughter, every morning when he had shaken off sleep to open the latticed casement and look out therefrom, that he might catch sight of her abode. So that day he arose and did as he was wont. But when he drew near the latticed casement of his palace and looked out at Aladdin's pavilion, he saw naught—nay, the site was smooth as a well-trodden highway and like unto what it had been aforetime, and he could find nor edifice nor offices. So astonishment clothed him as with a garment, and his wits were wildered and he began to rub his eyes, lest they be dimmed or darkened, and to gaze intently. But at last he was certified that no trace of the pavilion remained, nor sign of its being, nor wist he the why and the wherefore of its disappearance. So his surprise increased and he smote hand upon hand and the tears trickled down his cheeks over his beard, for that he knew not what had become of his daughter.

Then he sent out officials forthright and summoned the Grand Wazir, who at once attended, and seeing him in this piteous plight, said: "Pardon, O King of the Age, may Allah avert from thee every ill! Wherefore art thou in such sorrow?" Exclaimed the sovereign, "Methinketh thou wottest not my case." And quoth the Minister: "Oh no wise, O our lord. By Allah, I know of it nothing at all." "Then," resumed the Sultan, "'tis manifest thou hast not looked this day in the direction of Aladdin's pavilion." "True, O my lord," quoth the Wazir. "It must still be locked and fast shut," and quoth the King: "Forasmuch as thou hast no inkling of aught, arise and look out at the window and see Aladdin's pavilion, whereof thou sayest 'tis locked and fast shut." The Minister obeyed his bidding, but could not see anything, or pavilion or other place. So with mind and thoughts sore perplexed he returned to his liege lord, who asked him: "Hast now learned the reason of my distress, and noted yon locked-up palace and fast shut?" Answered the Wazir: "O King of the Age, erewhile I represented to thy Highness that this pavilion and these matters be all magical." Hereat the Sultan, fired with wrath, cried, "Where be Aladdin?" and the Minister replied, "He hath gone a-hunting," when the King commanded without stay or delay sundry of his agas and army officers to go and bring to him his son-in-law chained and with pinioned elbows.

So they fared forth until they found Aladdin, when they said to him: "O our lord Aladdin, excuse us, nor be thou wroth with us, for the King hath commanded that we carry thee before him pinioned and fettered, and we hope pardon from thee, because we are under the royal orders which we cannot gainsay." Aladdin, hearing these words, was seized with surprise, and not knowing the reason of this, remained tongue-tied for a time, after which he turned to them and asked: "O assembly, have you naught of knowledge concerning the motive of the royal mandate? Well I wot my soul to be innocent, and that I never sinned against King or against kingdom." "O our lord," answered they, "we have no inkling whatever." So Aladdin alighted from his horse and said to them: "Do ye whatso the Sultan bade you do, for that the King's command is upon the head and the eyes." The agas, having bound Aladdin in bonds and pinioned his elbows behind his back, haled him in chains and carried him into the city. But when the lieges saw him pinioned and ironed, they understood that the Sultan purposed to strike off his head, and forasmuch as he was loved of them exceedingly, all gathered together and seized their weapons, then, swarming out of their houses, followed the soldiery to see what was to do. And when the troops arrived with Aladdin at the palace, they went in and informed the Sultan of this, whereat he forthright commanded the sworder to cut off the head of his son-in-law.

Now as soon as the subjects were aware of this order, they barricaded the gates and closed the doors of the palace and sent a message to the King saying: "At this very moment we will level thine abode over the heads of all it containeth, and over thine own, if the least hurt or harm befall Aladdin." So the Wazir went in and reported to the Sultan: "O King of the Age, thy commandment is about to seal the roll of our lives, and 'twere more suitable that thou pardon thy son-in-law, lest there chance to us a sore mischance, for that the lieges do love him far more than they love us." Now the Sworder had already dispread the carpet of blood and, having seated Aladdin thereon, had bandaged his eyes. Moreover, he had walked round him three several times awaiting the last orders of his lord, when the King looked out of the window and saw his subjects, who had suddenly attacked him, swarming up the walls intending to tear them down. So forthright he bade the Sworder stay his hand from Aladdin and commanded the crier fare forth to the crowd and cry aloud that he had pardoned his son-in-law and received him back into favor.

But when Aladdin found himself free and saw the Sultan seated on his throne, he went up to him and said: "O my lord, inasmuch as thy Highness hath favored me throughout my life, so of thy grace now deign let me know the how and the wherein I have sinned against thee." "O traitor," cried the King, "unto this present I knew not any sin of thine." Then, turning to the Wazir, he said: "Take him and make him look out at the window, and after let him tell us where be his pavilion." And when the royal order was obeyed, Aladdin saw the place level as a well-trodden road, even as it had been ere the base of the building was laid, nor was there the faintest trace of edifice. Hereat he was astonished and perplexed, knowing not what had occurred. But when he returned to the presence, the King asked him: "What is it thou hast seen? Where is thy pavilion, and where is my daughter, the core of my heart, my only child, than whom I have none other?" Aladdin answered, "O King of the Age, I wot naught thereof nor aught of what hath befallen," and the Sultan rejoined: "Thou must know, O Aladdin, I have pardoned thee only that thou go forth and look into this affair and inquire for me concerning my daughter. Nor do thou ever show thyself in my presence except she be with thee, and if thou bring her not, by the life of my head I will cut off the head of thee." The other replied: "To hear is to obey. Only vouchsafe me a delay and respite of some forty days, after which, an I produce her not, strike off my head and do with me whatso thou wishest." The Sultan said to Aladdin: "Verily, I have granted thee thy request, a delay of forty days. But think not thou canst fly from my hand, for I would bring thee back even if thou wert above the clouds instead of being only upon earth's surface." Replied Aladdin: "O my lord the Sultan, as I said to thy Highness, an I fail to bring her within the term appointed, I will present myself for my head to be stricken off."

Now when the folk and the lieges all saw Aladdin at liberty, they rejoiced with joy exceeding and were delighted for his release, but the shame of his treatment and bashfulness before his friends and the envious exultation of his foes had bowed down Aladdin's head. So he went forth a wandering through the city ways, and he was perplexed concerning his case and knew not what had befallen him. He lingered about the capital for two days, in saddest state, wotting not what to do in order to find his wife and his pavilion, and during this time sundry of the folk privily brought him meat and drink. When the two days were done, he left the city to stray about the waste and open lands outlying the walls, without a notion as to whither he should wend. And he walked on aimlessly until the path led him beside a river, where, of the stress of sorrow that overwhelmed him, he abandoned himself to despair and thought of casting himself into the water. Being, however, a good Moslem who professed the unity of the Godhead, he feared Allah in his soul, and standing upon the margin, he prepared to perform the wuzu ablution.

But as he was bailing up the water in his right hand and rubbing his fingers, it so chanced that he also rubbed the ring. Hereat its Marid appeared, and said to him: "Adsum! Thy thrall between thy hands is come. Ask of me whatso thou wantest." Seeing the Marid, Aladdin rejoiced with exceeding joy and cried: "O Slave, I desire of thee that thou bring before me my pavilion and therein my wife, the Lady Badr al-Budur, together with all and everything it containeth." "O my lord," replied the Marid, "'tis right hard upon me that thou demandest a service whereto I may not avail. This matter dependeth upon the Slave of the Lamp, nor dare I even attempt it." Aladdin rejoined: "Forasmuch as the matter is beyond thy competence, I require it not of thee, but at least do thou take me up and set me down beside my pavilion in what land soever that may be." The slave exclaimed, "Hearing and obeying, O my lord," and uplifting him high in air, within the space of an eye glance set him down beside his pavilion in the land of Africa, and upon a spot facing his wife's apartment.

Now this was at fall of night, yet one look enabled him to recognize his home, whereby his cark and care were cleared away and he recovered trust in Allah after cutting off all his hope to look upon his wife once more. Then he fell to pondering the secret and mysterious favors of the Lord (glorified be His omnipotence!), and how after despair had mastered him the ring had come to gladden him, and how when all his hopes were cut off, Allah had deigned bless him with the services of its slave. So he rejoiced and his melancholy left him. Then, as he had passed four days without sleep for the excess of his cark and care and sorrow and stress of thought, he drew near his pavilion and slept under a tree hard by the building, which (as we mentioned) had been set down amongst the gardens outlying the city of Africa. He slumbered till morning showed her face, and when awakened by the warbling of the small birds, he arose and went down to the bank of the river which flowed thereby into the city, and here he again washed hands and face and after finished his wuzu ablution. Then he prayed the dawn prayer, and when he had ended his orisons he returned and sat down under the windows of the Princess's bower.

Now the Lady Badr al-Budur, of her exceeding sorrow for severance from her husband and her sire, the Sultan, and for the great mishap which had happened to her from the Maghrabi, the magician, the accursed, was wont to rise during the murk preceding dawn and to sit in tears, inasmuch as she could not sleep o' nights and had forsworn meat and drink. Her favorite slave girl would enter her chamber at the hour of prayer salutation in order to dress her, and this time, by decree of Destiny, when she threw open the window to let her lady comfort and console herself by looking upon the trees and rills, and she herself peered out of the lattice, she caught sight of her master sitting below, and informed the Princess of this, saying: "O my lady! O my lady! Here's my lord Aladdin seated at the foot of the wall!" So her mistress arose hurriedly and gazing from the casement, saw him, and her husband, raising his head, saw her, so she saluted him and he saluted her, both being like to fly for joy. Presently quoth she, "Up and come in to me by the private postern, for now the accursed is not here," and she gave orders to the slave girl, who went down and opened for him. Then Aladdin passed through it and was met by his wife, when they embraced and exchanged kisses with all delight until they wept for overjoy.

After this they sat down, and Aladdin said to her: "O my lady, before all things 'tis my desire to ask thee a question. 'Twas my wont to place an old copper lamp in such a part of my pavilion. What became of that same?" When the Princess heard these words, she sighed and cried, "O my dearling, 'twas that very lamp which garred us fall into this calamity!" Aladdin asked her, "How befell the affair?" and she answered by recounting to him all that passed, first and last, especially how they had given in exchange an old lamp for a new lamp, adding: "And next day we hardly saw one another at dawn before we found ourselves in this land, and he who deceived us and took the lamp by way of barter informed me that he had done the deed by might of his magic and by means of the lamp; that he is a Moorman from Africa; and that we are now in his native country."

When the Lady Badr al-Budur ceased speaking, Aladdin resumed: "Tell me the intent of this accursed in thy respect, also what he sayeth to thee and what be his will of thee." She replied: "Every day he cometh to visit me once and no more. He would woo me to his love, and he sueth that I take him to spouse in lieu of thee and that I forget thee and be consoled for the loss of thee. And he telleth me that the Sultan, my sire, hath cut off my husband's head, adding that thou, the son of pauper parents, wast by him enriched. And he sootheth me with talk, but he never seeth aught from me save weeping and wailing, nor hath he heard from me one sugar-sweet word." Quoth Aladdin: "Tell me where he hath placed the lamp, an thou know anything thereof," and quoth she: "He beareth it about on his body alway, nor is it possible that he leave it for a single hour. Moreover, once when he related what I have now recounted to thee, he brought it out of his breast pocket and allowed me to look upon it." When Aladdin heard these words, he joyed with exceeding joy and said: "O my lady, do thou lend ear to me. 'Tis my design to go from thee forthright and to return only after doffing this my dress, so wonder not when thou see me changed, but direct one of thy women to stand by the private postern alway, and whenever she espy me coming, at once to open. And now I will devise a device whereby to slay this damned loon."

Herewith he arose and, issuing from the pavilion door, walked till he met on the way a fellah, to whom he said, "O man, take my attire and give me thy garments." But the peasant refused, so Aladdin stripped him of his dress perforce and donned it, leaving to the man his own rich gear by way of gift. Then he followed the highway leading to the neighboring city and entering it, went to the perfumers' bazaar, where he bought of one some rarely potent bhang, the son of a minute, paying two dinars for two drachms thereof, and he returned in disguise by the same road till he reached the pavilion. Here the slave girl opened to him the private postern, wherethrough he went in to the Lady Badr al-Budur, and said: "Hear me! I desire of thee that thou dress and dight thyself in thy best and thou cast off all outer show and semblance of care. Also when the accursed, the Maghrabi, shall visit thee, do thou receive him with a 'Welcome and fair welcome,' and meet him with smiling face and invite him to come and sup with thee. Moreover, let him note that thou hast forgotten Aladdin, thy beloved, likewise thy father, and that thou hast learned to love him with exceeding love, displaying to him all manner joy and pleasure. Then ask him for wine, which must be red, and pledge him to his secret in a significant draught. And when thou hast given him two or three cups full and hast made him wax careless, then drop these drops into his cup and fill it up with wine. No sooner shall he drink of it than he will fall upon his back senseless as one dead." Hearing these words, the Princess exclaimed: "'Tis exceedingly sore to me that I do such deed, withal must I do it that we escape the defilement of this accursed who tortured me by severance from thee and from my sire. Lawful and right therefore is the slaughter of this accursed."

Then Aladdin ate and drank with his wife what hindered his hunger, then, rising without stay or delay, fared forth the pavilion. So the Lady Badr al-Budur summoned the tirewoman, who robed and arrayed her in her finest raiment and adorned her and perfumed her. And as she was thus, behold, the accursed Maghrabi entered. He joyed much seeing her in such case and yet more when she confronted him, contrary to her custom, with a laughing face, and his love longing increased, and his desire to have her. Then she took him and, seating him beside her, said: "O my dearling, do thou (an thou be willing) come to me this night and let us sup together. Sufficient to me hath been my sorrow, for were I to sit mourning through a thousand years or even two thousand, Aladdin would not return to me from the tomb. And I depend upon thy say of yesterday; to wit, that my sire, the Sultan, slew him in his stress of sorrow for serverance from me.

"Nor wonder thou an I have changed this day from what I was yesterday, and the reason thereof is I have determined upon taking thee to friend and playfellow in lieu of and succession to Aladdin, for that now I have none other man but thyself. So I hope for thy presence this night, that we may sup together and we may carouse and drink somewhat of wine each with other, and especially 'tis my desire that thou cause me taste the wine of thy natal soil, the African land, because belike 'tis better than aught of the wine of China we drink. I have with me some wine, but 'tis the growth of my country and I vehemently wish to taste the wine produced by thine."

When the Maghrabi saw the love lavisht upon him by the Lady Badr al-Budur, and noted her change from the sorrowful, melancholy woman she was wont to be, he thought that she had cut off her hope of Aladdin, and he joyed exceedingly and said to her: "I hear and obey, O my lady, whatso thou wishest and all thou biddest. I have at home a jar of our country wine, which I have carefully kept and stored deep in earth for a space of eight years, and I will now fare and fill from it our need and will return to thee in all haste." But the Princess, that she might wheedle him the more and yet more, replied: "O my darling, go not thou, leaving me alone, but send one of the eunuchs to fill for us thereof, and do thou remain sitting beside me, that I may find in thee my consolation." He rejoined: "O my lady, none wotteth where the jar be buried save myself, nor will I tarry from thee." So saying, the Moorman went out, and after a short time he brought back as much wine as they wanted, whereupon quoth the Princess to him: "Thou hast been at pains and trouble to serve me, and I have suffered for thy sake, O my beloved." Quoth he: "On no wise, O eyes of me. I hold myself enhonored by thy service."

Then the Lady Badr al-Budur sat with him at table, and the twain fell to eating, and presently the Princess expressed a wish to drink, when the handmaid filled her a cup forthright and then crowned another for the Moroccan. So she drank to his long life and his secret wishes, and he also drank to her life. Then the Princess, who was unique in eloquence and delicacy of speech, fell to making a cup companion of him and beguiled him by addressing him in the sweetest terms of hidden meaning. This was done only that he might become more madly enamored of her, but the Maghrabi thought that it resulted from her true inclination for him, nor knew that it was a snare set up to slay him. So his longing for her increased, and he was dying of love for when he saw her address him in such tenderness of words and thoughts, and his head began to swim and all the world seemed as nothing in his eyes. But when they came to the last of the supper and the wine had mastered his brains and the Princess saw this in him, she said: "With us there be a custom throughout our country, but I know not an it be the usage of yours or not." The Moorman replied, "And what may that be?" So she said to him: "At the end of supper each lover in turn taketh the cup of the beloved and drinketh it off." And at once she crowned one with wine and bade the handmaid carry to him her cup, wherein the drink was blended with the bhang.

Now she had taught the slave girl what to do, and all the handmaids and eunuchs in the pavilion longed for the sorcerer's slaughter and in that matter were one with the Princess. Accordingly the damsel handed him the cup and he, when he heard her words and saw her drinking from his cup and passing hers to him and noted all that show of love, fancied himself Iskandar, Lord of the Two Horns. Then said she to him, the while swaying gracefully to either side and putting her hand within his hand: "O my life, here is thy cup with me and my cup with thee, and on this wise do lovers drink from each other's cups." Then she bussed the brim and drained it to the dregs, and again she kissed its lip and offered it to him. Thereat he flew for joy and, meaning to do the like, raised her cup to his mouth and drank off the whole contents, without considering whether there was therein aught harmful or not. And forthright he rolled upon his back in deathlike condition and the cup dropped from his grasp, whereupon the Lady Badr al-Budur and the slave girls ran hurriedly and opened the pavilion door to their lord Aladdin, who, disguised as a fellah, entered therein.

He went up to the apartment of his wife, whom he found still sitting at table, and facing her lay the Maghrabi as one slaughtered. So he at once drew near to her and kissed her and thanked her for this. Then, rejoicing with joy exceeding, he turned to her and said: "Do thou with thy handmaids betake thyself to the inner rooms and leave me alone for the present, that I may take counsel touching mine affair." The Princess hesitated not but went away at once, she and her women. Then Aladdin arose, and after locking the door upon them, walked up to the Moorman and put forth his hand to his breast pocket and thence drew the lamp, after which he unsheathed his sword and slew the villain. Presently he rubbed the lamp and the Marid slave appeared and said: "Adsum, O my lord! What is it thou wantest?" "I desire of thee," said Aladdin, "that thou take up my pavilion from this country and transport it to the land of China and there set it down upon the site where it was whilom, fronting the palace of the Sultan." The Marid replied, "Hearing and obeying, O my lord."

Then Aladdin went and sat down with his wife and throwing his arms round her neck, kissed her and she kissed him, and they set in converse what while the Jinni transported the pavilion and all therein to the place appointed. Presently Aladdin bade the handmaids spread the table before him, and he and the Lady Badr al-Budur took seat thereat and fell to eating and drinking, in all joy and gladness, till they had their sufficiency, when, removing to the chamber of wine and cup converse, they sat there and caroused in fair companionship and each kissed other with all love liesse. The time had been long and longsome since they enjoyed aught of pleasure, so they ceased not doing thus until the wine sun arose in their heads and sleep gat hold of them, at which time they went to their bed in all ease and comfort. Early on the next morning Aladdin woke and awoke his wife, and the slave girls came in and donned her dress and prepared her and adorned her whilst her husband arrayed himself in his costliest raiment, and the twain were ready to fly for joy at reunion after parting. Moreover, the Princess was especially joyous and gladsome because on that day she expected to see her beloved father.

Such was the case of Aladdin and the Lady Badr al-Budur, but as regards the Sultan, after he drove away his son-in-law he never ceased to sorrow for the loss of his daughter, and every hour of every day he would sit and weep for her as women weep, because she was his only child and he had none other to take to heart. And as he shook off sleep morning after morning he would hasten to the window and throw it open and peer in the direction where formerly stood Aladdin's pavilion and pour forth tears until his eyes were dried up and their lids were ulcered. Now on that day he arose at dawn and, according to his custom, looked out, when lo and behold! he saw before him an edifice, so he rubbed his eyes and considered it curiously, when he became certified that it was the pavilion of his son-in-law. So he called for a horse without let or delay, and as soon as his beast was saddled, he mounted and made for the place, and

Aladdin, when he saw his father-in-law approaching, went down and met him halfway, then, taking his hand, aided him to step upstairs to the apartment of his daughter. And the Princess, being as earnestly desirous to see her sire, descended and greeted him at the door of the staircase fronting the ground-floor hall. Thereupon the King folded her in his arms and kissed her, shedding tears of joy, and she did likewise, till at last Aladdin led them to the upper saloon, where they took seats and the Sultan fell to asking her case and what had betided her.

The Lady Badr al-Budur began to inform the Sultan of all which had befallen her, saying: "O my father, I recovered not life save yesterday when I saw my husband, and he it was who freed me from the thraldom of that Maghrabi, that magician, that accursed, than whom I believe there be none viler on the face of earth. And but for my beloved, I had never escaped him, nor hadst thou seen me during the rest of my days. But mighty sadness and sorrow gat about me, O my father, not only for losing thee but also for the loss of a husband under whose kindness I shall be all the length of my life, seeing that he freed me from that fulsome sorcerer." Then the Princess began repeating to her sire everything that happened to her, and relating to him how the Moorman had tricked her in the guise of a lamp-seller who offered in exchange new for old, how she had given him the lamp whose worth she knew not, and how she had bartered it away only to laugh at the lampman's folly.

"And next morning, O my father," she continued, "we found ourselves and whatso the pavilion contained in Africa land, till such time as my husband came to us and devised a device whereby we escaped. And had it not been for Aladdin's hastening to our aid, the accursed was determined to enjoy me perforce." Then she told him of the bhang drops administered in wine to the African and concluded: "Then my husband returned to me, and how I know not, but we were shifted from Africa land to this place." Aladdin in his turn recounted how, finding the wizard dead-drunken, he had sent away his wife and her women from the poluted place into the inner apartments; how he had taken the lamp from the sorcerer's breast pocket, whereto he was directed by his wife; how he had slaughtered the villain; and finally how, making use of the lamp, he had summoned its slave and ordered him to transport the pavilion back to its proper site, ending his tale with: "And, if thy Highness have any doubt anent my words, arise with me and look upon the accursed magician." The King did accordingly and, having considered the Moorman, bade the carcass be carried away forthright and burned and its ashes scattered in air.

Then he took to embracing Aladdin and, kissing him, said: "Pardon me, O my son, for that I was about to destroy thy life through the foul deeds of this damned enchanter, who cast thee into such pit of peril. And I may be excused, O my child, for what I did by thee, because I found myself forlorn of my daughter, my only one, who to me is dearer than my very kingdom. Thou knowest how the hearts of parents yearn unto their offspring, especially when like myself they have but one and none other to love." And on this wise the Sultan took to excusing himself and kissing his son-in-law. Aladdin said to the Sultan: "O King of the time, thou didst naught to me contrary to Holy Law, and I also sinned not against thee, but all the trouble came from that Maghrabi, the impure, the magician." Thereupon the Sultan bade the city be decorated, and they obeyed him and held high feast and festivities. He also commanded the crier to cry about the streets saying: "This day is a mighty great fête, wherein public rejoicings must be held throughout the realm, for a full month of thirty days, in honor of the Lady Badr al-Budur and her husband Aladdin's return to their home."

On this wise befell it with Aladdin and the Maghrabi, but withal the King's son-in-law escaped not wholly from the accursed, albeit the body had been burnt and the ashes scattered in air. For the villain had a brother yet more villainous than himself, and a greater adept in necromancy, geomancy, and astromancy. And even as the old saw saith, "A bean and 'twas split," so each one dwelt in his own quarter of the globe that he might fill it with his sorcery, his fraud, and his treason. Now one day of the days it fortuned that the Moorman's brother would learn how it fared with him, so he brought out his sandboard and dotted it and produced the figures which, when he had considered and carefully studied them, gave him to know that the man he sought was dead and housed in the tomb. So he grieved and was certified of his disease, but he dotted a second time seeking to learn the manner of the death and where it had taken place. So he found that the site was the China land and that the mode was the foulest of slaughter. Furthermore, that he who did him die was a young man Aladdin hight. Seeing this, he straightway arose and equipped himself for wayfare, then he set out and cut across the wilds and wolds and heights for the space of many a month until he reached China and the capital of the Sultan wherein was the slayer of his brother.

He alighted at the so-called strangers' khan and, hiring himself a cell, took rest therein for a while, then he fared forth and wandered about the highways that he might discern some path which would aid him unto the winning of his ill-minded wish; to wit, of wreaking upon Aladdin blood revenge for his brother. Presently he entered a coffeehouse, a fine building which stood in the market place and which collected a throng of folk to play, some at the mankalah, others at the backgammon, and others at the chess and what not else. There he sat down and listened to those seated beside him, and they chanced to be conversing about an ancient dame and a holy, by name Fatimah, who dwelt away at her devotions in a hermitage without the town, and this she never entered save only two days each month. They mentioned also that she had performed many saintly miracles, which when the Maghrabi, the necromancer, heard he said in himself: "Now have I found that which I sought. Inshallah—God willing—by means of this crone will I win to my wish."

The necromancer went up to the folk who were talking of the miracles performed by the devout old woman and said to one of them: "O my uncle, I heard you all chatting about the prodigies of a certain saintess named Fatimah. Who is she, and where may be her abode?" "Marvelous!" exclaimed the man. "How canst thou be in our city and yet never have heard about the miracles of the Lady Fatimah? Evidently, O thou poor fellow, thou art a foreigner, since the fastings of this devotee and her asceticism in worldly matters and the beauties of her piety never came to thine ears." The Moorman rejoined: "'Tis true, O my lord. Yes, I am a stranger, and came to this your city only yesternight. And I hope thou wilt inform me concerning the saintly miracles of this virtuous woman and where may be her wone, for that I have fallen into a calamity, and 'tis my wish to visit her and crave her prayers, so haply Allah (to Whom be honor and glory!) will, through her blessings, deliver me from mine evil." Hereat the man recounted to him the marvels of Fatimah, the devotee, and her piety and the beauties of her worship, then, taking him by the hand, went with him without the city and showed him the way to her abode, a cavern upon a hillock's head. The necromancer acknowledged his kindness in many words and, thanking him for his good offices, returned to his cell in the caravanserai.

Now by the fiat of Fate on the very next day Fatimah came down to the city, and the Maghrabi, the necromancer, happened to leave his hostelry a-morn, when he saw the folk swarming and crowding. Wherefore he went up to discover what was to do, and found the devotee standing a-middlemost the throng, and all who suffered from pain or sickness flocked to her soliciting a blessing and praying for her prayers, and each and every she touched became whole of his illness. The Moroccan, the necromancer, followed her about until she returned to her antre. Then, awaiting till the evening evened, he arose and repaired to a vintner's store, where he drank a cup of wine. After this he fared forth the city, and finding the devotee's cavern, entered it and saw her lying prostrate with her back upon a strip of matting. So he came forward and mounted upon her belly, then he drew his dagger and shouted at her, and when she awoke and opened her eyes, she espied a Moorish man with an unsheathed poniard sitting upon her middle as though about to kill her.

She was troubled and sore terrified, but he said to her: "Hearken! And thou cry out or utter a word, I will slay thee at this very moment. Arise now and do all I bid thee." Then he sware to her an oath that if she obeyed his orders, whatever they might be, he would not do her die. So saying, he rose up from off her and Fatimah also arose, when he said to her, "Give me thy gear and take thou my habit," whereupon she gave him her clothing and head fillets, her face kerchief and her mantilla. Then quoth he, "'Tis also requisite that thou anoint me with somewhat shall make the color of my face like unto thine." Accordingly she went into the inner cavern, and bringing out a gallipot of ointment, spread somewhat thereof upon her palm and with it besmeared his face until its hue favored her own. Then she gave him her staff and, showing him how to walk and what to do when he entered the city, hung her rosary around his neck. Lastly she handed to him a mirror and said, "Now look! Thou differest from me in naught," and he saw himself Fatimah's counterpart as thou she had never gone or come. But after obtaining his every object he falsed his oath and asked for a cord, which she brought to him. Then he seized her and strangled her in the cavern, and presently, when she was dead, haled the corpse outside and threw it into a pit hard by and went back to sleep in her cavern. And when broke the day, he rose, and repairing to the town, took his stand under the walls of Aladdin's pavilion.

Hereupon flocked the folk about him, all being certified that he was Fatimah, the devotee, and he fell to doing whatso she was wont to do. He laid hands on these in pain and recited for those a chapter of the Koran and made orisons for a third. Presently the thronging of the folk and the clamoring of the crowd were heard by the Lady Badr al-Budur, who said to her handmaidens. "Look what is to do, and what be the cause of this turmoil!" Thereupon the aga of the eunuchry fared forth to see what might be the matter and, presently returning, said: "O my lady, this clamor is caused by the Lady Fatimah, and if thou be pleased to command, I will bring her to thee. So shalt thou gain through her a blessing." The Princess answered: "Go bring her, for since many a day I am always hearing of her miracles and her virtues, and I do long to see her and get a blessing by her intervention, for the folk recount her manifestations in many cases of difficulty."

The aga went forth and brought in the Moroccan, the necromancer, habited in Fatimah's clothing, and when the wizard stood before the Lady Badr al-Budur, he began at first sight to bless her with a string of prayers, nor did any one of those present doubt at all but that he was the devotee herself. The Princess arose and salaamed to him, then, seating him beside her, said: "O my Lady Fatimah, 'tis my desire that thou abide with me alway, so might I be blessed through thee, and also learn of thee the paths of worship and piety and follow thine example making for salvation." Now all this was a foul deceit of the accursed African, and he designed furthermore to complete his guile, so he continued: "O my Lady, I am a poor woman and a religious that dwelleth in the desert, and the like of me deserveth not to abide in the palaces of the kings." But the Princess replied: "Have no care whatever, O my Lady Fatimah. I will set apart for thee an apartment of my pavilion that thou mayest worship therein, and none shall ever come to trouble thee. Also thou shalt avail to worship Allah in my place better than in thy cavern." The Moroccan rejoined: "Hearkening and obedience, O my lady. I will not oppose thine order, for that the commands of the children of the kings may not be gainsaid nor renounced. Only I hope of thee that my eating and my drinking and sitting may be within my own chamber, which shall be kept wholly private. Nor do I require or desire the delicacies of diet, but do thou favor me by sending thy handmaid every day with a bit of bread and a sup of water, and, when I feel fain of food, let me eat by myself in my own room."

Now the accursed hereby purposed to avert the danger of haply raising his face kerchief at mealtimes, when his intent might be baffled by his beard and mustachios discovering him to be a man. The Princess replied: "O my Lady Fatimah, be of good heart, naught shall happen save what thou wishest. But now arise and let me show thee the apartment in the palace which I would prepare for thy sojourn with us." The Lady Badr al-Budur arose, and taking the necromancer who had disguised himself as the devotee, ushered him in to the place which she had kindly promised him for a home, and said: "O my Lady Fatimah, here thou shalt dwell with every comfort about thee and in all privacy and repose, and the place shall be named after thy name." Whereupon the Maghrabi acknowledged her kindness and prayed for her. Then the Princess showed him the jalousies and the jeweled kiosque with its four and twenty windows, and said to him, "What thinkest thou, O my Lady Fatimah, of this marvelous pavilion?" The Moorman replied: "By Allah, O my daughter, 'tis indeed passing fine and wondrous exceedingly, nor do I deem that its fellow is to be found in the whole universe. But alas for the lack of one thing which would enhance its beauty and decoration!" The Princess asked her: "O my Lady Fatimah, what lacketh it, and what be this thing would add to its adornment? Tell me thereof, inasmuch as I was wont to believe it wholly perfect." The Moroccan answered: "O my lady, all it wanteth is that there be hanging from the middle of the dome the egg of a fowl called the roc, and were this done, the pavilion would lack its peer all the world over." The Princess asked, "What be this bird, and where can we find her egg?" and the Moroccan answered, "O my lady, the roc is indeed a giant fowl which carrieth off camels and elephants in her pounces and flieth away with them, such is her stature and strength. Also this fowl is mostly found in Mount Kaf, and the architect who built this pavilion is able to bring thee one of her eggs."

They then left such talk, as it was the hour for the noonday meal, and when the handmaid had spread the table, the Lady Badr al-Budur sent down to invite the accursed African to eat with her. But he accepted not, and for a reason he would on no wise consent—nay, he rose and retired to the room which the Princess had assigned to him and whither the slave girls carried his dinner. Now when evening evened, Aladdin returned from the chase and met his wife, who salaamed to him, and he clasped her to his bosom and kissed her. Presently, looking at her face, he saw thereon a shade of sadness, and he noted that, contrary to her custom, she did not laugh, so he asked her: "What hath betided thee, O my dearling? Tell me, hath aught happened to trouble thy thoughts?" "Nothing whatever," answered she. "But, O my beloved, I fancied that our pavilion lacked naught at all. However, O eyes of me, O Aladdin, were the dome of the upper story hung with an egg of the fowl called roc, there would be naught like it in the universe." Her husband rejoined: "And for this trifle thou art saddened, when 'tis the easiest of all matters to me! So cheer thyself, and whatever thou wantest, 'tis enough thou inform me thereof, and I will bring it from the abysses of the earth in the quickest time and at the earliest hour."

Aladdin, after refreshing the spirits of his Princess by promising her all she could desire, repaired straightway to his chamber and taking the lamp, rubbed it, when the Marid appeared without let or delay saying, "Ask whatso thou wantest." Said the other: "I desire thee to fetch me an egg of the bird roc, and do thou hang it to the dome crown of this my pavilion." But when the Marid heard these words, his face waxed fierce and he shouted with a mighty loud voice and a frightful, and cried: "O denier of kindly deeds, sufficeth it not for thee that I and all the Slaves of the Lamp are ever at thy service, but thou must also require me to bring thee our Liege Lady for thy pleasure, and hang her up at thy pavilion dome for the enjoyment of thee and thy wife? Now, by Allah, ye deserve, thou and she, that I reduce you to ashes this very moment and scatter you upon the air. But inasmuch as ye twain be ignorant of this matter, unknowing its inner from its outer significance, I will pardon you, for indeed ye are but innocents. The offense cometh from that accursed necromancer, brother to the Maghrabi, the magician, who abideth here representing himself to be Fatimah, the devotee, after assuming her dress and belongings and murthering her in the cavern. Indeed he came hither seeking to slay thee by way of blood revenge for his brother, and 'tis he who taught thy wife to require this matter of me."

So saying, the Marid evanished. But when Aladdin heard these words, his wits fled his head and his joints trembled at the Marid's terrible shout. But he empowered his purpose and, arising forthright, issued from his chamber and went into his wife's. There he affected an ache of head, for that he knew how famous was Fatimah for the art and mystery of healing all such pains. And when the Lady Badr al-Budur saw him sitting hand to head and complaining of unease, she asked him the cause and he answered, "I know of none other save that my head acheth exceedingly." Hereupon she straightway bade summon Fatimah, that the devotee might impose her hand upon his head, and Aladdin asked her, "Who may this Fatimah be?" So she informed him that it was Fatimah, the devotee, to whom she had given a home in the pavilion. Meanwhile the slave girls had fared forth and summoned the Maghrabi, and when the accursed made act of presence, Aladdin rose up to him and, acting like one who knew naught of his purpose, salaamed to him as though he had been the real Fatimah and, kissing the hem of his sleeve, welcomed him and entreated him with honor, and said: "O my Lady Fatimah, I hope thou wilt bless me with a boon, for well I wot thy practice in the healing of pains. I have gotten a mighty ache in my head." The Moorman, the accursed, could hardly believe that he heard such words, this being all that he desired. The necromancer, habited as Fatimah, the devotee, came up to Aladdin that he might place hand upon his head and heal his ache. So he imposed one hand and, putting forth the other under his gown, drew a dagger wherewith to slay him. But Aladdin watched him and, taking patience till he had wholly unsheathed the weapon, seized him with a forceful grip and, wrenching the dagger from his grasp, plunged it deep into his heart.

When the Lady Badr al-Budur saw him do on this wise, she shrieked and cried out: "What hath this virtuous and holy woman done that thou hast charged thy neck with the heavy burthen of her blood shed wrongfully? Hast thou no fear of Allah that thou killest Fatimah, this saintly woman, whose miracles are far-famed?" "No," replied Aladdin, "I have not killed Fatimah. I have slain only Fatimah's slayer, he that is the brother of the Maghrabi, the accursed, the magician, who carried thee off by his black art and transported my pavilion to the Africa land. And this damnable brother of his came to our city and wrought these wiles, murthering Fatimah and assuming her habit, only that he might avenge upon me his brother's blood. And he also 'twas who taught thee to require of me a roc's egg, that my death might result from such requirement. But an thou doubt my speech, come forward and consider the person I have slain." Thereupon Aladdin drew aside the Moorman's face kerchief and the Lady Badr al-Budur saw the semblance of a man with a full beard that well-nigh covered his features.

She at once knew the truth, and said to her husband, "O my beloved, twice have I cast thee into death risk!" But he rejoined: "No harm in that, O my lady. By the blessing of your loving eyes, I accept with all joy all things thou bringest me." The Princess, hearing these words, hastened to fold him in her arms and kissed him, saying: "O my dearling, all this is for my love to thee and I knew naught thereof, but indeed I do not deem lightly of thine affection." So Aladdin kissed her and strained her to his breast, and the love between them waxed but greater. At that moment the Sultan appeared, and they told him all that had happened, showing him the corpse of the Maghrabi, the necromancer, when the King commanded the body to be burned and the ashes scattered on air, even as had befallen the wizard's brother.

And Aladdin abode with his wife, the Lady Badr al-Budur, in all pleasure and joyaunce of life, and thenceforward escaped every danger, and after a while, when the Sultan deceased, his son-in-law was seated upon the throne of the kingdom. And he commanded and dealt justice to the lieges so that all the folk loved him, and he lived with his wife in all solace and happiness until there came to him the Destroyer of delights and the Severer of societies.

And a tale is also told about

ALI BABA AND THE FORTY THIEVES

IN days of yore and in times and tides long gone before, there dwelt in a certain town of Persia two brothers, one named Kasim and the other Ali Baba, who at their father's demise had divided the little wealth he had left to them with equitable division, and had lost no time in wasting and spending it all. The elder, however, presently took to himself a wife, the daughter of an opulent merchant, so that when his father-in-law fared to the mercy of Almighty Allah, he became owner of a large shop filled with rare goods and costly wares and of a storehouse stocked with precious stuffs, likewise of much gold that was buried in the ground. Thus was he known throughout the city as a substantial man. But the woman whom Ali Baba had married was poor and needy. They lived, therefore, in a mean hovel, and Ali Baba eked out a scanty livelihood by the sale of fuel which he daily collected in the jungle and carried about the town to the bazaar upon his three asses.

Now it chanced one day that Ali Baba had cut dead branches and dry fuel sufficient for his need, and had placed the load upon his beasts, when suddenly he espied a dust cloud spiring high in air to his right and moving rapidly toward him, and when he closely considered it, he descried a troop of horsemen riding on amain and about to reach him. At this sight he was sore alarmed, and fearing lest perchance they were a band of bandits who would slay him and drive off his donkeys, in his affright he began to run. But forasmuch as they were near-hand and he could not escape from out the forest, he drove his animals laden with the fuel into a byway of the bushes and swarmed up a thick trunk of a huge tree to hide himself therein. And he sat upon a branch whence he could descry everything beneath him whilst none below could catch a glimpse of him above, and that tree grew close beside a rock which towered high abovehead.

The horsemen, young, active, and doughty riders, came close up to the rock face and all dismounted, whereat Ali Baba took good note of them, and soon he was fully persuaded by their mien and demeanor that they were a troop of highwaymen who, having fallen upon a caravan, had despoiled it and carried off the spoil and brought their booty to this place with intent of concealing it safely in some cache. Moreover, he observed that they were forty in number. Ali Baba saw the robbers, as soon as they came under the tree, each unbridle his horse and hobble it. Then all took off their saddlebags, which proved to be full of gold and silver. The man who seemed to be the captain presently pushed forward, load on shoulder, through thorns and thickets, till he came up to a certain spot, where he uttered these strange words: "Open, Sesame!" And forthwith appeared a wide doorway in the face of the rock. The robbers went in, and last of all their chief, and then the portal shut of itself.

Long while they stayed within the cave whilst Ali Baba was constrained to abide perched upon the tree, reflecting that if he came down, peradventure the band might issue forth that very moment and seize him and slay him. At last he had determined to mount one of the horses and driving on his asses, to return townward, when suddenly the portal flew open. The robber chief was first to issue forth, then, standing at the entrance, he saw and counted his men as they came out, and lastly he spake the magical words, "Shut, Sesame!" whereat the door closed of itself. When all had passed muster and review, each slung on his saddlebags and bridled his own horse, and as soon as ready they rode off, led by the leader, in the direction whence they came. Ali Baba remained still perched on the tree and watched their departure, nor would he descend until what time they were clean gone out of sight, lest perchance one of them return and look around and descry him.

Then he thought within himself: "I too will try the virtue of those magical words and see if at my bidding the door will open and close." So he called out aloud, "Open, Sesame!" And no sooner had he spoken than straightway the portal flew open and he entered within. He saw a large cavern and a vaulted, in height equaling the stature of a full-grown man, and it was hewn in the live stone and, lighted up with light that came through air holes and bull's-eyes in the upper surface of the rock which formed the roof. He had expected to find naught save outer gloom in this robbers' den, and he was surprised to see the whole room filled with bales of all manner stuffs, and heaped up from sole to ceiling with camelloads of silks and brocades and embroidered cloths and mounds on mounds of varicolored carpetings. Besides which, he espied coins golden and silvern without measure or account, some piled upon the ground and others bound in leathern bags and sacks. Seeing these goods and moneys in such abundance, Ali Bab determined in his mind that not during a few years only but for many generations thieves must have stored their gains and spoils in this place.

When he stood within the cave, its door had closed upon him, yet he was not dismayed, since he had kept in memory the magical words, and he took no heed of the precious stuffs around him, but applied himself only and wholly to the sacks of ashrafis. Of these he carried out as many as he judged sufficient burthen for the beasts, then he loaded them upon his animals, and covered his plunder with sticks and fuel, so none might discern the bags but might think that he was carrying home his usual ware. Lastly he called out, "Shut, Sesame!" and forthwith the door closed, for the spell so wrought that whensoever any entered the cave, its portal shut of itself behind him, and as he issued therefrom, the same would neither open nor close again till he had pronounced the words "Shut, Sesame!" Presently, having laden his asses, Ali Baba urged them before him with all speed to the city and reaching home, he drove them into the yard, and, shutting close the outer door, took down first the sticks and fuel and after the bags of gold, which he carried in to his wife.

She felt them, and finding them full of coin, suspected that Ali Baba had been robbing, and fell to berating and blaming him for that he should do so ill a thing. Quoth Ali Baba to his wife, "Indeed I am no robber, and rather do thou rejoice with me at our good fortune." Hereupon he told her of his adventure, and began to pour the gold from the bags in heaps before her, and her sight was dazzled by the sheen and her heart delighted at his recital and adventures. Then she began counting the gold, whereat quoth Ali Baba: "O silly woman, how long wilt thou continue turning over the coin? Now let me dig a hole wherein to hide this treasure, that none may know its secret." Quoth she: "Right is thy rede! Still would I weigh the moneys and have some inkling of their amount," and he replied, "As thou pleasest, but see thou tell no man." So she went off in haste to Kasim's home to borrow weights and scales wherewith she might balance the ashrafis and make some reckoning of their value. And when she could not find Kasim, she said to his wife, "Lend me, I pray thee, thy scales for a moment." Replied her sister-in-law, "Hast thou need of the bigger balance or the smaller?" and the other rejoined, "I need not the large scales, give me the little," and her sister-in-law cried, "Stay here a moment whilst I look about and find thy want."

With this pretext Kasim's wife went aside and secretly smeared wax and suet over the pan of the balance, that she might know what thing it was Ali Baba's wife would weigh, for she made sure that whatso it be, some bit thereof would stick to the wax and fat. So the woman took this opportunity to satisfy her curiosity, and Ali Baba's wife, suspecting naught thereof, carried home the scales and began to weigh the gold, whilst Ali Baba ceased not digging. And when the money was weighed, they twain stowed it into the hole, which they carefully filled up with earth. Then the good wife took back the scales to her kinswoman, all unknowing that an ashrafi had adhered to the cup of the scales. But when Kasim's wife espied the gold coin, she fumed with envy and wrath, saying to herself: "So ho! They borrowed my balance to weigh out ashrafis?" And she marveled greatly whence so poor a man as Ali Baba had gotten such store of wealth that he should be obliged to weigh it with a pair of scales.

Now after long pondering the matter, when her husband returned home at eventide, she said to him: "O man, thou deemest thyself a wight of wealth and substance, but lo! thy brother Ali Baba is an emir by the side of thee, and richer far than thou art. He hath such heaps of gold that he must needs weigh his moneys with scales, whilst thou, forsooth, art satisfied to count thy coin." "Whence knowest thou this?" asked Kasim. And in answer his wife related all anent the pair of scales, and how she found an ashrafi stuck to them, and shewed him the gold coin, which bore the mark and superscription of some ancient king. No sleep had Kasim all that night by reason of his envy and jealousy and covetise, and next morning he rose betimes and going to Ali Baba, said: "O my brother, to all appearance thou art poor and needy, but in effect thou hast a store of wealth so abundant that perforce thou must weigh thy gold with scales." Quoth Ali Baba: "What is this thou sayest? I understand thee not. Make clear thy purport." And quoth Kasim, with ready rage: "Feign not that thou art ignorant of what I say, and think not to deceive me." Then, showing him the ashrafi, he cried: "Thousands of gold coins such as these thou hast put by, and meanwhile my wife found this one stuck to the cup of the scales." Then Ali Baba understood how both Kasim and his wife knew that he had store of ashrafis, and said in his mind that it would not avail him to keep the matter hidden, but would rather cause ill will and mischief, and thus he was induced to tell his brother every whit concerning the bandits and also of the treasure trove in the cave.

When he had heard the story, Kasim exclaimed: "I would fain learn of thee the certainty of the place where thou foundest the moneys, also the magical words whereby the door opened and closed. And I forewarn thee, an thou tell me not the whole truth, I will give notice of those ashrafis to the wali, then shalt thou forfeit all thy wealth and be disgraced and thrown into gaol." Thereupon Ali Baba told him his tale, not forgetting the magical words, and Kasim, who kept careful heed of all these matters, next day set out, driving ten mules he had hired, and readily found the place which Ali Baba had described to him. And when he came to the aforesaid rock and to the tree whereon Ali Baba had hidden himself, and he had made sure of the door he cried in great joy, "Open, Sesame!" The portal yawned wide at once and Kasim went within and saw the piles of jewels and treasures lying ranged all around, and as soon as he stood amongst them the door shut after him, as wont to do. He walked about in ecstasy marveling at the treasures, and when weary of admiration, he gathered together bags of ashrafis, a sufficient load for his ten mules, and placed them by the entrance in readiness to be carried outside and set upon the beasts. But by the will of Allah Almighty he had clean forgotten the cabalistic words, and cried out, "Open, Barley!" Whereat the door refused to move. Astonished and confused beyond measure, he named the names of all manner of grains save sesame, which had slipped from his memory as though he had never heard the word, whereat in his dire distress he heeded not the ashrafis that lay heaped at the entrance, and paced to and fro, backward and forward, within the cave, sorely puzzled and perplexed. The wealth whose sight had erewhile filled his heart with joy and gladness was now the cause of bitter grief and sadness.

It came to pass that at noontide the robbers, returning by that way, saw from afar some mules standing beside the entrance, and much they marveled at what had brought the beasts to that place, for inasmuch as Kasim by mischance had failed to tether or hobble them, they had strayed about the jungle and were browsing hither and thither. However, the thieves paid scant regard to the estrays, nor cared they to secure them, but only wondered by what means they had wandered so far from the town. Then, reaching the cave, the captain and his troop dismounted, and going up to the door, repeated the formula, and at once it flew open.

Now Kasim had heard from within the cave the horse hoofs drawing nigh and yet nigher, and he fell down to the ground in a fit of fear, never doubting that it was the clatter of the banditti who would slaughter him without fail. Howbeit, he presently took heart of grace, and at the moment when the door flew open he rushed out hoping to make good his escape. But the unhappy ran full tilt against the captain, who stood in front of the band, and felled him to the ground, whereupon a robber standing near his chief at once bared his brand and with one cut clave Kasim clean in twain. Thereupon the robbers rushed into the cavern, and put back as they were before the bags of ashrafis which Kasim had heaped up at the doorway ready for taking away, nor recked they aught of those which Ali Baba had removed, so dazed and amazed were they to discover by what means the strange man had effected an entrance. All knew that it was not possible for any to drop through the skylights, so tall and steep was the rock's face, withal slippery of ascent, and also that none could enter by the portal unless he knew the magical words whereby to open it. However, they presently quartered the dead body of Kasim and hung it to the door within the cavern, two parts to the right jamb and as many to the left, that the sight might be a warning of approaching doom for all who dared enter the cave. Then, coming out, they closed the hoard door and rode away upon their wonted work.

Now when night fell and Kasim came not home, his wife waxed uneasy in mind, and running round to Ali Baba, said: "O my brother, Kasim hath not returned. Thou knowest whither he went, and sore I fear me some misfortune hath betided him." Ali Baba also divined that a mishap had happened to prevent his return. Not the less, however, he strove to comfort his sister-in-law with words of cheer, and said: "O wife of my brother, Kasim haply exerciseth discretion and, avoiding the city, cometh by a roundabout road and will be here anon. This I do believe is the reason why he tarrieth." Thereupon, comforted in spirit, Kasim's wife fared homeward and sat awaiting her husband's return, but when half the night was spent and still he came not, she was as one distraught. She feared to cry aloud for her grief, lest haply the neighbors, hearing her, should come and learn the secret, so she wept in silence and upbraiding herself, fell to thinking: "Wherefore did I disclose this secret to him and beget envy and jealousy of Ali Baba? This be the fruit thereof, and hence the disaster that hath come down upon me."

She spent the rest of the night in bitter tears, and early on the morrow hied in hottest hurry to Ali Baba and prayed that he would go forth in quest of his brother. So he strove to console her, and straightway set out with his asses for the forest. Presently, reaching the rock, he wondered to see stains of blood freshly shed, and not finding his brother or the ten mules, he forefelt a calamity from so evil a sign. He then went to the door and saying, "Open, Sesame!" he pushed in and saw the dead body of Kasim, two parts hanging to the right and the rest to the left of the entrance. Albeit he was affrighted beyond measure of affright, he wrapped the quarters in two cloths and laid them upon one of his asses, hiding them carefully with sticks and fuel that none might see them. Then he placed the bags of gold upon the two other animals and likewise covered them most carefully, and when all was made ready he closed the cave door with the magical words, and set him forth wending homeward with all ward and watchfulness. The asses with the load of ashrafis he made over to his wife, and bade her bury the bags with diligence, but he told her not the condition in which he had come upon his brother Kasim. Then he went with the other ass—to wit, the beast whereon was laid the corpse—to the widow's house and knocked gently at the door.

Now Kasim had a slave girl shrewd and sharp-witted, Morgiana hight. She as softly undid the bolt and admitted Ali Baba and the ass into the courtyard of the house, when he let down the body from the beast's back and said: "O Morgiana, haste thee and make thee ready to perform the rites for the burial of thy lord. I now go to tell the tidings to thy mistress, and I will quickly return to help thee in this matter." At that instant Kasim's widow, seeing her brother-in-law, exclaimed: "O Ali Baba, what news bringest thou of my spouse? Alas! I see grief tokens written upon thy countenance. Say quickly what hath happened." Then he recounted to her how it had fared with her husband and how he had been slain by the robbers and in what wise he had brought home the dead body. Ali Baba pursued: "O my lady, what was to happen hath happened, but it behooveth us to keep this matter secret, for that our lives depend upon privacy." She wept with sore weeping and made answer: "It hath fared with my husband according to the fiat of Fate, and now for thy safety's sake I give thee my word to keep the affair concealed." He replied: "Naught can avail when Allah hath decreed. Rest thee in patience until the days of thy widowhood be accomplisht, after which time I will take thee to wife, and thou shalt live in comfort and happiness. And fear not lest my first spouse vex thee or show aught of jealousy, for that she is kindly and tender of heart." The widow, lamenting her loss noisily, cried, "Be it as e'en thou please."

Then Ali Baba farewelled her, weeping and wailing for her husband, and joining Morgiana, took counsel with her how to manage the burial of his brother. So, after much consultation and many warnings, he left the slave girl and departed home driving his ass before him. As soon as Ali Baba had fared forth Morgiana went quickly to a druggist's shop, and that she might the better dissemble with him and not make known the matter, she asked of him a drug often administered to men when diseased with dangerous distemper. He gave it saying: "Who is there in thy house that lieth so ill as to require this medicine?" and said she: "My master Kasim is sick well nigh unto death. For many days he hath nor spoken nor tasted aught of food, so that almost we despair of his life." Next day Morgiana went again and asked the druggist for more of medicine and essences such as are adhibited to the sick when at door of death, that the moribund may haply rally before the last breath. The man gave the potion and she, taking it, sighed aloud and wept, saying: "I fear me he may not have strength to drink this draught. Methinks all will be over with him ere I return to the house."

Meanwhile Ali Baba was anxiously awaiting to hear sounds of wailing and lamentation in Kasim's home, that he might at such signal hasten thither and take part in the ceremonies of the funeral. Early on the second day Morgiana went with veiled face to one Baba Mustafa, a tailor well shotten in years whose craft was to make shrouds and cerecloths, and as soon as she saw him open his shop she gave him a gold piece and said, "Do thou bind a bandage over thine eyes and come along with me." Mustafa made as though he would not go, whereat Morgiana placed a second gold coin in his palm and entreated him to accompany her. The tailor presently consented for greed of gain, so, tying a kerchief tightly over his eyes, she led him by the hand to the house wherein lay the dead body of her master.

Then, taking off the bandage in the darkened room, she bade him sew together the quarters of the corpse, limb to its limb, and casting a cloth upon the body, said to the tailor: "Make haste and sew a shroud according to the size of this dead man, and I will give thee therefor yet another ducat." Baba Mustafa quickly made the cerecloth of fitting length and breadth, and Morgiana paid him the promised ashrafi, then, once more bandaging his eyes, led him back to the place whence she had brought him. After this she returned hurriedly home and with the help of Ali Baba washed the body in warm water and donning the shroud, laid the corpse upon a clean place ready for burial.

This done, Morgiana went to the mosque and gave notice to an imam that a funeral was awaiting the mourners in a certain household, and prayed that he would come to read the prayers for the dead, and the imam went back with her. Then four neighbors took up the bier and bore it on their shoulders and fared forth with the imam and others who were wont to give assistance at such obsequies. After the funeral prayers were ended four other men carried off the coffin, and Morgiana walked before it bare of head, striking her breast and weeping and wailing with exceeding loud lament, whilst Ali Baba and the neighbors came behind. In such order they entered the cemetery and buried him, then, leaving him to Munkar and Nakir— the Questioners of the Dead—all wended their ways. Presently the women of the quarter, according to the custom of the city, gathered together in the house of mourning and sat an hour with Kasim's widow comforting and condoling, presently leaving her somewhat resigned and cheered. Ali Baba stayed forty days at home in ceremonial lamentation for the loss of his brother, so none within the town save himself and his wife (Kasim's widow) and Morgiana knew aught the secret. And when the forty days of mourning were ended Ali Baba removed to his own quarters all the property belonging to the deceased and openly married the widow. Then he appointed his nephew, his brother's eldest son, who had lived a long time with a wealthy merchant and was perfect of knowledge in all matters of trade, such as selling and buying, to take charge of the defunct's shop and to carry on the business.

It so chanced one day when the robbers, as was their wont, came to the treasure cave that they marveled exceedingly to find nor sign nor trace of Kasim's body, whilst they observed that much of gold had been carried off. Quoth the captain: "Now it behooveth us to make inquiry in this matter, else shall we suffer much of loss, and this our treasure, which we and our forefathers have amassed during the course of many years, will little by little be wasted and spoiled." Hereto all assented and with single mind agreed that he whom they had slain had knowledge of the magical words whereby the door was made to open; moreover, that someone besides him had cognizance of the spell and had carried off the body, and also much of gold. Wherefore they needs must make diligent research and find out who the man ever might be. They then took counsel and determined that one amongst them, who should be sagacious and deft of wit, must don the dress of some merchant from foreign parts, then, repairing to the city, he must go about from quarter to quarter and from street to street and learn if any townsman had lately died, and if so where he wont to dwell, that with this clue they might be enabled to find the wight they sought. Hereat said one of the robbers: "Grant me leave that I fare and find out such tidings in the town and bring thee word anon, and if I fail of my purpose I hold my life in forfeit."

Accordingly that bandit, after disguising himself by dress, pushed at night into the town, and next morning early he repaired to the market square and saw that none of the shops had yet been opened save only that of Baba Mustafa, the tailor, who, thread and needle in hand, sat upon his working stool. The thief bade him good day and said: "'Tis yet dark. How canst thou see to sew?" Said the tailor: "I perceive thou art a stranger. Despite my years, my eyesight is so keen that only yesterday I sewed together a dead body whilst sitting in a room quite darkened." Quoth the bandit thereupon to himself, "I shall get somewhat of my want from this snip," and to secure a further clue he asked: "Meseemeth thou wouldst jest with me, and thou meanest that a cerecloth for a corpse was stitched by thee and that thy business is to sew shrouds." Answered the tailor: "It mattereth not to thee. Question me no more questions."

Thereupon the robber placed an ashrafi in his hand and continued: "I desire not to discover aught thou hidest, albeit my breast, like every honest man's, is the grave of secrets, and this only would I learn of thee—in what house didst thou do that job? Canst thou direct me thither, or thyself conduct me thereto?" The tailor took the gold with greed and cried: "I have not seen with my own eyes the way to that house. A certain bondswoman led me to a place which I know right well, and there she bandaged my eyes and guided me to some tenement and lastly carried me into a darkened room where lay the dead body dismembered. Then she unbound the kerchief and bade me sew together first the corpse and then the shroud, which having done, she again blindfolded me and led me back to the stead whence she had brought me and left me there. Thou seest then I am not able to tell thee where thou shalt find the house." Quoth the robber: "Albeit thou knowest not the dwelling whereof thou speakest, still canst thou take me to the place where thou wast blindfolded. Then I will bind a kerchief over thine eyes and lead thee as thou wast led. On this wise perchance thou mayest hit upon the site. An thou wilt do this favor by me, see, here another golden ducat is thine." Thereupon the bandit slipped a second ashrafi into the tailor's palm, and Baba Mustafa thrust it with the first into his pocket. Then, leaving his shop as it was, he walked to the place where Morgiana had tied the kerchief around his eyes, and with him went the robber, who, after binding on the bandage, led him by the hand.

Baba Mustafa, who was clever and keen-witted, presently striking the street whereby he had fared with the handmaid, walked on counting step by step, then, halting suddenly, he said, "Thus far I came with her," and the twain stopped in front of Kasim's house, wherein now dwelt his brother Ali Baba. The robber then made marks with white chalk upon the door, to the end that he might readily find it at some future time, and removing the bandage from the tailor's eyes, said: "O Baba Mustafa, I thank thee for this favor, and Almighty Allah guerdon thee for thy goodness. Tell me now, I pray thee, who dwelleth in yonder house?" Quoth he: "In very sooth I wot not, for I have little knowledge concerning this quarter of the city." And the bandit, understanding that he could find no further clue from the tailor, dismissed him to his shop with abundant thanks, and hastened back to the tryst place in the jungle where the band awaited his coming.

Not long after, it so fortuned that Morgiana, going out upon some errand, marveled exceedingly at seeing the chalk marks showing white in the door. She stood awhile deep in thought, and presently divined that some enemy had made the signs that he might recognize the house and play some sleight upon her lord. She therefore chalked the doors of all her neighbors in like manner and kept the matter secret, never entrusting it or to master or to mistress. Meanwhile the robber told his comrades his tale of adventure and how he had found the clue, so the captain and with him all the band went one after other by different ways till they entered the city, and he who had placed the mark on Ali Baba's door accompanied the chief to point out the place. He conducted him straightway to the house and shewing the sign, exclaimed, "Here dwelleth he of whom we are in search!" But when the captain looked around him, he saw that all the dwellings bore chalk marks after like fashion, and he wondered, saying: "By what manner of means knowest thou which house of all these houses that bear similar signs is that whereof thou spakest?" Hereat the robber guide was confounded beyond measure of confusion, and could make no answer. Then with an oath he cried: "I did assuredly set a sign upon a door, but I know not whence came all the marks upon the other entrances, nor can I say for a surety which it was I chalked." Thereupon the captain returned to the market place and said to his men: "We have toiled and labored in vain, nor have we found the house we went forth to seek. Return we now to the forest, our rendezvous. I also will fare thither."

Then all trooped off and assembled together within the treasure cave, and when the robbers had all met, the captain judged him worthy of punishment who had spoken falsely and had led them through the city to no purpose. So he imprisoned him in presence of them all, and then said he: "To him amongst you will I show special favor who shall go to town and bring me intelligence whereby we may lay hands upon the plunderer of our property." Hereat another of the company came forward and said, "I am ready to go and inquire into the case, and 'tis I who will bring thee to thy wish." The captain, after giving him presents and promises, dispatched him upon his errand, and by the decree of Destiny, which none may gainsay, this second robber went first to the house of Baba Mustafa the tailor, as had done the thief who had foregone him. In like manner he also persuaded the snip with gifts of golden coin that he be led hood-winked, and thus too he was guided to Ali Baba's door. Here, noting the work of his predecessor, he affixed to the jamb a mark with red chalk, the better to distinguish it from the others, whereon still showed the white. Then hied he back in stealth to his company.

But Morgiana on her part also descried the red sign on the entrance, and with subtle forethought marked all the others after the same fashion, nor told she any what she had done. Meanwhile the bandit rejoined his band and vauntingly said: "O our captain, I have found the house and thereon put a mark whereby I shall distinguish it clearly from all its neighbors." But, as aforetime, when the troop repaired thither, they saw each and every house marked with signs of red chalk. So they returned disappointed and the captain, waxing displeased exceedingly and distraught, clapped also this spy into gaol. Then said the chief to himself: "Two men have failed in their endeavor and have met their rightful meed of punishment, and I trow that none other of my band will essay to follow up their research. So I myself will go and find the house of this wight."

Accordingly he fared along, aided by the tailor Baba Mustafa, who had gained much gain of golden pieces in this matter, he hit upon the house of Ali Baba. And here he made no outward show or sign, but marked it on the tablet of his heart and impressed the picture upon the page of his memory. Then, returning to the jungle, he said to his men: "I have full cognizance of the place and have limned it clearly in my mind, so now there will be no difficulty in finding it. Go forth straightway and buy me and bring hither nineteen mules, together with one large leathern jar of mustard oil and seven and thirty vessels of the same kind clean empty. Without me and the two locked up in gaol ye number thirty-seven souls, so I will stow you away armed and accoutered each within his jar and will load two upon each mule, and upon the nineteenth mule there shall be a man in an empty jar on one side and on the other the jar full of oil. I for my part, in guise of an oil merchant, will drive the mules into the town, arriving at the house by night, and will ask permission of its master to tarry there until morning. After this we shall seek occasion during the dark hours to rise up and fall upon him and slay him." Furthermore, the captain spake, saying: "When we have made an end of him we shall recover the gold and treasure whereof he robbed us and bring it back upon the mules."

This counsel pleased the robbers, who went forthwith and purchased mules and huge leathern jars, and did as the captain had bidden them. And after a delay of three days, shortly before nightfall they arose, and oversmearing all the jars with oil of mustard, each hid him inside an empty vessel. The chief then disguised himself in trader's gear and placed the jars upon the nineteen mules; to wit, the thirty-seven vessels, in each of which lay a robber armed and accoutered, and the one that was full of oil. This done, he drove the beasts before him, and presently he reached Ali Baba's place at nightfall, when it chanced that the housemaster was strolling after supper to and fro in front of his home. The captain saluted him with the salaam and said: "I come from such-and-such a village with oil, and ofttimes have I been here a-selling oil, but now to my grief I have arrived too late and I am sore troubled and perplexed as to where I shall spend the night. An thou have pity on me, I pray thee grant that I tarry here in thy courtyard and ease the mules by taking down the jars and giving the beasts somewhat of fodder." Albeit Ali Baba had heard the captain's voice when perched upon the tree and had seen him enter the cave, yet by reason of the disguise he knew him not for the leader of the thieves, and granted his request with hearty welcome and gave him full license to halt there for the night. He then pointed out an empty shed wherein to tether the mules, and bade one of the slave boys go fetch grain and water. He also gave orders to the slave girl Morgiana, saying: "A guest hath come hither and tarrieth here tonight. Do thou busy thyself with all speed about his supper and make ready the guest bed for him."

Presently, when the captain had let down all the jars and had fed and watered his mules, Ali Baba received him with all courtesy and kindness, and summoning Morgiana, said in his presence: "See thou fail not in service of this our stranger, nor suffer him to lack for aught. Tomorrow early I would fare to the hammam and bathe, so do thou give my slave boy Abdullah a suit of clean white clothes which I may put on after washing. Moreover, make thee ready a somewhat of broth overnight, that I may drink it after my return home." Replied she, "I will have all in readiness as thou hast bidden." So Ali Baba retired to his rest, and the captain, having supped, repaired to the shed and saw that all the mules had their food and drink for the night, and finding utter privacy, whispered to his men who were in ambush: "This night at midnight, when ye hear my voice, do you quickly open with your sharp knives the leathern jars from top to bottom, and issue forth without delay." Then, passing through the kitchen, he reached the chamber wherein a bed had been dispread for him, Morgiana showing the way with a lamp. Quoth she, "An thou need aught beside, I pray thee command this thy slave, who is ever ready to obey thy say!" He made answer, "Naught else need I." Then, putting out the light, he lay down on the bed to sleep awhile ere the time came to rouse his men and finish off the work.

Meanwhile Morgiana did as her master had bidden her. She first took out a suit of clean white clothes and made it over to Abdullah, who had not yet gone to rest. Then she placed the pipkin upon the hearth to boil the broth and blew the fire till it burnt briskly. After a short delay she needs must see an the broth be boiling, but by that time all the lamps had gone out and she found that the oil was spent and that nowhere could she get a light. The slave boy Abdullah observed that she was troubled and perplexed hereat, and quoth he to her: "Why make so much ado? In yonder shed are many jars of oil. Go now and take as much soever as thou listest." Morgiana gave thanks to him for his suggestion, and Abdullah, who was lying at his ease in the hall, went off to sleep so that he might wake betimes and serve Ali Baba in the bath. So the handmaiden rose, and with oil can in hand walked to the shed where stood the leathern jars all ranged in rows.

Now as she drew nigh unto one of the vessels, the thief who was hidden therein, hearing the tread of footsteps, bethought him that it was of his captain, whose summons he awaited, so he whispered, "Is it now time for us to sally forth?" Morgiana started back affrighted at the sound of human accents, but inasmuch as she was bold and ready of wit, she replied, "The time is not yet come," and said to herself: "These jars are not full of oil, and herein I perceive a manner of mystery. Haply the oil merchant hatcheth some treacherous plot against my lord, so Allah, the Compassionating, the Compassionate, protect us from his snares!" Wherefore she answered in a voice made like to the captain's, "Not yet, the time is not come." Then she went to the next jar and returned the same reply to him who was within, and so on to all the vessels, one by one. Then said she in herself: "Laud to the Lord! My master took this fellow in believing him to be an oil merchant, but lo! he hath admitted a band of robbers, who only await the signal to fall upon him and plunder the place and do him die."

Then passed she on to the furthest jar and, finding it brimming with oil, filled her can, and returning to the kitchen, trimmed the lamp and lit the wicks. Then, bringing forth a large caldron, she set it upon the fire, and filling it with oil from out the jar, heaped wood upon the hearth and fanned it to a fierce flame, the readier to boil its contents. When this was done, she bailed it out in potfuls and poured it seething hot into the leathern vessels, one by one, while the thieves, unable to escape, were scalded to death and every jar contained a corpse. Thus did this slave girl by her subtle wit make a clean end of all, noiselessly and unknown even to the dwellers in the house. Now when she had satisfied herself that each and every of the men had been slain, she went back to the kitchen and, shutting to the door, sat brewing Ali Baba's broth.

Scarce had an hour passed before the captain woke from sleep and, opening wide his window, saw that all was dark and silent. So he clapped his hands as a signal for his men to come forth, but not a sound was heard in return. After a while he clapped again and called aloud, but got no answer, and when he cried out a third time without reply, he was perplexed and went out to the shed wherein stood the jars. He thought to himself: "Perchance all are fallen asleep, whenas the time for action is now at hand, so I must e'en awaken them without stay or delay." Then, approaching the nearest jar, he was startled by a smell of oil and seething flesh, and touching it outside, he felt it reeking hot. Then, going to the others one by one, he found all in like condition. Hereat he knew for a surety the fate which had betided his band and, fearing for his own safety, he clomb onto the wall, and thence dropping into a garden, made his escape in high dudgeon and sore disappointment. Morgiana awaited awhile to see the captain return from the shed but he came not, whereat she knew that he had scaled the wall and had taken to flight, for that the street door was double-locked. And the thieves being all disposed of on this wise, Morgiana laid her down to sleep in perfect solace and ease of mind.

When two hours of darkness yet remained, Ali Baba awoke and went to the hammam, knowing naught of the night adventure, for the gallant slave girl had not aroused him, nor indeed had she deemed such action expedient, because had she sought an opportunity of reporting to him her plan, she might haply have lost her chance and spoiled the project. The sun was high over the horizon when Ali Baba walked back from the baths, and he marveled exceedingly to see the jars still standing under the shed, and said: "How cometh it that he, the oil merchant, my guest, hath not carried to the market his mules and jars of oil?" She answered: "Allah Almighty vouchsafe to thee sixscore years and ten of safety! I will tell thee in privacy of this merchant." So Ali Baba went apart with his slave girl, who, taking him without the house, first locked the court door, then, showing him a jar, she said, "Prithee look into this and see if within there be oil or aught else."

Thereupon, peering inside it, he perceived a man, at which sight he cried aloud and fain would have fled in his fright. Quoth Morgiana: "Fear him not. This man hath no longer the force to work thee harm, he lieth dead and stone-dead." Hearing such words of comfort and reassurance, Ali Baba asked: "O Morgiana, what evils have we escaped, and by what means hath this wretch become the quarry of Fate?" She answered: "Alhamdolillah—praise be to Almighty Allah! —I will inform thee fully of the case. But hush thee, speak not aloud, lest haply the neighbors learn the secret and it end in our confusion. Look now into all the jars, one by one from first to last." So Ali Baba examined them severally and found in each a man fully armed and accoutered, and all lay scalded to death. Hereat, speechless for sheer amazement, he stared at the jars, but presently, recovering himself, he asked, "And where is he, the oil merchant?" Answered she: "Of him also I will inform thee. The villain was no trader, but a traitorous assassin whose honeyed words would have ensnared thee to thy doom. And now I will tell thee what he was and what hath happened, but meanwhile thou art fresh from the hammam and thou shouldst first drink somewhat of this broth for thy stomach's and thy health's sake." So Ali Baba went within and Morgiana served up the mess, after which quoth her master: "I fain would hear this wondrous story. Prithee tell it to me, and set my heart at ease." Hereat the handmaid fell to relating whatso had betided in these words:

"O my master, when thou badest me boil the broth and retiredst to rest, thy slave in obedience to thy command took out a suit of clean white clothes and gave it to the boy Abdullah, then kindled the fire and set on the broth. As soon as it was ready I had need to light a lamp so that I might see to skim it, but all the oil was spent, and, learning this, I told my want to the slave boy Abdullah, who advised me to draw somewhat from the jars which stood under the shed. Accordingly I took a can and went to the first vessel, when suddenly I heard a voice within whisper with all caution, 'Is it now time for us to sally forth?' I was amazed thereat, and judged that the pretended merchant had laid some plot to slay thee, so I replied, 'The time is not yet come.' Then I went to the second jar and heard another voice, to which I made the like answer, and so on with all of them. I now was certified that these men awaited only some signal from their chief, whom thou didst take to guest within thy walls supposing him to be a merchant in oil, and that after thou receivedst him hospitably the miscreant had brought these men to murther thee and to plunder thy good and spoil thy house.

"But I gave him no opportunity to win his wish. The last jar I found full of oil, and taking somewhat therefrom, I lit the lamp. Then, putting a large caldron upon the fire, I filled it up with oil which I brought from the jar and made a fierce blaze under it, and when the contents were seething hot, I took out sundry cansful with intent to scald them all to death, and going to each jar in due order, I poured within them, one by one, boiling oil. On this wise having destroyed them utterly, I returned to the kitchen, and having extinguished the lamps, stood by the window watching what might happen, and how that false merchant would act next. Not long after I had taken my station, the robber captain awoke and ofttimes signaled to his thieves. Then, getting no reply, he came downstairs and went out to the jars, and finding that all his men were slain, he fled through the darkness, I know not whither. So when he had clean disappeared I was assured that, the door being double-locked, he had scaled the wall and dropped into the garden and made his escape. Then with my heart at rest I slept."

And Morgiana, after telling her story to her master, presently added: "This is the whole truth I have related to thee. For some days indeed have I had inkling of such matter, but withheld it from thee, deeming it inexpedient to risk the chance of its meeting the neighbors' ears. Now, however, there is no help but to tell thee thereof. One day as I came to the house door I espied thereon a white chalk mark, and on the next day a red sign beside the white. I knew not the intent wherewith the marks were made, nevertheless I set others upon the entrances of sundry neighbors, judging that some enemy had done this deed, whereby to encompass my master's destruction. Therefore I made the marks on all the other doors in such perfect conformity with those I found that it would be hard to distinguish amongst them. Judge now and see if these signs and all this villainy be not the work of the bandits of the forest, who marked our house that on such wise they might know it again. Of these forty thieves there yet remain two others concerning whose case I know naught, so beware of them, but chiefly of the third remaining robber, their captain, who fled hence alive. Take good heed and be thou cautious of him, for shouldst thou fall into his hands, he will in no wise spare thee, but will surely múrther thee. I will do all that lieth in me to save from hurt and harm thy life and property, nor shall thy slave be found wanting in any service to my lord."

Hearing these words, Ali Baba rejoiced with exceeding joyance and said to her: "I am well pleased with thee for this thy conduct, and say me what wouldst thou have me do in thy behalf. I shall not fail to remember thy brave deed so long as breath in me remaineth." Quoth she: "It behooveth us before all things forthright to bury these bodies in the ground, that so the secret be not known to anyone." Hereupon Ali Baba took with him his slave boy Abdullah into the garden and there under a tree they dug for the corpses of the thieves a deep pit in size proportionate to its contents, and they dragged the bodies (having carried off their weapons) to the fosse and threw them in. Then, covering up the remains of the seven and thirty robbers, they made the ground appear level and clean as it wont to be. They also hid the leathern jars and the gear and arms, and presently Ali Baba sent the mules by ones and twos to the bazaar and sold them all with the able aid of his slave boy Abdullah. Thus the matter was hushed up, nor did it reach the ears of any. However, Ali Baba ceased not to be ill at ease, lest haply the captain or the surviving two robbers should wreak their vengeance on his head. He kept himself private with all caution, and took heed that none learn a word of what had happened and of the wealth which he had carried off from the bandits' cave.

Meanwhile the captain of the thieves, having escaped with his life, fled to the forest in hot wrath and sore irk of mind, and his senses were scattered and the color of his visage vanished like ascending smoke. Then he thought the matter over again and again, and at last he firmly resolved that he needs must take the life of Ali Baba, else he would lose all the treasure which his enemy, by knowledge of the magical words, would take away and turn to his own use. Furthermore, he determined that he would undertake the business singlehanded; and that after getting rid of Ali Baba, he would gather together another band of banditti and would pursue his career of brigandage, as indeed his forebears had done for many generations. So he lay down to rest that night, and rising early in the morning, donned a dress of suitable appearance, then, going to the city, alighted at a caravanserai, thinking to himself: "Doubtless the múrther of so many men hath reached the wali's ears, and Ali Baba hath been seized and brought to justice, and his house is leveled and his good is confiscated. The townfolk must surely have heard tidings of these matters." So he straightway asked of the keeper of the khan, "What strange things have happened in the city during the last few days?" And the other told him all that he had seen and heard, but the captain could not learn a whit of that which most concerned him. Hereby he understood that Ali Baba was ware and wise, and that he had not only carried away such store of treasure, but he had also destroyed so many lives and withal had come off scatheless. Furthermore, that he himself must needs have all his wits alert not to fall into the hands of his foe and perish.

With this resolve the captain hired a shop in the bazaar, whither he bore whole bales of the finest stuffs and goodly merchandise from his forest treasure house, and presently he took his seat within the store and fell to doing merchant's business. By chance his place fronted the booth of the defunct Kasim, where his son, Ali Baba's nephew, now traded, and the captain, who called himself Khwajah Hasan, soon formed acquaintance and friendship with the shopkeepers around about him and treated all with profuse civilities. But he was especially gracious and cordial to the son of Kasim, a handsome youth and a well-dressed, and ofttimes he would sit and chat with him for a long while. A few days after, it chanced that Ali Baba, as he was sometimes wont to do, came to see his nephew, whom he found sitting in his shop. The captain saw and recognized him at sight, and one morning he asked the young man, saying, "Prithee tell me, who is he that ever and anon cometh to thee at thy place of sale?" Whereto the youth made answer, "He is my uncle, the brother of my father." Whereupon the captain showed him yet greater favor and affection, the better to deceive him for his own devices, and gave him presents and made him sit at meat with him and fed him with the daintiest of dishes.

Presently Ali Baba's nephew bethought him it was only right and proper that he also should invite the merchant to supper, but whereas his own house was small, and he was straitened for room and could not make a show of splendor, as did Khwajah Hasan, he took counsel with his uncle on the matter. Ali Baba replied to his nephew: "Thou sayest well. It behooveth thee to entreat thy friend in fairest fashion even as he hath entreated thee. On the morrow, which is Friday, shut thy shop, as do all merchants of repute. Then, after the early meal, take Khwajah Hasan to smell the air, and as thou walkest lead him hither unawares. Meanwhile I will give orders that Morgiana shall make ready for his coming the best of viands and all necessaries for a feast. Trouble not thyself on any wise, but leave the matter in my hands." Accordingly on the next day—to wit, Friday—the nephew of Ali Baba took Khwajah Hasan to walk about the garden, and as they were returning he led him by the street wherein his uncle dwelt. When they came to the house, the youth stopped at the door and knocking, said: "O my lord, this is my second home. My uncle hath heard much of thee and of thy goodness meward, and desireth with exceeding desire to see thee, so shouldst thou consent to enter and visit him, I shall be truly glad and thankful to thee." Albeit Khwajah Hasan rejoiced in heart that he had thus found means whereby he might have access to his enemy's house and household, and although he hoped soon to attain his end by treachery, yet he hesitated to enter in and stood to make his excuses and walk away.

But when the door was opened by the slave porter, Ali Baba's nephew seized his companion's hand and after abundant persuasion led him in, whereat he entered with great show of cheerfulness as though much pleased and honored. The housemaster received him with all favor and worship and asked him of his welfare, and said to him: "O my lord, I am obliged and thankful to thee for that thou hast shewn favor to the son of my brother, and I perceive that thou regardest him with an affection even fonder than my own." Khwajah Hasan replied with pleasant words and said: "Thy nephew vastly taketh my fancy and in him I am well pleased, for that although young in years yet he hath been endued by Allah with much of wisdom."

Thus they twain conversed with friendly conversation, and presently the guest rose to depart and said: "O my lord, thy slave must now farewell thee, but on some future day—Inshallah—he will again wait upon thee." Ali Baba, however, would not let him leave, and asked: "Whither wendest thou, O my friend? I would invite thee to my table, and I pray thee sit at meat with us and after hie thee home in peace. Perchance the dishes are not as delicate as those whereof thou art wont to eat, still deign grant me this request, I pray thee, and refresh thyself with my victual." Quoth Khwajah Hasan: "O lord, I am beholden to thee for thy gracious invitation, and with pleasure would

I sit at meat with thee, but for a special reason must I needs excuse myself. Suffer me therefore to depart, for I may not tarry longer, nor accept thy gracious offer." Hereto the host made reply: "I pray thee, O my lord, tell me what may be the reason so urgent and weighty." And Khwajah Hasan answered: "The cause is this. I must not, by order of the physician who cured me lately of my complaint, eat aught of food prepared with salt." Quoth Ali Baba: "An this be all, deprive me not, I pray thee, of the honor thy company will confer upon me. As the meats are not yet cooked, I will forbid the kitchener to make use of any salt. Tarry here awhile, and I will return anon to thee." So saying, Ali Baba went in to Morgiana and bade her not put salt into any one of the dishes, and she, while busied with her cooking, fell to marveling greatly at such order and asked her master, "Who is he that eateth meat wherein is no salt?" He answered: "What to thee mattereth it who he may be? Only do thou my bidding." She rejoined: "'Tis well. All shall be as thou wishest." But in mind she wondered at the man who made such strange request, and desired much to look upon him.

Wherefore, when all the meats were ready for serving up, she helped the slave boy Abdullah to spread the table and set on the meal, and no sooner did she see Khwajah Hasan than she knew who he was, albeit he had disguised himself in the dress of a stranger merchant. Furthermore, when she eyed him attentively, she espied a dagger hidden under his robe. "So ho!" quoth she to herself. "This is the cause why the villain eateth not of salt, for that he seeketh an opportunity to slay my master, whose mortal enemy he is. Howbeit I will be beforehand with him and dispatch him ere he find a chance to harm my lord." Now when Ali Baba and Khwajah Hasan had eaten their sufficiency, the slave boy Abdullah brought Morgiana word to serve the dessert, and she cleared the table and set on fruit fresh and dried in salvers, then she placed by the side of Ali Baba a small tripod for three cups with a flagon of wine, and lastly she went off with the slave boy Abdullah into another room, as though she would herself eat supper. Then Khwajah Hasan—that is, the captain of the robbers—perceiving that the coast was clear, exulted mightily, saying to himself: "The time hath come for me to take full vengeance. With one thrust of my dagger I will dispatch this fellow, then escape across the garden and wend my ways. His nephew will not adventure to stay my hand, for an he do but move a finger or toe with that intent, another stab with settle his earthly account. Still must I wait awhile until the slave boy and the cookmaid shall have eaten and lain down to rest them in the kitchen."

Morgiana, however, watched him wistfully and divining his purpose, said in her mind: "I must not allow this villain advantage over my lord, but by some means I must make void his project and at once put an end to the life of him." Accordingly the trusty slave girl changed her dress with all haste and donned such clothes as dancers wear. She veiled her face with a costly kerchief, around her head she bound a fine turban, and about her middle she tied a waistcloth worked with gold and silver, wherein she stuck a dagger whose hilt was rich in filigree and jewelry. Thus disguised, she said to the slave boy Abdullah: "Take now thy tambourine, that we may play and sing and dance in honor of our master's guest." So he did her bidding and the twain went into the room, the lad playing and the lass following. Then, making a low congee, they asked leave to perform and disport and play, and Ali Baba gave permission, saying, "Dance now and do your best that this our guest may be mirthful and merry." Quoth Khwajah Hasan, "O my lord, thou dost indeed provide much pleasant entertainment."

Then the slave boy Abdullah, standing by, began to strike the tambourine whilst Morgiana rose up and showed her perfect art and pleased them vastly with graceful steps and sportive motion. And suddenly, drawing the poniard from her belt, she brandished it and paced from side to side, a spectacle which pleased them most of all. At times also she stood before them, now clapping the sharp-edged dagger under her armpit and then setting it against her breast. Lastly she took the tambourine from the slave boy Abdullah, and still holding the poniard in her right, she went round for largess as is the custom amongst merrymakers. First she stood before Ali Baba, who threw a gold coin into the tambourine, and his nephew likewise put in an ashrafi. Then Khwajah Hasan, seeing her about to approach him, fell to pulling out his purse, when she heartened her heart, and quick as the blinding levin she plunged the dagger into his vitals, and forthwith the miscreant fell back stone-dead.

Ali Baba was dismayed, and cried in his wrath: "O unhappy, what is this deed thou hast done to bring about my ruin?" But she replied: "Nay, O my lord, rather to save thee and not to cause thee harm have I slain this man. Loosen his garments and see what thou wilt discover thereunder." So Ali Baba searched the dead man's dress and found concealed therein a dagger.

Then said Morgiana: "This wretch was thy deadly enemy. Consider him well. He is none other than the oil merchant, the captain of the band of robbers. Whenas he came hither with intent to take thy life, he would not eat thy salt, and when thou toldest me that he wished not any in the meat, I suspected him, and at first sight I was assured that he would surely do thee die. Almighty Allah be praised, 'tis even as I thought." Then Ali Baba lavished upon her thanks and expressions of gratitude, saying, "Lo, these two times hast thou saved me from his hand," and falling upon her neck, he cried: "See, thou art free, and as reward for this thy fealty I have wedded thee to my nephew." Then, turning to the youth, he said: "Do as I bid thee and thou shalt prosper. I would that thou marry Morgiana, who is a model of duty and loyalty. Thou seest now yon Khwajah Hasan sought thy friendship only that he might find opportunity to take my life, but this maiden with her good sense and her wisdom hath slain him and saved us."

Ali Baba's nephew straightway consented to marry Morgiana. After which the three, raising the dead body, bore it forth with all heed and vigilance and privily buried it in the garden, and for many years no one know aught thereof. In due time Ali Baba married his brother's son to Morgiana with great pomp, and spread a bride feast in most sumptuous fashion for his friends and neighbors, and made merry with them and enjoyed singing and all manner of dancing and amusements. He prospered in every undertaking and Time smiled upon him and a new source of wealth was opened to him.

For fear of the thieves he had not once visited the jungle cave wherein lay the treasure since the day he had carried forth the corpse of his brother Kasim. But some time after, he mounted his hackney one morning and journeyed thither, with all care and caution, till finding no signs of man or horse, and reassured in his mind, he ventured to draw near the door. Then, alighting from his beast, he tied it up to a tree, and going to the entrance, pronounced the words which he had not forgotten, "Open, Sesame!" Hereat, as was its wont, the door flew open, and entering thereby he saw the goods and hoard of gold and silver untouched and lying as he had left them. So he felt assured that not one of all the thieves remained alive, and that save himself there was not a soul who knew the secret of the place. At once he bound in his saddlecloth a load of ashrafis such as his horse could bear and brought it home, and in after days he showed the hoard to his sons and sons' sons and taught them how the door could be caused to open and shut. Thus Ali Baba and his household lived all their lives in wealth and joyance in that city where erst he had been a pauper, and by the blessing of that secret treasure he rose to high degree and dignities.

CONCLUSION

Now during this time Scheherazade had borne the King three boy children, so when she had made an end of the story, she rose to her feet and kissing ground before him, said, "O King of the Time and unique one of the Age and the Tide, I am thine handmaid, and these thousand nights and a night have I entertained thee with stories of folk gone before and admonitory instances of the men of yore. May I then make bold to crave a boon of thy Highness?" He replied, "Ask, O Scheherazade, and it shall be granted to thee." Whereupon she cried out to the nurses and the eunuchs, saying, "Bring me my children." So they brought them to her in haste, and they were three boy children, one walking, one crawling, and one suckling. She took them, and setting them before the King, again kissed the ground and said: "O King of the Age, these are thy children, and I crave that thou release me from the doom of death, as a dole to these infants. For an thou kill me, they will become motherless and will find none among women to rear them as they should be reared."

When the King heard this, he wept, and straining the boys to his bosom, said: "By Allah, O Scheherazade, I pardoned thee before the coming of these children, for that I found thee chaste, pure, ingenuous, and pious! Allah bless thee and thy father and thy mother and thy root and thy branch! I take the Almighty to witness against me that I exempt thee from aught that can harm thee." So she kissed his hands and feet and rejoiced with exceeding joy, saying, "The Lord make thy life long and increase thee in dignity and majesty!" presently adding: "Thou marveledst at that which befell thee on the part of women; yet there betided the Kings of the Chosroes before thee greater mishaps and more grievous than that which hath befallen thee; and indeed I have set forth unto thee that which happened to caliphs and kings and others with their women, but the relation is longsome and hearkening groweth tedious, and in this is all-sufficient warning for the man of wits and admonishment for the wise."

Then she ceased to speak, and when King Shahryar heard her

speech and profited by that which she said, he summoned up his reasoning powers and cleansed his heart and caused his understanding revert and turned to Allah Almighty and said to himself: "Since there befell the Kings of the Chosroes more than that which hath befallen me, never whilst I live shall I cease to blame myself for the past. As for this Scheherazade, her like is not found in the lands, so praise be to Him who appointed her a means for delivering His creatures from oppression and slaughter!" Then he arose from his séance and kissed her head, whereat she rejoiced, she and her sister Dunyazade, with exceeding joy.

When the morning morrowed, the King went forth and sitting down on the throne of the kingship, summoned the lords of his land, whereupon the chamberlains and nabobs and captains of the host went in to him and kissed ground before him. He distinguished the Wazir, Scheherazade's sire, with special favor and bestowed on him a costly and splendid robe of honor and entreated him with the utmost kindness, and said to him: "Allah protect thee for that thou gavest me to wife thy noble daughter, who hath been the means of my repentance from slaying the daughters of folk. Indeed I have found her pure and pious, chaste and ingenuous, and Allah hath vouchsafed me by her three boy children, wherefore praised be He for his passing favor." Then he bestowed robes of honor upon his wazirs and emirs and chief officers, and he set forth to them briefly that which had betided him with Scheherazade and how he had turned from his former ways and repented him of what he had done and purposed to take the Wazir's daughter, Scheherazade, to wife and let draw up the marriage contract with her. When those who were present heard this, they kissed the ground before him and blessed him and his betrothed Scheherazade, and the Wazir thanked her. Then Shahryar made an end of his sitting in all weal, whereupon the folk dispersed to their dwelling places and the news was bruited abroad that the King purposed to marry the Wazir's daughter, Scheherazade.

Then he proceeded to make ready the wedding gear, and presently he sent after his brother, King Shah Zaman, who came, and King Shahryar went forth to meet him with the troops. Furthermore, they decorated the city after the goodliest fashion, and diffused scents from censers and burnt aloes wood and other perfumes in all the markets and thoroughfares, and rubbed themselves with saffron, what while the drums beat and the flutes and pipes sounded and mimes and mountebanks played and plied their arts and the King lavished on them gifts and largess. And in very deed it was a notable day. When they came to the palace, King Shahryar commanded to spread the tables with beasts roasted whole and sweetmeats and all manner of viands, and bade the crier cry to the folk that they should come up to the Divan and eat and drink, and that this should be a means of reconciliation between him and them. So high and low, great and small, came up unto him, and they abode on that wise, eating and drinking seven days with their nights.

Then the King shut himself up with his brother and related to him that which had betided him with the Wazir's daughter, Scheherazade, during the past three years, and told him what he had heard from her of proverbs and parables, chronicles and pleasantries, quips and jests, stories and anecdotes, dialogues and histories and elegies and other verses. Whereat King Shah Zaman marveled with the uttermost marvel and said: "Fain would I take her younger sister to wife, so we may be two brothers german to two sisters german, and they on like wise be sisters to us; for that the calamity which befell me was the cause of our discovering that which befell thee, and all this time of three years past I have taken no delight in woman, save that I lie each night with a damsel of my kingdom, and every morning I do her to death. But now I desire to marry thy wife's sister, Dunyazade."

When King Shahryar heard his brother's words, he rejoiced with joy exceeding and arising forthright, went in to his wife, Scheherazade, and acquainted her with that which his brother purposed, namely that he sought her sister, Dunyazade in wedlock, whereupon she answered: "O King of the Age, we seek of him one condition; to wit, that he take up his abode with us, for that I cannot brook to be parted from my sister an hour, because we were brought up together and may not endure separation each from other. If he accept this pact, she is his handmaid." King Shahryar returned to his brother and acquainted him with that which Scheherazade had said, and he replied: "Indeed, this is what was in my mind, for that I desire nevermore to be parted from thee one hour. As for the kingdom, Allah the Most High shall send to it whomso He chooseth, for that I have no longer a desire for the kingship." When King Shahryar heard his brother's words, he rejoiced exceedingly and said: "Verily, this is what I wished, O my brother. So Alhamdolillah—praised be Allah—who hath brought about union between us."

Then he sent after the kazis and ulema, captains and notables, and they married the two brothers to the two sisters. The contracts were written out and the two Kings bestowed robes of honor of silk and satin on those who were present, whilst the city was decorated and the rejoicings were renewed. The King commanded each emir and wazir and chamberlain and nabob to decorate his palace, and the folk of the city were gladdened by the presage of happiness and contentment. King Shahryar also bade slaughter sheep and set up kitchens and made bride feasts and fed all comers, high and low; and he gave alms to the poor and needy and extended his bounty to great and small. Then the eunuchs went forth, that they might perfume the hammam for the brides, so they scented it with rose-water and willow-flower water and pods of musk and fumigated it with Kakili eagle wood and ambergris. Then Scheherazade entered, she and her sister Dunyazade, and they cleansed their heads and clipped their hair.

When they came forth of the hammam bath, they donned raiment and ornaments such as men were wont prepare for the Kings of the Chosroes; and among Scheherazade's apparel was a dress purfled with red gold and wrought with counterfeit presentments of birds and beasts. And the two sisters encircled their necks with necklaces of jewels of price, in the like whereof Iskandar rejoiced not, for therein were great jewels such as amazed the wit and dazzled the eye. And the imagination was bewildered at their charms, for indeed each of them was brighter than the sun and the moon. Before them they lighted brilliant flambeaux of wax in candelabra of gold, but their faces outshone the flambeaux, for that they had eyes sharper than unsheathed swords and the lashes of their eyelids bewitched all hearts. Their cheeks were rosy red and their necks and shapes gracefully swayed and their eyes wantoned like the gazelle's. And the slave girls came to meet them with instruments of music. Then the two Kings entered the hammam bath, and when they came forth, they sat down on a couch set with pearls and gems, whereupon the two sisters came up to them and stood between their hands, as they were moons, bending and leaning from side to side in their beauty and loveliness.

Presently they brought forward Scheherazade and displayed her, for the first dress, in a red suit, whereupon King Shahryar rose to look upon her and the wits of all present, men and women, were bewitched for that she was even as saith of her one of her describers:

> A sun on wand in knoll of sand she showed,
> Clad in her cramoisy-hued chemisette.
> Of her lips' honeydew she gave me drink
> And with her rosy cheeks quencht fire she set.

Then they attired Dunyazade in a dress of blue brocade and she became as she were the full moon when it shineth forth. So they displayed her in this, for the first dress, before King Shah Zaman, who rejoiced in her and well-nigh swooned away for love longing and amorous desire. Yea, he was distraught with passion for her whenas he saw her, because she was as saith of her one of her describers in these couplets:

> She comes appareled in an azure vest,
> Ultramarine as skies are deckt and dight.
> I view'd th' unparalleled sight, which showed my eyes
> A summer moon upon a winter night.

Then they returned to Scheherazade and displayed her in the second dress, a suit of surpassing goodliness, and veiled her face with her hair like a chin veil. Moreover, they let down her side locks, and she was even as saith of her one of her describers in these couplets:

> O hail to him whose locks his cheeks o'ershade,
> Who slew my life by cruel hard despite.
> Said I, "Hast veiled the morn in night?" He said,
> "Nay I but veil moon in hue of night."

Then they displayed Dunyazade in a second and a third and a fourth dress, and she paced forward like the rising sun, and swayed to and fro in the insolence of beauty, and she was even as saith the poet of her in these couplets:

> The sun of beauty she to all appears
> And, lovely coy, she mocks all loveliness.
> And when he fronts her favor and her smile
> A-morn, the sun of day in clouds must dress.

Then they displayed Scheherazade in the third dress and the fourth and the fifth, and she became as she were a ban branch snell or a thirsting gazelle, lovely of face and perfect in attributes of grace, even as saith of her one in these couplets:

> She comes like fullest moon on happy night,
> Taper of waist with shape of magic might.
> She hath an eye whose glances quell mankind,
> And ruby on her cheeks reflects his light.
> Enveils her hips the blackness of her hair—
> Beware of curls that bite with viper bite!
> Her sides are silken-soft, that while the heart
> Mere rock behind that surface 'scapes our sight.
> From the fringed curtains of her eyne she shoots
> Shafts that at furthest range on mark alight.

Then they returned to Dunyazade and displayed her in the fifth dress and in the sixth, which was green, when she surpassed with her loveliness the fair of the four quarters of the world, and outvied with the brightness of her countenance the full moon at rising tide, for she was even as saith of her the poet in these couplets:

A damsel 'twas the tirer's art had decked with snare and sleight,
And robed with rays as though the sun from her had borrowed light.
She came before us wondrous clad in chemisette of green,
As veilèd by his leafy screen Pomegranate hides from sight.
And when he said, "How callest thou the fashion of thy dress?"
She answered us in pleasant way with double meaning dight:
"We call this garment *crèvecoeur,* and rightly is it hight,
For many a heart wi' this we brake and harried many a sprite."

Then they displayed Scheherazade in the sixth and seventh dresses and clad her in youth's clothing, whereupon she came forward swaying from side to side and coquettishly moving, and indeed she ravished wits and hearts and ensorceled all eyes with her glances. She shook her sides and swayed her haunches, then put her hair on sword hilt and went up to King Shahryar, who embraced her as hospitable host embraceth guest, and threatened her in her ear with the taking of the sword, and she was even as saith of her the poet in these words:

> Were not the murk of gender male,
> Than feminines surpassing fair,
> Tirewomen they had grudged the bride,
> Who made her beard and whiskers wear!

Thus also they did with her sister Dunyazade, and when they had made an end of the display, the King bestowed robes of honor on all who were present and sent the brides to their own apartments. Then Scheherazade went in to King Shahryar and Dunyazade to King Shah Zaman, and each of them solaced himself with the company of his beloved consort and the hearts of the folk were comforted.

When morning morrowed, the Wazir came in to the two Kings and kissed ground before them, wherefore they thanked him and were large of bounty to him. Presently they went forth and sat down upon couches of kingship, whilst all the wazirs and emirs and grandees and lords of the land presented themselves and kissed ground. King Shahryar ordered them dresses of honor and largess, and they prayed for the permanence and prosperity of the King and his brother.

Then the two sovereigns appointed their sire-in-law, the Wazir, to be Viceroy in Samarkand, and assigned him five of the chief emirs to accompany him, charging them attend him and do him service. The Minister kissed the ground and prayed that they might be vouchsafed length of life. Then he went in to his daughters, whilst the eunuchs and ushers walked before him, and saluted them and farewelled them. They kissed his hands and gave him joy of the kingship and bestowed on him immense treasures, after which he took leave of them and setting out, fared days and nights till he came near Samarkand, where the townspeople met him at a distance of three marches and rejoiced in him with exceeding joy. So he entered the city and they decorated the houses, and it was a notable day. He sat down on the throne of his kingship and the wazirs did him homage and the grandees and emirs of Samarkand, and all prayed that he might be vouchsafed justice and victory and length of continuance. So he bestowed on them robes of honor and entreated them with distinction, and they made him Sultan over them.

As soon as his father-in-law had departed for Samarkand, King Shahryar summoned the grandees of his realm and made them a stupendous banquet of all manner of delicious meats and exquisite sweetmeats. He also bestowed on them robes of honor and guerdoned them, and divided the kingdoms between himself and his brother in their presence, whereat the folk rejoiced. Then the two Kings abode, each ruling a day in turn, and they were ever in harmony each with other, while on similar wise their wives continued in the love of Allah Almighty and in thanksgiving to Him. And the peoples and the provinces were at peace and the preachers prayed for them from the pulpits, and their report was bruited abroad and the travelers bore tidings of them to all lands.

In due time King Shahryar summoned chroniclers and copyists and bade them write all that had betided him with his wife, first and last. So they wrote this and named it *The Stories of the Thousand Nights and a Night*. The book came to thirty volumes, and these the King laid up in his treasury. And the two brothers abode with their wives in all pleasaunce and solace of life and its delights, for that indeed Allah the Most High had changed their annoy into joy, and on this wise they continued till there took them the Destroyer of delights and the Severer of societies, the Desolator of dwelling places and Garnerer of graveyards, and they were translated to the ruth of Almighty Allah. Their houses fell waste and their palaces lay in ruins and the kings inherited their riches.

Then there reigned after them a wise ruler, who was just, keen-witted, and accomplished, and loved tales and legends, especially those which chronicle the doings of sovereigns and sultans, and he found in the treasury these marvelous stories and wondrous histories, contained in the thirty volumes aforesaid. So he read in them a first book and a second and a third and so on to the last of them, and each book astounded and delighted him more than that which preceded it, till he came to the end of them. Then he admired whatso he had read therein of description and discourse and rare traits and anecdotes and moral instances and reminiscences, and bade the folk copy them and dispread them over all lands and climes, wherefore their report was bruited abroad and the people named them *The Marvels and Wonders of the Thousand Nights and a Night*. This is all that hath come down to us of the origin of this book, and Allah is All-knowing. So Glory be to Him Whom the shifts of Time waste not away, nor doth aught of chance or change affect His sway, Whom one case diverteth not from other case and Who is sole in the attributes of perfect grace. And prayer and peace be upon the Lord's Pontiff and Chosen One among His creatures, our lord MOHAMMED, the Prince of mankind, through whom we supplicate Him for a goodly and a godly

FINIS.